600 - 600D

SEDAN AND MULTIPLA

SHOP MANUAL

DIREZIONE ASSISTENZA TECNICA AUTOVEICOLI

SECTION INDEX

Section	Section Page
GENERAL	1 — 3
ENGINE	2 — 11
FUEL SYSTEM LUBRICATION COOLING	3 — 75
CLUTCH - GEARBOX - DIFFERENTIAL	4 — 107
FRONT SUSPENSION AND WHEELS	5 — 145
REAR SUSPENSION AND WHEELS SHOCK ABSORBERS	6 — 175
STEERING SYSTEM	7 — 195
BRAKES WHEELS AND TIRES	8 — 213
AIR CONDITIONING WINDSHIELD WASHER TIGHTENING REFERENCE	9 — 237
ELECTRICAL	10 — 245
BODY	11 — 327
MAINTENANCE TOOL EQUIPMENT VEHICLE SPECIFICATIONS	12 — 345
MOD. 600 D	13 — 361

IMPORTANT

All the dimensions in metric units shown in this publication are the official ones.

Dimensions are also given in British and American units for prompt reference, and they have been calculated to a degree of approximation according to the need for accuracy in individual measurements.

Section 1
GENERAL INFORMATION

	Page
MAIN DATA OF ENGINE	5
MAIN DATA OF VEHICLES	5
FILL-UP DATA	7
UNIT IDENTIFICATION DATA	8
ORDERING SPARE PARTS	8
JACKING UP OR TOWING THE CAR	9
SERVICE HINTS	10

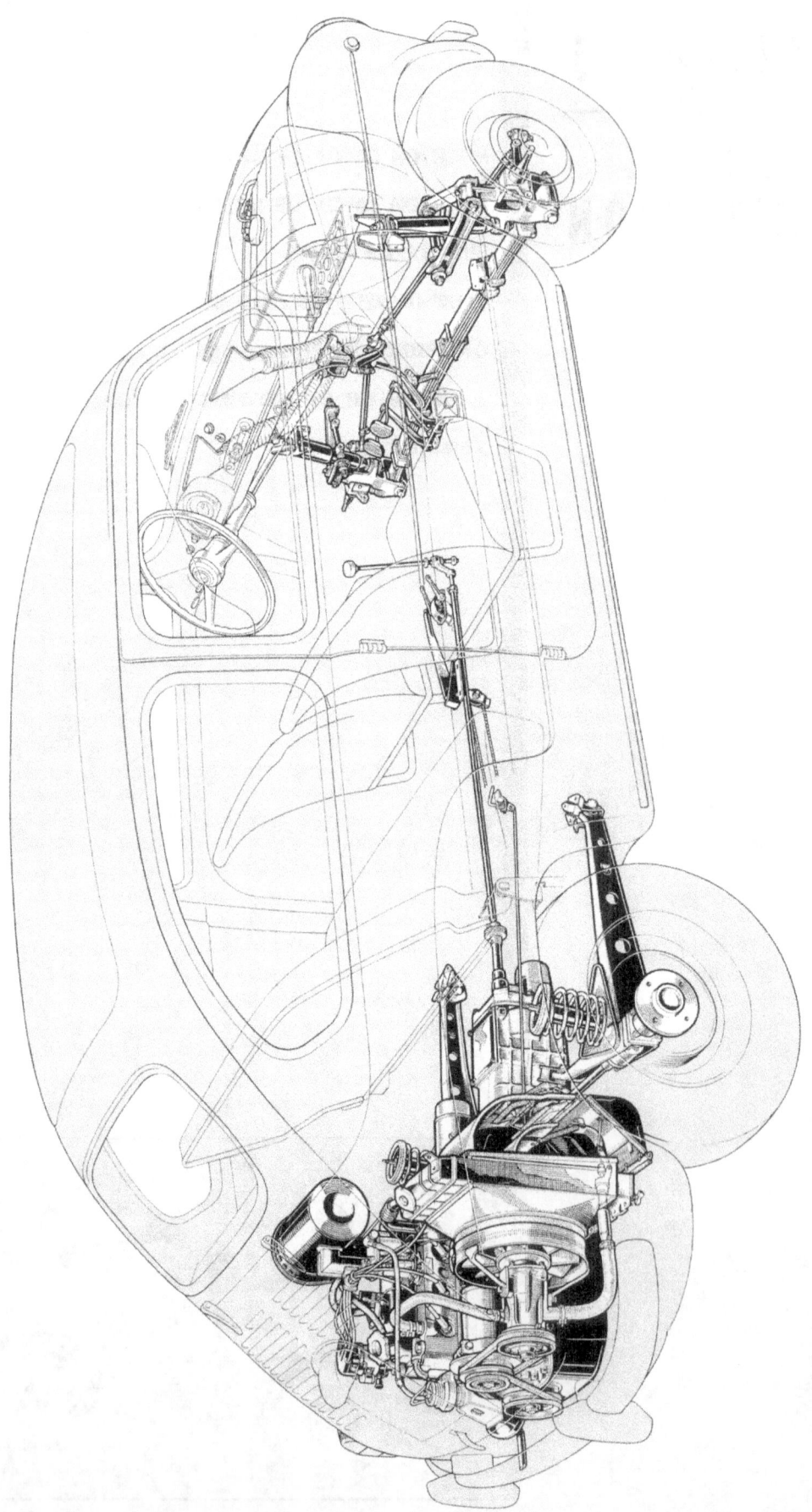

Fig. 1 - Phantom view of mechanical components (Sedan).

GENERAL INFORMATION

The «600» Model is manufactured in two different types: «4 passenger Sedan» and «Multipla».

The instructions contained in this Manual refer to both types. Any information or instruction specified only for one type or the other bears the indication «Sedan» or «Multipla»; also «Sedan version 140» or «Multipla version 141» relating to vehicles for export to U.S.A. and Canada.

ENGINE MAIN DATA

Type { Sedan	100.000
Type { Multipla	100.008
Number of cylinders, in line	4
Bore and stroke	2.36" x 2.20" (60 x 56 mm)
Total piston displacement	38.63 cu. in. (633 cc)
Compression ratio	7.5 to 1
Max. power (without exhaust silencer, fan and water pump)	24.5 HP
Max. power, S.A.E. standards	28.5 HP
at	4,600 r.p.m.
Max. torque (without exhaust silencer, fan and water pump)	28.9 ft.lbs (400 kgcm)
at	3,000 r.p.m.

DIMENSIONS AND WEIGHTS

	Sedan		Multipla	
Dimensions.	in.	mm	in.	mm
Overall length (with bumpers)	129.72 [1]	3.295 [1]	139.37 [2]	3.540 [2]
Overall width	54.33	1.380	57.09	1.450
Height (unladen)	55.32	1.405	62.21	1.580
Wheelbase	78.74	2.000	78.74	2.000
Front track	45.30	1.150	48.42	1.230
Rear track	45.67	1.160	45.55	1.157
Minimum ground clearance	6.30	160	5.9	150
Turning circle diameter	28 ft 6"	8.700	28 ft 10"	8.800
Weights.	lbs	kg	lbs	kg
Curb weight	1,334	605	1,653 [3]	750 [3]
Useful load	4 passengers plus 66	30	6 passengers or 5 passengers plus 154	70
Total weight, full load	2,017	915	2,579	1.170

[1] Version 140 = 130.51" (3.315 mm).   [2] Version 141 = 141.14" (3.585 mm).   [3] Version 141 = 1,664 lbs (755 kg).

MAIN DIMENSIONS OF VEHICLES

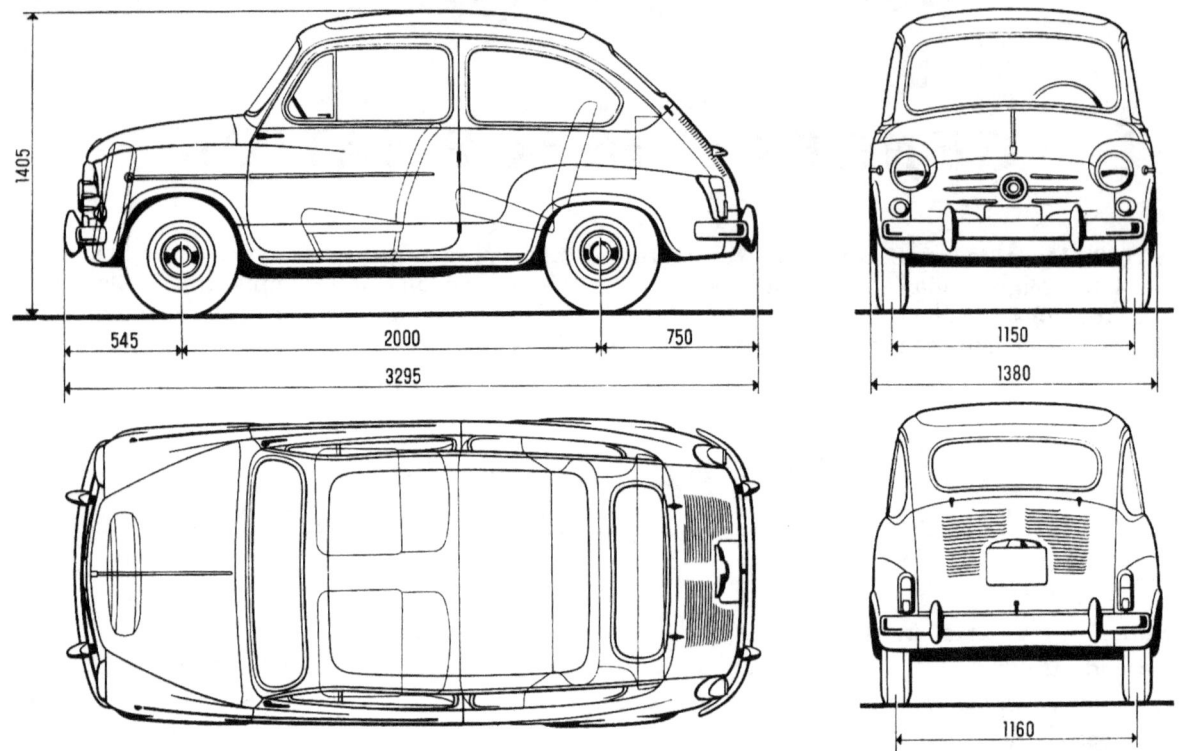

Fig. 2 - Sedan main dimensions.

545 mm = 21.46'' 750 mm = 29.53'' 1150 mm = 45.27'' 1160 mm = 45.67'' 1380 mm = 54.33''
2000 mm = 78.74'' 1405 mm = 55.32'' 3295 mm = 129.72''

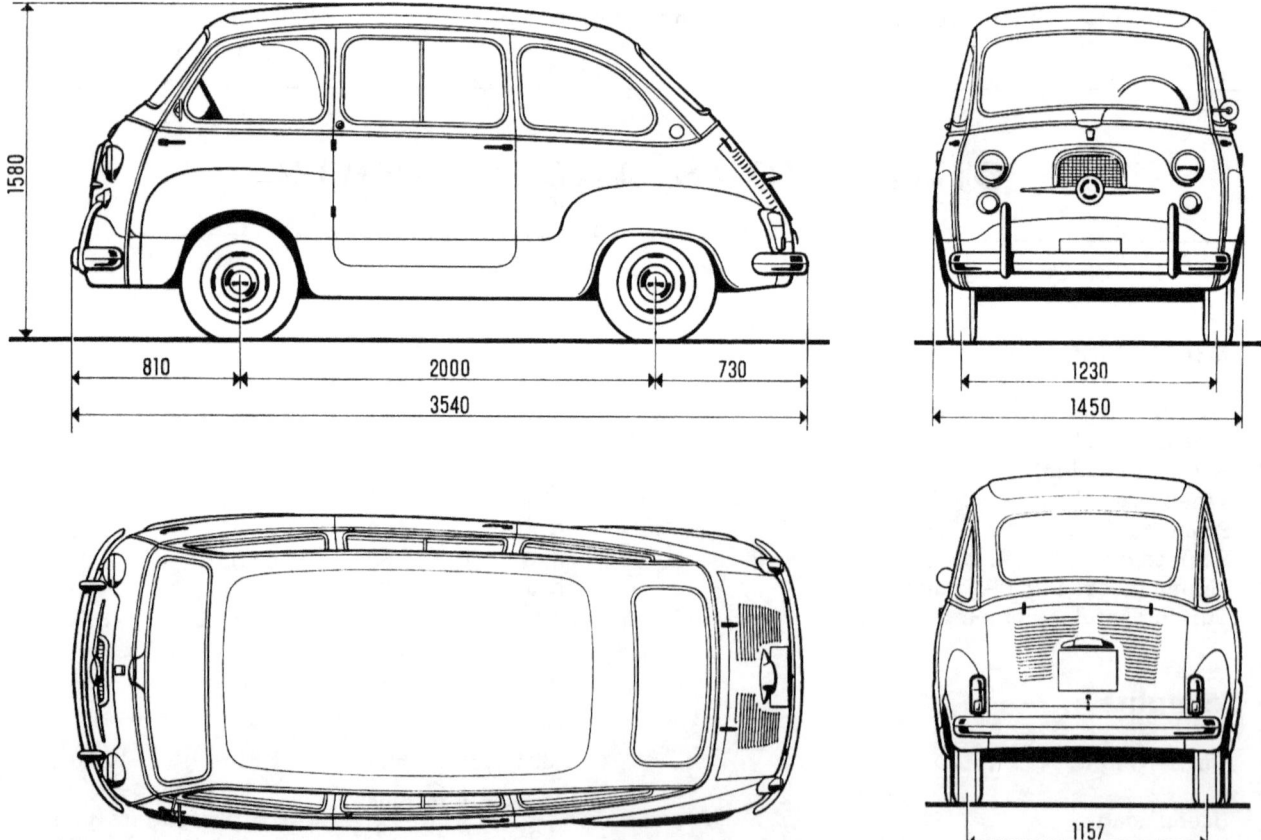

Fig. 3 - Multipla main dimensions.

810 mm = 31.89'' 730 mm = 28.74'' 3540 mm = 139.37'' 1230 mm = 48.42'' 1450 mm = 57.09''
2000 mm = 78.74'' 1580 mm = 62.21'' 1157 mm = 45.55''

(*) The maximum height is intended with unladen cars.

GENERAL: PERFORMANCES AND FILL-UP DATA

PERFORMANCES

	Sedan		Multipla	
Speeds.	m.p.h.	km/hr	m.p.h.	km/hr
Maximum permissible speeds after running-in (1800 miles = 3000 km)				
1st gear	15.5	25	12.5	20
2nd gear	25.0	40	22.0	35
3rd gear	40.3	65	34.0	55
4th gear	62.1	100	56.0	90
Climbable gradients.	%		%	
Maximum, with fully laden car:				
1st gear . . . abt.	27		23	
2nd gear . . . »	15		13	
3rd gear . . . »	9		7.5	
4th gear . . . »	5		4	
Reverse . . . »	30		29	

FILL-UP DATA

ITEM	SEDAN				MULTIPLA				REPLENISHMENT
	U.S. Units	G.B. Units	lt.	kg	U.S. Units	G.B. Units	lt.	kg	
Fuel tank	7.13 Gals.	5.94 Gals.	27	—	7.6 Gals.	6.4 Gals.	29	—	Gasoline: Oct. rat. 83 (Res. Meth.)
including reserve supply	{3.70 Qts. 5.28	{3.08 Qts. 4.4	3,5-5	—	{3.70 Qts. 5.28	{3.08 Qts. 4.4	3,5-5	—	
Radiator, water jackets [1]	4.50 »	3.76 »	4,300	—	6.87 »	5.72 »	6,500	—	Water [2]
Sump, lines and filter [3]	3.17 »	2.64 »	3,000	2,700	3.17 »	2.64 »	3,000	2,700	FIAT oil [5]
Gearbox and differential	1.64 »	1.36 »	1,550	1,400	1.64 »	1.36 »	1,505	1,400	FIAT W 90 oil (SAE 90 EP)
Steering box	.13 »	.11 »	0,120	0,110	.17 »	.15 »	0,165	0,150	FIAT W 90 oil (SAE 90 EP)
Brake fluid reservoir	.30 »	.25 »	0,280	0,275	.39 »	.33 »	0,370	0,365	FIAT special blue brake fluid or equivalent non-mineral HD type
Front shock absorbers (each)	.14 »	.12 »	0,135	0,120	.17 »	.15 »	0,165	0,150	FIAT S. A. I. oil
Rear shock absorbers (each)	.13 »	.11 »	0,120	0,110	.13 »	.11 »	0,120	0,110	FIAT S. A. I. oil
Windshield washer fluid bag	[4]	[4]	—	[4]	—	—	—	—	Water and FIAT D.P./1 fluid mixture (concentrated solution)

[1] Including the heating system for the « Multipla ».

[2] When temperature is close to 32° F (0° C) change to good commercial grade anti-freeze mixture (see page 102).

[3] Total capacity of oil pan, filter and lines 3.16 Imp. qts - 3.8 U. S. qts (3,25 kg). The figure specified in the chart is the amount recommended for periodical oil replacement, cartridge excluded.

[4] Pure water .66 Imp. qts - .79 U. S. qts (0,75 kg) plus .6 oz (0,017 kg) - Summer 1.2 (0,034 kg) - Winter solution.

[5] See following table for oil grades:

TEMPERATURE	SERVICE MS FIAT (API) OIL	FIAT « MULTIGRADO » OIL
Above 32° F (0° C) (minimum)	VS 30 (SAE 30)	10 W - 30
From 32° F to 5° F (0° to —15° C) (minimum)	VS 20 (SAE 20)	10 W - 30
Below 5° F (—15° C) (minimum)	VS 10 W (SAE 10 W)	—
Above 86° F (30° C) (average)	VS 40 (SAE 40)	20 W - 40

WARNING: Never top up with oils of other grades or Makes. - When starting to use these detergent oils on engines other then new the lubrication system must first the thoroughly flushed.

UNIT IDENTIFICATION DATA

Each car is identified by an **Engine number** and a **Chassis number**.

To complete the identification of the car when ordering parts also a **Number for spares** is provided.

These three numbers are repeated on the Identification plate.

Engine Number.

This number is punched on cylinder block, just above the timing cover. The number is preceded by lettering FIAT and engine type (fig. 4).

Fig. 4 - Location of engine number.

Chassis Number.

It is located on engine compartment bulkhead bottom, to the left of the Identification plate and is preceded by lettering « FIAT » and by the type number (fig. 5).

Number for Spares.

This number is stamped at centre on Identification plate lower edge (fig. 6).

Identification Plate.

This plate, giving engine and Chassis numbers and Number for spares, is located on engine compartment bulkhead left side.

NOTE - As far as « Sedan version 140 » and « Multipla version 141 » are concerned, unit Identification plate include also:

— body paint identification number;
— roof paint identification number.

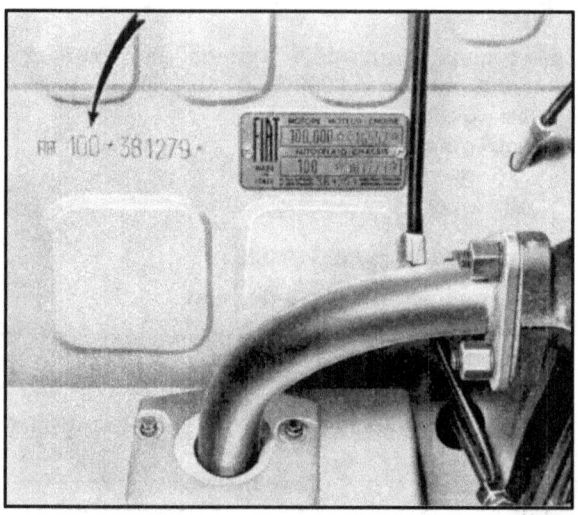

Fig. 5 - Location of chassis number and of identification plate.

NOTICE - A new type of unit identification plate is now adopted, which differs from the plates shown in figs. 5-6 as follows:

— addition of the series approval number as issued by the Motoring Inspectorate General (Italian);
— suppression of the engine serial number.

As a result, when the engine number must be quoted in orders for spare parts, read the number stamped on the engine block.

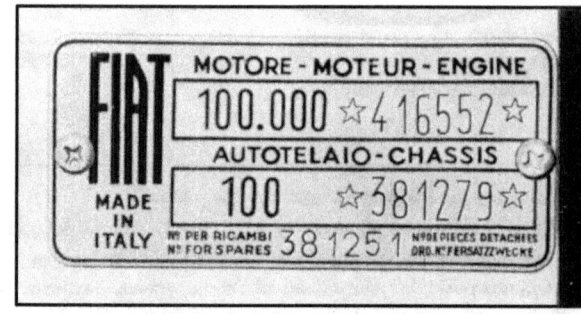

Fig. 6 - Unit identification plate.

ORDERING SPARE PARTS

Specify:
— Car Model;
— Engine Number;
— Chassis Number;
— Number for Spares;
— Part No. of the ordered spare.

JACKING UP OR TOWING THE CAR

To jack up or tow the car there are some particular recommendations to be followed which are outlined below.

Raising the car with the **tool kit jack** does not involve any difficulty. Anyhow the operations required are described under « Wheels and Tires ».

Fig. 7 - Using hydraulic jack Arr. 2027 under floor bracket to raise Sedan at front end.

Instead, when using a **garage jack**, proceed as follows:

— at front and at rear: place jack arm exclusively under the specially designed brackets on floor bottom (figs. 7 and 8). At rear always interpose a suitably thick (3 cm at least) wooden block between jack arm and bracket (fig. 8).

Fig. 8 - Raising Sedan rear end with hydraulic jack provided with wood block to be placed under the support bracket.

Fig. 9 - Raising Multipla front end with hydraulic jack Arr. 2027.

In case vehicle needs towing, the rope must be secured only to the front bracket which has been suitably shaped for this purpose.

To jack up first series vehicles (numbers less than 069847), not provided with said brackets, the hydraulic garage jack must be equipped with the specially designed cross member **Arr. 2072** so that vehicle weight will rest on leaf spring, (fig. 10) at front, or on swinging arms at rear. On these vehicles, tow rope must be attached exclusively to leaf spring end.

On first as well as second series cars, fixture **I. 31333** must be used to raise vehicle with an auto-hoist. The brackets of the fixture must be applied at front leaf spring ends and of rear swinging arm ends.

Fig. 10 - Raising Sedan front end with hydraulic jack Arr. 2027 provided with cross member Arr. 2072 (up to car No. 069847).

SERVICE HINTS

Before attempting any repair, adjustment, check, removal or installation of any part, take the necessary precautions to prevent damages to inner trim or body varnish by protecting parts involved with some suitable covering.

To ensure best possible results when servicing the different units of the car, aside from the skill of repairmen, it is essential to do the job in well-lighted, clean and dust-free shops.

The Shop must have available the general and special tools designed for the job and the type of car being serviced. To this end, consult the « Tool Catalogue » issued by the FIAT Service Department.

The importance of washing carefully all engine components and of freeing lubrication ducts from possible obstructions when disassembling or overhauling, cannot be over-emphasized.

An adequate lubrication of units and parts before re-assembly, is essential to eliminate the risk of seizure during the initial period of operation.

When disassembling an engine or other units proceed with order, do not mix up parts and handle them carefully.

When a unit has received proper care and best possible servicing, it must again operate as if it were new.

Use exclusively original FIAT spares: in fact, only these will restore the units to perfect efficiency.

Follow strictly the techniques outlined on succeeding pages and keep within the tabulated allowances, wear limits and torque specifications.

Remember that if an operation is not performed according to best shop practice, the unit serviced cannot give satisfactory results. In this case, it would require a second disassembly to remedy any trouble, with a deriving time waste and cost increase before it can be restored to full efficiency.

To obtain best results, without unnecessary wastes of material and time, perform each servicing operation methodically, with order, care and proper equipment.

CAR KEYS

Each new car is delivered with two sets of keys to suit:
— ignition;
— driver's side door lock and (Multipla only) fuel tank filler cap.

These keys bear an identification number stamped on key head.
To have car key duplications made through the cutting machine Ap. 5013, identify keys quoting code number and applicable use.

Section 2
ENGINE

	Page
DESCRIPTION OF COMPONENTS	13
TROUBLES AND REMEDIES	14
MISCELLANEOUS OPERATIONS	21
CYLINDER BLOCK AND CRANKCASE	27
PISTONS - PINS - RINGS	33
CONNECTING RODS AND ROD BEARINGS	37
CRANKSHAFT AND MAIN BEARINGS	42
CYLINDER HEAD - VALVES - VALVE GUIDES AND SPRINGS	50
TIMING GEAR	57
SPECIFICATIONS - REPAIR AND REBUILD STANDARDS	66
ENGINE TIGHTENING REFERENCE	71
ENGINE BRAKE TEST	72

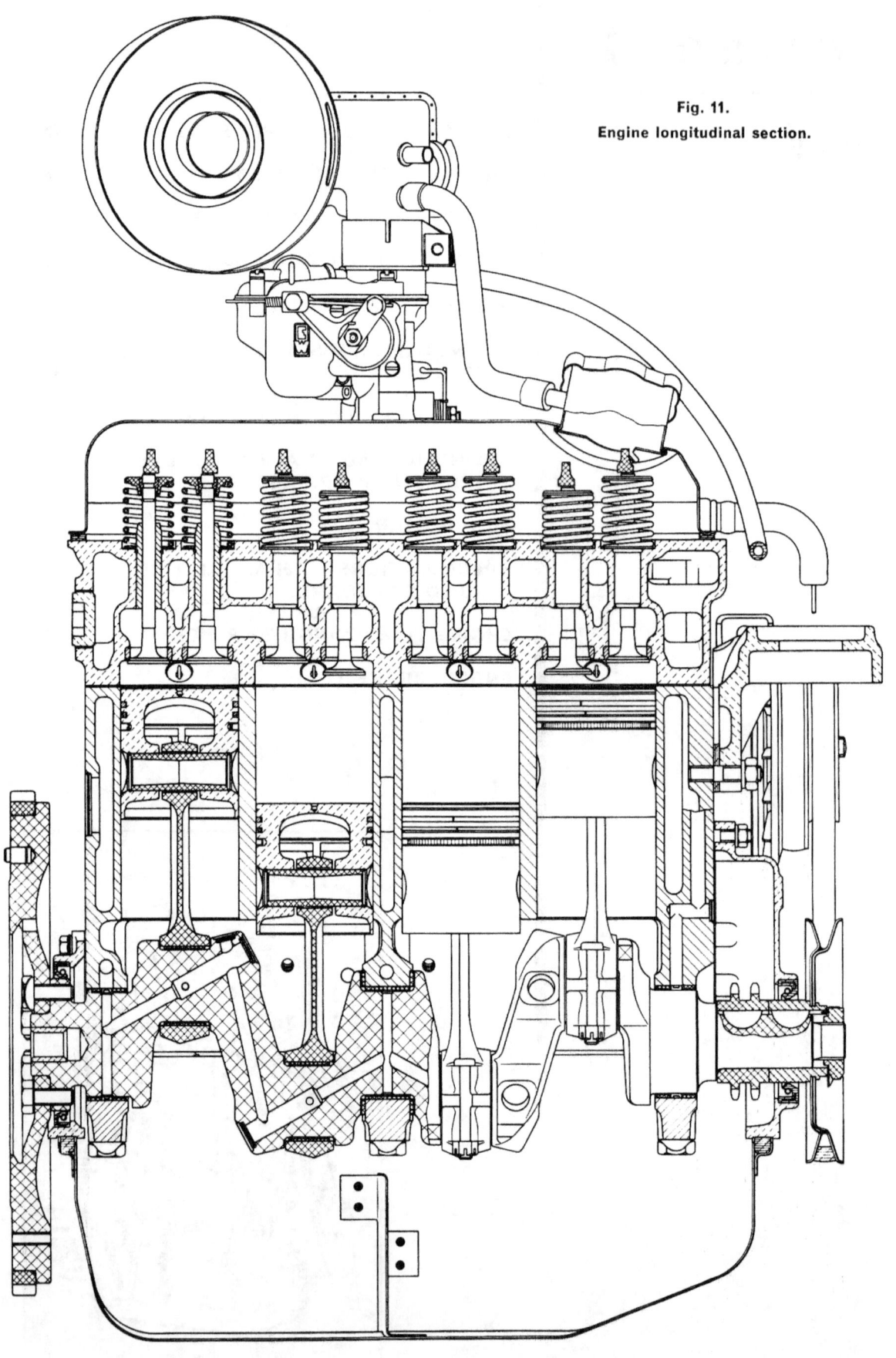

Fig. 11.
Engine longitudinal section.

ENGINE

Description of Components.

As the **100.000** engine installed on the **600 Sedan** and the **100.008** engine installed on the **600 Multipla** differ only in the cooling water temperature control system, the following description is applicable to both engines.

It is a four-stroke, Otto cycle, rear-mounted engine running on gasoline.

Cast-iron **cylinder block** integral with crankcase.

Aluminum **cylinder head** with cast-iron valve seat inserts and incorporated intake manifold.

Steel, three-bearing **crankshaft**; thin-wall **main bearings** and thrust washers on front support.

Steel **connecting rods**: thin-wall **big end bearings** and bronze **small end bushes**.

Aluminum-alloy, oval-tapered **pistons** (max. diameter at skirt bottom on axis perpendicular to gudgeon pin boss) with three cast-iron rings: a compression ring, a compression-oilscraper ring and an oilscraper ring with radial slots. The steel **gudgeon pin** is secured in position on bosses by two steel snap rings. Piston pin boss axis is .078" (2 mm) off center with respect to piston diameter, towards side opposite the skirt expansion slot.

Overhead **valves**, camshaft-controlled through tappets, pushrods and rockers.

The cast-iron **camshaft**, in crankcase, is chain-driven by the crankshaft.

Fuel feed: by mechanical, diaphragm type pump, controlled by a camshaft driven pushrod.

Fig. 13.
100.000 engine, left hand side (direction of drive).

Fig. 12.
100.000 engine, right hand side (direction of drive).

Downdraft carburetor. Carburetor air intake provided with air cleaner and silencer, and a warm air scoop for winter operation.

Lubrication: oil circulated under pressure by a gear-type pump. Oil pressure relief valve in main circuit.

By-pass cartridge filter.

Insufficient oil pressure indicator sending unit.

Cooling: forced circulation by centrifugal-type water pump. Upright-pipe radiator cooled by belt-driven fan.

«Sedan»: temperature control of water in radiator through thermostatic regulation of air flow in engine compartment.

«Multipla»: water temperature control by a thermostat in duct from cylinders to radiator.

A sending unit is provided to control the excessive water temperature indicator in instrument cluster on facia.

Ignition: by **battery**; ignition distributor, controlled by a camshaft-driven shaft, incorporating an automatic advance and additional manifold-vacuum operated diaphragm advance control.

Starting: by **electric starter**, on gearbox, hand-controlled by lever on floor tunnel.

Power plant suspension is obtained by a rear central rubber pad and two front rubber pads on gearbox sides, connected to a suitable cross member mounted on floor.

ENGINE TROUBLE DIAGNOSIS AND CORRECTIONS

Engine Will Not Start.

POSSIBLE CAUSES	REMEDIES
1) Weak battery.	1) Check and re-charge battery as recommended under « Battery ».
2) Corroded or loose battery terminal connections.	2) Clean, examine and tighten cable clamps to battery terminals, as recommended under « Battery ». Replace cables and clamps if they are too much corroded.
3) Weak coil.	3) Check coil and replace by a new one.
4) Loose or broken ignition cables from coil to distributor and from distributor to spark plugs.	4) Examine and re-set circuit or replace faulty cables.
5) Cracked distributor cap.	5) Replace cap.
6) Moisture or dirt deposits on distributor cap contact points.	6) Wipe and clean points.
7) Distributor breaker contact points dirty, oxidized or blackened; pitted points or excessive point gap.	7) Clean contacts and adjust point gap as recommended under « Ignition Distributor ».
8) Distributor rotor cracked, or showing signs of burning or wet.	8) Clean or replace rotor, if necessary.
9) Center distributor cap contact worn or broken or with distorted pressure spring.	9) Replace contact and contact spring.
10) Shorted condenser or with poor insulation.	10) Bench test condenser and replace it, if defective.
11) Fouled spark plugs or excessive spark plugs gap.	11) Clean spark plugs and set gap as recommended under « Spark Plugs ».
12) Improper timing (ignition).	12) Check and set timing, as recommended under « Ignition Timing ».
13) Defective starting motor.	13) Locate failure and correct it.

14) Carburetor flooded.
    a) due to too long starting with inserted choke without using accelerator;
    b) due to carburetor defect.
	14) Proceed as follows:
	    a) remove and wipe spark plugs or wait some minutes and start engine with choke out and all open throttle;
	    b) remove and rebuild carburetor, as recommended in covering chapter.

15) Dirt or water in fuel line or carburetor.	15) Remove and thoroughly clean carburetor; if trouble recurs, flush and blow fuel tank and lines.
16) Incorrect fuel level in carburetor bowl.	16) Check fuel level in bowl and adjust it, if necessary, as recommended under « Carburetor ».

(continued)

ENGINE: TROUBLE DIAGNOSIS AND CORRECTIONS

Engine Will Not Start (continuation).

POSSIBLE CAUSES	REMEDIES
17) Defective fuel pump.	17) Remove and rebuild fuel pump as recommended under « Fuel Pump ».
18) Poor compression.	18) Check compression (113.8 to 128 p.s.i. - 8 to 9 kg/cm^2) using a pressure gauge; rebuild engine if compression is too low.
19) Engine overheating.	19) Check water level in radiator, feu and water pump drive belt tension, water pump operation and proceed as required.

Engine Stalls.

POSSIBLE CAUSES	REMEDIES
1) Idling speed too low.	1) Increase throttle opening slightly and adjust mixture rating as recommended under « Carburetor ».
2) Idle mixture too lean or too rich.	2) Adjust mixture rating as recommended under « Carburetor ».
3) Carburetor flooding: a) due to too long starting with inserted choke withoug using accelerator; b) due to carburetor defect.	3) Proceed as follows: a) remove and wipe spark plugs or wait some minutes and start engine with choke out and all open throttle; b) remove and rebuild carburetor, as recommended in covering chapter.
4) Needle valve in carburetor stuck.	4) Rebuild, as recommended under « Carburetor ».
5) Dirt or water in fuel line or carburetor.	5) Remove and thoroughly clean carburetor; if trouble recurs, flush and blow fuel tank and lines.
6) Incorrect fuel level in carburetor bowl.	6) Check and adjust fuel level, as recommended under « Carburetor ».
7) Incorrect use of choke device.	7) Operate as recommended under covering paragraph of chapter « Carburetor ».
8) Loose or corroded battery terminals.	8) Clean terminals and tighten nuts as recommended under « Battery ». Replace cables and terminal clamps if they are too much worn.
9) Loose ignition cables from coil to distributor and from distributor to spark plugs.	9) Examine and re-set circuit.
10) Loose ignition swith connections.	10) Examine and re-set circuit.
11) Spark plugs dirty, damp or gaps incorrectly set.	11) Clean spark plugs and set gap as recommended under « Spark Plurgs ».

(continued)

Engine Stalls (continuation).

POSSIBLE CAUSES	REMEDIES
12) Distributor breaker contact points dirty, oxidized or blackened; pitted points or excessive point gap.	12) Clean contacts and adjust point gap as recommended under « Ignition Distributor ».
13) Distributor rotor contact worn.	13) Replace distributor rotor.
14) Distributor advance not operating.	14) Rebuild ignition distributor as recommended in covering chapter.
15) Defective coil and condenser.	15) Inspect and replace both of them, if necessary. Operate as recommended under « Ignition Coil » and « Ignition Distributor ».
16) Exhaust system restricted.	16) Thoroughly clean exhaust silencer, exhaust piping and manifold.
17) Incorrect valve tappet clearance.	17) Adjust tappet clearance as recommended under « Valve Tappets - Push Rods - Rocker Arms ».
18) Burned valves.	18) Replace valves.
19) Poor compression.	19) Check compression (113.8 to 128 p.s.i. - 8 to 9 kg/cm^2) using a pressure gauge; rebuild engine if compression is too low.
20) Engine overheating.	20) Check water level in radiator, fan and water pump drive belt tension, water pump operation and overhaul as required.

Engine Has No Power.

POSSIBLE CAUSES	REMEDIES
1) Incorrect ignition timing.	1) Inspect and set ignition timing, as recommended under « Ignition Timing ».
2) Weak coil or condenser.	2) Bench test coil and condenser, as recommended under « Ignition Coil » and « Ignition Distributor ». Replace both parts, if necessary.
3) Reduced accelerator pedal travel.	3) Locate failure and correct it.
4) Distributor rotor contact worn.	4) Replace distributor rotor.
5) Defective centrifugal or vacuum advance (distributor).	5) Rebuild ignition distributor and vacuum advance, as recommended in covering chapters.
6) Excessive play in distributor shaft.	6) Rebuild distributor and replace damaged parts.
7) Weak spring in contact points.	7) Replace distributor breaker arm, spring and point assembly.
8) Distributor cam worn.	8) Replace cam body.
9) Insufficient distributor point dwell.	9) Adjust point dwell angle as recommended under « Ignition Distributor ».

(continued)

ENGINE: TROUBLE DIAGNOSIS AND CORRECTIONS

Engine Has No Power (continuation).

POSSIBLE CAUSES	REMEDIES
10) Spark plugs dirty, damp or gaps incorrectly set.	10) Clean spark plugs and set gap as recommended under « Spark Plugs ».
11) Low grade fuel.	11) Use fuel with 83 Oct. Rating (Research Method).
12) Weak valve springs.	12) Check spring pressure on tester A. 11493 and compare figures with those tabulated under « Valve Springs ».
13) Valves sticking when hot, burned or twisted.	13) Overhaul valves and valve guides as recommended under « Cylinder Head »; replace as required.
14) Incorrect valve tappet clearance.	14) Adjust tappet clearance as recommended under « Valve Timing ».
15) Worn camshaft lobes.	15) Check valve timing and compare data with those in valve timing diagram, as shown under « Valve Timing »; replace camshaft, if necessary.
16) Valve timing incorrect.	16) Time valves as recommended in covering chapter.
17) Insufficient engine bench running-in.	17) If necessary, remove engine from car and test it on bench.
18) Poor compression.	18) Check compression (113.8 to 128 p.s.i. - 8 to 9 kg/cm^2) using a pressure gauge; if pressure is too low, locate failure and rebuild engine.
19) Blown cylinder head gasket.	19) Remove cylinder head, check cylinder head and block for even mating surfaces, replace head gasket.
20) Defective fuel pump.	20) Rebuild fuel pump and replace worn parts.
21) Too rich or lean fuel mixture.	21) Adjust carburetor.
22) Carburetor in poor condition.	22) Clean carburetor, blow jets and adjust carburetor as recommended.
23) Dirt or water in gas line or carburetor.	23) Remove and thoroughly clean carburetor; it trouble recurs, flush and blow fuel tank and lines.
24) Incorrect fuel level in carburetor bowl.	24) Check fuel level in bowl and adjust as recommended under « Carburetor ».
25) Engine overheating.	25) Check water level in radiator, fan and water pump drive belt tension, water pump operation and overhaul as required.
26) Clutch slipping.	26) Check throwout mechanism for correct operation, driven disk linings for absence of oil or grease, or wear. Operate as required.
27) Tight wheel bearings.	27) Locate origin of failure; replace as required and adjust correctly as recommended under « Front and Rear Suspension and Wheels ».
28) Brakes dragging.	28) Inspect and adjust brakes.

Engine «Lopes» or Misses at Idle.

POSSIBLE CAUSES	REMEDIES
1) Incorrect carburetor idle adjustment.	1) Adjust idle as recommended under « Carburetor ».
2) Dirty jets or plugged passages in carburetor.	2) Remove and clean jets; if necessary, remove carburetor and rebuild it thoroughly.
3) Dirt or water in fuel line or carburetor.	3) Remove and thoroughly clean carburetor; if trouble recurs, flush and blow fuel tank and lines.

4) Carburetor flooding:
   a) due to long starting with inserted choke without using accelerator;
   b) due to carburetor defect.
	4) Proceed as follows:
	   a) remove and wipe spark plugs or wait some minutes and start engine with choke out and all open throttle;
	   b) remove and rebuild carburetor, as recommended in covering chapter.

5) Leaking gasket between carburetor and intake manifold spacer.	5) Check mating surfaces for level, replace gasket and tighten nuts properly.
6) Blown cylinder head gasket.	6) Check mating surfaces for level, replace gasket and tighten screws at specified torque.
7) Incorrect valve tappet clearance.	7) Adjust clearance, as recommended under « Valve Timing ».
8) Burned, warped or pitted valves.	8) Rebuild cylinder head.
9) Worn camshaft lobes.	9) Check valve timing and compare data with those in valve timing diagram, as shown under « Valve Timing »; replace camshaft, if necessary.
10) Worn timing chain.	10) Replace chain.
11) Uneven compression rates.	11) Using pressure gauge, check compression in each cylinder (113.8 to 128 p.s.i. - 8 to 9 kg/cm^2) and rebuild engine, if required.
12) Engine overheating.	12) Check coolant level in radiator, fan and water pump drive belt tension, water pump operation and overhaul as required.
13) Weak battery.	13) Check state of charge of battery and recharge.
14) Incorrect ignition timing.	14) Set ignition timing.
15) Leaks in ignition wiring.	15) Locate leak and correct as necessary.
16) Moisture on electrical system wires.	16) Wipe cable terminals, if damp. If the whole cable insulation is soaked, replace the cable.
17) Defective mechanical and vacuum advance mechanisms.	17) Rebuild ignition distributor and vacuum advance, as recommended under « Ignition Distributor ».
18) Excessive play in distributor shaft.	18) Rebuild ignition distributor and replace worn parts.
19) Distributor cam worn.	19) Rebuild ignition distributor and replace cam body.
20) Spark plugs damp, dirt or the gaps set too wide.	20) Clean spark plugs and adjust gap, as recommended under « Spark Plugs ».

ENGINE: TROUBLE DIAGNOSIS AND CORRECTIONS

Engine Misses at High Speed.

POSSIBLE CAUSES	REMEDIES
1) Dirty jets in carburetor, especially the main jet and emulsion well.	1) Remove jets and blow then clean.
2) Dirt or water in fuel line or carburetor.	2) Remove and thoroughly clean carburetor; if trouble recurs, flush and blow fuel tank and lines.
3) Incorrect ignition timing.	3) Set ignition timing, as recommended in covering chapter.
4) Weak coil or condenser.	4) Bench test coil and condenser and replace by new ones, if necessary.
5) Distributor breaker points dirty or incorrectly spaced.	5) Clean and adjust points.
6) Distributor rotor contact worn.	6) Replace distributor rotor.
7) Loose ignition wiring.	7) Check wiring cables for secure fastening on nuts and spark plug inserts.
8) Excessive play in distributor shaft.	8) Rebuild ignition distributor and replace worn parts.
9) Spark plugs dirty, damp or the gaps set too wide.	9) Clean spark plugs and adjust gap, as recommended under « Spark Plugs ».
10) Weak distributor point contact.	10) Smooth distributor points and adjust gap.
11) Insufficient spring tension on contact breaker arm.	11) Replace breaker arm assembly.
12) Distributor cam lobe worn.	12) Rebuild ignition distributor and replace cam body.
13) Detonation or preignition.	13) Check spark advance and set ignition timing, where necessary. Make sure that spark plugs are the Factory recommended type and in serviceable condition. If piston and combustion chambers are carboned up, use higher grade fuel.
14) Weak valve springs.	14) Remove cylinder head and replace springs.
15) Worn camshaft lobes.	15) Check valve timing and compare data with those in valve timing diagram, as shown under « Valve Timing »; replace camshaft, if necessary.
16) Badly worn diaphragm in fuel pump.	16) Remove fuel pump and replace diaphragm, as recommended under « Fuel Pump ».
17) Engine overheating.	17) Check coolant level in radiator, fan and water pump drive belt tension, water pump operation and overhaul as required.
18) Low grade fuel.	18) Use fuel with 83 Oct. Rating (Research Method).

Engine Misses While Idling.

POSSIBLE CAUSES	REMEDIES
1) Spark plugs dirty, damp or the gaps set too wide.	1) Clean spark plugs and adjust gap, as recommended under « Spark Plugs ».
2) Broken or loose ignition wires.	2) Check wiring cables for secure fastening on nuts and spark plug inserts.
3) Burned or pitted breaker contact points, or set with insufficient gap.	3) Overhaul and adjust contact points, as recommended under « Ignition Distributor ».
4) Coil or condenser defective.	4) Bench test coil and condenser and replace them, if required.
5) Weak battery.	5) Check battery state of charge using a hydrometer and recharge battery, if necessary. Proceed as recommended under « Battery ».
6) Distributor cap cracked.	6) Replace cap.
7) Distributor rotor contact worn.	7) Replace distributor rotor.
8) Moisture on electrical system wires.	8) Wipe cable terminals, if damp. If the whole cable insulation is soaked, replace the cable.
9) Excessive play in distributor shaft or shaft cam worn.	9) Rebuild ignition distributor and replace worn parts.
10) Burned, warped or pitted valves.	10) Overhaul cylinder head and replace valves. Proceed as recommended under « Cylinder Head ».
11) Incorrect valve tappet clearance.	11) Adjust clearance, as recommended under « Rocker Arms ».
12) Incorrect carburetor idle adjustment.	12) Adjust idle speed, as recommended under « Carburetor ».
13) Improper carburetor float level.	13) Check and adjust float, as recommended under « Carburetor ».
14) Poor compression.	14) Check compression using a pressure gauge; if pressure is too low (below 113.8 to 128 p.s.i. - 8 to 9 kg/cm^2), locate causes and remove them.

NOTE - Compression check-up in each cylinder should be made in the following conditions:
- cold engine;
- correct valve tappet clearance;
- carburetor throttle valves wide open;
- fully charged battery;
- engine cranked by the starting motor.

MISCELLANEOUS OPERATIONS

ENGINE REMOVAL AND INSTALLATION . . . . page 21
ENGINE DISASSEMBLY . . . . » 23
ENGINE ASSEMBLY . . . . » 25

ENGINE REMOVAL AND INSTALLATION

Raise car rear end and rest on stands **Arr. 2002 bis**, placed under swinging arms.

Then proceed as follows:

— lift front compartment lid and disconnect battery positive terminal and fuel delivery pipe at tank;

— recline rear seat back forward over cushion;

— back out the two mounting screws of the floor covering behind rear seat and take off the covering;

— remove starter motor shroud by undoing its five mounting screws (fig. 15);

— undo the two upper short screws fixing gearbox-differential unit to engine;

— remove right central apron, under engine, then the flywheel cover secured to gearbox;

— disconnect silencer by freeing its pipe at exhaust manifold and the muffler at sump; remove the gasket;

Fig. 14 - Sedan engine compartment: the engine central rear support is visible in the foreground.

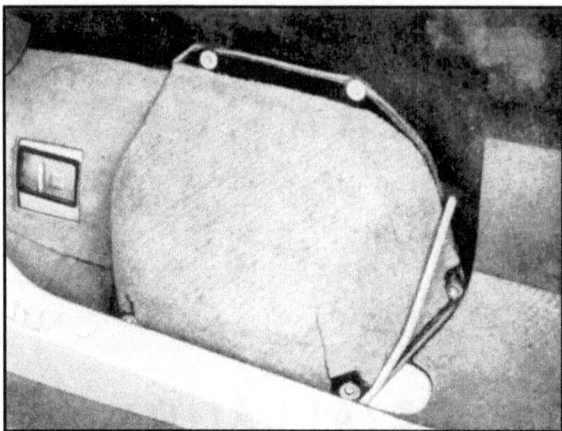

Fig. 15 - Starter shroud (accessible from inside the car).
To the left is visible the warm air inlet.

— drain cooling system by first taking off radiator filler cap and then opening the cocks under radiator and water pump. After this, remove the radiator-to-water pump hose;
— disconnect the delivery pipe at fuel pump;
— disconnect the insufficient oil pressure indicator sending unit cable and the excessive water temperature indicator sending unit cable;
— at air cleaner, remove vent hoses and vacuum advance line;
— take off cleaner and its gasket for carburetor mounting;

Fig. 17 - Taking off body rear end lower panel for engine removal.
1. Sling Arr. 2069. - 2. Body rear end lower panel.

— disconnect: throttle control bowden after removing its fastener and bowden cranked lever (on cylinder head) after disinserting the cotter pin;
— disconnect carburetor starting device (choke) bowden after slackening its nut;
— disconnect the High and Low tension cables at ignition coil, and the two generator cables;

Fig. 16 - Engine compartment left view.

Fig. 18 - Engine removal.

ENGINE: DISASSEMBLY

— disconnect the cylinder head water outlet-to-radiator hose, after slackening its collar;

— apply engine sling **Arr. 2069** and hook it up to a hoist.

— undo the two lower long screws securing engine to gearbox-differential unit;

— back out the engine rear central support mounting nut; take off the washer, the cup and the upper rubber pad;

— unscrew the two nuts, one on each side, securing the bumper bar and ornaments to the inner attachment brackets;

— back out the four nuts and two screws securing the body rear end lower panel and remove the latter (fig. 17).

The engine is now free and may be taken out (fig. 18).

The installation of engine does not involve any particular difficulty. Reverse the instructions outlined for removal. Utmost care must be taken in joining engine to gearbox-differential unit: the clutch shaft must be inserted into splined hub of driven member.

ENGINE DISASSEMBLY

For an easier performance of engine disassembly operations, engine should be placed on revolving stand **Arr. 2204** and secured with clamps **Arr. 2205/3** (figs. 19 and 22).

Operate as follows.

Arrange a suitable tray and remove the drain plug from oil pan, leaving lubrication oil to drain out thoroughly.

Drain the coolant from cylinder block, by screwing up the tap underneath the water pump.

Loosen both nuts securing generator mounting bracket to crankcase and slide off water pump and generator drive belts.

Disconnect: generator and generator bracket, water pump including fan and air conveyor (after sliding off water line from cylinder head connection - use wrench **A. 50013** to loosen collar retainer), by-pass oil filter and clutch from flywheel.

Slide off or remove: vent pipes, fuel pump-to-carburetor pipe, vacuum advance pipe, spark plug, ignition distributor and excessive water temperature warning light sending unit cables.

Disconnect: air cleaner and ignition system wiring harness assembly, carburetor, fuel pump (slide off the control rod) and the ignition distributor and vacuum advance assembly.

Slide off the oil dip stick.

Disconnect: cylinder head cover, exhaust manifold (using wrench **A. 8110**), rocker arm and shaft assembly, excessive water temperature warning light sending unit, oil pressure relief valve,

Fig. 19.

Engine installed on rotating stand.

Timing sprocket end view.

1. Rotating stand Arr. 2204. - 2. Arms Arr. 2205/3.

low oil pressure indicator sending unit and cylinder head water outlet elbow.

Slide off rocker arm push rods.

Disconnect: cylinder head (use socket **A. 8302** to withdraw center hold down screw) and gasket, then the oil pan from crankcase.

Using wrench **A. 50022**, remove spark plugs from cylinder head.

Turn the twin beams **Arr. 2204/1** of revolving stand by 180°, so to reverse the engine.

Disconnect: timing gear cover (after removing generator drive drive pulley), oil pump and shaft assembly, flywheel, flywheel end cover and crankshaft oil seal.

NOTE - To prevent the flywheel from rotating as crankshaft screws are removed, arrange tool **A. 60165** as shown in fig. 20.

Fig. 20 - Tool A. 60165 for flywheel retainment during installation on crankshaft.

1. Tool A. 60165. - 2. Flywheel.

Flywheel-to-crankshaft screws should be drawn up with 25.3 to 28.9 ft.lbs (3.500 to 4.000 kgmm) of torque.

Remove the timing gear and chain.

Turn the twin beams of revolving stand by 90°, so to set the cylinder block right side up.

Remove connecting rod bearing caps and rod bearing halves.

Slide off four piston-ring-pin-connecting rod and bearing assemblies.

Fig. 21 - Removing timing drive sprocket with universal puller.
1. Universal puller A. 40005. - 2. Timing sprocket.

Again, turn over the engine and set it upside down.

Remove main bearing caps, main bearing cap halves and thrust rings from center bearing cap.

Remove crankshaft and withdraw bearing halves from crankcase seats and thrust rings from center bearing.

NOTE - During engine disassembly and overhaul operations, take care to keep each set of rod and main bearings separately.

Remove camshaft chain side bushing dowel screw and withdraw camshaft and bushing. Center and flywheel end camshaft bushings are still in place on crankcase. Prior to removing these bushings, perform inspections as outlined on page 61.

Slide off tappets from tappet seats.

Unfasten the cylinder block-crankcase unit from revolving stand and advance it to the washing tank as outlined on page 27 under « Cleaning ».

NOTE - If necessary, remove the timing gear from crankshaft using all-purpose puller A. 40005.

ENGINE ASSEMBLY

Secure the crankcase to service revolving stand **Arr. 2204**, using clamps **Arr. 2205/3**.

If they had been removed, install on crankcase: both transmission case dowels, both crankshaft oil seal cover dowels, flywheel end, oil pressure relief valve components, the breather tube.

Install camshaft center and flywheel end bushings. Bushings should be press fitted into bores and reamed.

NOTE - For installation of bushings, follow procedure outlined on page 59.

Rotate the cylinder block on stand and set it upside down.

Thoroughly clean main bearing bores and inserts and position main bearing inserts in crankcase bores.

Install crankshaft, laying it on three bearings.

Install both thrust ring halves on center bearing. Ring babbitt coated side should be turned toward shaft shoulders.

Fit the center bearing cap together with the other two thrust ring halves and remaining two bearing caps.

Check clearance between main bearing halves and journals, as outlined on page 46.

When clearance has been set within assembly specifications, oil bearing halves and journals liberally.

Tighten main bearing cap screws with 44.8 ft.lbs (6.200 kgmm) of torque and secure screws with lock plates.

Attach connecting rods with pistons as outlined on page 42, install piston rings using ring installer **A. 10114** and set ring gaps 120° reciprocally apart.

With a brush, oil pistons and rings, then fit band **A. 60078**, which should be tightened just to allow piston to slide in.

Working from top of cylinder block, insert four connecting rod-piston-ring assemblies into cylinder bores.

Connecting rod identification number, to match with cylinder barrel, should be turned toward the camshaft.

Rotate the cylinder block on service stand and set it again upside down.

Slide in valve tappets.

NOTE - Rod bearing-to-crankpin journal clearance has been inspected previously with crankshaft on work bench, as directed on page 37.

Clean connecting rod bearing bores and inserts and position connecting rod bearing inserts in bores.

Oil connecting rod bearing inserts and crankpin journals liberally.

Fig. 22.
Engine installed on rotating stand.
Flywheel end view (clutch installed).

1. Rotating stand Arr. 2204. - 2. Arms Arr. 2205/3.

Fit connecting rod bearing caps and draw up cap screw nuts with 16 ft.lbs (2.200 kgmm) of torque, using a torque wrench.

See that connecting rod big end can move freely on journal.

Fit chain end bushing on camshaft and slide camshaft into crankcase bore and center and flywheel end bushings which have been installed previously.

Chain end bushing should be positioned in a way that the hole on the bushing is lined up with the hole on crankcase. When the bushing has been centered correctly, tighten relevant dowel screw.

Try the camshaft through some turns to make sure that it rotates freely on bushings.

Install the oil seal cover assembly, flywheel end, on crankshaft, with the gasket between crankcase and cover.

Install flywheel and draw up screws with 25.3 to 28.9 ft.lbs (3.500 to 4.000 kgmm) of torque, using a torque wrench. Secure screws with lock plates.

Fit gasket and assemble the oil pump, taking care to mesh pump drive shaft gear with camshaft gear. To facilitate assembly, smear the shaft gear end and the gear with FIAT Jota 3 grease.

Secure the oil pump to the crankcase and check the camshaft for free rotation and correct fit with the pump shaft.

Fit the timing chain to the camshaft driven gear and slide the driven gear on to the camshaft while engaging the chain on the drive gear.

Secure the gear to the camshaft by means of screw, plain washer and lock plate. Bend down the lock plate on the screw. Screw tightening torque: 38.3 ft.lbs (5.300 kgmm).

Place the timing gear cover gasket on crankcase and install the timing gear cover, complete with the crankshaft oil seal. Secure the cover with cover screws.

Force the drive pulley on to the crankshaft and secure with nut and lock plate.

Fit both oil pan gaskets on crankcase edge. Position flywheel end and chain end gaskets in place on oil pan, install the oil pan and secure with screws, lock plate and toothed washers.

Rotate the engine on service stand and set it right side up.

Fit the head gasket on crankcase and install the cylinder head assembly, including: valves, valve guides, valve springs, water outlet elbow, engine-to-water pump circuit connection, exhaust manifold and carburetor spacer with fuel discharge tube.

Secure the cylinder head, tightening in the order and at the torque recommended on page 56. The long screw in also to retain the excessive water temperature indicator sending unit on head (the plug-in socket should be turned toward the center engine bearing and the sending unit centerline should be parallel with the engine centerline). The short screw must be inserted inside the carburetor spacer.

Along with the screws are fitted the copper washer, in touch with the cylinder head, and the plain washer.

Install the rocker arm shaft assembly and secure with nuts, toothed washers and plain washers. Recommended torque of shaft support nuts: $14\frac{1}{2}$ ft.lbs (2.000 kgmm). Adjust valve tappet clearance as outlined on page 57.

Install the oil filter.

Fit the carburetor gasket, the carburetor shield, the other gasket and eventually the carburetor on carburetor spacer. Secure with nuts and toothed washers.

Install the water pump assembly, including fan, air conveyor, pulley and engine ground cable (which is located between the top screw and washer securing conveyor to water pump; conveyor screw tightening torque 18.1 ft.lbs (2.500 kgmm).

Place both seals between water pump and crankcase and secure with screws and plain washers.

Slide fuel pump drive rod into crankcase seat. Install the fuel pump, with interposition of gasket, insulator and second gasket. Secure the fuel pump with screws and toothed washers.

Install the generator, fit belt and tighten nuts.

Insert the distributor drive shaft and, after arranging the sector scale **C. 661**, set the timing mark on flywheel at 10° advance on scale.

Connect ignition cables with distributor cap and set distributor breaker with points beginning to open. Secure ignition distributor to cylinder head; the distributor screw is also to lock the fuel line clamp.

Install the fuel line and connect it to the fuel pump and carburetor. For easier mating of fuel line with connectors, just heat the length of line which will thread in. Tighten the fuel line-to-pump clip.

Install spark plugs and connect with distributor cables.

Install the cover gasket and place on cylinder head cover.

Fit vent sleeves and vacuum advance tube.

NOTE - Prior to tying the engine to transmission in place on vehicle, secure the clutch, including the driven plate, to the flywheel and fit the upper dust shield.

CYLINDER BLOCK AND CRANKCASE

Cleaning	page	27
Checking Barrel Wear	»	27
Reconditioning Cylinder Barrels	»	29
Reboring with Stationary Reamer	»	29
Reboring with Portable Reamer	»	30
Checking and Grinding Cylinder Head Seating Face	»	31
Checking Camshaft Bushing Seats and Bushings	»	31
Checking for Wear and Reaming Tappet Seats	»	31
Lining Cylinder Barrels	»	31

The cylinder block is one iron casting with the crankcase. Camshaft bushing bores, main bearing bores as well as valve tappet holes are machined on crankcase.

On crankcase are also machined jackets for coolant circulation and proper mountings for fuel pump, oil filter, water pump, oil pump and ignition distributor drive shaft, oil vapour settling chamber, oil dip stick, oil pressure relief valve and oil gauge sending unit.

Cleaning.

After the engine has been disassembled, clean the cylinder block-crankcase unit by immersing it into a wash tank containing a water and soda solution which has been heated to 176° to 185° F (80° to 85° C).

Next raise the block and, using a pump, submit it to a heavy jet of this solution to remove all oil sediments, calcar deposits and dirt from oil passages.

Place the cylinder block on service stand and complete cleaning by scraping any carbon deposits which may still be present on cylinder head mating surface.

Thoroughly blow the cylinder block and especially the internal oil passages with compressed air.

Checking Barrel Wear.

Inspect cylinder barrels: if light scoring marks are found, a reconditioning by very fine emery cloth wrapped around reamer will suffice.

Once this operation is over, check if clearance between maximum piston diameter and barrel

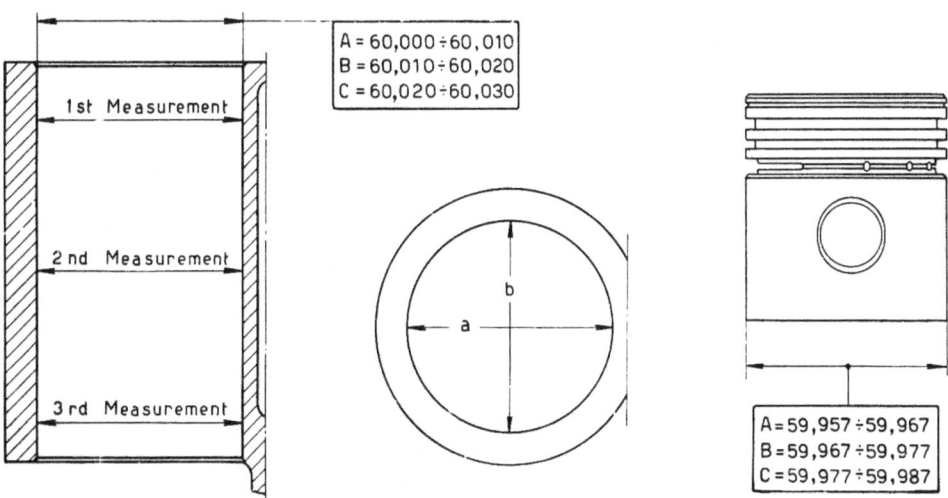

Fig. 23 - Diagram for checking cylinder and piston diameters.

(fig. 36) is still within maximun allowable limit of .0059" (0,15 mm).

The measurement of barrel diameter must be taken lengthwise and crosswise at three different heights (fig. 23).

The dial indicator must first be set to zero using ring gauge **C. 631**.

If max. wear or ovalization does not exceed .0059" (0,15 mm) barrels may be honed, otherwise they must be rebored.

Fig. 25 - Crankcase bottom view.
Arrows point to the letters stamped on crankcase bottom edge to indicate the barrel class in relation to diameter.

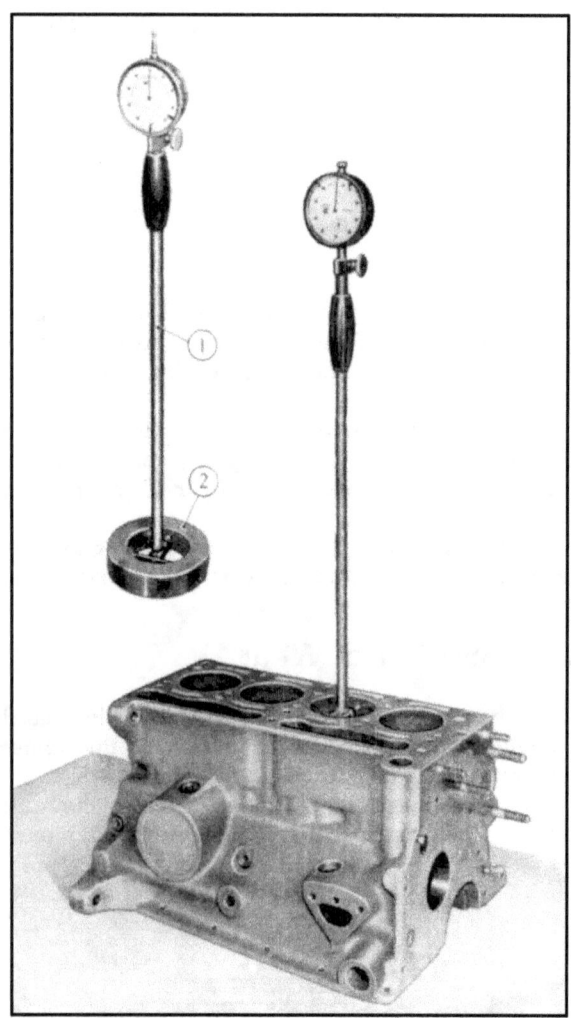

Fig. 24 - Measuring cylinder barrel diameter.
1. Dial indicator C. 687. - 2. Ring gauge C. 631 for dial indicator setting.

Both honing and reboring operations must be carried out to the values corresponding to spare piston oversizes, to ensure correct clearance between parts, i. e., .0013" to .0021" (0,033 to 0,053 mm) as tabulated on page 29.

As may be seen in the table, cylinder barrels are subdivided into three classes depending on their diameters: identification code letters A, B and C, must be stamped on crankcase lower edge near the cylinder to which they refer (fig. 25).

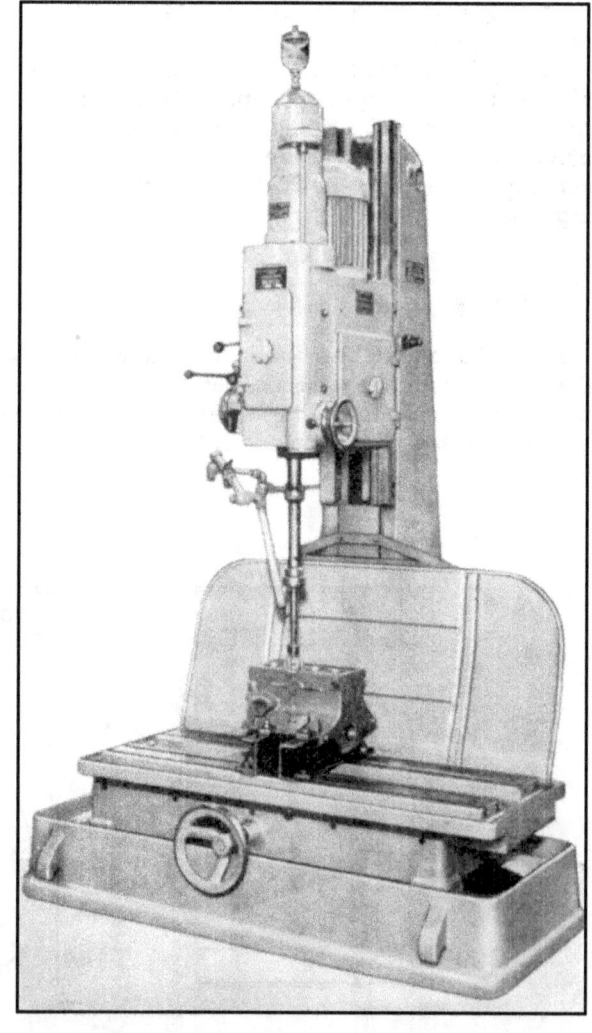

Fig. 26 - Grinding the cylinder on stationary grinder.

ENGINE: CYLINDER BLOCK AND CRANKCASE

CYLINDER BARREL DIAMETERS AND PISTON OVERSIZE DIAMETERS MATCHING DATA

OVERSIZE	CLASS	PISTON DIAMETER (at skirt bottom on axis perpendicular to pin)	CYLINDER BARREL DIAMETER	FIT CLEARANCE
Standard	A	2.3605" to 2.3609" (59,957 to 59,967 mm)	2.3622" to 2.3626" (60,000 to 60,010 mm)	.0013" to .0021" (0,033 to 0,053 mm)
	B	2.3609" to 2.3613" (59,967 to 59,977 mm)	2.3626" to 2.3630" (60,010 to 60,020 mm)	
	C	2.3613" to 2.3617" (59,977 to 59,987 mm)	2.3630" to 2.3634" (60,020 to 60,030 mm)	
.0078" (0,2 mm)	A	2.3684" to 2.3688" (60,157 to 60,167 mm)	2.3701" to 2.3705" (60,200 to 60,210 mm)	.0013" to .0021" (0,033 to 0,053 mm)
	B	2.3688" to 2.3692" (60,167 to 60,177 mm)	2.3705" to 2.3709" (60,210 to 60,220 mm)	
	C	2.3692" to 2.3696" (60,177 to 60,187 mm)	2.3709" to 2.3713" (60,220 to 60,230 mm)	
.0157" (0,4 mm)	A	2.3762" to 2.3766" (60,357 to 60,367 mm)	2.3779" to 2.3783" (60,400 to 60,410 mm)	.0013" to .0021" (0,033 to 0,053 mm)
	B	2.3766" to 2.3770" (60,367 to 60,377 mm)	2.3783" to 2.3787" (60,410 to 60,420 mm)	
	C	2.3770" to 2.3774" (60,377 to 60,387 mm)	2.3787" to 2.3791" (60,420 to 60,430 mm)	
.0236" (0,6 mm)	A	2.3841" to 2.3845" (60,557 to 60,567 mm)	2.3858" to 2.3862" (60,600 to 60,610 mm)	.0013" to .0021" (0,033 to 0,053 mm)
	B	2.3845" to 2.3849" (60,567 to 60,577 mm)	2.3862" to 2.3866" (60,610 to 60,620 mm)	
	C	2.3849" to 2.3853" (60,577 to 60,587 mm)	2.3866" to 2.3870" (60,620 to 60,630 mm)	
.0315" (0,8 mm)	A	2.3920" to 2.3924" (60,757 to 60,767 mm)	2.3937" to 2.3941" (60,800 to 60,810 mm)	.0013" to .0021" (0,033 to 0,053 mm)
	B	2.3924" to 2.3928" (60,767 to 60,777 mm)	2.3941" to 2.3945" (60,810 to 60,820 mm)	
	C	2.3928" to 2.3932" (60,777 to 60,787 mm)	2.3945" to 2.3949" (60,820 to 60,830 mm)	

Also pistons are subdivided into three classes. Therefore, every barrel and relevant piston must always be of the same class.

Max. reconditioning limit for barrels is .0315" (0,8 mm), after which barrels must be lined.

For details, refer to relevant chapter on page 31.

Reconditioning Cylinder Barrels.

When stock to be removed is not excessive, for instance .0059" (0,15 mm), lapping is sufficient.

After taking suitable measurements to establish the exact diameter to which barrels must be lapped, install and clamp the cylinder block on fixture on lapping machine table.

Lap barrels first with a set of medium-grain stones, then with a fine-grain stone set.

To obtain best possible smoothness, polish with very fine grade emery cloth wrapped around the honing tool.

Lapping must be carried out on all cylinders.

Reboring with Stationary Reamer.

If barrel wear is greater than .0059" (0,15 mm) cylinders must be rebored on a stationary reamer.

Install crankcase on reamer table and proceed as follows:

Insert the spindle tool holder head in barrel. This head is provided with a centering device (fig. 28) consisting of a lever linked to a dial gauge.

Lower tool carrier head into barrel while keeping the plunger depressed with fingers to prevent its striking against cylinder edge. Stop head when

Fig. 27 - Detail of cylinder barrel grinding.

plunger reaches the spot chosen for trueing, start tool spindle at minimum speed and check trueing on dial gauge (fig. 30).

By the horizontal table control handwheel reduce dial pointer fluctuations to a minimum and then, by the other handwheel, stabilize pointer on zero read-

Fig. 28 - Centering cylinder barrel before grinding.
1. Centering plunger. - 2. Tool projection adjustment screw.

ing or, in case barrel is out-of-true, bring reading down to the out-of-true value.

Having thus centered the spindle, lock table in position by its control lever; next, raise tool head, remove dial plunger and by the tool setting device adjust tool to the diameter chosen.

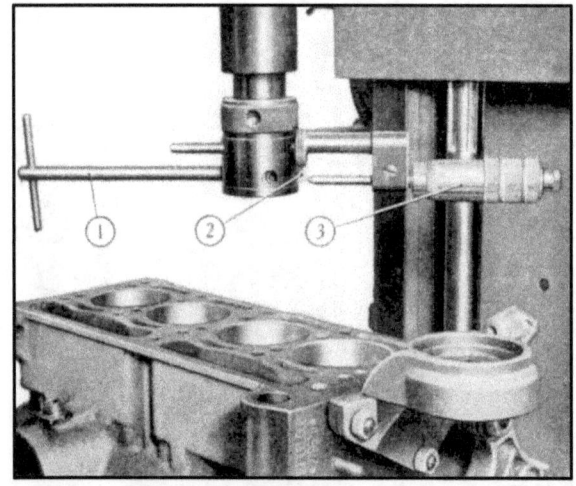

Fig. 29 - Measuring tool projection for barrel grinding.
1. Wrench for tool projection adjustment. - 2. Tool. - 3. Micrometer.

The tool setting device consists of a micrometric gauge having a long anvil which must be inserted in tool head up to the micrometer screw (fig. 29).

Holding gauge well against tool head, by turning gauge slowly bring its measuring plunger in contact with tool tip.

The micrometer reading plus the constant figure marked on tool head will give immediately the diameter obtainable with tool as it has been set.

To prevent clogging by boring cast-iron dust, the micrometer anvil hole in tool is blanked by a plug which should be removed only with the special wrench provided in the tool kit.

Tool adjustment to the desired diameter figure is controlled by screws; screws are also provided to lock tool in position.

Once tool has been set as described, start machine into operation.

When reboring is completed and .0015" to .0019" (0,04 to 0,05 mm) of stock has been left, hone and polish with very fine grade abrasives as described previously.

Fig. 30 - Cylinder reboring on stationary machine.

Reboring with Portable Reamer.

Install portable reamer M. 111 on cylinder block and lower into barrel the centering head fitted to reaming bar.

Expand head blades, center spindle to barrel, then set reamer on cylinder block.

As described previously, take measurements to determine to which diameter the barrel must be brought.

Adjust tool and set reamer into operation. After reaming, polish as already described.

ENGINE: CYLINDER BLOCK AND CRANKCASE

Checking and Grinding Cylinder Head Seating Face.

The cylinder block to cylinder head faying surface may be found deformed: hence, it is advisable to check its flatness by coating a surface plate with lampblack and dragging cylinder head along the coating. Spots needing grinding will thus show clearly.

The grinding of seating face should be done on a surface grinder.

If not available, filing will do.

Operate in such a way as to obtain proper flatness by removing the least possible amount of material.

NOTE - Cylinder head mating surface can be also inspected for level using a straightedge and a feeler gauge as shown in fig. 31.

Straightedge should be placed at both diagonal lines of cylinder block face; also centrally, in longitudinal direction.

Checking Camshaft Bushing Seats and Bushings.

Camshaft center and flywheel end bushings are installed into seat in crankcase with a **pinch fit**, whereas **clearance** is left when installing chain end bushing.

Center and flywheel end bushings are selected into three classes according to their outer diameter: A, B and C. The same applies to their crankcase seats. Whenever bushings are serviced, see that there is always pinch fit between parts to prevent bushings from floating in their bores in operation.

Moreover, check the inside face of bushings for wear and make sure that clearance between bushings and camshaft supports is not in excess of limits specified on page 61.

For procedure relating to this inspection and fitting specifications, see page 59 under the heading « Camshaft ».

Checking for Wear and Reaming Tappet Seats.

If while servicing the engine an excessive tappet-to-seat wear is noticed (.0031" - 0,08 mm) this calls for a reconditioning which must be carried out as follows:

— measure tappet seat diameter to find out the exact amount of reaming required. In fact, tappets are supplied as spares in two oversizes: .0020" and .0039" (0,05 and 0,10 mm).

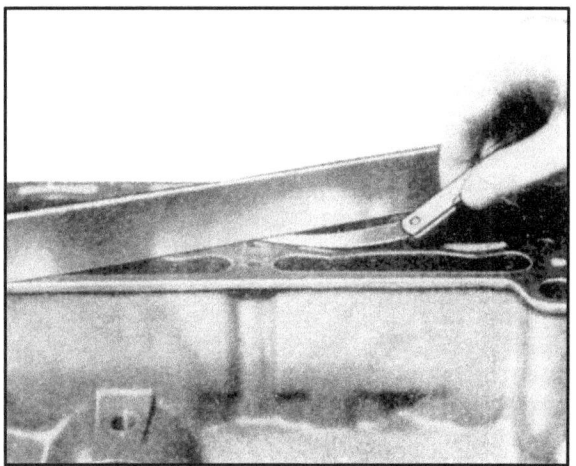

Fig. 31 - Checking crankcase top face.

If tappets to be fitted are .0020" (0,05 mm) oversize use reamer **U. 0318/1** while for the .0039" (0,10 mm) oversize tappets use reamer **U. 0318/2** (fig. 32).

By proceeding as outlined above, the recommended .00039" to .0018" (0,010 to 0,046 mm) clearance will be obtained.

For further data on tappets, refer to the relevant paragraph on page 63.

Lining Cilinder Barrels.

Max. reboring allowable for a cylinder in excess of standard diameter, also in relation to piston oversizes, is .0315" (0,8 mm).

Fig. 32 - Reaming pushrod seats with reamer U. 0318/1 (1st oversizing) or U. 0318/2 (2nd oversizing).

When this limit must necessarily be exceeded, the lining of cylinder barrels must be carried out in accordance with the following:

— rebore cylinder barrels to a diameter of 2.5169″ to 2.5177″ (63,93 to 63,95 mm) (fig. 34);

— press fit liners: these must have an O. D. of 2.4803″ to 2.5204″ (64,000 to 64,018 mm) and an I. D. of 2.3425″ to 2.3499″ (59,500 to 59,690 mm) (fig. 33);

— grind and polish liners: bring I. D. to 2,3622″ to 2.3634″ (60,000 to 60,030 mm) at the same time bearing in mind the classes - as for the standard crankcases - that is:

A = 2.3622″ to 2.3626″   (60,000 to 60,010 mm);
B = 2.3626″ to 2.3630″   (60,010 to 60,020 mm);
C = 2.3630″ to 2.3634″   (60,020 to 60,030 mm);

— hone slightly the cylinder block top after press-fitting the liners.

Liners must be press-fitted using an arbor with the aid of plate **A. 60082**, after cylinder walls and the outer face of liners have been oiled.

By fitting the liners, standard piston may again be used and subsequently, up to a max. wear of .0315″ (0,8 mm), oversize pistons can be used following a reboring of liners.

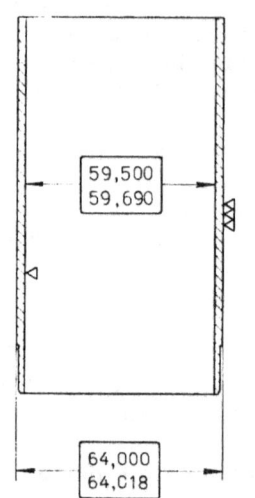

Fig. 33.
I. D. and O. D. of spare liner before assembly.

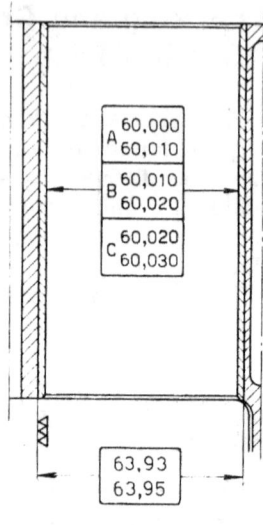

Fig. 34.
Barrel diameter for installation of spare liner and liner I. D. to be obtained after assembly.

Liners are also supplied as spares oversized by .00157″ (0,04 mm) on the outer diameter: 2.5212″ to 2.5220″ (64,040 to 64,058 mm).

Fit clearance between liner and barrel should be: .0019″ to .0035″ (0,050 to 0,088 mm).

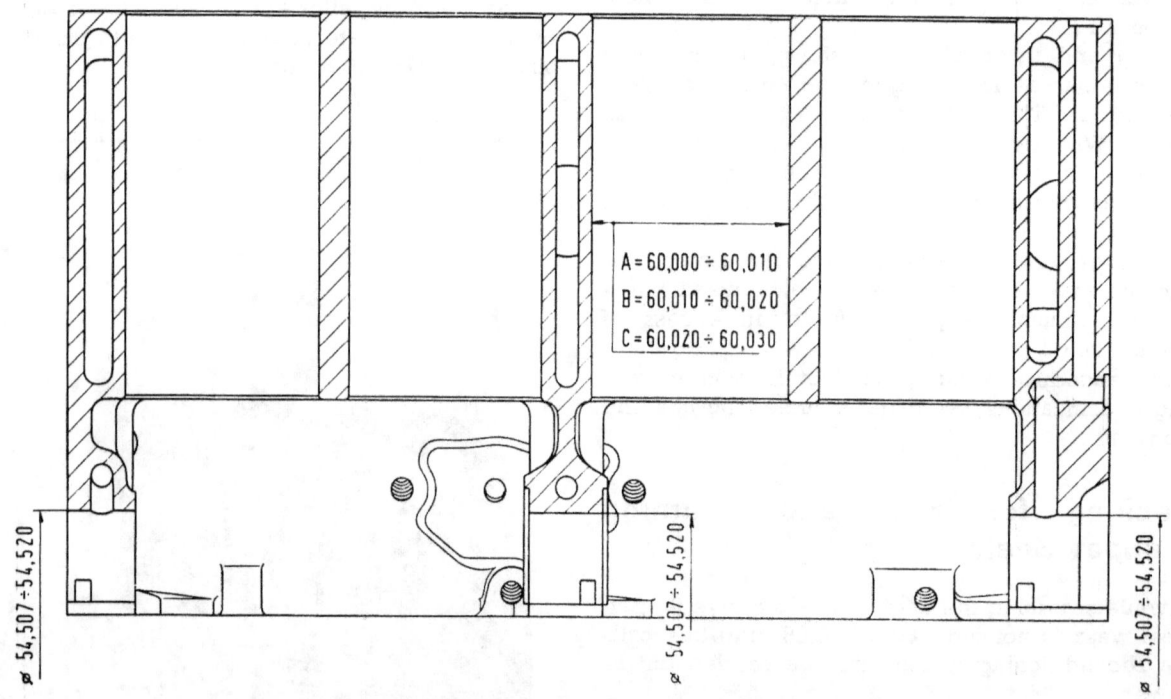

Fig. 35 - Longitudinal section of crankcase through cylinder barrels.

ENGINE: PISTONS - PINS - RINGS

PISTONS - PINS - RINGS

Cleaning, Inspection and Repair . . . . page 33
Installation . . . . » 36

Light alloy pistons are of the flat top, oval taper design.

Max. diameter is at skirt base on axis perpendicular to piston pin hole.

Also pistons, as liners, are subdivided into three classes, based on their skirt diameter: A, B and C (fig. 37); pistons must always be fitted in liners of the same class.

First compression ring and second oil scraper ring are of special cast iron; third radialslot oil scraper ring is of steel.

Steel piston pin. Fit clearance between barrel and piston, measured on axis perpendicular to piston pin bore, must be:

— at skirt top: .0025" to .0033" (0,065 to 0,085 mm);

— at skirt bottom: .0013" to .0020" (0,033 to 0,053 mm).

When servicing pistons, always remember to decarbonize piston tops, ring grooves and rings; check barrel to piston clearances which must never exceed .0059" (0,15 mm); if clearance is greater, in which case liners need reboring, install oversized pistons.

As spares, pistons are supplied in the following oversize classes:

.0078"   .0157"   .0236"   .0315"
(0,2 mm) (0,4 mm) (0,6 mm) (0,8 mm)

Fig. 36 - Checking piston-to-barrel clearance with feeler gauge C. 316.

Cleaning, Inspection and Repair.

Piston skirt wear must always be added to barrel (or liner) wear to find the actual clearance between the two parts.

Clearance may be checked either by measuring piston and barrel diameters or by using one of the blades of feeler gauge **C 316** (fig. 36).

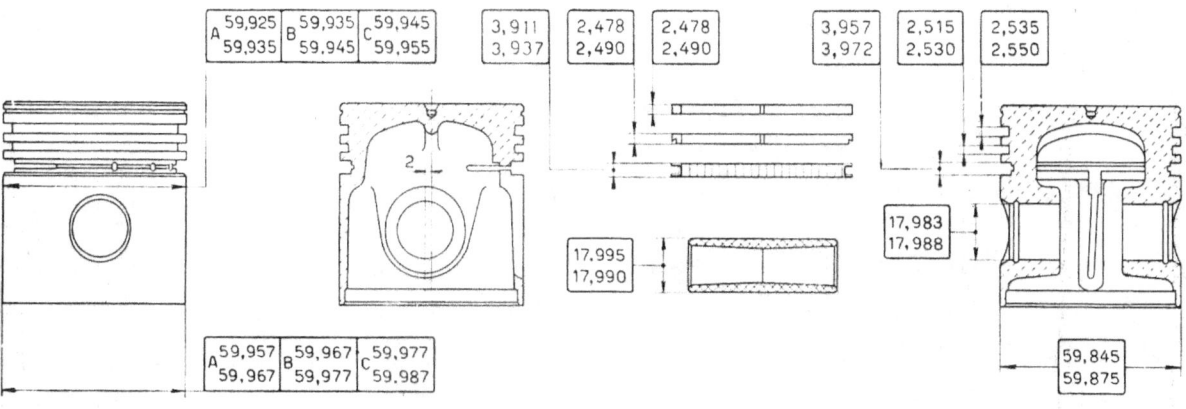

Fig. 37 - Piston, piston pin and piston rings main data.

Fig. 38 - Checking piston ring-to-groove clearance with gauge C. 316.

When pistons need not be replaced, check ring-to-groove clearance (fig. 38) after decarbonizing, and make sure it still falls within the values tabulated on page 35.

Before fitting rings on pistons, with the specially designed installer **A. 10114**, it is essential to place rings in cylinder to check gap clearance (fig. 39) which must result as tabulated on page 35; should this not be true, a reconditioning must be carried out using grinder **A. 10650** (fig. 40). If found necessary, replace.

The slotted oilscraper ring ends must instead be in contact.

The first two rings are supplied as spares in the same oversize classes as pistons, i. e.:

.0078"   .0157"   .0236"   .0315"
(0,2 mm) (0,4 mm) (0,6 mm) (0,8 mm)

The radially slotted oilscraper ring is supplied also in the .0157" (0,4 mm) oversizes.

Check that piston pin-to-boss is a pinch fit assembly. Should a clearance be found, restore bore roundness using expansible reamer **U. 0320** to adapt bore to oversize of piston pin being installed (fig. 41).

Pins are supplied as spares with .0078" and .0197" (0,2 and 0,5 mm) O. D.

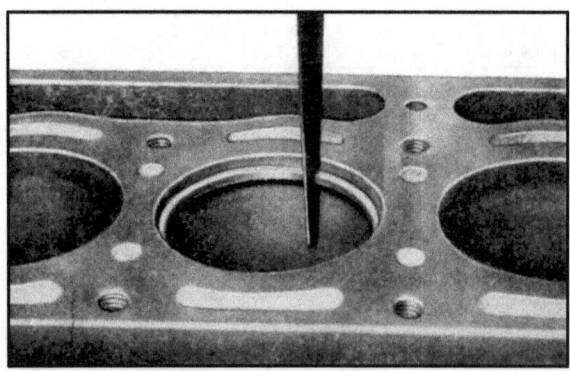

Fig. 39 - Checking ring gap, with ring in cylinder, using feeler gauge C. 316.

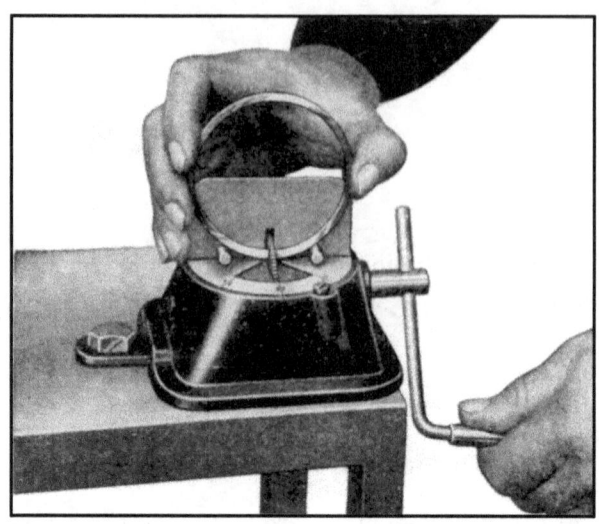

Fig. 40 - Grinding piston ring ends with grinder A. 10650.

PISTON PIN OUTER DIAMETERS

Standard	Oversizes	
	.0078" (0,2 mm)	.0197" (0,5 mm)
.7085" (17,995 mm)	.7164" (18,196 mm)	.7282" (18,496 mm)
.7084" (17,990 mm)	.7162" (18,190 mm)	.7280" (18,490 mm)

Pin-to-bore pinch fit must be: .000078" to .00051" (0,002 to 0,013 mm).

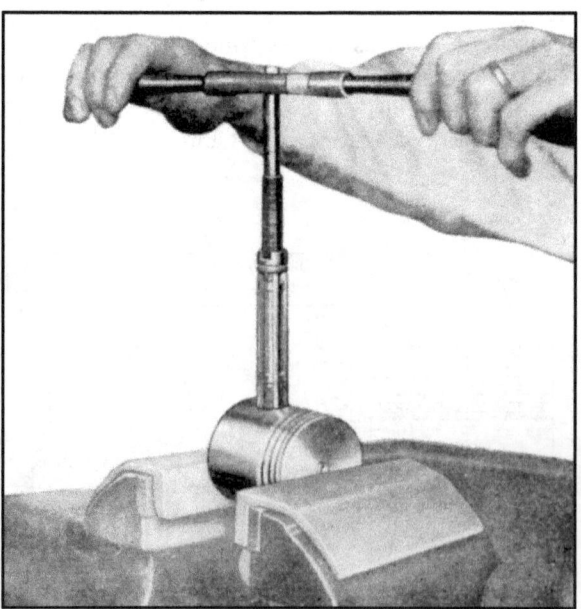

Fig. 41 - Reboring piston boss by means of expansible reamer U. 0320.

ENGINE: PISTONS - PINS - RINGS

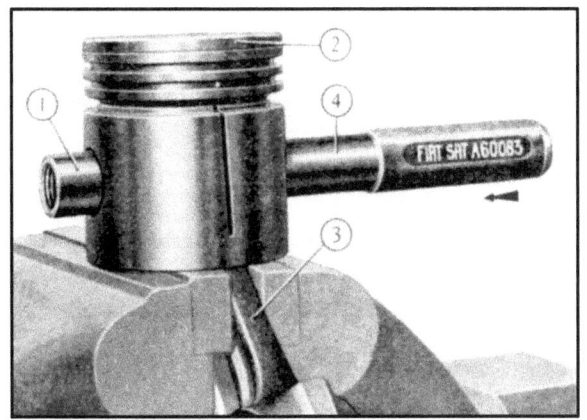

Fig. 42 - Removing piston with striker A. 60083.
1. Piston pin. - 2. Piston. - 3. Connecting rod. - 4. Striker A. 60083 for pin installation and removal.

Install pins after heating pistons in an oven or in hot water at 176° F (80° C) to expand boss bore and facilitate pin insertion.

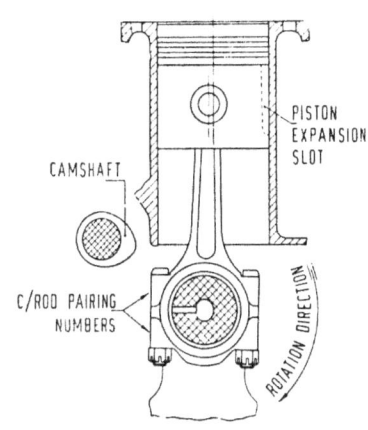

Fig. 44.
Diagram for connecting-rod-piston set matching and installation in engine.

To install and remove pins, use special striker A. 60083 (fig. 42).

The four pistons installed in an engine must have the same weight within a tolerance of .14 oz (4 grams) otherwise engine running balance is compromised.

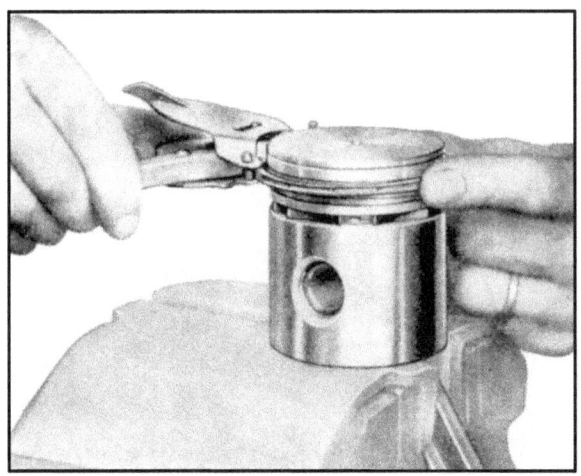

Fig. 43 - Fitting piston rings with installer A. 10114.

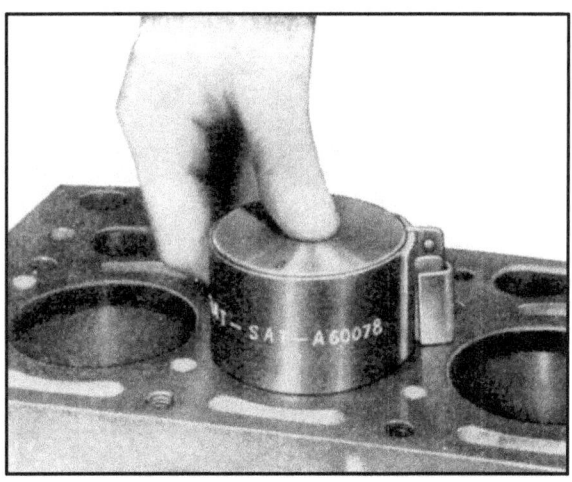

Fig. 45 - Inserting piston in barrel with inserter A. 60078.

PISTONS - PISTON RINGS - PINS AND CYLINDER BARRELS DATA

	FIT CLEARANCES	WEAR LIMITS
Piston diameter to cylinder barrel, on plane perpendicular to pin:		
— at skirt top	.0025″ to .0033″ (0,065 to 0,085 mm)	.0098″ (0,25 mm)
— at skirt bottom	.0013″ to .0020″ (0,033 to 0,053 mm)	.0059″ (0,15 mm)
Piston pin-to-bore	Pinch fit of .0078″ to .0005″ (0,02 to 0,013 mm) at all times	—
Rings-to-groove lands:		
— 1st ring: compression	.0017″ to .0028″ (0,045 to 0,072 mm)	.0059″ (0,15 mm)
— 2nd ring: oilscraper	.0010″ to .0020″ (0,025 to 0,052 mm)	.0059″ (0,15 mm)
— 3rd ring: oilscraper with radial slots	.00078″ to .0024″ (0,020 to 0,061 mm)	.0059″ (0,15 mm)
Ring gap, with rings in barrel { compression and oilscraper	.0078″ to .0137″ (0,20 to 0,35 mm)	.0197″ (0,50 mm)
{ radially slotted oilscraper	none	—

Installation.

Piston must always be installed with slot turned toward engine right side (as seen from timing drive end), i. e. on side opposite the camshaft (fig. 44).

The installation of pistons is facilitated by using piston inserter **A. 60078** (fig. 45) which keeps rings tight in their grooves.

To match pistons with connecting rods, see instructions under « Connecting Rods » (page 37); the piston-connecting rod set must be checked for correct alignment on fixture **C. 627**: if any incorrectness is found, check connecting rod ends center-to-center parallelism as directed on page 41.

Pistons must always be removed or installed from cylinder block top, otherwise the operation will be impeded by crankshaft supports.

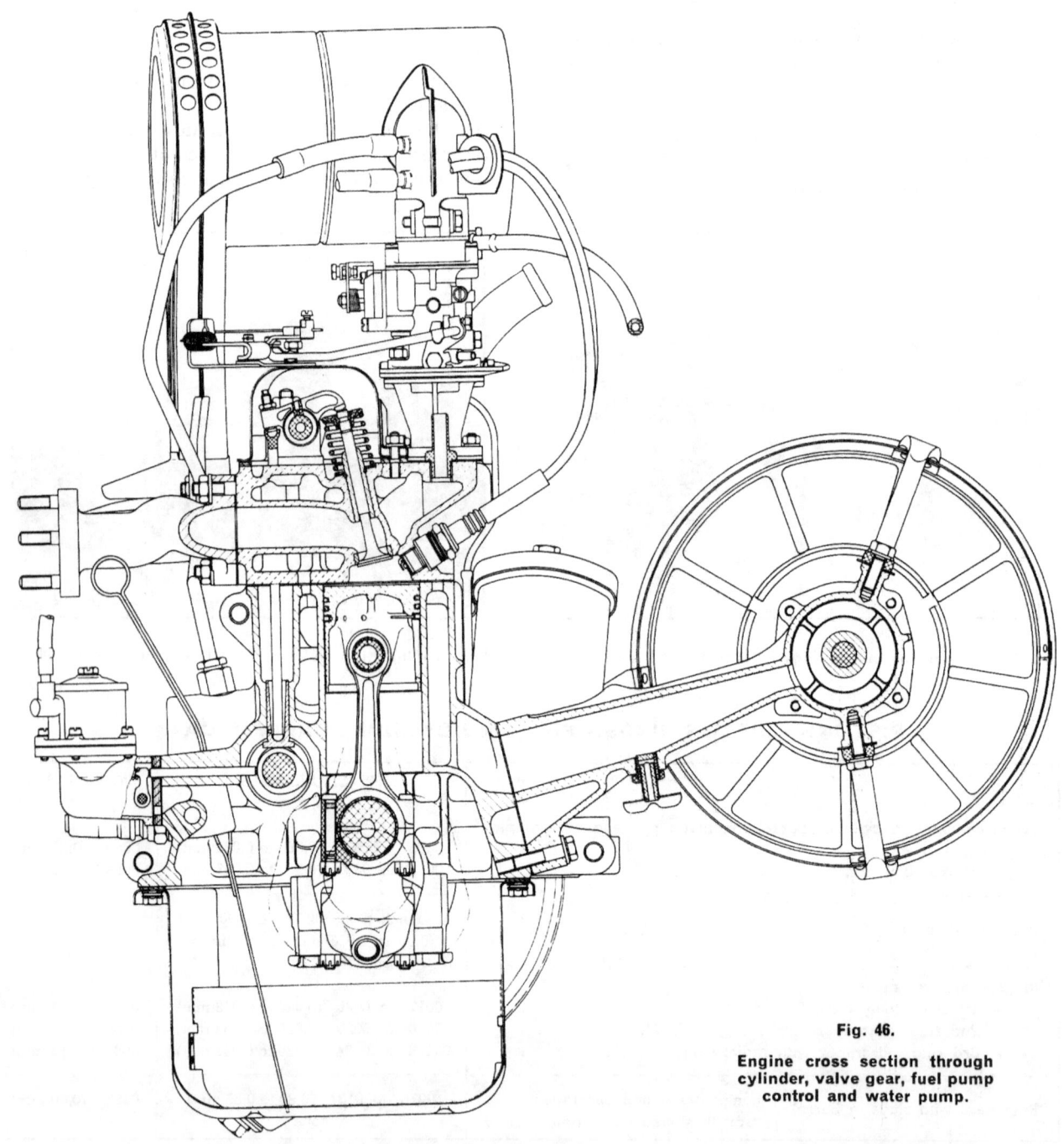

Fig. 46.

Engine cross section through cylinder, valve gear, fuel pump control and water pump.

ENGINE: CONNECTING RODS AND ROD BEARINGS

CONNECTING RODS AND ROD BEARINGS

Checking Rod Bearings and Bearing-to-Crankpin Journal Clearance . . . . page 37
Connecting Rod Identification . . . . » 39
Checking and Replacing Bushes . . . . » 39
Checking Connecting Rod Weight . . . . » 40
Checking Alignment . . . . » 41
Piston-Connecting Rod Assembly and Installation . . . . » 42

Connecting rods must be checked for:

— condition of bearings and clearance of bearings to crankpins;
— condition of bushes and clearance of bushings to piston pins;
— weight;
— alignment of big end to small end bores.

Checking Rod Bearings and Bearing-to-Crankpin Journal Clearance.

Examine the internal face of bearing halves. If light scratches are noticed, it will be possible to remove them using an extremely refined grinding wheel. Conversely, should bearings show deep notches or evident signs of wear, they must be replaced. As a matter of fact, according to a well known motoring service rule, it is not possible refacing babbitt layer in thin wall bearings.

After bearing halves have been ascertained to be in good condition, inspect clearance between rod bearings and crankpin journals.

A new method of bearing clearance inspection has been lately introduced in workshop procedure, namely the « Plastigage » calibrated thread, for replacement of cigarette paper method.

Clearance is determined through the amount of thread flattening.

« Plastigage » calibrated thread is supplied in several diameters according to the value of clearance

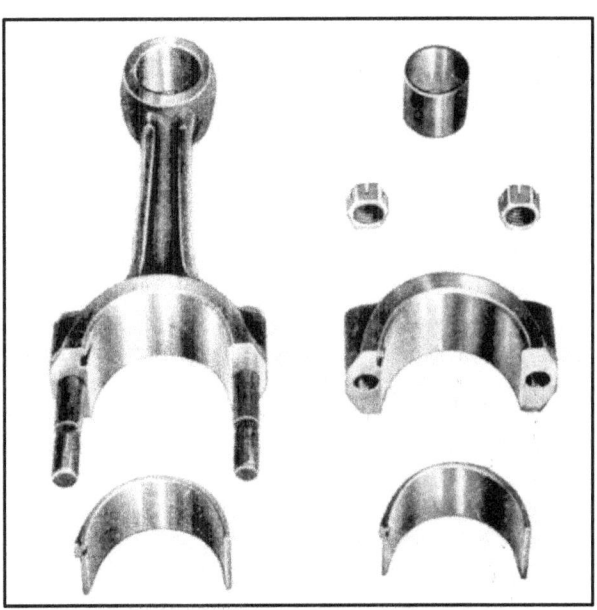

Fig. 47 - Detail of connecting rod.

under inspection. Thread is contained in proper envelopes (fig. 48) on which the following data are stamped: the type of thread, the clearance range and the graduation scale of the flattened strip at its widest point, to determine the amount of clearance.

To check clearance, proceed as follows:

— wipe the oil from all crankpin journals and rod bearing inserts;

CALIBRATED STRIP

Fig. 48 - « Plastigage » calibrated strip for bearing insert-to-crankpin journal clearance inspection, and envelope with graduation scale.

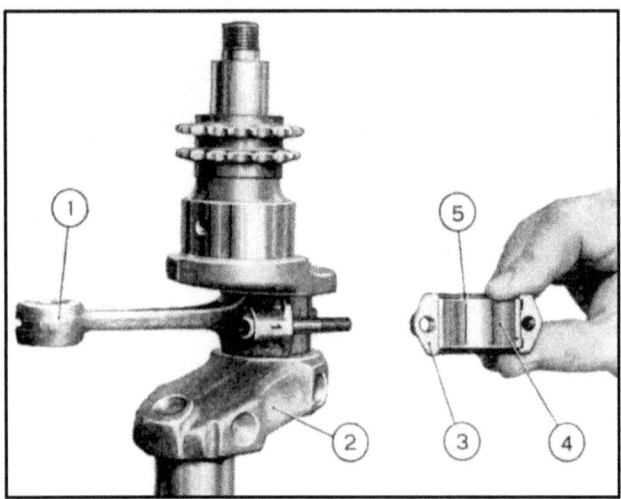

Fig. 49 - « Plastigage » position for bearing insert-to-crankpin journal clearance inspection.
1. Connecting rod. - 2. Crankshaft. - 3. Connecting rod cap. - 4. Bearing insert. - 5. Plastigage strip.

— install bearing inserts on connecting rods and rod caps;

— match connecting rods with crankpin journals, according to their identification numbers;

— place a piece of Plastigage type PG-1 the full width of the bearing insert, along the crankshaft longitudinal axis (fig. 49);

— fit the bearing cap and draw up the nuts with 16 ft.lbs (2.200 kgmm) of torque, using a torque indicating wrench;

— remove the bearing cap. The Plastigage will be found adhering to either the bearing shell or the crankpin and it will have developed a rectangular section as it was flattened from tightening action (fig. 50);

— to determine the actual clearance between crankpin and bearing shell, compare the width of the flattened Plastigage **at its widest point** with the graduations on the envelope (fig. 51). The number within the graduation on the envelope indicates the bearing clearance in thousandths of a mm.

If clearance is within the tolerance range of .0005" to .0022" (0,012 to 0,057 mm) which is the assembly

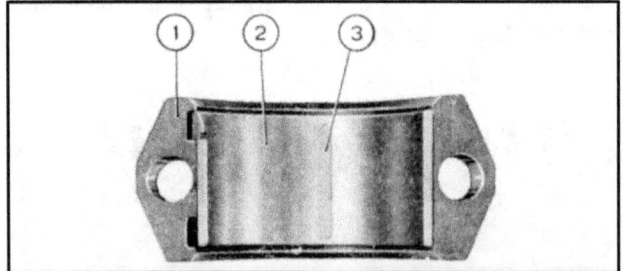

Fig. 50 - Evidence of « Plastigage » strip flattening after assembly of rod cap to connecting rod and crankpin journal.
1. Rod cap. - 2. Bearing insert. - 3. Plastigage strip.

clearance, or it reads less than .0039" (0,10 mm), max. wear limit, bearing shells can still be used without touching crankpin journals.

Conversely, should clearance be in excess of the above, bearing inserts must be replaced by undersized ones and crankpin journals ground as outlined on page 42.

THICKNESS OF CONNECTING ROD BEARING HALVES

Standard bearing	Undersizes			
	.01" (0,254 mm)	.02" (0,508 mm)	.03" (0,762 mm)	.04" (1,016 mm)
.0605" (1,537 mm)	.0655" (1,664 mm)	.0705" (1,791 mm)	.0755" (1,918 mm)	.0805" (2,045 mm)
.0607" (1,543 mm)	.0657" (1,670 mm)	.0707" (1,797 mm)	.0757" (1,924 mm)	.0807" (2,051 mm)

Connecting rod bearing bore diameter: 1.5003" to 1.5008" (38,106 to 38,119 mm).

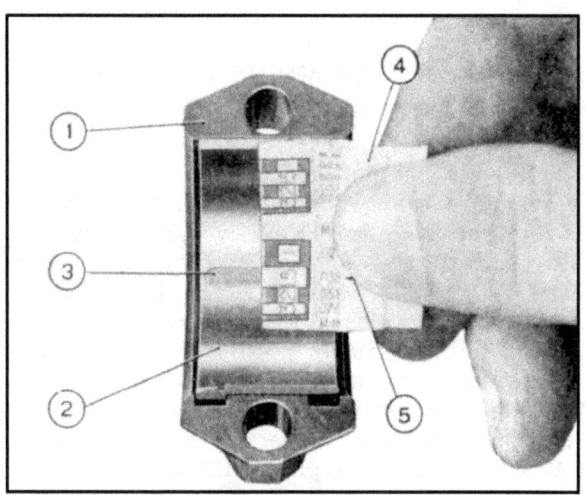

Fig. 51 - Checking bearing insert-to-crankpin journal clearance by comparing width of flattened « Plastigage »
1. Rod cap. - 2. Bearing insert. - 3. Plastigage strip. - 4. Piece of envelope with graduation scale. - 5. Bearing insert-to-crankpin journal clearance reading.

CRANKPIN DIAMETERS

Standard	Undersizes			
	.01" (0,254 mm)	.02" (0,508 mm)	.03" (0,762 mm)	.04" (1,016 mm)
1.3775" (34,988 mm)	1.3675" (34,734 mm)	1.3575" (34,480 mm)	1.3474" (34,226 mm)	1.3376" (33,972 mm)
1.3783" (35,008 mm)	1.3683" (34,754 mm)	1.3583" (34,500 mm)	1.3482" (34,246 mm)	1.3384" (33,992 mm)

ENGINE: CONNECTING RODS AND ROD BEARINGS

NOTICE

Plastigage type PG-1 enables clearance inspection up to .0030" (0,076 mm). Therefore, should inspection indicate no flattening of Plastigage strip, the procedure should be repeated using Plastigage type PR-1, which enables clearance inspection up to .0060" (0,152 mm).

It will be thus possible to determine whether actual wear is or not in excess of .0039" (0,10 mm) limit.

Connecting Rod Identification.

Each connecting rod of a set is stamped both on cap and on stem (fig. 53) with a number relating to the cylinder in which it is to be fitted.

When installing replacement rods stamp them with numbers from 1 to 4 in the position shown in fig. 52. On connecting rods 1 and 3 numbers 1 and 3 must be stamped on one side while on connecting rods 2 and 4 numbers must be stamped on the opposite side. At assembly, all numbers must face the camshaft side of engine (fig. 44).

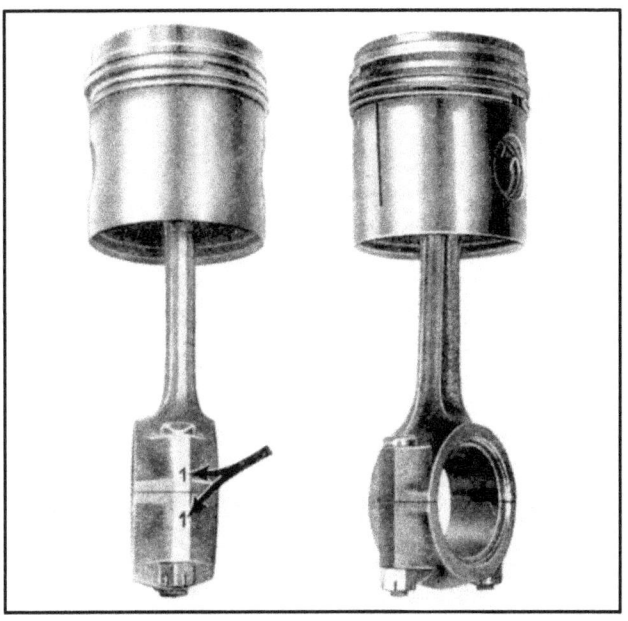

Fig. 53 - Connecting rod-piston set.

Note position of piston expansion slot with respect to connecting rod numbering indicated by arrows.

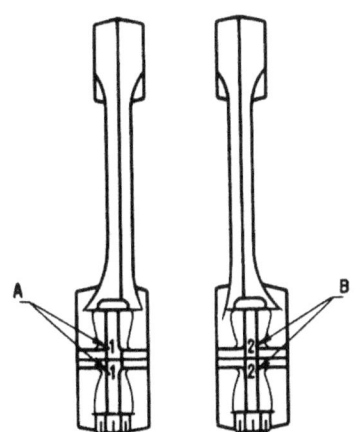

Fig. 52.

Numbering connecting rods.

Letter A indicates the side where numbers must be stamped for connecting rods of cylinder Nos. 1 and 3. - B, the side where numbers must be stamped for connecting rods of cylinder Nos. 2 and 4.

Note the offset position of bearing bores to connecting rod arm.

Checking and Replacing Bushes.

Small end bushes must be press fitted and interference between bush O. D. and small end bore must be .0011" to .0036" (0,028 to 0,091 mm).

Check inner surface: if any sign of ovalization or damage is noticed, recondition the bush.

Clamp tool A. 60077 in a vise and secure the connecting rod big end to it. Reface small end bush using expansion reamer U. 0320 (fig. 56).

The inner diameter must be brought to .7164" - .7166" (18,197 - 18,203 mm) or to .7283" - .7285" (18,497 - 18,503 mm) according to whether an .0078" (0,2 mm) or .0197" (0,5 mm) oversize piston pin must be fitted.

CONNECTING ROD SMALL END-TO-BUSH PINCH FIT

Connecting rod small end diameter	Bush outer diameter	Pinch fit
.7850" to .7863" (19,939 to 19,972 mm)	.7874" to .7882" (20,00 to 20,03 mm)	.0011" to .0036" (0,028 to 0,091 mm)

BUSH-TO-PISTON PIN FIT CLEARANCE

	I. D. OF PRESS FITTED AND REAMED BUSH	PISTON PIN DIAMETER	CLEARANCE
Standard	.7087" to .7088" (17,997 to 18,003 mm)	.7086" to .7084" (17,996 to 17,990 mm)	.00004" to .00051" (0,001 to 0,013 mm)
.0078" oversize (0,2 mm)	.7164" to .7166" (18,197 to 18,203 mm)	.7163" to .7162" (18,196 to 18,190 mm)	.00004" to .00051" (0,001 to 0,013 mm)
.0197" oversize (0,5 mm)	.7283" to .7285" (18,497 to 18,503 mm)	.7282" to .7280" (18,496 to 18,490 mm)	.00004" to .00051" (0,001 to 0,013 mm)

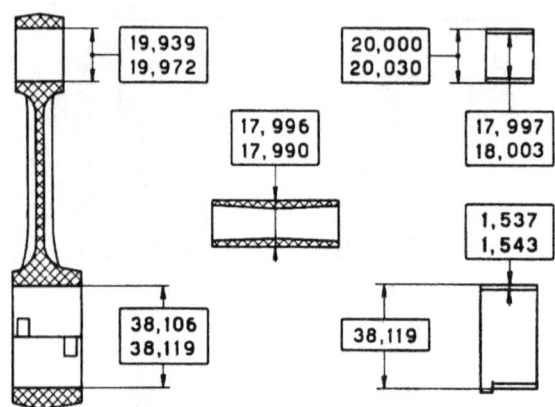

Fig. 54 - Main data for connecting rod, bearing, bush and pin.

At the above values, the standard piston pin-to-bush fit clearance of .00004" to .00051" (0,001 to 0,013 mm) will be maintained.

In case bushes must be replaced, operate as follows:

— Take off old bush using remover **A. 60076**.

— With the same tool install new bush (fig. 55).

— Using reamer **U. 0320** ream bushing I.D. to .7087" to .7088" (17,997 to 18,003 mm). With such an I.D. a standard piston pin may be fitted.

Checking Connecting Rod Weight.

All four connecting rods in an engine must have the same weight, with a ± .1 oz (± 3 grams) tolerance.

The checking must be carried out on a double-scale balance with zero at center.

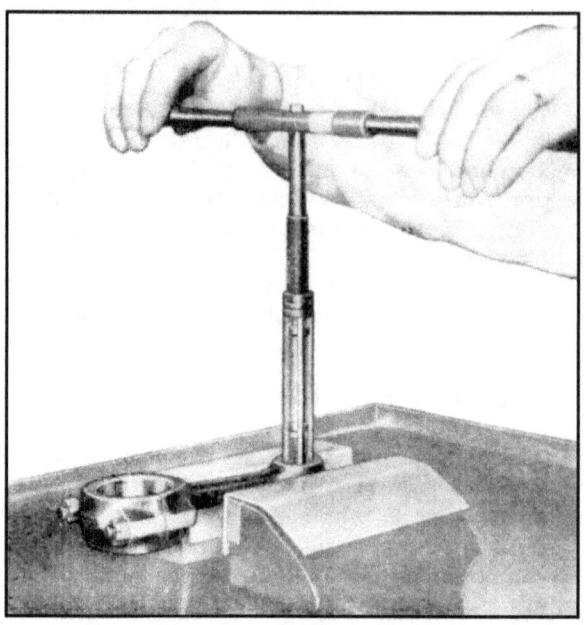

Fig. 56 - Reboring connecting rod small end bush with expansible reamer U. 0320.

Max. permissible weight difference between lightest and heaviest connecting rods is .2 oz (6 grams).

If the weight difference does not fall within the tolerance range remove excess material by grinding on cap lower end.

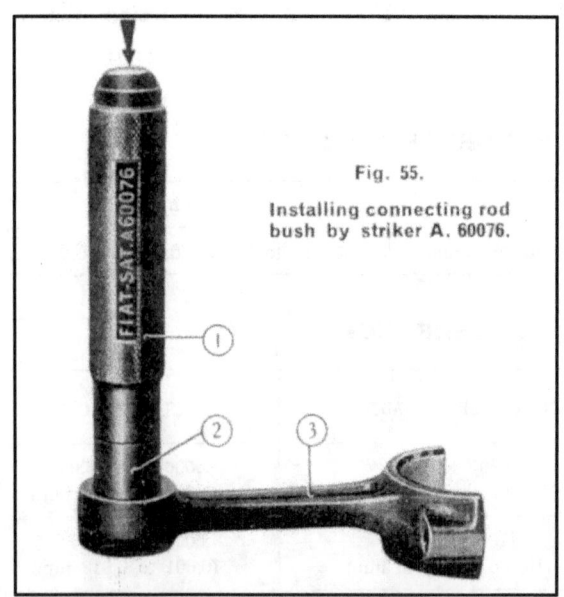

Fig. 55. Installing connecting rod bush by striker A. 60076.

1. Striker A. 60076, bush installation and removal. - 2. Small end bush. - 3. Connecting rod.

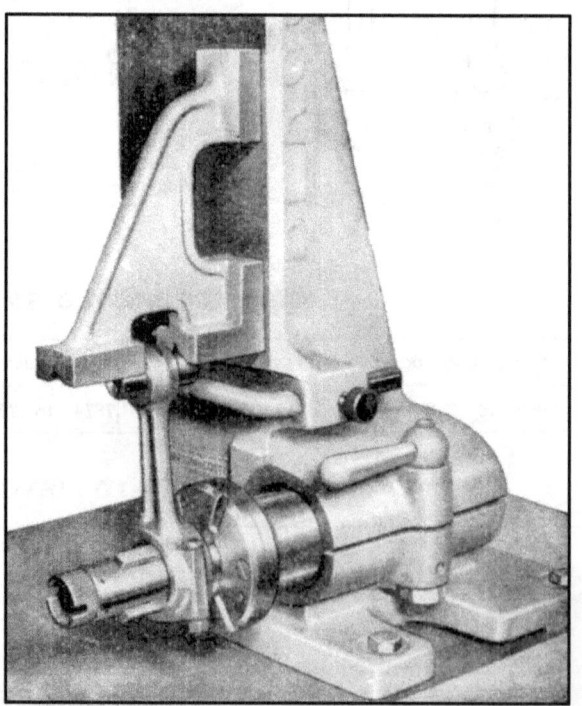

Fig. 57 - Checking the connecting rod alignment on fixture C. 627.

The shaft on which connecting rod big end is fitted is expansible.

ENGINE: CONNECTING RODS AND ROD BEARINGS

Checking Alignment.

Use fixture **C. 627**. Insert connecting rod big end on stub shaft of fixture, insert piston pin in small end bore end then rest checking square on piston pin (fig. 57).

Misalignment is revealed by the gap existing between square and vertical plane of fixture.

If connecting rod is found misaligned, straighten by clamping rod in a vice and using forked lever **A. 10029** (fig. 58).

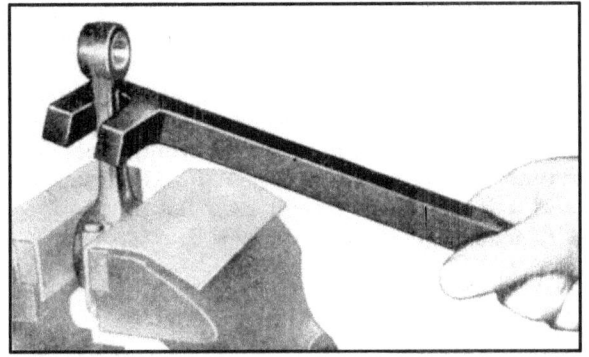

Fig. 58 - Straightening connecting rod stem with forked lever A. 10029.

Replace connecting rod if misalignment is excessive.

Before installing connecting rods in engine it is advisable to check the connecting-rod-piston assembly (fig. 59) by the same fixture used to check alignment of connecting rod alone.

Fig. 59 - Checking the alignment of piston-connecting rod set on fixture C. 627.

Tightening torque for connecting rod cap bolts is **16 ft lbs (2.200 kgmm)**.

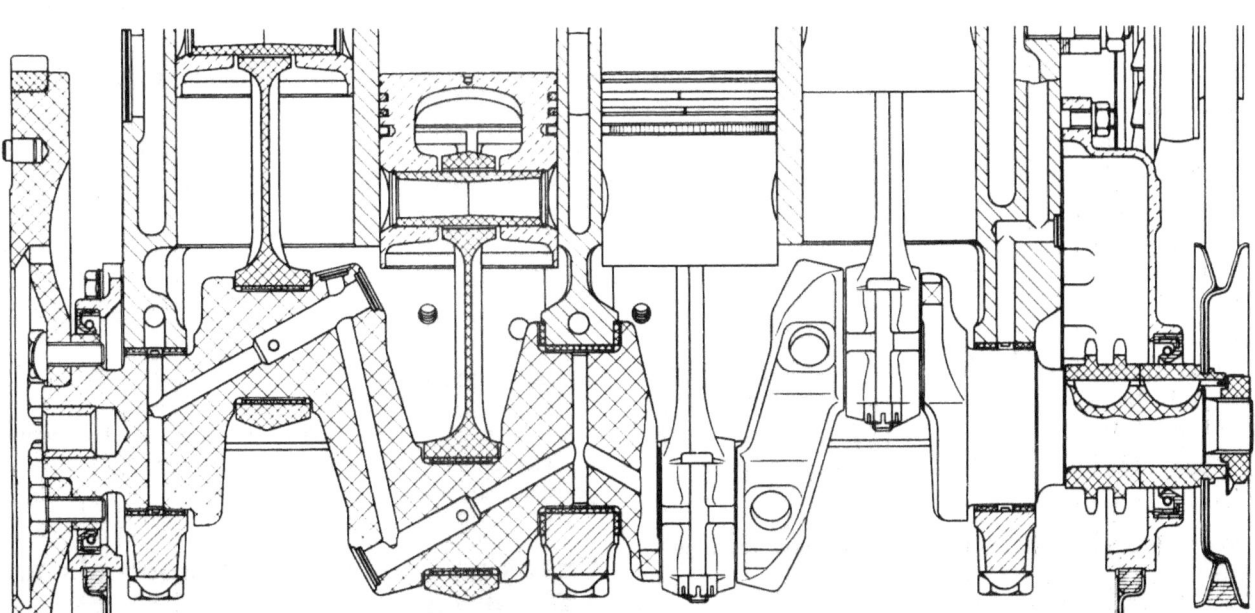

Fig. 60 - Crankcase longitudinal section through crankshaft.
Note the relative positions of connecting rods and main bearings.

Fig. 61.
Tightening connecting rod cap nuts by means torque wrench.

Torque specification: 16 ft.lbs (2.200 kgmm).

Piston-Connecting Rod Assembly and Installation.

Connecting rod and piston must be assembled in such a way that the number stamped on connecting rod stem and cap faces the side opposite the slot in piston skirt.

Since the connecting rod bush centerline is .0984" (2,5 mm) out of center with respect to connecting rod stem centerline, the connecting rod must be so installed that the portion out of center is positioned opposite the main bearing (fig. 60).

Correct assembly is assisted by the number bearing reference to the cylinder, stamped on the connecting rod. This number must face camshaft.

This stresses the importance of a correct stamping of connecting rods with the cylinder reference number (see page 38 and figs. 52-53). This way, the slot in piston skirt will face the side opposite the camshaft (fig. 44).

CRANKSHAFT AND MAIN BEARINGS

Soundness	page 42
Checking and Grinding Journals and Crankpins	» 42
Flywheel and Ring Gear	» 45
Checking Crankshaft Balance	» 45
Checking Journals and Crankpins Alignment	» 45
Cleaning Oil Galleries	» 46
Checking Main Bearing Shells and Main Bearing-to-Crankshaft Bearing Journal Clearance . .	» 46
Checking End Play	» 48
Bearing Installation	» 48
Tightening Procedure	» 49
Oil Seal Gaskets	» 49
Pilot Bush	» 49

Steel, three-bearing crankshaft with babbitt-lined thin-wall main bearings and two thrust washers on front support.

Wash crankshaft carefully and inspect for:

— soundness;

— roundness and wear, of journals and crankpins;

— balancing;

— alignment of crankpins and journals;

— cleanliness of oil galleries.

Soundness.

Replace shaft if cracked in any point because soundness is an essential requisite for safe and good operation.

Checking and Grinding Journals and Crankpins.

Inspect journals and crankpins: if light scoring marks are noticed, reface by a very fine stone

ENGINE: CRANKSHAFT AND MAIN BEARINGS

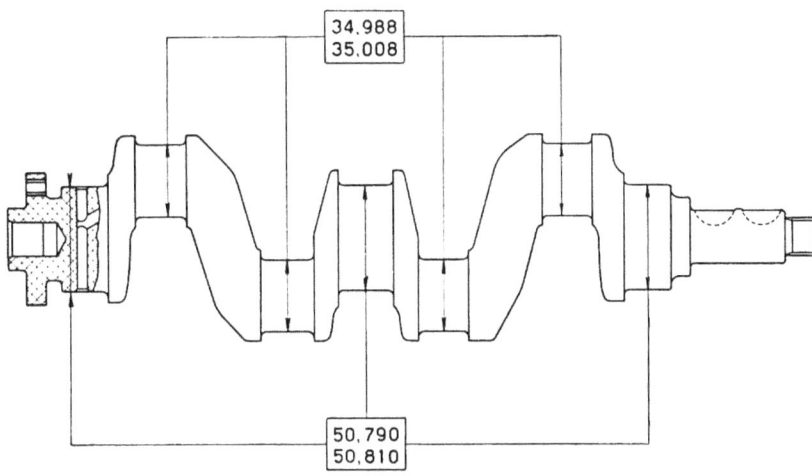

Fig. 62.
Data of crankshaft and main bearings.

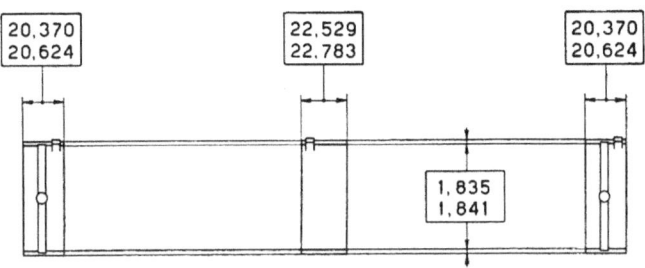

(carborundum); if remarkable out-of-round (more than .0020″ = 0,05 mm) or deep scoring marks are noticed, regrind journals and crankpins using the specially designed grinder (fig. 63) and fit suitable undersize bearings.

Undersize bearing classes are charted on page 46.

Before regrinding, measure each journal and crankpin by micrometer to determine the diameter to which journals and crankpins must be reduced.

Fit clearances are:
— crankpin-to-connecting rod bearing: .00047″ to .00225″ (0,012 to 0,057 mm);
— journal-to-main bearing: .00059″ to .0023″ (0,015 to 0,060 mm).

Replacement main and rod bearing half undersize range: .01″ - .02″ - .03″ - .04″ (0,254 - 0,508 - 0,762 - 1,016 mm).

CRANKPIN DIAMETERS

Standard	Undersizes			
	.01″ (0,254 mm)	.02″ (0,508 mm)	.03″ (0,762 mm)	.04″ (1,016 mm)
1.3775″ (34,988 mm)	1.3675″ (34,734 mm)	1.3575″ (34,480 mm)	1.3474″ (34,226 mm)	1.3376″ (33,972 mm)
1.3783″ (35,008 mm)	1.3683″ (34,754 mm)	1.3583″ (34,500 mm)	1.3482″ (34,246 mm)	1.3384″ (33,992 mm)

JOURNAL DIAMETERS

Standard	Undersizes			
	.01″ (0,254 mm)	.02″ (0,508 mm)	.03″ (0,762 mm)	.04″ (1,016 mm)
1.9996″ (50,790 mm)	1.9894″ (50,536 mm)	1.9796″ (50,282 mm)	1.9696″ (50,028 mm)	1.9595″ (49,774 mm)
2.0004″ (50,810 mm)	1.9902″ (50,556 mm)	1.9804″ (50,302 mm)	1.9704″ (50,048 mm)	1.9603″ (49,794 mm)

Fig. 63 - Reconditioning crankpins and journals on grinder.

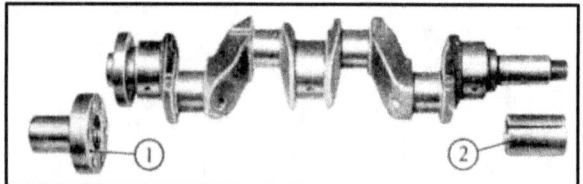

Fig. 64 - Crankshaft and adaptors for mounting on grinder.
1 and 2. Flange and bush set of fixture A. 60080.

Journal and crankpin regrinding must be performed to obtain, depending on extent of wear, the corresponding diameters given in the two tables aside without altering crankshaft radii (see figs. 66 through 69).

After regrinding install the corresponding undersized bearing halves.

To load crankshaft on grinding machine, use fixture **A. 60080** consisting of two adaptor items (fig. 64):

— one must be inserted on crankshaft front end tang, to avoid possible damages caused by the tool clamp;

— the other must be applied on flywheel mounting flange and carries the seat accomodating the tail center.

Make sure crankshaft is perfectly centered as this is an essential condition to obtain the correct alignment of crankpins and journals (fig. 65).

Grinding with a rather fine grain stone should result in perfectly smooth surfaces and must give diameters falling within the tolerance ranges specified in the tables.

Fig. 65 - Crankshaft centering on grinder.
On central journal is fitted the dial indicator to check centering.
1 and 2. Flange and bush of fixture A. 60080 for crankshaft installation on grinder.

After the subsequent honing of said surfaces, wash crankshaft very carefully to remove all possible abrasive metal particles.

CRANKSHAFT RADII DATA

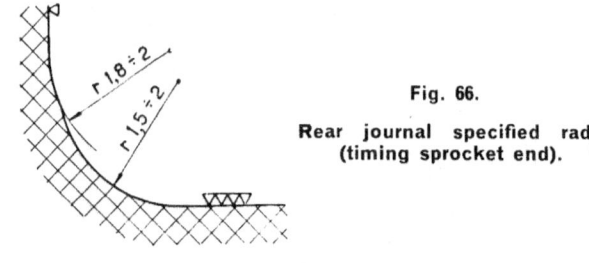

Fig. 66.
Rear journal specified radii (timing sprocket end).

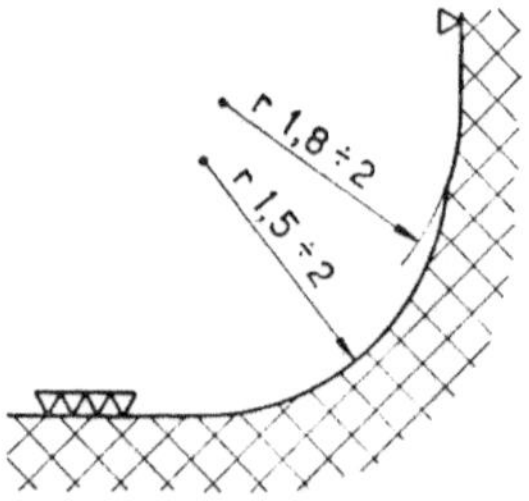

Fig. 67.
Front journal specified radii (flywheel end).

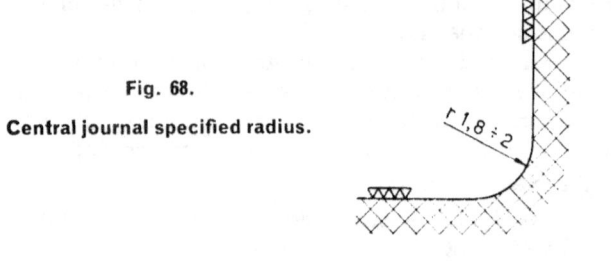

Fig. 68.
Central journal specified radius.

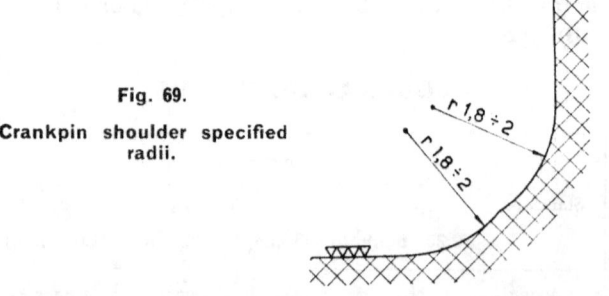

Fig. 69.
Crankpin shoulder specified radii.

Crankshaft oil galleries must be washed repeatedly with gasoline pushed through under pressure.

ENGINE: CRANKSHAFT AND MAIN BEARINGS

Flywheel and Ring Gear.

Inspect ring gear teeth.

If these are excessively worn or damaged remove ring gear and fit a replacement as follows:

— heat new ring gear in oil bath at 176° F (80° C);

— place immediately flywheel and ring gear under the press and force ring gear on flywheel.

Check flywheel areas in contact with clutch facing and with attachment flange to crankshaft: they must show a mirror-like surface, free of any scoring mark.

The areas must be perfectly flat and square to flywheel rotation axis. In case of doubt, check this condition using a dial gauge.

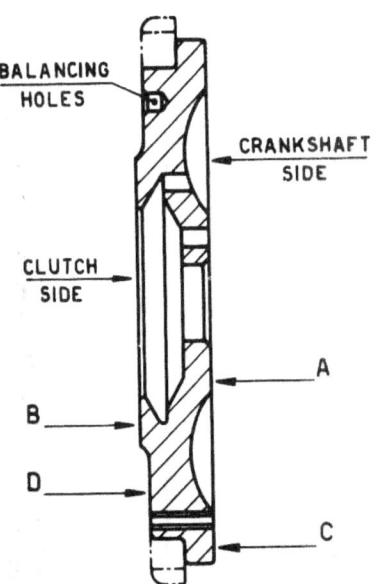

Fig. 70 - Diagram for inspection of flywheel driven plate contact and crankshaft mounting faces.

Rotate the flywheel with indicators resting on A (fig. 70), some 1.3" (33 mm) apart from rotation axis, and on B, clutch end; dial should register no runout in excess of .0039" (0,1 mm). With the indicator resting on C (fig. 70), runout should not exceed .0079" (0,2 mm).

For flywheel removal from or installation on crankshaft in crankcase, use tool A. 60165 which thwarts flywheel rotation (fig. 20).

Flywheel mounting screws must be tightened using a torque wrench with 25.3 to 28.9 ft.lbs (3.500 to 4.000 kgmm) of torque.

Maximum flywheel out-of-balance, with flywheel in place: .868 ft.lbs (120 grmm). Balancing holes should be drilled along plane D, in suitable position to restore balance.

Checking Crankshaft Balance.

Arrange V blocks C. 732 on a level plane. Level blocks by suitable shims and then place crankshaft complete with flywheel on V blocks. If crankshaft tends to rotate around its axis stick some putty on flywheel half going up until balance is obtained.

Remove putty; its weight is the amount of material to be removed from flywheel portion opposite that on which putty was applied.

To remove excess material, drill holes in the flywheel heavier half (along plane D, fig. 70).

Checking Journals and Crankpins Alignment.

After grinding journals and crankpins, and after balancing crankshaft, check alignment of journals and crankpins.

Place crankshaft on V blocks C. 731 or between centers and using a dial indicator check:

— Alignment of journals. Maximum permissible tolerance is ± .00098" (± 0,025 mm) (fig. 71).

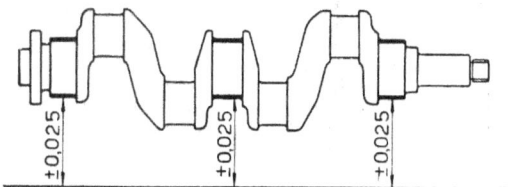

Fig. 71 - Crankshaft journal alignment maximum permissible tolerances.

— Out-of-round on both journals and crankpins. Maximum permissible tolerance is ± .00039" (± 0,01 mm).

— Alignment of crankpins with journals:

a) axes of both crankpins and journals must lie on the same plane; maximum permissible tolerance square to said plane, is ± .0098" (± 0,25 mm) (fig. 72);

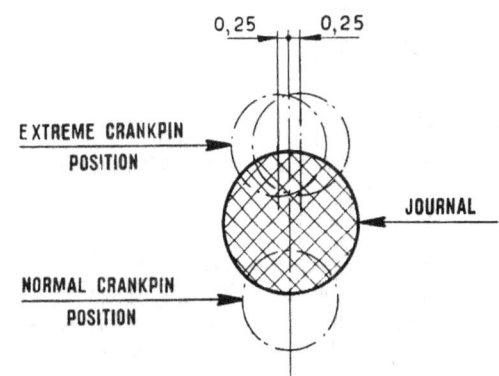

Fig. 72 - Crankpins versus journals alignment maximum permissible tolerances.

b) maximum permissible tolerance on the distance between crankshaft axis and crankpin outer surface is ± .00098″ (± 0,025 mm) (fig. 73).

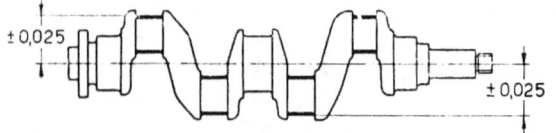

Fig. 73 - Crankpins to crankshaft centerline alignment maximum permissible tolerances.

— Squareness of crankshaft axis to flywheel resting face; when resting a dial indicator plunger laterally, at a minimum distance of 1.221″ (31 mm) from crankshaft axis and rotating slowly the crankshaft, out-of-square must not exceed ± .00098″ (± 0,025 mm).

If misalignments are detected, straighten by means of a press.

Cleaning Oil Galleries.

After the above operations, clean carefully all oil galleries in crankshaft by removing the gallery plugs and then recondition the seats with cutter **A. 60091** driven by spindle **A. 60066**.

Wash out the galleries with gasoline or kerosene.

Blow compressed air in the ducts to eliminate any foreign matter and any residue of gasoline or kerosene.

After the above operations, press-fit the new plugs using punch **A. 60092** to ensure oil-tightness and finish the job with staking punch **A. 60075**.

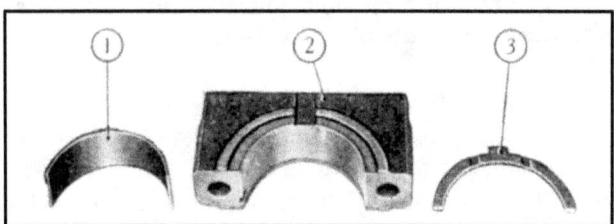

Fig. 74 - Central main bearing support cap.
1. Semi-bearing. - 2. Cap. - 3. Half thrust ring.

Checking Main Bearing Shells and Main Bearing-to-Crankshaft Bearing Journal Clearance.

Examine main bearing halves. If light scratches are noticed, remove them by using an extremely refined grinding wheel. In case of deep scores, signs of seizure or of important wear, bearings must be replaced. As a matter of fact, it is not possible refacing or adapting thin-wall bearings.

Main bearing bore diameter: 2.1460″ to 2.1465″ (54,507 to 54,520 mm).

Thickness of main bearing halves, both standard and undersizes, are tabulated hereafter.

THICKNESS OF MAIN BEARING HALVES

Standard	Undersizes			
	.01″ (0,254 mm)	.02″ (0,508 mm)	.03″ (0,762 mm)	.04″ (1,016 mm)
.0723″ (1,835 mm)	.0772″ (1,962 mm)	.0822″ (2,089 mm)	.0872″ (2,216 mm)	.0923″ (2,343 mm)
.0725″ (1,841 mm)	.0774″ (1,968 mm)	.0824″ (2,095 mm)	.0874″ (2,222 mm)	.0925″ (2,349 mm)

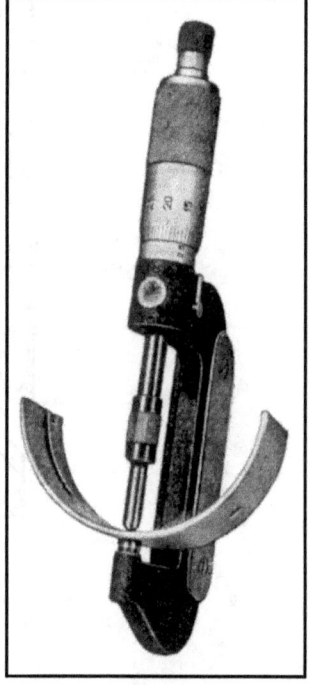

Fig. 75.
Checking the thickness of a semibearing by micrometer provided with plunger C. 318.

If examination evidences the possibility o still using main bearing halves, check clearance between them and bearing journals.

As already outlined in detail for connecting rod bearings (see page 37), « Plastigage » calibrated thread is used to check bearing clearance.

With engine on service stand and upside down so that bearing caps are relieved from crankshaft and flywheel weight, it will be possible to inspect all crankshaft bearings at the same time.

After cleanliness has been assured and oil thoroughly wiped, proceed as follows:

— arrange bearing halves in place on transverse members;

— install crankshaft;

ENGINE: CRANKSHAFT AND MAIN BEARINGS

— arrange bearing halves in place on bearing caps;

— place a piece of Plastigage type PG-1 the full width of the bearing insert, along the crankshaft longitudinal axis;

— fit the bearing caps, complete with bearing half and Plastigage strip, on main bearings;

— install mounting screws on bearing caps and draw up with prescribed torque, or 44.8 ft.lbs (6.200 kgmm);

Fig. 76 - « Plastigage » position for bearing insert-to-crankshaft bearing journal clearance inspection.
1. Main bearing cap. - 2. Thrust ring. - 3. Bearing insert. - 4. Plastigage strip. - 5. Center main bearing journal. - 6. Bearing insert. - 7. Thrust ring.

— remove the bearing caps. The Plastigage will be found adhering to either the bearing shells or the crankshaft journals and it will have developed a rectangular section as it was flattened from tightening action;

— to determine the actual clearance between main bearing shells and three bearing journals, compare the width of the flattened Plastigage at **its widest point** with the graduations on the envelope. The number within the graduation on the envelope indicates the bearing clearance in thousandths of a mm (fig. 78).

Main bearing half-to-crankshaft bearing journal assembly clearance: .0006" to .0024" (0,015 to 0,060 mm). Wear limit: .0059" (0,10 mm).

Fig. 77 - Evidence of « Plastigage » strip flattening after assembly of bearing cap to main bearing and crankshaft bearing journal.
1. Center main bearing journal. - 2. Plastigage strip.

Should the Plastigage strip have been flattened lightly or not at all and any comparison with the envelope graduation be impossible, this means that clearance is in excess of .0030" (0,076 mm) (maximum graduation reading), although actual clearance cannot be measured. If so, repeat the procedure using Plastigage type PR-1.

Fig. 78 - Checking bearing insert-to-center main bearing journal clearance by comparing width of flattened « Plastigage ».
1. Crankshaft bearing journal. - 2. Plastigage strip. - 3. Piece of envelope with graduation. - 4. Bearing insert-to-main bearing journal clearance reading.

Fig. 79 - Tightening main bearing cap mounting screws to 44.8 ft.lbs (6200 kgmm) with a torque wrench.

It will be thus possible to determine whether bearing wear exceeds or not .0039" (0,10 mm) limit.

If the latter condition is experienced, replace bearing inserts by undersizes and grind crankshaft bearing journals.

In case, for any reason, it is impossible to place the engine upside down and therefore the main bearing caps are supporting the weight of the crankshaft and the flywheel, inspect clearance at one bearing at a time by relieving the cap of inspected bearing from above load.

After all checks, install all caps on supports, tighten with torque wrench to the specified value and rotate crankshaft: an unimpeded rotation means that fit clearance are correct and, also, that crankpins and journals are aligned.

Checking End Play.

After checking clearance between bearings and journals, check clearance between thrust washers and crankshaft shoulder lands. Clearance must range within .0102" (0,26 mm) (fig. 81).

Fig. 80 - Checking crankshaft bearing journals for rocking on main bearings.

If clearance is greater, replace thrust washers with .0039" (0,1 mm) oversize washers. Standard and oversize washer thicknesses are tabulated below:

THRUST WASHER	THICKNESS
Standard	Oversize .0039" (0,1 mm)
.0910" to .0930" (2,31 to 2,36 mm)	.0948" to .0968" (2,41 to 2,46 mm)

For thrust washer installation see the following paragraph.

Fig. 81 - Checking clearance between thrust washers and crankshaft shoulder lands.

Bearing Installation.

When installing bearings hold strictly to the following:

— absolutely never trim the seating planes and the bearing seats;

— make sure parts to be assembled are perfectly clean;

— check that bearing stop dog is free to move radially in its seat (otherwise a forced assembly may occur at the faying edges of the two semibearings);

— since bearing O. D. is larger than the bearing seat I. D., assembly must be such that semibearings project of equal amounts beyond the matching planes;

— install upper thrust semiwashers when crankshaft is already in crankcase. Insert them in grooves so that the babbitt metal lined face in which grooves are machined abuts against crankshaft shoulder;

— fit lower semiwashers in cap and install as an assembly with cap.

ENGINE: CRANKSHAFT AND MAIN BEARINGS

Fig. 82 - Rear view of installed crankshaft.
1. Cover. - 2. Oil seal. - 3. Flywheel mounting flange. - 4. Clutch pilot bush.

Tightening Procedure.

Use a torque wrench and tighten nuts and screws to specified torques.

Tighten gently and continuously until reaching the specified torque, being careful not to overtighten.

Both resting faces and threads must be absolutely clean.

Do not lubricate threads.

Oil Seal Gaskets.

Two rubber seals, with inner garter spring, located one in the timing gear cover and one in the flywheel end cover (fig. 82), ensure oil tightness.

Fig. 83 - Centering the flywheel end oil seal cover.
1. Cover. - 2. Flywheel mounting flange. - 3. Tool A. 60166.

Fig. 84 - Pilot bush removal using puller A. 6515.

When servicing the engine see that these gaskets are properly seated, their inner surface is not worn, and matches shaft perfectly; otherwise replace.

To install the flywheel end seal, use tool **A. 60166** (fig. 83) which is designed to ensure the perfect centering of cover on crankshaft flange mounting the flywheel. This will exclude any possibility of incorrect assembly and consequent oil leakage.

Pilot Bush.

Is located inside the flywheel end of crankshaft and is of self-lubricating bronze. If bush is excessively worn, fit a new one.

To remove old bush use puller **A. 6515** (fig. 84) or puller **A. 40006/1** with adapter **A. 40006/2**.

Do not ream bush I. D. after press-fitting.

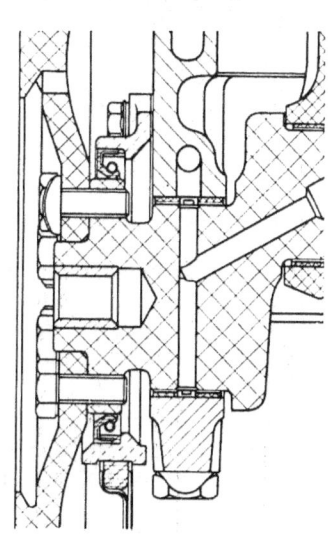

Fig. 85.

Longitudinal section of engine through rear oil seal and clutch shaft pilot bushing.

CYLINDER HEAD

VALVES, VALVE GUIDES AND SPRINGS

Cylinder Head Removal and Disassembly	page 50
Cylinder Head Inspection and Servicing	» 50
Valve Guide Inspection and Servicing	» 51
Valve Seat Removal, Inspection and Servicing	» 52
Valve Removal, Inspection and Servicing	» 54
Inspecting the Springs	» 55
Valve Seal Test	» 56
Cylinder Head Assembly and Installation	» 56

Cylinder Head Removal and Disassembly.

The cylinder head must be removed and disassembled whenever compression losses are experienced due to valve leakage, or after a certain period of operation, with a view to eliminating carbon deposits from combustion chambers.

Take off: air cleaner, carburetor, ignition distributor with vacuum advance device, cylinder head cover, the two water outlet pipes from cylinder head, exhaust pipe from exhaust manifold, exhaust manifold, spark plug and excessive water temperature indicator sending unit cables.

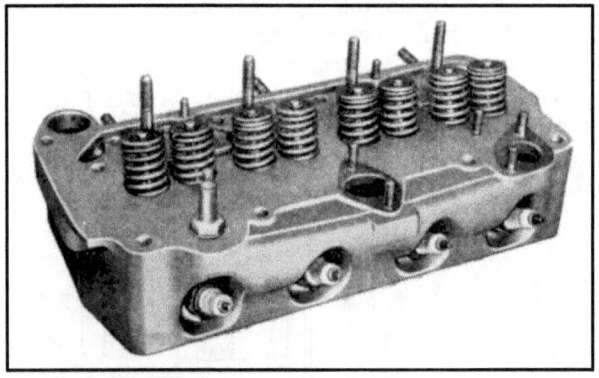

Fig. 86 - Cylinder head with valves, springs and spark plugs.

Remove cylinder head hold-down screws.
Disassembly of cylinder head is not particularly difficult; however, the following chapters will deal with this operation, indicating also the required tooling.
Cylinder head disassembly must be performed on work bench after securing the head with supporting fixture **A. 60041** and plate **A. 60045** (figs. 87 and 104).

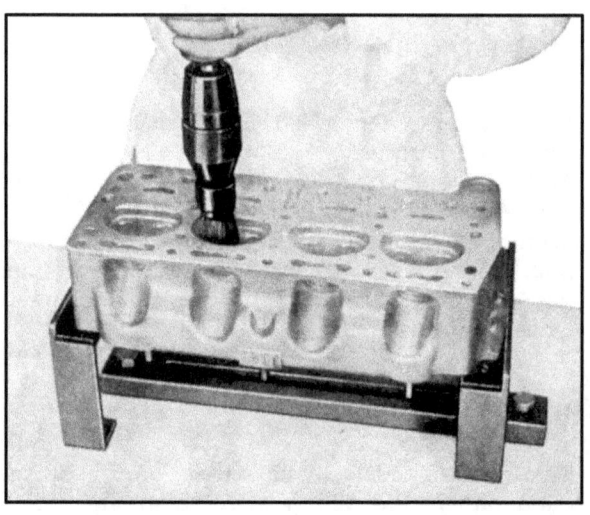

Fig. 87 - Decarbonizing combustion chambers with wire brush **A. 11416**.
Cylinder head is installed on supporting fixture **A. 60041**.

Cylinder Head Inspection and Servicing.

First, remove carbon deposits using wire brush **A. 11416** driven by an electric, portable drill (fig. 87).
Check that seating plane is not deformed.

— Coat a surface plate with a film of lampblack.
— Place cylinder head on surface plate, slide it back and forth and check the marks left by the lampblack (fig. 88).

If surface results irregular, recondition on surface grinder **M. 30** (fig. 89) or, if this is not available, with a file. Be careful to remove the least possible amount of material so as not to alter the compression ratio.

ENGINE: CYLINDER HEAD - VALVES - VALVE GUIDES AND SPRINGS

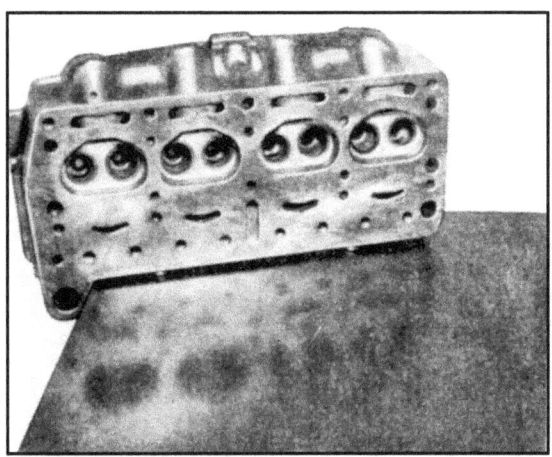

Fig. 88 - Checking on a surface plate the cylinder head-to-block seating face.

After flattening, clean carefully by washing, to remove all traces of abrasive material.

If it is suspected that water passages are cracked, carry out a hydraulic test as follows:

— Install fixture **A. 60081** on cylinder head as shown in figs. 90-91 and connect pipe 1 (fig. 91) to hand pump **A. 60060**.

Heat the water in tank to 185° to 194° F (85° to 90° C) by switching on the electric resistances of the heating apparatus.

Open the handwheel and pump water into cylinder head until building up a 24.4 to 42.6 psi (2 to 3 kg/cm²) pressure.

If cylinder head leaks, pressure gauge pointer will be seen to return to zero. In this case, replace cylinder head.

Valve Guide Inspection and Servicing.

Clean carefully valve guides and recondition with brush **A. 11417** (fig. 92) and reamer **U. 0313** (fig. 93).

Fig. 89 - Flattening out cylinder head seating face on surface grinder M. 30.

Valve guides are press fitted with a .0009'' to .0031'' (0,023 to 0,080 mm) pinch fit.

Fig. 90 - Installation of fixture A. 60081 for cylinder head hydraulic sealing test.

Arrows point to plate mounting nuts.

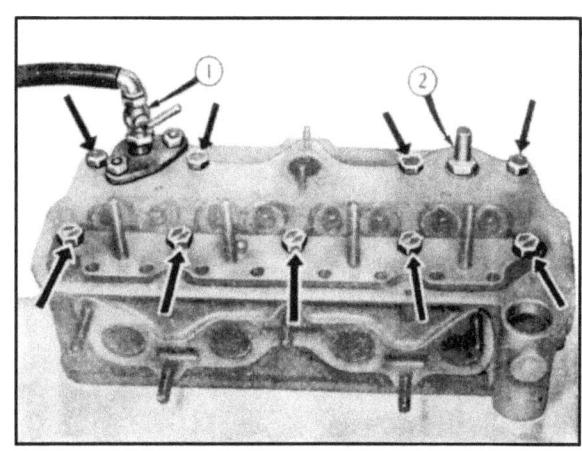

Fig. 91 - Hydraulic sealing test.

1. Pipe with connection and cock. - 2. Water outlet plug.

Arrows point to mounting screws of fixture shown in fig. 90.

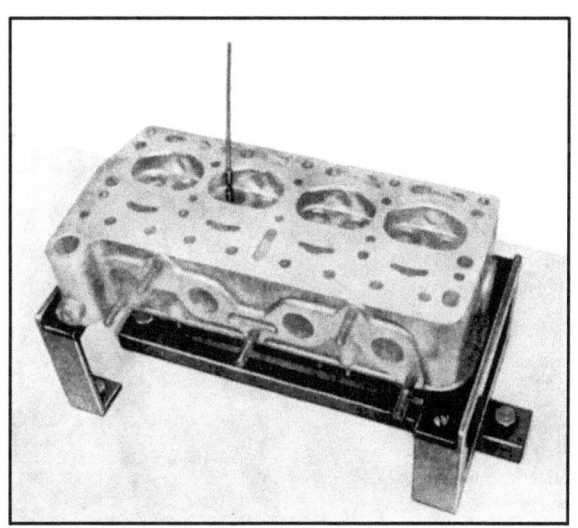

FIAT - 600 - 600 D SEDAN AND MULTIPLA

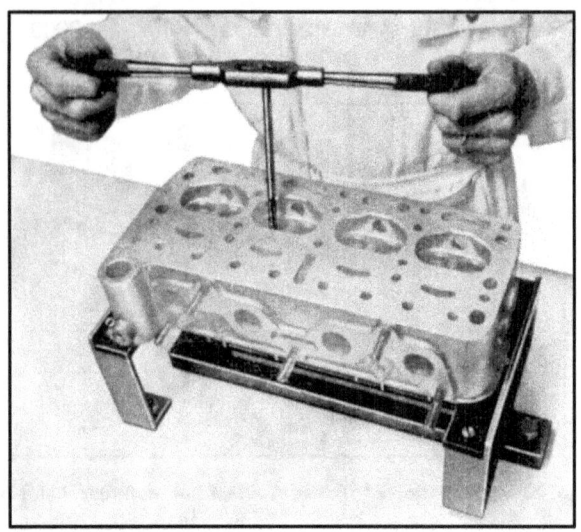

Fig. 93 - Reconditioning valve guides with reamer U. 0313.

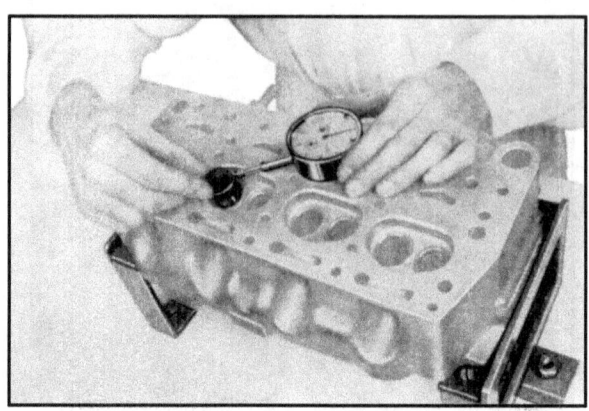

Fig. 95 - Checking valve stem-to-guide clearance.

VALVE GUIDE-TO-VALVE GUIDE SEAT PINCH FIT

Valve guide seat diameter	Valve guide outer diameter	Pinch fit
.5098" to .5110" (12,950 to 12,977 mm)	.5118" to .5130" (13,000 to 13,030 mm)	.0009" to .0031" (0,023 to 0,080 mm)

To remove and install valve guides use drift rod **A. 60059** (fig. 94).

Replace valve guides when clearance between valve and guide is excessive and replacement of valve alone is not sufficient to overcome the trouble.

Fit clearance between valve stem and guide is .00086" to .00216" (0,022 to 0,055 mm); maximum permissible wear limit is .0059" (0,15 mm).

Replace valve guide lock ring, if defective.

Valve Seat Removal, Inspection and Servicing.

Recondition valve seats in cylinder head, after decarbonizing.

Seat angle must be 45°±5'.

To recondition seats use cutters **A. 60096** (having an inclination of 20°) and **A. 60159** (with an inclination of 75°); one removes material at top, the other at bottom.

— Insert pilot **A. 60058** in valve guide (fig. 96) and then apply the cutter, driving it by spindle **A. 11482** (fig. 97). Pilot **A. 60058** must be selected among the three allotted, so as to obtain the correct matching to valve guide with the least possible clearance.

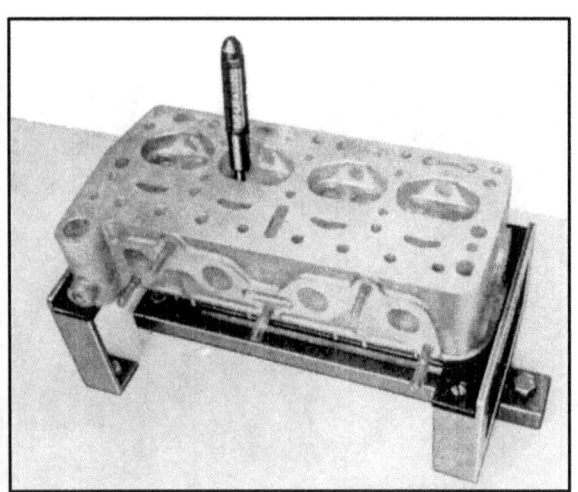

Fig. 94 - Removal of valve guides, using drift rod A. 60059 (which serves also for installation).

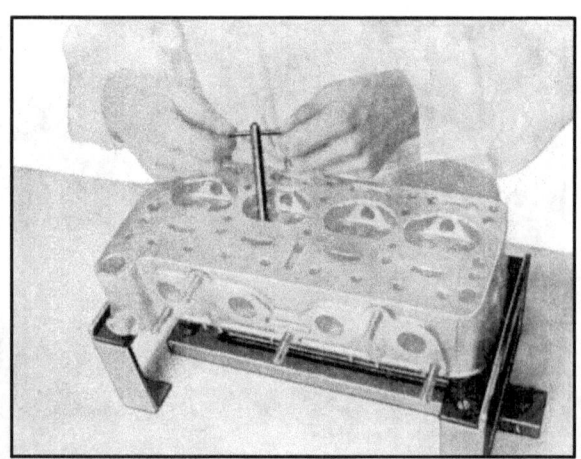

Fig. 96 - Inserting pilot A. 60058 in valve guide, for cutter or grinder centering.

ENGINE: CYLINDER HEAD - VALVES - VALVE GUIDES AND SPRINGS

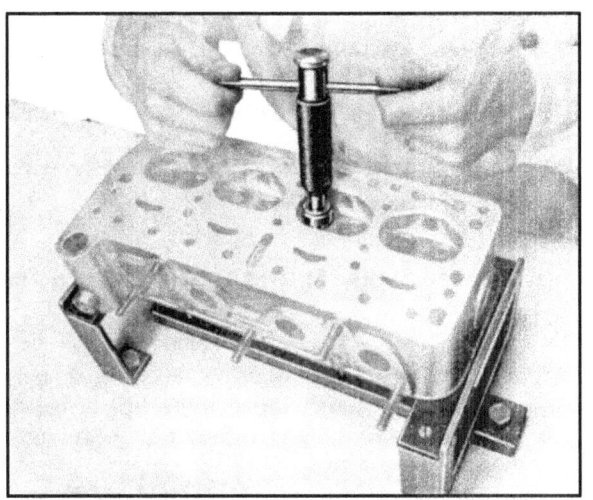

Fig. 97 - Reducing valve seats with cutter A. 60096 (20°) and spindle A. 11482.

The 20° cutter removes material at seat top.

After reconditioning, grind seats with taper grinder **A. 60057** (fig. 103), using the Vibrocentric tool **A. 11460** and spindle **A. 11475**.

The grinder must be fitted on pilot **A. 60058** same as for the cutters.

Much care must be exercised in grinding the valve seats: the grinder must remain in contact with the seat for short instants and during this time the current to the Vibrocentric tool must be cut off (tool working only by inertia) to prevent vibrations which might lead to incorrect grinding.

Never allow grinder to stop while it is still in contact with the ground seat.

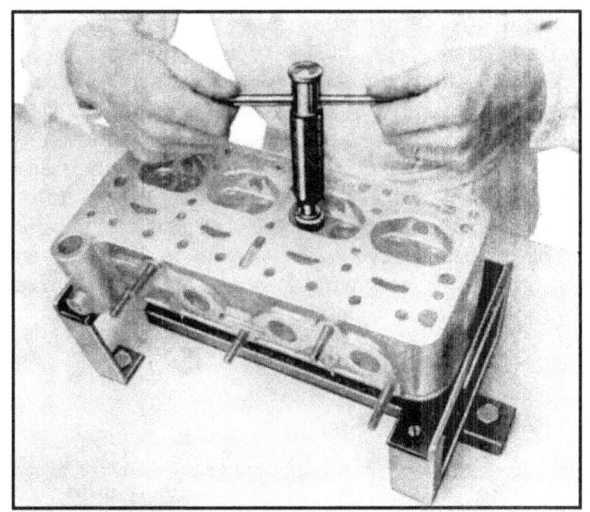

Fig. 98 - Reducing valve seats, with cutter A. 60159 (75°) and spindle A. 11482.

The 75° cutter removes material at seat bottom.

VALVE AND VALVE SEAT REFACING DIAGRAMS

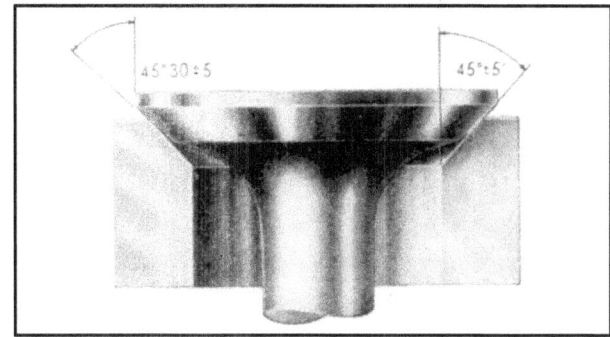

Fig. 99 - Inclination angle of seats on cylinder head and on valves.

Fig. 100 - Reducing valve seat at top with 20° cutter.

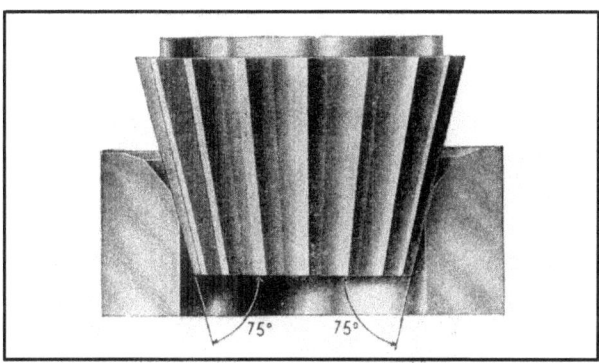

Fig. 101 - Reducing valve seat at bottom with 75° cutter.

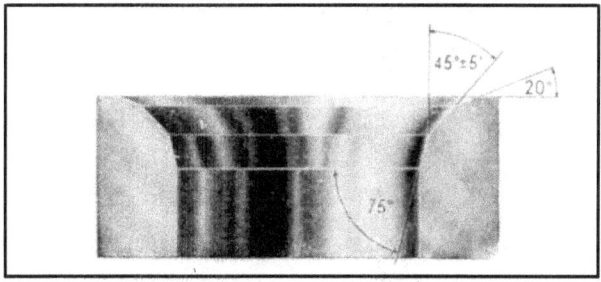

Fig. 102 - Valve seat after reduction.

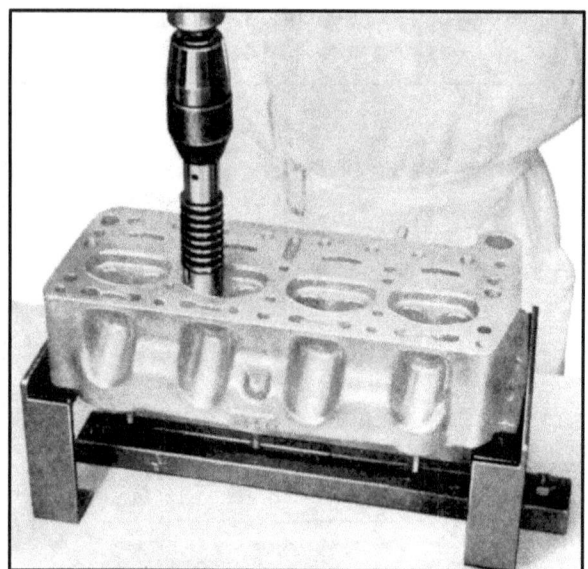

Fig. 103 - Reconditioning valve seats with taper grinder A. 60057.

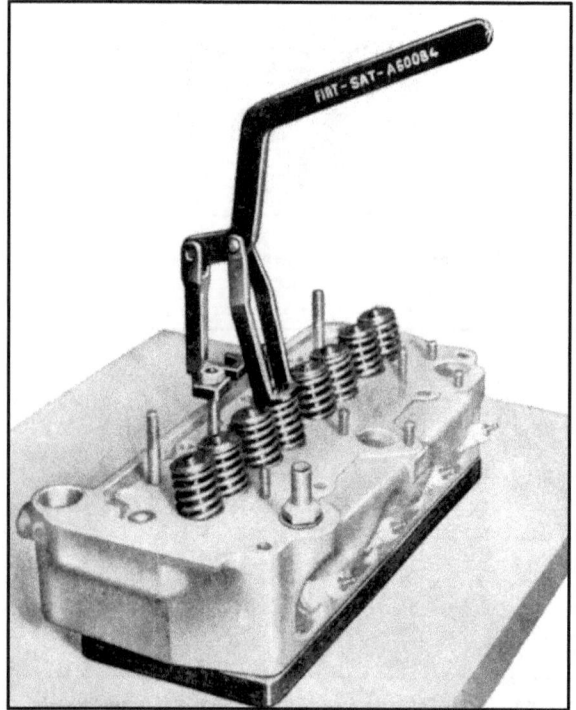

Fig. 104 - Removing valves with tool A. 60084.

Cylinder head must rest on supporting plate A. 60045.

To obtain a good work dress quite often the grinder with a diamond point dresser, installing grinder on tool **A. 11480**.

The above tool allows also of restoring grinder to correct taper of 45°±5′.

When grinding seats, wet grinder slightly with a few drops of kerosene.

Valve Removal, Inspection and Servicing.

Place cylinder head on plate **A. 60045** and, using tool **A. 60084** (fig. 104), depress the upper cup so as to free the valves by removing their locks. Remove also snap rings.

Fig. 105 - Reconditioning valve seating face on universal grinder A. 11401.

Check valve soundness and then the clearance between stem and guide (fig. 95); as already mentioned on page 52 fit clearance should be .00086″ to .00216″ (0,022 to 0,055 mm) and maximum permissible wear limit .0059″ (0,15 mm).

Valve cleaning should be performed using electrical twin polisher **M. 112** or wire brush **A. 11419**.

Recondition valve seating face after having checked that stem is not distorted. Replace if necessary.

Introduce valve stem in self-centering spindle of universal grinder **A. 11401** (fig. 105) and position support so that valve will have an inclination, with respect to grinder wheel, such that the correct refacing angle is ensured: 45° 30′ ± 5′.

VALVE-TO-VALVE GUIDE DATA

Valve guide inner diameter	Valve stem diameter	Fit clearance	Wear limit
.2765″ to .2772″ (7,022 to 7,040 mm)	.2756″ to .2750″ (7,000 to 6,985 mm)	.00087″ to .00216″ (0,022 to 0,055 mm)	.0059″ (0,15 mm)

ENGINE: CYLINDER HEAD - VALVES - VALVE GUIDES AND SPRINGS

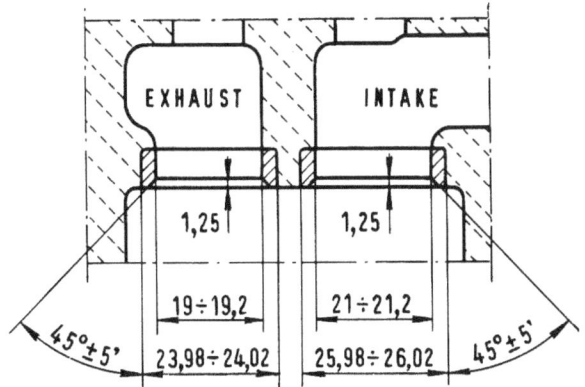

Fig. 106 - Main specifications of intake and exhaust valve seats on cylinder head.

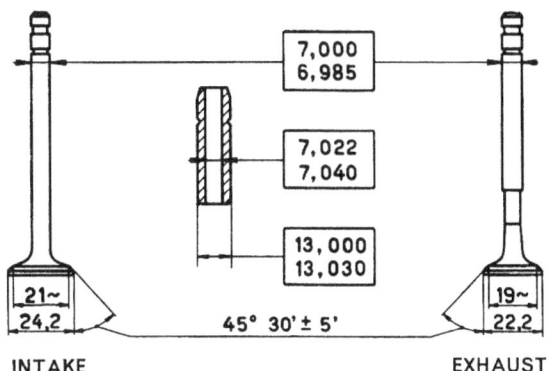

Fig. 109 - Intake-exhaust valves and guides checking data.

Check to see that after reconditioning, valve thickness in correspondence with maximum mushroom head diameter is not less than .0197″ (0,5 mm).

Inspecting the Springs.

Check to see that valve springs are not cracked or have not weakened. Spring flexibility should be checked with tester **A. 11493**, comparing the load and give-in characteristics recorded with the data tabulated for new springs in valve spring data table on page 56.

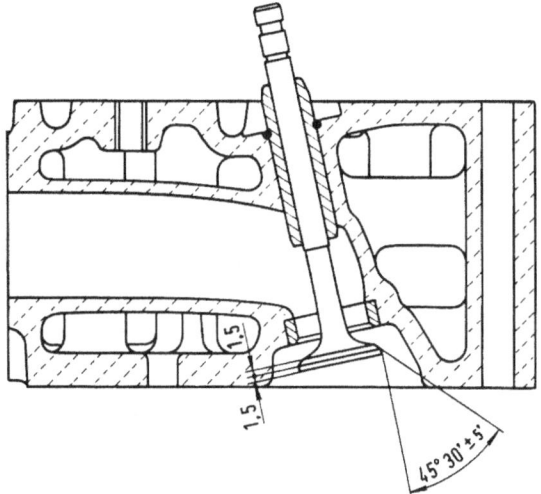

Fig. 107 - Main specifications of intake valve face.

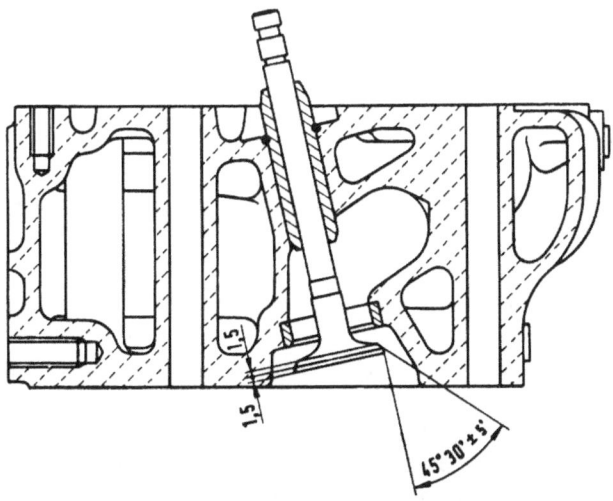

Fig. 108 - Main specifications of exhaust valve face.

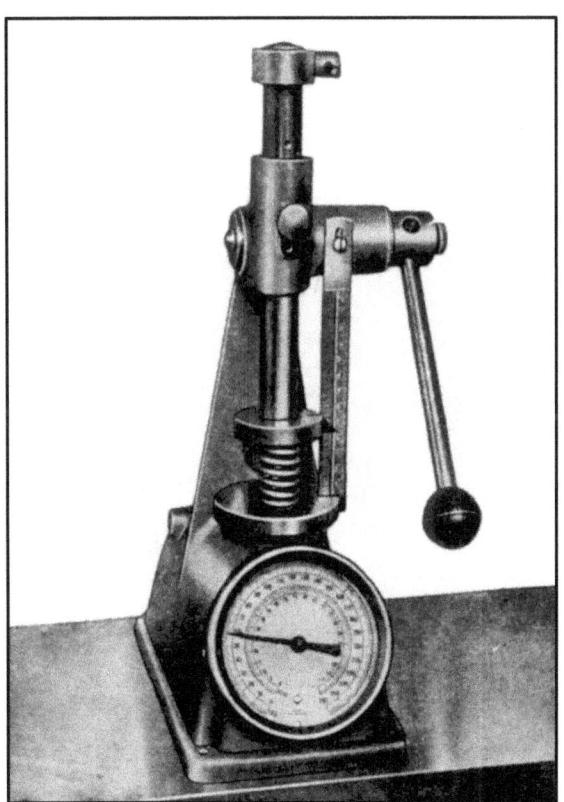

Fig. 110 - Valve spring check on tester A. 11493.

ENGINE VALVE SPRINGS

Active coils No.	Inner diameter	Wire diameter	A	B		C		Minimum permissible load referre to B
6	.7953″ (20,2 mm)	.1181″ (3 mm)	2.0354″ (51,7 mm)	1.2598″ (32 mm)	53.36 lbs (24,2 kg)	.9646″ (24,5 mm)	73.64 lbs (33,4 kg)	41.9 lbs (19 kg)

A = Spring free height.   B = Seated spring height.   C = Minimum working spring height.

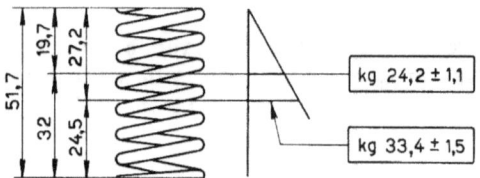

Fig. 111 - Valve spring check data.
See table above.

Valve Seal Test.

After having accurately ground and cleaned both the valves and valve seats, proceed with the compression seal test using tester **A. 60079** after blanking spark plug seat with tool **A. 60018** (fig. 112).

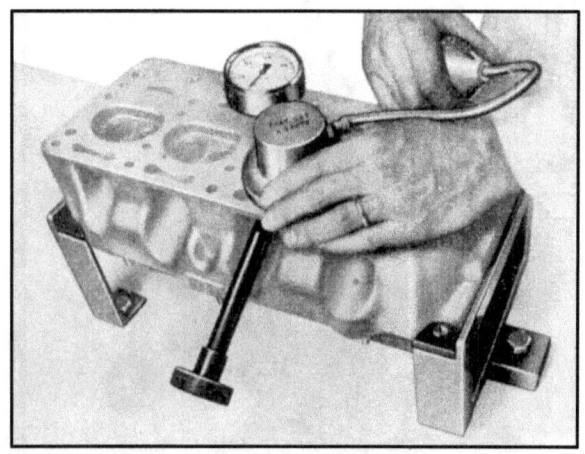

Fig. 112 - Valve compression sealing check with tester A. 60079.
Note tool A. 60018 blanking spark plug seat.

This tester, which must be placed over valve seats of each cylinder, consists of:
— a compression chamber;
— a rubber sealing gasket;
— a rubber bulb;
— a pressure gauge.

Compress air by rubber bulb until pointer in gauge moves close to last reading on dial.

If matching between valve and seat is not perfect, escaping air will immediately be revealed by pointer which will move back toward zero.

Many engine operation troubles are caused by faulty valves; it is therefore essential to ensure perfect compression tightness of valves and specified valve-to-guide clearance.

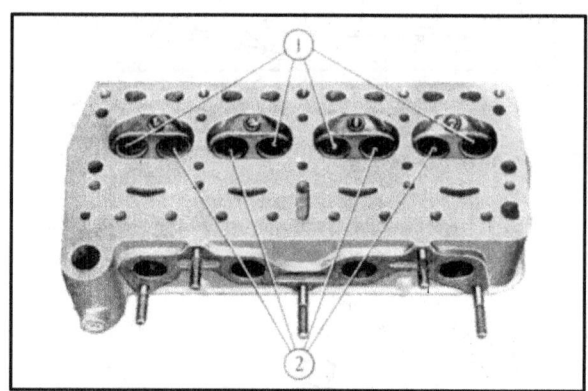

Fig. 113 - Cylinder head bottom view.
1. Exhaust valves. - 2. Intake valves.

Cylinder Head Assembly and Installation.

For this operation, and the equipment required, refer to the pertinent chapters on preceding pages.

The cylinder head must be installed on block as follows:

— Position head, complete with valves and springs, on block and interpose the gasket.

— Fit washers and fixing screws, which should be turned in slightly.

ENGINE: VALVE TIMING GEAR

— Using torque wrench, tighten cylinder head screws in three passes, following the sequence shown in fig. 114:

first pass: draw up screws with 10.8 to 18.1 ft.lbs (1.500 to 2.500 kgmm) of torque;

second pass: lock screws to specified torque, or 20.3 to 21.7 ft.lbs (2.800 to 3.000 kgmm);

third pass: check screws 1 and 2, fig. 114, for correct torque.

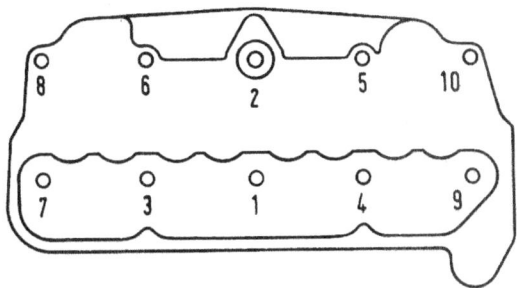

Fig. 114 - Head hold-down screws torque sequence.

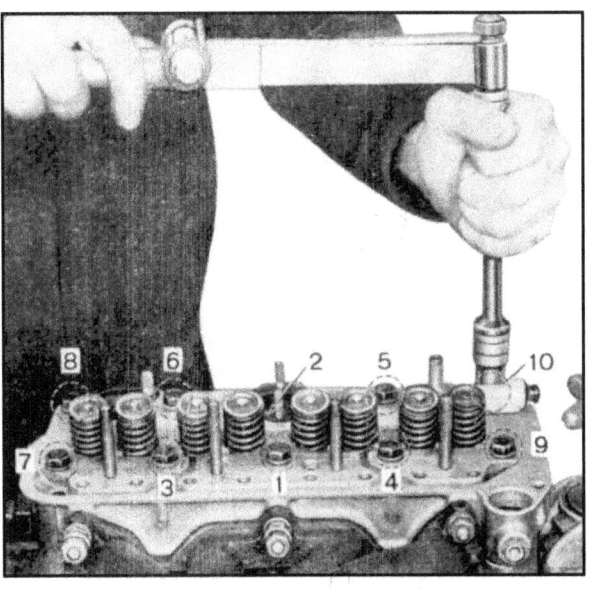

Fig. 115 - Tightening head hold-down screws with torque wrench.

Recommended torque: 20.3 to 21.7 ft.lbs (2.800 to 3.000 kgmm).

VALVE TIMING GEAR

Camshaft and Camshaft Bushes	page 59
Check-up and Service of Camshaft and Bushes	» 60
Valve Tappets	» 63
Pushrods	» 64
Rockers	» 64
Tappet-to-Rocker Clearance Adjustment	» 64
Valve Gear Timing	» 65

Valves are controlled through tappets, pushrods and rockers by camshaft in crankcase, which is in turn chain-driven by crankshaft (fig. 132).

Timing data, as referred to a valve-to-rocker tappet adjustment clearance of .0177" (0,45 mm) is:

Intake:
— opens: BTDC . . . . 4°
— closes: ABDC . . . . 34°

Exhaust:
— opens: BBDC . . . . 29°
— closes: ATDC . . . . 1°

Final tappet operation clearance adjustment, with cold engine intake and exhaust .0059" (0,15 mm).

NOTE - Up to engine No. 466800, the following engines excepted:

from N. 437546 to N. 437595;
  »   459191 » » 462191;
  »   462959 » » 465055;

timing data, as referred to a valve-to-rocker tappet adjustment clearance of .0082" (0,21 mm), should be as specified hereafter:

Intake:
— opens: BTDC . . . . 10°
— closes: ABDC . . . . 35°

Exhaust:
— opens: BBDC . . . . 35°
— closes: ATDC . . . . 2°

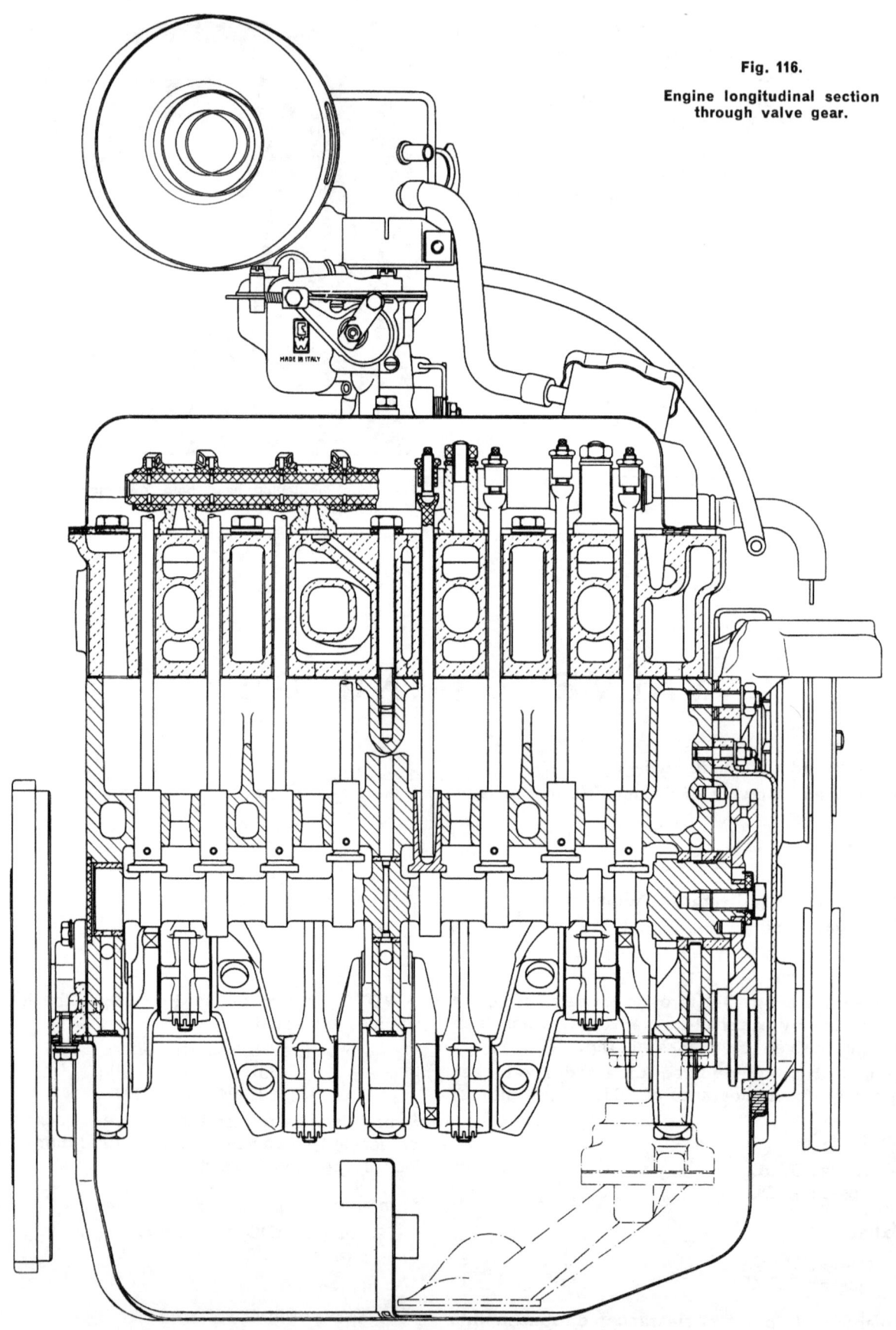

Fig. 116.
Engine longitudinal section through valve gear.

ENGINE: VALVE TIMING GEAR

Final tappet operation clearance adjustment, with cold engine:
— intake and exhaust .0039" (0,10 mm).

Camshaft and Camshaft Bushes.

Camshaft is borne on three bushings: two end bushings and a center one.

The features of three camshaft bushings are the following:

— The chain end bushing is a bronze alloy. It is selected, on the ground of its outside diameter, in three size classes:

A = 1.8886" to 1.8890" (47,970 to 47,980 mm);
B = 1.8890" to 1.8894" (47,980 to 47,990 mm);
C = 1.8894" to 1.8898" (47,990 to 48,000 mm).

Therefore, on fitting bushing on crankcase, make sure to which class the bore belongs and install a bushing of the same class. To prevent the bushing from floating, it is secured through a dowel screw.

— Center and flywheel end bushings are made of a steel back and inner babbitt coating. They are installed by pressure into crankcase bores.

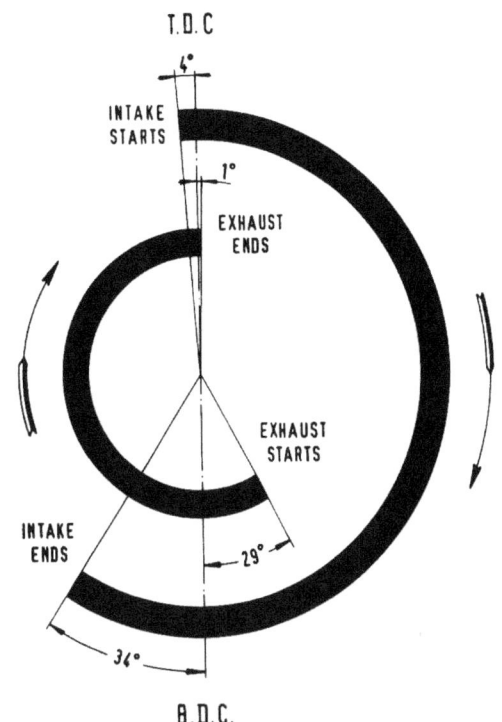

Fig. 117 - Timing diagram.
Data refer to .0177" (0,45 mm) valve stem-to-rocker arm clearance adjustment.

BUSHING BORE - BUSHING AND CAMSHAFT DIAMETERS

BEARINGS	CHAIN END	CENTER	FLYWHEEL END
Crankcase bore diameter	A = 1.8890" to 1.8894" (47,980 to 47,990 mm) B = 1.8894" to 1.8898" (47,990 to 48,000 mm) C = 1.8898" to 1.8902" (48,000 to 48,010 mm)	1.6504" to 1.6516" (41,920 to 41,950 mm)	1.4143" to 1.4154" (35,921 to 35,951 mm)
Bushing outside diameter: Free	A = 1.8886" to 1.8890" (47,970 to 47,980 mm) B = 1.8890" to 1.8894" (47,980 to 47,990 mm) C = 1.8894" to 1.8898" (47,990 to 48,000 mm)	1.6550" to 1.6565" (42,037 to 42,075 mm)	1.4175" to 1.4190" (36,030 to 36,068 mm)
Press fitted	—	1.6504" to 1.6516" (41,920 to 41,950 mm)	1.4143" to 1.4154" (35,921 to 35,951 mm)
Bushing inside diameter: Seated bushing	1.4870" to 1.4910" (37,770 to 37,871 mm)	1.4870" to 1.4910" (37,770 to 37,871 mm)	1.2070" to 1.2110" (30,658 to 30,759 mm)
Reamed bushing	1.4971" to 1.4976" (38,025 to 38,037 mm)	1.4971" to 1.4976" (38,025 to 38,037 mm)	1.2215" to 1.2220" (31,026 to 31,038 mm)
Camshaft journal diameter	1.4961" to 1.4951" (38,000 to 37,975 mm)	1.4961" to 1.4951" (38,000 to 37,975 mm)	1.2205" to 1.2195" (31,000 to 30,975 mm)

Fig. 118 - Crankcase, timing sprocket end view.

a. Screw, securing chain end bush (1) of camshaft.

When bushings are seated in crankcase bores, their inner faces should be reamed to the following diametrical sizes:

— chain end bushing . . = 1.4971" to 1.4976" (38,025 to 38,037 mm);
— center bushing . . . = 1.4971" to 1.4976" (38,025 to 38,037 mm);
— flywheel end bushing = 1.2215" to 1.2220" (31,026 to 31,038 mm).

NOTE - Size class letter of chain end bushing and bushing crankcase bore is stamped at following locations:

— bushing . . . on bushing outer face;
— bore . . . . on lower face of crankcase near bushing dowel screw hole.

NOTE - Install bushes in seats so that oil passage holes are in line with lubrication holes in crankcase.

For location of bushings in crankcase bores, see fig. 125 showing alignment of bearing bores with oil passages in crankcase.

Check-up and Service.

Camshaft journals and cams must be the smoothest possible and in good condition.

If any traces of seizure or scoring marks are observed, replace the camshaft. If these are light, an attempt may be made to smooth out parts with a fine-grain hone.

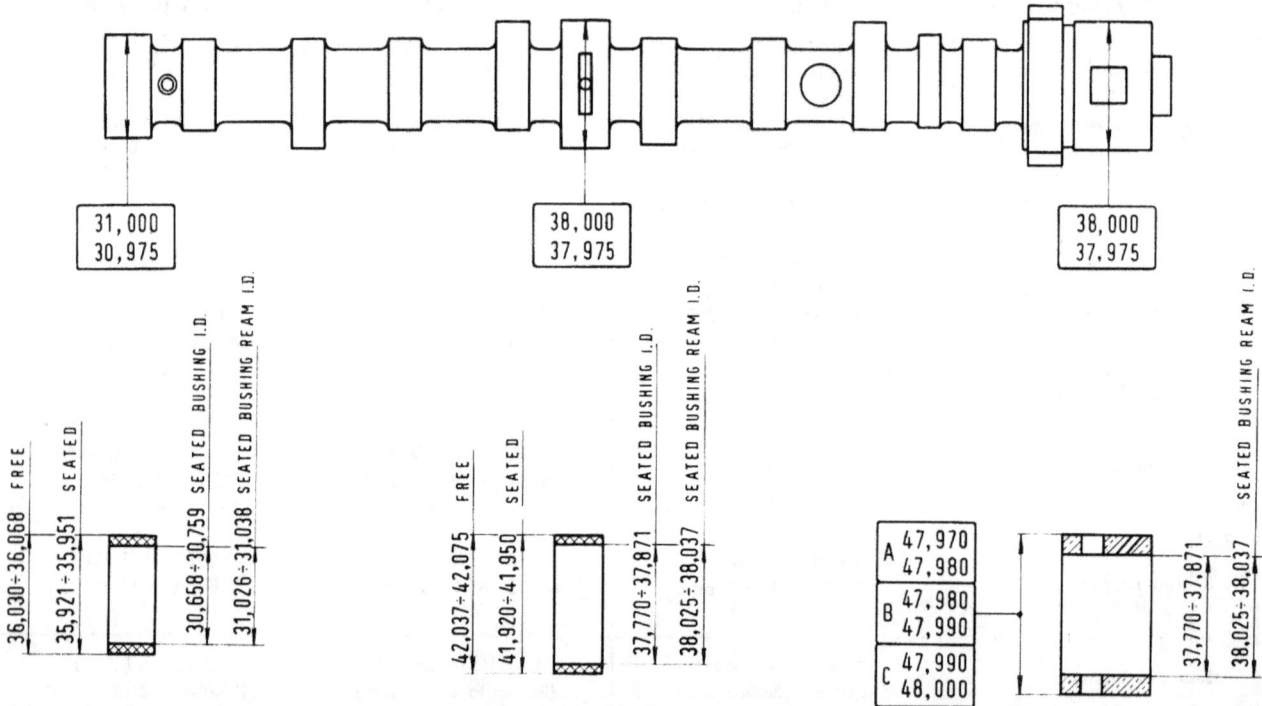

Fig. 119 - Main specifications of camshaft journals and bushings.

(From engine No. 758493, Sedan, and from engine No. 765151, Multipla).

ENGINE: VALVE TIMING GEAR

Check to see that in each cylinder valves open and close as specified; instructions for this check are outlined under « Valve Gear Timing » (page 65). Adjust valve tappet clearance at .0177" (0,45 mm).

Centering check: place camshaft between centers of gauge **C. 603**, rotate shaft by hand and with a dial indicator check for out-of-true which, if found greater than .0039" (0,10 mm) will call for a straightening of camshaft by a fly press.

Camshaft journal to bush fit clearances and wear limits are tabulated below. No undersized I. D. camshaft bush is available as spare.

In case of excessive camshaft wear, replace the camshaft and fit new bushes. New camshaft bushes should be reamed in the inner face to the bore diameter tabulated on page 62.

CAMSHAFT BUSHING - BUSHING SEAT AND CAMSHAFT REPAIR AND REBUILD STANDARDS

	FITS OF NEW PARTS	WEAR LIMITS
Camshaft bushing-to-crankcase bore:		
— chain end	.0000" to .0078" (0,000 to 0,020 mm)	.0039" (0,10 mm)
— center	pinch fit at all times	—
— flywheel end		
Camshaft journal-to-camshaft bushing:		
— chain end journal	.00098" to .00244" (0,025 to 0,062 mm)	.0039" (0,10 mm)
— center journal	.00098" to .00244" (0,025 to 0,062 mm)	.0039" (0,10 mm)
— flywheel end journal	.00102" to .00248" (0,026 to 0,063 mm)	.0039" (0,10 mm)

NOTICE

Up to engine No. 758492, « Sedan », and up to engine No. 765150, «Multipla», center and flywheel end camshaft bushings were selected, on the ground of their outer diameter value, in three size classes; chain end bushing was not classified. Crankcase bores to suit center and flywheel end bushings, too, were selected in three classes.

Bushing class identification letter was stamped on outer face of bushing; crankcase bore class identification letters were stamped at areas shown in fig. 121.

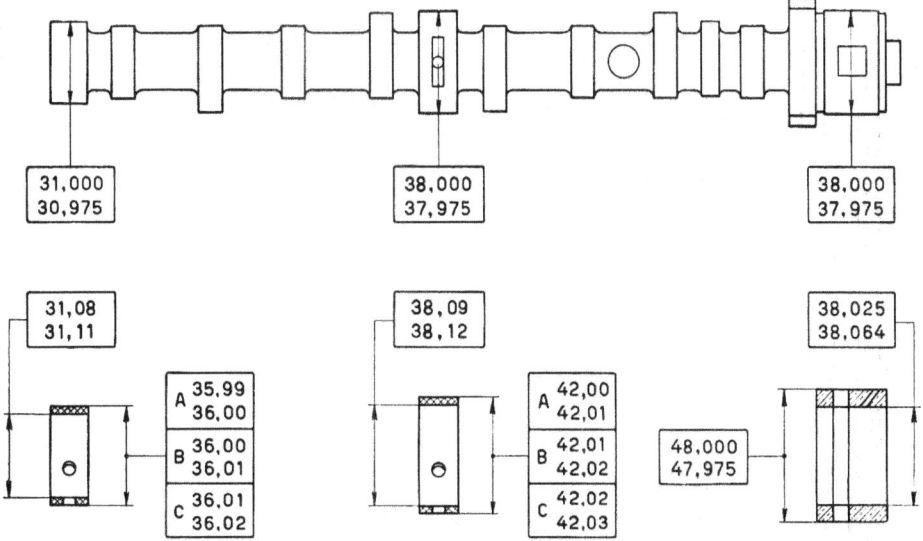

Fig. 120 - Camshaft bushes and journals check data *.
(Up to engine No. 758492, Sedan, and up to engine No. 765150, Multipla).

(*) Values are given for bushes before installation. Press fitted bush data are as follows:
1.2221" to 1.2243" (31,040 to 31,070 mm),
1.4976" to 1.4988" (38,040 to 38,070 mm).

BUSHING SEAT - CAMSHAFT BUSHING AND CAMSHAFT DIAMETERS

BEARINGS	CHAIN END	CENTER	FLYWHEEL END
Crankcase bore diameter	1.8898" to 1.8908" (48,000 to 48,025 mm)	A = 1.6504" to 1.6508" (41,920 to 41,930 mm) B = 1.6508" to 1.6512" (41,930 to 41,940 mm) C = 1.6512" to 1.6516" (41,940 to 41,950 mm)	A = 1.4142" to 1.4146" (35,920 to 35,930 mm) B = 1.4146" to 1.4150" (35,930 to 35,940 mm) C = 1.4150" to 1.4154" (35,940 to 35,950 mm)
Bushing outside diameter	1.8888" to 1.8898" (47,975 to 48,000 mm)	A = 1.6535" to 1.6539" (42,000 to 42,010 mm) B = 1.6539" to 1.6544" (42,010 to 42,020 mm) C = 1.6544" to 1.6548" (42,020 to 42,030 mm)	A = 1.4169" to 1.4173" (35,990 to 36,000 mm) B = 1.4173" to 1.4177" (36,000 to 36,010 mm) C = 1.4177" to 1.4181" (36,010 to 36,020 mm)
Bushing inside diameter	1.4971" to 1.4986" (38,025 to 38,064 mm) (free fit)	1.4977" to 1.4989" (38,040 to 38,070 mm) (press fit)	1.2221" to 1.2233" (31,040 to 31,070 mm) (press fit)
Camshaft journal diameter	1.4961" to 1.4951" (38,000 to 37,975 mm)	1.4961" to 1.4951" (38,000 to 37,975 mm)	1.2205" to 1.2195" (31,000 to 30,975 mm)

Three camshaft bushings were secured to crankcase seats by means of dowel screws (figs. 118 and 122).

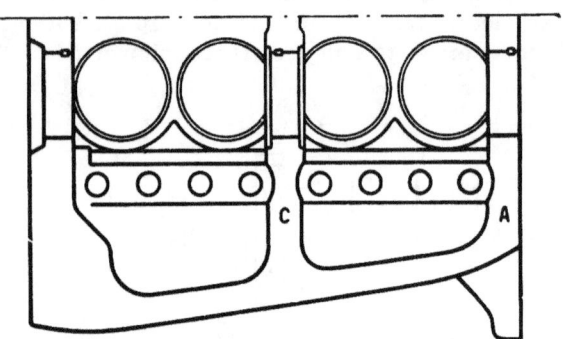

Fig. 121 - Central and flywheel end bush seat class identification letters.

(up to engine No. 758492, Sedan, and up to engine No. 765150, Multipla).

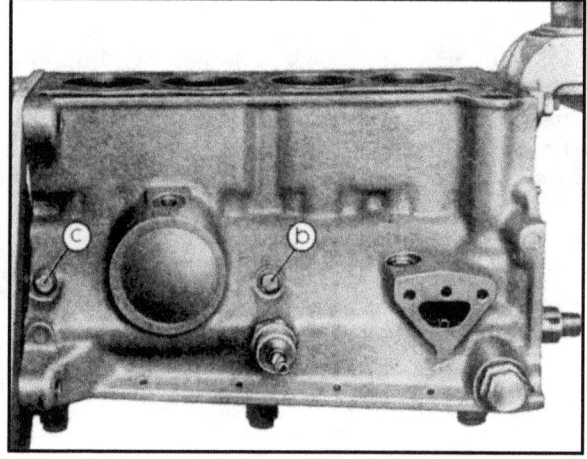

Fig. 122 - Crankcase, left side, early type.

b and c. Screws securing camshaft central and flywheel end bushes (up to engine No. 758492, Sedan, and up to engine No. 765150, Multipla).

	FIT CLEARANCE	WEAR LIMITS
Camshaft chain end bush-to-seat on crankcase	0.000" to .0020" (0,000 to 0,050 mm)	.0059" (0,15 mm)
Camshaft central and flywheel end bushes-to-seats on crankcase . .	Pinch fit at all times	—
Camshaft journal-to-bushes: — chain end journal . . . . — central journal . . . . — flywheel end journal	.0009" to .0035" (0,025 to 0,089 mm) .0016" to .0037" (0,040 to 0,095 mm) .0016" to .0037" (0,040 to 0,095 mm)	.0059" (0,15 mm)

ENGINE: VALVE TIMING GEAR

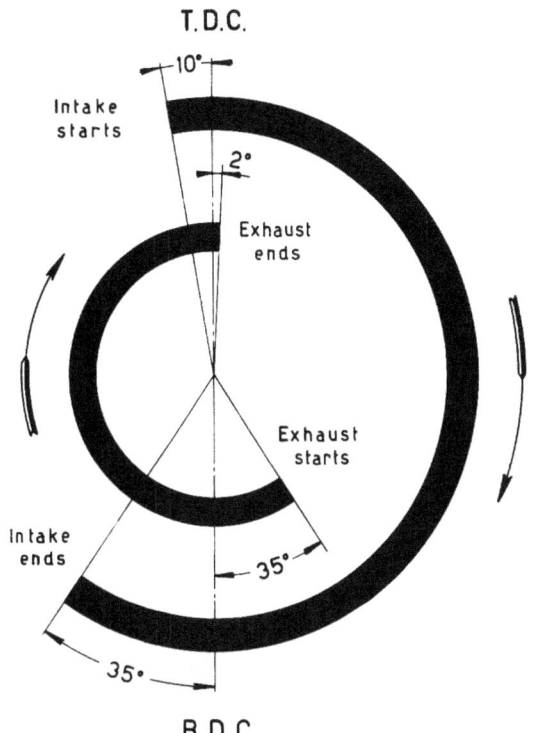

Fig. 123 - Timing diagram-early type camshaft, up to engine No. 466800.

Data intended with timing adjustment of valve-to-rocker clearance at .0082" (0,21 mm).

VALVE TAPPETS

Check also that tappet end surfaces, in contact with cams on shaft, are at all times as smooth as possible. Any indent or imprint, if not too deep, may be removed with the aid of a fine-grain abrasive stone.

The external surface of tappets and the guide bore in cylinder block must not be excessively worn, out-of-round or in any way scored. If the clearance between these two parts is greater than .0031" (0,08 mm) **a new oversized tappet must be fitted**, making sure first that guide bore is not out-of-round. If necessary, recondition guide bore with a reamer as outlined on page 31 under paragraph « Checking for Wear and Reaming Tappet Seats ».

Tappets are also supplied as spares in the .0020" and .0040" (0,05 - 0,10 mm) **O. D. oversizes**.

Standard tappet-to-seat fit clearance is .0004" to .0018" (0,010 to 0,046 mm).

Fit data is given in fig. 124 and table on page 64.

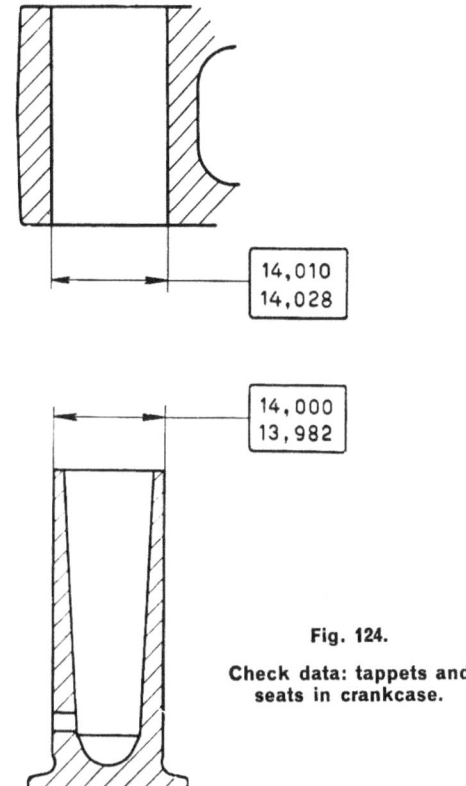

Fig. 124.

Check data: tappets and seats in crankcase.

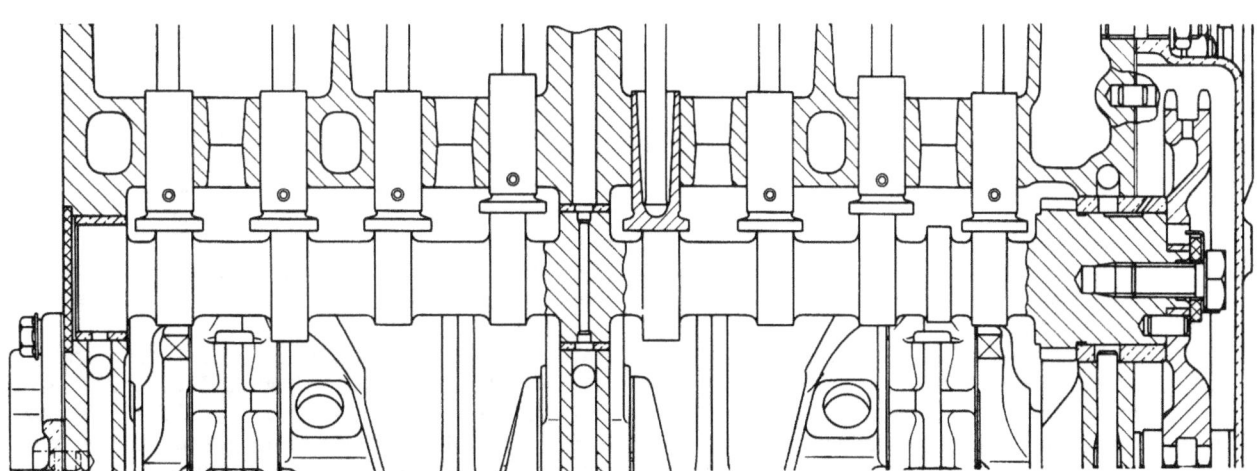

Fig. 125 - Detail of engine longitudinal section through camshaft and tappets.

TAPPETS AND SEATS FIT DATA

OVERSIZES	SEAT DIAMETER	VALVE TAPPET OUTER DIAMETER	FIT CLEARANCES
Standard	.5516" to .5523" (14,010 to 14,028 mm)	.5512" to .5505" (14,000 to 13,982 mm)	.00039" to .00181" (0,010 to 0,046 mm)
.0019" (0,05 mm)	.5535" to .5542" (14,060 to 14,078 mm)	.5531" to .5524" (14,050 to 14,032 mm)	
.0039" (0,10 mm)	.5555" to .5562" (14,110 to 14,128 mm)	.5551" to .5544" (14,100 to 14,082 mm)	

PUSHRODS

Check to see that pushrods show no sign of distortion, that spherical end in contact with rocker is not seized or rough.

Should any of these faults be present, replace parts.

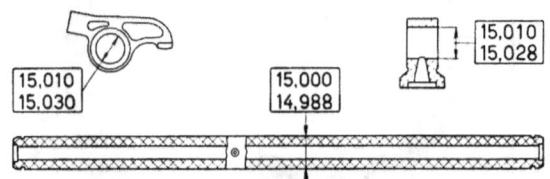

Fig. 127 - Main data of rockers, and their shaft and support.

NOTE - Rocker arm shaft support nuts should be drawn up with 14 1/2 ft.lbs (2.000 kgmm) of torque, using a torque wrench.

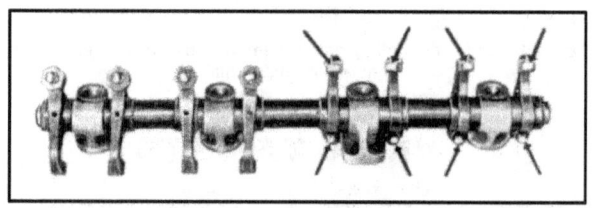

Fig. 128 - Rockers assembly.

Arrows show points to be checked on rockers.

Tappet-to-Rocker Clearance Adjustment.

This clearance must be kept reasonably constant as much as possible in order not to alter any of the data given in the timing diagram (fig. 117) as would occur when clearance is greater or smaller than specified.

In fact, if clearance is excessive noises will develop; instead, if clearance is much less than specified, valves will keep on staying a bit open with consequent lack of compression, reduced life of valves and seats.

Adjustment must be performed using the recommended wrenches: **A. 50023** and **A. 8262/bis** (fig. 129).

Rocker-to-valve clearance, when cold, both for intake and exhaust valves, should be .0039" (0,10 mm) up to engine No. 466800, and .0059" (0,15 mm) from engine No. 466801. Use respectively feeler gauge **C. 110** and **C. 111** to check clearance (see note page 57).

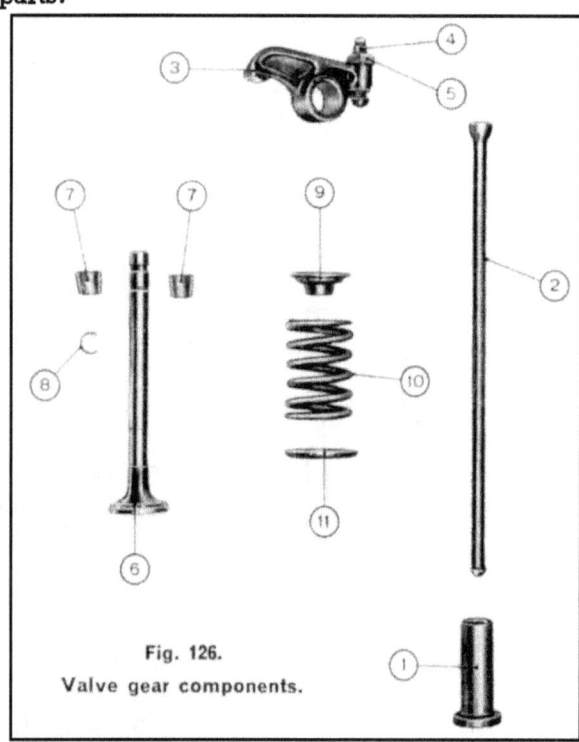

Fig. 126.
Valve gear components.

1. Tappet. - 2. Pushrod. - 3. Rocker. - 4-5. Rocker adjusting screw and nut. - 6. Valve. - 7. Cone retainers. - 8. Lock ring. - 9. Cup. - 10. Spring. - 11. Cup.

ROCKERS

Check rocker carrier shaft-to-rocker hole clearance: fit clearance is .00039" to .0017" (0,010 to 0,042 mm) and max. wear limit .0059" (0,15 mm). Replace parts if necessary.

If any contacting surface is found scored or scuffed, replace parts.

Accurately check the condition of the rocker-to-valve and rocker ball head-to-pushrod contact surfaces (fig. 128), which must at all times be polished to a mirror-like finish.

ENGINE: VALVE TIMING GEAR

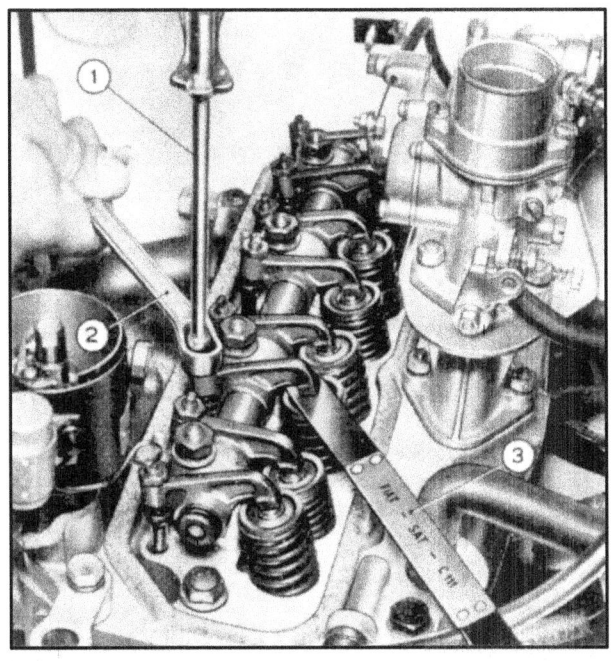

Fig. 129 - Adjusting tappet clearance.

1. Wrench A. 50023. - 2. Wrench A. 8262/bis. - 3. Feeler gauge C. 110 or C. 111.

VALVE GEAR TIMING

Proceed as follows:

— Install graduated sector C. 661 (fig. 131).

— Rotate flywheel and bring the timing mark to 4° (or 10°, up to engine No. 466800) advance position which corresponds to the beginning of intake stroke in cylinder No. 1.

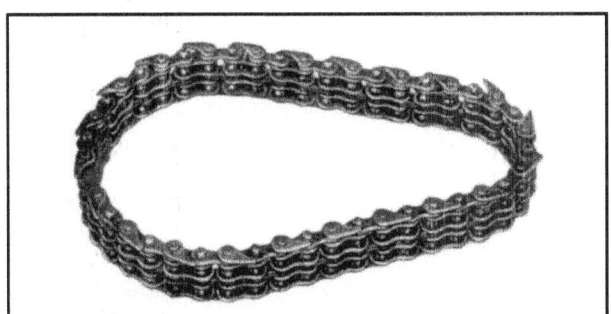

Fig. 130 - Timing drive self-stretching chain.

— Temporarily adjust cylinder No. 1 valve-to-rocker clearance to .0177″ (0,45 mm) (or .0082″ - 0,21 mm, up to engine No. 466800).

Turn camshaft until cylinder No. 1 intake valve begins to open.

Next, check timing marks on crankshaft and camshaft sprockets (fig. 132). If they register, install timing chain and, by turning flywheel, check on

Fig. 131 - Graduated sector C. 661 installed for valve gear timing.

graduated sector that advance and retard angles are as specified in timing diagram (figs. 117 - 123).

Once these operations are completed, adjust final valve-to-rocker operation clearance to .0059″ (0,15 mm) (or .0039″ - 0,10 mm, up to engine No. 466800), with engine cold.

To adjust clearance, use wrenches A. 50023 and A. 8262/bis, and feeler gauge C. 111 (or C. 110, up to engine No. 466800) (fig. 129).

Fig. 132 - Timing marks on crankshaft and camshaft sprockets. When marks register timing is correct.

SPECIFICATIONS - REPAIR AND REBUILD STANDARDS

CYLINDER BLOCK AND CRANKCASE

		in.	mm
Cylinder barrel diameter	Class A Class B Class C	2.3622 to 2.3626 2.3626 to 2.3630 2.3630 to 2.3634	60,000 to 60,010 60,010 to 60,020 60,020 to 60,030
Cylinder liner seat diameter		2.5169 to 2.5177	63,93 to 63,95
Replacement cylinder liner O. D.		2.5197 to 2.5204	64,000 to 64,018
Replacement cylinder liner I. D.		2.3425 to 2.3500	59,500 to 59,690
Cylinder barrel-to-liner pinch fit		.0020 to .0035	0,050 to 0,088

NOTE - Valve tappet seat and camshaft bushing bore data are tabulated on pages 70 and 71.

CONNECTING RODS - BEARING INSERTS - BUSHINGS

	in.	mm
Connecting rod bearing bore diameter	1.5002 to 1.5007	38,106 to 38,119
Connecting rod small end bushing bore diameter	.7850 to .7863	19,939 to 19,972
Standard con rod bearing half thickness	.0605 to .0607	1,537 to 1,543
Replacement connecting rod bearing half undersize range	.0100 - .0200 .0300 - .0400	0,254 - 0,508 0,762 - 1,016
Connecting rod small end bushing O. D.	.7874 to .7882	20,00 to 20,03
Connecting rod small end bushing I. D. (bushing in place)	.7086 to .7088	17,997 to 18,003
Piston pin-small end bushing fit: assembly clearance wear limit	.000039 to .0005 .0019	0,001 to 0,013 0,05
Small end bushing-to-bushing bore	pinch fit at all times (.0011 to .0036)	(0,028 to 0,091)
Con rod bearing half-to-crankpin journal fit: — assembly clearance — wear limit	.00047 to .00225 .0039	0,012 to 0,057 0,10
Maximum misalignment of connecting rod axes: — 4 $^{59}/_{64}$" (125 mm) apart from rod centerline	±.0020	±0,05
Weight tolerance in the same set of connecting rods	±.1 oz	±3 gr.

ENGINE: SPECIFICATIONS - REPAIR AND REBUILD STANDARDS

PISTONS - PISTON PINS - PISTON RINGS

		in.	mm
Standard piston diameter, square to pin axis			
— at skirt top	Class A	2.3592 to 2.3596	59,925 to 59,935
	Class B	2.3596 to 2.3600	59,935 to 59,945
	Class C	2.3600 to 2.3604	59,945 to 59,955
— at skirt bottom	Class A	2.3605 to 2.3609	59,957 to 59,967
	Class B	2.3609 to 2.3613	59,967 to 59,977
	Class C	2.3613 to 2.3617	59,977 to 59,987
Piston pin bore diameter		.7080 to .7082	17,983 to 17,988
Piston ring groove height	1st groove	.0998 to .1004	2,535 to 2,550
	2nd groove	.0990 to .0996	2,515 to 2,530
	3rd groove	.1557 to .1563	3,957 to 3,972
Piston pin diameter, standard		.7085 to .7084	17,995 to 17,990
Replacement piston pin oversizes		.0078 - .0197	0,2 - 0,5
Piston ring thickness:			
— first compression ring and second oil ring		.0976 to .0980	2,478 to 2,490
— third radial-slot oil ring		.1539 to .1550	3,911 to 3,937
Piston-to-cylinder barrel fit, measured square to pin axis:			
— at skirt top	assembly clearance	.0025 to .0033	0,065 to 0,085
	wear limit	.0098	0,25
— at skirt bottom	assembly clearance	.0013 to .0020	0,033 to 0,053
	wear limit	.0059	0,15
Piston pin-to-pin boss fit		pinch fit at all times (.00008 to .00050)	(0,002 to 0,013)
Piston ring-to-groove land fit (vertically):			
— first compression ring	assembly clearance	.0017 to .0028	0,045 to 0,072
	wear limit	.0059	0,15
— second oil ring	assembly clearance	.0009 to .0020	0,025 to 0,052
	wear limit	.0059	0,15
— third radial-slot oil ring	assembly clearance	.0008 to .0024	0,020 to 0,061
	wear limit	.0059	0,15
Gap of piston rings in cylinder barrel:			
— first and second ring	assembly clearance	.0078 to .0137	0,20 to 0,35
	wear limit	.0197	0,50
— third ring		touch fit at all times	
Piston oversize range		.0078 - .0157 .0236 - .0315	0,2 - 0,4 - 0,6 - 0,8
Piston ring oversize range:			
— first and second ring		.0078 - .0157 .0236 - .0315	0,2 - 0,4 - 0,6 - 0,8
— third ring		.0157	0,4

CRANKSHAFT - MAIN BEARING INSERTS

	in.	mm
Crankpin journal diameter, standard	1.3775 to 1.3783	34,988 to 35,008
Main bearing bore diameter	2.1459 to 2.1464	54,507 to 54,520
Main bearing half thickness	.0722 to .0725	1,835 to 1,841
Replacement main bearing half undersize range	.0100 - .0200 .0300 - .0400	0,254 - 0,508 0,762 - 1,016
Crankshaft bearing journal diameter, standard	1.9996 to 2.0004	50,790 to 50,810
Main bearing half-to-bearing journal fit: — assembly clearance . . . . — wear limit	.00059 to .0023 .0039	0,015 to 0,060 0,10
Center bearing journal length, shoulder-to-shoulder . . .	1.1055 to 1.1071	28,08 to 28,12
Center main bearing bore and cap width: — between thrust ring seats	.9249 to .9273	23,24 to 23,30
Center main bearing thrust ring thickness	.0909 to .0929	2,31 to 2,36
Center main bearing thrust ring oversize	.0039	0,10
Crankshaft end fit: — assembly clearance . . . . — wear limit	.0102 .0138	0,26 0,35
Maximum misalignment of crankshaft bearing journals (fig. 71)	± .00098	± 0,025
Misalignment of crankpin journals to bearing journals (fig. 72)	± .00980	± 0,25
Maximum out-of-round of crankpin and bearing journals, after grinding	± .00039	± 0,01
Misalignment of crankpin journals to crankshaft centerline (fig. 73)	± .00098	± 0,025
Flywheel: — parallel relationship of clutch disk face and crankshaft mounting face: max. out-of-true . . . . — squareness of above faces to rotation axis	up to .0039 up to .0039	≤ 0,1 ≤ 0,1
Squareness of flywheel resting face to crankshaft centerline: max. out-of-true with indicator plunger set laterally at least 1 7/32" (31 mm) apart from crankshaft	up to .00098	≤ 0,025

ENGINE: SPECIFICATIONS - REPAIR AND REBUILD STANDARDS

CYLINDER HEAD - VALVES - GUIDES - SPRINGS

	in.	mm
Valve guide cylinder head seat diameter	.5098 to .5110	12,950 to 12,977
Valve guide O. D.	.5118 to .5130	13,000 to 13,030
Valve guide I. D., valves in head	.2765 to .2772	7,022 to 7,040
Valve guide-to-cylinder head fit	pinch fit at all times (.00091 to .0031)	(0,023 to 0,080)
Valve stem diameter	.2756 to .2750	7,000 to 6,985
Valve-to-valve guide fit: — assembly clearance — wear limit	.00087 to .00217 .0059	0,022 to 0,055 0,15
Valve seat angle	45° ± 5′	
Valve face angle	45° 30′ ± 5′	
Intake valve head diameter: — face top end — face bottom end	abt. .8268 .9449 to .9528	~ 21 24 to 24,2
Exhaust valve head diameter: — face top end — face bottom end	abt. .7480 .8661 to .8740	~ 19 22 to 22,2
Maximum run-out of valve turning on stem, with dial plunger on center of outside face	.00078	0,02
Valve seat height	.0492	1,25
Valve seat smaller diameter: — intake — exhaust	.8268 to .8346 .7480 to .7559	21 to 21,2 19 to 19,2
Valve spring I. D.	.7953	20,2
Free spring height	2.0353	51,7
Spring height under 53.3 lbs (24,2 kg) of load (valves closed)	1.2992	32
Spring height under 73.6 lbs (33,4 kg) of load (valves open)	.9646	24,5
Axial lift of valves { intake exhaust	.2972 .2776	7,55 7,05
Minimum load for spring height of 1.2992″ (32 mm)	41.9 lbs	19 kg

CAMSHAFT - CAMSHAFT BUSHINGS

			in.	mm
Bushing crankcase bore diameter (*):				
— chain end bearing		Class A	1.8890 to 1.8894	47,980 to 47,990
		Class B	1.8894 to 1.8898	47,990 to 48,000
		Class C	1.8898 to 1.8902	48,000 to 48,010
— center bearing			1.6504 to 1.6516	41,920 to 41,950
— flywheel end bearing			1.4143 to 1.4154	35,921 to 35,951

		free		press fitted	
Bushing O. D. (*):		in.	mm		
— chain end	Class A	1.8886 to 1.8890	47,970 to 47,980	—	—
	Class B	1.8890 to 1.8894	47,980 to 47,990	—	—
	Class C	1.8894 to 1.8898	47,990 to 48,000	—	—
— center		1.6550 to 1.6565	42,037 to 42,075	1.6504 to 1.6516	41,920 to 41,950
— flywheel end		1.4175 to 1.4190	36,030 to 36,068	1.4143 to 1.4154	35,921 to 35,951

	seated		reamed	
Bushing I. D. (*):				
— chain end	1.4870 to 1.4910	37,770 to 37,871	1.4971 to 1.4976	38,025 to 38,037
— center	1.4870 to 1.4910	37,770 to 37,871	1.4971 to 1.4976	38,025 to 38,037
— flywheel end	1.2070 to 1.2110	30,658 to 30,759	1.2215 to 1.2220	31,026 to 31,038

Bushing-to-bushing crankcase bore fit (*):				
— chain end	assembly clearance		.0000 to .0078	0,000 to 0,020
	wear limit		.0039	0,10
— center		pinch fit	.00343 to .00610	0,087 to 0,155
— flywheel end		pinch fit	.00311 to .00579	0,079 to 0,147

Camshaft journal diameter:		
— chain end	1.4961 to 1.4951	38,000 to 37,975
— center	1.4961 to 1.4951	38,000 to 37,975
— flywheel end	1.2205 to 1.2195	31,000 to 30,975

Camshaft journal-to-camshaft bushing (*):			
— assembly clearance	chain end bearing	.00098 to .00244	0,025 to 0,062
	center bearing	.00098 to .00244	0,025 to 0,062
	flywheel end bearing	.00102 to .00248	0,026 to 0,063
— wear limit		.0039	0,10

(*) As concerns camshaft and camshaft bushing data to suit engines up to No. 758492, Sedan, and up to No. 765150, Multipla, see covering tables on page 62.

IMPORTANT NOTICE ON THE USE OF TORQUE WRENCHES

Never forget that tightening of screws and nuts with torque wrenches to the recommended torques, must always be performed with threads and seating faces (screw or nut head seating faces, lockplates) absolutely dry, perfectly free of any rust, grease, dirt, etc.

ENGINE: **SPECIFICATIONS - REPAIR AND REBUILD STANDARDS** 71

TAPPETS - ROCKER ARMS - ROCKER ARM SHAFT AND SUPPORTS

	in.	mm
Valve tappet crankcase seat diameter	.5516 to .5523	14,010 to 14,028
Valve tappet O.D., standard	.5512 to .5505	14,000 to 13,982
Valve tappet oversize range	.0020 - .0040	0,05 - 0,10
Valve tappet-to-tappet seat fit: assembly clearance .. wear limit	.00039 to .00181 .00315	0,010 to 0,046 0,08
Rocker arm shaft support bore diameter	.5910 to .5917	15,010 to 15,028
Rocker arm shaft diameter	.5906 to .5901	15,000 to 14,988
Rocker arm shaft support-to- assembly clearance .. rocker arm shaft fit: wear limit	.00039 to .00157 .0059	0,010 to 0,040 0,15
Rocker arm bore diameter	.5910 to .5918	15,010 to 15,030
Rocker arm-to-rocker arm assembly clearance .. shaft fit: wear limit	.00039 to .00165 .0059	0,010 to 0,042 0,15

ENGINE TIGHTENING REFERENCE

ITEM	DRWG. OR STD. PART No.	THREAD PITCH	MATERIAL	TIGHTENING TORQUE
Flywheel-to-crankshaft screw	1/47517/30	8 MA (x1,25)	R 100	25.3 to 28.9 ft.lbs (3500 to 4000 kgmm)
Main bearing cap-to-crankcase screw .	0.04.141/ 873821	10 x 1,25 M	R 100	44.8 ft.lbs (6200 kgmm)
Cap-to-connecting rod bolt nut ...	1/25662/20	7 MB (x0,75)	R 80 (Bolt R 100)	16 ft.lbs (2200 kgmm)
Sprocket-to-crankshaft screw	1/59706/20	10 x 1,25 M	R 80	38.3 ft.lbs (5300 kgmm)
Cylinder head-to-cylinder block screw	1/47518/30 1/47519/30 1/47524/30	8 MA (x1,25)	R 100	20.3 to 21.7 ft.lbs (2800 to 3000 kgmm)
Rocker support-to-cylinder head stud nut	1/17016/20	8MA (x1,25)	R 80 (Stud R 100)	14.5 ft.lbs (2000 kgmm)
Fan drive pulley-to-crankshaft nut ..	0.32.333/ 4064759	18 MB (x1,5)	R 50 Znt (Crankshaft C 40 Bon.)	72.3 ft.lbs (10000 kgmm)
Air conveyor-to-water pump screw .	0.32.426/ 898514	8 MB (x1)	R 80	18.1 ft.lbs (2500 kgmm)

ENGINE BRAKE TEST

After overhauling, the engine must be bench and brake tested.

Engine Installation on Test Bench.

Place engine on stands (fig. 133), using the brackets shown for front and rear supports.

Connect: exhaust manifold to flanged exhaust pipe (fig. 133) and flywheel to input shaft by the suitable flange (fig. 134). Connect fuel and coolant lines.

Remove the insufficient oil pressure indicator sending unit and, in its place, connect the pipe to the test bench pressure gauge.

Connect ignition distributor and generator cables.

Preliminary Operations.
— Check oil in sump for correct level.
— Open fuel and coolant cocks.
— Send current to ignition system.
— Start engine.

Test Procedure.

After starting the engine see if:
— oil, coolant or fuel leaks occur at faying surfaces, connections and gaskets;
— oil circulates correctly and test bench oil gage reads the specified pressure of 35.5 to 42.6 psi (2,5 to 3 kg/cm²);

Fig. 134 - Engine on test bench.
Arrow points to flange connecting engine flywheel to input shaft of test bench.

— engine runs correctly.

In case of irregular operation, stop engine at once and remedy the trouble before proceeding with the test.

It should be noted, however, that during the initial test period engine operation is still rough due to friction between contact surfaces of moving parts which still need breaking in, specially when pistons, bearings or cylinder liners have been replaced, or barrels rebored.

Bench Test Range of Rebuilt Engines.

A rebuilt engine should be submitted to a proper testing range on test bench. To do so, comply with the data tabulated hereafter.

Test Speed Rate r.p.m.	Time - Min.	Brake Load
500	15'	No load
2,000	15'	Half load
2,000	5'	Full load
Total	35'	

When bench testing a rebuilt engine, take care not to run the engine to top speed limits, but comply with the figures given in the table.

Engine break-in will be completed by the Owner who is bound not to drive the car beyond the speed rates specified for the initial use period.

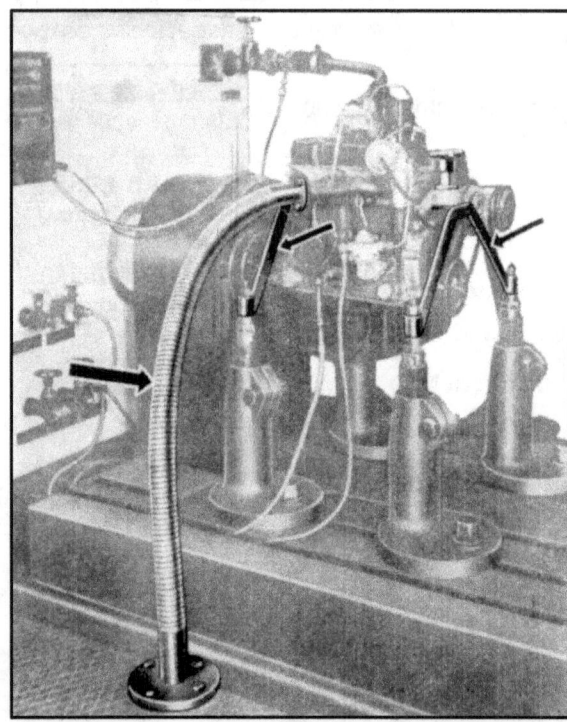

Fig. 133 - Engine on test bench stands.
Arrows point to brackets for engine front and rear supports and flanged pipe for exhaust of combustion gases.

ENGINE: BRAKE TEST

Fig. 135 - Engine under running-in on test bench.

Power Test.

To know the power developed by the engine at the various speeds, the formula is:

$$HP = 0{,}001 \, P \cdot N$$

where:
- HP = Power in HP;
- P = Load in kg (reading of dynamometer or weight applied on brake arm end);
- N = R.P.M. (reading of tachometer);
- 0,001 = Constant for a brake arm of length = 0,716 m.

For brakes with arm length = 1,432 m the formula is: $HP = 0{,}002 \, P \cdot N$

Inspection after Brake Test.

Disassemble engine and inspect components after brake test only when:
— engine operation has shown irregular or engine has not developed the rated power.

In this occurrence, after remedying troubles and reassembling engine repeat brake test and make sure of correct engine operation.

Fig. 137 - Performance curves of the 100.000 and 100.008 engines (up to No. 644010 and 644440, respectively).

Data are the minimum for a fully run-in engine and are intended:
(1) without water pump, fan, generator, exhaust silencer;
(2) with water pump, fan, generator and w/o silencer;
(3) with water pump, fan, generator and exhaust silencer.

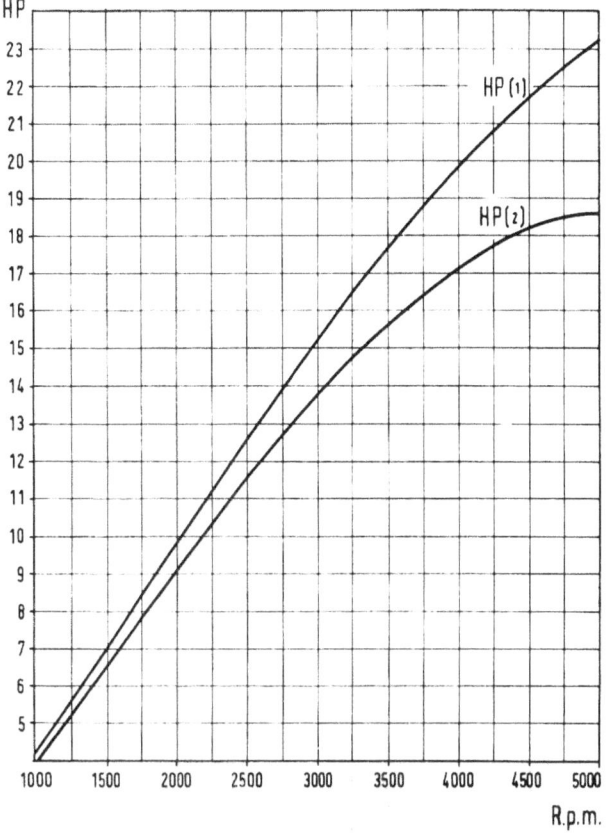

Fig. 136 - Performance curves of the 100.000 and 100.008 engines (from No. 644011 and 644441, respectively).

Data are the minimum for a fully run-in engine and are intended:
(1) without water pump, fan, generator, exhaust silencer;
(2) with water pump, fan, generator and exhaust silencer.

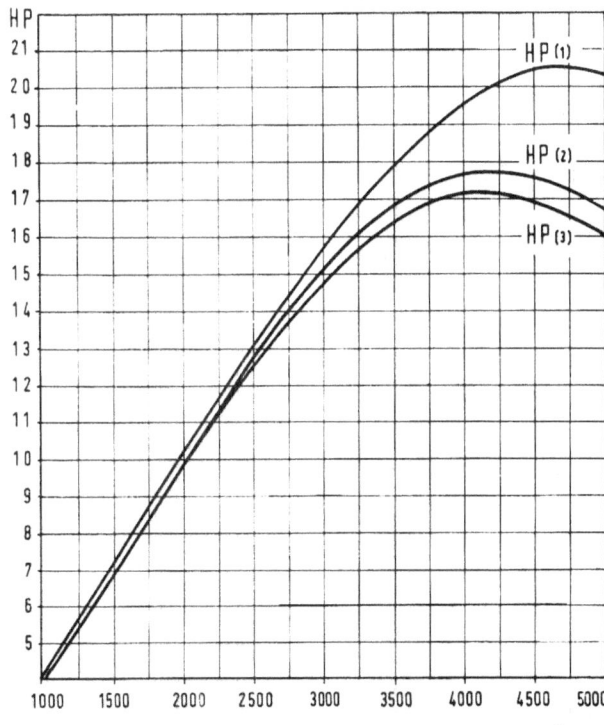

NOTES

Section 3

FUEL SYSTEM
LUBRICATION SYSTEM
COOLING SYSTEM
POWER PLANT MOUNTINGS

	Page
FUEL PUMP	77
FUEL TANK	78
DRY AIR CLEANER	78
OIL BATH AIR CLEANER	80
MANIFOLDS	80
WEBER 26 IM CARBURETOR	81
WEBER 22 IM CARBURETOR	88
LUBRICATION SYSTEM	91
OIL PUMP	91
OIL PRESSURE RELIEF VALVE	92
OIL FILTER	93
SUMP-TO-CRANKCASE SEAL GASKETS	93
LOW OIL PRESSURE INDICATOR SENDING UNIT	95
CRANKASE VENTILATION LINES	96
OIL PUMP FIT DATA	96
COOLING SYSTEM	97
WATER PUMP	98
AIR CONVEYOR	100
FAN	100
RADIATOR	101
ANTIFREEZE MIXTURE	102
THERMOSTAT	104
POWER PLANT MOUNTINGS	105

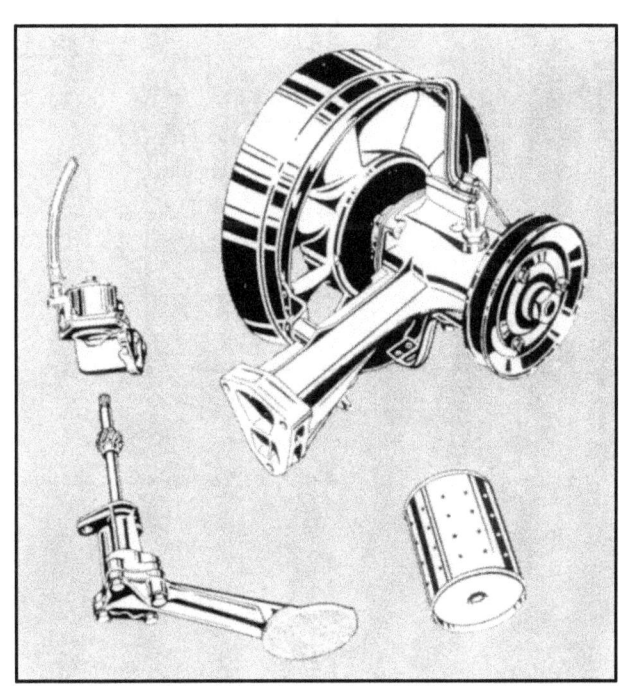

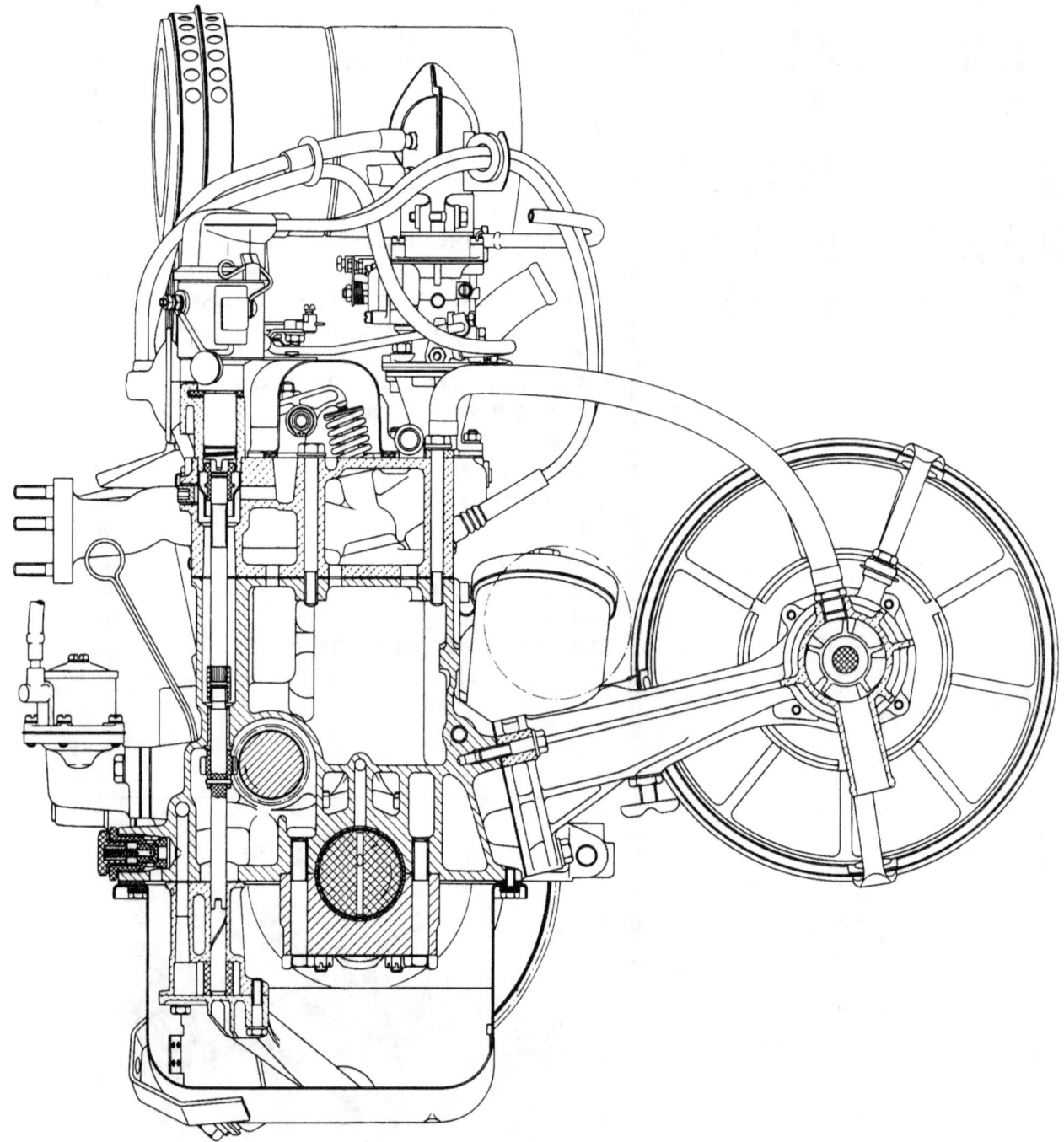

Fig. 138 - Engine cross section through drives.

ENGINE: FUEL SYSTEM

FUEL SYSTEM

Fuel Pump	page	77
Fuel Tank	»	78
Dry Air Cleaner	»	78
Oil Bath Air Cleaner	»	80
Manifolds	»	80
Weber 26 IM Carburetor	»	81
Weber 22 IM Carburetor	»	88

Fuel is drawn from tank by a diaphragm pump which then sends it on to carburetor.

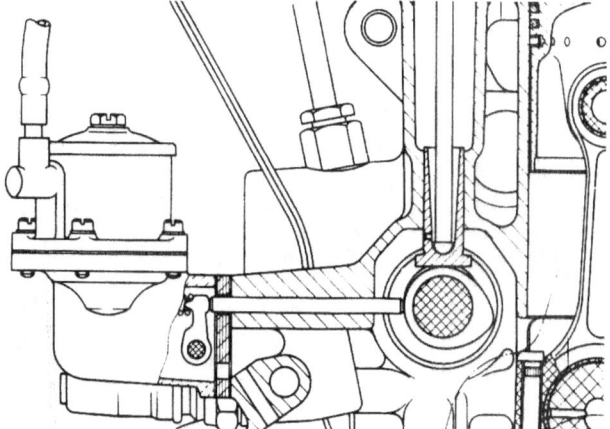

Fig. 139 - Detail of engine cut-away on fuel pump control.

FUEL PUMP

This pump is mounted on crankcase left side and is controlled by a camshaft cam lobe through a rod that acts on diaphragm operating rocker (fig. 139).

It consists of two elements:

— the upper element which incorporates the fuel chamber - which also serves for priming; filter gauze; inlet and outlet valves with relevant springs;

— the lower element which houses the pump diaphragm, and its camshaft-operated pushrod control (fig. 140).

The fuel pump requires no particular attention. Nevertheless, a periodical check is recommended.

By taking off pump cover, the sludge deposited in fuel chamber or on filter gauze may be removed.

The disassembly of inlet and outlet valves (13, 18, fig. 140) is performed after removing retaining plate (10, fig. 140). Wash these valves in gasoline. Replace if they are damaged.

Check springs for good condition: if weak or distorted, replace.

The inlet chamber diaphragm control mechanism must be washed in kerosene and wetted with some thin oil.

Fuel pump seals, even if slightly damaged, must be replaced. Apply grease sparingly on new seals before assembly. If a new diaphragm has to be fitted, keep it in kerosene for at least fifteen minutes before assembly.

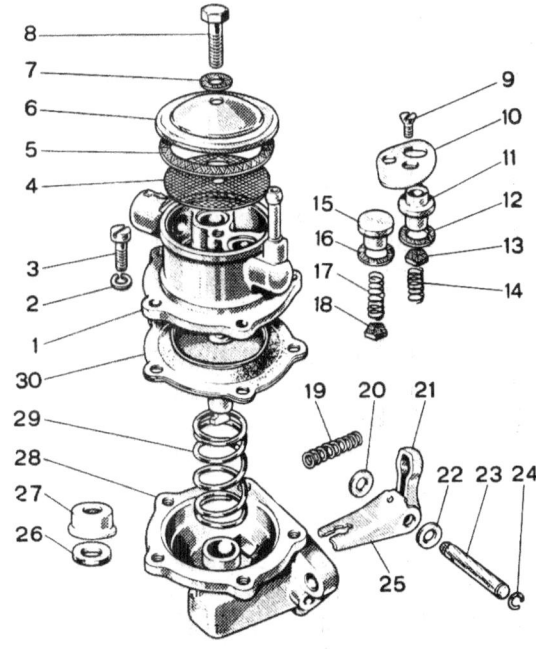

Fig. 140 - Fuel pump components.
(Alternative to pump shown in fig. 141).

1. Upper body. - 2. Lockwasher. - 3. Screw. - 4. Filter. - 5. Seal. - 6. Cover. - 7. Gasket. - 8. Screw. - 9. Screw. - 10. Plate. - 11. Plug. - 12. Gasket. - 13. Inlet valve. - 14. Spring. - 15. Plug. - 16. Gasket. - 17. Spring. - 18. Outlet valve. - 19. Spring. - 20. Washer. - 21. Control rocker. - 22. Washer. - 23. Pin. - 24. Snapring. - 25. Lever. - 26. Felt. - 27. Cup. - 28. Pump lower body. - 29. Spring. - 30. Diaphragm.

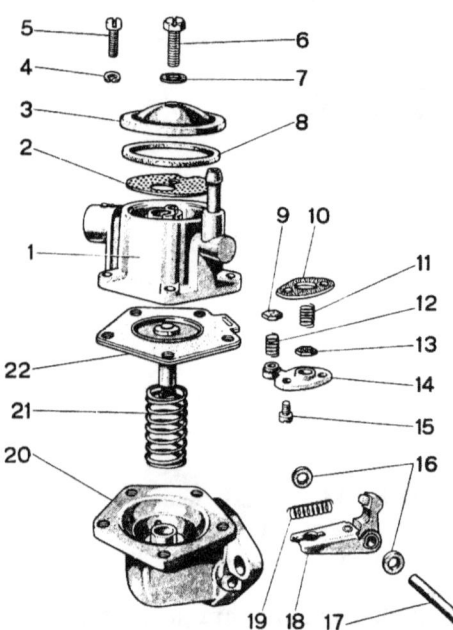

Fig. 141 - Fuel pump components.

(Alternative to pump shown in fig. 140).

1. Upper body. - 2. Filter. - 3. Cover. - 4. Lockwasher. - 5. Screw. - 6. Screw. - 7. Gasket. - 8. Gasket. - 9. Inlet valve. - 10. Gasket. - 11. Spring. - 12. Spring. - 13. Outlet valve. - 14. Cover. - 15. Screw. - 16. Washers. - 17. Pin. - 18. Control rocker. - 19. Spring. - 20. Lower body. - 21. Spring. - 22. Diaphragm.

NOTE - The fuel pump components may turn out to differ slightly from those shown in figs. 140-141, according to the source of the fuel pump.

When no gasoline reaches carburetor, check to see if this condition is due to one of the following possible causes:

a) empty tank;
b) loose fuel pump cover screws;
c) leaky pipes or connections;
d) bent or flattened pipes;
e) dirty filter gauze;
f) dirty or distorted valves;
g) weak springs;
h) fuel pump control pushrod excessively worn, shortened or seizing in its seat.

Correct the condition by eliminating the cause of trouble.

NOTE - Before removing pump and relevant lines for cleaning and checks, disconnect plastic pipe on tank to prevent the flow of fuel from tank through syphoning.

FUEL TANK

The tank is located on right side of front compartment.

The tank carries: the filler union with cap, fuel level gauge sending unit in conjunction with suction pipe with filter.

To remove tank for cleanings, proceed as follows: disconnect the plastic pipe between suction and pump pipes. Disconnect sending unit cables and remove sending unit in conjunction with the suction pipe and filter.

Eventually, remove the tank fastening strap. To do so, undo the upper screw and disengage the strap from the dash plate.

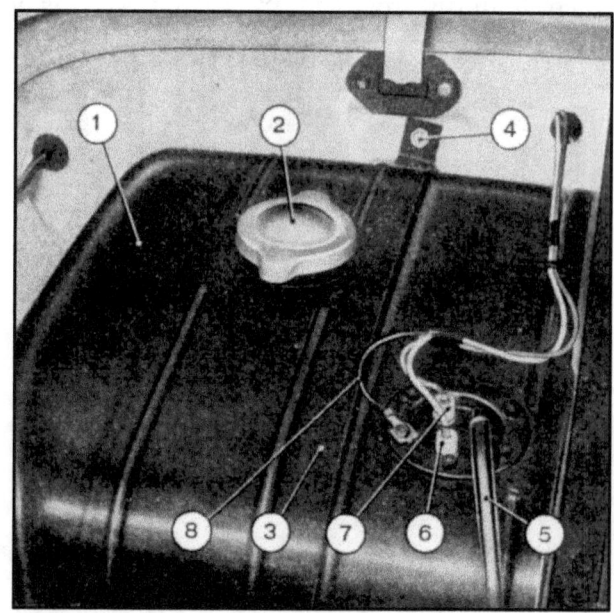

Fig. 142 - Fuel tank.

1. Tank. - 2. Fuel filler plug. - 3. Tank fastening band. - 4. Band screw. - 5. Fuel pump line. - 6. Fuel gauge cable terminal. - 7. Fuel reserve supply indicator terminal. - 8. Ground cable.

Withdraw the tank from the front compartment. Drain the fuel and clean accurately both tank and filter with gasoline.

DRY AIR CLEANER

The dry air cleaner is provided with silencer and a warm air intake scoop.

A special pleated paper cartridge is fitted.

The cover is slotted and may rotate on its fixing pin. By this arrangement a sort of climatic control is possible: in fact, in summer air is drawn in through the upper slots in cover while in winter, after suitably turning the cover 180° degrees, the heated air around exhaust manifold will enter through the lower scoop at cleaner base (fig. 143).

ENGINE: FUEL SYSTEM

Rotate cover by grabbing the two lugs after slackening the central mounting wing nut.

Move up **green lug** in summer and **red lug** in winter.

A continuous and constant air cleaner efficiency is of maximum importance to protect the engine and its components. In fact, if dust or any other foreign matter - suspended in the air drawn in by the engine - succeeds in flowing past the cleaner and reaching the engine inner components, dirt will mix with lube oil and form a strongly abrasive compound that will accelerate wear and shorten life of engine components.

The cartridge must be replaced every 6000 miles (10.000 km).

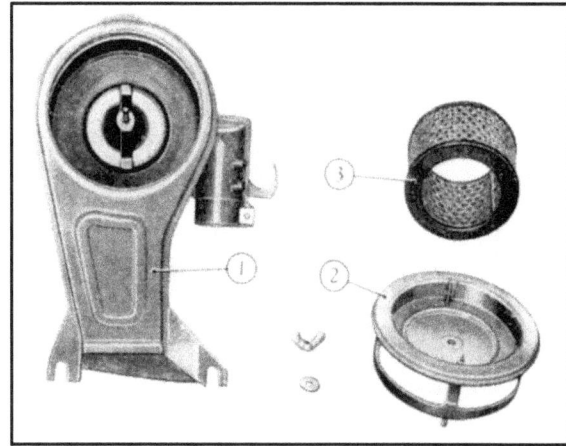

Fig. 144 - Air cleaner components.

1. Cleaner body. - 2. Cover with air intake openings. - 3. Filtering element.

It goes without saying, however, that if car has been driven mostly over dusty roads the cartridge must be replaced more often.

To take down air cleaner from engine, proceed as follows:

a) slacken the air cleaner-to-carburetor cover mounting screw in its hollow pad;

b) slacken the two cleaner lower end nuts from the studs on exhaust manifold (fig. 145);

c) at air cleaner, disconnect crankcase and cylinder head vent hoses;

d) remove air cleaner, and then the cleaner-to-carburetor mounting gasket.

Fig. 143 - Engine air intake.

1. Air cleaner with intake silencer. - 2. Wing nut. - 3. Cleaner cover rotation grab lugs to set air intake according to seasonal requirements. - 4. Warm air intake slots (summer, green lug up). - 5. Warm air intake (winter, red lug up). - 6. Exhaust manifold.

NOTE - It is of paramount importance that the filter element be given the proper routine care as recommended As a matter of fact a clogged air cleaner results in lower engine suction which brings about a reduction of engine power. Therefore, when engine performance is poor, inspect first of all is poor, inspect first of all the condition of the air cleaner.

Fig. 145 - Removal of air cleaner and exhaust manifold using wrench A. 8110.

1. Air cleaner. - 2. Wrench A. 8110. - 3. Exhaust manifold.

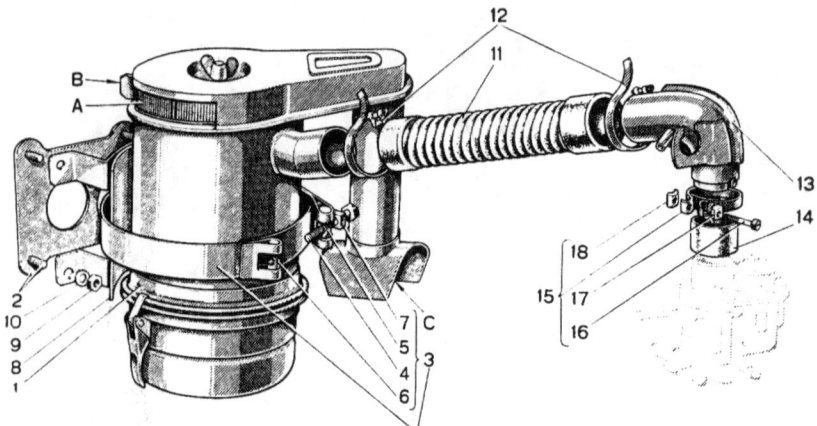

Fig. 146.
Oil bath air cleaner.

1. Air cleaner. - 2. Cleaner support bracket. - 3. Collar, cleaner to bracket. - 4. Collar screw. - 5. Bridge piece. - 6. Nut. - 7. Pad. - 8. Support plate. - 9. Nut. - 10. Lockwasher. - 11. Hose. - 12. Collar. - 13. Elbow. - 14. Adapter. - 15. Collar, adapter. - 16. Collar screw. - 17. Bridge piece. - 18. Nut. - A. Screened slots, air intake in summer. - B. Shutter lug. - C. Warm air intake scoop (winter).

OIL BATH AIR CLEANER

On cars intended for special service conditions, the standard paper cartridge air filter has been replaced by an oil bath air cleaner.

The latter consists of a cylindrical shell with cover having a by-pass shutter, filtering element with retaining ring and oil bowl with gasket.

According to seasonal requirements the by-pass may be set in two positions. During summer air enters through the screened slots (A, fig. 146). In winter the entrance of cold air may be impeded by rotating the by-pass 105° thus feeding warm air to the engine. The stream of incoming air is ducted around exhaust manifold through lower scoop (C, fig. 146) where it is heated.

To set the by-pass in the required position slacken the cover central wingnut and turn by-pass lug (B, fig. 146) then retightening the wingnut.

Oil level must never be allowed to drop more than .39" (1 cm) below fill mark on oil bowl. To check oil level release the two fasteners and take off the bowl. Usually the oil level should be checked every 900 miles (1500 km) topping up, if necessary, with engine lube oil.

Change the oil every 3,000 miles (5.000 km) after cleaning the filter as follows:

a) Wash bowl with kerosene or gasoline.

b) Take off the filtering element, after removing its retainment ring on central pipe.

c) Wash the element by immersion in kerosene or gasoline.

d) Let the element drip dry and reinstall.

The oil bowl capacity is .38 (U. S.) ar .32 (G. B.) qts (0,400 kg).

Every 6,000 miles (10.000 km) carry out a general cleaning of the cleaner.

To this purpose remove the cleaner from car by slackening the clamp screw (3, fig. 146) securing the unit to the support bracket (8) and collar (15, fig. 146) of cleaner connection to carburetor.

Dismantle the cleaner and wash all its components in kerosene or gasoline.

Reassemble, refill the bowl with engine oil and reinstall on car.

MANIFOLDS

Manifolds will rarely require attention as they are not subject to appreciable wear.

On engines 100.000 and 100.008 intake manifold is cast integral with the cylinder head.

The exhaust manifold may develop cracks or distortions as a result of intense heat to which it is subjected.

When servicing manifolds, remove carbon deposits and dirt having collected on both inside and outside of them; check the cylinder head mating face for level and, if necessary, smooth it out with a file; carefully inspect the manifold for evidence of cracks and if so, replace manifold; make sure that the gasket warrants perfect seal, otherwise replace the gasket.

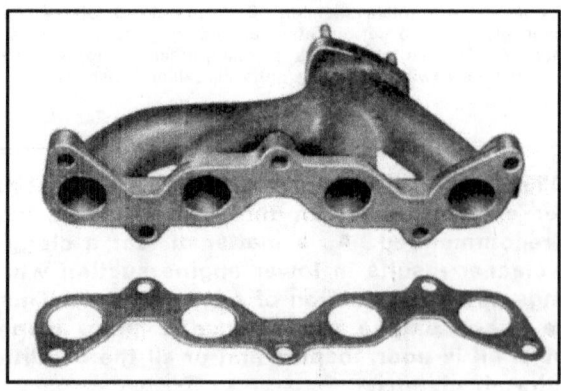

Fig. 147 - Exhaust manifold and gasket.

ENGINE: FUEL SYSTEM

CARBURETOR

WEBER CARBURETOR TYPE 26 IM

This carburetor has a throat diameter at the height of throttle of 1.02" (26 mm).

Carburetor is equipped with **progressive-action starting device** which enables the driver to suit the mixture richness to the most varied conditions of starting, until the engine has reached the rated operation temperature.

The dampened needle valve ensures a smoother engine running since thanks to its dampening device it is not affected by vibrations or shocks and, therefore, keeps more steadily constant the level in carburetor bowl.

Secondary Venturi diameter is .63" (16 mm) and is in a single casting with carburetor body. A fuel strainer is incorporated in carburetor cover.

At bottom, near the throttle control lever, the carburetor carries the connection for vacuum advance corrector.

Operation.

Referring to the diagram (fig. 150) the operation of Weber 26 IM carburetor can be outlined as follows: the air from above, flows through Venturi (24) where it mixes with the fuel issuing from nozzle (25) and is then conveyed to cylinders through primary Venturi (21) and throat where throttle (19) is adjusting the flow.

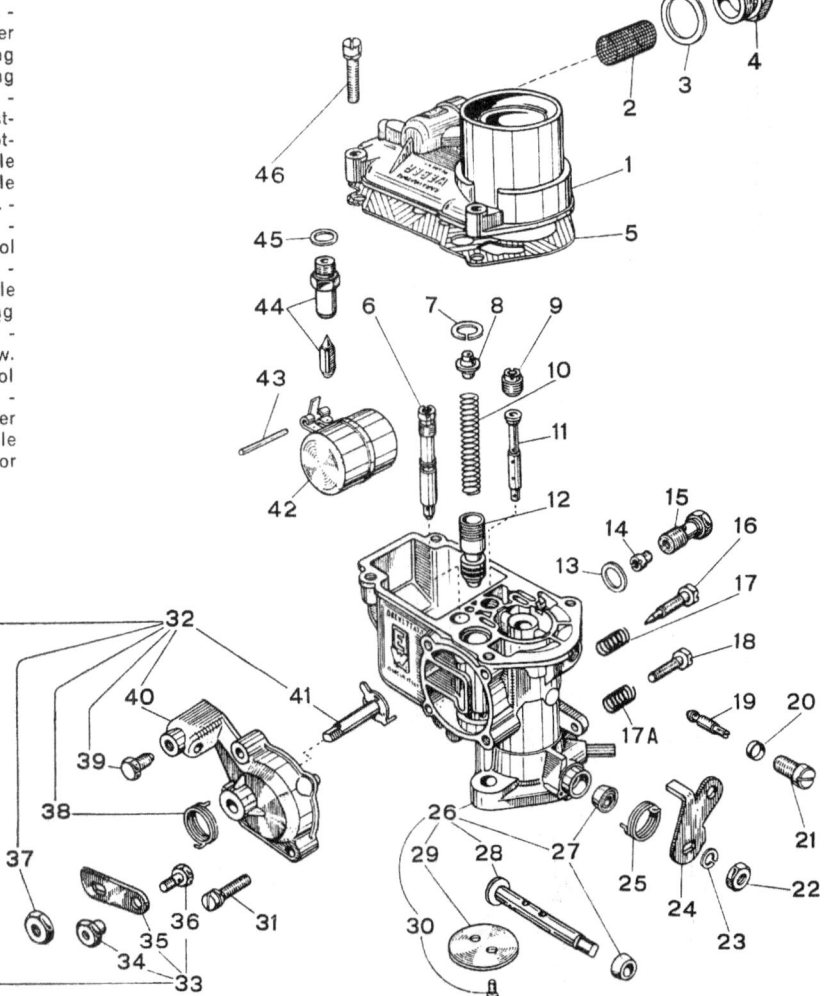

1. Cover. - 2. Strainer. - 3. Strainer plug gasket. - 4. Strainer plug. - 5. Cover gasket. - 6. Starting jet. - 7. Spring retainment snap ring. - 8. Spring retainer and guide. - 9. Air corrector screw. - 10. Starting valve spring. - 11. Emulsion well. - 12. Starting valve. - 13. Main jet holder gasket. - 14. Main jet. - 15. Main jet holder. - 16. Idle speed mixture adjusting screw. - 17. Screw friction spring. - 17 A. Throttle opening setscrew friction spring. - 18. Throttle opening setscrew. - 19. Idle speed jet. - 20. Idle speed jet holder gasket. - 21. Idle speed jet holder. - 22. Throttle control lever nut. - 23. Lockwasher. - 24. Throttle control lever. - 25. Throttle control lever spring. - 26. Body. - 27. Throttle shaft seal. - 28. Throttle shaft. - 29. Throttle. - 30. Throttle screw. - 31. Cover screw. - 32. Cover. - 33. Starting control lever. - 34. Bowden wire screw nut. - 35. Starting control lever. - 36. Bowden wire screw. - 37. Starting control lever nut. - 38. Starting control lever spring. - 39. Sheath screw. - 40. Cover. - 41. Starting valve control shaft. - 42. Float - either brass or nylon. - 43. Float pivot. - 44. Needle valve. - 45. Needle valve gasket. - 46. Carburetor cover screw.

Fig. 148.
Weber 26 IM carburetor.

FIAT - 600 - 600 D SEDAN AND MULTIPLA

Fig. 149 - Weber 26 IM carburetor.

1. Idle speed jet holder. - 2. Throttle control lever. - 3. Slow running adjustment screw. - 4. Vacuum advance line connection. - 5. Idle speed mixture adjustment screw. - 6. Main jet holder. - 7. Fuel inlet connection. - 8. Strainer plug.

From fuel line, joined to carburetor by connection (8), the fuel flows across strainer (7), through needle valve (9) into bowl (16) where float (12) hinged to pivot (11) controls the opening of needle (10) and maintains a constant fuel level.

From bowl (16) - via metered main jet (15) - fuel reaches emulsion well (23) whence, after having been mixed with the air coming from metered air corrector screw (1), through emulsion orifices (22) and spray nozzle (25) it finally reaches Venturis (24) and (21) where it blends with the air stream promoted by engine vacuum and is then drawn into cylinders.

While idling, through an appropriate passage fuel is carried from well (23) to idle speed jet (13) where it is mixed with the air coming from air orifice (5). Through duct (3) and idle speed orifice (18) - adjustable by taper-point screw (17) - the fuel reaches carburetor throat past throttle (19) where it is further mixed with the air stream drawn in by engine vacuum through the gap around the throttle in idling speed position.

From duct (3) the mixture can also reach the carburetor throttle chamber through transition hole (20), located in exact relation to the throttle; the purpose of this transition hole is to permit a smooth acceleration of engine from idling speed, proportionately to the increase in throttle opening.

Starting Device.

This device has the function of ensuring proper engine cold starting. It is controlled by means of the left lever (2, fig. 156) placed behind the gearbox lever and must be progressively set back to rest position as engine is reaching the rated operation temperature. The starting device (fig. 151) is made up of valve (33) actuated by the lug of rocker (38) connected, through a suitable shaft, to control lever (40). By pulling the device control to stroke end, valve (33) is lifted from its seat and brought in the « fully open » position (diagram « A », fig. 151). Under these conditions valve (33) closes air orifice (27) and transition mixture orifice (29) and uncovers

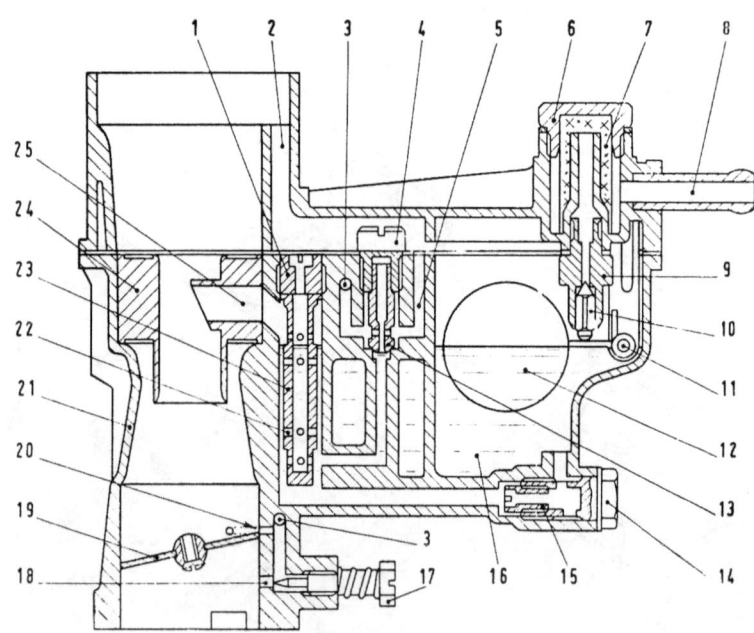

Fig. 150.

Diagrammatic section.

1. Air corrector screw. - 2. Air intake. - 3. Idle speed mixture duct. - 4. Idle speed jet holder. - 5. Idle speed air orifice. - 6. Strainer plug. - 7. Strainer. - 8. Fuel inlet connection. - 9. Needle valve. - 10. Valve needle. - 11. Float pivot. - 12. Float. - 13. Idle speed jet. - 14. Main jet holder. - 15. Main jet. - 16. Bowl. - 17. Idle speed mixture adjustment screw. - 18. Idle speed orifice. - 19. Throttle. - 20. Transition hole. - 21. Primary Venturi. - 22. Emulsion orifices. - 23. Emulsion well. - 24. Secondary Venturi. - 25. Main nozzle.

ENGINE: FUEL SYSTEM

mixture orifices (30) (32) [(which communicate with starting jet (48) through duct (26)] and air orifices (35) (which communicate with the outside through strainer (37) and slot (36).

With throttle in idling speed position, the vacuum of engine cranked by the starter causes the fuel contained in the recess of jet (48), in the jet and in reserve well (47), to be emulsioned with the air coming from orifices (45) and (46).

With valve (33) partially opened, orifice (29) may communicate with carburetor throat, through the valve central slot, duct (28) and orifice (31) drilled in Venturi (21) in correspondence with the restriction.

Through duct (26) and orifices (30) and (32) the mixture arrives - simultaneously with air from orifices (35) - past the throttle through duct (34), thus permitting prompt starting of the engine.

After engine fires the device delivers a mixture whose fuel/air ratio is such as to permit regular running of engine while still cold. But, as the engine warms up, this mixture would be excessive and too rich; therefore, it becomes necessary to exclude gradually the device as the engine is reaching the rated operation temperature. During this maneuver, valve (33) slowly uncovers orifice (27) which permits a greater amount of air to enter through the hole of spring guide (44) (to weaken the mixture) while, by closing progressively orifices (30) and (32) and air orifices (35), also the amount of mixture is reduced. This way, the mixture title and amount is reduced proportionally to the amount the device is inserted (see diagram «B», fig. 151).

Orifice (29), duct (28), and orifice (31), drilled in Venturi (21), have the task of permitting a regular progression of acceleration also with cold engine. By opening throttle (19) to speed up the engine the vacuum acting on duct (34) is reduced. This would cause a reduction in the amount of fuel delivered through said duct (34), with consequent irregular running of the engine, but, through orifice (31), duct (28) and orifice (29) (from which air is drawn when throttle is closed) some mixture is sucked in by the vacuum formed in the restriction of the Venturi consequent to the opening of the throttle, and this compensates for the reduction in delivery through duct (34).

When the starting device is excluded, valve (33) covers also orifice (29) and prevents the entrance of mixture (diagram «C», fig. 151).

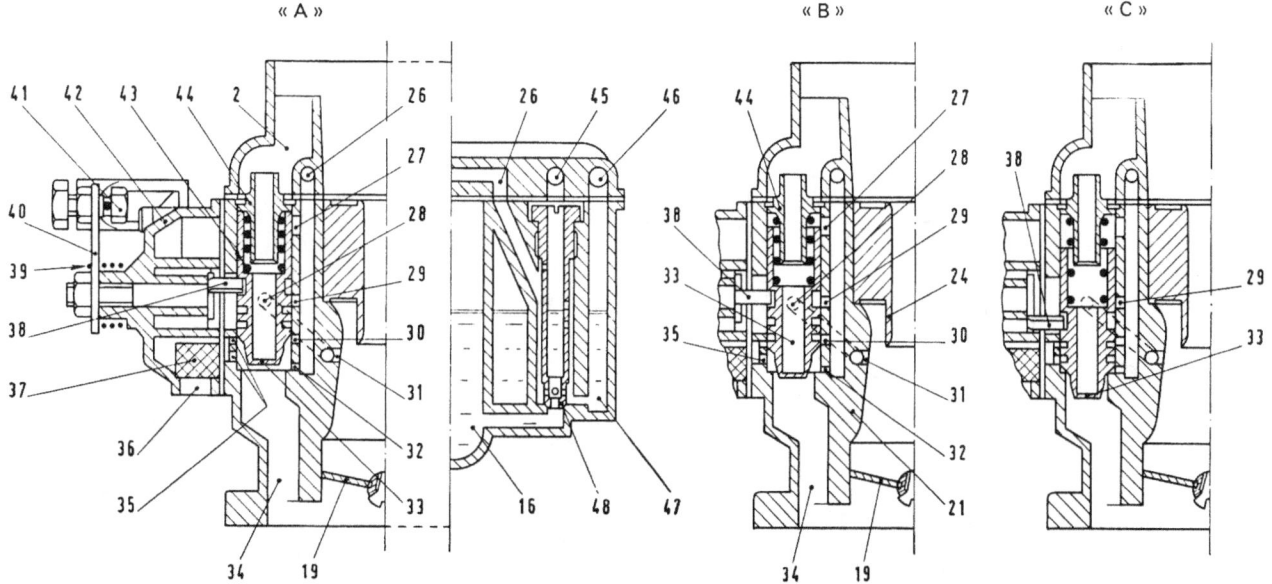

Fig. 151 - Starting device (choke) diagrammatic section.
«A»: Device fully inserted. - «B»: Device partially inserted. - «C»: Device disinserted.
2. Air inlet. - 16. Bowl. - 19. Throttle. - 21. Primary Venturi. - 24. Secondary Venturi. - 26. Mixture duct. - 27. Mixture leaning air orifice. - 28. Transition duct. - 29. Transition mixture orifice. - 30. Starting mixture orifice. - 31. Transition orifice. - 32. Starting mixture orifice. - 33. Starting valve. - 34. Starting mixture duct. - 35. Starting device air orifices. - 36. Air intake slot. - 37. Strainer. - 38. Rocker. - 39. Lever return spring. - 40. Starting device control lever. - 41. Control wire screw. - 42. Cover with support for starting device control bowden. - 43. Starting valve spring. - 44. Spring casing. - 45. Starting jet emulsion air orifice. - 46. Air emulsion reserve well orifice. - 47. Starting reserve well. - 48. Starting jet.

NOTE - Slot 36 and filter strainer 37 are fitted only on carburetor 22 IM as described on page 88.

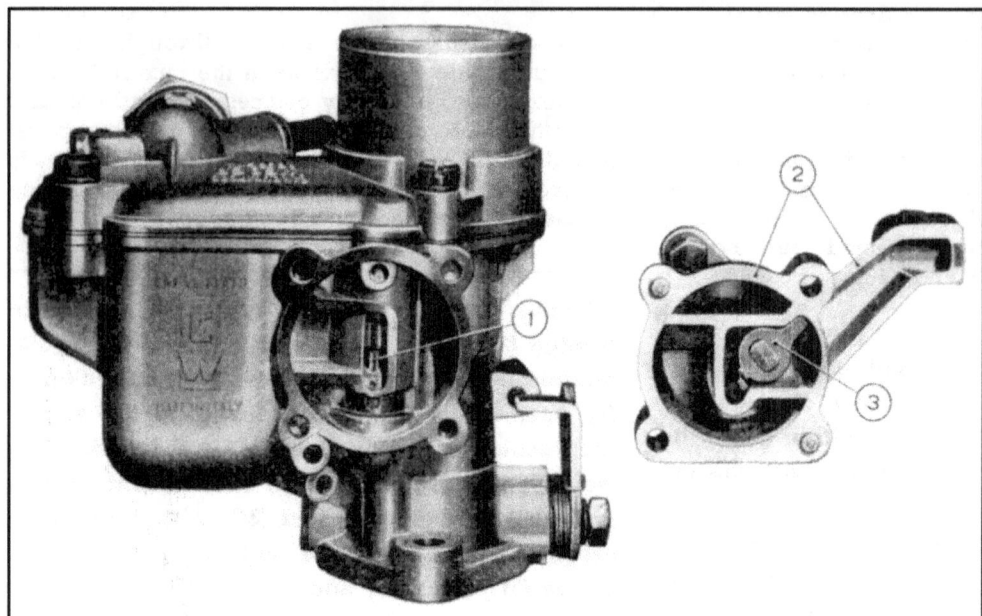

Fig. 152.
Weber 26 IM carburetor with choke device cover removed.

1. Choke valve. - 2. Choke device cover. - 3. Choke valve shaft.

Use of the Starting Device.

To profit by all the advantages the progressive-action starting device may offer, use it as follows:

ENGINE STARTING

Cold starts - fully throw in the device (position A, fig. 153); after engine fires push in slightly the control.

Hot starts - throw in the device only partially (position B, fig. 153).

ENGINE WARM-UP

During engine warming-up period, even with car running, push home gradually the starting device lever through successive stages so as to supply the engine with the supplementary amount of mixture indispensable for a regular and smooth engine operation (position B, fig. 153).

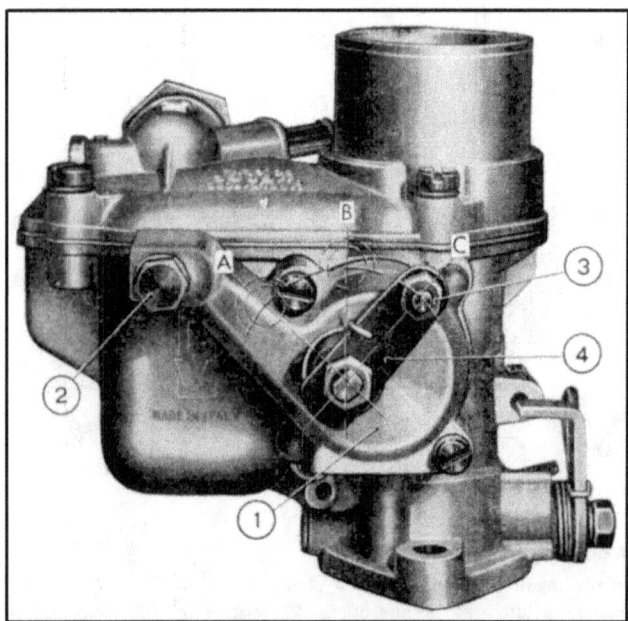

Fig. 153 - Weber 26 IM carburetor, starting device (choke) end.

1. Choke device cover. - 2. Bowden mounting screw. - 3. Nut and screw, choke bowden wire. - 4. Choke control lever. - A. Position of lever 4 for « fully inserted » choke. - B. « Partially inserted » choke. - C. « Disinserted » choke.

Fig. 154 - Weber 26 IM carburetor.

1. Bowden mounting screw. - 2. Choke control lever. - 3. Screw and nut, choke bowden wire. - 4. Starting mixture duct. - 5. Throttle. - 6. Idle speed passage.

ENGINE: FUEL SYSTEM

NORMAL CAR DRIVING

As soon as the engine has reached the rated operation temperature exclude completely the starting device by bringing the control lever to position C (fig. 153).

Idling Speed Adjustment.

Idling speed may be adjusted by throttle setscrews (8, fig. 155) and mixture setscrew (11).

Screw (3) allows of adjusting the throttle opening screw (11), conical, has the task of metering the amount of mixture coming from idling speed passage which will then blend with the air flowing past the gap around the throttle when in idle speed position. This makes possible a rating of mixture best suited to engine requirements and smooth operation.

Always adjust idling speed with engine running and warm by first setting throttle to minimum opening by setscrew (8) so as to insure steady operation.

Next, by turning screw (11) in or out set mixture richness to the most suitable ratio for said throttle opening, thus accomplishing a fast and steady idling; reduce minimum throttle opening somewhat more until best idling speed rate is obtained.

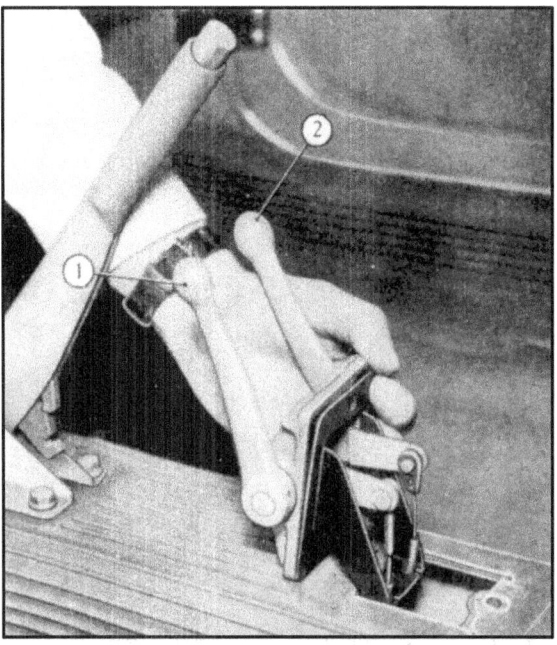

Fig. 156 - Control levers on floor tunnel (during removal).
1. Starter motor lever. - 2. Choke lever.

Carburetor Trouble Shooting Instructions.

Carburetor should be serviced only if carburetion is definitely at fault.

Some possible causes may be:

Flooded carburetor: improperly seated needle valve.

Engine does not start when cold: starting device operation is irregular because starting jet is obstructed or starting device control travel has shortened.

Engine does not start when warm: clogged jets or passages, misadjusted idle speed circuit.

Engine does not idle: clogged jets or passages, misadjusted idle speed circuit.

Engine pick up is poor: obstructed main jet or emulsion orifices.

Increased gasoline consumption: foreign matter in air corrector screw intake and in emulsion well orifices.

This trouble may also be due to altered calibration of metered parts (main jet diameter larger than standard, air corrector screw O. D. smaller than standard).

Engine does not develop the rated power: improper throttle opening caused by binding of throttle valve shaft in its seat or by a stiffening or locking of throttle controls.

Fig. 155 - Weber 26 IM carburetor in place on engine.

1. Accelerator control cable. - 2. Relay lever. - 3. Cable screw. - 4. Terminal. - 5. Rod. - 6. Clip. - 7. Throttle control lever. - 8. Throttle closing set screw. - 9. Idle jet holder. - 10. Main jet holder. - 11. Idle speed mixture metering screw. - 12. Choke control cable. - 13. Choke control lever. - 14. Fuel inlet line. - 15. Filter inspection plug. - 16. Fuel drain shield and tube. - 17. Spacer. - 18. Vacuum advance tube.

Carburetor Servicing Instructions.

FUEL LEVEL IN BOWL

The needle valve and float are easily accessible for inspection by removing the carburetor cover with which they form an assembly.

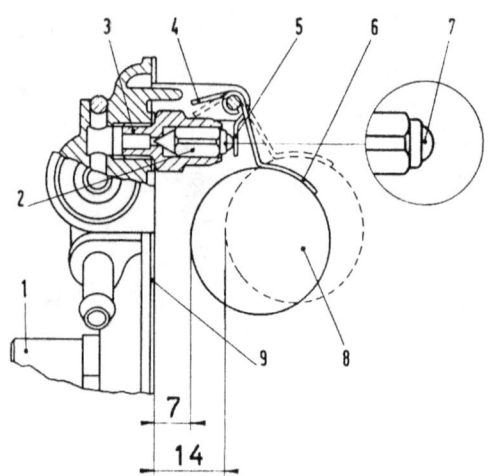

Fig. 157 - Float adjustment data.

BRASS FLOAT

1. Carburetor cover. - 2. Needle. - 3. Needle valve. - 4. Lug. - 5-6. Arms. 7. Needle ball. - 8. Float. - 9. Cover gasket.

Before checking level in bowl, see that:
— needle valve is well screwed in and aluminum gasket is in place;
— calibrated orifice in valve seat is unobstructed, not worn or deformed;
— the needle slides freely in its guide.

In case sealing is imperfect, replace the complete valve:
— the float is not distorted or broken and moves on its pivot without drag or excessive play; replace if these conditions are not met.

Now, check the level and preceed as directed hereafter (fig. 157):

a) Check that needle valve (3) is screwed tight in its seat.

b) Keep carburetor cover (1) upright or else the weight of float (8) would lower ball (7) fitted on needle (2).

c) Check that with cover held vertical and float arm (5) in slight contact with ball (7) of needle (2), the float is .28" (7 mm) away from cover with gasket (9) flat against cover face.

d) Check that float travel is .28" (7 mm); if necessary, bend lug (4) as required.

e) If float (8) is not correctly positioned, bend float arms (6) until the correct adjustment is obtained. See that arm (5) is perpendicular to needle axis and does not show rough spots or indents which might impair free sliding of the needle.

f) Check that float rotates freely around its pivot pin.

As a rule, the above adjustment operations must be performed every time a new float is installed.

CAUTION - Should a replacement of the needle valve be required, make sure first that the new valve is screwed tight in its seat with a new seal interposed. This will mean that the level check must be repeated.

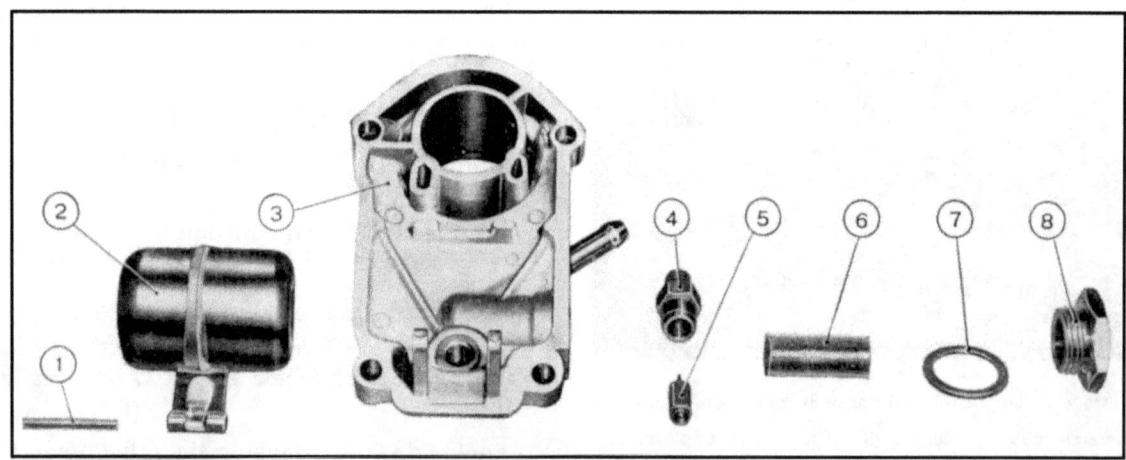

Fig. 158 - Carburetor cover components.

1. Float pivot. - 2. Float. - 3. Carburetor cover. - 4 -5. Needle valve seat and needle valve. - 6. Filter strainer. - 7. Gasket. - 8. Filter inspection plug.

ENGINE: FUEL SYSTEM

Fig. 159.

Weber 26 IM carburetor, open.

1. Secondary Venturi. - 2. Nozzle tube. - 3. Choke valve spring lock ring. - 4. Spring retainer and guide. - 5. Choke jet. - 6. Fuel bowl. - 7. Emulsion well with air bleed jet. - 8. Gasket and carburetor cover. - 9. Cover locating dowel. - 10. Float.

THROTTLE VALVE COMPONENTS

Throttle valve shaft should rotate freely in its guides even when engine is very warm. Excessive clearances caused by wear must not be tolerated since they account for irregular engine operation at idling speed.

Replace shaft if necessary.

Throttle must not be in any way distorted and must be tightly secured on its spindle.

CARBURETOR CLEANING INSTRUCTIONS

A general cleaning of carburetor should be carried out periodically, in accordance with the following:

Passages. - All fuel passages have a diameter that is the most appropriate to insure best operating conditions: it is therefore essential to remove any dirt or scale deposited by fuel, which would alter

Fig. 160.

Jets, jet holders and choke valve.

NOTE

The .0394" (1,00 mm) main jet is fitted on carburetors up to engine No. 876482; starting from engine No. 876483, carburetors have a .0382" (0,97 mm) main jet.

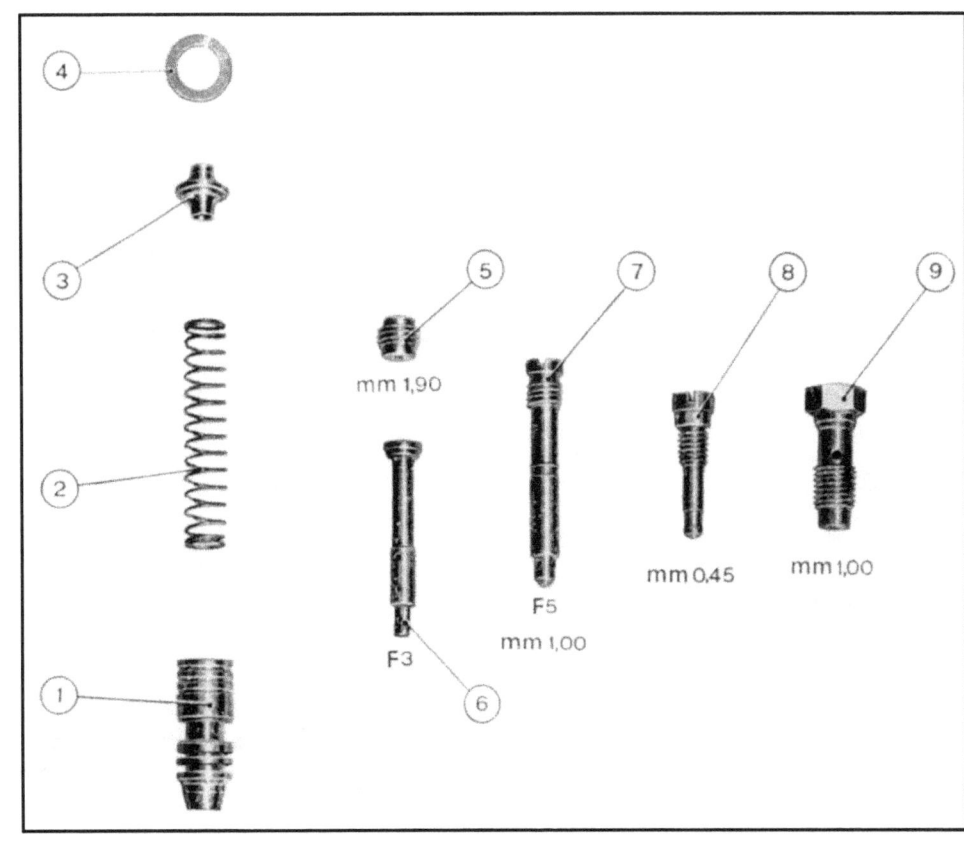

1. Choke valve. - 2. Spring. - 3. Spring retainer and guide. - 4. Lock ring. - 5. Air bleed jet. - 6. Emulsion well. - 7. Choke jet. - 8. Idling jet holder and jet. - 9. Main jet holder and jet.

mm 1,90 = .0748"
mm 1,00 = .0394"
mm 0,45 = .0177"

undesirably the conditions of operation. Clean with gasoline and blow dry with compressed air all passages in castings. Do not pass drills or other metal points through jets and passages because these would be altered in their calibrated diameters.

Calibrated parts. - Idling and max. rated speed jet holders, and relevant bayonet-coupled jets, are easily removed by using a wrench or a screwdriver.

To clean the different calibrated parts, wash in gasoline and blow with a compressed air blast. We strongly advise against the use of metallic points or other unsuitable tools which may irreparably upset the pre-established calibration of orifices.

Should it be necessary to remove carburetor adjustment components for inspection of some parts, make sure that after re-assembly parts are again well tight in their seats to avoid possible operating troubles.

STRAINER

To clean the strainer, unscrew and take off its plug, with gasket, on carburetor cover and then pull out the strainer.

Clean strainer seat carefully. Wash strainer in gasoline and blow clean with an air blast.

WEBER 26 IM CARBURETOR SETTING DATA

		in.	mm
Body diameter		1.0236	26
Primary Venturi diameter		.7480	19
Secondary Venturi diameter		.1772	4,50
Main jet diameter { up to engine No. 876482		.0394	1,00
{ from engine No. 876483		.0382	0,97
Idling jet diameter		.0177	0,45
Choke jet diameter	F 5/	.0394	1,00
Air bleed jet diameter		.0748	1,90
Needle valve diameter		.0591	1,50
Float setting		.2756	7
Float weight		.32 oz	9 gr.
Emulsion Tube		F 3	F 3

WEBER 22 IM CARBURETOR

The 22 IM Weber carburetor has been installed in production up to engine No. 644010, «Sedan», and up to engine No. 644440, «Multipla».

Setting data covering above carburetor are tabulated on next page.

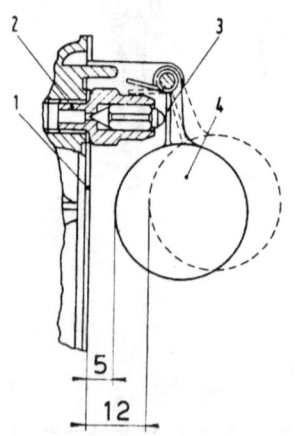

Fig. 161.

Float adjustment data.

NYLON FLOAT

1. Cover gasket. - 2. Needle valve. - 3. Arm. - 4. Float.

Both brass and nylon floats are used in 22 IM carburetor. See the exact type of float prior to setting the float level.

For the nylon float the adapting operations outlined on page 86, covering the brass float, are not required inasmuch as after assembly the float (4) is located at .20" (5 mm) from the cover face, in vertical position (with gasket in place), and may move through a .28" (7 mm) travel.

Therefore, simply check that:

a) needle valve (2) is screwed tight in its seat;

b) arm (3) does not have any indents on its contacting face;

c) float (4) rotates freely around its pivot pin.

NOTE - For description, operation, trouble shooting and service procedures, see Weber 26 IM carburetor.

ENGINE: FUEL SYSTEM

WEBER 22 IM CARBURETOR SETTING DATA

	in.	mm
Body diameter	.8661	22
Primary Venturi diameter	.6299	16
Secondary Venturi diameter	.1772	4,50
Main jet diameter	.0315	0,80
Idling jet diameter	.0177	0,45
Choke jet diameter	F 6/ .0472	1,20
Air bleed jet diameter	.0847	2,15
Needle valve diameter	.0591	1,50
Float setting { brass float (fig. 157)	.2756	7
{ nylon float (fig. 161)	.1969	5
Float weight { brass float	.32 oz	9 gr.
{ nylon float	.19 oz	5,5 gr.
Emulsion well	F 2	F 2

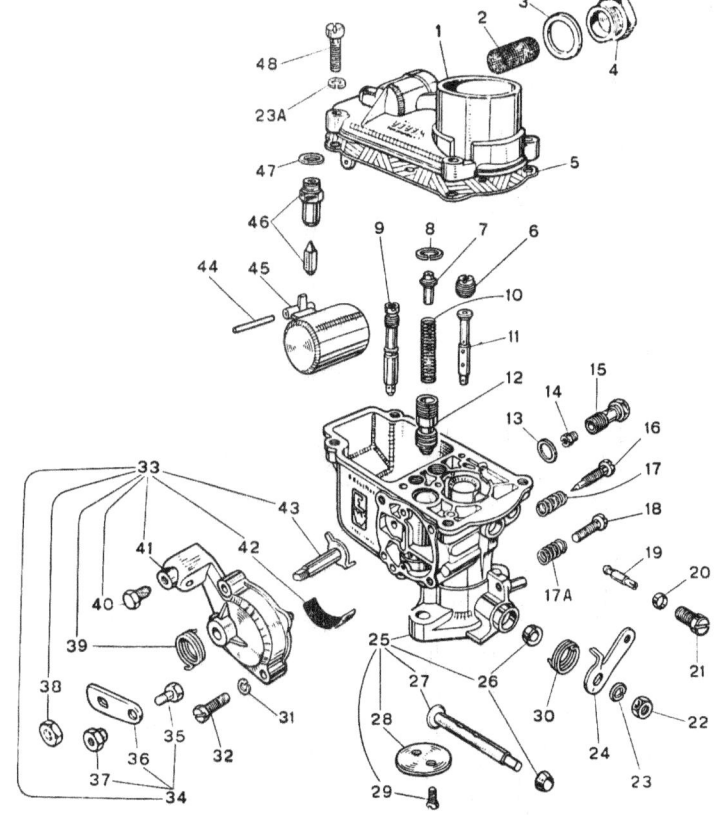

Fig. 162.

Weber 22 IM carburetor.

1. Cover. - 2. Strainer. - 3. Strainer plug gasket. - 4. Strainer plug. - 5. Cover gasket. - 6. Air corrector screw. - 7. Spring retainer and guide. - 8. Spring retainment snap ring. - 9. Starting jet. - 10. Starting valve spring. - 11. Emulsion well. - 12. Starting valve. - 13. Main jet holder gasket. - 14. Main jet. - 15. Main jet holder. - 16. Idle speed mixture adjusting screw. - 17. Screw friction spring. - 17 A. Throttle opening setscrew friction spring. - 18. Throttle opening setscrew. - 19. Idle speed jet. - 20. Idle speed jet holder gasket. - 21. Idle speed jet holder. - 22. Throttle control lever nut. - 23. Lockwasher. - 23 A. Cover screw lockwasher. - 24. Throttle control lever. - 25. Body. - 26. Throttle shaft seal. - 27. Throttle shaft. - 28. Throttle. - 29. Throttle screw. - 30. Throttle control lever spring. - 31. Cover screw lockwasher. - 32. Cover screw. - 33. Cover. - 34. Starting control lever. - 35. Bowden wire screw. - 36. Starting control lever. - 37. Bowden wire screw nut. - 38. Starting control lever nut. - 39. Starting control lever spring. - 40. Sheath screw. - 41. Cover. - 42. Starting air filter. - 43. Starting valve control shaft. - 44. Float pivot. - 45. Float. - either brass or nylon. - 46. Needle valve. - 47. Needle valve gasket. - 48. Carburetor cover screw.

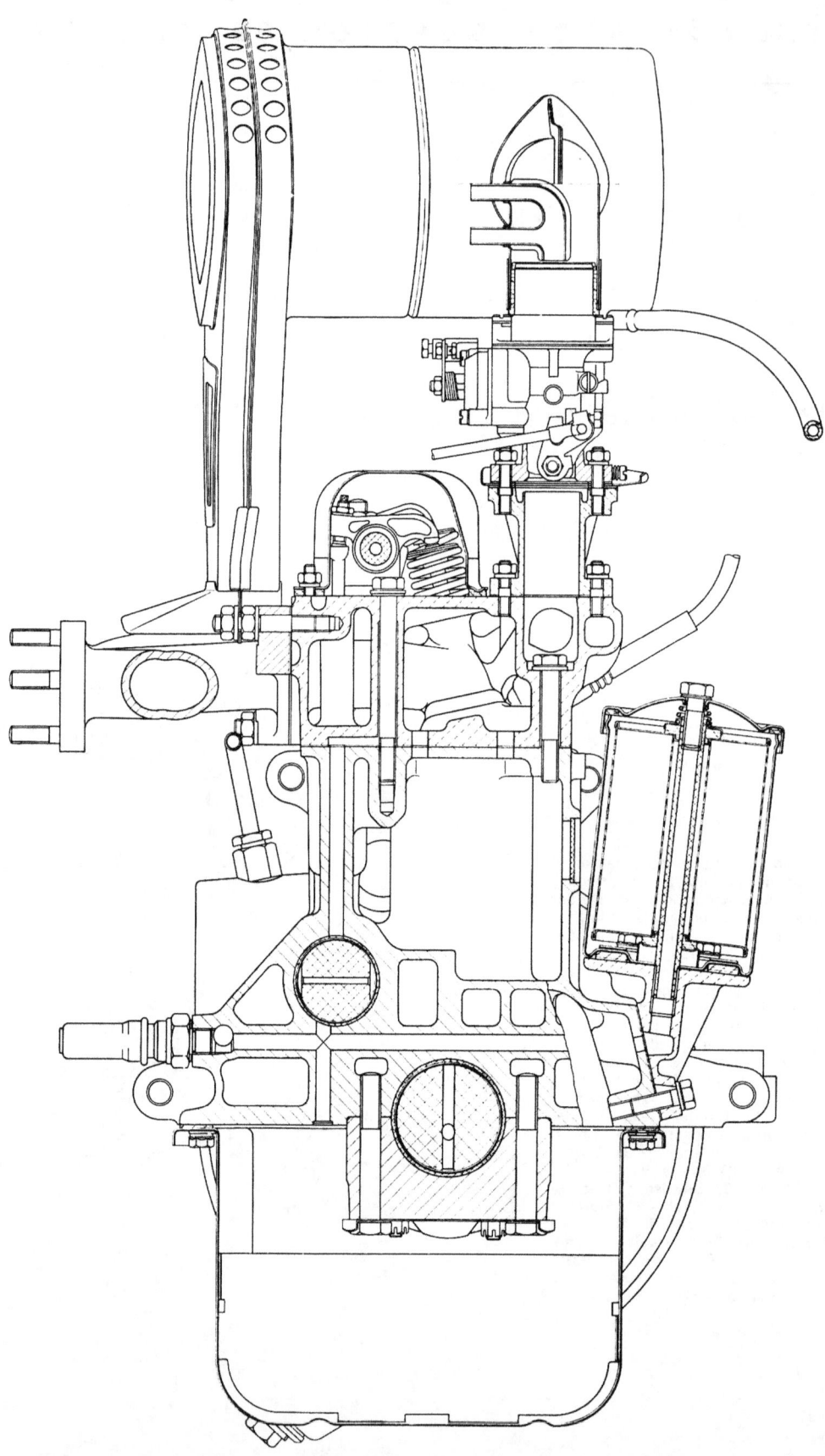

Fig. 163 - Engine cross-section.

LUBRICATION SYSTEM

Oil Pump	page 91
Oil Pressure Relief Valve	» 92
Oil Filter	» 93
Sump-to-Crankcase Seal Gaskets	» 93
Low Oil Pressure Indicator Sending Unit	» 95
Crankcase Ventilation and Vacuum Advance Device Lines	» 96

Engine lubrication is of the forced pressure type. Pressure is promoted by a gear pump mounted below crankcase (fig. 164) which is driven off the camshaft by a helical gear couple.

The lubrication system also includes the following:

— a suction intake with incorporated filtering screen;

— a by-pass cartridge-type oil filter mounted on engine right side;

— an oil pressure relief valve on crankcase lower left side;

— a sending unit, signalling insufficient oil pressures.

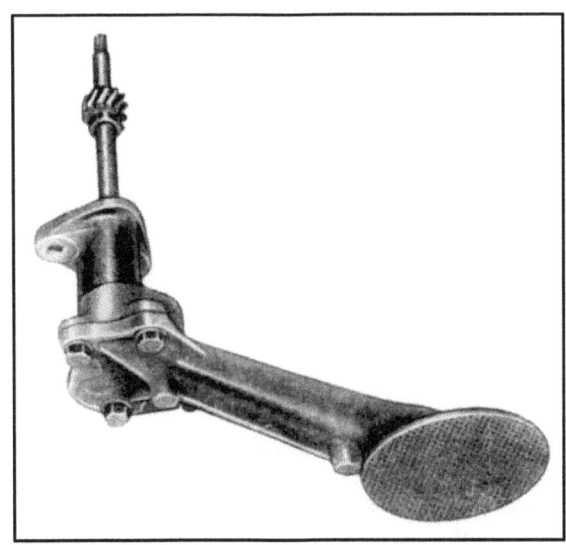

Fig. 165 - Oil pump, complete with intake horn and drive shaft.

The correct gear backlash is .0032" (0,08 mm). Check clearance between gears and pump body which should not exceed .0059" (0,15 mm).

Fig. 164 - Capsized engine on rotating stand.
Oil pump mounting is clearly visible.

OIL PUMP

The oil pump is mounted on crankcase lower end and is secured by two screws. It consists of a body, a driving gear, a driven gear, a suction intake provided with filtering screen and a drive shaft with relevant bush (fig. 166).

When servicing the pump, inspect teeth of both driving and driven gears; replace gear if teeth are found worn or damaged.

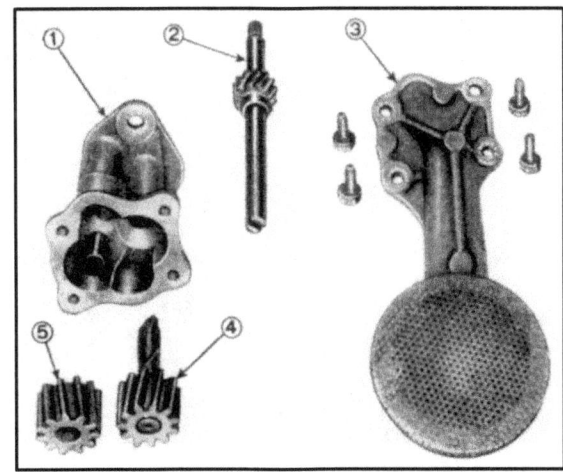

Fig. 166 - Oil pump components.

1. Body. - 2. Drive shaft. - 3. Suction intake, with screen. - 4. Driving gear. - 5. Driven gear.

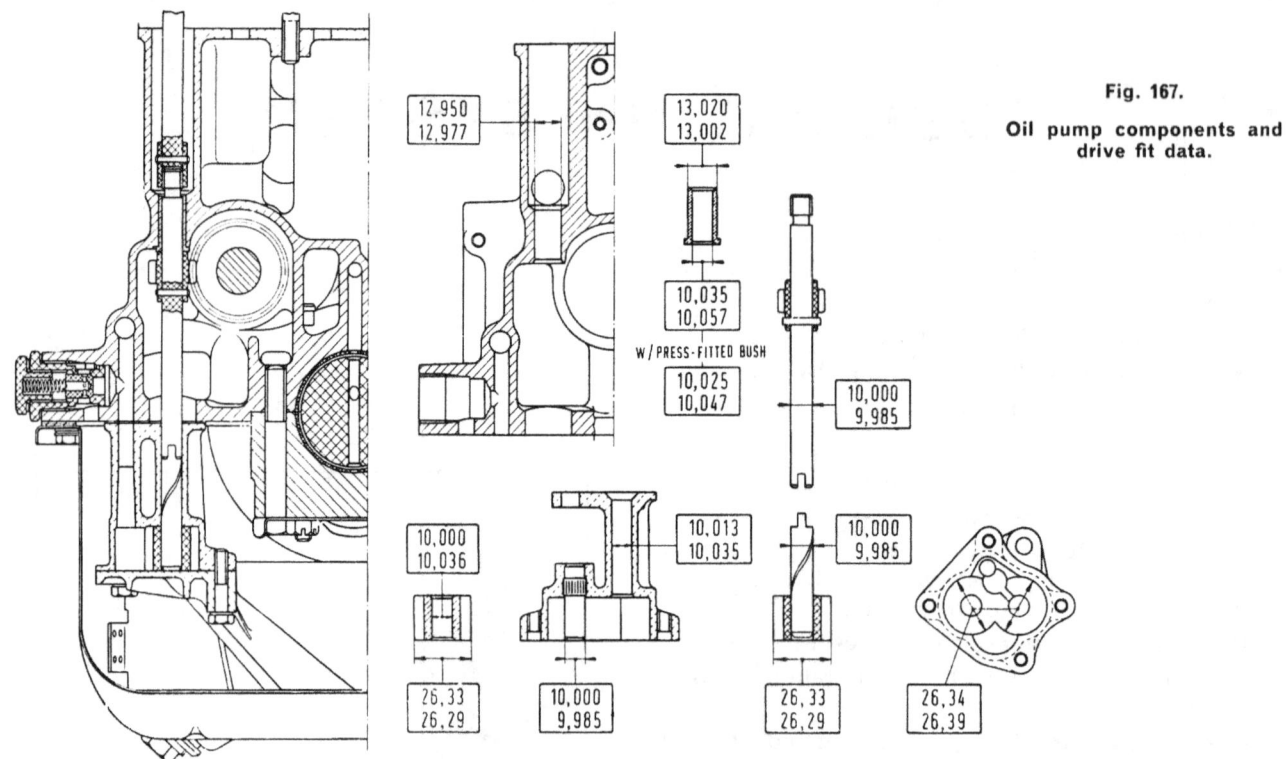

Fig. 167. Oil pump components and drive fit data.

Use a feeler gauge. Fit clearance is .0004" to .0039" (0,01 to 0,10 mm).

Check clearance between driving gear and its guide which must not be greater than .0059" (0,15 mm). Fit clearance: .00051" to .00196" (0,013 to 0,050 mm).

Check that clearance between shaft and driven gear is .0000" to .0020" (0,000 to 0,051 mm) and does not exceed .0039" (0,10 mm).

Check that drive shaft bush pinch fit in crankcase is .00098" to .00276" (0,025 to 0,070 mm).

Check pump drive shaft-to-crankcase bush clearance: it must not be greater than .0059" (0,15 mm). Fit clearance is .00098" to .0024" (0,025 to 0,062 mm).

Oil pump drive shaft gear-to-camshaft gear assembly clearance: .00236" (0,06 mm) - wear limit: .0039" (0,10 mm).

Check filtering screen for any clogging or tear: replace if necessary.

OIL PRESSURE RELIEF VALVE

This unit is directly screwed in crankcase, on left lower end.

It consists of: body, valve, spring, threaded casing, spring adjustment shims and seal.

Engine oil pressure regulation is accomplished as follows:

— unscrew the plug performing as a casing for spring;
— add or remove shims in plug as required;
— screw in plug and tighten.

With engine running at rated speed, the lube oil pressure reading at test gauge **A. 60162** fitted in place of the insufficient oil pressure indicator should be 35.5 to 42.6 psi (2,5 to 3 kg/cm^2).

Fig. 168 - Cutaway of oil pump and oil pressure relief valve.

1. Oil pressure relief valve assembly. - 2. Oil pump body. - 3. Oil pump drive gear. - 4. Driven gear. - 5. Lube oil delivery duct.

ENGINE: LUBRICATION SYSTEM

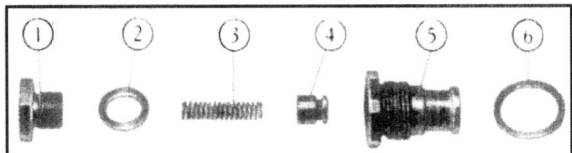

Fig. 169 - Oil pressure relief valve components.

1. Casing. - 2. Gasket, plug. - 3. Spring. - 4. Valve. - 5. Body. - 6. Seal.

OIL FILTER

The filter consists of a sheet metal container enclosing a cartridge type filtering element (fig. 171).

Check color of sump oil: if dark, check filter operation by running the engine for a few minutes so as to bring oil to operating temperature.

If filter body remains cool, the filter is obviously inefficient. In this case, check to see if trouble originates from clogged ducts or from a dirty cartridge.

Correct this condition, by cleaning ducts or replacing cartridge, as required.

Also, check for tightness the two seals (5, fig. 171) - one above and one below the filtering element - and, if required, replace. Make sure that new seals installed are a snug fit, to prevent oil from seeping into filter body without passing through the cartridge.

Filter cleaning must receive particular care considering the importance of an efficient and diligent engine lubrication at all times.

Regardless of its condition, the filtering element should be replaced every 6000 miles (10.000 km) and the oil renewed.

In new engines, oil must be replaced after the first 900 to 1200 miles (1500 to 2000 km) and 1800 to 2400 miles (3000 to 4000 km); during the third oil renewal at 5000 to 5600 miles (8000 to 9000 km) replace also the filtering cartridge.

Never run engine when cartridge is not in filter for, otherwise, in addition to troubles arising from

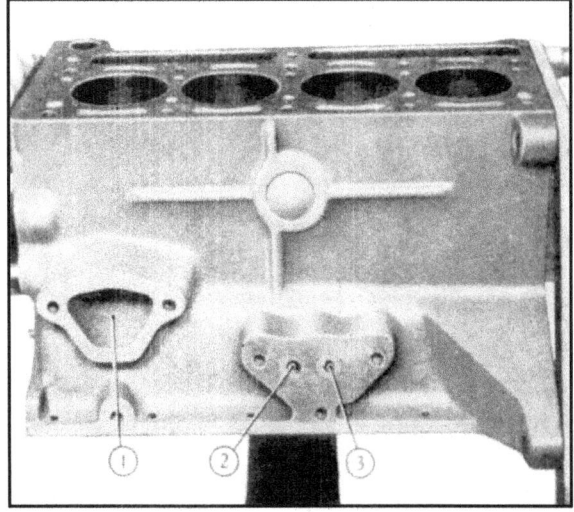

Fig. 170 - Crankcase, right side.

1. Inlet duct, for water from pump. - 2. Orifice, oil outlet from crankcase and inlet to filter. - 3. Orifice, oil inlet to crankcase from filter.

non-filtered oil, an excessive drop in oil pressure would take place.

CAUTION - When servicing the lubrication system wash all oil passages and ducts and then blow dry with compressed air.

SUMP-TO-CRANKCASE SEAL GASKETS

To ensure perfect oil-tightness, the two longitudinal half gasket and the flywheel and timing gear end gaskets must be applied on sump as follows:

— brush on some bonding compound on sump edges;

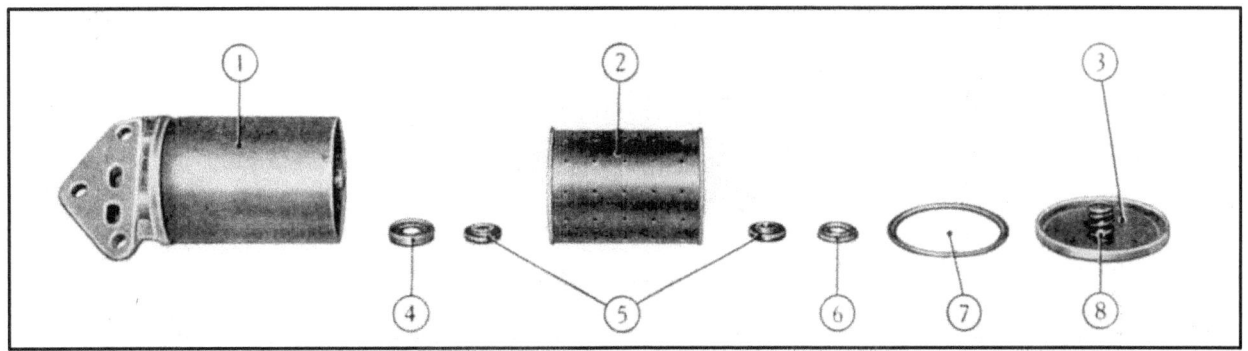

Fig. 171 - Components of by-pass oil filter.

1. Container. - 2. Filtering element. - 3. Cover. - 4. Base, seal carrier. - 5. Seal, filtering element. - 6. Washer, spring seat. - 7. Seal, cover. - 8. Spring, pressure.

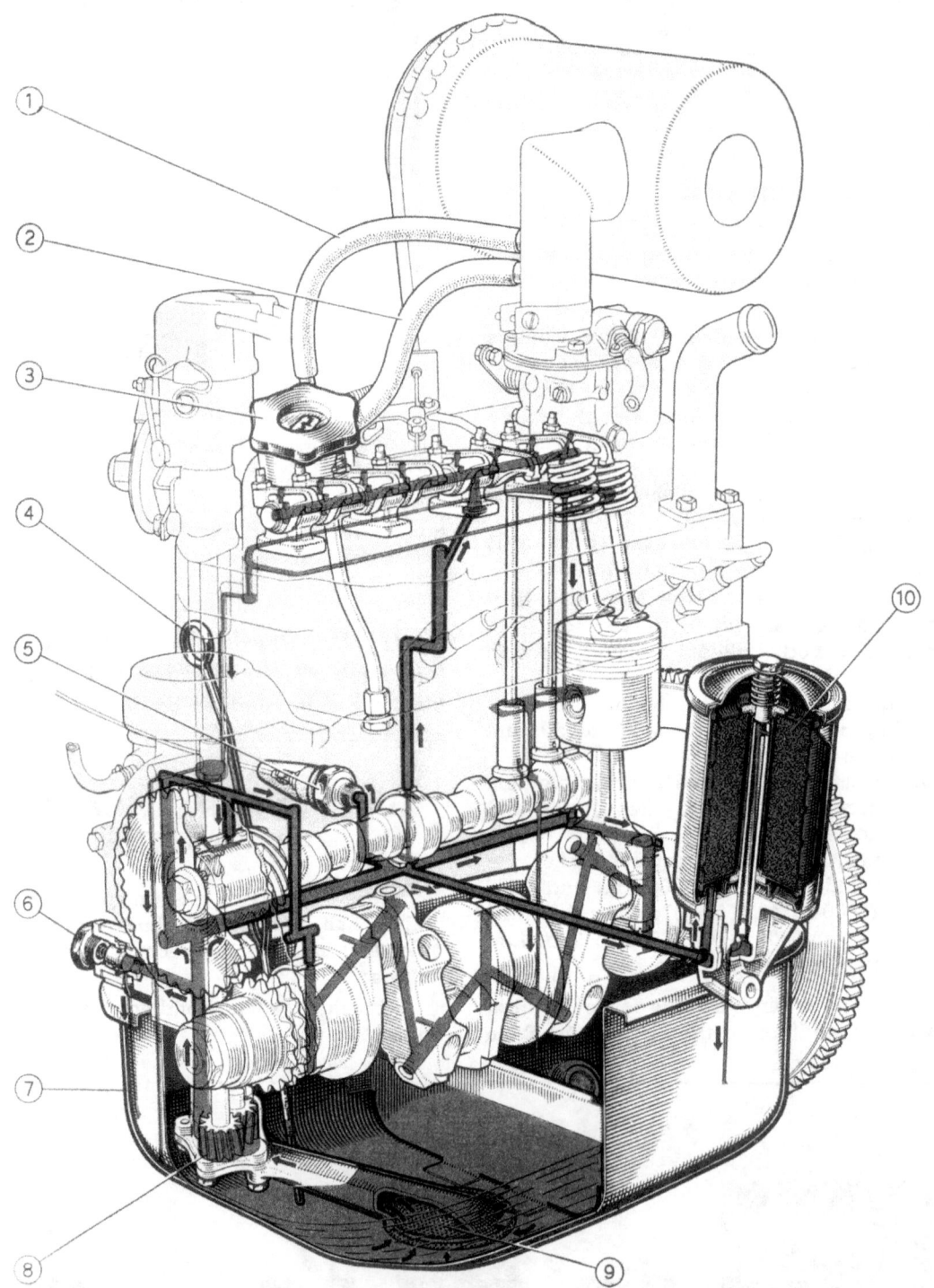

Fig. 172 - Engine lubrication diagram.

1. Crankcase ventilation hose. - 2. Rocker chamber ventilation hose. - 3. Oil filler neck. - 4. Level rod. - 5. Insufficient oil pressure indicator sending unit. - 6. Oil pressure relief valve. - 7. Sump. - 8. Oil pump. - 9. Oil pump intake screen. - 10. Replaceable-cartridge, by-pass oil filter.

ENGINE: LUBRICATION SYSTEM

— fit the four seal gaskets and flatten out accurately;

— install fixture **A. 60163** and secure on sump so as to exert the necessary pressure on gaskets in their seats (fig. 173).

It is recommended to leave gaskets under the pressure of said fixture for at least 45 minutes.

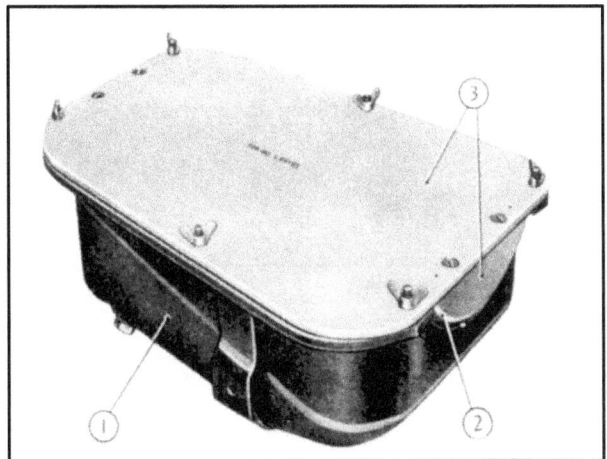

Fig. 173 - Bonding the gaskets on sump faying face.
1. Sump. - 2. Gasket. - 3. Fixture A. 60163 for gasket compression.

LOW OIL PRESSURE INDICATOR SENDING UNIT

The sending unit is located on the left side of cylinder block and, by electric cable, is connected to the optical indicator in instrument cluster on facia.

With very warm engine, at an r.p.m. rate lower than 1000 the indicator may light up even if pressure is under control and operation regular.

The indicator signals when oil pressure drops to less than 14 to 8.5 psi (1 to 0,6 kg/cm^2).

Fig. 174 - Low oil pressure indicator sending unit.
1. Unit body. - 2. Connector, for cable to indicator. - 3. Seal.

Fig. 175 - Vent and vacuum advance device lines.

1. Air cleaner. - 2. Hose. - 3. Crankcase-to-cleaner line. - 4. Oil vapour condensing chamber. - 5. Cylinder head cover-to-cleaner hose. - 6. Cylinder head cover. - 7. Carburetor. - 8. Carburetor-to-vacuum advance line. - 9. Vacuum advance. - 10. Ignition distributor.

NOTE - Any accidental short circuit, as, for instance, the indicator light bulb being shorted, might cause damage to the sending unit.

This should be borne in mind in case of switch failure. Of course, the short must be eliminated prior to replacing switch.

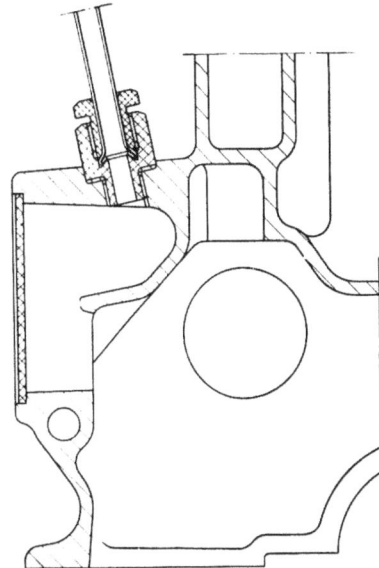

Fig. 176 - Detail of engine cross section through oil vapour condensing chamber and through the line to air cleaner.

The indicator lights up (2,5-Watt red bulb) only when ignition is turned ON and goes OUT when oil pressure is sufficient for adequate lubrication.

CRANKCASE VENTILATION AND VACUUM ADVANCE DEVICE LINES

Venting of crankcase is obtained through an oil vapor condensing chamber (fig. 176) connected to air cleaner elbow on carburetor via an external piping (2 and 3, fig. 175). A second line (5, fig. 175) connects to the air cleaner elbow also the rocker chamber.

The vacuum promoted by engine suction actuates the advance device through hose (8, fig. 175), connecting the vacuum advance device to carburetor throat.

During servicing, remove the three lines and inspect pipings for obstruction and/or cracks.

All line connections must be a snug fit to ensure tightness.

If any are leaky, replace faulty parts.

OIL PUMP FIT DATA

ITEM	CLEARANCES AND FITS		WEAR LIMITS	
	in.	mm	in.	mm
Drive shaft guide bush-to-seat in crankcase	Pinch fit of .00098 to .0027 at all times	0,025 to 0,070	—	—
Drive shaft-to-crankcase bush ...	.00098 to .0024	0,025 to 0,062	.0059	0,15
Driving gear shaft-to-seat in pump body	.00051 to .00196	0,013 to 0,050	.0059	0,15
Driven gear-to-its shaft	.0000 to .0020	0,000 to 0,051	.0039	0,10
Gears-to-pump body	.0004 to .0039	0,010 to 0,100	.0059	0,15
Driving-to-driven gears backlash ..	.00315	0,08	.0059	0,15
Drive shaft gear-to-camshaft gear ..	.00236	0,06	.0039	0,10

COOLING SYSTEM

Water Pump (Description)	page 98
Water Pump Removal and Disassembly	» 99
Inspection, Assembly and Installation of Water Pump	» 99
Air Conveyor	» 100
Fan	» 100
Radiator	» 101
Antifreeze Mixtures	» 102
Thermostat	» 104
Excessive Water Temperature Indicator Sending Unit	» 104
Generator and Water Pump Drive Belt Tension Adjustment	» 104

Cooling systems are different for the two models.

« Sedan ».

Forced water circulation by centrifugal pump.
Upright pipe radiator cooled by fan keyed on pump shaft. Radiator equipped with thermostat controlling through a lever the air flow adjustment butterfly valve (fig. 177).
Thermostatic adjustment of water temperature by the air flow control.

« Multipla ».

Forced water circulation by centrifugal pump.
Upright pipe radiator cooled by fan keyed on pump shaft. Thermostat in pipe from cylinder head to radiator.

Fig. 178 - Engine compartment: cooling system components of engine 100.000 (Sedan).
1. Water temperature indicator sending unit. - 2. Hose, water circulation from cylinder head to pump. - 3. Hose, water circulation from cylinder head to radiator. - 4. Radiator and filter cap. - 5. Fan. - 6. Engine ground strap. - 7. Water pump.

On both models, a sending unit installed on cylinder head controls an « excessive cooling water temperature indicator » to warn the driver when engine overheating occurs.
The two cooling systems are described in detail for both models in the following paragraphs.

Fig. 177 - Detail of engine compartment ventilation and car interior heating system.

1. Side linings. - 2. Radiator. - 3. Radiator water drain cock. - 4. Baffle for warm air entrance into car. - 5. Return spring. - 6 and 8. Lever and pushrod for shutter control. - 7. Shutter, air draft control in engine compartment.

« Sedan ».

The centrifugal pump, belt-driven by the generator pulley - which in turn is driven by the acces-

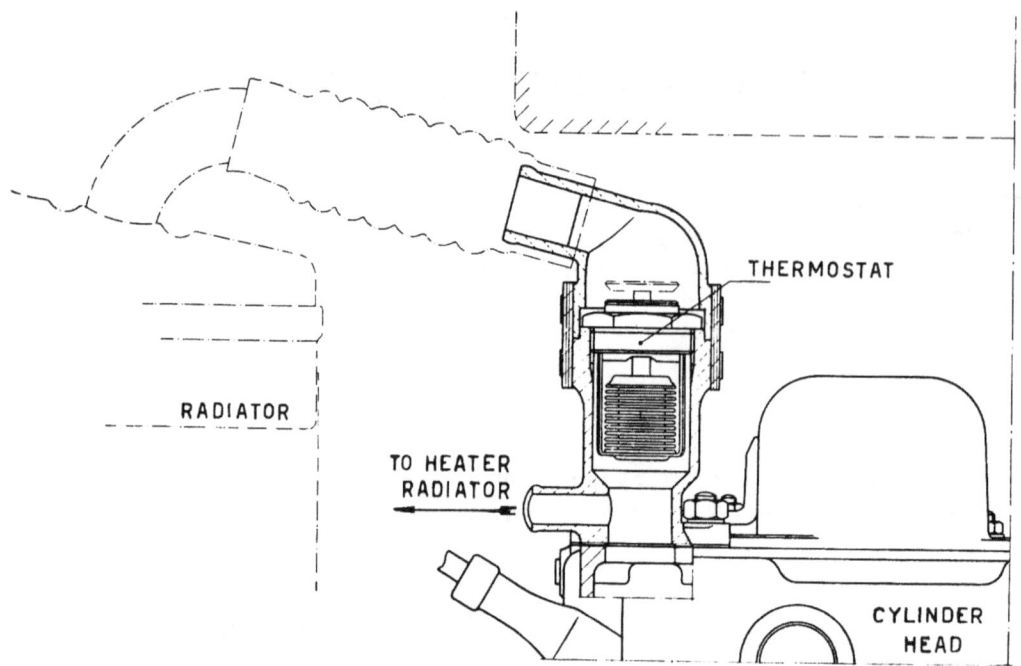

Fig. 179 - Section through thermostat and diagram of connection to radiator (engine 100.008 for Multipla).

sory pulley on crankshaft - forces water into the cylinder block jackets and in the cylinder head water pockets; from cylinder head the water passes to radiator and to upper central portion of pump body through two stub pipes connected by hoses.

From radiator, the water returns to the pump.

When water temperature exceeds 167° to 176° F (75° to 80° C) the thermostat (fig. 188) operates lever (6, fig. 177) and opens shutter (7, fig. 177); this way, fresh air passes through the radiator core and cools the water therein circulating; the shutter is wide open at 221° F (105° C).

In other words, the thermostat governs the air draft through engine compartment according to the temperature of engine water.

« Multipla ».

In this model water circulation is as follows:

The centrifugal pump - which as on the « Sedan » is belt driven by generator pulley - forces the water into cylinder block jackets and cylinder head water pockets. Until the engine is cold and water temperature below 161° to 170° F (72° to 77° C) the water returns directly to the pump from cylinder head, through a hose. When the above temperature is exceeded, the thermostat (fig. 179) in cylinder head water outlet union opens, and the water circulates in the radiator then returning to the pump through a hose.

WATER PUMP

The water pump is of the centrifugal, impeller type (fig. 182). The impeller is integral with its shaft which revolves on two ball bearings housed in pump body. The rear bearing is retained, on outer face, by a circlip fitting in a groove in pump body. On the inner face, both bearings are shouldered by spacers retained by snap rings fitting in grooves machined in the impeller shaft.

The pump is made watertight by two special rubber seals (9, fig. 182) encased in a metal shell.

Fig. 180 - Engine compartment right bottom view.

1. Shutter, air draft control. - 2. Radiator drain cock. - 3. Radiator. - 4. Hose collars. - 5. Water hose, radiator to pump. - 6. Water pump and cylinder block drain cock. - 7. Water pump.

ENGINE: COOLING SYSTEM

Water Pump Removal and Disassembly.

Removal.

Remove front, lower right apron.
Drain water by opening cock (2, fig. 180) under radiator and pump cock (6, fig. 180).
Remove drive belt from pulley.
Loosen collars (4), of pump inlet hose and remove hose. To loosen collars, use wrench A. 50013.
Slacken collar and remove hose (2, fig. 178) from pump.
Disconnect engine ground cable (6, fig. 178) from body lower rear panel.
Undo the three water pump mounting screws and remove pump assembly complete with fan and air conveyor.

Disassembly.

Secure pump assembly in a vice and remove conveyor, drive pulley and fan.
Remove rear ball bearing retaining circlip.
Undo the screws joining the two body halves and remove front body half from impeller shaft.
From impeller remove: front bearing, thrust ring and relevant retaining ring, water seal.
Take off front body half and from it remove rear ball bearing and thrust ring.
Finally, from impeller remove: rear bearing thrust ring retainment ring and water seal.

Inspection, Assembly and Installation.

During overhauls check that:
— the gasket between the two pump body halves is sound;
— the two ball bearings are in good condition and have no axial play; holding fast with one hand the outer ring and rocking back and forth the inner ring, no roughness or noisiness must be noticed;
— rear bearing and thrust ring retainment rings have not lost their elasticity;

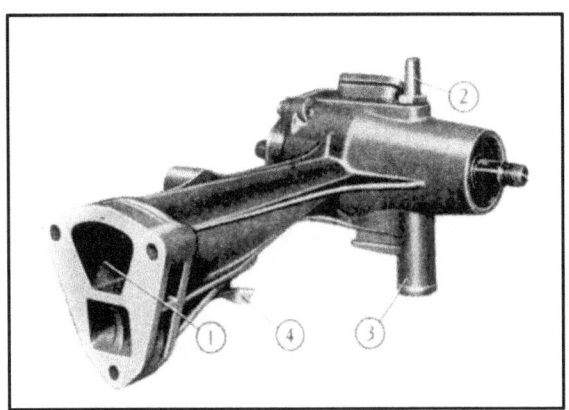

Fig. 181 - Water pump assembly.

1. Water duct from pump to crankcase. - 2. Connection for water hose from engine to pump. - 3. Water inlet from radiator. - 4. Drain cock.

— impeller shaft shows no seizing marks nor out-of-true; impeller is securely fixed on shaft;
— thrust rings of the two bearings are not excessively worn;
— the two encased water seals are perfectly efficient and undamaged. Usually these seals must be replaced when disassembly has proven highly difficult.

If damages or wear are detected, replace the parts involved.
To reassemble and reinstall the pump, reverse the disassembly and removal operation order.

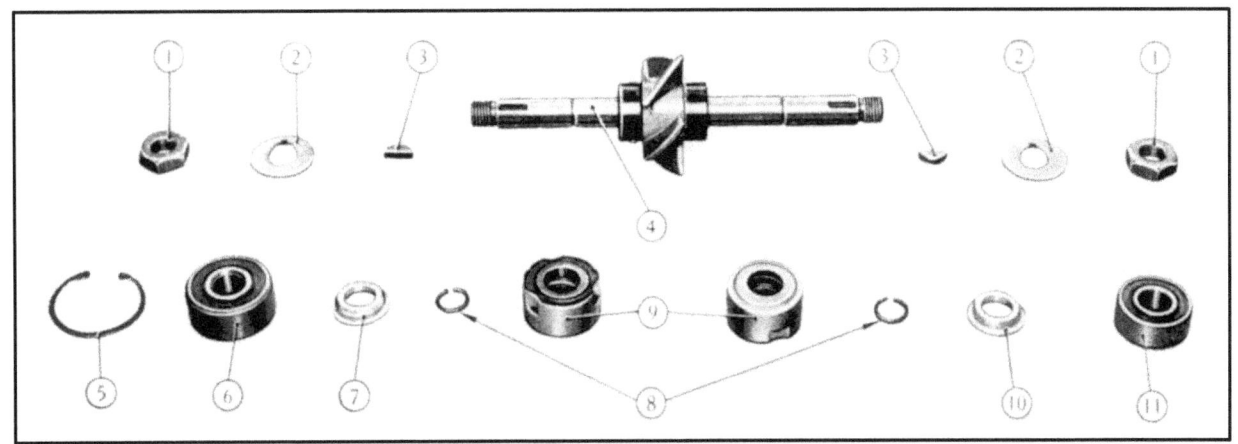

Fig. 182 - Water pump nner components.

1. Nuts. - 2. Plates. - 3. Keys. - 4. Impeller shaft. - 5. Circlip. - 6. Pulley end ball bearing. - 7. Spacer. - 8. Spacer retaining rings. 9. Seals. - 10. Thrust washer. - 11. Fan end ball bearing.

AIR CONVEYOR

To inspect and check air conveyor operate as follows:

— install conveyor on water pump body, tightening the mounting screws to a torque of 23.14 ft.lbs (3200 kgmm). Place a dial indicator plunger against conveyor inner face (point «A» shown in fig. 183), and rotate conveyor around water pump body axis: maximum permissible out-of-round is .078″ (2 mm).

FAN

The fan is secured to water pump shaft by a key. To remove fan, unscrew the mounting nut.
Inspect blades to see that they are not deformed.
Straighten if necessary.

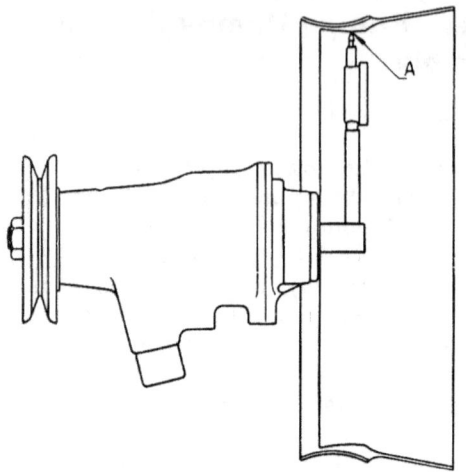

Fig. 183 - Checking air conveyor.
A. Point to be checked.

Rotate fan on its axis while resting a dial indicator plunger or a scriber on tip of blades: the length

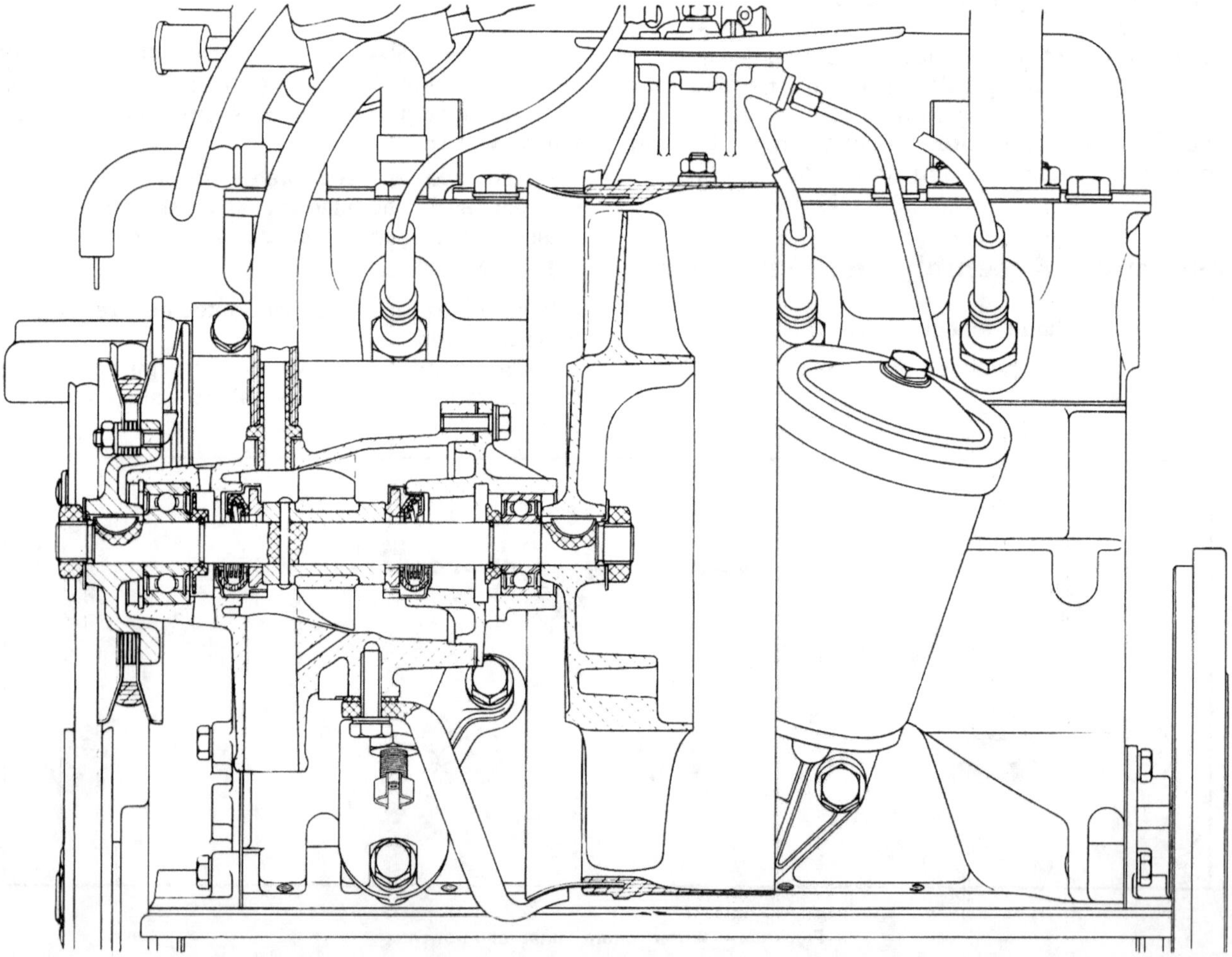

Fig. 184 - Section through water pump, fan and air conveyor.

ENGINE: COOLING SYSTEM

of each blade must not differ from that of the other blades by more than .0394" (1 mm) (fig. 185).

NOTE - Starting from engine No. 764729, « Sedan », and No. 765151, « Multipla », the fan made up of welded sheet metal elements has been replaced by an aluminum cast fan.

Fig. 185 - Checking fan, welded metal element type (up to engine No. 764728, Sedan, and No. 765150, Multipla).

RADIATOR

« Sedan ».

The radiator is of the upright pipe, three-row type (fig. 186).

If overheating is noticed during operation, check the thermostat mounted inside radiator lower bowl.

The thermostat should begin to actuate lever (4, fig. 188) when the temperature reaches 167° to 176° F (75° to 80° C) and should be fully extended when temperature is about 221° F (105° C).

If not so, check thermostat and inspect operating linkages and shutter to see that articulations are not binding.

To check thermostat, see page 104.

If both thermostat and operating linkages with shutter are efficient, overheating is probably due

Fig. 186 - Sedan radiator front view.

to poor cooling ability of the radiator. Therefore, check that excessive scale or rust has not formed in radiator core.

Otherwise, clean both radiator and water jackets with a water and sodium bicarbonate solution as follows:

— Open the cocks under radiator and pump, and drain water.

— Fill cooling system with 9 U.S. pints or 7.6 G.B. pints (4,30 liters) of water containing 7 oz (200 grams) of sodium bicarbonate.

— Run engine at idling speed for about 10 minutes.

— Stop engine and leave the solution in cooling system for about half an hour.

— Run engine and at the same time drain system. Stop engine immediately after all the solution has been drained.

— Let engine cool down and then flush with clean water for some minutes, leaving drain cocks open.

NOTE - The operation described above must be performed also before shifting to antifreeze mixtures since these compounds have a tendency to loosen scale and rust.

— Close cocks, fill with clean water, run again engine and drain.

— Close cocks and fill system to correct level.

If radiator is leaking, locate the crack(s) and repair by soldering.

To locate leaky points, operate as follows:

— Close water outlet pipe and connect a hose to inlet pipe.

— Fill radiator with water.

— Send compressed air in the hose connected to inlet pipe at a pressure of about 14.22 psi (1 kg/cm²).

If radiator is cracked, water will issue at leaky points.

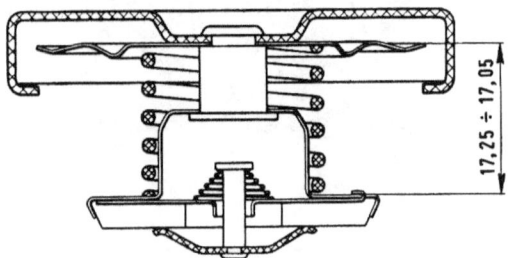

Fig. 187 - Sedan and Multipla radiator filler cap.

If too frequent top-ups are required, the trouble may originate from:

a) Defective radiator filler neck valve.

— Check the gasket installed under the valve: if damaged, it causes the sticking of the valve either in the closed or open position. In this second case the water may overflow freely from radiator.

b) Leaking hoses.

— Check clamping collars. If hoses are damaged, replace.

c) Defective water pump inner seals.

— Check if water issues from the body halves drain holes; if so, disassemble the pump and replace seals.

« Multipla ».

The radiator of the « Multipla » differs from the « Sedan » radiator in that:

The thermostat is mounted in the connection from cylinder head to radiator. This thermostat is serviced as described under « Thermostat » on page 104.

To wash the radiator, proceed as follows:

— to drain the water, besides the two cocks placed under radiator and pump, open also the cock permitting the passage of water to the heater radiator and the drain cock placed in car, behind front seat, to the right of tunnel;

— the amount of flushing water to be poured in radiator for cleaning is 13.7 U.S. pts - 11.50 G.B. pts (6,50 liters), containing 8.8 oz. (250 grams) of sodium bicarbonate.

CAUTION - When refilling the cooling system after total draining, fill the radiator to correct level, run the engine at idling speed for some minutes and then top up. As far as the Multipla is concerned, check also, during this operation, that the cock permitting the passage of water into heater radiator is open.

ANTIFREEZE MIXTURES

When outer temperature approaches 32° F (0° C) an antifreeze mixture must be used in radiator to prevent freezing.

FIAT ANTIFREEZE MIXTURE AND WATER SOLUTION

	ANTIFREEZE				WATER			FREEZING POINT	
% in volume	U.S. pints	G.B. pints		Liters	U.S. pints	G.B. pints	Liters	°F	°C
Sedan									
20	1.80	1.50		0,85	7.20	6.07	3,45	17	— 8
30	2.75	2.29		1,30	6.35	5.28	3,00	5	—15
40	3.60	3		1,70	5.40	4.57	2,60	—13	—25
Multipla									
20	2.75	2.29		1,30	10.95	9.16	5,20	17	— 8
30	4.10	3.43		1,95	9.60	8.02	4,55	5	—15
40	5.40	4.58		2,60	8.30	6.87	3,90	—13	—25

ENGINE: COOLING SYSTEM

The preferred mixtures are those of water and glycerine or glycol (ethyl- propyl-, etc.) provided suitable corrosion inhibitors are added.

The use of the special antifreeze FIAT mixture which is synthetic, inalterable, free from volatile components, and anticorrosive is recommended.

Percentages in relation to freezing points are tabulated on page 102.

However, in case FIAT antifreeze mixture is not available, use exclusively mixtures based on neutral glycerine or ethyl alcohol.

The composition of the above mixtures is tabulated here below.

NOTE - Alcohol solutions must be topped up often with alcohol additions after checking the solution specific gravity with a hydrometer since alcohol evaporates rapidly at temperatures around 158° F (70° C).

MIXTURE OF NEUTRAL GLYCERINE AND WATER

Specific gravity at 59° F (15° C)	GLYCERINE				WATER			FREEZING POINT	
	% in volume	U.S. pints	G.B. pints	Liters	U.S. pints	G.B. pints	Liters	°F	°C
Sedan									
1,049	15	1.40	1.15	0,65	7.60	6.45	3,65	24	− 4
1,070	25	2.12	1.85	1,05	6.88	5.75	3,25	17	− 8
1,115	35	3.15	2.65	1,50	5.85	4.95	2,80	7	−14
1,129	40	3.60	3.00	1,70	5.40	4.60	2,60	2	−17
1,144	45	4.10	3.45	1,95	4.90	4.15	2,35	− 4	−20
1,160	50	4.50	3.80	2,15	4.50	3.80	2,15	−10	−23
Multipla									
1,049	15	2.00	1.65	0,95	11.70	9.85	5,55	24	− 4
1,070	25	3.40	2.80	1,60	10.30	8.70	4,90	17	− 8
1,115	35	4.75	3.90	2,25	8.95	7.60	4,25	7	−14
1,129	40	5.40	4.60	2,60	8.30	6.90	3,90	2	−17
1,144	45	6.12	5.00	2,90	7.58	6.50	3,60	− 4	−20
1,160	50	6.85	5.75	3,25	6.85	5.75	3,25	−10	−23

MIXTURE OF ETHYL ALCOHOL AND WATER

Specific gravity at 59° F (15° C)	ALCOHOL				WATER			FREEZING POINT	
	% in volume	U.S. pints	G.B. pints	Liters	U.S. pints	G.B. pints	Liters	°F	°C
Sedan									
0,969	26,50	2.40	2.00	1,15	6.60	5.60	3,15	16	− 9
0,965	30,00	2.75	2.30	1,30	6.25	5.30	3,00	10	−12
0,959	35,25	3.15	2.65	1,50	5.85	4.95	2,80	7	−14
0,956	37,40	3.40	2.80	1,60	5.60	4.80	2,70	5	−15
Multipla									
0,969	26,50	3.60	3.00	1,70	10.10	8.50	4,80	16	− 9
0,965	30,00	4.10	3.45	1,95	9.60	8.05	4,55	10	−12
0,959	35,25	4.85	4.00	2,30	8.85	7.50	4,20	7	−14
0,956	37,40	5.20	4.30	2,45	8.50	7.20	4,05	5	−15

THERMOSTAT

« Sedan ».

As already said under « Radiator », the thermostat (contained in radiator lower bowl) must start expanding when water temperature reaches 167° to 176° F (75° to 80° C) and be completely extended at around 221° F (105° C).

To remove the thermostat undo the ring nut securing it to radiator using wrench A. 12201 (fig. 188).

If the thermostat is found defective [it may be checked by immersion in water whose temperature is increased from 167° F (75° C) up], replace it.

Fig. 188 - Sedan radiator rear view.

1. Gaskets. - 2. Felts. - 3. Drain cock. - 4. Air draft shutter tie rod control lever. - 5. Roller in contact with thermostat. - 6. Wrench A. 12201 for thermostat mounting nut.

« Multipla ».

The thermostat is mounted on the water outlet pipe at front of cylinder head. It should start opening when cooling water reaches a temperature of 161° to 170° F (72° to 77° C) and should be completely extended at 176° to 185° F (80° to 85° C).

The thermostat is adjusted by the Manufacturer and no further adjustments are required.

Should the bellows be damaged (cracking or piercing), the valve would open and water would normally circulate through the radiator.

To remove the thermostat unscrew it with wrench A. 50021.

To check thermostat operation immerse the thermostat in water at 176° F (80° C) up. The complete stroke of valve, with fully expanded thermostat is .256″ ± .020″ (6,5 ± 0,5 mm).

Replace the thermostat if found defective.

EXCESSIVE WATER TEMPERATURE INDICATOR SENDING UNIT

This unit (1, fig. 178) is mounted at rear end of cylinder head. At assembly, check that the seating surface for sending unit on cylinder head is perfectly flat and smooth.

Sending unit setting data: with temperature increments of 1.8° F (1° C) per minute the contact of terminal with ground must take place at a temperature of 230° to 248° F (110° to 120° C).

In case of defective operation of the sending unit, if the trouble is not ascribable to the wiring or to the bulb, replace the unit.

GENERATOR AND WATER PUMP DRIVE BELT TENSION ADJUSTMENT

Both generator and water pump with fan are driven by Vee belts.

The drive is taken from a single-groove pulley mounted on crankshaft and transmitted to a twin-groove pulley on generator shaft; from this pulley, another belt carries the drive to the pump pulley.

Check that tension is such that under 22 lbs. (10 kg) pressure belts sag .39″ to .59″ (1 to 1,5 cm) (fig. 189).

If belts are slack, they slip, generator and water pump are not driven at the required speed and belts wear rapidly; on the contrary, too tight belts induce an excessive strain on generator and water pump bearings.

To adjust belts:

— Adjust first tension of belt between crankshaft pulley and generator pulley by slackening the two generator mounting nuts (2, fig. 189): the upper one anchoring generator to crankcase and the lower one for generator position adjustment.

— Rotate generator as required to stretch the belt and then retighten mounting nuts (lover nut first).

Adjust tension of belt from generator to water pump as follows:

Back out the three pulley-to-hub mounting nuts (5, fig. 189).

ENGINE: POWER PLANT MOUNTINGS

Remove rear semi-pulley, take out one (or more, depending on belt slackness) of the spacer rings (6, fig. 189) forming pulley groove and re-fit ring(s) outside of pulley; this way, pulley groove will be narrower and belt will move towards pulley periphery.

Re-install the semi-pulley, with spacer ring(s) on its outer face, and secure to hub by the three mounting nuts.

Fig. 189 - Adjusting water pump, fan and generator drive belt tension.

1. Adjustable generator support. - 2. Support fixing nuts. - 3. Generator pulley. - 4. Water pump and fan drive pulley. - 5. Pulley-to-hub mounting nuts. - 6. Spacer rings, belt tension adjustment.

POWER PLANT MOUNTINGS

The power plant is elastically mounted on three supports.

At front the plant rests on a cross member secured under car floor through two rubber cushions fixed to gearbox casing (fig. 191). Position of cush-

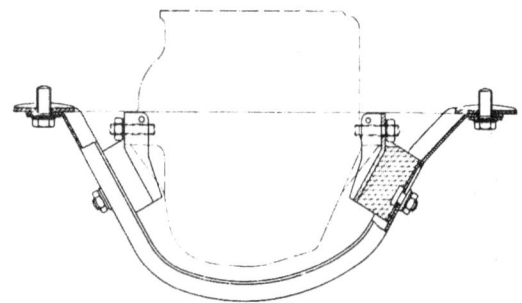

Fig. 191 - Cross section of power plant front support.

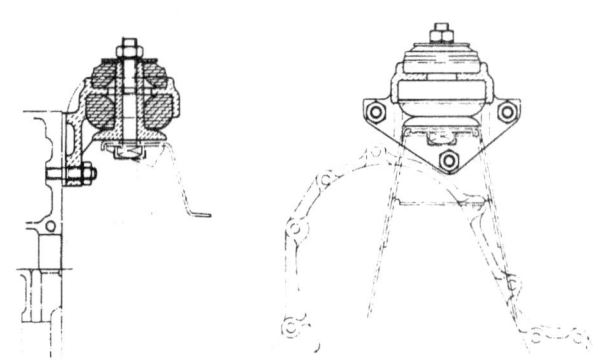

Fig. 190 - Lengthwise and crosswise section of power plant rear central support.

ions on cross member is adjustable to ensure alignment of the assembly.

At rear the engine crankcase rests on body rear lower panel through a suitable support and two interposed rubber cushions (fig. 190).

When removing or installing power plant on car, observe that rubber cushions are in good condition and that power plant alignment is correct.

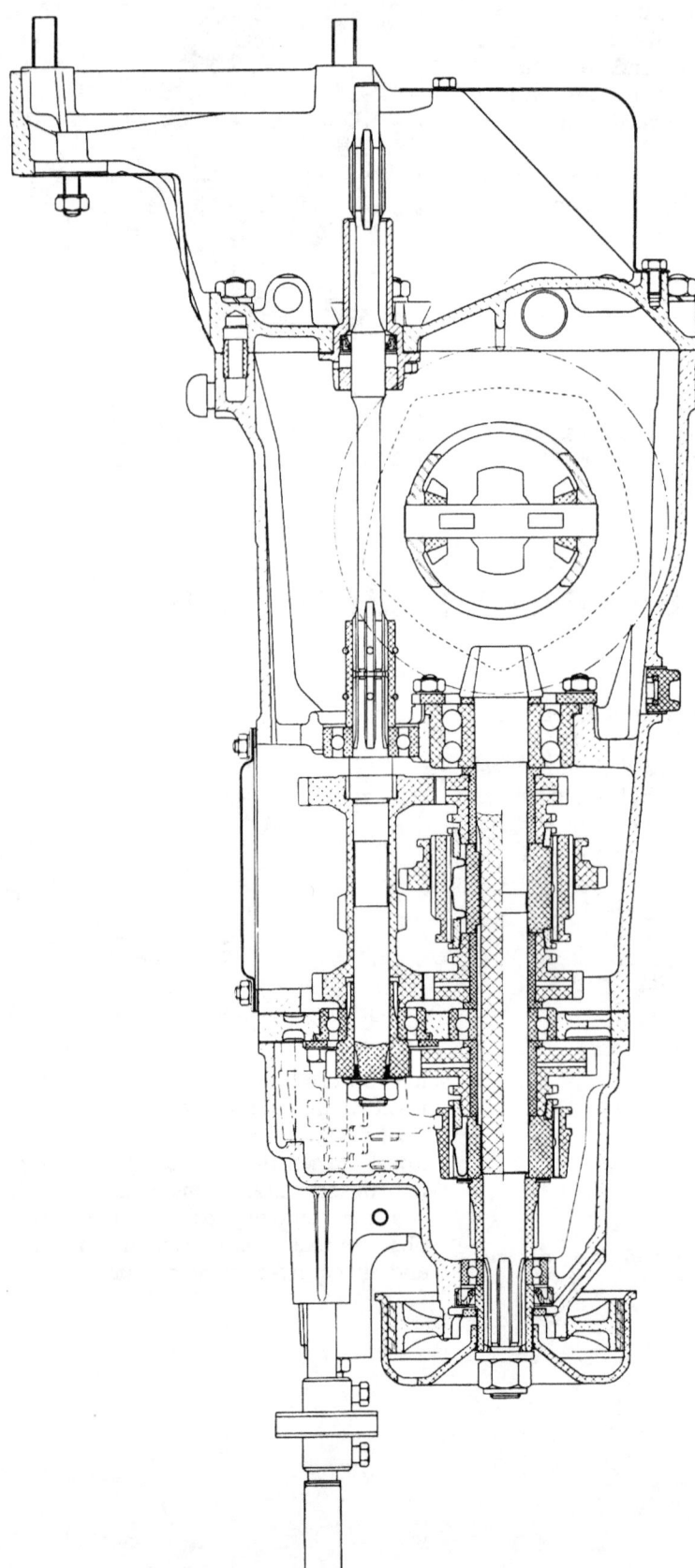

Fig. 192 - Longitudinal section of gearbox-differential-parking brake assembly (early type).

NOTE - The gearbox-differential unit shown in this picture was installed: up to engine No. 758492, Sedan; up to engine No. 765150, Multipla.

Section 4
CLUTCH
GEARBOX
DIFFERENTIAL

	Page
CLUTCH	108
WITHDRAWAL MECHANISM	110
GEARBOX - DIFFERENTIAL UNIT	115
GEARBOX	120
DIFFERENTIAL AND FINAL DRIVE	126
SWING AXLE SHAFTS AND SLIP JOINTS	137
GEARSHIFT CONTROL MECHANISM	138

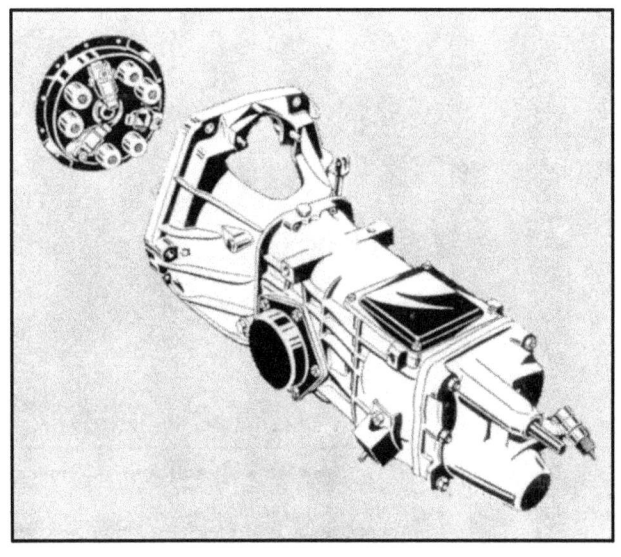

CLUTCH

Description of Components	page 108
Removal and Disassembly	» 109
Inspecting Disassembled Components	» 109
Pressure Spring Data	» 109
Assembly and Adjustment	» 110
Withdrawal Mechanism	» 110
Pedal Free Play	» 111
Installation	» 111
Clutch Trouble Diagnosis and Corrections	» 112
Specifications and Data	» 114
Servicing Equipment	» 114

Description of Components.

The clutch is the same for both « Sedan » and « Multipla »: single plate, with spring cushioned hub, working dry.

The outer diameter of the driven plate is 6.10" (155 mm).

The clutch consists of the following parts:

Driven plate. - This plate is provided with annular facings and spring cushioned hub (i.e. with springs arranged around the hub and cushion discs having the purpose of dampening the acceleration and deceleration torques thus, rendering smooth and gradual the engagement).

Pressure plate. - Accurately machined, this plate presses the driven plate against the flywheel.

Withdrawal levers. - Every lever is mounted on a pin screwed in the pressure plate and projecting from the cover; the lever, resting on the cover, is held in place by a retainment spring and a plate, and is secured by a nut and lockplate.

The height of the lever inner end may be adjusted by screwing or unscrewing the locking nut.

Engagement springs. - Six powerful springs force the pressure plate on driven plate.

Sliding sleeve with thrust bearing. - The sleeve, controlled by a fork lever, may slide until it presses, with the thrust bearing, on the withdrawal lever inner ends.

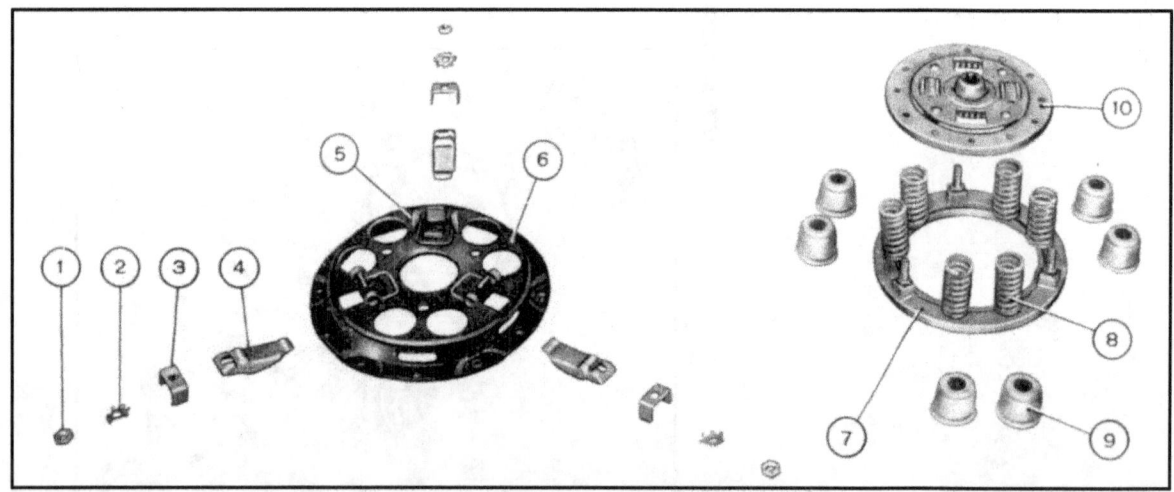

Fig. 193 - Clutch and driven plate components.

1. Withdrawal lever nut. - 2. Lock plate. - 3. Lever mounting plate. - 4. Withdrawal lever. - 5. Lever spring retainer. - 6. Clutch cover. - 7. Pressure plate. - 8. Pressure spring. - 9. Spring cup. - 10. Driven plate.

CLUTCH

Cover. - Of pressed sheet steel and with 6 holes for passage of the engagement springs with cups. The cover is fixed to flywheel by six screws (figure 199).

When depressing the clutch pedal, the clutch is disengaged by the action of the withdrawal levers that lift the pressure plate, thus permitting the driven plate to clear the flywheel. The control is transmitted from pedal to pressure plate via a linkage formed by levers, bowden, control shaft, fork and sleeve.

NOTE - The driven plate shown in fig. 193 is with cushion discs.

Driven plates have been equipped with cushion discs as follows:

« Sedan » - From engine No. 505990 to No. 505993;
From engine No. 508399 to No. 508401;
From engine No. 512811 onward.
« Multipla » - Starting from engine No. 513141.

Removal and Disassembly.

To remove the clutch, remove first the gearbox differential unit as described on page 119.

After removal of the gearbox/differential unit, detach the clutch by undoing the six mounting screws holding the clutch to flywheel.

Place unit on fixture **A. 62022** as shown in fig. 195, and lock cover by the three studs.

Straighten the lockplate tabs and unscrew the withdrawal lever retaining nuts; take off the plates and the levers and then slacken gradually the three T-handles of the fixture until releasing all pressure. Remove the cover and take off the spring cups and the springs.

Inspecting Disassembled Components.

Check springs for perfect efficiency, seeing if they conform to the data tabulated on bottom of this page. Replace the springs if they are weakened beyond the limits indicated in the table.

Check that: withdrawal levers are not worn, plates are not deformed, lever retainment springs are not deformed or weak and pin threads are undamaged. Replace any defective part.

Check pressure plate for damages and for smoothness of friction surface with driven plate, which must be absolutely flat and free from distortions of any kind. Otherwise, clutch will be noisy. If deformations or nicks found are not too severe, the trouble is remedied by lapping on a surface grinder.

Similarly, check also the flywheel friction surface.

Check that pilot bush is not chipped or excessively worn. To replace the bush, if required, use puller **A. 6515** or ram puller **A. 40006/1/2**.

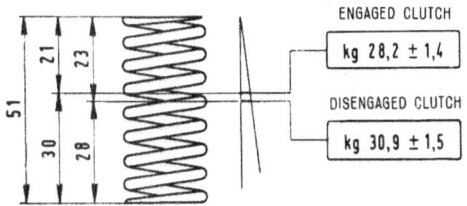

Fig. 194 - Clutch spring characteristics.

Inspect driven plate facings and replace if worn. If facings are greasy and only the surface is involved, wash with turpentine while scrubbing with a wire brush. Instead, if facings are soaked with oil, replace them.

Any time facings are replaced check balancing and trueness of the driven plate. To this purpose place the plate on the splined shaft and rest on V blocks **C. 732**: remove material from the heavier spots.

Check trueness by rotating the plate slowly while resting on V blocks.

Out-of-true, checked with a scriber, must not exceed .016" (0,4 mm).

Check that the rivets securing the facings on the plate are perfectly clenched and flush with the facings because otherwise the flywheel and pressure plate friction faces might be scored and damaged.

To prevent rattling: clutch shaft splines should not have any clearance in excess of .012" (0,30 mm) with respect to driven plate and hub-to-shaft splines side clearance should not exceed .0039" (0,10 mm).

Check that the plate slides freely on splined shaft. Inspect also the sleeve and the thrust bearing and replace if damaged.

PRESSURE SPRING DATA

PART No.	WIRE dia.	OUTER dia.	ACTIVE coils	TOTAL coils	FREE height	SEATED SPRING		
						Height	Corresp. load	Min. load
874239	.118 in. (3 mm)	.945 in. (24 mm)	7 1/4	8 3/4	2 in. (51 mm)	1.18 in. (30 mm)	62.18±3 lbs (28,2±1,4 kg)	53 lbs. (24 kg)

Assembly and Adjustment.

— Place clutch pressure plate, complete with pins, on fixture **A. 62022** (fig. 195).

— On clutch cover, install the three withdrawal levers, arranging their retainment springs as shown in fig. 195.

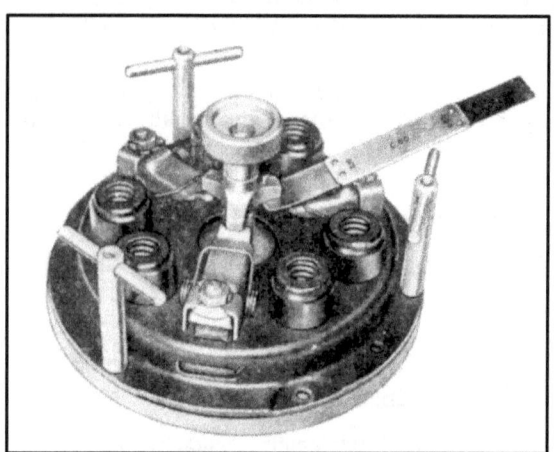

Fig. 195 - Assembling and adjusting clutch on fixture **A. 62022**.

Use feeler gauge **C. 110**.

— Place the six clutch withdrawal springs in their bosses on pressure plate.

— Insert cups on springs and install clutch cover.

— Using fixture **A. 62022** press clutch cover down at the same time making sure that levers and their supporting pins are properly guided into their seating holes in cover.

— Fit the three lever backing plates and screw in nuts and lockplate on supporting pins.

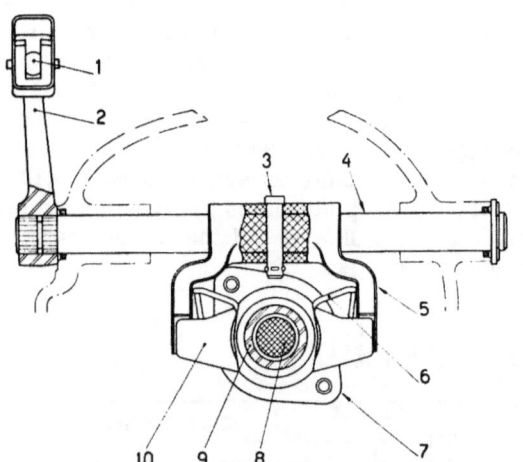

Fig. 196 - Clutch rear throwout control.

1. Bowden. - 2 and 4. Lever with control shaft. - 3. Forked lever securing pin. - 5. Forked lever. - 6. Spring. - 7 and 9. Support for throwout control sleeve. - 8. Clutch shaft. - 10. Clutch throwout control sleeve.

— After fully tightening tool T-handles, adjust end play between withdrawal levers and central lobes of tool by screwing in or out backing plate nuts until a .0039″ (0,10 mm) clearance - checked with gauge - is obtained (see fig. 195).

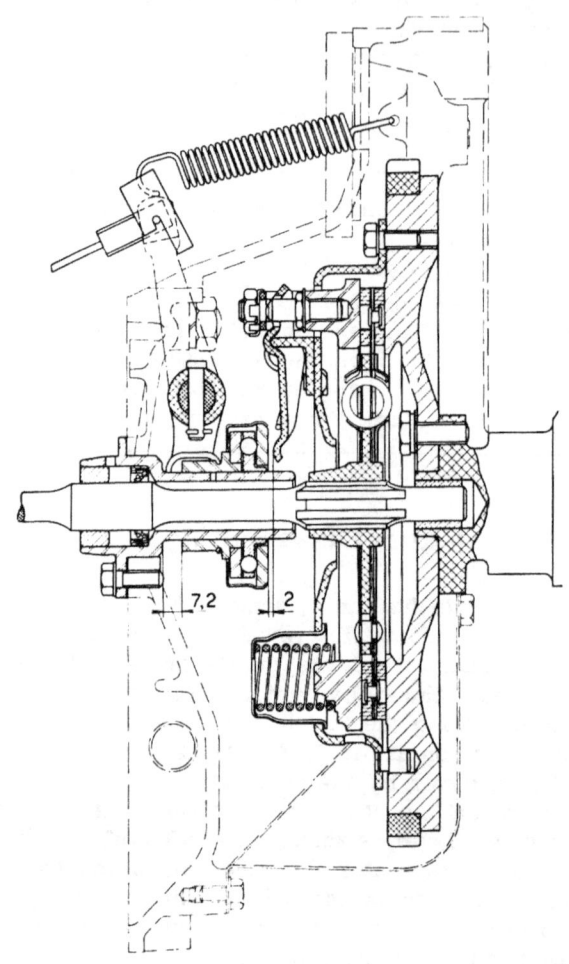

Fig. 197 - Longitudinal section of clutch through throwout control (clutch shaft and driven plate are of the early type).

Indicated clearances (.078″ and .283″ = 2 and 7,2 mm) must be obtained by adjusting the clutch release bowden cable.

Following end play adjustment, lock withdrawal lever supporting pin nuts to prevent any subsequent misadjustment.

In order not to affect clutch unit balance, clutch pressure plate and cover must be reinstalled exactly in the same position as before disassembly.

WITHDRAWAL MECHANISM

This mechanism consists of:

1) a forked lever, integral with a shaft (passing through clutch housing) on which is keyed the outer operating lever (fig. 196);

CLUTCH

2) a return spring, connected to outer operating lever and anchored on gearbox casing (fig. 197) which, when in normal position, keeps throwout bearing away from the three withdrawal levers.

The throwout bearing is pressed against withdrawal levers by a sleeve connected to forked lever (fig. 196).

Pedal Free Play.

Under normal operating conditions, the clutch pedal should have a free travel of approximately

Fig. 199 - Installing the clutch assembly and driven plate on flywheel.

Centering of driven plate with pilot bush is obtained by using alignment bar **A. 62023** shown above.

25/32" (20 mm) before acting on withdrawal levers.

When this free travel is reduced or annulled on account of facing wear (in which case clutch would slip), a correct pedal play must be restored by the necessary adjustment, proceeding as follows:

— Remove front suspension leaf spring apron.

— Unscrew locknut (2, fig. 198) and then screw in or back out stretcher (3, fig. 198) of clutch control tie rod, according to whether pedal free travel must be reduced or increased.

— Check the pedal travel obtained, tighten locknut (2), and re-install front apron.

Installation.

This is a simple operation.

Before tightening the screws securing the clutch, align the driven plate with respect to pilot bush on crankshaft using alignment bar **A. 62023**, as shown in fig. 199.

Fig. 198 - Clutch front throwout control.
1. Bowden. - 2. Counternut. - 3. Stretcher. - 4. Control shaft. - 5. Pedal stem.

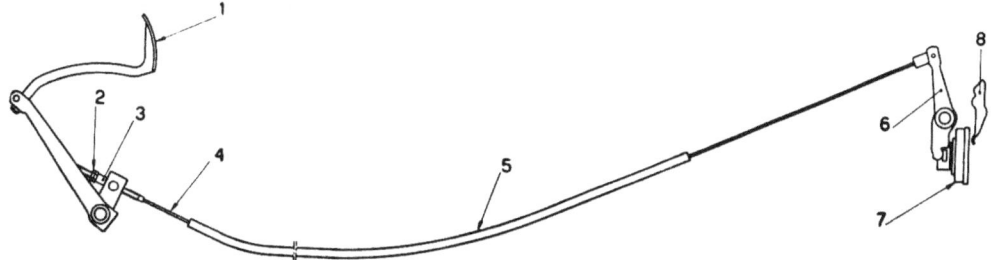

Fig. 200 - Diagram of clutch throwout control assembly.
1. Clutch pedal. - 2. Counternut. - 3. Stretcher. - 4-5. Bowden assembly. - 6. Throwout control forked lever arm. - 7. Throwout bearing. - 8. Throwout lever.

CLUTCH TROUBLE DIAGNOSIS AND CORRECTIONS

Noises when Clutch Pedal is Depressed.

POSSIBLE CAUSES	REMEDIES
1) Thrust bearing excessively worn, damaged, broken or dry.	1) Replace bearing. Lubrication is not possible as bearing is metal cased.
2) Seizure of thrust bearing and withdrawal levers.	2) Replace thrust bearing. Clean lever ends with metal brush and smooth out bearing contact faces with felt polishers.
3) Withdrawal levers striking against clutch cover.	3) Examine lever mounting and adjust levers.
4) Insufficient pedal free play.	4) Set pedal free play at 25/32" (20 mm).
5) Broken or weak pedal return spring.	5) Replace spring.
6) Broken or weak forked lever return spring.	6) Replace spring.
7) Excessive play of driven plate hub to clutch shaft causes rattles.	7) Replace the driven plate and check that clearance between hub of new driven plate and clutch shaft is within .0039" (0,10 mm) endwise and .0118" (0,30 mm) crosswise. Should clearance exceed above limits, replace also the clutch shaft.

Noises when Clutch Pedal is Released.

POSSIBLE CAUSES	REMEDIES
1) Misalignment of driven plate to flywheel causes slight movement of driven plate hub in respect of facings. This noise is particularly audible with engine idling or running at low speed.	1) Set level of driven plate. With driven plate locked on clutch shaft, set it under slight rotation and check for no runout in excess of .0157" (0,4 mm), using a scriber.
2) Driven plate springs broken or weak.	2) Replace driven plate.
3) Insufficient pedal free play.	3) Set clutch pedal free play at 25/32" (20 mm).
4) Pedal return spring broken or weak.	4) Replace the spring.
5) Forked lever return spring broken or weak.	5) Replace the spring.

The Clutch Drags.

POSSIBLE CAUSES	REMEDIES
1) Excessive pedal free play.	1) Set free play at 25/32" (20 mm).
2) Driven plate warped.	2) Set level of driven plate. Maximum plate runout: .0157" (0,4 mm).

(continued)

CLUTCH

The Clutch Drags (continuation).

POSSIBLE CAUSES	REMEDIES
3) Roughness on driven plate facings.	3) Rub facings with a metal brush or replace them, if necessary.
4) Driven plate facings improperly fitted, loose or broken.	4) Replace facings. Facing rivets should be clenched, to avoid damage to pressure plate and flywheel.
5) Driven plate hub forcing on clutch shaft.	5) Locate cause of trouble and remove it, if possible. Otherwise replace the driven plate.
6) Damaged clutch shaft splines prevent the driven plate from sliding.	6) Replace the clutch shaft; also the driven plate, if required.

The Clutch Slips.

POSSIBLE CAUSES	REMEDIES
1) Insufficient clutch pedal return travel, due to the flexible cable being stuck or the pedal return spring being too weak.	1) Locate cause of failure and replace spring or eliminate sticking of control cable.
2) Damage throwout mechanism.	2) Overhaul throwout mechanism; also clutch, if required.
3) Clutch pressure springs weak or broken.	3) Overhaul clutch and replace springs.
4) Oil or grease or driven plate facings.	4) Remove cause of oil leakage and replace facings, if they cannot be reconditioned by rubbing with turpentine and metal brush.
5) Driven plate facings worn or burned.	5) Replace facings.

The Clutch Grabs.

POSSIBLE CAUSES	REMEDIES
1) Oil or grease on flywheel, pressure plate and driven plate facings.	1) Remove cause of leakage, clean flywheel and pressure plate thoroughly, replace driven plate facings.
2) Loose facings at driven plate hub due to poor rivet tightness.	2) If facings are not worn, replace defective rivets. Otherwise, replace facings and clench rivets securely.
3) Driven plate hub does not slide freely on clutch shaft.	3) Remove any foreign matter or dirt deposits from shaft splines. Should trouble still be present, replace damaged part.
4) Pressure plate deeply cracked or broken.	4) Replace pressure plate.
5) Improper adjustment of withdrawal levers.	5) Adjust withdrawal levers as specified on page 110, under « Assembly and Adjustment of Clutch ».

Excessive Facing Wear.

POSSIBLE CAUSES	REMEDIES
1) Insufficient pedal free play.	1) Set clutch pedal free play at 25/32'' (20 mm).
2) Driver steps unnecessarily on pedal; this causes facing wear and damage to throwout bearing.	2) Advise driver to discontinue wrong practice and step on clutch pedal only when necessary.
3) Pressure springs weak or broken.	3) Check pressure springs for tension as specified on page 109 and replace springs, if they are unserviceable.
4) Driven plate facings installed incorrectly.	4) Replace facings by new ones and install them correctly. Check driven plate for center.

SPECIFICATIONS AND DATA

Type	Single plate, working dry
Driven plate with facings of	Ferodo
Facing O.D.	6.10'' (155 mm)
Facing I.D.	4.48'' (114 mm)
Clutch springs:	
Part No.	874239
Free height	2.00'' (51 mm)
Seated height	1.18'' (30 mm)
Corresponding load	62.18 $\pm$ 3 lbs (28,2 $\pm$ 1,4 kg)
Minimum load	53 lbs (24 kg)
Pedal free travel	25/32'' (20 mm)
Clearance between central ring of fixture A. 62022 and withdrawal levers	.0039'' (0,10 mm)
Driven plate facing max. permissible out-of-true	.0078'' to .0157'' (0,20 to 0,40 mm)
Clearance between clutch shaft and clutch hub splines:	
longitudinally	.00197'' to .0039'' (0,05 to 0,10 mm)
crosswise	.0059'' to .0118'' (0,15 to 0,30 mm)

SERVICING EQUIPMENT

A. 40006/1/2   Puller for pilot bush.
A. 62022   Fixture for clutch assembly, disassembly and adjustment.
A. 62023   Alignment bar for driven plate centering at assembly of clutch on flywheel.

GEARBOX - DIFFERENTIAL UNIT

Description of Components . . . . page	115
Gearbox and Road Wheel Ratios . . . . »	117
Removal of Gearbox - Differential Unit from Car . . . . »	119
Installation of Gearbox - Differential Unit . . . . »	137
Unit Adjustment and Tightening Reference . . . . »	141
Technical Specifications . . . . »	142
Service Equipment . . . . »	143
GEARBOX . . . . »	120
Disassembly . . . . »	120
Inspecting Disassembled Components . . . . »	121
Assembly . . . . »	122
Trouble Diagnosis and Corrections . . . . »	124
DIFFERENTIAL AND FINAL DRIVE . . . . »	126
Noise Diagnosis and Remedies . . . . »	126
Disassembly . . . . »	127
Inspection and Repair of Parts . . . . »	129
Installation and Adjustment of Bevel Drive Pinion . . . . »	130
How to Determine Bevel Drive Pinion Thrust Ring Thickness . . . . »	132
Assembly of Inner Case . . . . »	133
Preload of Ring Gear Bearings and Bevel Ring Gear-to-Pinion Backlash Adjustment . . »	134
Checking Tooth Contact Between Pinion and Ring Gear . . . . »	135
SWING AXLE SHAFTS AND SLIP JOINTS . . . . »	137
Description and Repair . . . . »	137
GEARSHIFT CONTROL MECHANISM . . . . »	138
Adjustment . . . . »	138
Removal . . . . »	139
Disassembly and Inspection of Gearshift Lever Components . . . . »	140

Description of Components.

Gearbox and differential unit are incorporated in a single casing.

The drive is transmitted to rear wheels through two swing axle shafts which are linked to differential via slip joints.

Gearbox provides four forward speeds and one reverse.

Fourth speed is actually an overdrive. Constant mesh second, third and fourth speeds, all synchromeshed by synchronizer rings.

The gearbox-differential unit mounted on the « Multipla » differs from the standard « Sedan » unit in the following: casing, 3rd and 4th speed gear ratios, final drive ratio and its pinion adjustment shim. For ratios, table below.

NOTE

Due to the parking brake having been shifted from the gearbox-differential unit to the rear wheels, as follows:

— starting from engine No. 758493, « Sedan »,

— starting from engine No. 765151, « Multipla »;

the gearbox-differential unit has undergone some modifications which can be easily traced by comparing fig. No. 192 with No. 201 and fig. No. 219 with No. 220.

Description and service procedure apply to new type units. For old type units, particular information has been given whenever necessary.

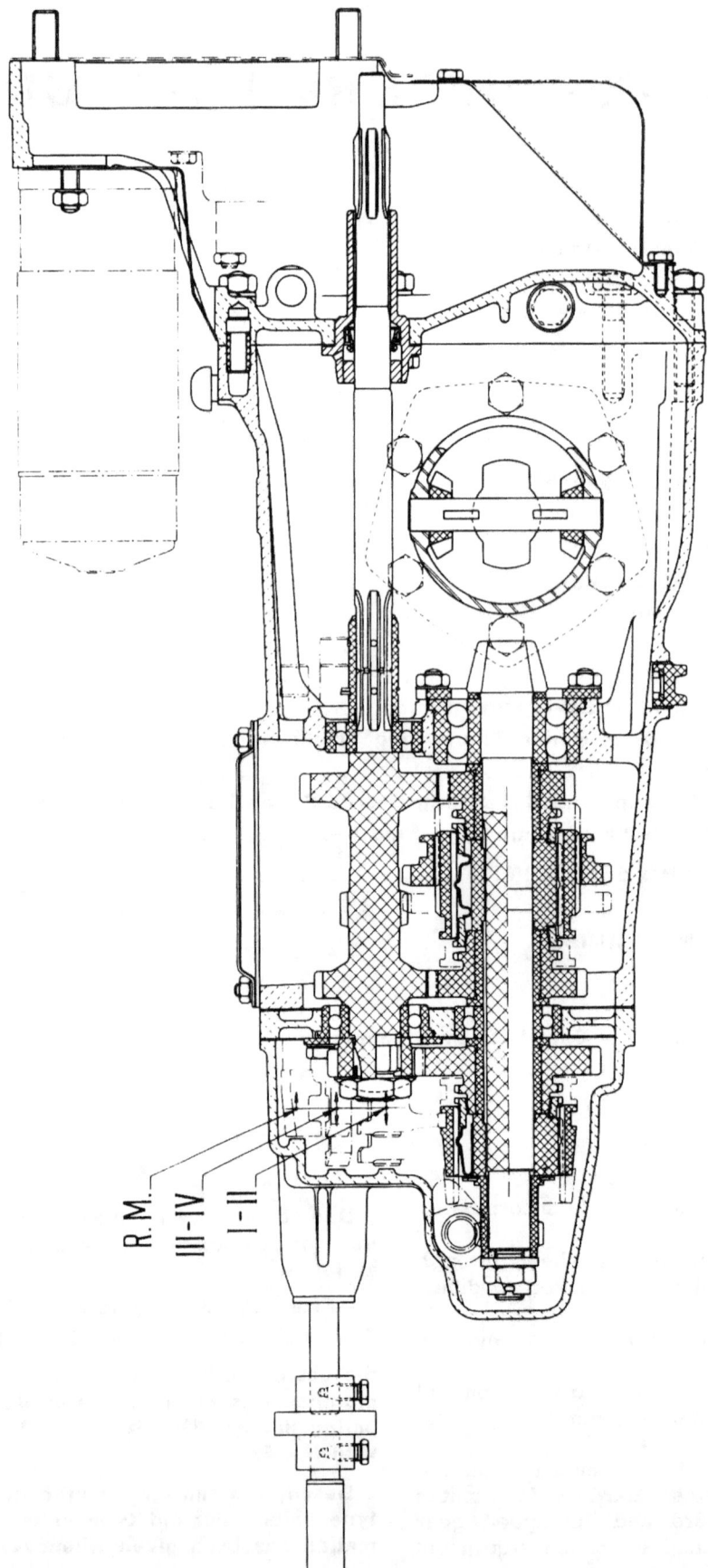

Fig. 201 - Longitudinal section of gearbox - differential unit (late type).

NOTE: This gearbox - differential unit has been adopted starting from engine No. 758493, «Sedan»; and from engine No. 765151, «Multipla».

GEARBOX - DIFFERENTIAL UNIT

GEARBOX AND ROAD WHEEL RATIOS

GEARS	1st	2nd	3rd	4th	REVERSE
Gear ratios:					
Sedan	$\frac{44}{13} = 3,384$	$\frac{37}{18} = 2,055$	$\frac{32}{24} = 1,333$	$\frac{26}{29} = 0,896$	$\frac{24}{13} \times \frac{44}{19} = 4,275$
Multipla	$\frac{44}{13} = 3,384$	$\frac{37}{18} = 2,055$	$\frac{32}{25} = 1,280$	$\frac{26}{31} = 0,838$	$\frac{24}{13} \times \frac{44}{19} = 4,275$
Ratio to wheels with final drive ratio:					
8 to 43 - Sedan .	18,189	11,045	7,164	4,818	22,978
7 to 45 - Multipla .	21,754	13,210	8,228	5,387	27,482

The aluminum gearbox-differential casing is mounted on engine by four screws and rests in front (fig. 206) on a sheet metal mounting attached to body floor and provided with rubber pads.

The unit consists of three separable elements:

— a central body, divided into two compartments: the front one contains the first, third, fourth and reverse speed gears, the layshaft and reverse shaft, and relevant striker rods and selector forks; the rear compartment, instead, houses the differential unit and the final drive ring gear and pinion set; first, third, fourth and reverse speed drive gears, being one unit, make up the primary shaft;

— a front extension, housing the second speed gear and selector fork, the gearshift control lever and speedometer drive gears;

— a rear housing mounted on engine which has a dual function: in front it shrouds the differential unit and, at rear, it performs as a clutch housing; the flywheel cover is attached to the rear housing.

An inspection lid is provided on central body; a seat for starter motor is provided on gearbox rear housing.

The primary shaft is joined to clutch shaft by a sleeve and two pins with snap rings.

The second speed drive gear is arranged on primary shaft, outside the central body.

Primary shaft is supported at its ends by ball bearings, while the clutch shaft rear end is supported by a bronze bush press-fitted in a sleeve (fig. 201) fixed to rear housing.

The layshaft, integral with final drive pinion, is supported on two ball bearings: a front bearing press-fitted in the mounting plate for central body cover and a rear double-row ball bearing press-fitted and locked in central body partition between gearbox and differential.

The layshaft carries: the fourth speed driven gear, the fourth speed synchronizer ring, the third and fourth speed sliding sleeve with sliding gear for first and reverse speeds, the third speed synchronizer, the third speed driven gear, the second speed gear with synchronizer, the hub and sliding sleeve for 2nd speed gear engagement and the speedometer drive gear.

Gearshifting is controlled by a lever on floor tunnel which, through a control rod, operates the selector lever in front extension housing.

The locking of all three rods, both in neutral or engaged position, is obtained through a ball that is pressed against specially machined notches in the rods themselves by the action of a spring (fig. 216).

The simultaneous engagement of two speeds is prevented by a device consisting of a ball and two rollers sliding in seats in the rods.

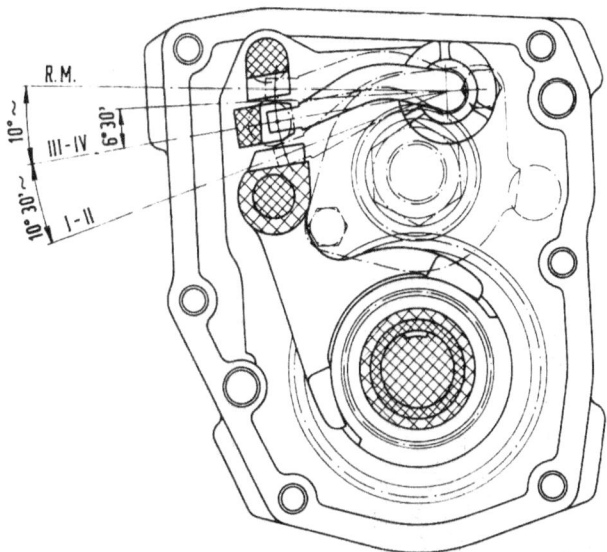

Fig. 202 - Gearbox cross section through striker rods and 2nd gear fork.

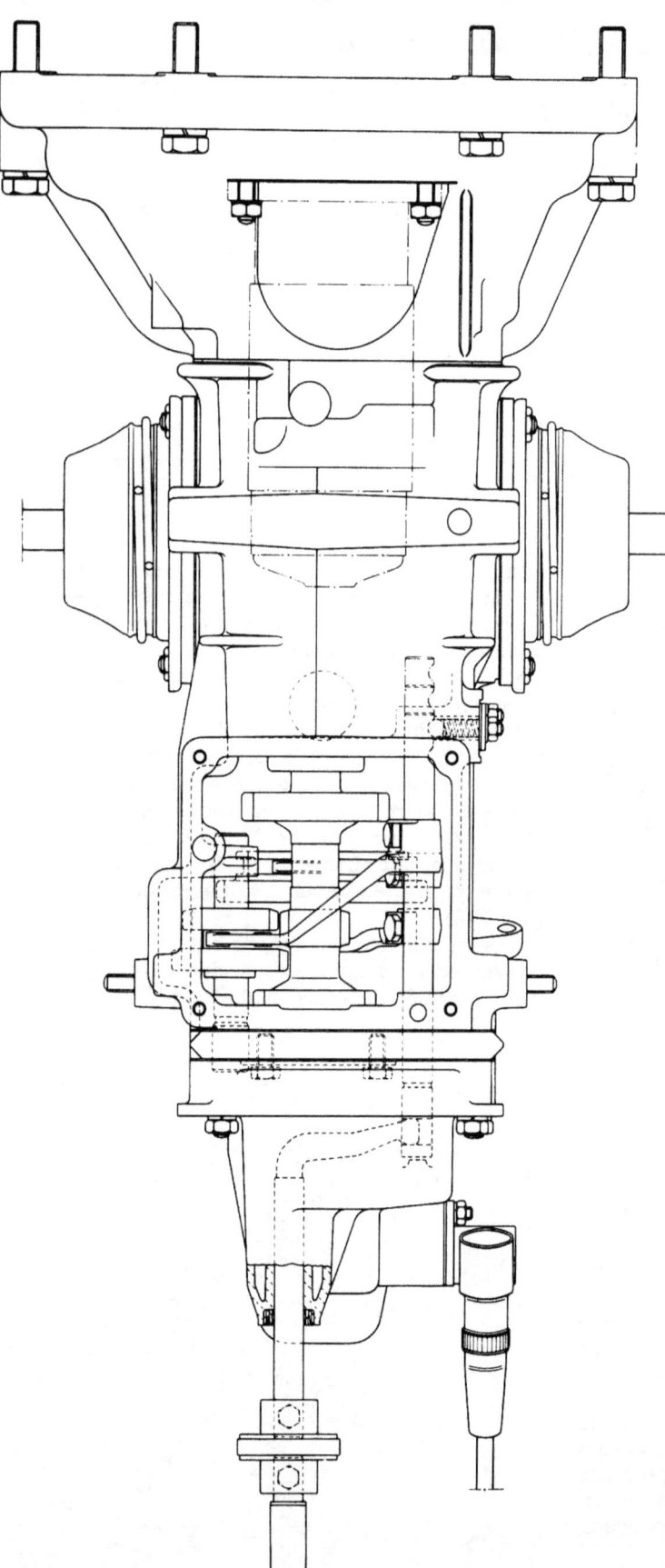

Fig. 203 - **Gearbox-differential assembly without inspection cover (late type).**

NOTE: This gearbox-differential unit has been adopted starting from engine No. 758493, «Sedan»; and from engine No. 765151, «Multipla».

CAUTION

Gearbox may be serviced without having to disassemble the differential unit, unless the layshaft - drive pinion assembly must be replaced.

To service the differential unit, instead, the disassembly of gearbox is inevitable since to obtain perfect final drive gear teeth mesh there are some operations involved which require the removal of layshaft - drive pinion assembly.

GEARBOX - DIFFERENTIAL UNIT

Differential unit and final drive ring gear and pinion set are housed in the rear end compartment of the gearbox central body.

Bevel drive pinion is integral with layshaft.

The differential case consists of two halves: the bevel drive ring gear is installed on one of the halves and secured by the same screws that join the two case halves.

Differential side gears have an inner splining in which the splined axle shaft ends slide by means of a specially designed slip joint (figs. 219 and 220).

Differential case is supported by two taper roller bearings secured in position by adjuster rings.

The Gleason final drive couple ratio is 8 to 43 (Sedan) and 7 to 45 (Multipla).

Gearbox ratios and drive ratios at wheels, in the different speeds, are tabulated on page 117.

Fig. 205 - Engine held by sling Arr. 2067 (as shown by arrows) during the gearbox-differential unit removal.

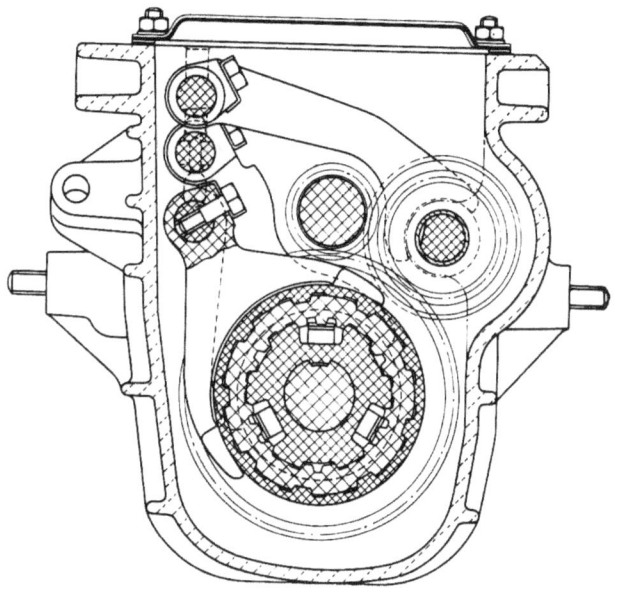

Fig. 204 - Gearbox cross section through 3rd and 4th gear engagement sleeves.

Removal of Gearbox-Differential Unit from Car.

Disconnect cable terminal on battery positive post, then raise car rear end and place on stands.

Lower rear seat back and remove floor bottom behind seat and starter cover.

Disconnect the two cables at starter, the control tie rod and remove starter.

Next, disconnect the clutch control bowden, the reaction spring, and disinsert rod from hole in gearbox support.

Undo the two upper short screws fixing the gearbox-differential unit to engine.

Support engine by sling **Arr. 2067** (fig. 205). Slacken the engine rear central support nut and the plate fixing the accelerator and carburetor starting device bowdens.

Undo the four screws fixing axle shaft splined sleeves-to-flexible joint on wheels (fig. 247) and take off inner spring.

Disconnect:

— gearshift control rod from speed selector lever joint;

— speedometer drive flexible shaft;

— clutch lower apron;

— rear apron.

Under gearbox-differential unit, place support **Arr. 2076** mounted on a hydraulich garage jack.

Unscrew the two lower long bolts fixing the gearbox-differential unit to engine.

Detach the gearbox-differential front support from body floor (fig. 206) and, by pushing the unit forward, slide out clutch shaft from its seat on crankshaft.

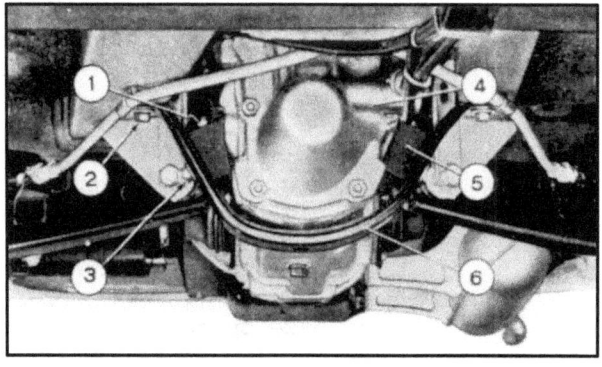

Fig. 206 - Front support of gearbox-differential unit.

1. Gearbox-differential unit mounting pad nuts. - 2. Screws securing bracket to body bottom. - 3. Rubber pad position adjustment nuts. - 4. Gearbox-differential unit. - 5. Rubber pads. - 6. Mounting bracket.

GEARBOX

Disassembly.

The following preliminary operations are necessary before disassembling the gearbox:
— disconnection of front support;
— removal of upper cover and casing lower plug, drain oil;
— washing of nuit.

Next, disassemble unit proceeding as follows:
Place unit on rotating stand **Arr. 2204**, and fix on support **Arr. 2206/6**.

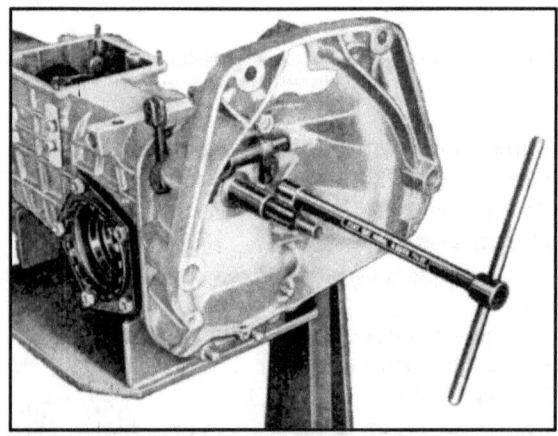

Fig. 207 - Removal of gearbox-differential unit bell-mounthed support.

Take off support with speedometer drive pinion.
Disassemble front housing and from it extract the speed selector lever and its gasket. Lock the layshaft-drive pinion in position, remove the cotter pin and unscrew the nut.
Disinsert speedometer drive gear from layshaft and then remove: the retainer cover, springs and balls for safety locking of stricker rods.
Open fasteners, and undo the selector fork-to-striker rod fixing screws (fig. 209).
Slide out reverse control upper rod and fork, the rod locking ball, the intermediate rod and safety roller, and third and fourth speeds control fork.
Pull outh the second speed sliding sleeve with fork and striker rod; take off hub, with relevant springs.
Remove synchronizer ring, second speed driven gear and relevant bush.
Unscrew primary shaft fixing nut and slide off lock washer; then remove the second speed drive

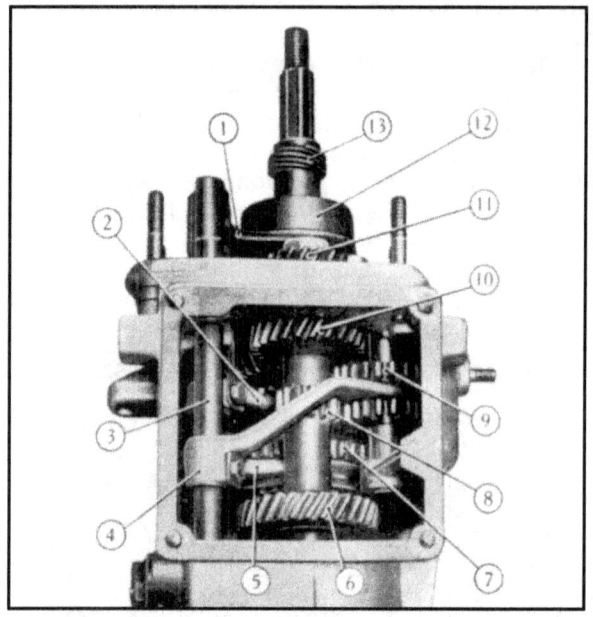

Fig. 208 - Gearbox without upper cover and front housing.

1. 2nd gear fork. - 2. 3rd and 4th gear fork. - 3 and 4. Reverse fork and striker rod. - 5. 1st gear fork. - 6. 4th speed driving gear. - 7. 1st speed and reverse sliding gear. - 8. 1st speed and reverse driving gear. - 9. Reverse gear. - 10. 3rd speed driving gear. - 11. 2nd speed driving gear. - 12. 2nd gear engagement sliding sleeve. - 13. Speedometer drive gear.

gear, ball bearing and reverse shaft retaining plate, and slide out reverse shaft with gear.
Remove the front housing-to-central body mounting plate, with relevant gaskets; from plate, take out the primary shaft front bearing and the layshaft front bearing.

Fig. 209 - Removing screws securing forks to striker rods.

From layshaft, slide out: the third speed driven gear with bushing, the synchronizer, the third and fourth speed sliding sleeve and hub, the first speed and reverse driven gear, the fourth speed synchronizer and driven gear with relevant bush.

Through front end, take off the primary shaft, which is one unit with first, third, fourth and reverse speed drive gear, the rear bearing, together with clutch shaft; next, take out the clutch release control assembly from rear housing.

After all these operations, the seal ring and clutch shaft intermediate support bush still remain in gearbox rear housing.

Inspecting Disassembled Gearbox Components.

After properly washing and cleaning all components, check that:

— Gearbox casing is not cracked and bearing seats are neither worn nor damaged to prevent bearing outer ring rotation in ring seats.

— Ball bearings are in perfect condition and axial play is not greater than maximum allowable limit of .0196'' (0,5 mm); radial play must not exceed .00196'' (0,05 mm) (figs. 211 and 214).

To check if inner ring revolves smoothly as it should in outer ring, hold bearing firmly by outer race, at the same time rock inner race back and forth: sliding must be free and noiseless.

Always replace bearings, unless their efficiency is sure beyond the slightest doubt.

— Primary shaft and layshaft, checked between centers and with dial gauge, are perfectly centered, the out-of-true readings for bearing seats being less than .0008'' (0,02 mm); splines must not be indented.

— Reverse shaft is perfectly smooth. Clearance between shaft and bush seated in sliding gear must not exceed .0059'' (0,15 mm).

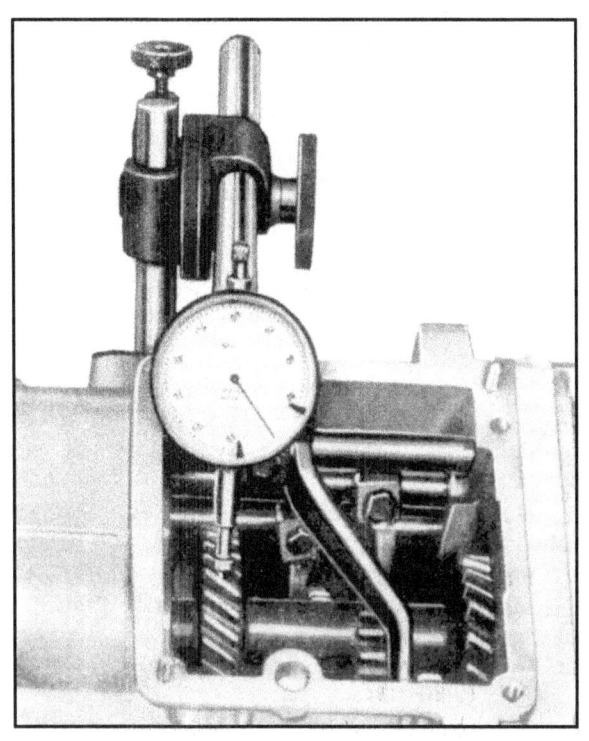

Fig. 210 - Checking backlash of gears.
Fit clearance: .0039'' (0,10 mm).

— Gear teeth show no sign of damage or excessive wear. Teeth of each pair in mesh must mate on their entire length.

Contact surfaces are smooth and show no indent marks.

Fig. 211.

Checking radial play in primary shaft rear bearing.

Max. permissible limit: .0019'' (0,05 mm).

NOTE - Primary and clutch shaft shown in this figure are of the early type.

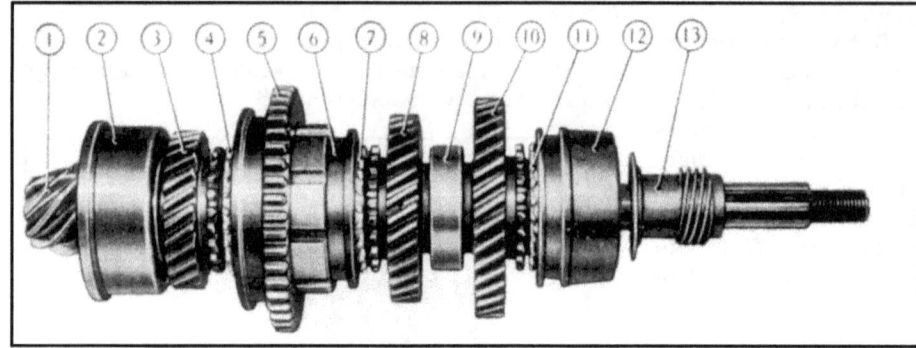

Fig. 212.

Layshaft gear cluster (early type).

Late type layshaft-drive pinion assembly is shorter, due to the absence of parking brake drum.

1. Layshaft bevel pinion. - 2. Rear bearing. - 3. 4th speed gear. - 4. 4th gear engagement synchronizer ring. - 5. 1st speed and reverse sliding gear. - 6. 3rd and 4th speed engagement sliding sleeve. - 7. 3rd speed engagement synchronizer ring. - 8. 3rd speed gear. - 9. Intermediate bearing. - 10. 2nd speed gear. - 11. 2nd speed engagement synchronizer ring. - 12. 2nd speed engagement sliding sleeve. 13. Speedometer drive gear.

— Clearances between gears are not greater than .0039″ (0,10 mm) when new; maximum wear limit is .0078″ (0,20 mm) (fig. 210).

— No appreciable clearance must exist between bushes and gears and between bushes and layshaft.

— Sleeves, both sliding and fixed, and relevant hubs are perfectly smooth on working surfaces and clearance between mating parts is not greater than .0039″ to .0059″ (0,10 to 0,15 mm). Wear limit is .0078″ (0,20 mm).

— Synchronizer rings are neither damaged on inner surfaces nor on splines in mesh with sliding sleeves.

The synchronizer rings must show a resistance to rotation on the tapering surface of the gears to which they are coupled.

— Gear shifting selector forks are not distorted and striker rods slide freely in their holes in casing.

— Oil seals are in perfect condition: replace as required.

— Striker rod locking balls, and safety rollers, slide freely in their seats. Their improper operation could cause troubles in the engagement and disengagement of speeds.

Assembly.

Arrange gearbox, complete with differential unit and final drive, on rotating stand **Arr. 2204** and secure to support **Arr. 2206/6**.

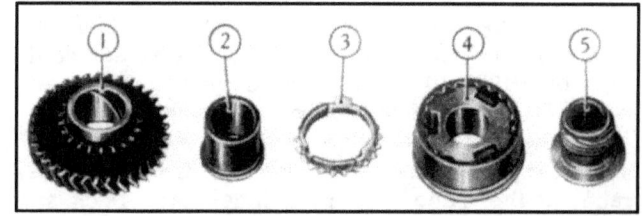

Fig. 213 - Components installed on layshaft for 2nd speed and speedometer drive.

1. 2nd speed driven gear. - 2. Gear bush. - 3. 2nd gear engagement synchronizer ring. - 4. 2nd gear engagement sliding sleeve and hub. - 5. Speedometer drive gear.

Through casing front end, insert the primary shaft and first, third, fourth and reverse speed drive gear assembly, complete with its rear bearing and clutch shaft.

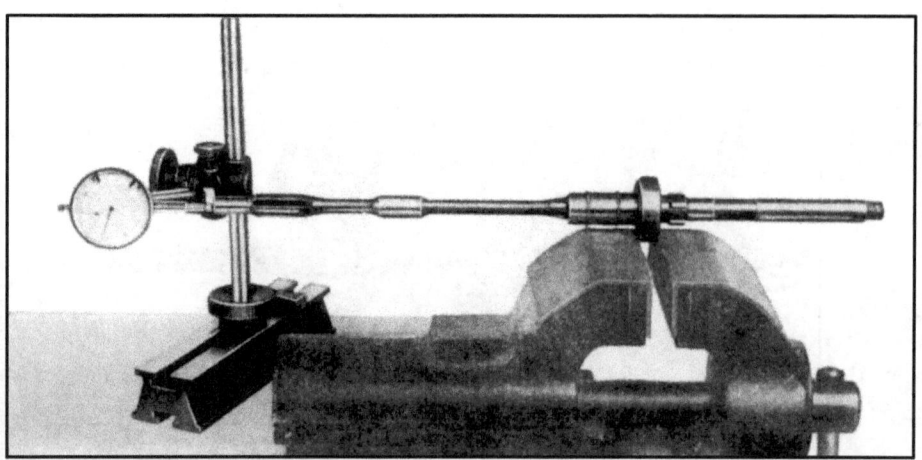

Fig. 214.

Checking axial play of primary shaft rear bearing.

Max. permissible limit: .0196″ (0,5 mm).

NOTE - Primary and clutch shaft shown in this figure are of the early type.

GEARBOX

Fig. 215 - **Components installed on layshaft for 1st, 3rd and 4th speeds.**

1. 4th speed driven gear. - 2. Gear bush. - 3. 4th gear engagement synchronizer ring. - 4. 3rd and 4th gear engagement sliding sleeve and hub. - 5. 1st speed and reverse sliding gear. - 6. 3rd gear engagement synchronizer ring. - 7. Gear bush. - 8. 3rd speed driven gear.

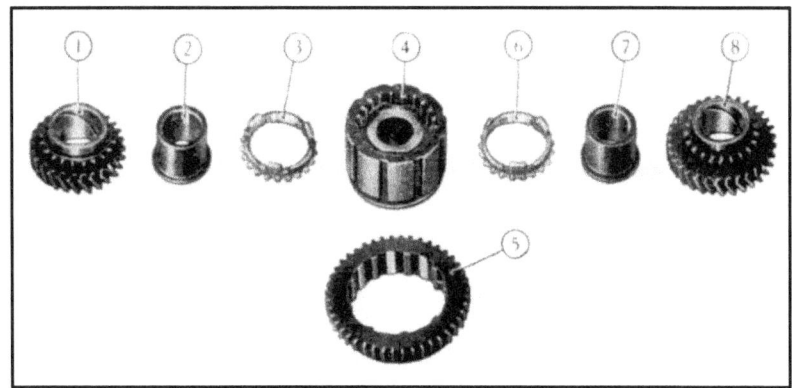

Fit on layshaft: the fourth speed gear and bush, the third and fourth speed gears synchronizer unit, the hub and the 3rd and 4th speed sliding sleeve to which must then be keyed the first speed driven gear; fit the third speed synchronizer ring and driven gear with relevant bush.

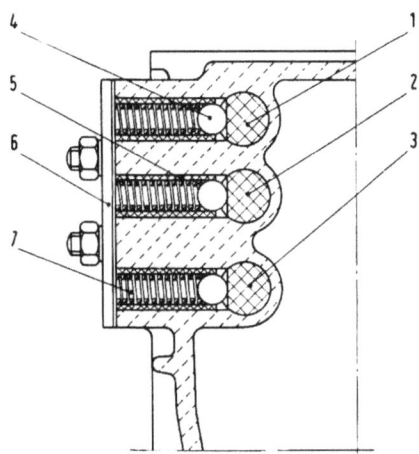

Fig. 216 - **Cross section detail on positioning balls.**

1. Reverse striker rod. - 2. 3rd and 4th speed striker rod. - 3. 1st and 2nd speed striker rod. - 4. Striker rod positioning balls. - 5. Ball and spring guide bushes. - 6. Cover. - 7. Ball springs.

Install the front housing-to-central body mounting plate, with relevant gaskets, and then the primary shaft front bearing and the layshaft front bearing.

Fit the reverse shaft with gear and bush, and then the retaining plate; key the second speed driving gear in position and secure by nut and lockwasher.

This nut must be tightened with a torque wrench to 43.4 ft.lbs (6000 kgmm) in early type gearboxes and to 72.3 to 79.6 ft.lbs (10.000 to 11.000 kgmm) in late type gearboxes.

On layshaft, fit: the second speed driven gear with bush, synchronizer ring and sliding sleeve hub.

Install the sliding sleeve with first and second speed striker rod and fork; position the three synchronizer inner springs. In its hole on central body, insert the striker rod safety roller.

Slide in position: the third and fourth speed intermediate striker rod and fork, and the safety roller and ball set; then, the reverse speed upper striker rod and fork.

Lock forks on rods by screws and fasteners.

Install the three positioning balls and relevant springs for striker rods (fig. 216) and secure the assembly by the cover provided with gasket; on layshaft, insert the speedometer driven gear.

Screw nut in place on layshaft and tighten by torque wrench to 39.8 ft.lbs (5500 kgmm).

In gearbox front housing, fit: the speed selector lever and gasket.

Next, fix front housing to central body at the same time inserting the speed selector lever on striker rod dogs.

Install: the speedometer drive pinion and support.

Should no slot on nut correspond to the cotter pin hole on shaft, tighten up the nut a further amount until alignment is obtained. Then install the cotter pin.

Fig. 217 - **Disassembled clutch and primary shafts.**

1. 4th speed driving gear. - 2. 1st speed and reverse driving gear. - 3. 3rd speed driving gear. - 4. 2nd speed driving gear. - 5. Clutch shaft. - 6. Sleeve, clutch shaft to primary shaft. - 7. Sleeve locking snap rings. - 8. Primary shaft rear bearing. - 9. Gear cluster driving gear. - 10. Primary shaft.

NOTE - Shafts and gears shown in this figure refer to gearbox adopted up to:
— engine No. 758492, «Sedan»;
— engine No. 765150, «Multipla».

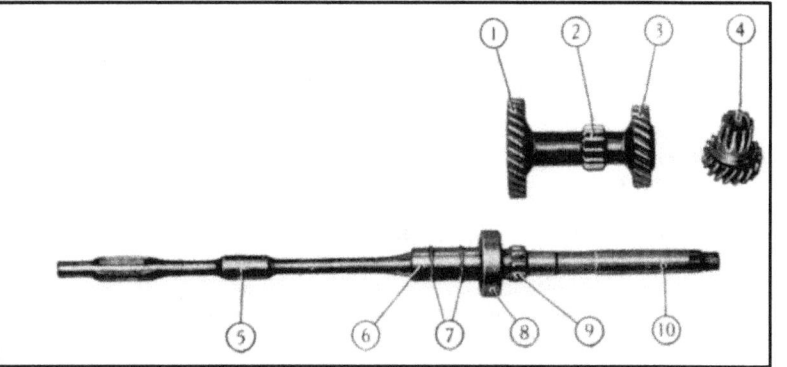

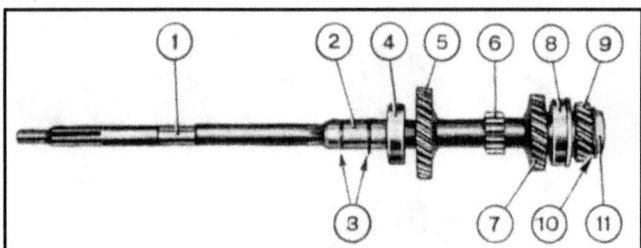

Fig. 218 - Clutch shaft, gearbox primary shaft and gear cluster.

1. Clutch shaft. - 2. Clutch shaft-to-primary shaft sleeve. - 3. Snap rings. - 4. Primary shaft rear bearing. - 5. 4th speed driving gear. - 6. 1st speed and reverse driving gear. - 7. 3rd speed driving gear. - 8. Primary shaft front bearing. - 9. 2nd speed driving gear. - 10. Lock washer. - 11. Nut.

NOTE

To facilitate in-or-out turning operation of primary shaft nut and drive pinion nut, tool A. 70072 has been designed, which locks the shafts in place.

On early type gearbox-differential units, if new tool is not available, use wrench A. 62024 (fig. 236).

On early type gearbox-differential units, the self-locking nut securing the brake drum on pinion shaft, should be drawn up with 47 ft.lbs (6.500 kgmm) of torque.

For reinstallation of gearbox-differential unit, see page 137.

TRANSMISSION TROUBLE DIAGNOSIS AND CORRECTIONS

Noisy Transmission.

POSSIBLE CAUSES	REMEDIES
1) Excessive backlash of gears in mesh due to gear wear.	1) Rebuild transmission and replace worn gears.
2) Gears, bearings, synchronizers or gear bushings damaged.	2) Rebuild transmission and replace worn parts.
3) Shafts misaligned or out of center due to loose mounting nuts.	3) Disassemble transmission and check components, repair and replace as required. On reassembly, tighten nuts to specified torque (page 141).
4) Dirt or metal chips in the lubricant.	4) Disassemble transmission, clean all components and make sure that they are sound. Replace lubricant.
5) Insufficient oil level in transmission case.	5) Add FIAT W 90 (SAE 90 EP) oil up to lower brim of filler plug seat.

Transmission Shifts Hard.

POSSIBLE CAUSES	REMEDIES
1) Defective link of gearshift lever to internal front lever.	1) Disassemble gearshift mechanism and inspect lever ball cap, cup and spring. Replace damaged parts.
2) Internal front lever rubber bushing and plates damaged.	2) Disassemble gearshift mechanism and replace bushing and plates.
3) Speed selector and engagement lever control rod twisted.	3) Remove rod and straighten.
4) Control rod-to-speed selector and engagement lever joint damaged.	4) Remove and replace flexible joint.

continued

GEARBOX: TROUBLE DIAGNOSIS AND CORRECTIONS

Transmission Shifts Hard (continuation).

POSSIBLE CAUSES	REMEDIES
5) Speed selector and engagement lever worn.	5) Remove front extension and replace lever.
6) Stiffened striker rods in case seats.	6) Remove rods, locate cause of stiffening and repair as required.
7) Sliding sleeves and gears bound in their seats due to the presence of dirt in splines or breakage of synchronizer springs.	7) Locate cause of binding, clean and replace damaged parts.
8) Improper quality of transmission lubricant.	8) Drain case and clean thoroughly. Refill with **FIAT W 90** (SAE 90 EP) oil.
9) Misadjusted clutch linkage and clutch make declutching impossible.	9) Rebuild clutch throwout mechanism and check height of clutch fingers. Adjust as directed under «Clutch» (page 110).

Transmission Jumps out of Gear.

POSSIBLE CAUSES	REMEDIES
1) Improper shifting.	1) Be sure the gears are conpletely engaged before releasing the clutch pedal.
2) Gearshift lever mounting bracket out of adjustment.	2) Adjust as outlined on page 138.
3) Incorrect assembly or wear of striker rod positioning balls and springs.	3) Remove cover and overhaul parts. Assemble the proper way.
4) Excessive end play caused by wear in the shift forks, sliding gear or sleeve grooves, or ball bearings.	4) Rebuild transmission and replace worn parts.
5) Striker rod rollers or balls worn or assembled incorrectly.	5) Disassemble and replace worn parts and assemble the correct way as outlined on page 123.
6) Worn synchronizer rings.	6) Overhaul sliding gears and sleeves and replace bumped ones. Replace synchronizer rings.

Oil Leakage.

POSSIBLE CAUSES	REMEDIES
1) Overfilled transmission case.	1) Check oil level for lower brim of filler plug seat.
2) Front extension, upper cover and clutch housing nuts loose.	2) Check tension and tighten nuts where required. Clutch housing nuts should be drawn up with $27^1/_2$ ft.lbs (3.800 kgmm) of torque, using a torque wrench.
3) Speed selector and engagement lever seal at front extension damaged.	3) Remove extension and lever, replace gasket and install on extension.
4) Clutch throwout bearing sleeve support seal damaged.	4) Remove and replace bearing sleeve support by a new one.
5) Gaskets: upper cover-to-case, front extension-to-bearing plate, bearing plate-to-case, throwout bearing sleeve support-to-clutch housing, damaged.	5) Replace gaskets which do not warrant oil tightness.

DIFFERENTIAL AND FINAL DRIVE

For an easier location of differential unit troubles, follow the directions outlined below which make a methodical diagnosis of operation troubles possible.

Noise Diagnosis and Remedies.

The following test are essential to establish whether noises are actually located in differential unit or caused by some other unit.

Test No. 1. - Drive car at a speed of about 12 m.p.h. (20 km/h) to determine the nature of noises present. Then, gradually increase the speed to about 45 m.p.h. (70 km/h). As the car picks up speed, record any noise that might develop at the different speeds as well as the moment in which they are audible and in which they fade away.

Release accelerator pedal and, without braking, let the car slow down to a dead stop. During this deceleration, check once more every change in the noises noticed and the speeds at which noises are most audible.

Generally, all noises will appear and disappear at the same speeds both when accelerating and decelerating.

Test No. 2. - Run the car up to about 50 m.p.h. (80 km/h).

Then, shift to neutral, switch off ignition, and coast until car comes to a dead stop. Again, record all noises heard at the different deceleration speeds.

All noises noticed in test No. 1 and still present in this test cannot be attributed to the differential inasmuch as this unit, not being under load, cannot originate any noise other than that due to bearings.

On the contrary, any noise recorded in the first test but absent in the second, may be ascribed to differential, axle shafts or wheel bearings.

These noises may be singled out by the following test:

Test No. 3. - Park the car, apply the brake, and start the engine. Next, increase engine r.p.m. gradually. Compare all noises appearing in this test with the ones recorded during test No. 1 and 2. Any noise developed in test No. 1 and still present can be disregarded. Such noises are most probably due to units which have nothing to do with diffeential unit, such as the air cleaner, silencer, engine or body.

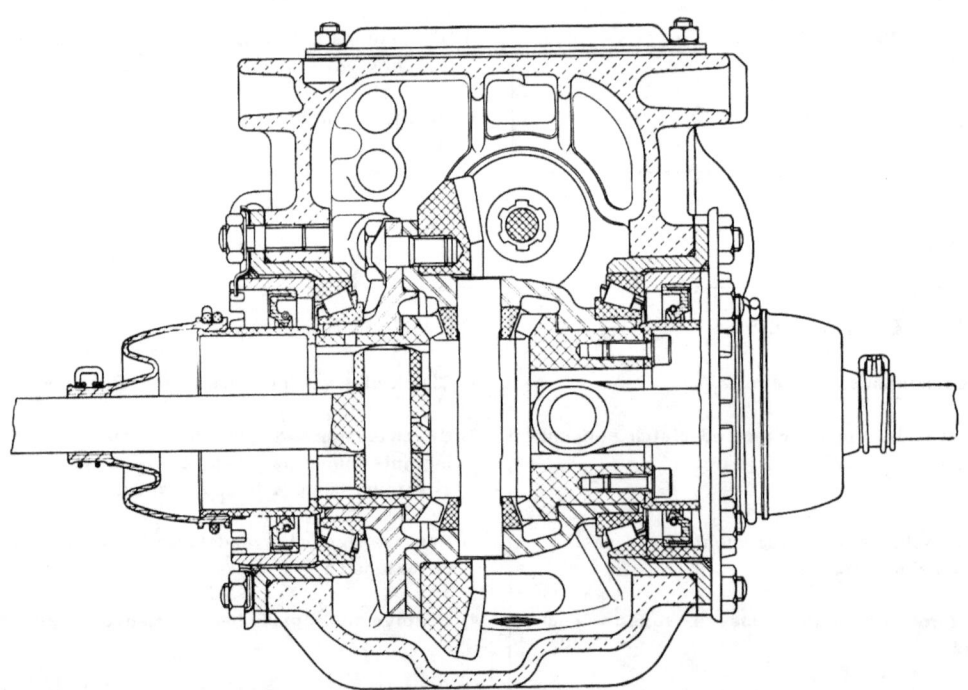

Fig. 219 - Cross section through differential case, bevel gear and axle shaft slip joints.

NOTE - The gearbox-differential unit shown in this picture was installed: up to engine No. 758492, Sedan; up to engine No. 765150, Multipla.

DIFFERENTIAL UNIT

Test No. 4. - Noises experienced in test No. 1 which, by elimination are still present in the two further tests (2 and 3) may be attributed to the differential.

To check on this assumption, raise rear wheels clear of ground, run the engine and engage fourth gear. It will now be possible to ascertain whether the noises ascribed to differential are actually caused by it.

Once noises have been located, proceed as follows for their elimination:

Noisiness on pull.

Check adjustment of differential case bearings.
Check ring gear-to-pinion backlash.

Noisiness on coast.

Check meshing depth of bevel pinion teeth which may need to be moved away from or toward ring gear.

Thumping.

Make sure that no gear teeth or bearing rings are chipped or excessively worn.

Noises due to excessive backlash.

Check and, if necessary, adjust ring gear-to-pinion backlash.

Make sure drive pinion axial play is not excessive.

Noisiness on turns.

Check that: idle pinions are not too tightly fitted on their shaft, idle pinion shaft surface is perfectly smooth, side gears are not too tightly fitted on their supports, all gears are neither chipped nor damaged in any other way, and wear of differential unit gears and thrust washers is not excessive.

Disassembly of Differential Unit.

After having disassembled the gearbox, as described on page 120, proceed with the disassembly of differential unit.

On both ends, remove: side gear lateral sleeves by undoing the two mounting screws with wrench **A. 8560** (fig. 221) (early type units only) bearing adjuster lockplate, bearing adjuster (and oil seals, early type units only) (fig. 222), bearing housing with seals.

Using tool **A. 62027**, pull out roller bearing outer ring (fig. 228).

Remove rear body of central casing (fig. 207) and then take out differential case (fig. 226).

If gearbox has already been disassembled, extract bevel pinion and relevant bearing, after taking off retaining plate.

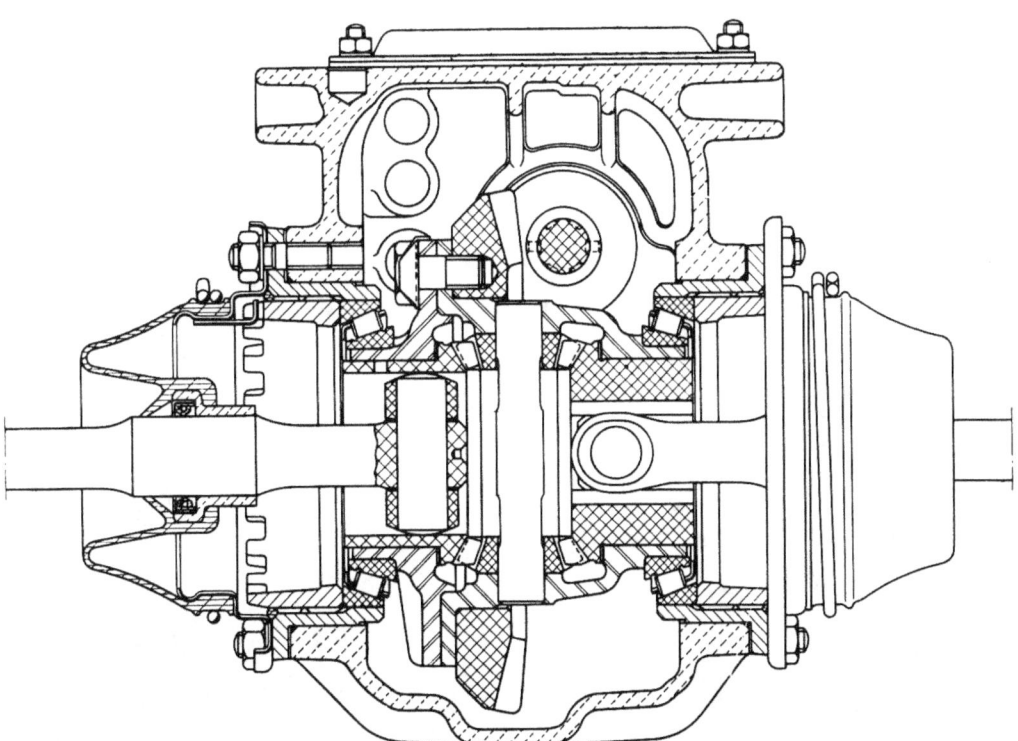

Fig. 220 - Cross sectional view through differential case, ring gear and axle shaft slip joints.

NOTE: The differential unit shown in this figure was adopted starting from engine No. 758493, « Sedan »; and engine No. 765151, « Multipla ».

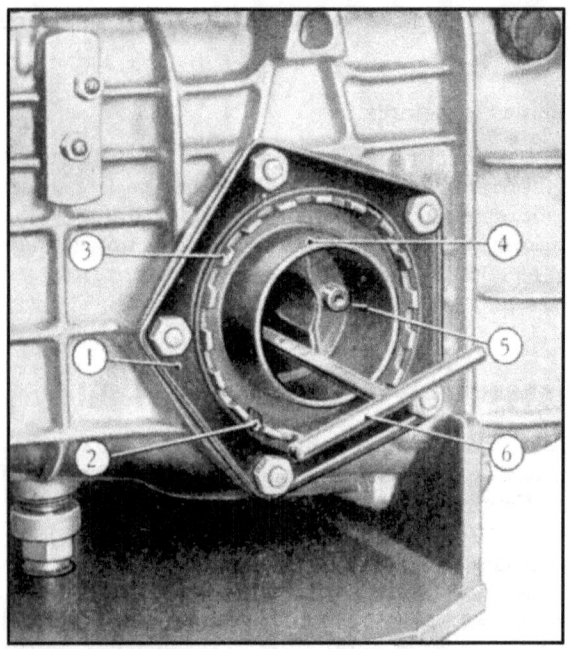

Fig. 221 - Removal of side gear sleeves (early type gearbox-differential unit).

1. Plate. - 2. Adjuster retainment plate tab. - 3. Adjuster. - 4. Side gear sleeve. - 5. Side gear sleeve fixing screw. - 6. Wrench A. 8560 for screw 5.

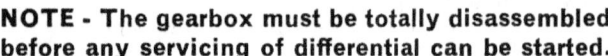

NOTE - The gearbox must be totally disassembled before any servicing of differential can be started.

Using an arbor and remover:
— **A. 42013** for 8-to-43 ratio «Sedan»;
— **A. 42016** for 7-to-45 ratio «Multipla»;
disassemble bevel pinion bearing (fig. 223).

Fig. 222 - Removing roller bearing adjuster.

1. Stand Arr. 2204. - 2. Support Arr. 2206/6. - 3. Wrench A. 52020 for early type gearboxes and A. 55034 for late type gearboxes.

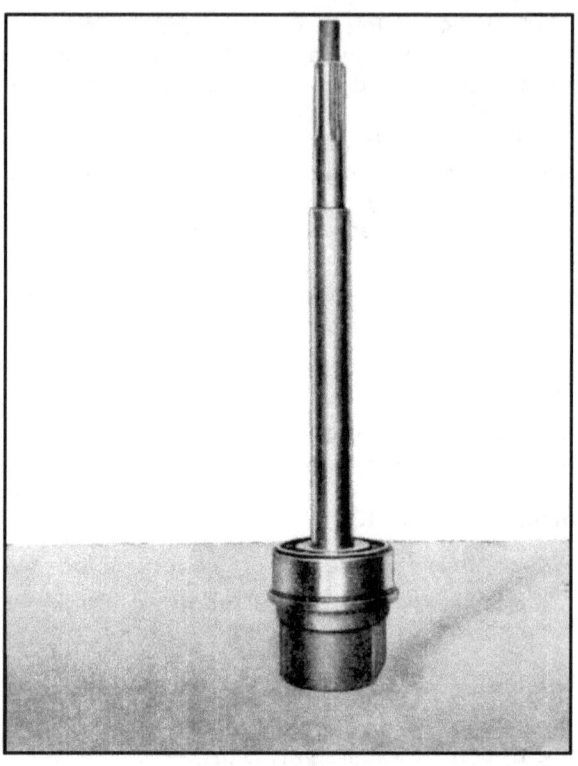

Fig. 223 - Removal of rear ball bearing after inserting the bevel drive pinion in remover A. 42013 (Sedan) or A. 42016 (Multipla).

Fig. 224 - Removal of differential case roller bearing inner ring by puller provided with plate A. 42014.

DIFFERENTIAL UNIT

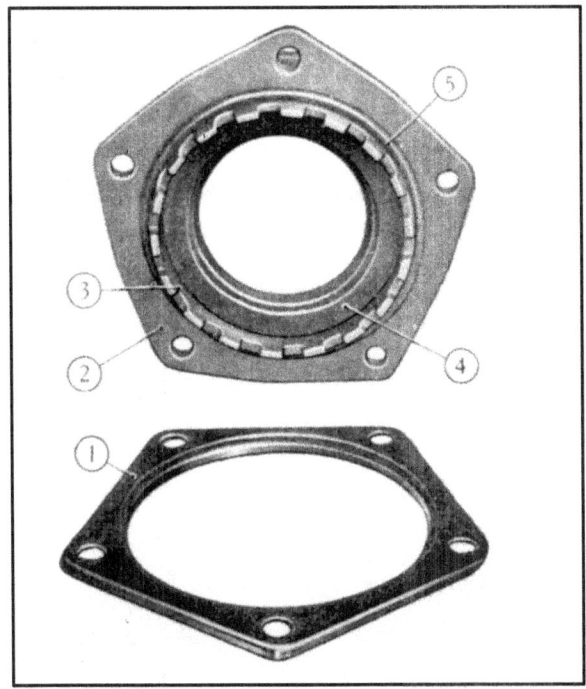

Fig. 225 - Differential case bearing housing assembly (early type).

1. Adjuster retainment plate. - 2. Bearing housing. - 3. Adjuster. - 4. Bearing seal. - 5. Gasket for plate «1».

From differential case, pull out roller bearing inner rings using puller **A. 40005** and plate **A. 42014** (fig. 224).

Undo the screws joining the two differential halves and the bevel ring gear.

Disinsert idle pinion carrier shaft, remove idle pinions and side gears with relevant thrust washers.

Fig. 226 - Disassembling differential inner case with bevel ring gear.

Inspection and Repair of Differential Parts.

After disassembly, the components of differential unit must be accurately checked for proper efficiency and to determine the presence of wear, damages or other irregularities.

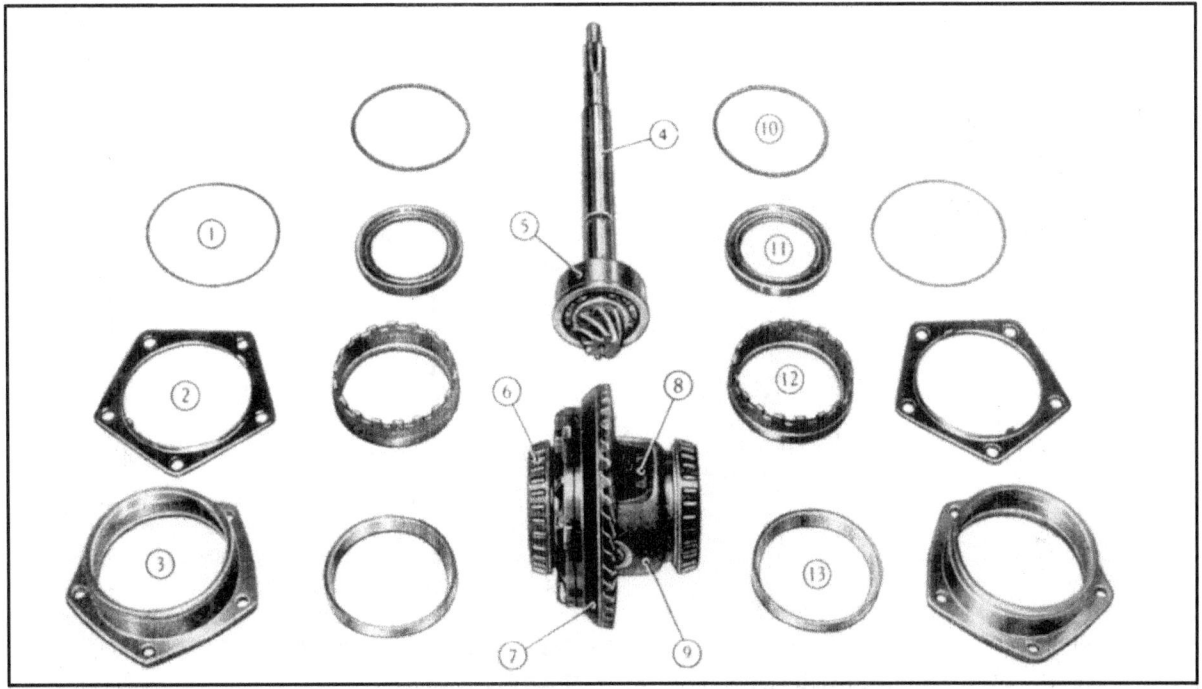

Fig. 227 - Differential and final drive set components (early type).

1. Gasket for plate 2. - 2. Plate securing adjuster 12. - 3. Roller bearing housing. - 4. Bevel drive pinion. - 5. Rear ball bearing for bevel drive pinion. - 6. Roller bearing inner ring. - 7. Final drive ring gear. - 8. Side gear. - 9. Differential case. - 10. Bearing housing seal ring. - 11. Oil seal. - 12. Roller bearing adjuster. - 13. Bearing outer ring.

The **idle pinion carrier shaft**, which is heavily stressed when car negotiates a turn, must be carefully checked for undesirable roughness or excessive wear and, if required, replaced.

Fig. 228 - Removal of differential case roller bearing outer ring using tool A. 62027.

The **ring gear and pinion set**, the **side gears and idle pinions** must be checked for broken, chipped or excessively worn teeth.

Check the condition of ball and roller bearings: rollers, balls and rings must not be damaged or worn.

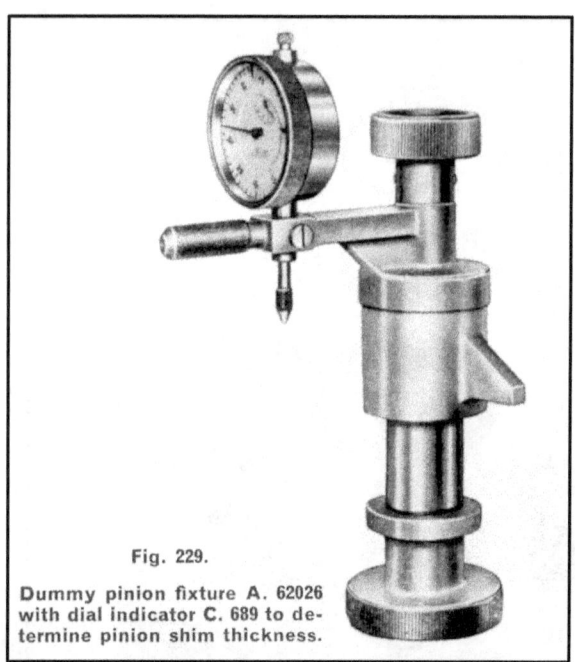

Fig. 229.
Dummy pinion fixture A. 62026 with dial indicator C. 689 to determine pinion shim thickness.

If damages to idle pinion thrust ring contact surfaces are slight, recondition rings; if necessary, replace rings with new ones or rings oversized in thickness as required.

Thrust rings are supplied as spares in the following thicknesses:

.0394" - .0512" - .0591" (1 - 1,3 - 1,5 mm).

Assembling and Adjusting Differential Unit.

INSTALLATION AND ADJUSTMENT OF BEVEL DRIVE PINION

A shim of suitable thickness must be installed between pinion and rear ball bearing to obtain the correct backlash between bevel ring gear and drive pinion.

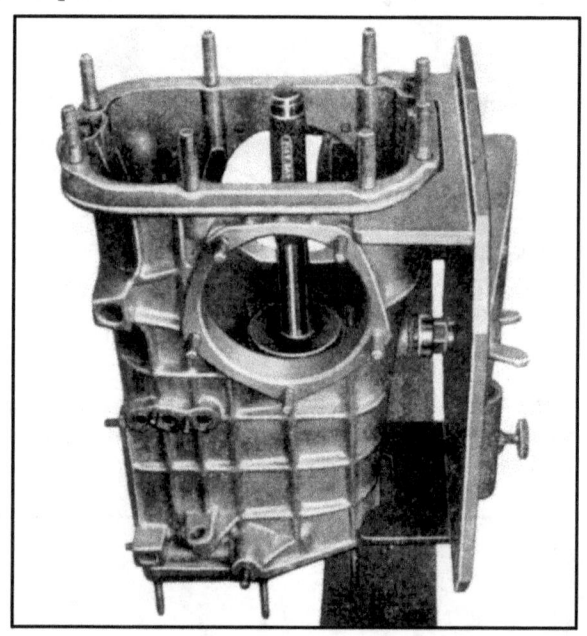

Fig. 230 - Installing bevel drive pinion rear ball bearing with tool A. 62028.

Spare shims are supplied in the following thicknesses:

.108" - .110" - .112" - 114" - .116"
(2,75 - 2,80 - 2,85 - 2,90 - 2,95 mm)
.118" - .120" - .122" - .124" - .126"
(3,00 - 3,05 - 3,10 - 3,15 - 3,20 mm)
.128" - .130" - .132" - .134"
(3,25 - 3,30 - 3,35 - 3,40 mm).

It should be noted that the shims for « Sedan » and for « Multipla » are not identified by the same Part No. which varies depending on whether the final drive ratio is 8 to 43 or 7 to 45.

To determine the exact thickness required, use dummy pinion fixture **A. 62026** (fig. 229), proceeding as follows:

— Place gearbox-differential unit central body on rotating stand **Arr. 2204** and secure on support **Arr. 2206/6**

DIFFERENTIAL UNIT

— Press-fit, in its seat, the bevel drive pinion rear ball bearing using tool **A. 62028** (fig. 230); fit the lockplate and tighten nuts to 18 ft.lbs (2500 kgmm).

— Then, proceed with the **determination of the thickness required for bevel pinion thrust ring on rear bearing**, to obtain a perfect adjustment of the pinion.

— Install fixture **A. 62026** (fig. 231) and lock it in position on pinion rear bearing by the knurled knob.

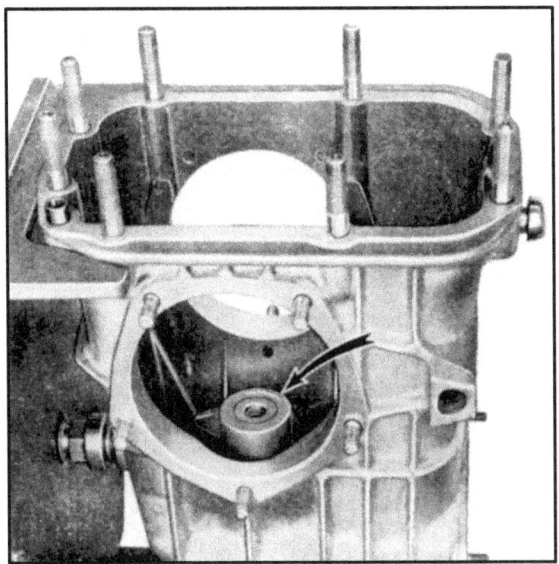

Fig. 231 - Fitting fixture A. 62026 on bevel pinion rear bearing.
Arrow indicates fixture top where indicator C. 689 must be fitted.

— On a surface plate (fig. 232) set centesimal and millimetric scales of dial indicator **C. 689** to zero. Next, fit dial indicator on fixture (fig. 233) and make sure indicator plunger rests on roller bearing housing seat.

— Move back and forth horizontally the indicator sliding support and note the indications of dial pointers; block dial indicator in position where pointers indicate minimum values.

The thickness of thrust ring to be fitted between pinion and bearing, is obtained by subtracting the dial indicator reading from the figure punched in the factory on bevel pinion, keeping in due account the sign preceding the number on pinion.

A serial number is stamped during production on both ring gear and drive pinion; moreover, on drive pinion is stamped also the variation between actual and nominal assembly distances.

Fig. 232 - Setting to zero indicator C. 689 on a surface plate.

In fact, the number on pinion is preceded by a (+) plus sign when positive and a (—) minus sign when negative.

Remove tool **A. 62026** and dial indicator **C. 689** and install:

Early-type gearbox-differential units:

— the drive pinion with thrust ring having the required thickness;

— the first dummy spacer **A. 62025/1**, the front housing-to-central body mounting plate;

Fig. 233 - Determining the thickness of pinion shim.
Shim thickness is obtained by subtracting the value stamped on bevel pinion from dial indicator reading.
1. Fixture A. 62026. - 2. Indicator C. 689.

HOW TO DETERMINE
BEVEL DRIVE PINION THRUST RING THICKNESS

If «a» is the value stamped on pinion and «b» the reading on dial indicator of fixture **A. 62026** (figs. 234-235), thickness «**S**» of thrust ring to be fitted is obtained as follows:

$$S = b - (+ a) = b - a$$
$$\text{or } S = b - (- a) = b + a$$

In other words:

— if number on pinion is preceded by **sign plus** (+), the thickness of thrust ring is obtained by **subtracting** the number from dial indicator reading;

— instead, if number on pinion is preceded by **sign minus** (—) the thickness of thrust ring is obtained by **adding** the number to dial indicator reading.

Example: if b = 3,10 mm, dial indicator reading,
if a = —10 (0,10 mm), number on pinion,
then S = 3,10 — (—0,10) = 3,10 + 0,10 = 3,20.

Hence, in a case as this, a 3,20 mm thick thrust ring should be fitted.

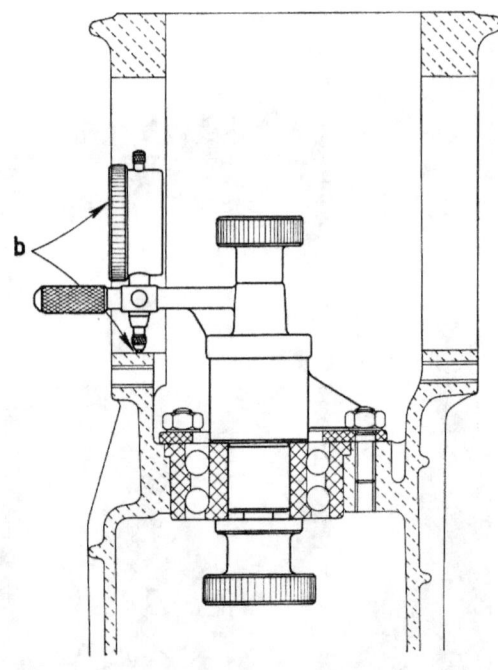

Fig. 234 - Schematic view of how fixture A. 62026 and dial indicator C. 689 must be installed to determine shim thickness.

b = Dial indicator reading from which the value stamped on bevel pinion must be subtracted.

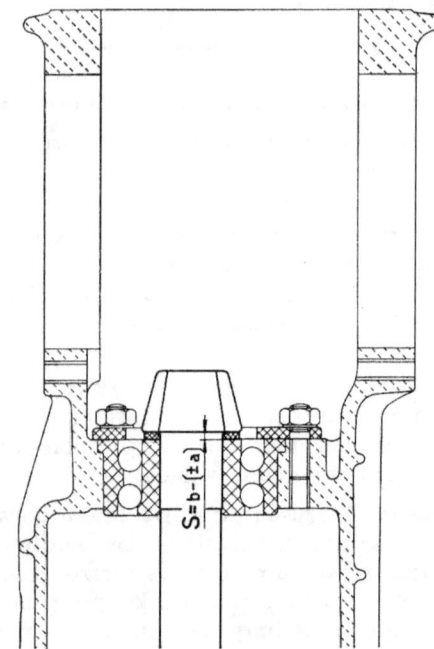

Fig. 235 - Schematic view on pinion assembly with shim on bearing.

Where: S = Thrust ring thickness;
b = Dial indicator reading;
a = Value stamped on bevel pinion.

DIFFERENTIAL UNIT

— the drive pinion intermediate bearing;
— the second dummy spacer **A. 62025/2**;
— the front housing with drive pinion front bearing and seal;
— the parking brake drum and secure it with the self-locking nut which should be tightened to 47 ft.lbs (6500 kgmm), using a torque wrench.

Late-type gearbox-differential units:

— the drive pinion with thrust ring having the required thickness;
— the first dummy spacer **A. 62025/1**;
— the front housing-to-central body mounting plate;
— the drive pinion front bearing;
— the second spacer **I. 31801/76**;
— the drive pinion shaft lock washer and nut; the nut should be drawn up with 72.3 ft.lbs (10.000 kgmm) of torque.

Fig. 236 - **Tightening parking brake drum-to-layshaft nut (early type gearbox-differential unit).**

Tightening torque must be 47 ft.lbs (6500 kgmm).

1. Support Arr. 2206/6. - 2. Stop pin for tool 3. - 3. Tool A. 62024, parking brake drum retainment. - 4. Torque wrench.

NOTE

Installation of dummy spacers in the place of gearbox gearings is made to avoid that any gearbox component may influence or alter tests for differential unit noise on bench.

Dummy spacers A. 62025/1/2 and I. 31801/76 are included in the kit supplied with gearbox and differential test bench I. 31801.

To facilitate in-or-out turning operation of primary shaft nut and drive pinion nut, tool A. 70072 has been designed, which locks the shafts in place.

On early type gearbox-differential units, if new tool is not available, use wrench A. 62024 (fig. 236).

Fig. 237 - **Installing differential case roller bearing inner ring by tool A. 62027.**

ASSEMBLY OF DIFFERENTIAL INNER CASE

In the two case halves, fit the side gears with thrust rings, idle pinions and their carrier shaft.

Insert bevel drive ring gear in left half-case, join the two case halves and then tighten with torque wrench to 44.8 ft.lbs (6200 kgmm).

Side gears must be so adjusted, by means of

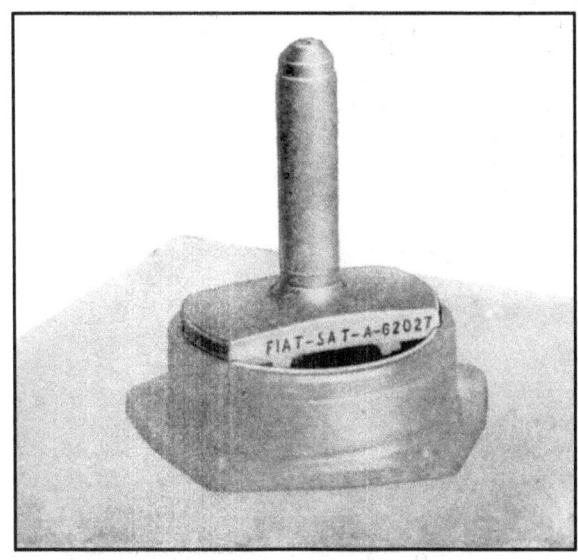

Fig. 238 - **Installing differential case roller bearing outer ring by tool A. 62027.**

the thrust rings, that the rotation torque specified below be obtained after assembly.

Check rotation torque by leaving free the case and locking one of the side gears. The torque required to rotate the other side gear must not be greater than 3.6 ft.lbs (0,5 kgm).

Side gear thrust rings are supplied in the following thicknesses:

.0394" - .0512" - .0591"
(1 - 1,3 - 1,5 mm).

Using tool **A. 62027** (fig. 237) install the two roller bearing inner rings.

Insert the assembly thus obtained in the gearbox-differential unit case, on rotating stand, and complete the assembly as follows:

Install the two bearing housings with relevant seals and roller bearing outer rings (using tool **A. 62027** - fig. 238), the two oil seals (early type gearboxes only) using installer **A. 62031**, bearing adjusters and seals (early type gearboxes only).

Secure bearing housing and draw up housing nuts with 18 ft.lbs (2.500 kgmm) of torque. Bearing adjuster lock plates should be installed after setting operation.

Preload of Ring Gear Bearings and Bevel Ring Gear-to-Pinion Backlash Adjustment.

These two operations must be carried out simultaneously using fixture **C. 688** equipped with two dial gauges, and wrench **A. 52020** (early type gearbox - differential units), or **A. 55034** (late-type gearbox - differential units) (fig. 239).

The fixture is fixed to differential unit by screwing stud (3, fig. 239); move support (4) until cranked lever (5) contacts the differential case outer side face, then turn in fixing knob and adjust support (6) until plunger of gauge (7) touches the flank of one ring gear tooth; next, tighten the fixing knob.

Note that fixture **C. 688** must be fitted with bearing adjuster rings slightly in touch with bearings, that is, without preload.

Using proper wrench (8, fig. 239), tighten one of the two adjuster rings: in so doing, the differential case is lightly divaricated, and this is recorded through lever (5), on dial gauge (9) previously set to zero.

Adjuster ring must be tightened until a divarication of .0039" to .0047" (0,10 to 0,12 mm), is obtained.

Slacken the opposite adjuster ring: the pointer of dial gauge (9) must return to zero; tighten again this adjuster ring until divarication results .0039" to .0047" (0,10 to 0,12 mm).

After thus obtaining the predetermined preload of bevel ring gear bearings, **check also ring gear-to-pinion backlash which must range from .0031" to .0051" (0,08 to 0,13 mm).**

Lock drive pinion rotation and manually move ring gear of the amount permitted by lash between teeth.

This lash will be recorded on dial gauge (7, fig. 239).

Preloading of bearings must be carried out only after rotating the bevel gear through a number of revolutions sufficient to ensure the final setting of bearings

---

If the reading is either lower or greater than the specified limits, move ring gear either in or out from pinion by slackening one of the adjuster rings and tightening the other of the same amount.

Fig. 239.

Adjustment of pinion-to-gear backlash and preloading of differential bearings by fixture C. 688 and wrench A. 52020 or A. 55034.

1. Support Arr. 2204/6. - 2 and 3. Support and stud for mounting fixture C. 688 on case. - 4. Dial gauge (9) support. - 5. Cranked lever. - 6. Dial gauge (7) support. - 7. Dial gauge for backlash checking. - 8. Wrench A. 52020 (early type gearbox-differential units), or A. 55034 (late-type gearbox-differential units) for bearing adjustment. - 9. Dial gauge, for checking the case halves divarication during bearing preloading.

DIFFERENTIAL UNIT

To prevent any alteration of the previously established preload, it is essential to rotate one adjuster ring of the same amount as the other, but in opposite directions.

To perform this operation with accuracy, check the reading on dial gauge (9, fig. 239).

In fact, as one of the adjuster rings is slackened, the distance between differential case halves will be less than the one previously established, as will be recorded on dial gauge.

Then, on tightening the other adjuster ring, follow the dial gauge pointer until it again reads the original value.

Next, by dial gauge (7, fig. 239), check to see if the correct backlash has been obtained. If not, screw adjuster rings in or out once more until the desired results are obtained. If the shop is equipped with differential test bench I. 13801 (fig. 240), the above preloading and adjustment operations may be performed on this bench, where also differential noise and final drive set tooth contact tests and checks shall be performed.

Checking Tooth Contact Between Pinion and Ring Gear.

The final inspection of tooth contact pattern must be carried out with the differential unit mounted on differential test bench.

Paint some of the ring gear teeth with red lead, then start the differential into rotation and brake it by acting on the levers so as to have the unit working under load.

A contact impression will be left on the teeth of the ring gear and the contact will be correct when the pinion gear tooth contact pattern will be evenly distributed on the ring gear teeth. Should tooth contact be improper the following cases, illustrated on page 136 in figs. from 242 to 245, may be met:

a) Excessive contact **on tooth flank** (fig. 242): **move pinion out from ring gear by reducing thickness of thrust ring under pinion head.**

b) Excessive contact **on tooth heel** (fig. 243): **move pinion in towards ring gear, by increasing thickness of thrust ring under pinion head.**

c) Excessive contact **on tooth face** (fig. 244): **move pinion in towards ring gear by increasing thickness of thrust ring under pinion head.**

d) Excessive contact **on tooth toe** (fig. 245): **move pinion out from ring gear by reducing thickness of thrust ring under pinion head.**

In all the above mentioned cases, to adjust pinion by replacing the shim, the differential unit must again be disassembled.

When unit is subsequently reassembled, all preloading and backlash adjustment operations will have to be repeated.

Once all operations are over, install adjuster lock plates. If the plate tabs do not fit into seat, tighten adjusters a further amount but try and keep movement within minimum limits to avoid varying the setting.

Remove dummy spacers A. 62025/1/2 or I. 31801/76, again place the differential case on revolving stand and complete the assembly of gearbox proceeding as outlined on page 122.

Note that the clutch housing-to-gearbox center body mounting nuts should be tightened with 27½ ft.lbs (3.800 kgmm) of torque.

Fig. 240.

Adjustment of pinion-to-gear backlash and preloading of differential bearings on test bench I. 31801 using fixture C. 688 and wrench A. 52020 for early-type gearbox-differential units or A. 55034 for late-type units.

ADJUSTING TOOTH CONTACT

IMPORTANT

If the operations for the determination of final drive pinion thrust ring thickness have been carried out correctly, a new disassembly and adjustment on account of faulty tooth contact will hardly be needed.

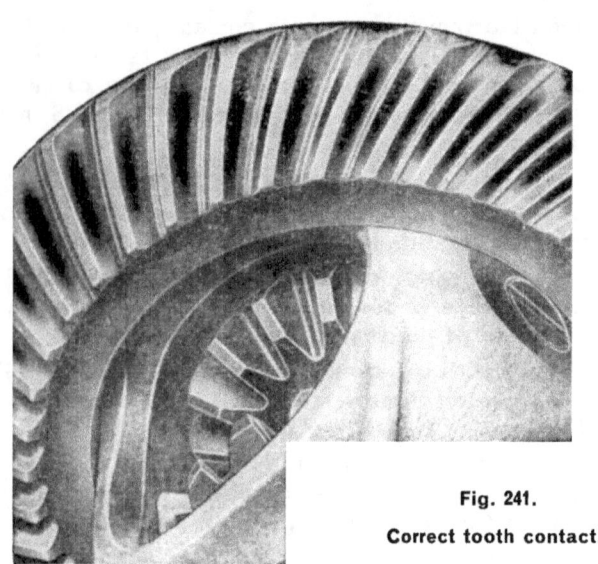

Fig. 241.

Correct tooth contact.

Excessive contact on tooth flank:

move pinion out from gear by reducing thrust ring thickness.

Fig. 242.

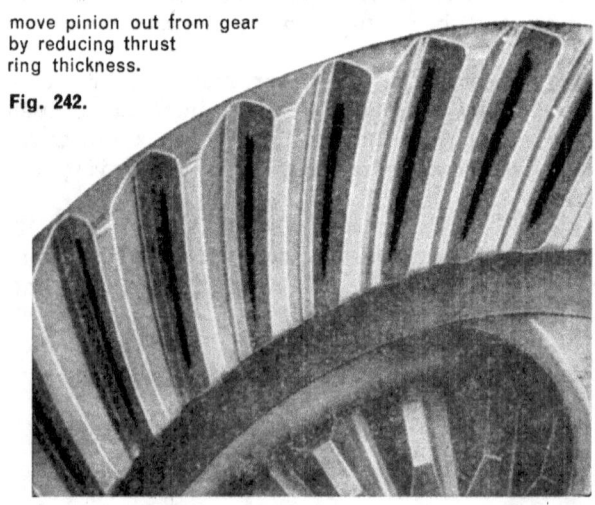

Excessive contact on tooth face:

move pinion in toward gear by increasing thrust ring thickness.

Fig. 244.

Excessive contact on tooth heel:

move pinion in toward gear by increasing thrust ring thickness.

Fig. 243.

Excessive contact on tooth toe:

move pinion out from gear by reducing thrust ring thickness.

Fig. 245.

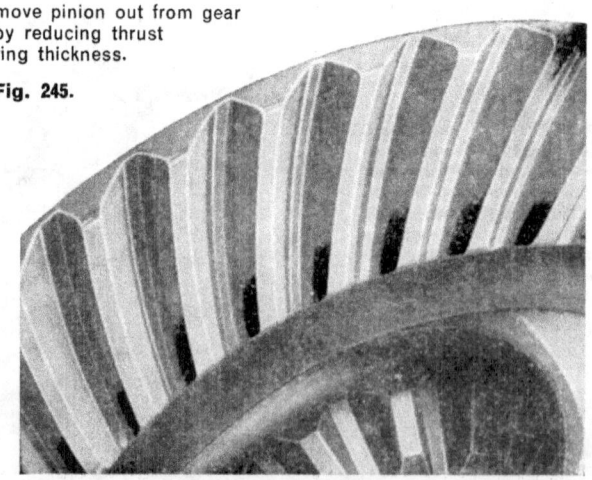

INSTALLATION OF GEARBOX-DIFFERENTIAL UNIT

Raise car rear end and rest on stands.

Check that: the engine central rear support nut is backed off a few turns to permit an adequate movement of power plant, the accelerator and carburetor starter device bowden sheathing lock plate is also slackened, the rear lower shield is removed.

Using alignment bar **A. 62023** (fig. 199) check that clutch driven disc hub is aligned with clutch shaft pilot bush.

Support gearbox-differential unit assembly with a garage jack and support **Arr. 2076** and, by pushing it towards engine, insert clutch shaft in driven disc hub splines and into pilot bush.

Couple gearbox rear housing to engine by the two centering dowels.

From inside car, screw in the two short upper bolts fixing gearbox on engine crankcase. Next, working under car, screw in the two long lower fixing bolts. Tighten these bolts by a torque wrench to 57.9 ft.lbs (8000 kgmm).

Place a jack under gearbox-differential unit, raise, and screw in the two bolts fixing the front support to body, interposing the fiber washers between parts.

Install speedometer bowden.

Insert clutch control tie rod into hole in gearbox support and fit into clutch withdrawal control lever yoke.

Insert gearshift selector lever into gearshift control rod joint, pulling gearshift hand lever backward, and fix with bolt.

If this operation has not been performed on bench, install axle shafts and insert slip joint into splines in side gear.

Interpose the spring between outer shaft end and inner axle shaft and connect splined sleeve to flexible joint. Fit oil seal boots already in place on axle shafts (as outlined in figs. 219 and 220) and secure with collars.

From inside car: connect clutch control tie rod to lever, install retracting spring by hooking it up at tie rod and at gearbox, install starter motor after connecting the control tie rod and the two cables and, finally, install the shroud, felt bottom and mat.

From under car: install rear apron and, after properly centering the power plant assembly by the rubber pads of front mounting, tighten fully the rear support mounting nut.

Take off engine hoist sling **Arr. 2067** (fig. 205).

Secure accelerator and starting device bowden sheathings by lockplates.

Connect cable to battery positive terminal.

SWING AXLE SHAFTS AND SLIP JOINTS

Description and Repair.

The two axle shafts are connected to differential through slip joints which allow shafts to swing and slide in a specially designed splined housing in differential side gear. At the other end, axle shafts are connected to wheel drive shaft flexible joints with the intermediary of a sliding sleeve (fig. 247).

While servicing axles, check the condition of slip joint sliding surfaces and housing in differential side gears; if clearance has become greater than .0078" (0,20 mm) on account of wear, replace slip joints and, if necessary, also differential side gear. Check also the clearance between slip joint pivots and runners: if found excessive, replace the axle shaft (joint pivot is not supplied as a separate spare) and runners.

Axle shaft-to-sliding sleeve spline clearance must not be greater than .0059" (0,15 mm).

Observe the sliding sleeve snap ring for snug fit in its groove-seat on shaft.

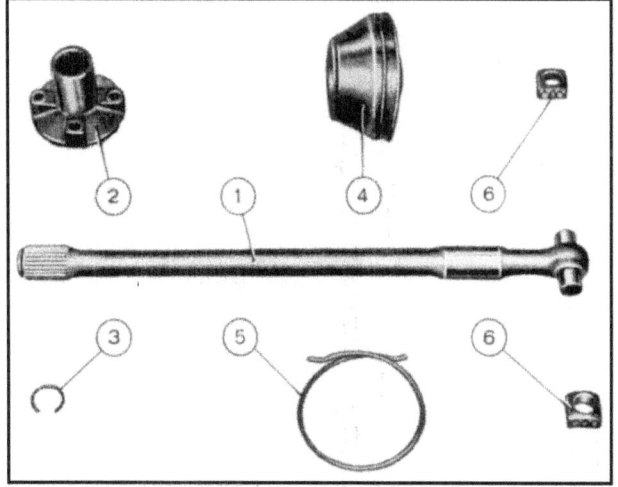

Fig. 246 - Components of axle shaft and slip joint.

1. Axle shaft with pivot. - 2. Flexible joint coupling sleeve. - 3. Boot spring fastener. - 4. Oil boot. - 5. Elastic collar securing the boot. - 6. Runners for axle shaft pivot.

Check the efficiency of the spring mounted between axle shaft end and wheel shaft tang: the spring must not be found weakened.

If oil seal boots show signs of cracks or cuts, replace. If seal boot collars are found defective, replace them. To remove and install seal boot collars, use expander **A. 62030**.

The inner face of axle shaft bushing gaskets should show no sign of wear. Bushing gaskets should adhere perfectly to their polished seat on axle shafts. If not so, replace gaskets.

On assembly, see that gaskets are positioned correctly in bushing seat, as oil leakage may occur if they are installed the wrong way.

Fig. 247 - Detail of axle shaft (right wheel drive).

1. Boot collar. - 2. Oil boot. - 3. Axle shaft. - 4. Axle shaft-to-flexible joint coupling sleeve. - 5. Coupling sleeve screws. - 6. Axle shaft flexible joint.

GEARSHIFT CONTROL MECHANISM

Adjustment.

When an unsatisfactory engagement of gears is noticed, the gearshifting control mechanism must be adjusted.

Operations to perform are:

— Undo the screws fixing cover (1, fig. 249) to tunnel and raise cover along gearshift lever stem.

— Slacken the lever support fixing screws, two upper and three lateral (fig. 249); as may be seen in fig. 252, slots have been machined in support to allow its longitudinal displacement.

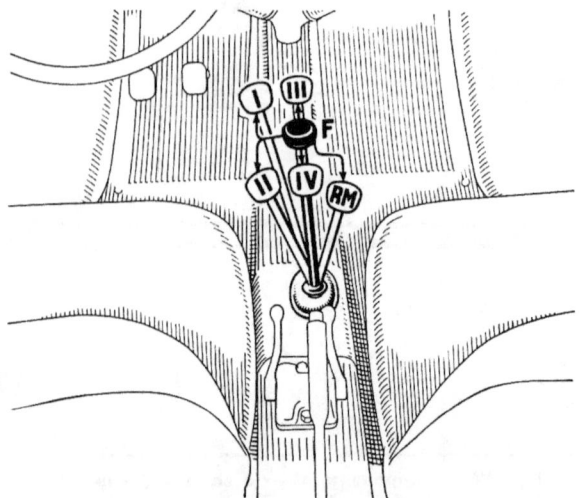

Fig. 248 - Positions of gearshift lever.
RM = Reverse. - F = Neutral.

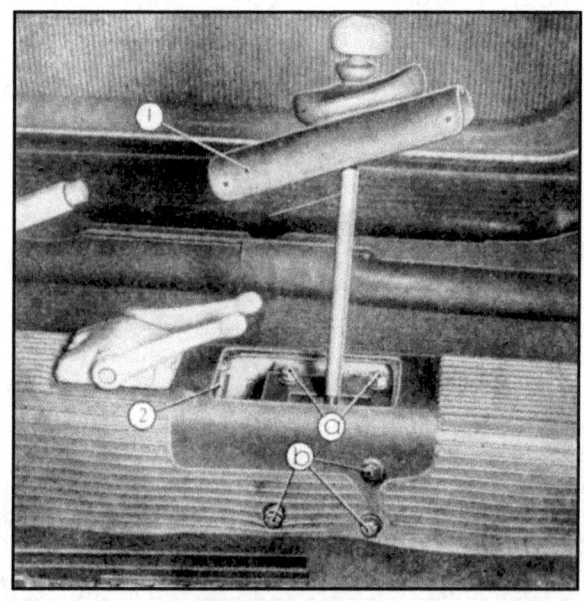

Fig. 249 - Gearshift control.

1. Protection cover. - 2. Gearshift control rod spring. — a and b. Gearshift support fixing screws.

— Push support forward, if first and third speed engagement is improper, and backward if 2nd, 4th and reverse speed engagements need adjustment. Next, tighten the mounting screws.

When adjustment is over, set components back in their initial positions.

DIFFERENTIAL UNIT

139

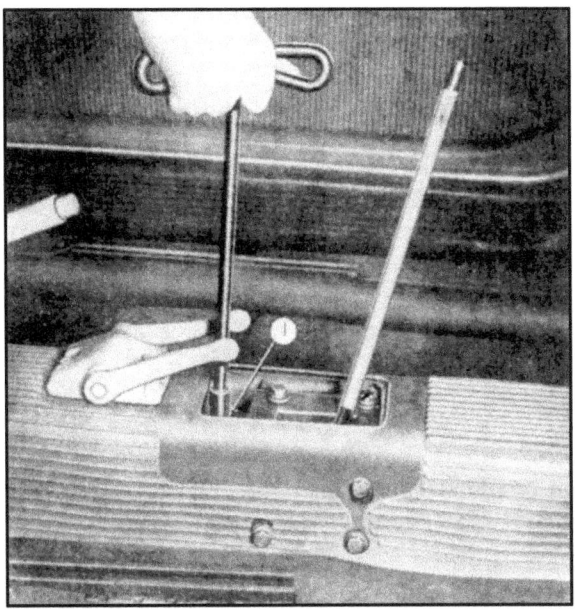

Fig. 250 - Removal of gearshift control assembly.

1. Removal of the screw securing inner lever to gearshift control rod.

Removal of Gearshift Control Mechanism.

To remove this assembly from car, proceed as follows:

— Unscrew the gearshift control lever knob,

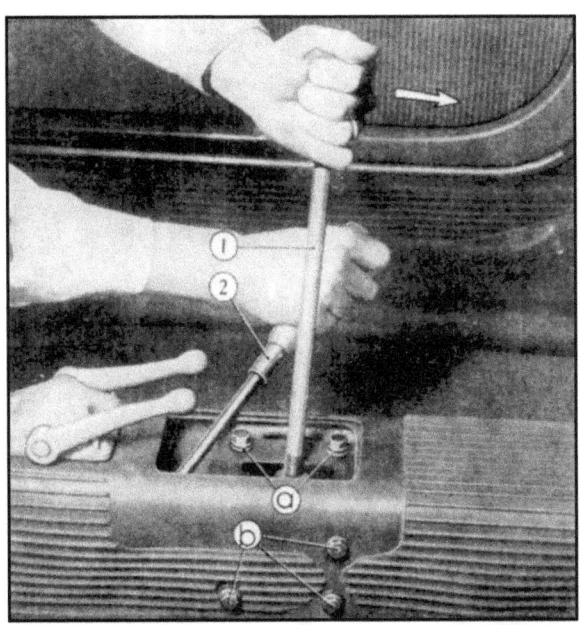

Fig. 251 - Removal of gearshift control assembly.

1. Gearshift lever: push forward. - 2. Screwdriver: pry on gearshift rod so as to disconnect inner lever. — a and b. Gearshift lever support securing screws.

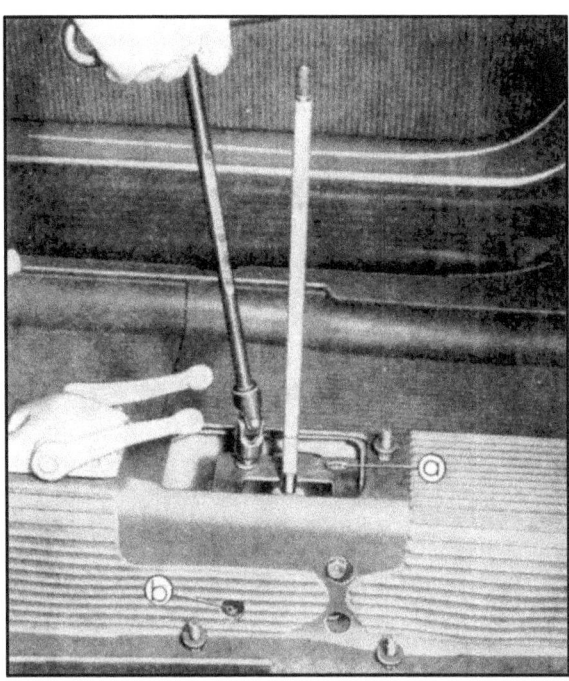

Fig. 252 - Removal of gearshift control assembly.

a. Slots, on support and tapped holes in seat. - b. Tapped holes in support and slots on seat.

then remove the cover fixing screws and slide cover out of hand lever.

— Unhook the gearshift control rod retracting spring (2, fig. 249).

— Take off brass lock wire and undo the set screw fixing the gearshift control rod to inner lever (fig. 250).

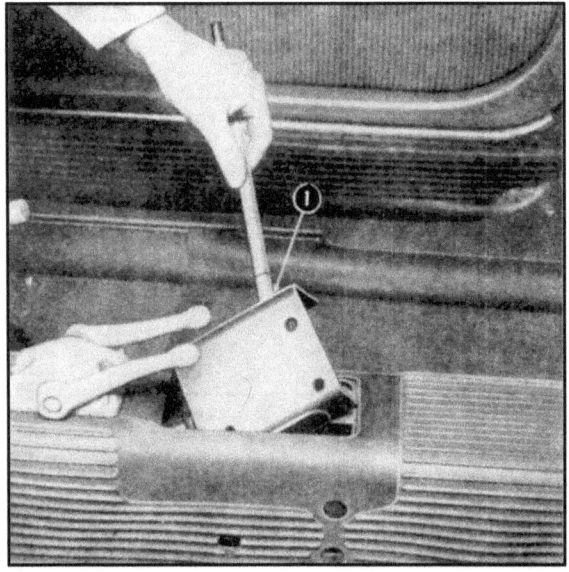

Fig. 253 - Removal of gearshift control assembly.

1. Removal of assembly: gearshift lever, support and inner lever.

Fig. 254 - Removal of gearshift control rod.
1. Starter control and choke control levers assembly: raise to remove from rod 2. - 2. Gearshift control rod.

— Push gearshift hand lever forward, and by pressing on gearshift control rod (fig. 251) disinsert the inner lever.

— Undo the five screws fixing the hand lever support, two upper and three lateral (fig. 252) and disinsert the assembly from its seat (fig. 253).

— Lift carburetor starting device and starter motor levers assembly, after having removed the two fixing screws.

This procedure facilitates the removal of the gearshift control rod (fig. 254) which had previously been disconnected at the elastic joint on selector lever.

Disassembly and Inspection of Gearshift Lever Components.

Gearshift hand lever is removed by backing out lower mounting nut (fig. 256).

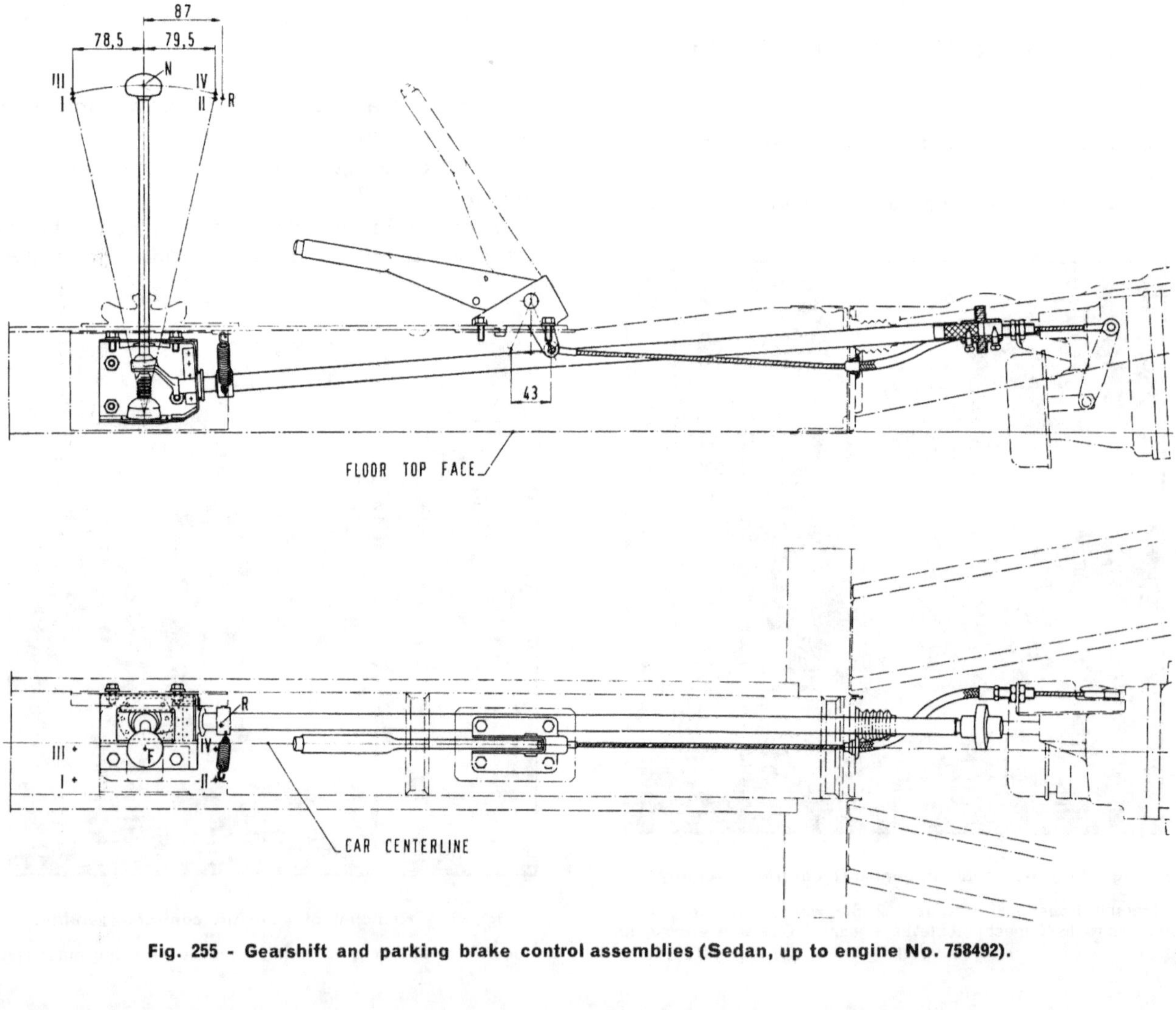

Fig. 255 - Gearshift and parking brake control assemblies (Sedan, up to engine No. 758492).

GEARBOX - DIFFERENTIAL UNIT

Observe that lever ball and socket are in good condition.

Replace spring if weakened.

Check resilient bush for soundness and the three plates for correct positioning; if wear or deformations are detected replace the bush and, if necessary, also the plates.

Fig. 256 - Gearshift control assembly.
Arrow points to the self-locking nut securing the gearshift hand lever to support.

GEARBOX - DIFFERENTIAL ADJUSTMENT AND TIGHTENING REFERENCE

ITEM	DRWG. OR STD. PART No.	THREAD	MATERIAL	TIGHTENING TORQUE
Pinion shaft nut ([1])	1/07934/11	14 MB (x1,5)	R 50 Cdt (shaft 14 CN 5 Cmt 5)	39.8 ft.lbs (5.500 kgmm)
Brake drum-to-layshaft nut ([2])	1/25748/11	14 MB (x1,5)	R 50 Cdt (shaft 14 CN 5)	47 ft.lbs (6.500 kgmm)
Primary shaft gear nut ([1])	1.28.113 981581	20 MC (x1)	R 50 (shaft 14 CN 5 Cmt 5)	72.3 ft.lbs (10.000 kgmm)
Primary shaft gear nut ([2])	1.28.113/ 977844	14 MC (x1)	R 50 (shaft 38 NCD 4 Bon)	43.4 ft.lbs (6.000 kgmm)
Ring gear-to-differential case screw	1.45.145/ 869734	10 x 1,25 M	R 100	44.8 ft.lbs (6.200 kgmm)
Differential bearing housing-to-gearbox casing nut	1/17016/11	8 MA (x1,25)	R 50 Cdt (stud R 80 Cdt)	18 ft.lbs (2.500 kgmm)
Layshaft rear bearing retainment plate nut	1/17016/11	8 MA (x1,25)	R 50 Cdt (stud R 80 Cdt)	18 ft.lbs (2.500 kgmm)
Gearbox casing rear housing-to-central body nut	1/21647/11	10 x 1,25 M	R 50 Cdt (stud R 50 Cdt)	27.5 ft.lbs (3.800 kgmm)
Gearbox-to-engine bolts: lower / upper	1.28.067/ 870058 / 1.28.068/ 870059	12 MB (x1,5)	R 80 Cdt	57.9 ft.lbs (8.000 kgmm)
Differential roller bearing preload (gearbox differential case divarication)				.0039" to .0047" (0,10 to 0,12 mm)
Final drive pinion-to-gear backlash				.0031" to .0051" (0,08 to 0,13 mm)

([1]) Sedan - starting from engine No. 758493; Multipla - starting from engine No. 765151.
([2]) Sedan - up to engine No. 758492; Multipla - up to engine No. 765150.

GEARBOX - DIFFERENTIAL TECHNICAL SPECIFICATIONS

Speeds	4 forward and 1 reverse
Synchronizer rings, for quick mesh of	2nd, 3rd and 4th speeds

Type of gears:
    2nd, 3rd, 4th speeds . . . . . .
    1st and reverse . . . .
	helical, constant mesh
	straight spur sliding gears

Gear ratios:	**Sedan** **Multipla**
1st gear	3,384 to 1 3,384 to 1
2nd gear	2,055 to 1 2,055 to 1
3rd gear	1,333 to 1 1,280 to 1
4th gear	0,896 to 1 0,838 to 1
Reverse	4,275 to 1 4,275 to 1
Gear backlash	.0039" (0,10 mm)
Ball bearing radial play	max. limit: .0020" (0,05 mm)
Ball bearing axial play	max. limit: .020" (0,5 mm)
Alignment of shafts (max. allowable out-of-true)	.0008" (0,02 mm) (on bearing seats)

Spiral final drive gear ratios:
    Sedan . . . .
    Multipla . . . .
	8 to 43
	7 to 45

Differential case bearings . . . .
    Type . . . .
    Adjustment . . . .
    Preload:
        gearbox-differential case divarication . . . . .
	2
	taper roller
	by adjusters
	
	.0039" to .0047" (0,10 to 0,12 mm)

Final drive pinion and ring gear (mated): backlash	.0031" to .0051" (0,08 to 0,13 mm)
Transmission of drive to rear wheels	by two axle shafts coupled to differential through slip joints

Lube oil:
    grade . . . .
    quantity { lt. . . . .
              kg . . . .
              qts. . . . .
	FIAT W 90 (SAE 90 EP)
	1,550
	1,400
	(U. S.) 1.64 - (G. B.) 1.36

SERVICE EQUIPMENT - GEARBOX - DIFFERENTIAL

Servicing must be carried out on rotating stand Arr. 2204 provided with support Arr. 2206/6.

A. 8560	Wrench - sleeve-to-side gear screw (early type).
A. 42013	Remover - final drive pinion ball bearing (Sedan).
A. 42014	Plate - differential case bearing inner ring removal (to be used with puller A. 40005).
A. 42016	Remover - final drive pinion ball bearing (Multipla).
A. 52020	Wrench - differential bearing adjuster rings (early type).
A. 55034	Wrench - differential bearing adjuster rings (late type).
A. 62024	Tool - parking brake drum retainment during tightening of final drive pinion nut (early type).
A. 62026	Fixture - drive pinion thrust ring thickness determination (to be used with C. 689).
A. 62027	Tool - differential case roller bearing outer ring remover and installer and inner ring installer.
A. 62028	Tool - bevel drive pinion rear ball bearing.
A. 62030	Expander - differential boot retainer collar installation and removal.
A. 62031	Installer - differential bearing oil seal.
A. 70071	Rubber boot (Qty. 2), to prevent oil leakage from gearbox casing with axle shaft removed (late type).
Arr. 2067	Sling - engine support during differential/gearbox removal.
Arr. 2076	Support - to be mounted on garage jack for gearbox-differential installation and removal.
Arr. 2206/6	Support - gearbox-differential unit retainment on rotating stand Arr. 2204.
C. 688	Fixture, with dial indicators - for bevel drive pinion-to-ring gear backlash adjustment and differential bearing preload checks.
C. 689	Dial indicator - for thrust ring thickness determination (to be used with A. 62026).

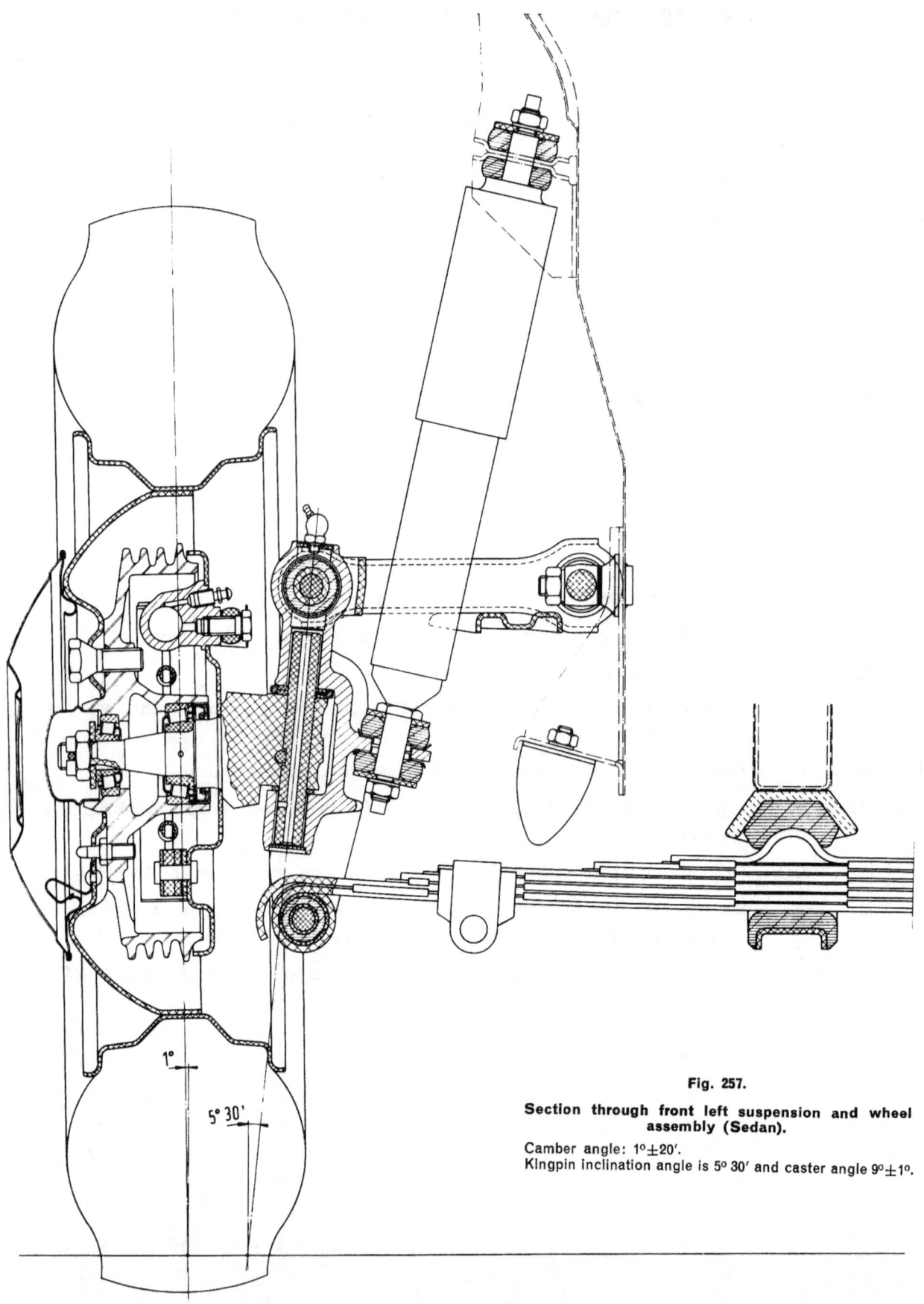

Fig. 257.

Section through front left suspension and wheel assembly (Sedan).

Camber angle: 1°±20'.
Kingpin inclination angle is 5° 30' and caster angle 9°±1°.

Section 5

FRONT SUSPENSION AND WHEELS

	Page
SEDAN	146
REMOVAL AND DISASSEMBLY	147
LEAF SPRING	148
SWINGING ARM	149
STEERING KNUCKLE PILLAR	150
STEERING KNUCKLE AND WHEEL HUB	152
ASSEMBLY AND INSTALLATION	155
CHECKING AND ADJUSTING FRONT END GEOMETRY	156
TIGHTENING REFERENCE	159
SPECIFICATIONS AND DATA	160
SERVICE EQUIPMENT	161
MULTIPLA	162
REMOVAL AND INSTALLATION	162
DISASSEMBLY	164
UPPER AND LOWER SWINGING ARMS	164
STEERING KNUCKLE PILLAR	167
ASSEMBLY	167
COIL SPRING	168
STABILIZER BAR	169
TIGHTENING REFERENCE	169
CHECKING AND ADJUSTING FRONT END GEOMETRY	171
SPECIFICATIONS AND DATA	171
SERVICE EQUIPMENT	172
TROUBLE DIAGNOSIS AND CORRECTIONS	172

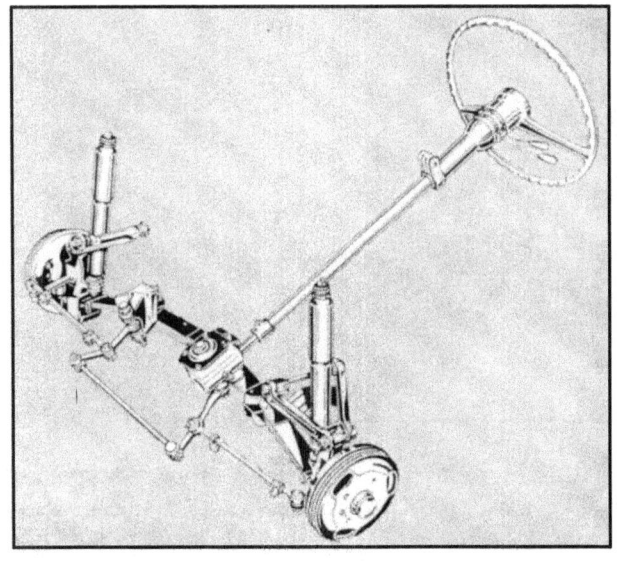

FRONT SUSPENSION AND WHEELS

The front suspension is substantially different on «Sedan» and «Multipla» models.

The operations for removal, installation, disassembly, service and reassembly are outlined separately for each model.

«Sedan» - independent wheels, transversal leaf spring and upper swinging arms. The leaf spring performs also as stabilizer.

Hydraulic, double-acting, telescopic shock absorbers.

«Multipla» - independent wheels, swinging arms connected to wheels and counteracted by coil springs and hydraulic, double-acting, telescopic shock absorbers (not the same as on «Sedan»). Transversal stabilizer bar anchored on lower swinging arms.

FRONT SUSPENSION AND WHEELS

600 SEDAN

The independent-wheel front suspension consists of a transversal leaf spring anchored to body through two rubber mountings and to kingpins through «estendblocks».

The leaf spring performs also as stabilizer.

Upper articulation of kingpins in swinging arms is obtained by «estendblocks»; arms are in turn anchored on body and swing on their pin through rubber bushes. The suspension system includes telescopic, double-acting, hydraulic shock absorbers, which are anchored to body (top end) and to knuckle pillar (bottom end).

Two rubber bumpers, secured to body-mounted brackets, limit leaf spring oscillations.

Fig. 258 - Front suspension bottom view.

1. Knuckle pillar. - 2. Swinging arm. - 3. Shock absorber. - 4. Steering knuckle. - 5. Leaf spring. - 6. Leaf spring elastic mountings. - 7. Rubber bumper.

FRONT SUSPENSION AND WHEELS

Front Suspension Removal and Disassembly.

— Raise front of car on stands and then remove wheels and leaf spring apron (1, fig. 261).

— Disconnect steering linkages from knuckle arms, relay lever and from pitman arm, using puller **A. 46022**.

Back out shock absorber upper mounting nut (4, fig. 261) and push down the outer cylinder.

Disconnect brake lines at wheel cylinders; before doing this, blank brake fluid reservoir outlet by inserting a suitable wooden peg through reservoir filler opening.

Fig. 259 - Front end bottom view.
The brake and clutch control apron is visible at center.

Fit cross beam **Arr. 2072** under leaf spring and support by hydraulic garage jack **Arr. 2027**.

Remove self-locking nut securing leaf spring to knuckle pillar and take off spring mounting bolt.

Remove nuts (5, fig. 261) securing swinging arm pin to studs welded on body and remove swinging arm assembly.

Remove adjusting shims and spacers from studs.

Remove nuts securing leaf spring elastic mountings to body (6, fig. 258); lower hydraulic jack slowly and take off the spring.

Disconnect hydraulic shock absorber from knuckle pillar.

Back out swinging arm pin mounting nuts and disinsert pin.

To remove kingpin operate as follows:
Take off lubricator.
Drive the « estendblock » out of knuckle pillar, using tool **A. 66042**.
By a drift rod, drive off lockpin of kingpin.
Remove the upper plug, with lubrication fitting, and lower plug, and take off kingpin.

Fig. 260 - Front left suspension detail.

NOTE - When removing quarter-elliptic spring from car, observe the quantity of adjusting shims between lower rubber mountings and upper plates.

On installation, proceed as recommended on page 155.

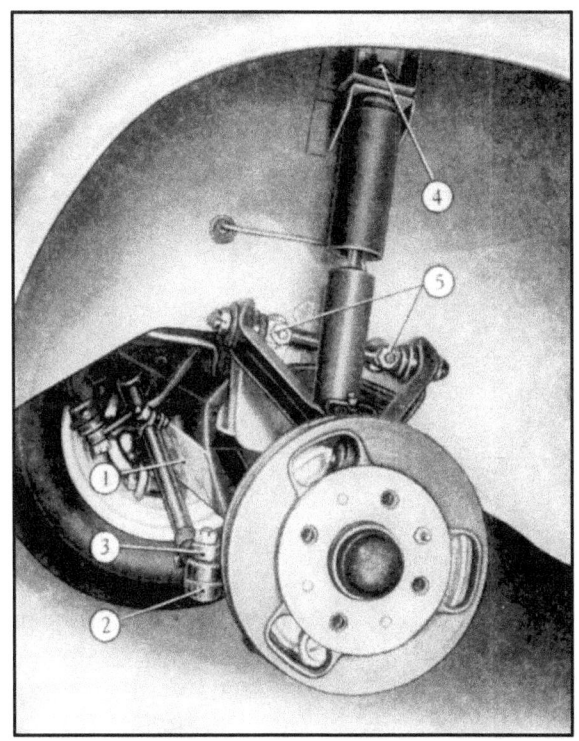

Fig. 261 - Front left suspension detail.
1. Apron. - 2. Track rod end. - 3. Knuckle arm. - 4. Shock absorber upper mounting nut. - 5. Swinging arm pin body nuts.

LEAF SPRING

Features.

The spring consists of a main leaf and five other leaves. Polyethylene insulating strips are sandwiched between leaves.

Leaves are held together by a center bolt and two elastically-mounted side clips.

For attachment to knuckle pillars, «estendblocks» are fitted in main leaf eyes.

Spring data is given in tables below as well as on next page and in figs. 263 and 264.

Inspection and Repair of Spring and «Estendblocks».

Disassemble leaf spring by taking off the side clips and center bolt. Next, wash all parts carefully.

Check the following:

a) Leaves are not broken or cracked; replace if required.

Third and fifth leaf do not come for replacement separately. If they are damaged, substitute the whole spring pack.

b) No paint is present between leaves; remove any trace of paint.

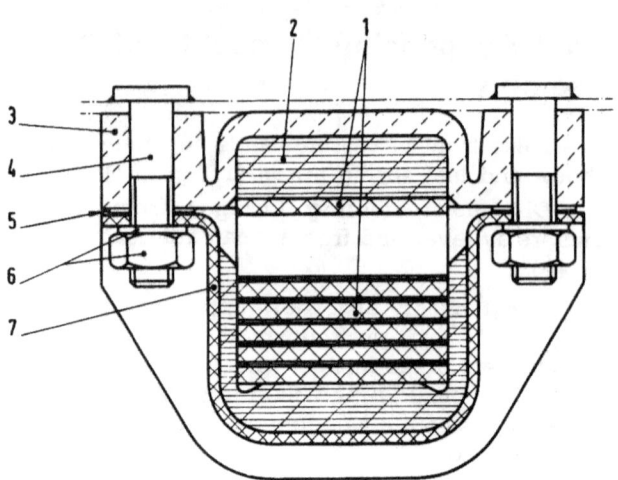

Fig. 262 - Sectional view of leaf spring rubber mounting.
1. Leaf spring. - 2. Mounting pad. - 3. Upper plate. - 4. Screw. - 5. Shims. - 6. Toothed washer and nut. - 7. Lower rubber mounting.

c) Mating faces of leaves must be perfectly smooth and clean; with a file or other suitable means, eliminate any indentation or rough areas.

d) Camber of leaves; if necessary, restore the required camber (see the setting data given for reassembled springs in the following tables).

e) Condition of «estendblocks» force-fitted in main leaf eyes. Some of the troubles they cause (noise or squeaks) are detectable when spring is mounted on car.

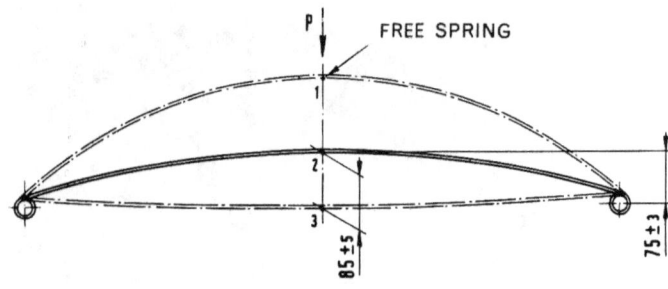

Fig. 263.
Diagram of centrally loaded spring main leaf.

SPECIFICATIONS

	FRONT LEAF SPRING, LOADED AT CENTER								
Position		Load P		Rise		Elastic give-in from pos. 2		Flexibility	
		lbs	kg	in	mm	in	mm	in/100 lbs	mm/100 kg
2	Initial load for flexibility checks.	331	150	2.95±.12	75±3	—	—	—	—
3		551	250*	—	—	3.35±.20	85±5	1.52±.09	85±5
* When testing the spring never exceed this load.									

FRONT SUSPENSION AND WHEELS

Position		Load P		Rise		Elastic give-in from pos. 1		Flexibility	
		lbs	kg	in	mm	in	mm	in/100 lbs	mm/100 kg
1	Initial load for flexibility checks	220	100	—	—	—	—		
2	Static load	375	170	.30±.12	7,5±3	2.17±.16	55±4	1.38±.09	78±5
3	Metal-to-bumper deflection load	573	260	—	—	4.33	110		

FRONT LEAF SPRING, INSTALLED ON CAR

Spring characteristics are intended at assembly conditions, i. e. with pre-compressed rubber pads.
Give-in checks must be carried out by loading both eyes simultaneously.

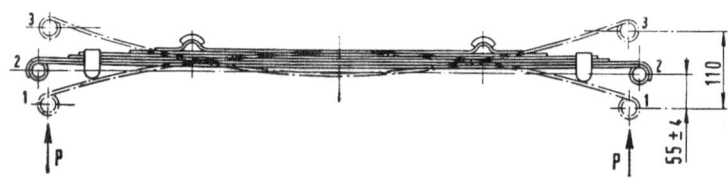

Fig. 264.
Diagram of spring installed on car.

If the above troubles are noticed, or excessive wear, traces of seizure and dryness of rubber parts, replace the «estendblocks».

Removal and installation of «estendblocks» is done using special tool **A. 66039**.

f) Good condition of all rubber pads, supports, clips and polyethylene linings. Replace parts as required.

SWINGING ARM

Features.

Of pressed sheet steel, joined by two pins: one on knuckle pillar and one on body.

«Flanblock» rubber bushes are press-fitted in the arms for the attachment of swinging arm pin to body (fig. 265).

Disassembly.

— Install swinging arm on fixture **A. 66038**.

— Remove cotter pins (7, fig. 265) and unscrew two nuts (8) securing pin (14) anchoring swinging arm to body.

— Remove cups (9) and withdraw rubber bushes (10) using all purpose puller **A. 40005/V**. Remove pin (14) with washers (11).

Inspection of Arm, Rubber Bushings and Pin.

a) Install swinging arm on fixture **A. 66038** and check that pin bores are aligned and not out-

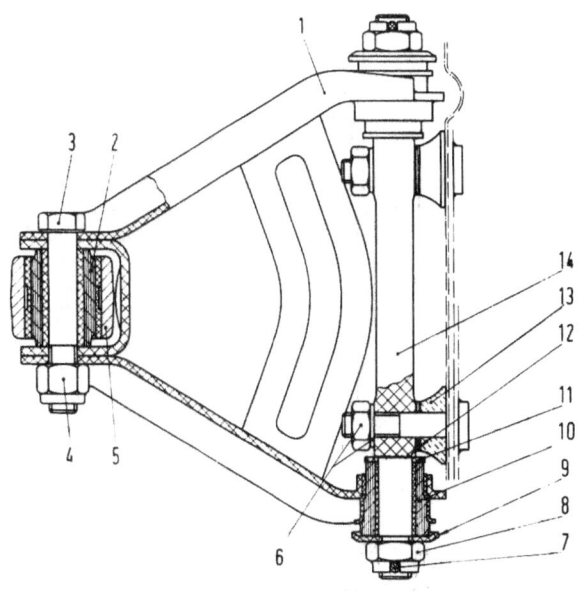

Fig. 265 - Partial schematic section of swinging arm.

1. Swinging arm. - 2. Rubber bushing (Estendblock). - 3. Screw. - 4. Self-locking nut. - 5. Pillar. - 6. Anchor pin-to-body toothed washer and nut. - 7. Split pin. - 8. Anchor pin nut. - 9. Outer cup. - 10. Rubber bushing (Flanblock). - 11. Inner washer. - 12. Camber and caster adjusting shims. - 13. Spacer. - 14. Swinging arm anchor pin.

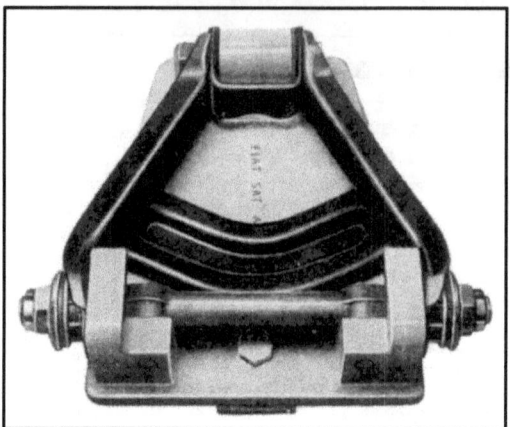

Fig. 266 - Checking swinging arm assembly on fixture A. 66038.

of-round. Check that swinging arm contacts shoulders of fixture.

If swinging arm is deformed, straighten as required.

The above check may be performed also on the swinging arm assembly inserting the holes of pin (14, fig. 265) on the fixture pins.

b) With bushes installed the arm must swing freely without any appreciable play.

c) Check that pin contact surfaces with caster and camber adjusting shims are not dented or scored to such an extent as to affect accuracy of adjustment; if denting or scoring is so serious that surfaces cannot be reconditioned, replace pin.

d) Check the condition of arm bushes; inner surface must not show signs of seizure and clearance to pin must not be greater than .0157" (0,40 mm); fit clearance: .002" to .01" (0,050 to 0,250 mm).

Observe that rubber parts of bush are not torn, cracked or weak. Otherwise, replace bushes.

Reassembly.

— Insert pin (4, fig. 267) provided with two washers (5) in swinging arm bores.
— Install pin and arm on fixture A. 66038.
— Press fit rubber bushes using installer A. 66044 and install cups and nuts. Secure nuts by cotter pins.

STEERING KNUCKLE PILLAR

Inspection and Repair of «Estendblock», Steering Knuckle Pillar and Kingpin.

Remove the «estendblock» with tool A. 66042 (which serves also as an installer) as directed on page 147.

Make sure the «estendblock» is not worn, that is, it has no sign of seizure on its inner surface or its rubber has not hardened. Replace if required.

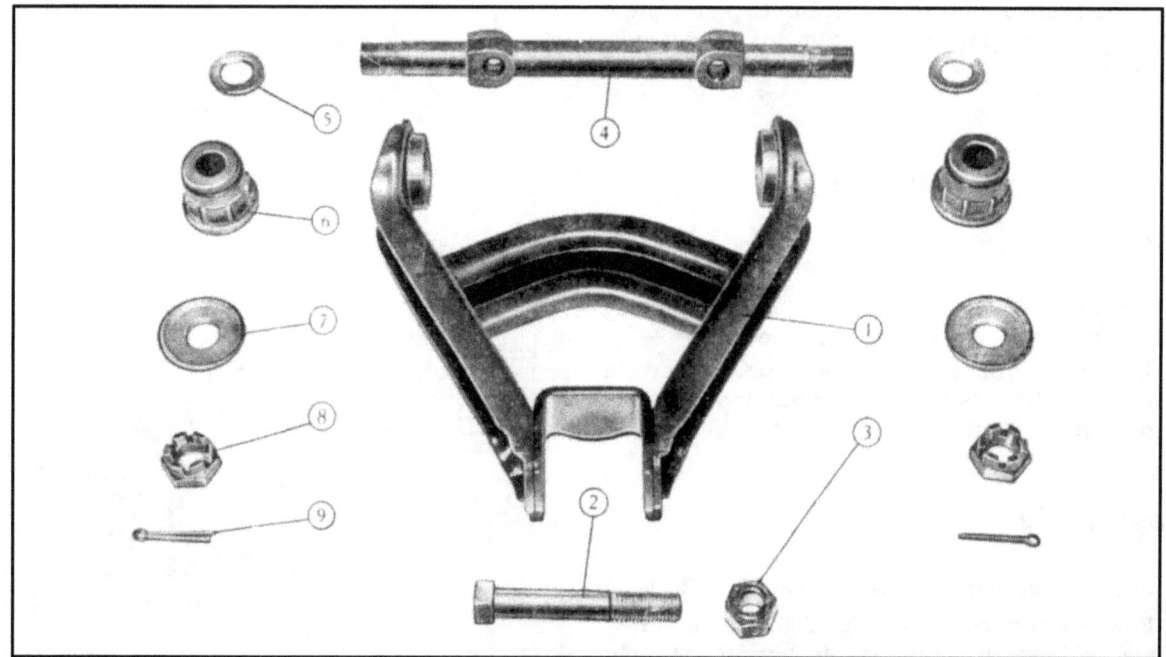

Fig. 267 - Swinging arm components.

1. Swinging arm. - 2. Bolt, swinging arm-to-kingpin. - 3. Self-locking nut. - 4. Swinging arm anchor pin. - 5. Inner washer for bush. - 6. Rubber bush. - 7. Cup for bush. - 8. Nut, securing pin 4 to swinging arm. - 9. Cotter pin for nut.

FRONT SUSPENSION AND WHEELS

Check that kingpin-to-bush clearance is not greater than .0079" (0,20 mm) (fit clearance, when new, is .00063" to .00213" [0,016 to 0,054 mm]).

If clearance is excessive, replace the two bushes and, if necessary, also the kingpin.

Kingpin bush installation and removal are carried out using tool **A. 66016**; after assembly, bushes must be accurately smoothened with reamer **U. 0360/25 B** (fig. 268) to a diameter of .5912" to .5922" (15,016 to 15,043 mm).

Using fixture **C. 1003** check that knuckle pillar has not been distorted, proceeding as follows:

a) Place pin (1, fig. 269) in knuckle pillar upper hole and lower pin (2) with square (3) in lower holes.

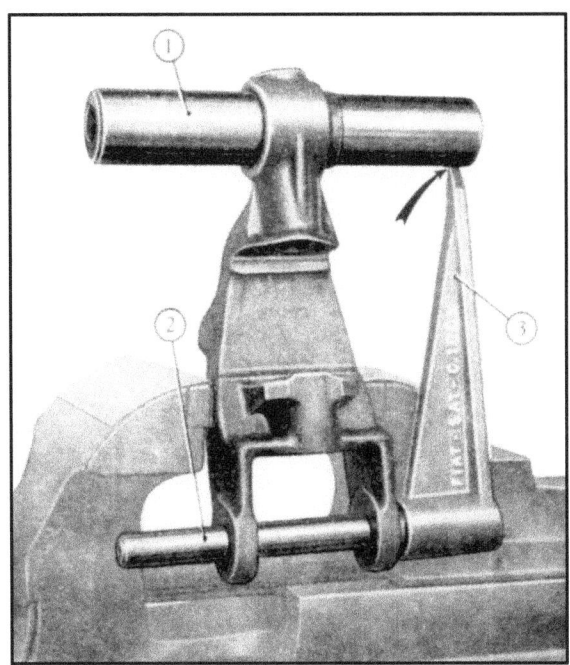

Fig. 269 - Checking parallelism of knuckle pillar axes with fixture C. 1003.

1. Upper pin. - 2. Lower pin with square 3.

Arrow points to square tip which must barely contact pin 1.

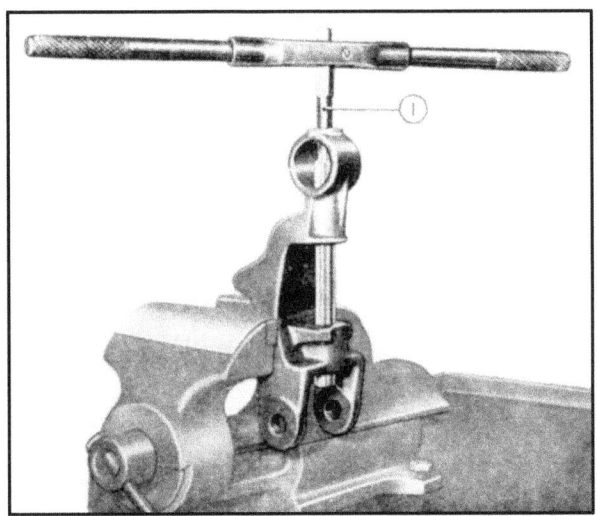

Fig. 268 - Smoothening inner surfaces of kingpin bushes.
1. Reamer U. 0360/25 B.

— Check that square tip just contacts upper pin (1).

— Repeat this operation on the other side. This will check knuckle pillar alignment.

If misaligned, on one side the square tip will clear pin (1) with a wide gap while on the other it will force against the pin.

It this is the case, replace the pillar.

b) Remove upper pin (1), and in its place, insert bar (4, fig. 270). If knuckle pillar is in good condition, the lower end of bar (4) should place itself tangentially to lower pin (2).

Should this not be the case, i. e., if the gap between the two parts is excessive or the parts strike each other, the knuckle pillar is evidently distorted.

If this is the case, replace the pillar.

While servicing progresses, check also kingpin lubricator squirt hole which must be unobstructed; clean if required.

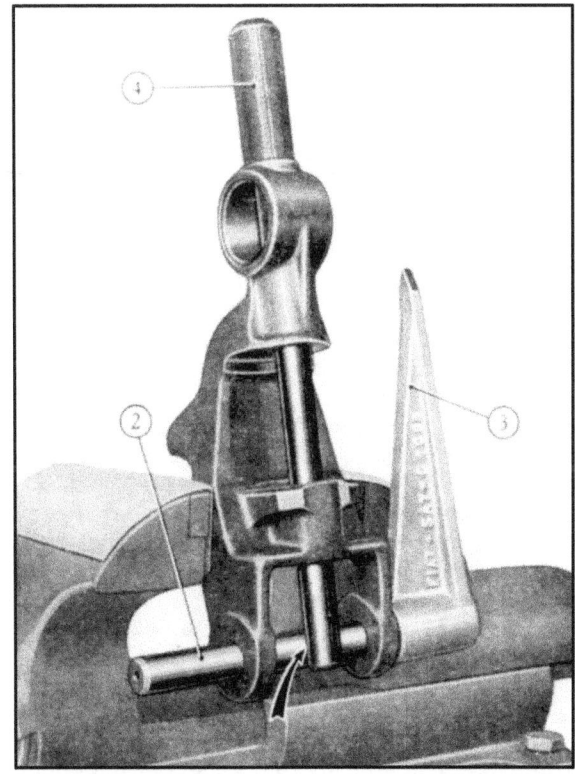

Fig. 270 - Checking knuckle pillar inclination with fixture C. 1003.

2. Lower pin with square 3. - 4. Bar.

Arrow points to bar 4 which must be tangential to pin 2.

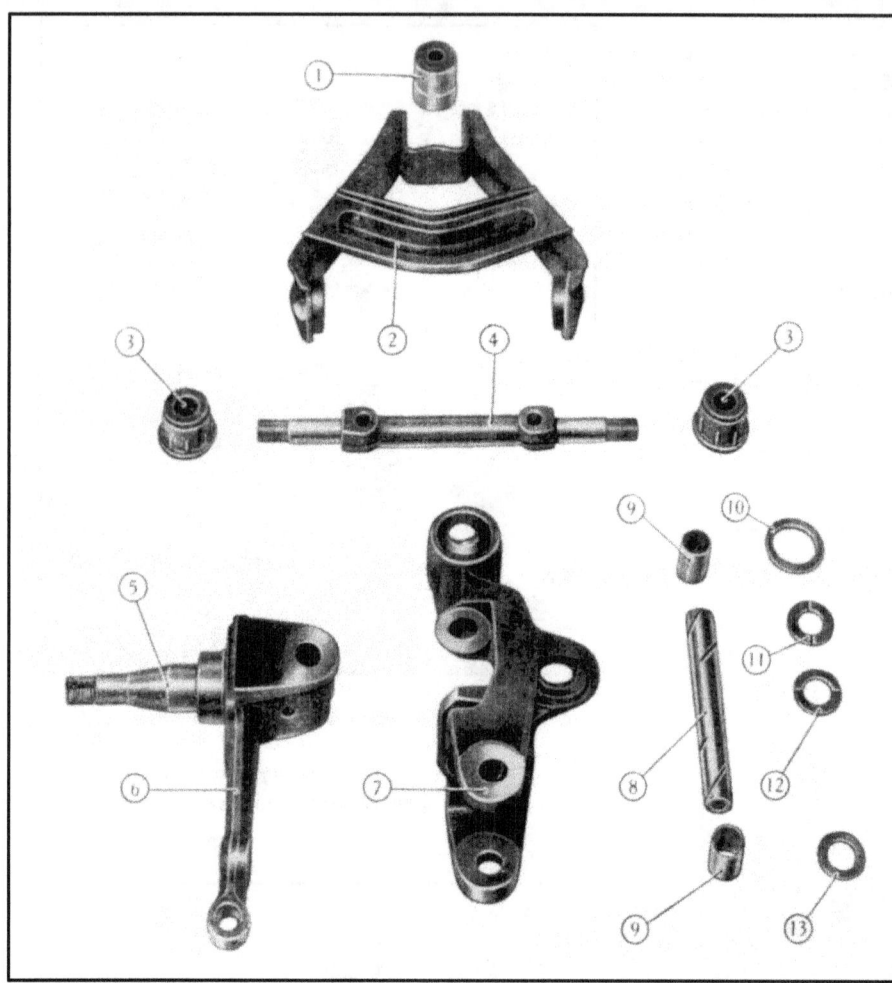

Fig. 271.

Components of swinging arm, steering knuckle, kingpin and knuckle pillar.

1. « Estendblock » on kingpin for swinging arm attachment. - 2. Swinging arm. - 3. Rubber bushes. - 4. Pin for swinging arm. - 5 and 6. Steering knuckle with arm. - 7. Steering knuckle pillar. - 8. Kingpin. - 9. Bushes for kingpin. - 10. Rubber ring for kingpin. - 11 and 12. Thrust rings for kingpin. - 13. Lower packing ring for kingpin.

STEERING KNUCKLE AND WHEEL HUB

Disassembly.

Use puller **A. 46014** (fig. 272) to drive off wheel hub caps and installer **A. 66008** (fig. 274) for their installation.

To remove the wheel hub/drum assembly, after removal of hub cap, split pin and nut, use universal puller **A. 40005** or puller **A. 6469** (fig. 275).

From drum remove the outher roller bearing inner ring, oil seal, snap ring and inner roller bearing inner ring.

Roller bearing outer rings are removed by puller **A. 6511** with which item **A. 6463** must be used when removing inner bearing outer ring.

Back out the drum-to-steering knuckle mounting nuts (two) and remove the complete brake housing flange.

The disassembly of steering knuckle from knuckle pillar is carried out as follows (see also description page 147):

— drive the « estendblock » out of knuckle pillar, using tool **A. 66042**;

— by a drift rod, drive off lockpin of kingpin;

— remove the upper plug, with lubrication fitting, and lower plug, and take off kingpin.

The steering knuckle can thus be removed, along with the snap ring, both thrust washers and lower shoulder ring.

Fig. 272 - Removing right front wheel hub cap by puller A. 46014.

FRONT SUSPENSION AND WHEELS

Inspection.

Inspect carefully all components. Particularly:

a) See that steering knuckle and steering arm are not cracked, otherwise replace.

b) Inspect steering knuckle surfaces in contact with roller bearing inner races which must not show any scoring or seizing signs.

c) Inspect the condition of the two upper thrust rings and of lower packing ring. Replace if worn.

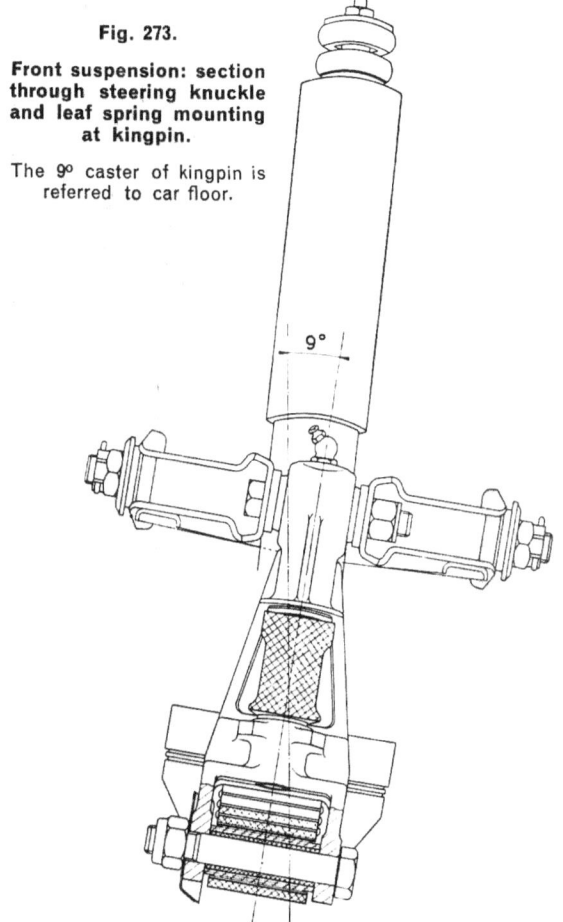

Fig. 273.

Front suspension: section through steering knuckle and leaf spring mounting at kingpin.

The 9° caster of kingpin is referred to car floor.

Spare lower packing rings are supplied in the following thicknesses:

After reassembly no appreciable clearance must result between steering knuckle and knuckle pillar. This is obtained by installing the lower packing ring of the proper thickness.

Fig. 274 - Installing right front wheel hub cap by installer A. 66008.

d) Check that seats on drums for roller bearing outer rings are perfectly smooth. No clearance is permitted between rings and seats. See that bearing cages and rollers are not chipped or broken.

Fig. 275 - Removing wheel brake drum by puller A. 6469.

e) The seal must not be torn and adhere perfectly to both drum and steering knuckle.

f) The snap ring between seal and inner bearing must not be deformed.

RING	STAND.	OVERSIZE				UNDERSIZE	
	in.	.002	.004	.008	.012	.002	.004
	mm	0,05	0,10	0,20	0,30	0,05	0,10
Thkss	in. .0977	.0997	.1016	.1056	.1095	.0957	.0938
	mm 2,482	2,532	2,582	2,682	2,782	2,432	2,382
	in. .098	.100	.102	.106	.110	.096	.094
	mm 2,50	2,55	2,60	2,70	2,80	2,45	2,40

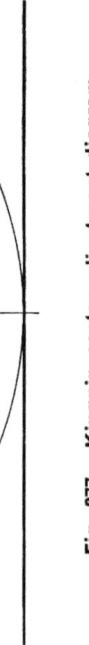

Fig. 277 - Kingpin caster adjustment diagram.

$\beta = 9° \pm 1°$ Kingpin caster.
D and E = Points where shims «S» must be installed.

NOTE - To prevent abnormal torsion of the «estendblock» press-fitted in knuckle pillar, the pillar-to-swinging arm pin nut must be tightened arranging the parts so that the angle between swinging arm plane and pillar axes is about 95° (fig. 276).

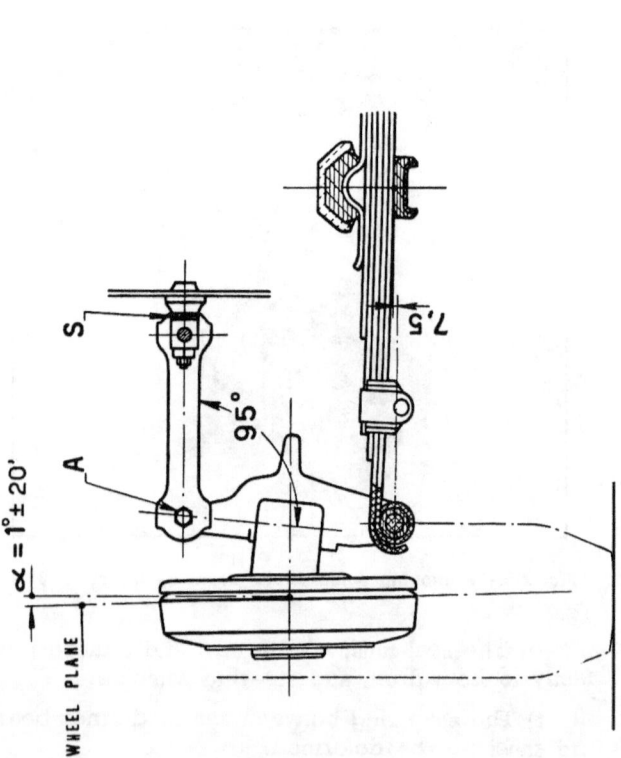

Fig. 276 - Front wheel camber checking diagram.

$\alpha = 1° \pm 20'$. Wheel camber.
A = Upper swinging arm pin nut.
S = Shims.
.30" (7,5 mm) = Measure corresponding to «fully-laden».

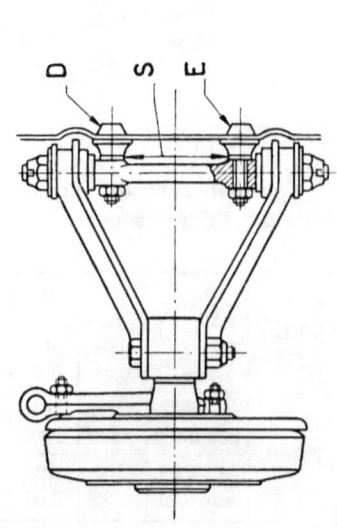

Fig. 278.
Front wheel camber adjustment diagram.

S = Shims.
D and E = Points where shims must be installed.

FRONT SUSPENSION ASSEMBLY AND INSTALLATION

Before reassembling the front suspension, determine the number of thickness shims to be fitted between leaf spring upper supports and caps for a correct assembly.

The amount of shims required is established by measuring the maximum thickness of the spring pack at the point where it is clamped between lower rubber mountings and upper plates, according to the following table:

Pack thickness found	Shims required
1.62" to 1.65" (41,2 to 41,8 mm)	None
1.65" to 1.69" (41,8 to 42,8 mm)	1
1.69" to 1.73" (42,8 to 44 mm)	2

Standard thickness shims are .039" (1 mm) thick.

Install the spring on fixture **A. 66061** and load it with the proper screw of the fixture until the reference index appears below cross beam lower edge.

In this position the spring attains the «full static load» setting same as on car; the sag between the plane through eye centers and spring lower face is approximately .30" (7,5 mm) (fig. 276).

Insert the spring so set and provided with upper plates and pads on the studs projecting from body bottom.

Fit the required amount of shims, both lower rubber mountings and screw on the stud nuts to a torque of 28.9 ft.lbs (4000 kgmm).

On bench assemble:

— the steering knuckle on knuckle pillar, interposing the two upper thrust rings, the snap ring and lower packing ring whose thickness shall be selected as specified above to take up any play between knuckle and knuckle pillar. Secure steering knuckle pin with elastic cotter;

— the brake housing flange on steering knuckle and tighten nuts to 14.5 ft.lbs (2000 kgmm);

— the roller bearings and seal on drum hub; pack liberally with FIAT MR grease the pocket between the two bearings;

— the drum hub on steering knuckle;

— the nut with washer securing the wheel hub to steering knuckle; **tighten nut to 21.7 ft.lbs (3000 kgmm)**.

Back out the nut one cotter slot (60°) and fit the cotterpin;

— the cap to hub using installer **A. 66008**.

NOTE

Starting from car No. **530630**, «Sedan», and car No. **036027**, «Multipla», the right steering knuckle nut has a counterclockwise threading and is identified by a circle groove on outside face.

Conversely, the left steering knuckle nut is still threading clockwise and brings no identification mark.

Above variation has been introduced as a prudential measure, like what already existing at left hand steering knuckles, to avoid that, should wheel bearings seize accidentally, right hand steering knuckle nuts are dragged to lock bearings and, consequently, road wheels.

This should be borne in mind when servicing front hubs, so that right hand steering knuckle nuts be not inadvertently screwed out by counterclockwise rotation, thus causing overtightness on the nut.

Connect now the swinging arm to the wheel assembly by bolt and nut.

The nut must be screwed onto the bolt (A, fig. 276) by arranging the parts in such a way that between the arm plane and the knuckle pillar the angle results about 95° (fig. 276). By this provision the swinging arm-to-knuckle pillar fit will be perfectly elastic and undue torsional stresses on knuckle pillar «estendblock» during operation will be prevented. Tightening torque is 43.4 to 50.6 ft.lbs (6000 to 7000 kgmm).

Insert the swinging arm pin on the two studs welded on body sides so as to support the suspension/wheels assembly.

Connect knuckle pillar to spring eye by inserting the bolt and tightening the self-locking nut to 43.4 to 50.6 ft.lbs (6000 to 7000 kgmm). During this operation the spring must be kept always «set» by fixture **A. 66061** to ensure correct assembly and to prevent abnormal stresses on the «estendblocks».

Slide off the swinging arm and insert spacers and shims (S, fig. 278) on studs, seeing that the resulting thickness is the same as found at disassembly. Again connect the swinging arm.

Screw on the nuts securing the pin to body and tighten to 32.6 ft.lbs (4500 kgmm).

Install shock absorber securing it to knuckle pillar and to body, inserting the plain washer between rubber pad and nut toothed washer.

Remove fixture **A. 66061**, connect steering rods, brake fluid pipes and install wheels. Raise car by hydraulic jack **Arr. 2027**, remove stands and lower car to ground.

After installing both right and left suspensions adjust front end geometry according to the directions contained in the following chapter.

NOTE - See page 190 for front and rear hydraulic shock absorber servicing.

CHECKING AND ADJUSTING FRONT WHEEL CAMBER AND CASTER

Values of front end setting (with car under static load, i. e., with 4 passengers plus 66 lbs [30 kg] of luggage distributed 44 lbs [20 kg] at front and 22 lbs [10 kg] at rear) are:

— camber $1° \pm 20'$;
— caster $9° \pm 1°$.

Camber (α, fig. 276) and caster (β, fig. 277) adjustments are performed by interposing shims (S, fig. 278) between swinging arm pin and body (at points D and E, figs. 277 and 278).

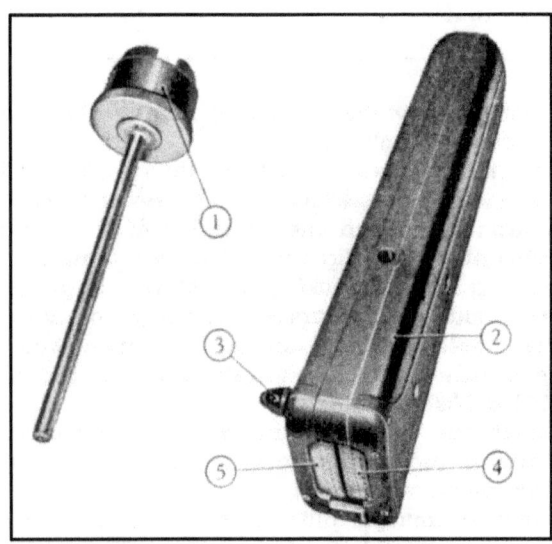

Fig. 279 - Items of fixture **C. 694**.

1. Magnetic device, gauge anchoring to wheel hub. - 2. Gauge. - 3. Caster scale zeroing knob. - 4. Camber scale. - 5. Caster scale.

Shims and spacers come for replacement in the following thicknesses:

— shims = .0197″ (0,5 mm);
— spacers = .3937″ (10 mm) and .4724″ (12 mm).

Front wheel alignment adjustment becomes necessary should an excessive tire wear or irregular steering performance (stiffening, etc.) be noticed.

Camber and caster are checked by fixture **C. 694** (figs. 279 and 280); toe-in (page 206) by gauge **C. 692**.

Fixture **C. 694** consists of:

— 1 gauge;
— 1 gauge magnetic anchoring device for attachment to wheel rim;
— 2 turntables.

The gauge is made up of a pendulum goniometer whose dial (fig. 279) has two scales of which one is fixed and the other adjustable by a knob.

The first scale is used to determine the camber angle magnitude, the second is for caster measurements.

Turntables (on which wheels rest and swivel) are made up of a sheet metal quadrangular base carrying the turntable disc. Besides around its axis, the turntable disc may move in any horizontal direction by means of a system of roller plates sliding orthogonally to each other.

The turntable disc carries also an adjustable, graduated sector which may be set to zero on an index of the turntable (fig. 280).

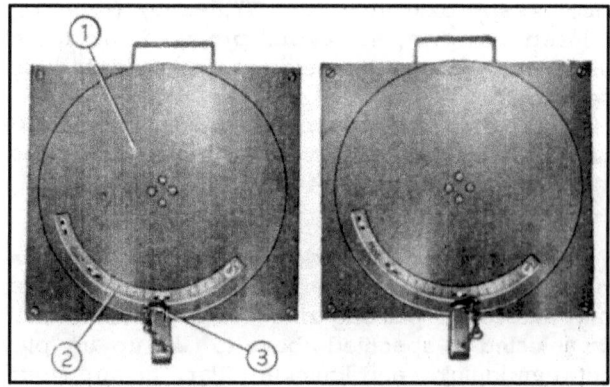

Fig. 280 - Turntables.

1. Turntable plate. - 2. Graduated sector. - 3. Turntable plate lock pin.

Use of the Fixture.

First, inspect all car components involved in front end geometry so as to correct any possible slight defect likely to lead to erroneous readings during checks and adjustments.

FRONT SUSPENSION AND WHEELS

Check:

— tire pressures (which should be 14.2 p.s.i. [1 kg/cm^2] for front wheels, and 22.8 p.s.i. [1,6 kg/cm^2] for rear wheels);

— tire installation (max. out-of-true not more than .1181" [3 mm]);

— play in wheel bearings: adjust if necessary;

— clearance between pin and bushes of steering knuckle: replace parts if worn;

— backlash of worm-to-sector set; adjust if necessary (see page 198);

— loose pins in steering rod articulation heads: replace heads as required;

— shock absorbers efficiency; replace or service, as required.

Fig. 282 - **Compressing rear coil spring to obtain fully laden condition.**

1. Rear left swinging arm. - 2. Fixture A. 66052. - 3. Wrench A. 74003.

— Raise front wheels and rest them at center of turntables. This way wheels can be aimed more easily at angles required for caster inspection.

Fig. 281 - **Compressing front leaf spring to obtain fully laden condition.**

1. Fixture A. 66051/1/2. - 2. Wrench A. 74003.

After performing the above checks:

— Place car on level ground. Car must be under « static load », i.e. with a load corresponding to the weight of four passengers, plus 66 lbs (30 kg) of luggage. Under this condition the height of spring supports above ground (measured at lowermost point) must be about 6.65" (169 mm) and the height of oil sump lowest point about 6.93" (176 mm).

To set the car in the « static load » condition it is sufficient to apply fixtures A. 66051/1/2 (right and left) on front suspension (fig. 281) and the set of fixture A. 66052 on rear suspension (fig. 282).

— Set steering wheel in half-travel position, with spokes horizontal.

— Place two wooden blocks having the same thickness as the turntables of fixture **C. 694** under rear wheels, so that car is level.

Fig. 283 - **Checking front wheel camber.**

The wheel must be in straightahead position; graduated sector must be set at 0°. Camber scale must read 1° (tolerance is ±20').
(Multipla: front wheel camber is 0° 30' ±20').

158 FIAT - 600 - 600 D SEDAN AND MULTIPLA

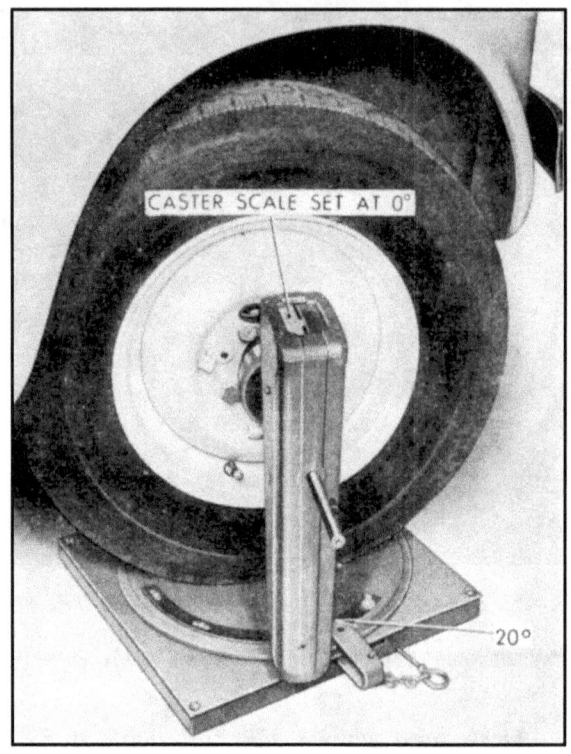

Fig. 284 - Checking front wheel caster.
1st operation: with wheel steered 20° out, set «Caster» scale at zero.
(Multipla: same as Sedan)

Fig. 285 - Checking front wheel caster.
2nd operation: with wheel steered 20° in, the «Caster» scale must read 9°; tolerance ± 1°.
(Multipla: caster must be 6°±30').

Set the graduated sector of turntable disc by lining up 0° mark with the pointer of the turntable.

— Install gauge of fixture **C. 694** on the wheel involved and perform the checks described below.

Checking Camber.

With fixture anchored on wheel and gauge set normally to car centerline (fig. 283), read value of camber angle on the «Camber» scale, which should be 1°±20'.

NOTE - To compensate for a possible small out-of-true of the wheel, deriving from slight differences in thickness of rim sheet, or stress warpage of the rim itself, it is advisable to repeat checking after rotating the wheel 180°. Should a different reading be had, sum the two readings and divide the resulting value by two. This will ensure correct results.

Checking Caster.

Use fixture **C. 694** and set gauge normally to car centerline.

Steer out wheel 20° and bring caster scale to «zero» (fig. 284).

Fig. 286 - Adjusting front wheel camber and caster.
A and B: studs on which swinging arm is mounted.
Arrows point to shims.

FRONT SUSPENSION AND WHEELS

Steer wheel 20° out and read «caster» angle value on «caster» scale: reading should be 9°±1° (fig. 285).

Should caster and camber not comply with specified values, adjust as outlined hereafter.

Adjusting Front Wheel Camber and Caster.

To adjust caster, slacken the two nuts securing swinging arm pin to body and then:

— **if caster angle must be increased** (β, fig. 277) move shims from rear screw (B) to front screw (A) (fig. 286);

— **if caster angle must be reduced** (β, fig. 277) move shims from front screw (A) to rear screw (B) (fig. 286).

To adjust camber, slacken the two nuts securing swinging arm pin to body and then:

— **if camber angle must be increased** (α, fig. 276) add the same number of shims on both screws (A and B, fig. 286);

— **if camber angle must be reduced** (α, fig. 276) remove the same number of shims from both screws (A and B, fig. 286).

The addition or removal of shims at points A and B permits camber adjustments without disturbing caster.

FRONT SUSPENSION AND WHEEL TIGHTENING REFERENCE
SEDAN

ITEM	DRWG. OR STD. PART No.	THREAD	MATERIAL	TIGHTENING TORQUE
Leaf spring-to-body nut	1/21647/11	10 x 1,25 M	R 50 Cdt (Screw C 21 R)	28.9 ft.lbs (4.000 kgmm)
Knuckle pillar-to-swinging arm . .	1/25747/11	12 MB (x1,5)	R 50 Cdt (Screw R 50 Cdt)	43.4 to 50.6 ft.lbs (6.000 to 7.000 kgmm)
Brake housing flange-to-steering knuckle nut	1/17016/11	8 MA (x1,25)	R 50 Cdt (Screw R 50)	14.5 ft.lbs (2.000 kgmm)
Leaf spring-to-knuckle pillar nut .	1/25748/11	14 MB (x1,5)	R 50 Cdt (Screw R 50 Znt)	43.4 to 50.6 ft.lbs (6.000 to 7.000 kgmm)
Front swinging arm-to-body nut . .	1/21647/11	10 x 1,25 M	R 50 Cdt (Screw R 80)	32.6 ft.lbs (4.500 kgmm)
Bearing-on-steering knuckle nut . .	1.58.220/ 980498	14 MB (x1,5)	R 50 (Steering knuckle 38NCD4 Bon)	21.7 ft.lbs (3.000 kgmm)
Wheel-to-hub screw	1.49.012/ 996225	12 MB (x1,5)	C 35 R (Bon Cdt)	43.4 to 50.6 ft.lbs (6.000 to 7.000 kgmm)

FRONT SUSPENSION AND WHEEL SPECIFICATIONS AND DATA
SEDAN

Leaf Spring	1
Leaves	1 main plus 5
Sag, with set spring	.30″±.12″ (7,5±3 mm) under a 375 lbs (170 kg) load
Bushes for connection to knuckle pillar	« estendblock »
Connection to body bottom	by 2 supports with rubber pads
Position of spring to tighten the nut of pin for connection to knuckle pillar	static load setting
Swinging Arms	2
Connection to body	by pin and rubber bushes
Position of arm and of pin hole axes for pin nut tightening	on the same plane
Steering Knuckle Pillars.	
Connection to leaf spring and to swinging arm . .	by « estendblocks »
Kingpin angle	5° 30′
Caster	9°±1°
Caster adjustment	by shims .0197″ (0,5 mm) thick
Position of knuckle pillar with respect to swinging arm plane for tightening the pin nut	95°
Steering Knuckles.	
Steering knuckle-to-knuckle pillar play adjustment .	by packing rings: thkss .098″ (2,50 mm) oversizes: .100 - .102 - .106 - .110 in. (2,55 - 2,60 - 2,70 - 2,80 mm); undersizes: .096 - .094 in. (2,45 - 2,40 mm) (see table page 153)
Wheels.	
Camber	1°±20′
Camber adjustment	by shims .02″ thk (0,5 mm)
Toe-in (see page 206)	.00″ to .08″ (0 to 2 mm)
Toe-in adjustment	by adjustable sleeves on track rods
Bearing lubrication	FIAT MR grease
Shock Absorbers	2
Type	hydraulic, telescopic, double acting
Diameter (inner cylinder)	1.063″ (27 mm)
Fluid	FIAT S. A. I. oil
Capacity	135±5 cc (0,120 kg)

FRONT SUSPENSION AND WHEEL SERVICE EQUIPMENT

SEDAN

A. 6463	Item (to be used with puller A. 6511) - wheel inner roller bearing outer ring removal.	
A. 6469	Puller - wheel drums.	
A. 6511	Puller - wheel bearing outer rings.	
A. 40005/V	Puller - swinging arm rubber bushes and wheel drums.	
A. 46014	Puller, ram - wheel hub caps.	
A. 56020	Wrench - shock absorber installation and removal.	
A. 57034	Wrench - shock absorber stem aligning nut.	
A. 66008	Installer - wheel hub caps.	
A. 66016	Installer and remover - bushes on knuckle pillar.	
A. 66038	Fixture - swinging arm checks, assembly and disassembly.	
A. 66039	Installer and remover - front suspension leaf spring « estendblocks ».	
A. 66041	Installer - front wheel inner bearing inner ring and front wheel inner and outer bearing outer rings.	
A. 66042	Installer and remover - « estendblock » in knuckle pillar.	
A. 66044	Installer - bushes on swinging arms.	
A. 66051/1/2	Fixture - leaf spring setting during front end geometry checks.	
A. 66052	Fixture (set) - rear springs compression and rear wheels holding in vertical position during front and rear end geometry checks.	
A. 66061	Fixture - leaf spring flexing to static load setting.	
A. 74003	Spanner wrench (to be used with A. 66051/1/2 and A. 66052).	
Arr. 2072	Cross beam - car front end lifting with hydraulic jack Arr. 2027.	
C. 692	Gauge - wheel toe-in checks.	
C. 694	Fixture - wheel camber and caster checks.	
C. 1003	Fixture - knuckle pillar alignment checks.	
U. 0360/25 B	Reamer - knuckle pillar bushes.	

NOTE ON SELF-LOCKING NUTS

When the threads, on which self-locking nuts of the nylon ring insert type must be screwed, are in good condition (free of burrs, rust, indents) or when they are not cross milled, the self-locking nuts may be screwed on and off more than once until practicable.

However, it is advisable to check the unscrewing torque and replace the nuts when said torque falls below specified limits.

On the contrary, should the above mentioned threads be cross milled, or even show burrs, rust or indents, nuts must be used once only since nylon ring is liable to be damaged with consequent loss of self-locking ability.

If when servicing is in progress it becomes necessary to screw and unscrew nuts on threads provided with milled slit or in the above mentioned conditions, it is recommended to use dummy nuts which should be replaced by the self-locking nuts proper, as soon as servicing terminates.

The self-locking nuts of the castellated type may be screwed and unscrewed indefinitely since, owing to their special design, their locking ability is never impaired.

FRONT SUSPENSION AND WHEELS
MULTIPLA

The independent-wheel front suspension consists of swinging arms connected to steering knuckle by rubber bush-mounted spiders and to body by supports mounted on arms through pins and rubber bushes.

Swinging arm oscillations are controlled by coil springs and hydraulic shock absorbers.

Rubber pad-mounted stabilizer bar anchored on lower swinging arms and body floor bottom.

Removal and Installation.

To remove right and left front assemblies, proceed as follows.

Raise car front end and place on stands located under side jack brackets.

Remove caps and wheels.

Inside car, under instrument panel, remove spare wheel to gain access to brake fluid reservoir.

Remove reservoir filler cap and introduce a suitably sized wooden peg to blank reservoir fluid outlet.

Disconnect steering rod heads at steering knuckle arms: remove split pin, back out the nut, apply puller **A. 46022** and free the knuckle arm head stem.

Disconnect stabilizer bar at lower swinging arms and body floor. Disconnect: the two brake fluid hoses at connections for lines from master cylinder and the shock absorber mounting at lower swinging arms.

Inside car, roll over the front floor mats to uncover the access opening of shock absorber upper mountings: insert special wrench **A. 56021** or **A. 57035** (respectively for early type and late type), and back out the mounting nuts.

Under car, pull down shock absorber complete with lower mounting; if required, the two parts may be separated by unscrewing the self-locking nut and the screw and by removing the spacer and the two lateral rubber bushes.

In place of the shock absorber, fit fixture **A. 66003** and, through the opening in front floor, screw in the mounting nut and two washers; turn lower handle and compress the coil spring.

Straighten out the plates and remove the two screws securing lower swinging arm supports to body floor.

Adjustment plates are inserted between the two swinging arm lower supports and body floor: record the number of these plates in both front and rear supports.

Fig. 287 - Bottom view of front suspension.

1. Steering knuckle. - 2. Rubber bumper. - 3. Coil spring. - 4. Steering rods. - 5. Shock absorber. - 6. Upper swinging arm. - 7. Lower swinging arm. - 8. Stabilizer bar.

FRONT SUSPENSION AND WHEELS

Back out the two screws and the two nuts securing the upper support to body. This permits the removal of the suspension on the side one has worked and of fixture **A. 66003**, which must then be used for removal of suspension on the other side.

Once fixture **A. 66003** has been taken off, the coil spring and the two arm rubber rings may be removed.

For re-installation, reverse the removal operations outlined above, starting off by compressing the coil spring between the two arms while suspension is on floor.

The wheel alignment adjustment plates must be fitted in the same number as recorded during the removal operations, excepting possible corrections which might prove necessary after installation when final checks are carried out using gauge **C. 694**, as described on page 171.

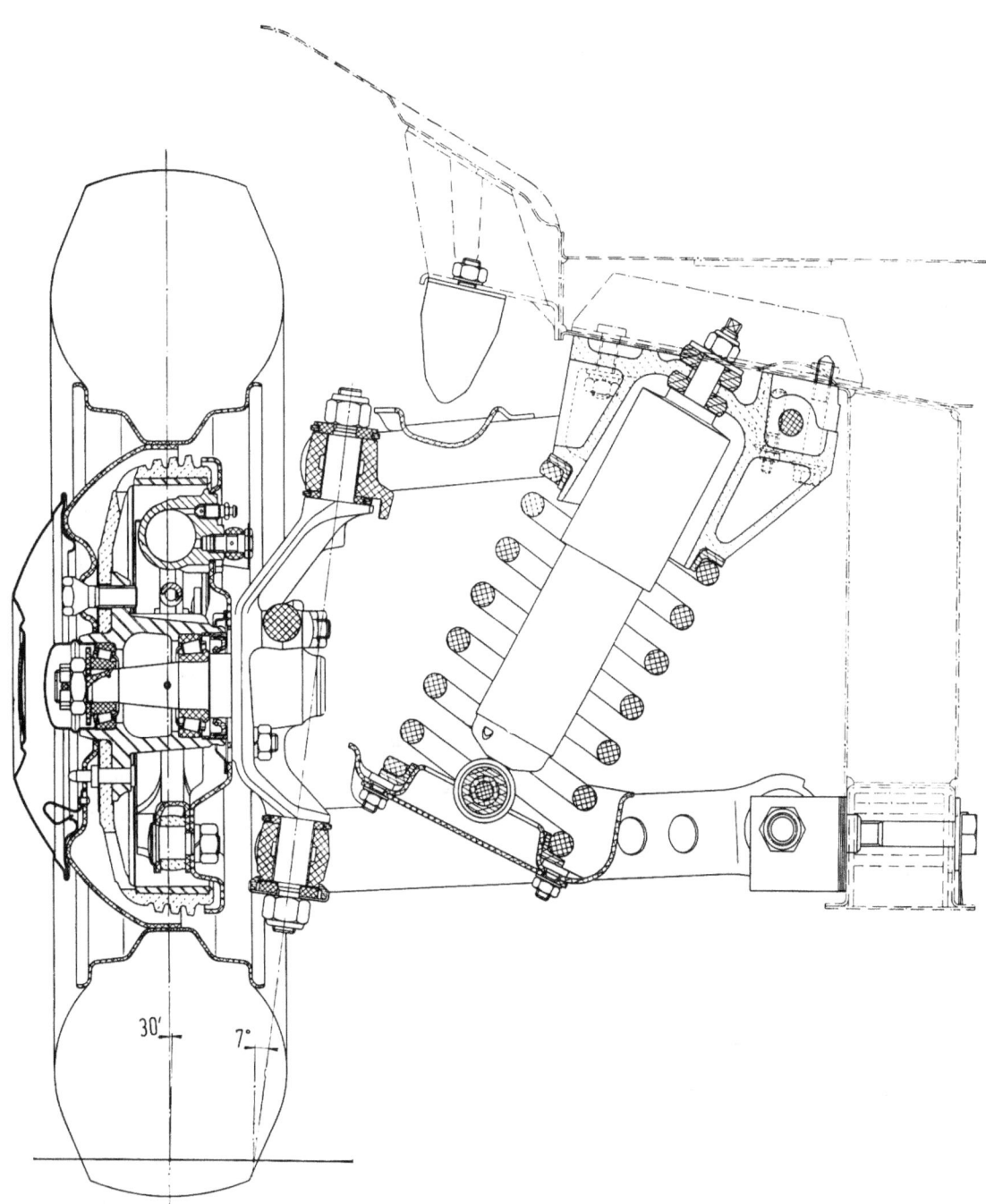

Fig. 288 - Section through front left suspension and wheel assembly.
Camber angle: 0° 30' ±20'. Steering knukcle inclination angle is 7° and caster angle 6° ±30'.

Disassembly.

Secure the left (or right) suspension assembly on rotating stand **A. 66029** (fig. 290).

Disconnect hose at wheel cylinder and remove hub caps using ram puller **A. 46014**.

Remove split pin, nut and washer, and then pull out the drum/hub assembly complete with outer roller bearing, inner roller bearing, spacer and seal gasket.

Back out the four nuts and remove the complete brake housing flange from steering knuckle.

Loosen out the upper swinging arm-to-steering knuckle pillar nut; slide off both rings; raise the swinging arm to disengage the pillar, then slide off the shim and snap ring.

Turn over the suspension stand and repeat the same steps as above outlined, thus disengaging the knuckle pillar also from lower swinging arm.

Disconnect the upper and lower swinging arms from rotating stand **A. 66029**.

To disassemble swinging arms, use fixture **A. 66023**.

UPPER AND LOWER SWINGING ARMS

Description, Disassembly and Service.

The upper and lower swinging arms allow the movement of knuckles and hence of the wheel assemblies on the vertical plane only.

The lower swinging arms are longer than the upper ones to allow for the variations of wheel camber during oscillations.

This way, the front wheel track variations ascribable to swinging arm oscillations are compensated.

Both the lower and the upper swinging arms are connected to their respective articulation pins and spiders by self-tapping bushes.

These bushes are threaded innerly throughout their length, so that they may be scewed on the threaded ends of pins or spiders, while, on their outer surface, the first portion is plain and the second threaded.

During the assembly of pins and spiders on swinging arms, this particular design initially per-

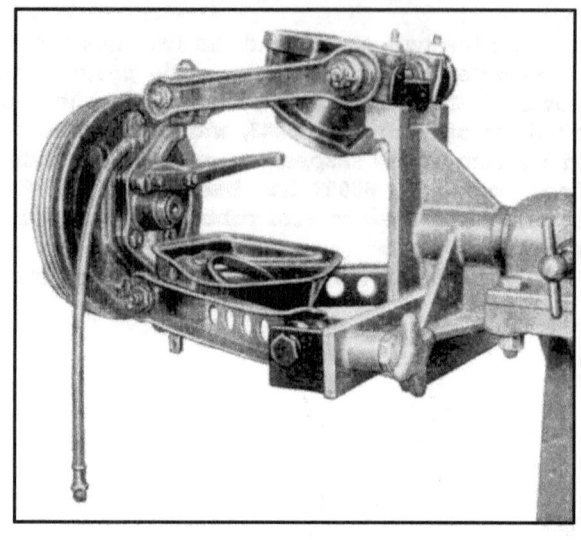

Fig. 289 - Front right suspension assembly on rotating stand A. 66029.

Fig. 290.

Front right suspension assembly on rotating stand A. 66029.

1-2. Studs and nuts, upper mounting of suspension assembly on stand. - 3. Knob, lower mounting. - 4. T-handle, support locking and unlocking.

FRONT SUSPENSION AND WHEELS

mits proper coupling of bush inner thread with pin thread and, subsequently, screwing of bush into the hole provided in the swinging arm.

The bush outer thread is of the self-tapping type inasmuch as, when screwed into the swinging arm, it must tap the hole.

Clearances originating from wear during operation are thus effectively minimized making possible the elimination of eventual undesirable clearances by replacing the self-tapping bushes, which are also supplied in the following outer diameter oversizes:

0.0098" and 0.0197" (0,25 and 0,50 mm).

Therefore, if during overhauls an insufficient grip of the new bush in the swinging arm is noticed, the bush must be replaced by an oversized one. When even the last oversize has been used, the swinging arm must be replaced.

If an excessive clearance is found between upper and lower swinging arms and steering knuckle, replace the spider inner bushes.

After fitting new bushes in spiders, ream their inner diameter to specified dimension using reamer **U. 0361**.

To remove and install spider bushes use tool **A. 66015**.

During overhauls, inspect swinging arms for distortions. This may be easily checked because, if deformed, arms will no longer fit on fixture A. 66023 (figs. 293 and 294). If deformations are slight, remedy by straightening; otherwise, replace the swinging arm.

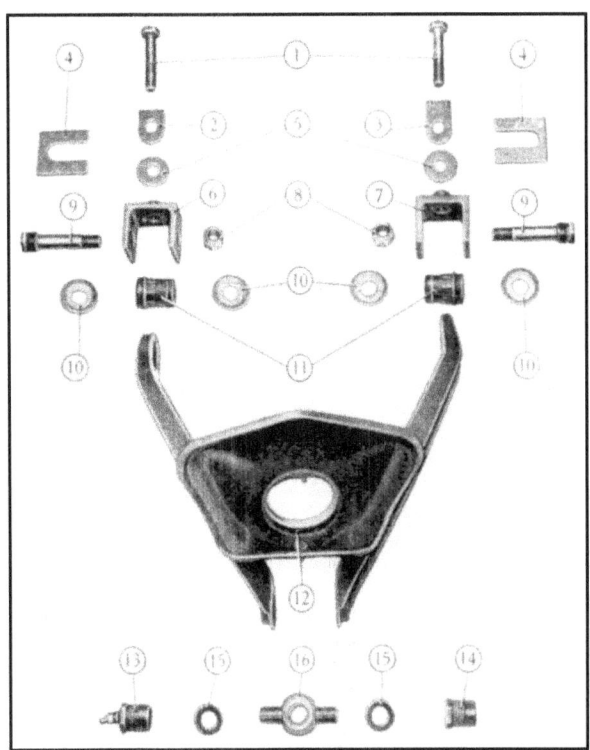

Fig. 291 - Lower swinging arm and attaching parts.

1. Screws, supports to body. - 2. Plate for front screw. - 3. Plate for rear screw. - 4. Shims. - 5. Plain washers. - 6-7. Supports for arm attachment to body. - 8. Self-locking nuts, arm pins to supports. - 9. Pins, arm to supports. - 10. Cups for rubber bushes. - 11. Rubber bushes. - 12. Lower swinging arm. - 13. Front self-tapping bush with lubricator. - 14. Rear self-tapping bush. - 15. Rubber rings for spider. - 16. Spider, with bushing, swinging arm to steering knuckle.

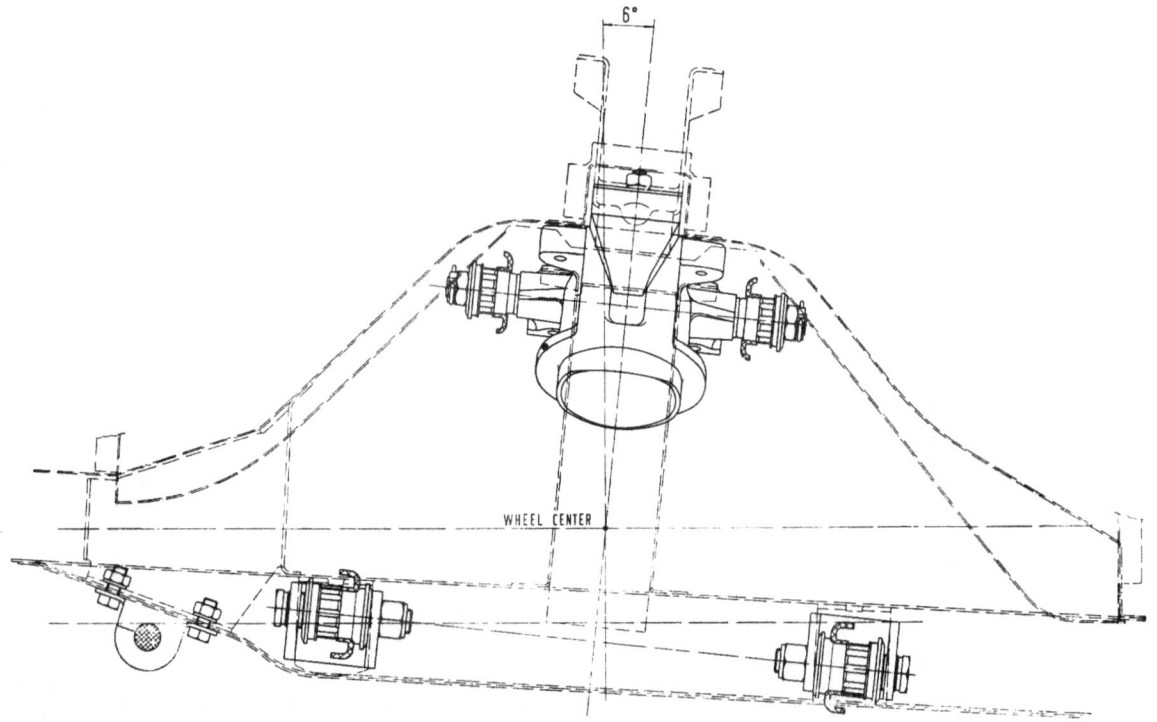

Fig. 292 - Detail of longitudinal section through the front suspension and steering knuckle caster angle.

Fig. 293 - Tightening the pin-to-upper swinging arm nuts.

1. Fixture A. 66023. - 2. Swinging arm. - 3. Support. - 4. Pin for spider location. - 5-6. Stud and nut, support to fixture A. 66023. - 7. Nut, pin to swinging arm. - 8. Wrench A. 8035 for nut tightening.

Check the condition of «Flanblock» rubber bushes press-fitted in swinging arms for connection to body: bush inner surface must not show any sign of seizure and the pin-to-bush clearance must be .0157" (0,40 mm) (fit clearance is .0002" to .0098" – 0,005 to 0,250 mm) for both upper and lower swinging arms.

Fig. 294 - Installing the self-tapping bushes on upper swinging arm and on spider.

The swinging arm is mounted on tool A. 66023.

1. Spider, arm to steering knuckle. - 2. Rubber ring for spider. - 3. Self-tapping bush for spider. - 4. Wrench A. 56015 for bush tightening.

Make sure bush rubber is not torn or excessively hardened.

Replace bushes, if required.

The removal of rubber bushes from swinging arms is done using all purpose puller A. 40005/V.

Installation of Upper and Lower Swinging Arms.

To fit the upper swinging arm, proceed as follows:

Mount rubber bushes into swinging arm holes using installer A. 66044.

On fixture A. 66023 install the support for attachment to body.

On spider threaded ends fit the two washers and seat the spider in swinging arm.

Install swinging arm on fixture A. 66023 and center the spider using the location pin (4, fig. 293).

Interpose the two washers, one on each side, between the support and arm inner shoulder contacts and insert the pin.

Fit the two pin centering keys and secure by nuts and washers.

Mount rubber bush cups on pin, one on each side, and screw in nuts without tightening.

Slightly tighten the self-tapping bushes on the pin and on the spider until a good initial mating of threads is obtained.

Then, tighten fully the self-tapping bushes with wrench A. 56015 (fig. 294) so that the bushes will thread their way into the swinging arms.

The tightening of these bushes will be over when their hexagonal head will bottom against swinging arm outer surface.

Next, fully tighten the rear pin nuts and fit the split pins.

To fit the lower swinging arm, proceed as follows:

Seat the spider and rings in swinging arm, proceeding as described for the upper arm.

NOTE - The special design of fixture A. 66023 permits:

— the tightening of upper swinging arm pin nuts (A, figs. 299-300), when angle δ formed by planes «b» and «c» equals approximately 16° (fig. 299);

— the tightening of lower swinging arm pin nuts (D, fig. 300), when angle γ formed by plane «e» with the axes of screws F and G equals approximately 3° (fig. 299).

This arrangement is essential because it prevents swinging arms from being submitted to abnormal torsional stresses during arm oscillations.

FRONT SUSPENSION AND WHEELS

Fit the arm on fixture **A. 66023** and center the spider.

To tighten the bushes, proceed as already described for the upper arm with the exception that wrench **A. 56001** must be used.

Mount rubber bushes in seats for attachment of arm supports on body and remove swinging arm from fixture.

On arm, fit the two supports with relevant pins and cups and tighten the self-locking nuts.

STEERING KNUCKLE PILLAR

Disassembly and reassembly are described on page 164 and opposite column, respectively.

Inspection.

Check carefully all components as directed below.

The two inner thrust rings and the packing ring must be sound, burless and perfectly elastic.

Check the condition of the lower cup and of the upper and lower rings: replace if defective.

Upper and lower washers must not be worn, otherwise they must be replaced with others of suitable thickness.

Washers are supplied in the following thicknesses:

.155" - .157" - .159" - .161"
(3,95 - 4,00 - 4,05 - 4,10 mm).

Inspect carefully the steering knuckle pillar, making sure that it is neither cracked nor deformed.

Outer and inner roller bearings must have both races and rollers in perfect condition.

Operation must be free from roughness.

Bearing oil seal must be elastic and undamaged. Spacer must not be deformed.

Replace any defective parts.

ASSEMBLING FRONT SUSPENSION

This operation is carried out on stand **A. 66029** proceeding as described below.

To simplify the disassembly and assembly operations the stand may be set in the most suitable position; as shown in figs. 289 and 295 the suspension assembly is installed on the stand in two different positions varying by 180°.

Procedure.

Secure the lower swinging arm by the fixture knobs.

Install upper swinging arm and mounting assembly on the two studs of the fixture and secure by two nuts.

On the lower and upper pins of steering knuckle install the thrust ring and the washers and then insert the pins in the spiders of the upper and lower swinging arms.

Install the upper thrust and packing rings and secure with a dummy nut (see note on next page); fit the lower ring and cup and secure with a dummy nut.

Check that steering knuckle swings freely but without appreciable play.

If the movement is too free or excessively stiff change the washers with others of suitable thickness.

After obtaining the correct adjustment, replace the dummy nuts with new self-locking nuts and tighten to 86.8 ft.lbs (12 kgm).

Fig. 295 - Front right suspension assembly mounted upside down on rotating stand **A. 66029**.

Install brake housing flange, complete with shoes and wheel cylinder, on steering knuckle and secure by bolts and nuts. Install steering knuckle arm.

The upper nuts are provided with a single lockplate and must be tightened to 32.5 - 39.8 ft.lbs (4,5 - 5,5 kgm). The lower nuts are secured by a lockwasher and tightening torque in still the same.

In the hub with drum install: the outer and inner roller bearing outer rings using tool **A. 66000**, the inner roller bearing inner ring, the spacer and the seal.

Pack the hub with FIAT MR grease and then insert the hub with drum on the steering knuckle.

Install outer roller bearing inner ring, the washer and then the nut which must be tightened to 21.7 ft.lbs (3 kgm). Back out the nut one cotter pin slot (about 60°) and secure with cotter pin.

Pack hub cap with FIAT MR grease and install cap with installer **A. 66008**.

Connect brake fluid hose to wheel cylinder.

Adjust brake shoe-to-drum clearance as described further on under « BRAKES ».

Remove the suspension assembly from the stand and proceed in the same way for the other.

COIL SPRING

Description, Inspection and Repair.

Front suspension coil springs are selected and divided in two classes:

— Class A: these springs are identified by a stripe of yellow paint on central coils and under a 970 lbs (440 kg) load their give-in is greater than 7.34" (186,5 mm).

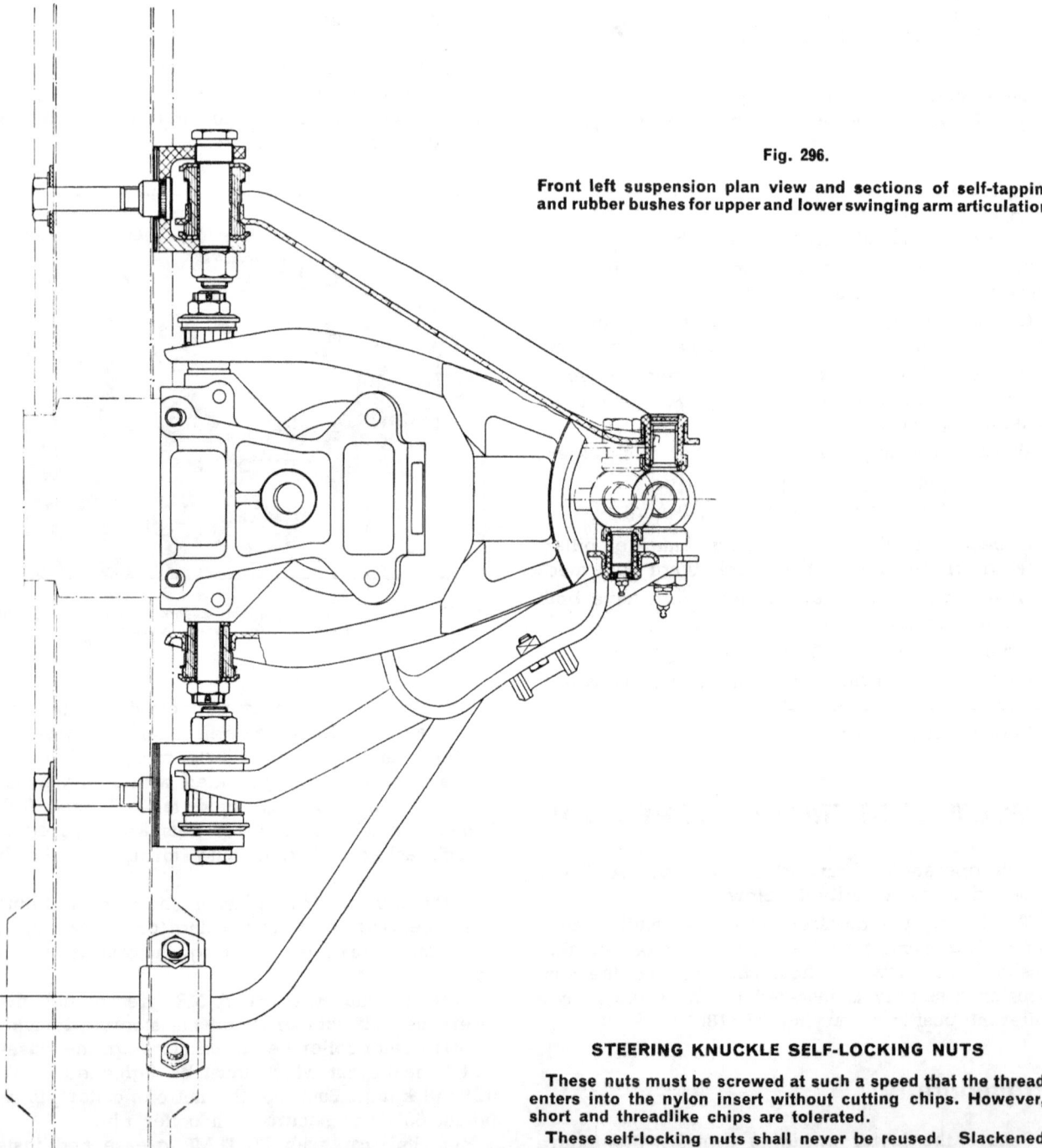

Fig. 296.
Front left suspension plan view and sections of self-tapping and rubber bushes for upper and lower swinging arm articulation.

STEERING KNUCKLE SELF-LOCKING NUTS

These nuts must be screwed at such a speed that the thread enters into the nylon insert without cutting chips. However, short and threadlike chips are tolerated.

These self-locking nuts shall never be reused. Slackened nuts must be replaced with new nuts. During the preliminary adjustment and setup operations use dummy nuts.

FRONT SUSPENSION AND WHEELS

— Class B: these springs are identified by a slight grinding on their upper portion and by a stripe of green paint on central coils. Under a 970 lbs (440 kg) load these springs have a give-in up to and not greater than 7.34" (186,5 mm).

During suspension overhaul check that both springs are of the same class. Inspect springs for cracks, weakening and other damages, replacing if necessary.

Inspect also the spring cups and replace if damaged.

COIL SPRING DATA

Wire diameter	.53 ± .0020 in. (13,5 ± 0,05 mm)
Inner diameter	3.54 ± .035 in. (90 ± 0,9 mm)
Total number of coils	7 1/2
Active coils	6
Direction of helix	clockwise
Free height	abt. 10.68 in. (271,5 mm)
Height under load of 970 ± 48.5 lbs (440 ± 22 kg)	7.34 in. (186,5 mm)
Flexibility	.35 ± .011 in/100 lbs (19,3 ± 0,6 mm/100 kg)

FRONT STABILIZER BAR

Description, Inspection and Repair.

The purpose of the front stabilizer bar is that of ensuring a greater stability of the car, especially on turns.

No particular overhaul operations are necessary for the bar, whose only parts subject to wear are the pads and the elastic bushes through which the bar is connected to the body and to the lower swinging arms.

During overhaul of front suspension inspect the bushes for wear and replace if necessary.

Check also that the bar has not undergone distortions, otherwise replace the bar as an assembly.

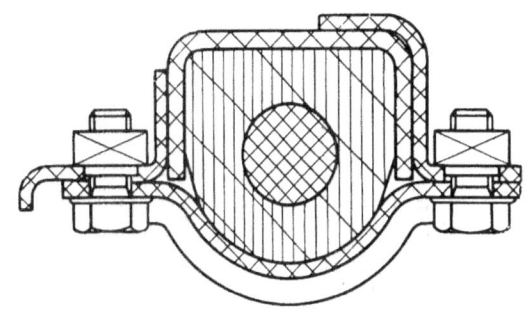

Fig. 297 - Section of stabilizer bar through the support with rubber bush connecting the lower swinging arm.

FRONT SUSPENSION TIGHTENING REFERENCE
MULTIPLA

ITEM	DRWG. OR STD. PART No.	THREAD	MATERIAL	TIGHTENING TORQUE
Steering knuckle-to-swinging arms self-locking nut	1/25748/11	14 MB (x1,5)	R 50 Cdt (Steer.knuck. 38NCD4 Bon)	86.8 ft.lbs (12.000 kgmm)
Brake housing flange and knuckle arm to steering knuckle bolt nut	1/21647/11	10 x 1,25 M	R 50 Cdt (Screws R 50 and R 80)	32.5 to 39.8 ft.lbs (4.500 to 5.500 kgmm)
Brake housing flange to steering knuckle bolt nut	1/21647/11	10 x 1,25 M	R 50 Cdt (Bolt R 50)	32.5 to 39.8 ft.lbs (4.500 to 5.500 kgmm)
Front wheel bearing retainment nut on steering knuckle	1/07246/11	18 MB (x1,5)	R 50 Cdt (Steer.knuck. 38 CD4 Bon)	21.7 ft.lbs (3.000 kgmm) (see page 167)

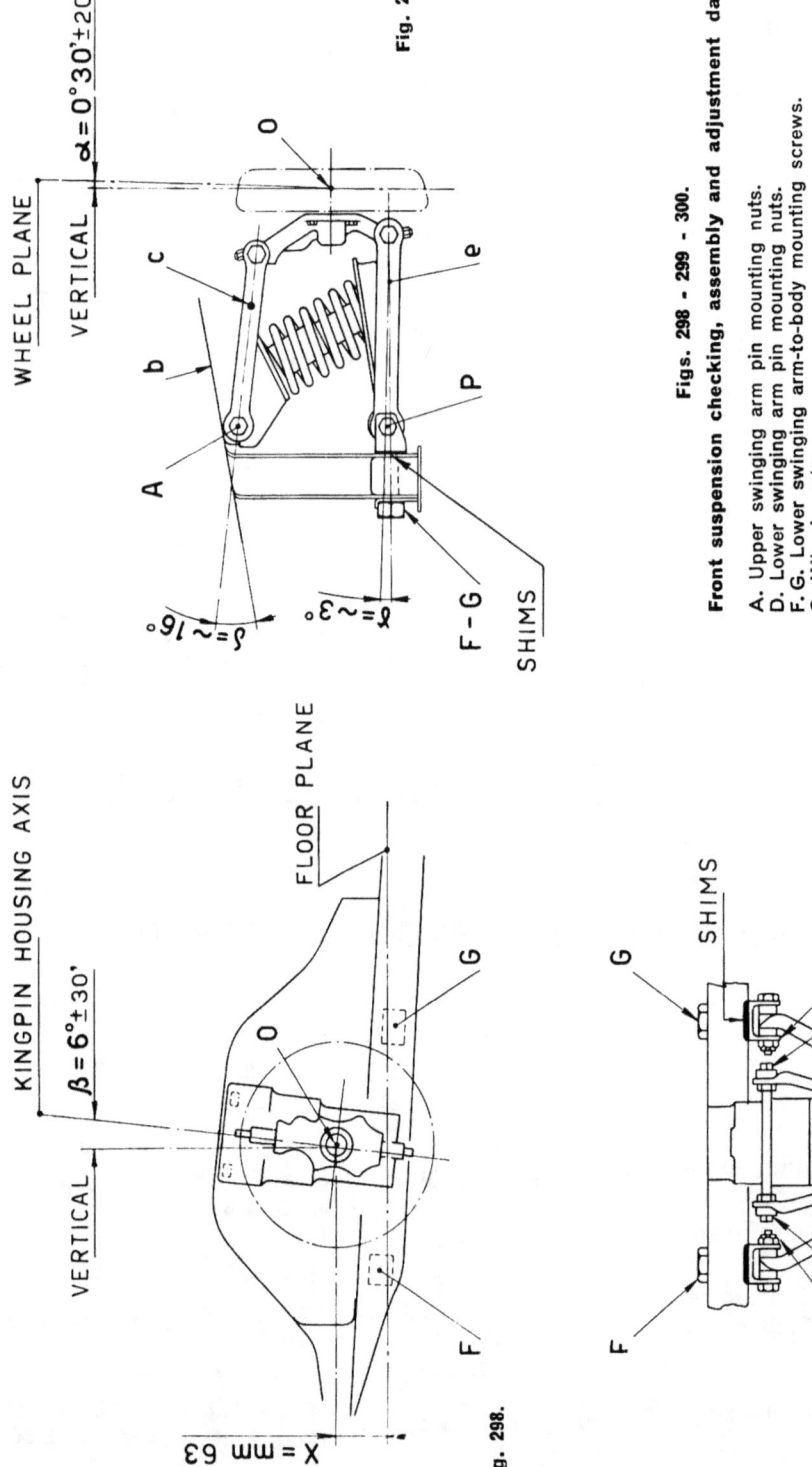

Figs. 298 - 299 - 300.
Front suspension checking, assembly and adjustment data.

A. Upper swinging arm pin mounting nuts.
D. Lower swinging arm pin mounting nuts.
F. G. Lower swinging arm-to-body mounting screws.
O. Wheel center.
P. Lower swinging arm pin axis.
b and c. Planes forming angle δ.
e. Lower swinging arm plane forming angle γ with axes of screws F and G.

NOTE – Nuts A should be tightened home when angle δ is about 16°.
Nuts D should be tightened home when angle γ is about 3°.

FRONT SUSPENSION AND WHEELS

CHECKING AND ADJUSTING FRONT WHEEL CAMBER AND CASTER

Front end geometry angles, with vehicle fully laden (6 persons plus fuel, oil, water) are:

— wheel camber: 0° 30′ ± 20′;
— caster: 6° ± 30′.

For toe-in data, see page 206.

Camber angles (α, fig. 299) and caster angles (β, fig. 298) are adjusted by interposing shims (figs. 299-300) on screws (F and G) between lower swinging arm supports and body bottom.

As already mentioned for «Sedan», the above angles are checked using gauge **C. 694** as described on page 156.

Preliminary inspections of the different components that might influence the geometry checks are the same as given for the «Sedan» on page 157, excepting tire pressures which for the Multipla are:

— front 24.2 p.s.i. - 1,70 kg/cm²;
— rear 28.5 p.s.i. - 2,00 kg/cm².

For Camber and Caster checks, follow the same instructions as outlined on page 158 for «Sedan» and remember that:

— to increase angle α (fig. 299): reduce the number of shims on both screws F and G (fig. 300); to reduce the angle, increase the shims;

— to increase angle β (fig. 298) shift a number of shims from screw F to screw G; to reduce the angle, shift shims from G to F.

IMPORTANT - Under fully laden conditions:

— the distance between axes of pins (P, fig. 299) and ground (measured at front end of vehicle) must be approximately 8.26″ (210 mm);

— the distance between engine sump bulge and ground must be approximately 7.20″ (183 mm);

— the distance (X, fig. 298) between wheel center (O, fig 298) and car floor must be 2.48″ (63 mm).

FRONT SUSPENSION SPECIFICATIONS AND DATA
MULTIPLA

Type	Independent-wheel, with shock absorbers and coil springs	
Stabilizer bar	Transversal, installed on rubber bushes	
Camber	0° 30′ ± 20′	Values to be checked with fully laden car (6 passengers + replenishments)
Caster	6° ± 30′	
Kingpin angle	7°	
Toe-in	0″ ± .039″ (0 ± 1 mm)	
Front track (on ground)	48.4″ (1230 mm)	
Wheelbase	78.7″ (2000 mm)	

Shock absorbers
    Type
    Diameter
    Fluid
    Capacity
	2
	Hydraulic, telescopic, double acting
	1.26″ (32 mm)
	FIAT S. A. I. oil
	165 cc (0,150 kg)	

FRONT SUSPENSION AND WHEEL SERVICE EQUIPMENT
MULTIPLA

Front suspension servicing must be carried out on rotating stand A. 66029.

A.	6469	Puller - wheel hubs.
A.	6511	Puller - wheel bearing outer rings.
A.	40005/V	Puller - swinging arm rubber bushes and wheel hubs.
A.	46014	Puller - wheel hub caps.
A.	46022	Puller - steering rod head pins.
A.	56001	Wrench - lower swinging arm spider self-tapping bush installation.
A.	56015	Wrench - upper swinging arm spider self-tapping bush installation.
A.	56021	Wrench - shock absorber removal and installation (early type).
A.	56024	Wrench - front shock absorber plug.
A.	57035	Wrench - shock absorber removal and installation (late type).
A.	66000	Installer - wheel outer and inner roller bearing outer rings.
A.	66003	Fixture - coil spring compression.
A.	66008	Installer - wheel hub caps.
A.	66015	Tool - spider bush remover and installer.
A.	66023	Fixture - installation and removal of swinging arm pins and spiders.
A.	66044	Installer - bushes on swinging arms.
C.	694	Gauge - wheel alignment checks.
U.	0361	Reamer - swinging arm spider bushes.

TROUBLE DIAGNOSIS AND CORRECTIONS
FRONT SUSPENSION AND WHEELS
(Sedan and Multipla)

Wheel Bounce.

POSSIBLE CAUSES	REMEDIES
1) Tire cracked.	1) Repair tire, if possible, or replace it by a new one.
2) Uneven tire pressure.	2) Check tire pressure and inflate correctly.
3) Unbalanced wheel rim or tires.	3) Proceed as recommended on page 234.
4) Weak coil spring.	4) Check against data on page 169 and replace spring if unserviceable.
5) Semi-elliptic spring mounting worn.	5) Replace mounting and upper rubber pad.
6) Inoperative shock absorber.	6) Check shock absorber on test equipment and overhaul it.
7) Wheel rim or tire misaligned.	7) Proceed as recommended on page 234.

FRONT SUSPENSION AND WHEELS

Excessive Tire Wear.

POSSIBLE CAUSES	REMEDIES
1) Failure to rotate tires.	1) For uniform tire wear, interchange tires crosswise every 3,000 miles (5.000 km).
2) Incorrect camber.	2) Check camber angle and adjust as recommended on pages 158 and 171.
3) Incorrect toe-in.	3) Check toe-in and adjust as recommended on page 206.
4) Improper tire inflation.	4) Proceed as directed on page 234.
5) Turning corners too fast.	5) Advise owner to negotiate curves at moderate speed to reduce tire wear.
6) Pick-ups too quick.	6) Advise gradual acceleration.
7) Sustained high-speed driving on gravel roads.	7) Advise moderate speed on roads of this kind.
8) Too much play at wheel bearings.	8) Adjust clearance and lubricate bearings as outlined on pages 155 and 167.
9) Wheel wobble.	9) Locate origin of failure as outlined under the following heading and proceed as required.
10) Stiffened suspension arms.	10) Disassemble suspension arms and replace damaged rubber bushings.
11) Brakes out of adjustment.	11) Set brake shoe-to-drum clearance as directed on page 222.

Wheel Wobble.

POSSIBLE CAUSES	REMEDIES
1) Uneven tire pressure.	1) Inflate to correct pressure.
2) Loose or worn wheel bearings.	2) Remove, inspect and replace bearings as required. Lubricate and reassemble as outlined on pages 155 and 167.
3) Inoperative shock absorbers.	3) Disassemble, overhaul and refill with FIAT S.A.I. fluid.
4) Loose steering knuckle or knuckle pillar.	4) Remove and replace: knuckle pillar bushings or control arm spider bushings, if worn; the kingpin and washers or shims as outlined on pages 150 - 151 - 152 - 153 and 167.
5) Incorrect front wheel alignment.	5) Check and adjust: caster, camber, and toe-in.
6) Control arm rubber bushings, or pillar and semi-elliptic spring «estendblocks», worn.	6) Check and replace bushings as directed in covering chapters.

Suspension Noise.

POSSIBLE CAUSES	REMEDIES
1) Lack of lubrication.	1) Lubricate: steering knuckle pillars, tie rods, control arm spider journals and wheel bearings, following lubrication diagrams in Section «Maintenance».
2) Noisy or inoperative shock absorbers.	2) Overhaul shock absorbers and refill with FIAT S.A.I. fluid as recommended on page 190.
3) Loose sway bar at lower control arm and body mountings.	3) Provided rubber bushings and cushions are not worn, tighten sway bar screws.
4) Dislodged coil spring.	4) Check: — upper and lower rubber seats for damage; — steering knuckle and upper control arm mounting nuts for a loose condition. After the origin of failure has been located and worn parts replaced, install spring in place and tighten nuts to prescribed torque.
5) Worn or loose wheel bearings.	5) Remove wheels and wheel hub drum and check bearing operation. Replace and lubricate as required and reassemble as outlined on pages 155 and 167.

Pull to One Side.

POSSIBLE CAUSES	REMEDIES
1) Low or uneven tire pressure.	1) Check tire pressure and inflate correctly.
2) Incorrect front wheel alignment.	2) Check and adjust: caster, camber and toe-in.
3) Suspension arms distorted.	3) Check suspension arms on test equipment and replace if they are distorted beyond repair.
4) Inoperative shock absorbers.	4) Disassemble, overhaul and refill with FIAT S.A.I. fluid.
5) Brake binding.	5) Service and adjust brakes as directed on page 222.

Section 6

REAR SUSPENSION AND WHEELS SHOCK ABSORBERS

	Page
DESCRIPTION	179
REMOVAL	179
SWINGING ARM	180
COIL SPRINGS	183
INSTALLATION	183
CHECKING AND ADJUSTING REAR WHEEL TOE-IN	187
SPECIFICATIONS AND DATA	188
TIGHTENING REFERENCE	189
SERVICE EQUIPMENT	189
HYDRAULIC SHOCK ABSORBERS	190

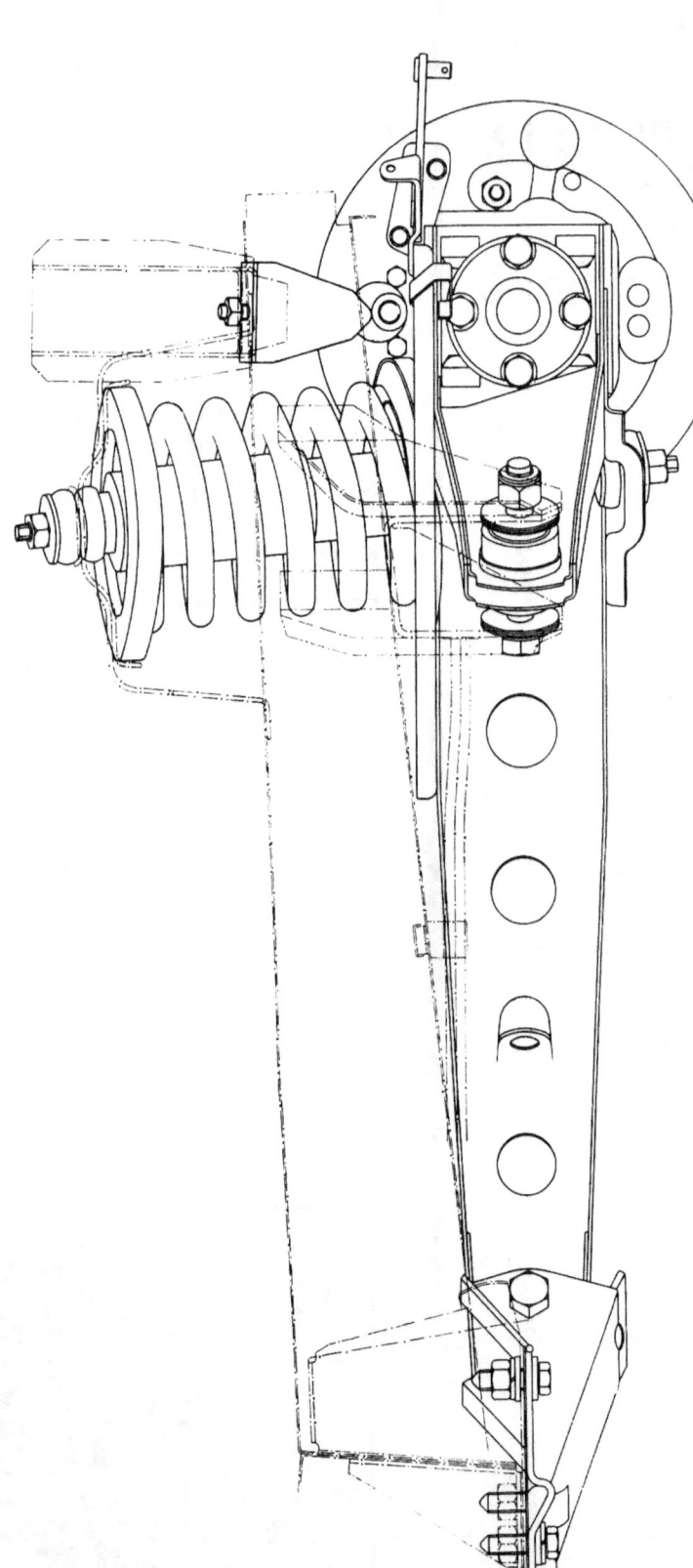

NOTE - Nuts securing swinging arm to front and rear supports must be tightened with wheel set vertically.
This will prevent « estendblocks » being stress-twisted during operation.
To set wheel plane vertical use fixture A. 66052.

Fig. 301 - Inner view of rear right suspension.

REAR SUSPENSION AND WHEELS

Description	page 179
Removal of Suspension Assembly	» 179
Swinging Arm	» 180
Disassembly, Inspection and Repair	» 180
Assembly	» 181
Preloading Wheel Bearings	» 181
Adjusting Swinging Arm	» 183
Coil Springs	» 183
Inspection	» 183
Installation of Rear Suspension	» 183
Checking and Adjusting Rear Wheel Toe-in	» 187
Specifications and Data	» 188
Tightening Reference	» 189
Service Equipment	» 189

Fig. 302 - Rear suspension assembly.

1. Parking brake control cable. - 2. Coil spring. - 3. Swinging arm internal mounting bracket. - 4. Swinging arm. - 5. Shock absorber lower mounting nut. - 6. Screws, swinging arm external mounting to body floor. - 7. Gearbox-differential unit mounting cross member. - 8. Swinging arm external support mounting self-locking nut. - 9. Oil boot. - 10. Differential shaft. - 11. Sleeve, coupling differential shaft to flexible joint. - 12. Flexible joint. - 13. Sleeve mounting screws.

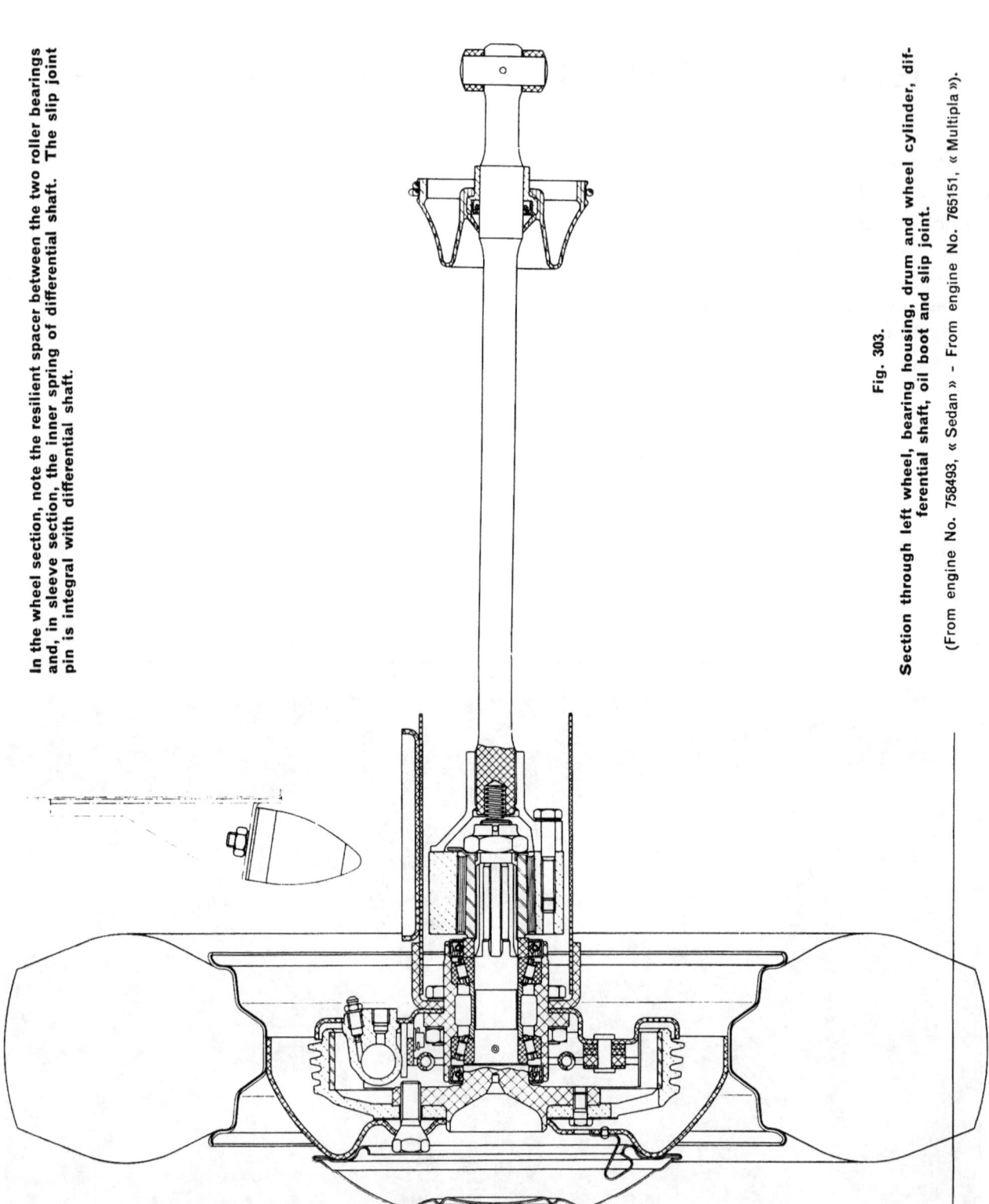

Fig. 303.

Section through left wheel, bearing housing, drum and wheel cylinder, differential shaft, oil boot and slip joint.

(From engine No. 758493, « Sedan » - From engine No. 765151, « Multipla »).

In the wheel section, note the resilient spacer between the two roller bearings and, in sleeve section, the inner spring of differential shaft. The slip joint pin is integral with differential shaft.

REAR SUSPENSION AND WHEELS

Description.

Rear wheels are independently sprung, with swinging arms, coil springs and telescopic, double acting, hydraulic shock absorbers.

Swinging arms are mounted on floor by « estendblocks ».

Coil springs are provided with rubber rings at both end mountings under body floor and on swinging arms.

Shock absorbers are of the same type as for front suspension; see page 190 for their operation and servicing.

At its vertex, the swinging arm carries the bearing housing - secured by screws and nuts - which also performs as a hub for wheel shaft (outer axle shaft).

Externally, wheel shaft carries the brake drum; at the inner end, it is keyed to splined flexible joint in which differential shaft (inner axle shaft) is inserted.

NOTE - « Sedan » and « Multipla » rear suspensions differ only in some swinging arm data and coil spring properties.

Removal of Rear Suspension Assembly.

Raise car on stands and take off wheel on side of suspension to be removed.

Support swinging arm by placing a jack underneath.

Inside car, remove floor lining behind rear seat and unscrew the shock absorber mounting nut on floor using wrench **A. 56020** (Sedan) or **A. 56021** (Multipla).

Fig. 304 - Detail of left rear suspension.

Unscrew the four mounting screws of sleeve coupling the flexible joint to differential shaft, pull back sleeve on to axle shaft, and take off inner spring.

Remove brake fluid reservoir cap, take out filtering screen, blank delivery hole as specified on page 225, and then disconnect brake line at connection on body floor.

With jack, lower the swinging arm, press in shock absorber by lowering the outer casing and pull out coil spring together with its two mounting rubber rings.

Back out the self-locking nut securing swinging arm to internal support welded on floor.

Disinsert mountig pin, and note the number and arrangement of « estenblock » side shims.

Next, remove the two screws and the screw nut securing swinging arm external support and take off swinging arm.

A rubber plate is interposed between support and body bottom.

Fig. 305.

Rear swinging arm and wheel shaft components.

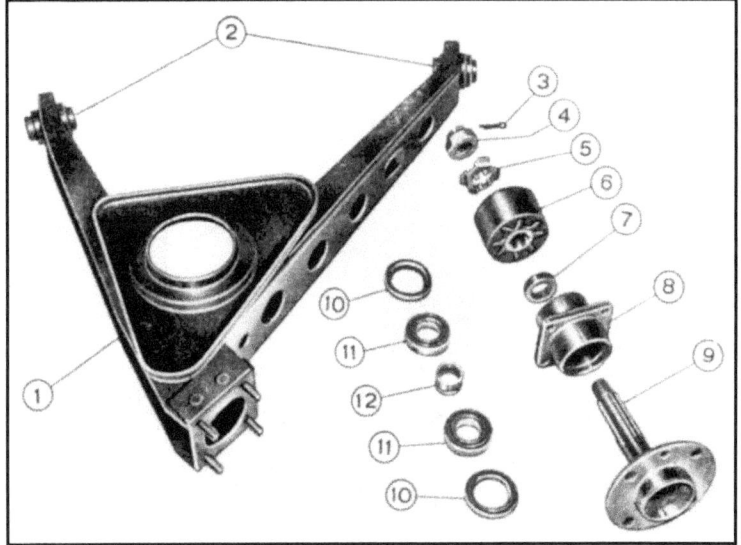

1. Swinging arm. - 2. « Estendblock », arm mounting on body floor. - 3. Cotter pin. - 4. Wheel shaft mounting nut. - 5. Lock plate. - 6. Flexible joint. - 7. Spacer, bearing housing-to-joint. - 8. Bearing housing. - 9. Wheel shaft. - 10. Bearing housing oil seals. - 11. Roller bearings. - 12. Resilient spacer.

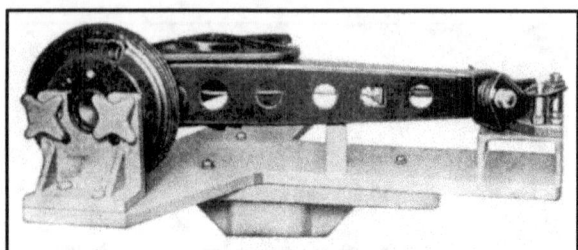

Fig. 306 - Swinging arm assembly, on adjustment fixture A. 66037.

SWINGING ARM

Disassembly, Inspection and Repair.

After disconnecting the shock absorber, install swinging arm on fixture A. 66037 (fig. 306).

If swinging arm has not been distorted, its installation on fixture should be easily carried out by proceeding as follows:

— Tighten the clamp screws (1, fig. 307) on wheel shaft.

— Couple swinging arm inner member to seat (2, fig. 307) of fixture alignment bracket.

— Fit swinging arm external support holes on pins (3) and stud (4) of fixture (fig. 307).

If somehow these three operations cannot be performed, the swinging arm needs straightening in the spots where it is distorted.

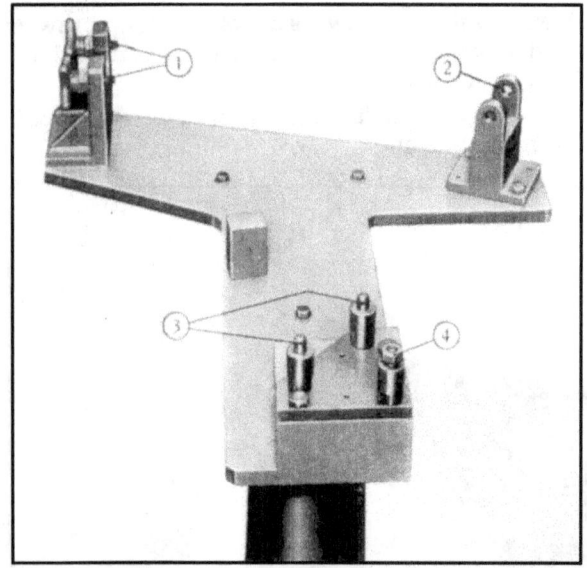

Fig. 307 - Fixture A. 66037, for swinging arm check and adjustment.

1. Clamp screws, securing wheel shaft on fixture. - 2. Alignment bracket, swinging arm member check. - 3. Swinging arm external support centering pins. - 4. Nut, to secure swinging arm external support on fixture stud.

Swinging arm components are disassembled as follows:

— Take off cotter pin and back out nut (4, fig. 305) fixing flexible joint (6) to wheel shaft; disinsert lock plate and joint.

— Pull out wheel shaft (9, fig. 305) and brake drum, using all-purpose puller A. 40005/1/9 or puller A. 6469, then the two oil seals (10), both outer and inner bearing inner rings, spacing ring (7) of flexible joint and resilient spacer (12, fig. 305).

— Remove the two bearing outer rings using remover A. 66034 (fig. 308).

Fig. 308 - Driving out inner and outer bearing outer rings using remover A. 66034.

If necessary, remove swinging arm external support, disconnect brake line at wheel cylinder, then the bearing housing and complete brake housing flange.

Check that:

a) « estendblocks » are a tight fit in their respective seats in swinging arm and arm mounting pins slide in freely without any excessive play: if « estendblocks » must be replaced, use tool A. 66045 which is suitable both for installation and removal;

b) inner and outer bearing outer rings have no play in their seats and roller cages are not broken or worn;

c) oil seals fit snugly on wheel shaft, bearing housing spacer and seats on bearing housing;

d) resilient spacer is not permanently distorted; whenever new bearings or bearing housings are fitted, always install a new spacer;

REAR SUSPENSION AND WHEELS

e) the mating surface of bearings on wheel shaft is perfectly smooth; shaft splines-to-flexible joint splines clearance must never exceed .0059" (0,15 mm);

f) flexible joint is not damaged to the point where metal-to-rubber bonding is compromised.

Assembly.

To assemble swinging arm, reverse the disassembly operations and use the following tools:

— **A. 66035** (fig. 309), to install roller bearing inner and outer rings;

— **A. 66045,** to install « estendblock » on swinging arms.

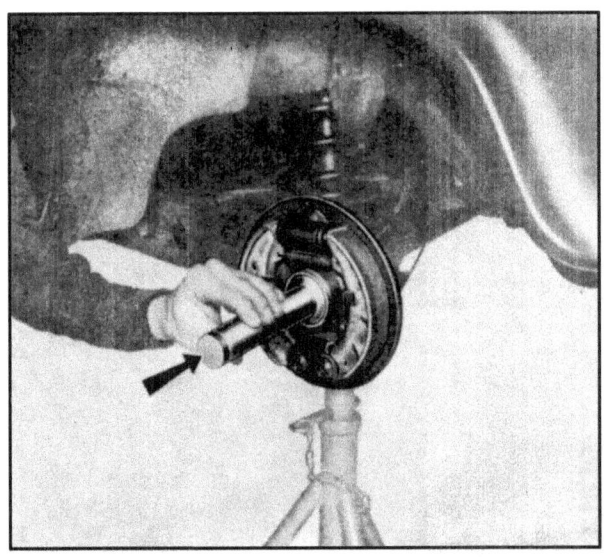

Fig. 309 - Installing inner and outer bearing inner and outer rings using tool A. 66035.

The bearing housing and brake housing mounting nuts must be tightened with a torque wrench to 43.4 ft.lbs (6000 kgmm).

During assembly, pack bearings with FIAT MR grease.

Preload the bearings and adjust the swinging arm as directed below.

Preloading Wheel Bearings.

To prevent either excessive play or rotational stiffness, the flexible joint-to-wheel shaft hub nut must be tightened gradually, so that bearing rotation torque will not exceed 0.36 ft.lbs (50 kgmm).

To check the rotation torque, proceed as follows.

Install support **A. 95697/3** on wheel drum. Insert the shank (2, fig. 311) of dynamometer **A. 95697** in support and grasp lever (3).

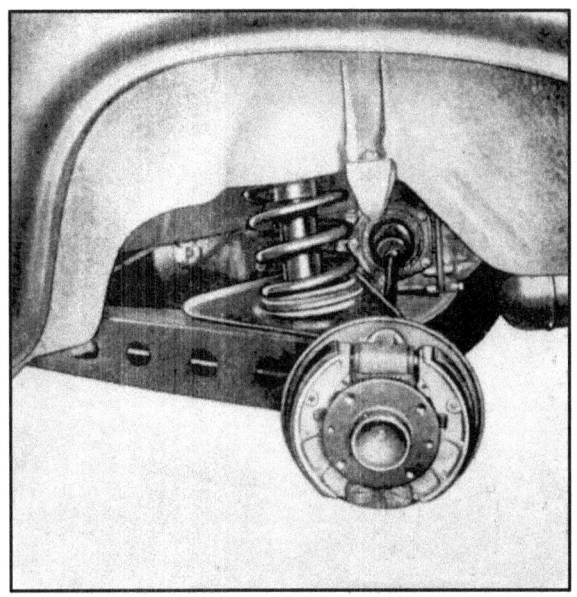

Fig. 310 - Left rear suspension, drum removed (early type brakes).

The presence of the resilient spacer between the two bearings ensures a constant adjustment and reduces the possibility of axial yields during operation.

Move the needle (4) to register .36 ft.lbs (5 kgcm) on dynamometer scale, as shown in fig. 311 and, using the lever (6), rotate the dynamometer and the wheel shaft some turns, clockwise.

During rotation, check that the needle (5) does not exceed the setting index (4).

If the rotation torque proves to be over .36 ft.lbs (5 kgcm), which indicates high bearing preload, remove the wheel shaft and replace the resilient spacer by a new one.

Next repeat the rotation torque test.

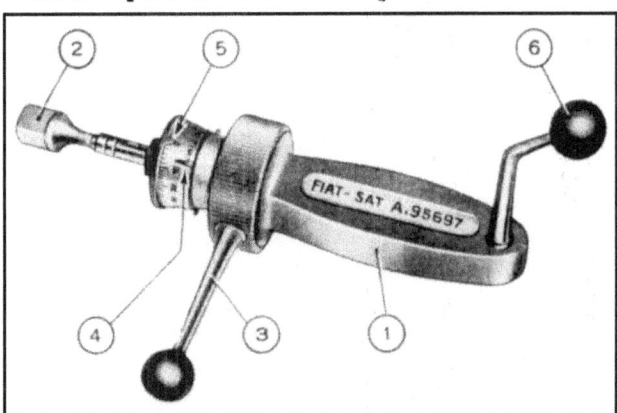

Fig. 311 - Bearing rotation torque dynamometer.

1. Dynamometer A. 95697. - 2. Dynamometer shank to insert in item A. 95697/3, fitted to wheel drum. - 3. Dynamometer grip lever. - 4. Rotation torque setting index. - 5. Adjustable needle. - 6. Dynamometer operating lever.

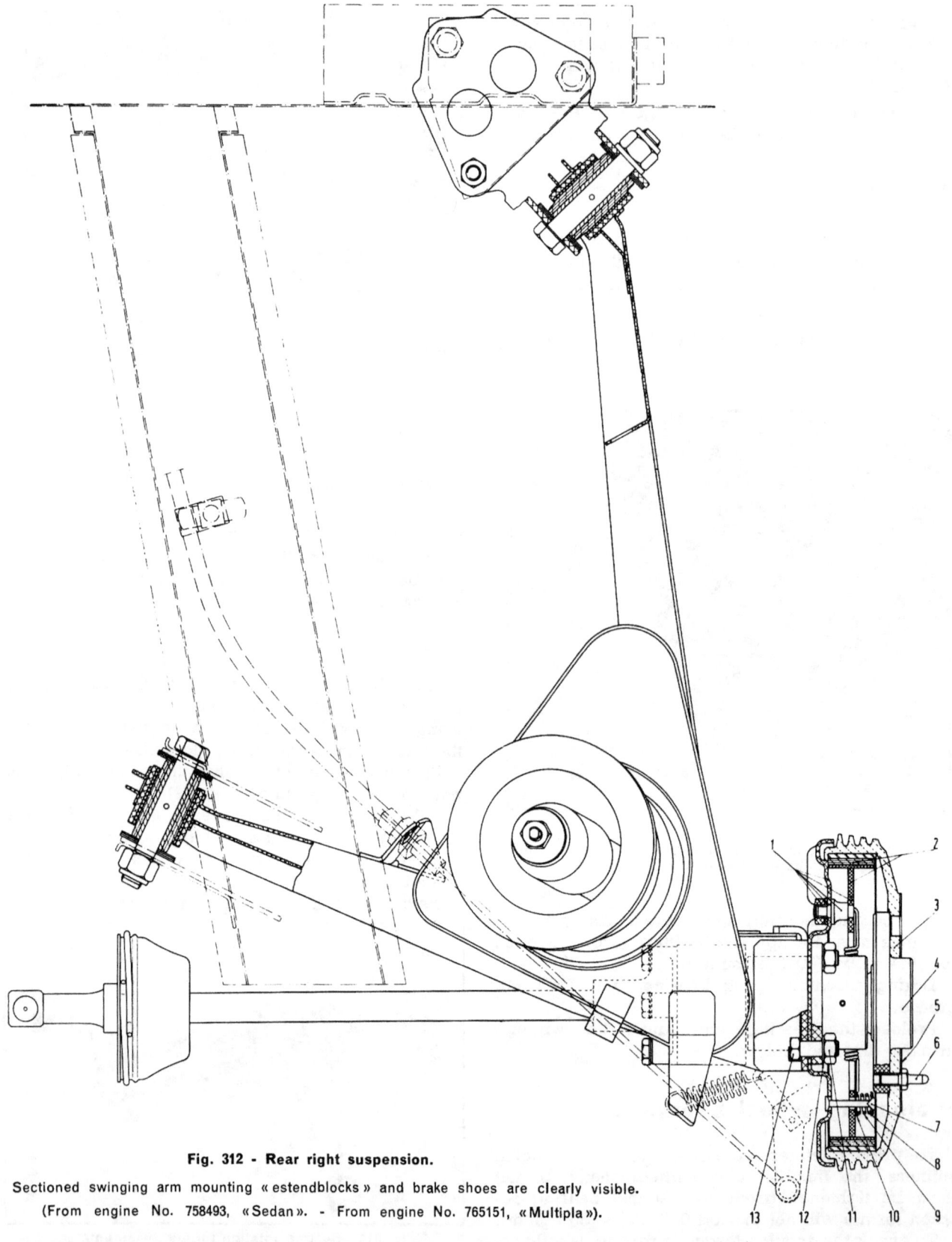

Fig. 312 - Rear right suspension.

Sectioned swinging arm mounting «estendblocks» and brake shoes are clearly visible.
(From engine No. 758493, «Sedan». - From engine No. 765151, «Multipla»).

1. Brake housing flange and shoe adjusting cam assembly. - 2. Brake shoe with lining. - 3. Drum. - 4. Wheel shaft. - 5. Plate. - 6. Wheel dowel. - 7. Shoe guide pin. - 8. Outer cup. - 9. Spring. - 10. Inner cup. - 11-12. Roller bearing support toothed washer and nut. - 13. Screw, welded to swinging arm.

REAR SUSPENSION AND WHEELS

Adjusting Swinging Arm.

Use fixture **A. 66037** (fig. 313).

In points A and B (fig. 313), between the «estendblock» and the swinging arm-to-body front mounting bracket, fit six shims (three on each side). For shim centering use alignment bar **A. 66033**; next, while removing the alignment bar, slip in the mounting pin and screw in the nut. After rear wheel geometry adjustments, this nut shall be tightened to 43.4 - 50.6 ft.lbs (6000 to 7000 kgmm).

In points C and D (fig. 313), insert the number of shims required to fill in the gap between the «estendblock» and the two fixture shoulders.

The number of shims, so determined - in both points C and D - must later be fitted between the «estendblock» and the shoulders on the swinging arm-to-body mounting bracket.

COIL SPRINGS

Coil springs mounted on the «Sedan» and «Multipla» models are of different design. Spring data are given below for each car.

«Sedan».

— Wire diameter .5433"±.0019" (13,8±0,05 mm)
— inner diameter . . 3.91"±.039" (99,4±1 mm)
— active coils . . . . 5 ½
— total No. of coils 7
— flexibility:
  .3802"±.0107"/100 lbs (21,3±0,6 mm/100 kg)
— direction of helix . . . . . . clockwise
— free height . . . . 9.63" (244,5 mm)
— height under a load of
  937±44 lbs (425±20 kg) . . 6" (154 mm)
— height under a load of
  1334±66 lbs (605±30 kg) . . 4.6" (116 mm)

«Multipla».

— Wire diameter .5866"±.0019" (14,9±0,05 mm)
— inner diameter . . 3.88"±.039" (98,6±1 mm)
— active coils 5
— total No. of coils . . . . 6 ½
— flexibility:
  2.553"±.0071"/100 lbs (14,3±0,4 mm/100 kg)
— direction of helix . . . . . . clockwise
— free height . . . . 8.85" (225 mm)
— height under a load of
  1094±55 lbs (496±25 kg) . . 6" (154 mm)
— height under a load of
  1712±86 lbs (776±39 kg) . . 4.49" (114 mm)

The «Multipla» coil springs are selected and subdivided into two classes:

a) Springs identified by a yellow stripe on central coils: «give-in» (or deflection) under a load of 1094 lbs (496 kg) of more than 6" (154 mm).

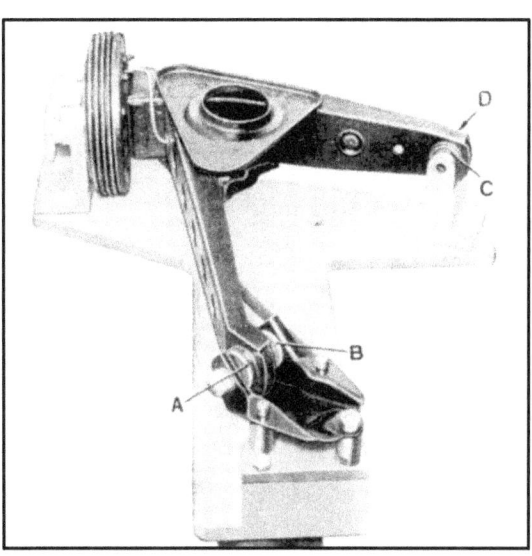

Fig. 313 - Adjusting rear suspension swinging arm on fixture A. 66037.

A and B. Swinging arm external support adjustment shims. - C and D. Swinging arm internal support adjustment shims.

b) Springs identified by a grinding mark on top coil and by a green stripe on central coils: «give-in» (or deflection) under a load of 1094 lbs (496 kg) of not more than 6" (154 mm).

Paired coil springs installed must be of the same class.

Inspection.

Inspect springs carefully to check on their efficiency.

In any cracks are found, replace springs.

Check condition of rings: replace if damaged.

INSTALLATION OF REAR SUSPENSION

To reinstall the rear suspension, operate as follows:

Raise suspension assembly by means of a jack and place assembly in alignment with attachments on body floor.

Screw in - without tightening - the two screws and the screw nut securing the swinging arm external bracket to body floor; screws and nut will have to be tightened to the specified final torque of 29 to 36.2 ft.lbs (4000 to 5000 kgmm) only after having adjusted rear wheel geometry.

Insert swinging arm inner member attachment end in the mounting bracket welded on body floor; place between the «estendblock» and bracket, the number of adjustment shims deter-

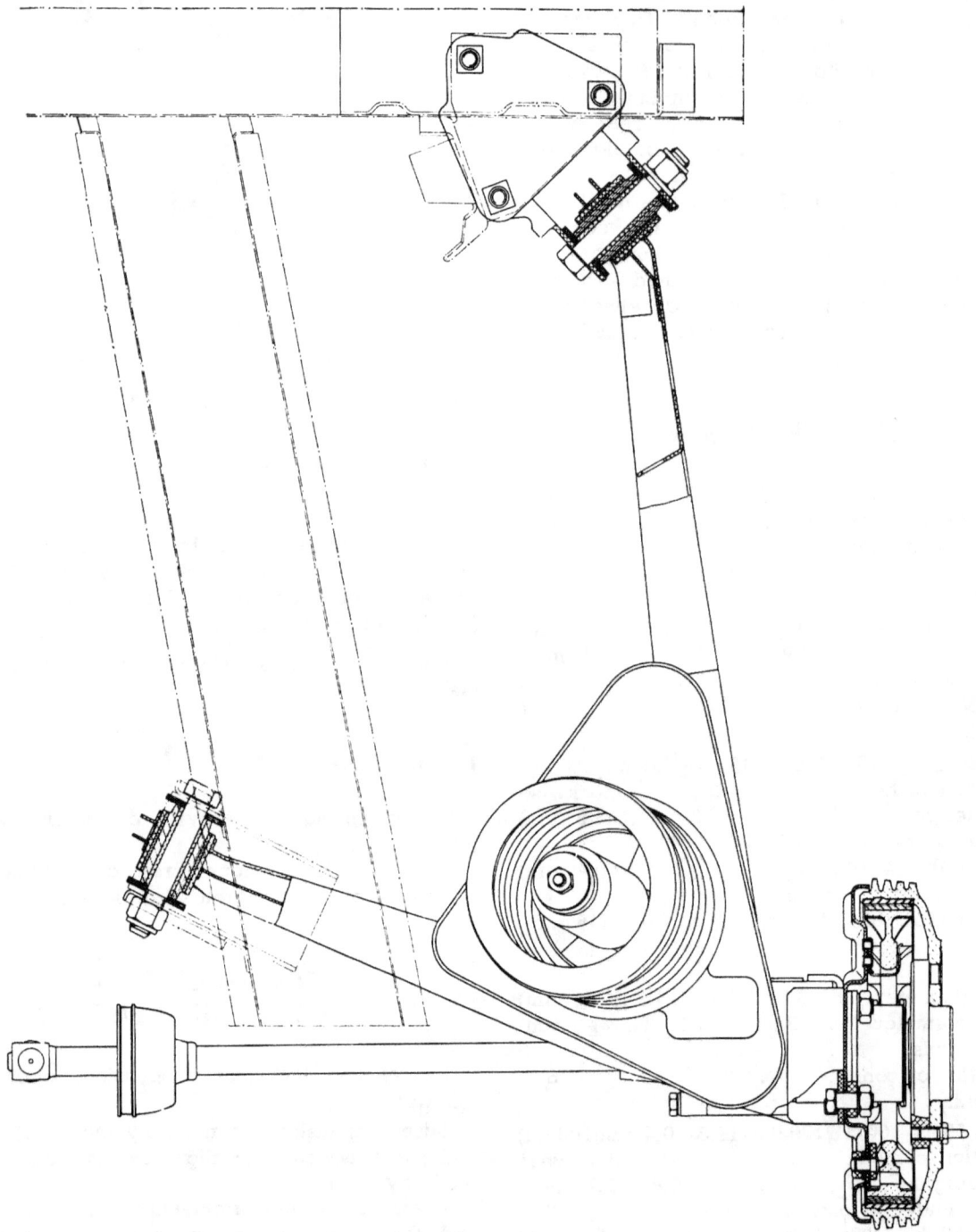

Fig. 314 - Rear right suspension.

Sectioned swinging arm mounting «estendblocks» and brake shoes are clearly visible
(up to engine No. 758492, «Sedan» - up to engine No. 765150, «Multipla»).

REAR SUSPENSION AND WHEELS

mined previously on fixture **A. 66037** (fig. 313). Then, insert the alignment bar **A. 66033** through «estendblock» and adjustment shims, aligning them with holes in mounting bracket.

Next, holding fast the entire assembly, while removing the alignment bar, slip in the mounting pin proper.

Finally, screw in the self-locking nut which, after wheel geometry adjustment, must be tightened to 43.4 - 50.6 ft.lbs (6000 - 7000 kgmm) with a torque wrench.

Seat properly, on swinging arm, the coil spring lower seating ring; insert spring on shock absorber (previously secured to arm) and position spring in its seat on arm. On spring, place the upper ring. Raise suspension assembly by means of a jack or fixture **A. 66052** and insert spring in its seat on body floor.

Make sure shock absorber-to-floor rubber ring has been fitted, then extend shock absorber until its upper mounting pin protrudes into car through the hump behind rear seat; working from inside of car, secure shock absorber by its mounting nut and toothed washer after having interposed rubber ring and plain washer.

To tighten nut, use wrench **A. 56020** (Sedan) or wrench **A. 56021** (Multipla).

Re-install floor lining behind rear seat.

Connect brake line to the connection on body floor.

Remove the wooden peg from brake fluid reservoir. Bleed brake system.

Between axle shaft and wheel shaft insert the inner spring; then couple the splined sleeve to the joint and tighten the screws to 22 ft.lbs (3000 kgmm).

Install wheels and lower the car to ground.

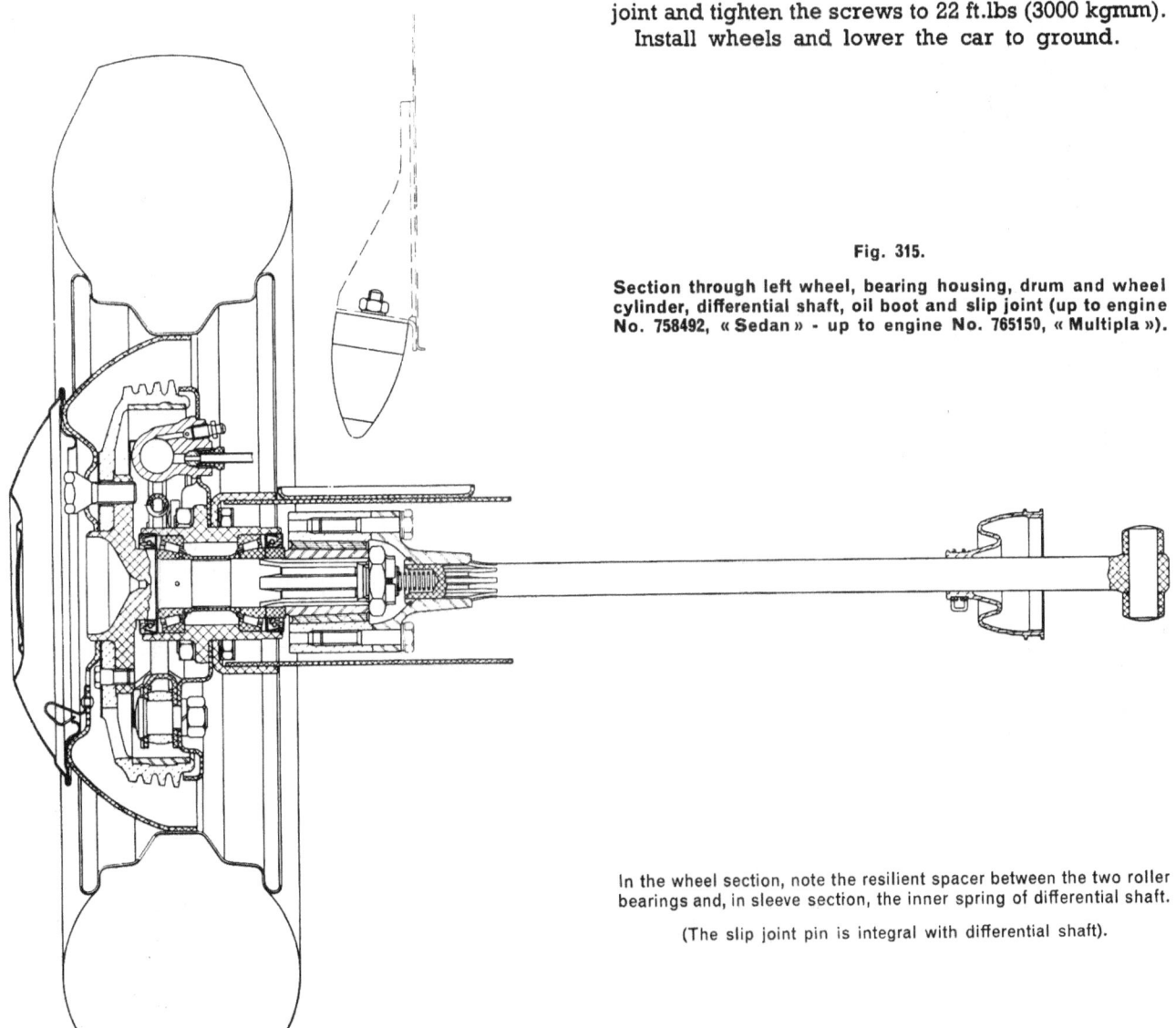

Fig. 315.

Section through left wheel, bearing housing, drum and wheel cylinder, differential shaft, oil boot and slip joint (up to engine No. 758492, «Sedan» - up to engine No. 765150, «Multipla»).

In the wheel section, note the resilient spacer between the two roller bearings and, in sleeve section, the inner spring of differential shaft.

(The slip joint pin is integral with differential shaft).

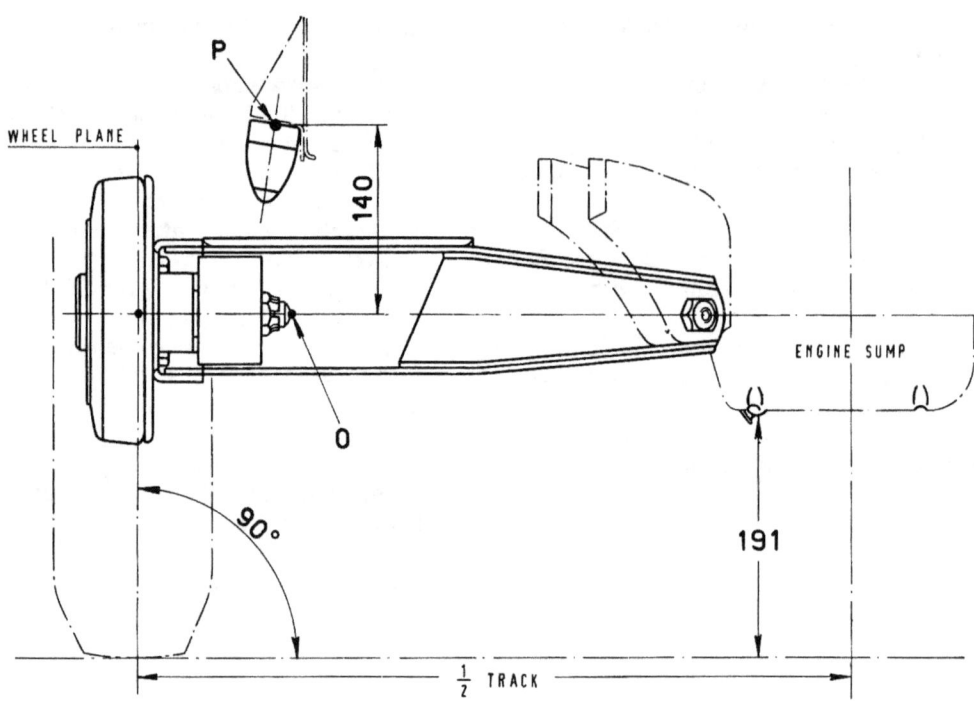

Fig. 316 - Position of rear suspension components, for rear wheel toe-in checking and adjustment.

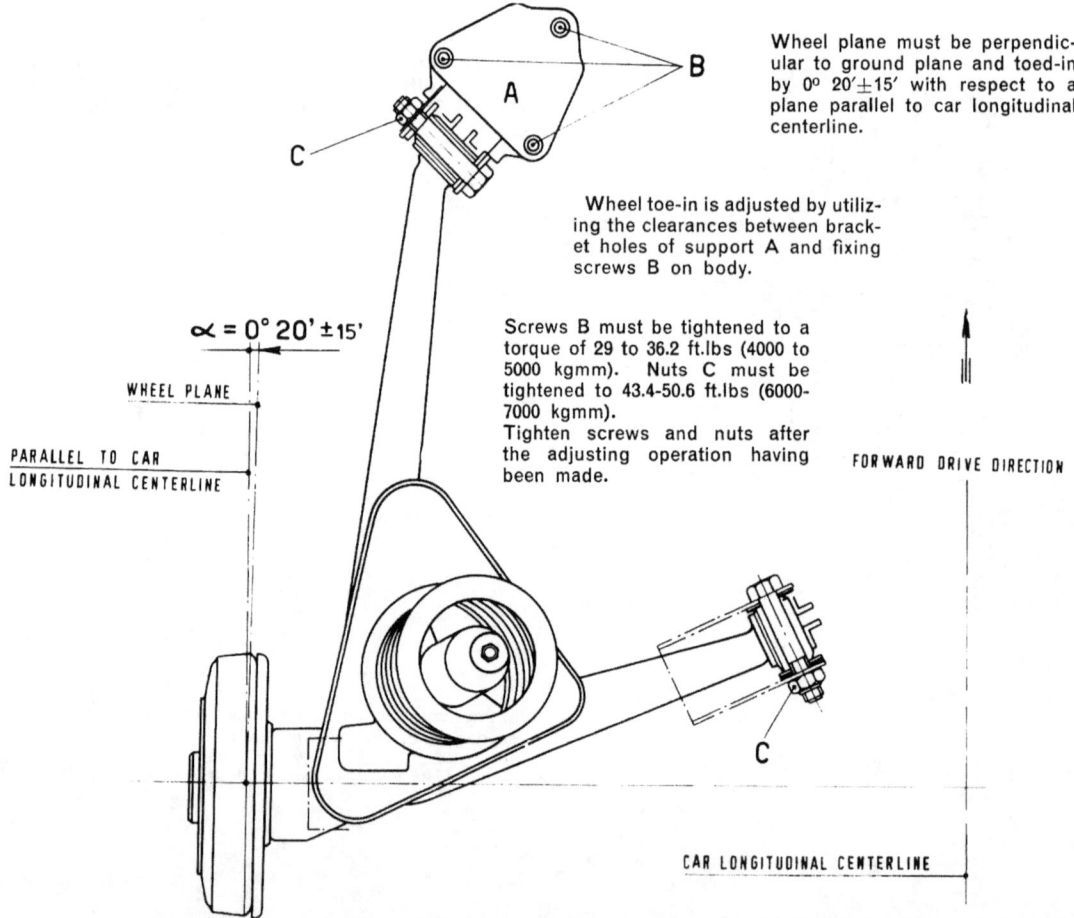

Wheel plane must be perpendicular to ground plane and toed-in by 0° 20'±15' with respect to a plane parallel to car longitudinal centerline.

Wheel toe-in is adjusted by utilizing the clearances between bracket holes of support A and fixing screws B on body.

Screws B must be tightened to a torque of 29 to 36.2 ft.lbs (4000 to 5000 kgmm). Nuts C must be tightened to 43.4-50.6 ft.lbs (6000-7000 kgmm).
Tighten screws and nuts after the adjusting operation having been made.

Fig. 317 - Adjusting rear wheel geometry.

CHECKING AND ADJUSTING REAR WHEEL TOE-IN

For correct toe-in, the rear wheels must be set with their plane:

— perpendicular to ground;

— toed in by 0° 20'±15' (angle α, fig. 317) to a parallel line to car longitudinal centerline;

— 22.56"±.059" (573±1,5 mm) (Sedan) and 22.58"±.059" (573,5±1,5 mm) (Multipla) apart from car longitudinal centerline (half track, fig. 316).

To adjust rear wheel geometry move suitably the swinging arm outer support.

Slight movements are permitted by the play existing between the support holes (A, fig. 317) and the mounting screws (B).

It should be noted that to a toe-in angle variation of 0° 15' (α, fig. 317) corresponds a displacement of about .3346 (8,5 mm) measured at 78.7" (2 m) from wheel center (distance equal to car wheelbase).

To check and adjust rear wheel geometry:

a) Place the car on stands and remove rear wheels.

b) Install the set of fixture **A. 66052** for spring compression and wheel retainment in vertical position (fig. 318).

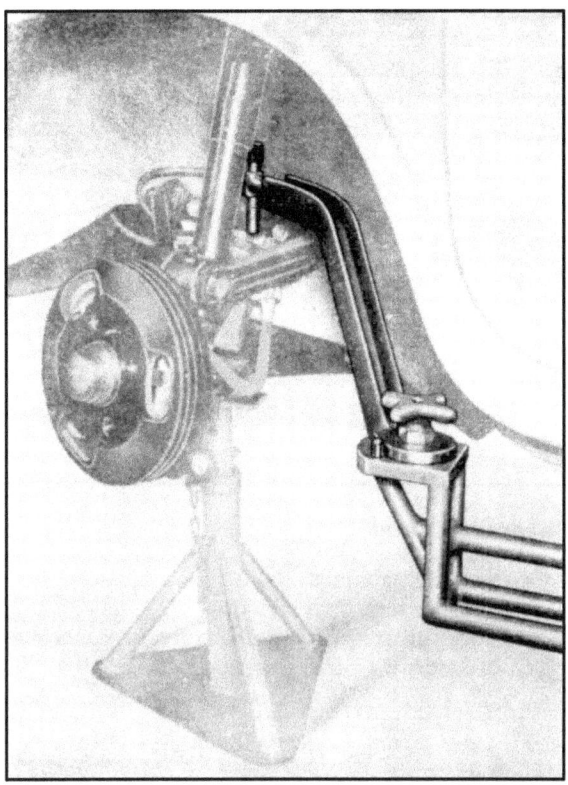

Fig. 319 - Checking rear wheel toe-in with gauge C. 696 (Sedan).
If rear wheel toe-in is correct (0° 20'), the vertical rod on gauge front end must contact front suspension swinging arm pin.

c) Lift rear suspensions by compressing the coil springs and shock absorbers. Screw on the fixture lower shank, using wrench **A. 74003**, until the index registers with the mark stamped on bracket. In this position the wheel plane is vertical and the center (0, fig. 316) of wheel shaft results at 5.51" (140 mm) from center of hole P in bumper resting plane.

The oil sump well will result 7.52" (191 mm) above ground.

d) Secure gauge **C. 696** to wheel shaft (fig. 318) by the two clamp screws (for the «Multipla», replace front bracket of gauge **C. 696** with bracket **C. 696/2**).

e) Check that the rod at front end of gauge **C. 696** (fig. 319) contacts, for the «Sedan», the pin of front suspension upper swinging arm. For the «Multipla», the rod of bracket **C. 696/2** must contact the body bottom frame. If this condition is not complied with, operate as follows (point f).

f) Slacken screws B (fig. 317) securing swinging arm external support A (fig. 317) to body bot-

Fig. 318 - Installation of the fixtures required for rear wheel toe-in checks.

1. Fixture A. 66052, coil spring compression and wheel retainment in vertical position. - 2. Wrench A. 74003. - 3. Gauge C. 696.

tom and set arm in the position in which condition indicated in point e) in satisfied; this position gives a 0° 20' toe-in of wheel plane with respect to vertical plane through the car longitudinal centerline.

After performing the adjustment tighten screws B (fig. 317) to 29-36.2 ft.lbs (4000-5000 kgmm) and then tighten nuts C (fig. 317) of the two swinging arm pins to 43.4-50.6 ft.lbs (6000-7000 kgmm).

As already said, a toe-in tolerance of ± 15 over angle α (0° 20') is permitted, provided such value is the same also for the other rear wheel. Rear wheels, in fact, must both be toed-in of the same angle.

Take off gauge **C. 696**; repeat the check and adjustment operations on the other wheel, minding that the gauge front bracket must be located in the other position provided.

REAR SUSPENSION AND WHEEL SPECIFICATIONS AND DATA

	SEDAN		MULTIPLA (paired)	
Swinging Arms.				
Connection to body	by « estendblocks »			
Adjustment	by shims			
Position of arm for tightening nuts to mounting pins and screws on body floor	wheels vertical and toed-in by 0° 20' ± 15'			
	in	mm	in	mm
Coil Springs.				
Free height	9.63	244,5	8.85	225
Height under a 937 ± 44 lbs (425 ± 20 kg) load . .	6.00	154	—	—
Height under a 1094 ± 55 lbs (496 ± 25 kg) load . .	—	—	6.00	154
Height under a 1334 ± 66 lbs (605 ± 30 kg) load . .	4.57	116	—	—
Height under a 1712 ± 86 lbs (776 ± 39 kg) load . .	—	—	4.49	114
Flexibility	.3802 ± .0107 in/100 lbs	21,3 ± 0,6 mm/100kg	.2553 ± .0071 in/100 lbs	14,3 ± 0,4 mm/100 kg
Wheels.				
Roller bearing adjustment	by resilient spacer			
Bearing rotation torque	below .36 ft.lbs (50 kgmm)			
Toe-in (both wheels)	0° 20' ± 15'			
Bearing lubrication	FIAT MR grease			
Shock Absorbers	two			
Type	hydraulic, telescopic			
Diameter (inner cylinder)	1.063'' (27 mm)			
Fluid grade	FIAT S. A. I. oil			
Capacity	120 ± 5 cc (0,110 kg)			

REAR SUSPENSION AND WHEEL TIGHTENING REFERENCE

ITEM	DRWG. OR STD. PART No.	THREAD	MATERIAL	TIGHTENING TORQUE
Rear swinging arm mounting pin-to-floor nut	1/25748/11 1/21640/11	14 MB (x1,5)	R 50 Cdt (Screw R 80 Cdt)	43.4 to 50.6 ft.lbs (6.000 to 7.000 kgmm)
Rear swinging arm support-to-floor screw	1.56.589/ 832632	10 x 1,25 M	R 80	29 to 36.2 ft.lbs (4.000 to 5.000 kgmm)
Hub and brake housing flange-to-swinging arm nut	1/21647/11	10 x 1,25 M	R 50 Cdt (Screw R 80)	43.4 ft.lbs (6.000 kgmm)
Differential shaft sleeve-to-flexible joint screw	1.45.579/ 988118	8 MA (x1,25)	R 80 Cdt	22 ft.lbs (3.000 kgmm)
Wheel-to-hub screw Sedan	1.49.012/ 996225	12 MB (x1,5)	C 35 R (Bon Cdt)	43.4 to 50.6 ft.lbs (6.000 to 7.000 kgmm)
Multipla	1.49.110/ 4052840	12 MB (x1,5)	C 35 R (Bon Cdt)	43.4 to 50.6 ft.lbs (6.000 to 7.000 kgmm)
Rear wheel bearing rotation torque				.36 ft.lbs (50 kgmm)

REAR SUSPENSION AND WHEEL SERVICE EQUIPMENT

A. 6469   Puller - wheel hub.
A. 40005/1/9   Puller - wheel drums.
A. 56020   Wrench - shock absorber installation and removal (Sedan).
A. 56031   Wrench - shock absorber plug.
A. 57035   Wrench - shock absorber installation and removal (Multipla).
A. 66033   Alignment bar - shims on swinging arm.
A. 66034   Remover - wheel bearing outer rings.
A. 66035   Installer - wheel bearing inner and outer rings.
A. 66037   Fixture - swinging arm checks and adjustments.
A. 66045   Tool - swinging arm « estendblock » removal and installation.
A. 66052   Fixture (set) - coil spring compression and wheel retainment in vertical position.
A. 74003   Spanner wrench (to be used with A. 66052).
A. 95697   Dynamometer - wheel bearing rotation torque measurement.
A. 95697/3   Support - wheel bearing rotation torque measurement (to be used with dynamometer A. 95697).
C. 696   Gauge - wheel alignment checking.
C. 696/2   Front bracket - wheel alignment check gauge (use with C. 696 only for Multipla).

HYDRAULIC SHOCK ABSORBERS

Description	page 190
Specifications and Data	» 190
Operation	» 191
Disassembly, Inspection, Reassembly	» 192
Checking Dampening Diagrams	» 192

Description.

Front and rear shock absorbers are of the telescopic, double-acting type; rear shock absorbers are identical for both «Sedan» and «Multipla» models (see data and specifications here below).

These shock absorbers are also termed «direct acting», since their dampening action takes place directly on suspensions without the intermediary of levers.

They are fitted with thermostatic valves ensuring steady dampening action regardless of temperature variations.

Essentially, a shock absorber of this type consists of a cylindrical body formed by two coaxial tubes (14 and 15, fig. 320) of which the inner one acts as a working cylinder and the outer one as a casing. The annular interstice between these two elements performs as a fluid reservoir.

A third outer cylinder (13) shields rod (2) from mud and stones.

On top, cylinder body is closed by bush (11), oil seal (5) and gasket (9), and seal housing (4).

Rod (2) slides through the plug and annexed parts: its upper end is fixed to body floor, and its lower end carries piston (22) on which rebound (26) and inlet (21) valves are arranged.

Two concentric rows of orifices are provided in piston.

The internal row is blanked underneath by the rebound valve which opens downwards. The external row is blanked by inlet valve which opens upwards.

At bottom, the shock absorber is closed by plug (35) with welded shank (36) for shock absorber mounting on suspensions.

At cylinder (15) bottom, plug (23) is mounted with compression (33) and compensating (30) valves.

Hydraulic shock absorbers, both front and rear, (starting from vehicles manufactured in the month of March 1959) are provided with a vapour pocket bleeder from cylinder interior.

SHOCK ABSORBER SPECIFICATIONS AND DATA

	SEDAN				MULTIPLA			
	Front		Rear		Front		Rear	
	in	mm	in	mm	in	mm	in	mm
Inner cylinder diameter	1.063	27	1.063	27	1.26	32	1.063	27
Length (between rubber ring mountings):								
— telescoped in	8.661	220	7.913	201	8.228	209*	7.913	201
— telescoped out	13.819	351	12.323	313	12.323	313*	12.323	313
Stroke	5.157	131	4.409	112	4.094	104	4.409	112
	cc	kg	cc	kg	cc	kg	cc	kg
Oil capacity	135±5	0,120	120±5	0,110	165±5	0,150	120±5	0,110

* These lengths are intended as measured from lower mounting eye center to rubber ring and on upper mounting plane.

HYDRAULIC SHOCK ABSORBERS

The bleeder device consists of a capillary hole (12, fig. 320) interconnecting the inner cylinder (15) with the upper chamber (10), and of a passage tube (16) from upper chamber to fluid reservoir.

Any vapour pockets in pressure cylinder are evacuated past the capillary hole (12) into the chamber (10), whence they flow down, during shock absorber operation, through passage (16) in a light fluid stream and up to top reservoir with the reservoir fluid.

This system definitely does away with any vapour lock in shock absorber hydraulic circuit, which is isolated from air contained in fluid reservoir.

Operation.

The shock absorber described above may be considered as divided in three sections:

— top portion of cylinder above piston (always full of fluid);

— bottom portion of cylinder below piston (always full of fluid);

— fluid reservoir, i. e. the annular interstice between cylinders (14) and (15) (never completely full).

REBOUND PHASE

This is the phase in which shock absorber extends. The fluid above piston finds the external row of orifices (24) closed and is forced through the internal row (25), thus acting on rebound valve (26) and passing to cylinder lower portion.

During its upward travel the piston produces a vacuum which draws fluid from the reservoir through annular passage (31) of lower plug (32) and compensating valve (30). The amount of fluid passing from reservoir to cylinder will be volumetrically equal to the portion of piston rod that has slid out.

Therefore in this phase only the rebound and compensating valves are active while the compression and inlet valves are inactive.

COMPRESSION PHASE

In this phase shock absorber telescopes in and the piston travels downwards.

The fluid in the lower chamber lifts inlet valve (21) and part of it passes into cylinder upper portion.

Some of the fluid, instead, rams compression valve (33), and through its orifices (34) passes into the reserve.

The dampening effect in this phase is the result of the displacement of an amount of fluid volumetrically equal to the portion of rod entering the cylinder.

SECTION OF SHOCK ABSORBER

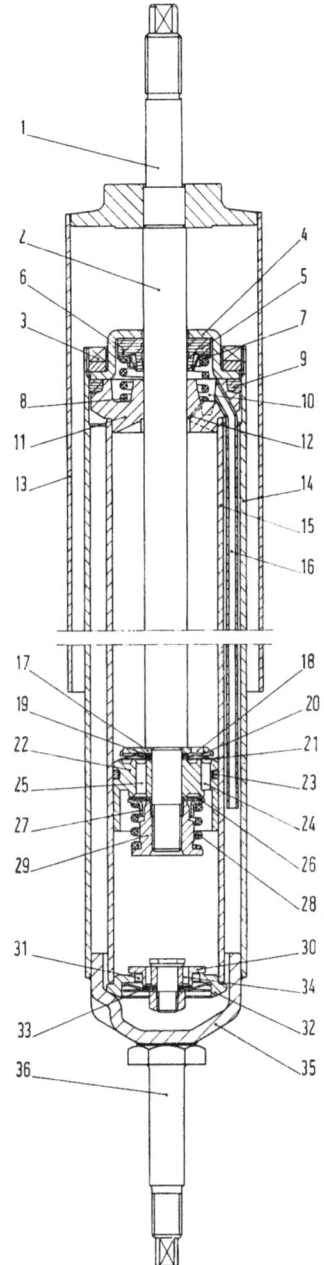

Fig. 320 - Section of shock absorber.

1. Threaded shank, floor mounting. - 2. Rod. - 3. Cylinder upper blanking threaded ring. - 4. Seal housing. - 5. Rod seal. - 6. Tab spring. - 7. Spring cup. - 8. Gasket packing spring. - 9. Casing gasket. - 10. Vapour pocket drain chamber. - 11. Rod guide bush. - 12. Vapour pocket drain capillary hole. - 13. Dust shield. - 14. Casing. - 15. Working cylinder. - 16. Vapour pocket drain passage. - 17. Valve lift limiting disc. - 18. Fluid passage orifice. - 19. Valve lift adjustment washer. - 20. Valve star shaped spring. - 21. Inlet valve. - 22. Piston. - 23. Compression ring. - 24. Inlet valve holes in piston. - 25. Rebound valve holes in piston. - 26. Rebound valve. - 27. Valve guide cup. - 28. Rebound valve spring. - 29. Piston mounting plug. - 30. Compensating valve. - 31. Compensating valve annular passage. - 32. Compensating-and-compression valve carrier plug. - 33. Compression valve. - 34. Compression valve orifices. - 35. Lower plug. 36. Threaded shank, lower mounting.

During this phase both the compensating (30) and rebound (26) valves remain closed and only the compression (33) and inlet (21) valves are operative.

Disassembly, Inspection, Reassembly.

Wash outer casing with warm water or kerosene. Clamp lower shank in a vise and telescope-up outer casing. Using wrench **A. 57034**, unscrew upper threaded ring (3).

Remove from vise and take out inner cylinder (15); by a screwdriver inserted in cylinder bottom chamfer, remove lower plug (32) carrying compression and compensating valves.

Push rod into cylinder (15), and clamp upper shank in a vise, unscrew plug (29), remove piston (22) with inlet and rebound valves.

Withdraw rod (2) from cylinder (15) and remove seal gasket, cup, threaded ring, etc.

Wash all components in kerosene or gasoline and then inspect parts carefully to see that:

a) inlet, rebound and compensating valve discs are not deformed;

b) the sliding surfaces of piston, seal ring and compression valve are smooth and are fluidtight;

c) rebound and compression valve springs, and upper spring for seal gasket are not weakened or broken;

d) the two seal gaskets are not worn or damaged; it is advisable to replace them in any case;

e) rod and cylinders are not deformed;

f) air pocket evacuating passage is not plugged. Take care not to kink the passage during disassembly and assembly operations. Replace passage, if damaged;

g) capillary hole (12, fig. 320) is not plugged.

Replace all damaged parts.

To reassemble shock absorber reverse order of disassembly operations.

Special care shall be taken in refilling the shock absorber.

In a graduated cylinder, measure the following amounts of **FIAT-SAI** oil:

Front shock absorbers { Sedan . . . 135±5 cc
                       Multipla . . 165±5 cc

Rear shock absorbers { Sedan . . . 120±5 cc
                      Multipla . . 120±5 cc

Then proceed as follows:

Mount piston on rod, insert rod and piston assembly into cylinder (15).

Push piston against bush (11), then pour fluid up to about 1/2 inch from the edge.

Press fit plug (32) and pour the remaining fluid in casing (14). Finally, insert cylinder (15) in casing (14) and tighten upper threaded ring (3).

IMPORTANT - The amount of **FIAT-SAI** oil introduced in shock absorbers, must always correspond exactly to recommendations.

A too high level would not allow the shock absorber to telescope in completely and would cause irreparable damages, while a too low level would reduce the dampening effect and might cause noisy operation.

CHECKING DAMPENING DIAGRAMS

Before disassembling the shock absorber for overhauls, it will be advisable to check its operation on shock absorber tester **A. 76003** (fig. 321) to determine dampening efficiency. Set up tester for the type of shock absorber to be checked.

To this purpose, and in accordance with the tester instruction book, proceed as follows:

a) Adjust reaction arm length at 9.843" (250 mm) (fig. 323).

b) Adjust test stroke at 3.937" (100 mm) (fig. 322).

c) Adjust distance between shock absorber mounting pins by bringing the two indexes in line with the reference marks on plate fitted on tester

Fig. 321.

Shock absorber operation tester A. 76003.

HYDRAULIC SHOCK ABSORBERS

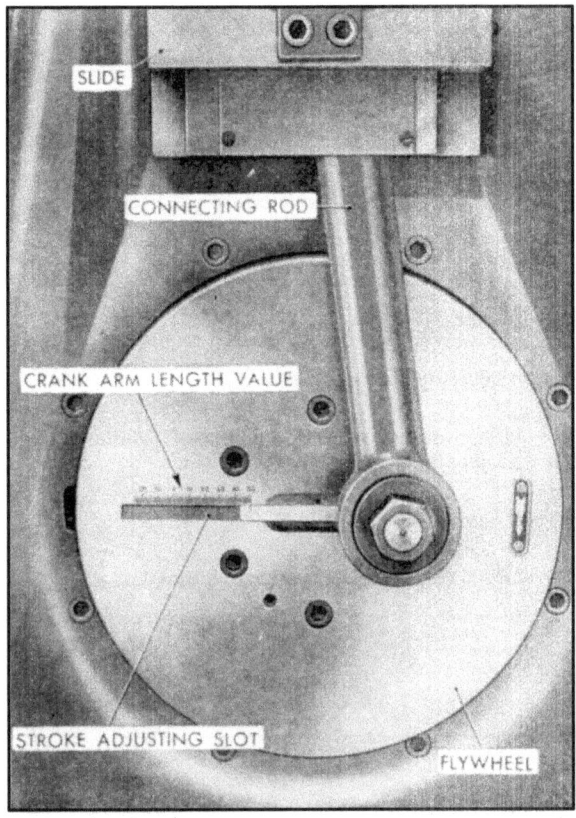

Fig. 322 - Detail of the shock absorber operation tester A. 76003.
In the figure the tester is set for a stroke of 100 mm, suitable for checking front and rear shock absorber of both the Sedan and the Multipla.

the master diagram have been computed according to this test condition.

Let shock absorber complete four or five cycles before tracing the dampening diagram by lowering the scriber to contact the paper sheet rolled on the drum (fig. 323).

Remove the traced paper from drum and place it under the plexiglass master diagram and check shock absorber diagram.

Diagram interpretation.

a) The values of the rebound and compression reactions are referred to the maximum ordinates of the corresponding diagrams.

b) The peak of the curve must be included between the master diagram ordinates.

c) The diagram must be regular and, in the inversion point, must in no spot be parellel to the base line.

After checking operation, disassemble shock absorber, inspect and replace parts as required.

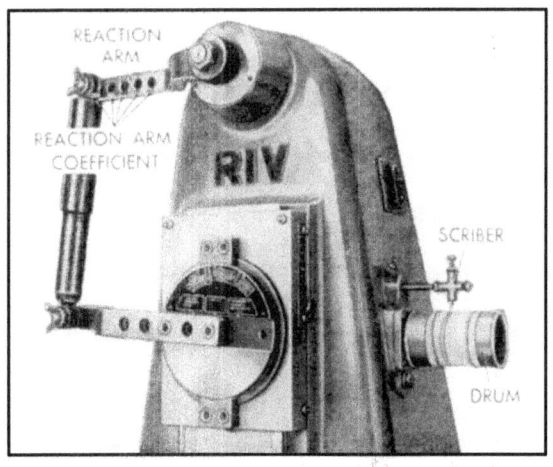

Fig. 323 - Detail of the A. 76003 shock absorber tester head.

slide side (fig. 323) relevant to shock absorber under test.

d) Wind the sheet of paper on the drum and scribe the base line by running the tester unloaded.

Install shock absorber on the tester, making sure that articulations are free. Test must be carried out at room temperature since the ordinates on

REAR SUSPENSION TROUBLE DIAGNOSIS AND CORRECTIONS

Sag at One Wheel.

POSSIBLE CAUSES	REMEDIES
1) Incorrect tire pressure.	1) Check pressure of tires and inflate as specified on page 234.
2) Weak or broken coil spring.	2) Check spring rise under load and replace spring if not within specifications (page 183), or broken.
3) Wear of shock absorber causes poor dampening action.	3) Overhaul shock absorber and replace worn parts.

Irregular or Abnormal Tire Wear.

POSSIBLE CAUSES	REMEDIES
1) Incorrect tire pressure.	1) Tires should be inflated, front and rear, to recommended pressure. Pressure specifications are given on page 234.
2) Wheels out of balance.	2) Inspect and fix as directed on page 234.
3) Wheels off center.	3) Inspect and fix as directed on page 234.
4) Misadjusted brakes.	4) Adjust brakes as outlined on page 222.
5) Weak or broken coil springs.	5) Check spring rise under load and replace spring if not within specifications (page 183), or broken.
6) Excessive load.	6) See load specifications, page 5.
7) Incorrect wheel alignment.	7) Check and adjust rear wheel toe-in as outlined on page 187.

Squeaks, Thumps, or Rattles.

POSSIBLE CAUSES	REMEDIES
1) Wheels out of balance.	1) Inspect and fix as directed on page 234.
2) Wheels off center.	2) Inspect and fix as directed on page 234.
3) Misadjusted brakes.	3) Adjust brakes as outlined on page 222.
4) Weak or broken coil springs or spring seats dislodged.	4) Check spring rise under load and replace spring if not within specifications (page 183), or broken. Replace upper and lower rubber seats, if damaged.
5) Wear of shock absorbers causes poor dampening action.	5) Overhaul shock absorbers and replace worn parts.
6) Worn rubber bushings in control arms.	6) Replace bushings by new ones.
7) Poor lubrication of wheel bearings.	7) Proceed as directed on page 181 and under « Maintenance ».

Pull to One Side.

POSSIBLE CAUSES	REMEDIES
1) Incorrect tire pressure.	1) Check pressure of tires and inflate as prescribed on page 234.
2) Misadjusted brakes.	2) Adjust brakes as directed on page 222.
3) Distorted suspension arm.	3) Remove, check on test equipment (see page 180), straighten arm, if possible, and set correctly on installation.

Section 7
STEERING GEAR AND LINKAGE

	Page
STEERING GEAR AND LINKAGE, « SEDAN »	196
STEERING GEAR AND LINKAGE, « MULTIPLA »	202
FRONT WHEEL TOE-IN	206
TIGHTENING REFERENCE	207
TOOL EQUIPMENT	207
STEERING GEAR SPECIFICATIONS AND DATA	208
TROUBLE DIAGNOSIS AND CORRECTIONS	209

7

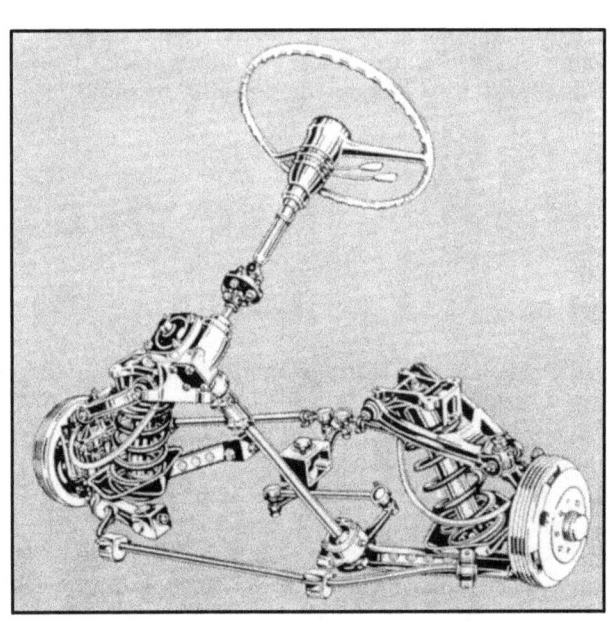

STEERING GEAR AND LINKAGE

SEDAN

Description	page 196
Steering Wheel Removal	» 196
Steering Box Removal	» 197
Steering Box Disassembly	» 198
Inspection and Adjustment	» 198
Steering Box Assembly and Installation	» 200
Support and Relay Lever	» 201
Steering Rods	» 201

MULTIPLA

Description	» 202
Steering Box Removal	» 202
Steering Box Disassembly	» 203
Inspection and Repair	» 203
Steering Box Assembly and Adjustment	» 204
Operating Rod	» 204
Support and Relay Lever	» 205
Steering Rods	» 205

CHECKING AND ADJUSTING FRONT WHEEL TOE-IN .... » 206
TIGHTENING REFERENCE .... » 207
TOOL EQUIPMENT .... » 207
SPECIFICATIONS AND DATA .... » 208
TROUBLE DIAGNOSIS AND CORRECTIONS .... » 209

The steering mechanism and box of the «Sedan» and «Multipla» are substantially different. The two systems, therefore, are dealt with separately. Here below is the description of the «Sedan» steering gear. For «Multipla», refer to the chapter on page 202.

SEDAN

Description.

Steering control is by worm screw and sector, ratio being 2 to 26.

Steering box is located on front left side of bulkhead (fig. 324) near the battery housing.

Steering linkage consists of two symmetrical side track rods, and a central link rod connecting pitman arm (fig. 324) to relay lever (fig. 336).

Steering circle diameter is 28 ft 7" (8,70 mm).

Steering Wheel Removal.

First remove horn control button by prying off with screwdriver placed between button and steering wheel hub; the button is simply held in place by spring fasteners (fig. 325).

Disinsert cable from pushbutton.

Back out the steering wheel-to-shaft nut using wrench **A. 8279** (fig. 326).

Extract steering wheel from shaft.

STEERING GEAR AND LINKAGE

Fig. 324 - Steering box and linkages (on car).
1. Steering box. - 2. Pitman arm. - 3. Central link rod. - 4. Left track rod. - 5. Brake fluid reservoir.

NOTE

The central link rod and relay lever have been fitted on «Sedan» starting from car No. 377801. Before this, steering linkage consisted of a short track rod on steering box end and a long track rod on opposite end: the two track rods, like the current ones, were fitted with adjustable end heads.

Fig. 326 - Removal of steering wheel mounting nut, using wrench A. 8279.

Steering Box Removal.

— Inside car, back off the steering column shaft-to-worm screw mounting nut.

— Under car, remove split pins and mounting nuts of track rods and disconnect rods at Pitman arm.

— Pull battery out of its seat, to gain access to upper self-locking nut (2, fig. 327) securing steering box to body.

— Unscrew the lower self-locking nut (3, fig. 327) and the lateral nut on the opposite side.

— Disinsert worm screw from steering column and take out steering box.

Fig. 325 - Horn pushbutton control (removed).
1. Steering wheel mounting nut. - 2. Pushbutton assembly. - 3. Horn cable.

Fig. 327 - Detail of steering box mounting.
1. Steering box. - 2. Upper self-locking nut. - 3. Lower self-locking nut. - 4. Battery tray.

Steering Box Disassembly.

Proceed as follows:

Secure steering box to servicing support **A. 66032**, remove mounting self-locking nut, and disinsert pitman arm using puller **A. 46021** (fig. 328).

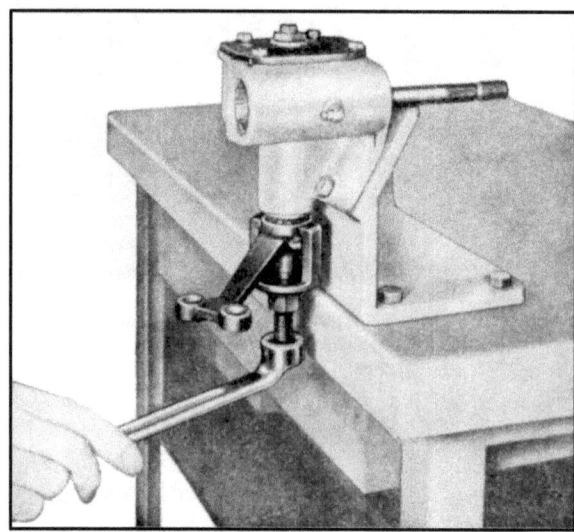

Fig. 328 - Disassembly of pitman arm, using puller **A. 46021**.
Steering box is mounted on servicing support **A. 66032**.

Remove the cotter pin and back out worm screw adjuster and bearing retainer lower sleeve, using wrench **A. 8065** (fig. 329).

Take off cover provided with screw and nut for worm sector adjustment and, after removing

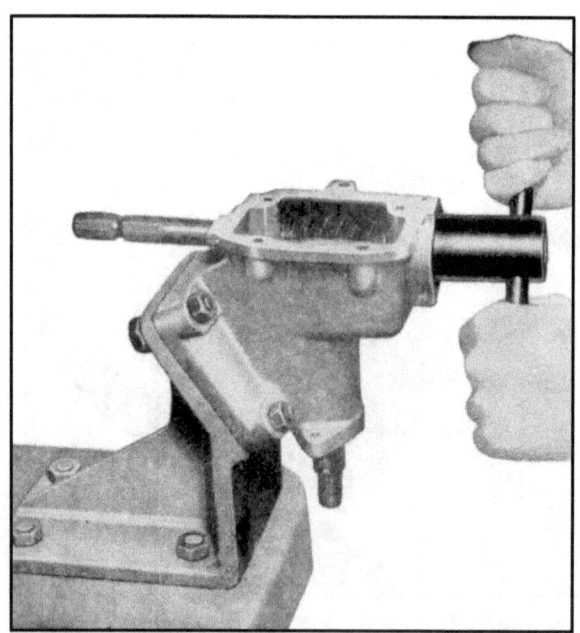

Fig. 329 - Removing adjuster sleeve of worm screw using wrench **A. 8065**.

Fig. 330 - Removing oil seal with tool **A. 10110**.

lower gasket from sector shaft, back out screw securing the eccentric bush adjusting plate and take off plate and upper gasket.

Disinsert worm sector, thrust washer and shims.
Remove worm screw by pulling from below (upper bearing outer ring will remain in housing).
The bearing inner rings will remain on worm screw; to take them off, use puller **A. 46019**.

— Remove: oil seal with tool **A. 10110** (fig. 330) and then worm screw upper bearing outer ring with puller **A. 66040** (fig. 331).

Inspection and Adjustment.

Check parts accurately to see that sector teeth and worm screw threads show no sign of seizing, indents or deep scoring.

Check contact surfaces to make sure that meshing between the two parts takes place at center; this, to have a basis for adjustments during assembly.

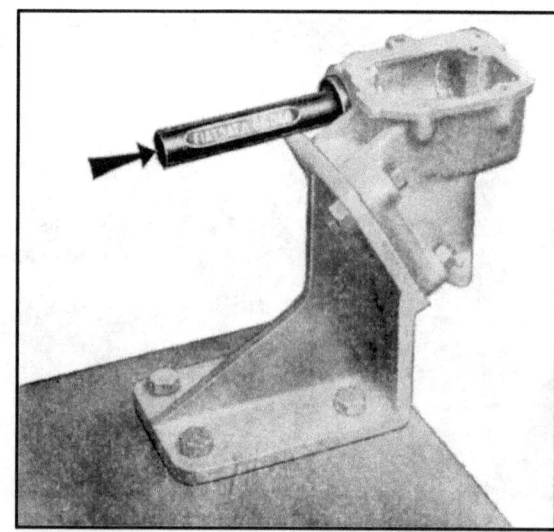

Fig. 331 - Removing worm screw upper bearing outer ring by puller **A. 66040**.

STEERING GEAR AND LINKAGE

Check clearance between eccentric bush (5, fig. 332) and worm sector shaft (10, fig. 332) which must not exceed .0039" (0,10 mm). Fit of new parts is .00000" to .00165" (0,000 to 0,042 mm).

It is advisable to check also worm screw centering: max. permissible out-of-true is .00197" (0,05 mm).

As to the adjustments, to be performed when servicing steering gear, proceed as follows.

NOTE - Steering worm and sector are assembled with a touch fit at tooth flank.

Adjustment is made by rotating the worm sector mounting eccentric bushing.

If backlash between worm screw and sector is excessive, adjust as follows:

Disconnect pitman arm and relevant gasket.

Back out screw (7, fig. 332) fixing adjustment plate (6).

Rotate eccentric bush (5) by the adjustment plate and move sector in toward worm screw. Secure plate again by using the second fixing hole.

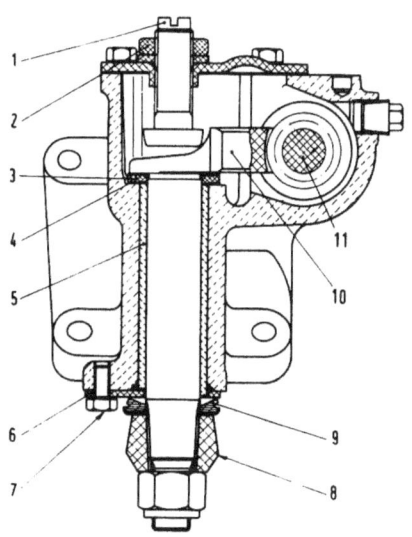

Fig. 332 - Section of steering box, through worm sector.

1. Sector adjusting screw. - 2. Mounting nut. - 3. Thrust washer. - 4. Shim. - 5. Eccentric bush. - 6. Bush adjusting plate. - 7. Plate fixing screw. - 8. Pitman arm. - 9. Sector seal. - 10. Worm sector. 11. Worm screw.

Should adjusting plate be already fixed in second hole (which would impede repositioning after rotation) remove plate from bush, rotate one or more serrations and secure.

If play in worm screw rollers in excessive, screw up lower adjuster ring (4, fig. 333). Once adjustment is over, adjuster ring must be secured by cotter: to this end, position ring in such a way that hole in steering box lines up with one of the spaces between ring castellations.

As already mentioned, worm screw and sector must mesh in their central portion: if off center, this condition may be corrected by moving sector axially by adding or removing the shims (4, fig. 332) against eccentric bush shoulder.

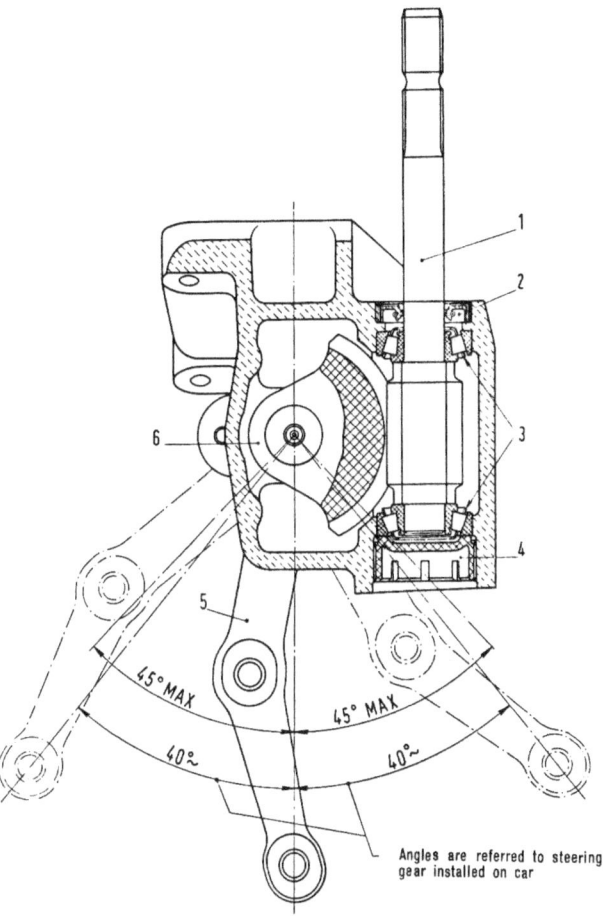

Fig. 333 - Section of steering box, through worm screw.

1. Worm screw. - 2. Oil seal. - 3. Roller bearings. - 4. Worm screw adjuster and bearing retainer. - 5. Pitman arm. - 6. Worm sector.

The next adjustment must be carried out by means of adjustment screw (1, fig. 332) on cover, then locking screw by nut (2).

Shims are supplied as spares with .0039" (0,10 mm) thickness.

Both the above adjustments must eliminate any play and blacklash in steering gear without rendering steering too stiff.

Replace any seal found damaged.

Inspect roller bearings: rollers, cages and outer races must neither be damaged nor excessively worn.

Steering Box Assembly and Installation.

Steering box is assembled by reversing disassembly operations.

Tools to be used:

A. 66043 to assemble and disassemble eccentric bush;
A. 66046 to install both worm screw roller bearing inner rings and upper bearing outer ring;
A. 8065 wrench, for worm screw adjuster sleeve.

It is essential that before re-assembly and subsequent adjustment, all components be perfectly clean and well lubricated.

For correct pitman arm positioning on assembly, the sector shaft and the pitman arm are marked with notches, or a tooth is omitted in the sector

NOTE - Steering box self-locking nuts must be tightened, with a torque wrench to 14.5 - 18 ft.lbs (2.000-2.500 kgmm).

Steering wheel mounting nut should be drawn up with 28.9 to 36.2 ft.lbs (4.000 to 5.000 kgmm) of torque.

Fig. 334 - Adjusting worm sector.

toothing whereas the pitman arm has a double tooth, which prevents incorrect assembly.

Pitman arm mounting nut must be tightened by torque wrench to 72-80 ft.lbs (10.000-11.000 kgmm).

For steering box reinstallation, reverse removal operations.

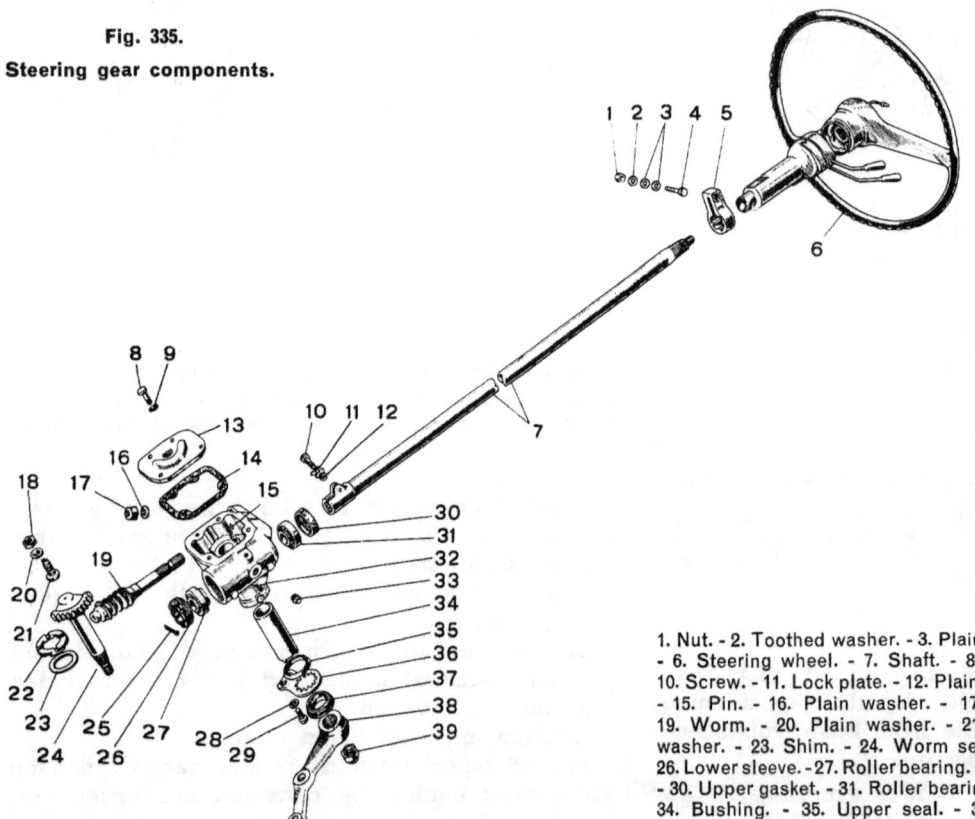

Fig. 335. Steering gear components.

1. Nut. - 2. Toothed washer. - 3. Plain washer. - 4. Screw. - 5. Support. - 6. Steering wheel. - 7. Shaft. - 8. Screw. - 9. Toothed washer. - 10. Screw. - 11. Lock plate. - 12. Plain washer. - 13. Cover. - 14. Gasket. - 15. Pin. - 16. Plain washer. - 17. Self-locking nut. - 18. Nut. - 19. Worm. - 20. Plain washer. - 21. Adjusting screw. - 22. Thrust washer. - 23. Shim. - 24. Worm sector and shaft. - 25. Split pin. - 26. Lower sleeve. - 27. Roller bearing. - 28. Toothed washer. - 29. Screw. - 30. Upper gasket. - 31. Roller bearing. - 32. Steering box. - 33. Plug. - 34. Bushing. - 35. Upper seal. - 36. Adjusting plate. - 37. Lower gasket. - 38. Pitman arm. - 39. Self-locking nut.

STEERING GEAR AND LINKAGE

Support and Relay Lever.

Relay lever support is mounted in front of bulkhead on side opposite the steering box.

Removal and disassembly.

Removal is accomplished as follows:

— take out cotter pins and unscrew the side track rod and central link rod end pin nuts;

— remove relay lever pins;

— back out the three support self-locking nuts (fig. 336) and take off support from studs.

Fig. 336 - Detail of steering relay linkage.
1. Side track rod lock clamp. - 2. Side track rod head. - 3. Relay lever. - 4. Relay lever support. - 5. Central link rod.

Arrows point to steering rod head lubricators.

Disassembly is accomplished as follows:

— secure support in a vise;

— back out the nut and disinsert pin, thus freeing the lever.

Inspection.

Check the clearance between pin and rubber bushes: if greater than .0118″ (0,30 mm) replace the most worn part or, if required, both.

Check the condition of rubber bushes press-fitted in support: the inner surface of bushes must not show any sign of seizure and the rubber must neither be torn or hard.

NOTE - Before carrying out any adjustment of steering gear, check that no other steering component is affected by play or maladjustment; otherwise, proceed first with its adjustment.

Reassembly.

The only special recommendation is the locking of the pin nut which must be tightened (after front wheel toe-in adjustment with wheels symmetrically located with respect to car centerline) to 40 - 43.4 ft.lbs (5500-6000 kgmm).

Steering Rods.

The steering linkage assembly consists of a pitman arm mounted on worm sector shaft and a relay lever supported on bulkhead on side opposite steering box: arm and lever are connected by a central non-adjustable link rod.

Two side track rods connect the pitman arm and relay lever (one each) to knuckle arms on wheels. These two rods are provided with adjustable end heads to permit wheel geometry adjustments as described on page 206 under « Front Wheel Toe-in ».

If play in ball pins is excessive, or ball pin is damaged, the track rod head assembly must be replaced.

For instructions on how to position and tighten track rod clamps see page 206.

Track rod ball pin mounting nuts must be tightened to 18.1 - 21.7 ft.lbs (2.500-3.000 kgmm).

Fig. 337.

Section through relay lever support (early type).

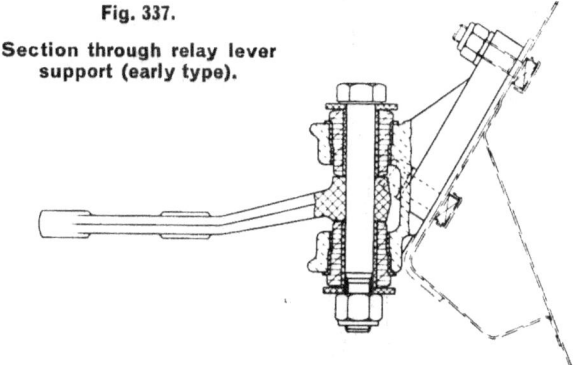

NOTE - On « Sedan », starting from car No. 698915 (including some vehicles from No. 696325 to No. 698914; excluding vehicles No. 699655 - 699656 - 699658 - 699662 - 699693 - 699805 - 700506 - 700507), a variation has been introduced to the tilt of side tie rod end heads, tilt of end head steering knuckle mounting eye, and front wheel geometry. As a result, front wheel toe-in with vehicle under full load, should be .0000″ to .0787″ (0 to 2 mm).

MULTIPLA

Description.

Steering control is by worm screw and roller, ratio being 1 to 16 4.

Steering box is located inside car on a horizontal bracket on the left side of dashboard.

Steering linkage consists of: a pitman arm (which is connected to steering box through an operating rod mounted in a ball-and-socket joint at arm end and on worm roller shaft at the other end), a non-adjustable rod from pitman arm to relay lever, anchored in a body-mounted support, and two track rods from relay lever yoke end to knuckle arms on wheels.

Turning circle diameter is 28 ft 10'' (8,80 m).

Steering Box Removal.

Remove steering wheel as described for the «Sedan» on page 196.

Remove steering column sheet metal cover and support.

Loosen flexible joint yoke mounting screw and take off steering shaft from worm screw shaft.

Slide down rubber boot of operating rod and slacken the nuts of the two screws locking the operating rod-to-roller shaft sleeve joint.

Unscrew the three self-locking nuts and remove relevant screws.

Steering box is now free.

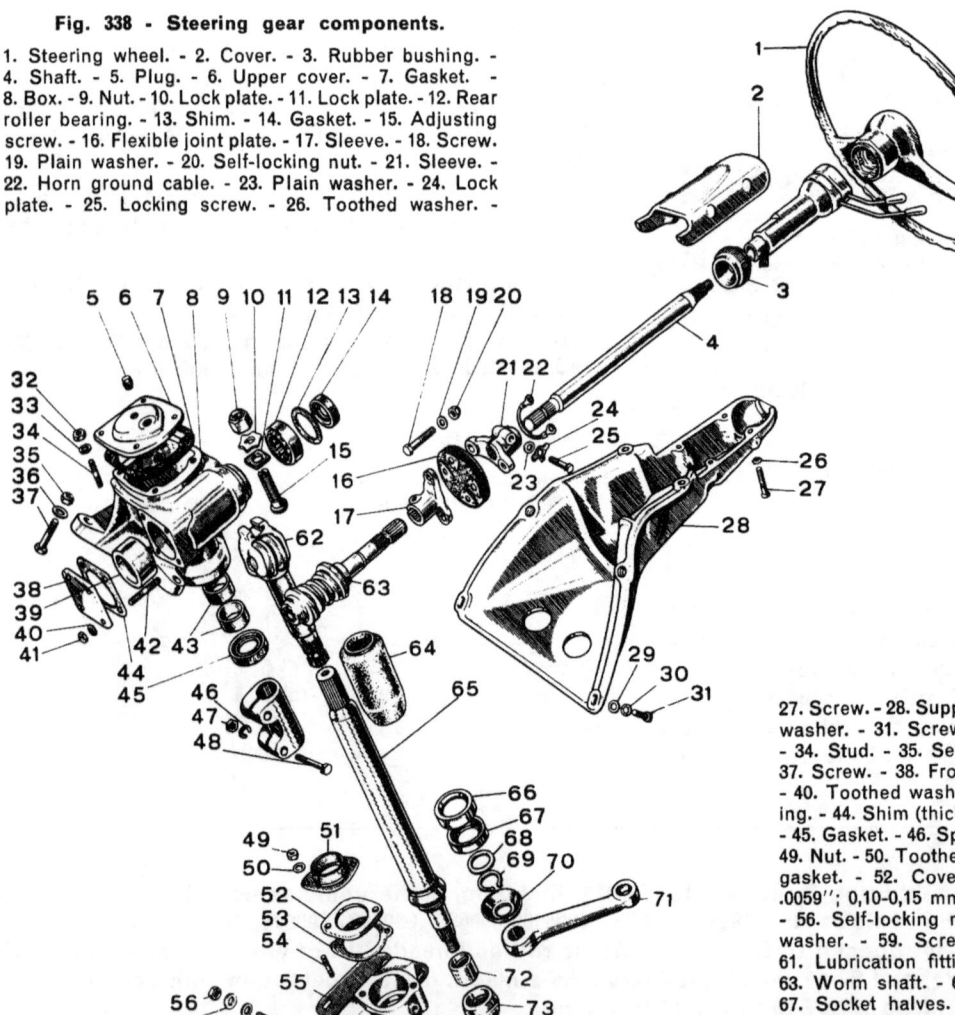

Fig. 338 - Steering gear components.

1. Steering wheel. - 2. Cover. - 3. Rubber bushing. - 4. Shaft. - 5. Plug. - 6. Upper cover. - 7. Gasket. - 8. Box. - 9. Nut. - 10. Lock plate. - 11. Lock plate. - 12. Rear roller bearing. - 13. Shim. - 14. Gasket. - 15. Adjusting screw. - 16. Flexible joint plate. - 17. Sleeve. - 18. Screw. - 19. Plain washer. - 20. Self-locking nut. - 21. Sleeve. - 22. Horn ground cable. - 23. Plain washer. - 24. Lock plate. - 25. Locking screw. - 26. Toothed washer. - 27. Screw. - 28. Support. - 29. Plain washer. - 30. Toothed washer. - 31. Screw. - 32. Nut. - 33. Toothed washer. - 34. Stud. - 35. Self-locking nut. - 36. Plain washer. - 37. Screw. - 38. Front cover. - 39. Front roller bearing. - 40. Toothed washer. - 41. Nut. - 42. Stud. - 43. Bushing. - 44. Shim (thickness .0039'' - .0059''; 0,10-0,15 mm). - 45. Gasket. - 46. Spring washer. - 47. Nut. - 48. Screw. - 49. Nut. - 50. Toothed washer. - 51. Operating rod upper gasket. - 52. Cover. - 53. Shim (thickness .0039'' - .0059''; 0,10-0,15 mm). - 54. Stud. - 55. Adjusting plate. - 56. Self-locking nut. - 57. Plain washer. - 58. Plain washer. - 59. Screw. - 60. Operating rod support. - 61. Lubrication fitting. - 62. Roller shaft assembly. - 63. Worm shaft. - 64. Boot. - 65. Operating rod. - 66. Socket halves. - 68. Washer. - 69. Snap ring. - 70. Lower gasket. - 71. Pitman arm. - 72. Bushing. - 73. Joint. - 74. Spring washer. - 75. Nut.

STEERING GEAR AND LINKAGE

Steering Box Disassembly.

Lock servicing support **A. 66050** in a vise and fix the steering box in support (fig. 340).

Remove nut (3, fig. 341) and then the upper cover, turn in the adjustment screw (4, fig. 341) and remove the worm roller shaft adjustment plate.

Take off the front thrust cover (6, fig. 339) and the vorm screw roller bearing shims (8).

Fig. 340.

Steering box mounted on service support A. 66050.

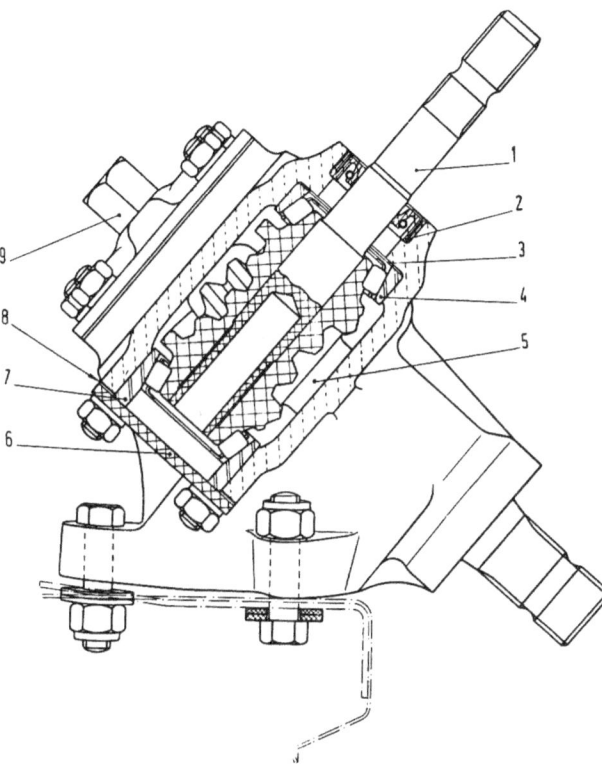

Fig. 339 - Steering box section through worm screw.
1. Worm screw. - 2. Seal, worm. - 3. Adjuster shims. - 4. Upper roller bearing. - 5. Roller shaft. - 6. Thrust cover. - 7. Lower roller bearing. - 8. Shims, worm bearing adjustment. - 9. Nut, roller shaft adjustment screw.

Pull out roller shaft (5, fig. 339) and push down worm screw (1): this will push out lower roller bearing and the upper roller bearing inner ring.

Remove worm screw oil seal (2, fig. 339) and roller shaft oil seal (8, fig. 341).

Fit puller **A. 46004** and remove the outer ring of the worm screw upper bearing (4, fig. 339) together with its adjuster shims (3) located between the bearing and the box.

If roller shaft bushes (6 and 7, fig. 341) are excessively worn, replace them using replacer **A. 66009**.

Inspection and Repair.

Check parts accurately to see that sector teeth and worm screw threads show no sign of seizure, indents or deep scoring.

Check contact surfaces to make sure that meshing between the two parts takes place at center; this, to have a basis for adjustment during assembly.

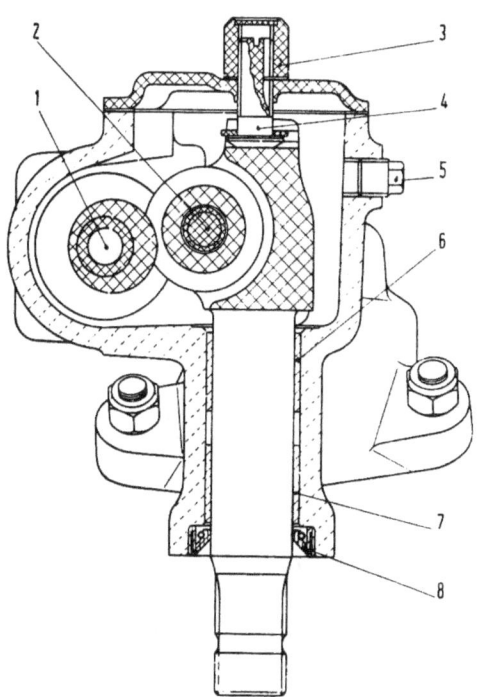

Fig. 341 - Steering box section through steering shaft.
1. Worm screw. - 2. Roller. - 3 and 4. Nut and screw, roller shaft adjustment. - 5. Oil filler and drain plug. - 6 and 7. Roller shaft bushes. 8. Roller shaft seal.

Check clearance between eccentric bushes (6 and 7, fig. 341) and roller shaft. Maximum allowable clearance is .0039″ (0,10 mm).

If found greater, remove the bushes and fit new ones using tool **A. 66009**.

After press-fitting, the bush inner diameter must be brought to the recommended size of 1.1297″ to 1.1306″ (28,698 to 28,720 mm) using reamer **U. 0336**. Fit clearance between roller shaft and bush is .0003″ to .0020″ (0,008 to 0,051 mm).

Roller shaft diameter is 1.1294″ to 1.1286″ (28,690 to 28,669 mm).

Check worm screw centering: maximum allowable off-center is .0019″ (0,05 mm).

The two roller bearings must slide smoothly and have no play between inner and outer rings.

Check the worm screw and roller seals for soundness.

Replace any part found damaged.

Steering Box Assembly and Adjustment.

Clamp servicing support **A. 66050** in a vise and fix the steering box in support.

Mount the worm screw shims and its upper roller bearing outer ring: the number of shims must be the same as found at disassembly, if the roller-to-worm screw mating was perfectly centered.

Place the roller bearing inner rings on worm screw.

Mount: the worm screw and the lower bearing outer ring, then the front thrust cover, interposing the shims between cover and box.

Shims are supplied as spares in the .0039″ and .0059″ (0,10 and 0,15 mm) thicknesses.

Check the play of worm screw bearings: reduce shim thickness if play is excessive and increase thickness if insufficient.

Install roller shaft and fit the upper cover with adjustment screw and plate.

Check worm screw-to-roller backlash: turn in screw (4, fig. 341) until all backlash is taken-up.

After this, screw in and tighten nut (3, fig. 341) to lock adjustment screw in position.

Said adjustment must be made when the roller is centered on worm screw.

If the mating of worm screw and roller is not perfectly centered, add or remove shims (6 and 9, fig. 342) and turn in or out the adjuster (according to need) of worm screw until perfect centering with roller is obtained.

In this case, repeat the adjustment of worm screw-to-roller backlash and then install the worm screw and roller shaft oil seals.

Operating Rod.

Operating rod upper end is connected to roller shaft while its lower end is connected to relay lever through the pitman arm and a link rod. At its lower end, the operating rod is supported in a ball-and-socket joint rotating in a spherical seat lined with half-bearings. The play between ball and half bearings of joint is adjusted by means of shims which are placed between joint and cover.

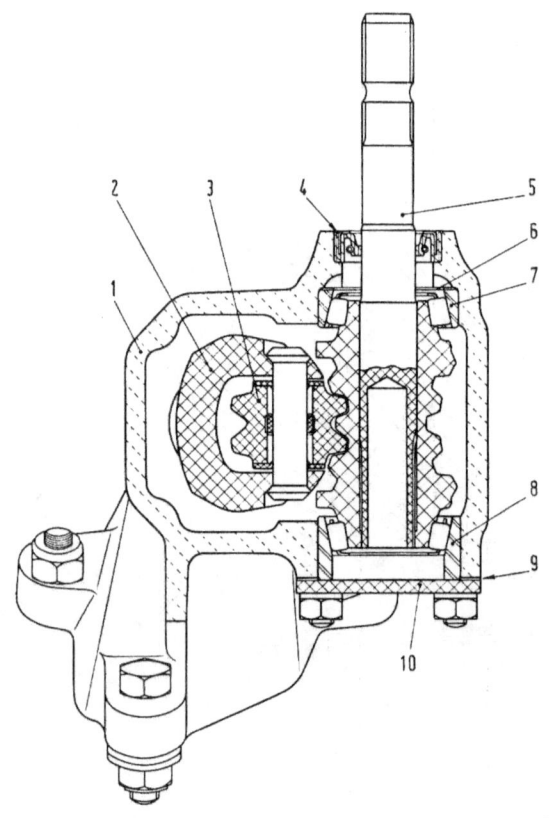

Fig. 342 - Steering box section through worm screw and roller.
1. Steering box. - 2. Roller shaft. - 3. Roller. - 4. Worm screw seal. - 5. Worm screw and shaft. - 6. Adjuster shims. - 7. Upper roller bearing. - 8. Lower roller bearing. - 9. Lower bearing shims. - 10. Thrust cover.

The following operations must be performed when servicing the operating rod assembly:

a) check the rod-to-joint bush clearance which must never exceed .0059″ (0,15 mm). Fit clearance is .00047″ to .0021″ (0,012 to 0,054 mm);

b) inspect the condition of joint half-bearings and replace if found worn;

c) check joint snap ring and replace if its flexibility is inadequate;

d) check the soundness of the upper and lower seals;

e) adjust the clearance between ball and half-bearings: the shims interposed between joint and

STEERING GEAR AND LINKAGE

cover are supplied as spares in the .0039" and .0059" (0,10 and 0,15 mm) thickness sizes.

At assembly, remember that the operating rod-to-pitman arm nut must be tightened with a torque wrench to 80 ft.lbs (11.000 kgmm).

Support and Relay Lever.

The relay lever support is anchored to a cross-member of body floor (fig. 287). For its removal, first disconnect the link rod pin and then the track rod pins. Next, unscrew the four self-locking nuts and back out the screws from cross-member.

To disassemble components, proceed as follows:

— clamp the support (1, fig. 343) in a vise;

— disinsert cotter pin (11) and back out relay lever mounting nut (10);

— pull out relay lever (12) and remove the rubber ring (13);

— remove upper cover (3), its gasket, spring (4) and cup (5);

— take off lockplate (6) and then disinsert pivot (8).

After disassembly:

— Inspect spring (4, fig. 343) and, if weak or distorted, fit a new spring. This will prevent the development of axial play between pivot and its support.

— Check the condition of bushes (9, fig. 343): if ovalized or if play with pivot is excessive, remove and replace with new bushes. Specified bush-to-pivot fit clearance is .00047" to .0021" (0,012 to 0,054 mm).

The recommended bush I. D. of .8666" to .8674" (22,012 to 22,033 mm) must be obtained after press-fitting, using a reamer.

No particular difficulty will be experienced for reassembly: just remember that the relay lever-to-pivot mounting nut must be tightened to a 101 ft.lbs (14.000 kgmm) torque.

Steering Rods.

The steering linkage assembly has already been described on page 202.

For servicing instructions, follow the same as outlined for «Sedan» on page 201.

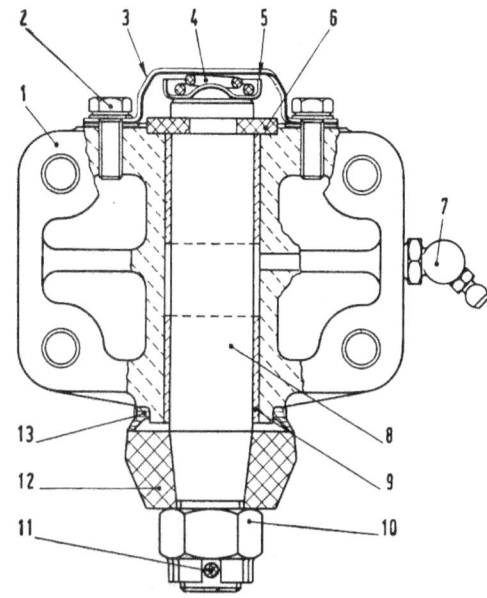

Fig. 343 - Section through relay lever support.
1. Support. - 2. Lower screw. - 3. Upper cover. - 4. Pivot spring. - 5. Lower cup. - 6. Pivot retainment plate. - 7. Lubricator. - 8. Relay lever pivot. - 9. Bushes. - 10. Lever-to-pivot nut. - 11. Cotter pin. 12. Relay lever. - 13. Rubber ring.

Remember that the ball pin-to-relay lever and to pitman arm mounting nuts must be tightened to 21.7 ft.lbs (3.000 kgmm) of torque.

NOTE - Steering box-to-horizontal bracket mounting nut must be tightened to 27.5 ft.lbs (3.800 kgmm).

CHECKING AND ADJUSTING FRONT WHEEL TOE-IN

Before starting the check, see that:

— tire pressures are as recommended:

Sedan p.s.i. kg/cm²

   front 14.2 1

   rear 22.8 1,60

Multipla

   front 24.2 1,70

   rear 28.5 2,00

— steering wheel spokes are horizontal;
— wheels are in straightahead position;
— car is fully laden.

Proceed as follows:

Adjust height of **C. 692** gauge plungers until they coincide with the wheel horizontal centerline, then set plungers against the outer edge of rim rear portion (fig. 345) and mark off with chalk.

Next, bring gauge in front of wheels, move car forward and stop when chalk marks line up with gauge plungers. Set one plunger in contact with wheel. The gap between the other plunger and the other wheel must be:

Fig. 345 - Checking front wheel toe-in.
Use gauge C. 692.

Sedan

— up to car No. 071086 . . . .2362'' to .3149''
    (6 to 8 mm) toe-in
— from car No. 071087 . . . .1181'' to .1968''
   up to No. 377800 (3 to 5 mm) toe-in
— from car No. 377801 . . . .0787'' (2 mm)
   up to No. 698914 toe-out
— from car No. 698915 . . . .0000'' to .0787''
    (0 to 2 mm) toe-in

Multipla

— wheels in straightahead position ± .0394''
    (1 mm) tolerance

If toe-in or toe-out need correction, slacken the four clamps fixing the sleeves on track rod heads. Rotate track rods in opposite directions and of an equal amount. Since track rods have one right-hand and one left-hand threaded end, when turned in one direction both heads are screwed out and when turned in the opposite direction both heads are screwed in. The result of this is a variation in track rod length.

When a perfect adjustment has been obtained, tighten the four clamps; with fully tightened clamp nuts, check that expansion slot in the sleeve registers with clamp joint; with fully tightened clamp, joint faces must not be in contact, otherwise the faulty clamp must be replaced.

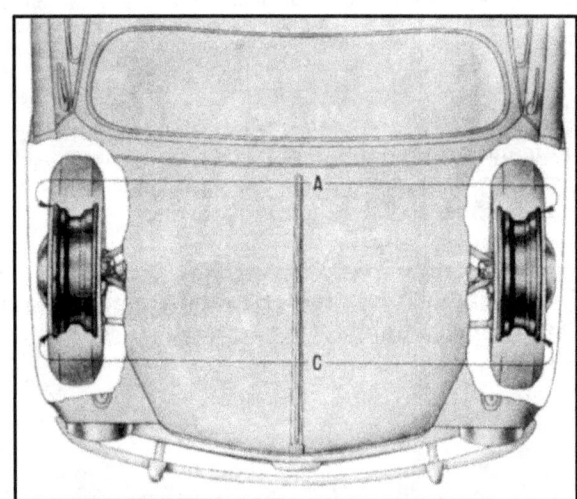

Fig. 344 - Front wheel toe-in check data.
C must be smaller than A by .0000'' to .0787'' (0 to 2 mm).

STEERING GEAR AND LINKAGE

STEERING MECHANISM TIGHTENING REFERENCE

ITEM		DRWG. OR STD. PART No.	THREAD	MATERIAL	TIGHTENING TORQUE
Steering box mounting self-locking nut (and relay lever support, Sedan only)	Sedan	1/25743/11	8 MA (x1,25)	R 50 Cdt (Screw R 80 Cdt)	14.5 to 18 ft.lbs (2.000 to 2.500 kgmm)
	Multipla	1/25745/11	10 x 1,25 M	R 50 Cdt (Screw R 80 Cdt)	27.5 ft.lbs (3.800 kgmm)
Pitman arm self-locking nut (Sedan)		1/25748/11	14 MB (x1,5)	R 50 Cdt (Sector 19CN5 Cmt3)	72 to 80 ft.lbs (10.000 to 11.000 kgmm)
Pitman arm nut (Multipla)		1/21641/21	16 MB (x1,5)	R 80 Cdt (Rod 38NCD4 Bon)	80 ft.lbs (11.000 kgmm)
Relay lever pin (or pivot) nut	Sedan	1/25747/11	12 MB (x1,5)	R 50 Cdt (Pin R 80 Cdt)	40 to 43.4 ft.lbs (5.500 to 6.000 kgmm)
	Multipla	1/07924/11	16 MB (x1,5)	R 50 Cdt (Pivot R 100)	101 ft.lbs (14.000 kgmm)
Track rod articulation head ball pin nut	Sedan	1/25756/11	10 x 1,25 M	R 50 Cdt (Pin 15 CND 3 Cmtl)	18.1 to 21.7 ft.lbs (2.500 to 3.000 kgmm)
	Multipla	1/07933/11	12 MB (x1,5)	R 50 Cdt (Pin 15 CND 3R)	21.7 ft.lbs (3.000 kgmm)
Steering wheel mounting nut		1.62.025 743601	18 MB (x1,5)	R 50 Cdt (Shaft C 12 tube)	28.9 to 36.2 ft.lbs (4.000 to 5.000 kgmm)

STEERING MECHANISM TOOL EQUIPMENT

	SEDAN	MULTIPLA
Support - steering box servicing	A. 66032	A. 66050
Puller - pitman arm	A. 46021	
Wrench - worm screw bearing adjuster sleeve	A. 8065	
Puller - worm screw bearing inner rings	A. 46019	
Puller - worm screw upper bearing outer ring	A. 66040	A. 46004
Tool - worm screw seal remover	A. 10110	
Tool - installer, roller (or sector) shaft bushes	A. 66043	A. 66009
Installer - worm screw roller bearing inner rings and upper bearing outer ring	A. 66046	
Wrench - steering wheel-to-shaft nut	A. 8279	
Puller - steering rod head pins	A. 46022	A. 46022
Reamer - roller shaft bushings		U. 0336

STEERING GEAR SPECIFICATIONS AND DATA

	SEDAN	MULTIPLA
Steering control	by worm screw and helical sector	by worm screw and roller
Reduction ratio	2 to 26	1 to 16.4
Worm screw bearings	taper roller	taper roller
Sector (or roller) shaft bushes	1, bronze	2, bronze
Bearing adjustment by	adjuster sleeve	rings at top shims at bottom
Adjustment of backlash between worm screw and sector (or roller)	by turning the adjuster in or out	by screw with plate acting on roller carrier shaft
Sector (or roller) shaft bush diameter	.7874" to .7882" (20,000 to 20,021 mm)	1.1297" to 1.1306" (28,698 to 28,720 mm)
Sector (or roller) shaft diameter	.7874" to .7865" (20,000 to 19,979 mm)	1.1294" to 1.1286" (28,690 to 28,669 mm)
Sector (or roller) shaft-to-bush clearance	.0000" to .0016" (0,000 to 0,042 mm)	.0003" to .0020" (0,008 to 0,051 mm)
Operating rod-to-bush in socket joint fit clearance .	—	.00047" to .0021" (0,012 to 0,054 mm)
Relay lever pivot-to-bush fit clearance	—	.00047" to .0021" (0,012 to 0,054 mm)
Turning circle diameter	28 ft. 7" (8,70 m)	28 ft. 10" (8,80 m)
Track rods	with adjustable heads	with adjustable heads
Pitman arm-to-relay lever rod	non-adjustable heads	non-adjustable heads

Cramping angles:
  inner wheel ....
  outer wheel ....
	32º
	25º 50'
		35º
		28º 30'

Front wheel toe-in	.0000" to .0787" (0 to 2 mm)	straight with a ± .039" (1 mm) tolerance

Steering gear lubricant:
  type ....
  quantity { litres ....
            kg ....
	Fiat W 90 (SAE 90 EP) oil
	0,120
	0,110
		Fiat W 90 (SAE 90 EP) oil
		0,165
		0,150

STEERING GEAR AND LINKAGE TROUBLE DIAGNOSIS AND CORRECTIONS

Jerky Steering.

POSSIBLE CAUSES	REMEDIES
1) Incorrect front wheel alignment.	1) Inspect and adjust as recommended on page 156.
2) Incorrect front wheel bearing adjustment.	2) Adjust as recommended on page 155.
3) Wheels out of balance.	3) Inspect and correct as recommended on page 234.
4) Loose steering linkage connections.	4) Inspect, replace worn parts, if any, and tighten nuts with torque recommended on page 207.
5) Loose or incorrect fitting of worm to sector or roller.	5) Adjust as recommended on pages 198 and 204.
6) Front suspension swinging arm spider bushings worn (Multipla).	6) Replace bushings as outlined on page 164.

Hard Steering.

POSSIBLE CAUSES	REMEDIES
1) Incorrect tire pressure.	1) Inflate tires to correct pressure as outlined on page 234.
2) Incorrect front wheel alignment.	2) Check wheel alignment and adjust as outlined and tubulated on page 156.
3) Incorrect adjustment of steering worm to worm sector or roller.	3) Adjust steering gear as recommended on pages 198 and 204.

Hard Turning when Stationary.

POSSIBLE CAUSES	REMEDIES
1) Incorrect tire pressure.	1) Check pressure of tires and inflate to correct value as specified on page 234.
2) Incorrect adjustment of steering worm to worm sector or roller.	2) Adjust steering gear as recommended on pages 198 and 204.
3) Front suspension swinging arm spider bushings worn (Multipla).	3) Replace bushings; self-threading bushings should be replaced by others of oversized dimensions. Proceed as outlined on page 164.

Loose Steering.

POSSIBLE CAUSES	REMEDIES
1) Incorrect front wheel bearing adjustment.	1) Adjust as recommended on page 155.
2) Loose steering linkage connections.	2) Inspect, replace worn parts, if any, and tighten nuts with torque recommended on page 207.
3) Loose steering gear mountings.	3) Tighten mounting nuts with recommended torque (page 207).
4) Incorrect adjustment of steering worm to worm sector or roller.	4) Adjust steering gear as recommended on pages 198 and 204.
5) Operating rod linking loose on bearings (Multipla).	5) Replace bearings and, if necessary, operating rod link.

Pull to One Side.

POSSIBLE CAUSES	REMEDIES
1) Incorrect tire pressure.	1) Inspect and inflate tires as specified on page 234.
2) Incorrect front wheel alignment.	2) Inspect and adjust front wheel alignment as specified on page 156.
3) Incorrect front wheel bearing adjustment.	3) Adjust bearings as specified on page 155.
4) Distorted steering knuckle pillar or swinging arms.	4) Disassemble suspensions and check knuckle pillar and swinging arms on test equipment, as outlined under « Front Suspension and Wheels ».
5) Unequal brake adjustment.	5) Adjust brakes as specified on page 222.
6) Semi-elliptic springs or coil springs weak or broken.	6) Check springs against data on pages 148, 149 and 169, and replace damaged or broken springs.

Tire Squeal on Turns.

POSSIBLE CAUSES	REMEDIES
1) Incorrect tire pressure.	1) Check tire pressure and inflate as specified on page 234.
2) Incorrect wheel alignment.	2) Check and correct as specified on pages 156 and 171.
3) Distorted steering knuckle pillar or swinging arms.	3) Check knuckle pillar and swinging arms on test equipment as shown under « Front Suspension and Wheels »; replace knuckle pillar, if distorted, and swinging arms which cannot be straightened correctly.

STEERING GEAR AND LINKAGE

Front Wheel Shimmy.

POSSIBLE CAUSES	REMEDIES
1) Incorrect tire pressure.	1) Inspect tire pressure and inflate as recommended on page 234.
2) Incorrect front wheel alignment.	2) Inspect and correct front wheel alignment as outlined on page 156.
3) Loose front wheel bearings.	3) Adjust bearings as outlined on page 155.
4) Wheels out of balance.	4) Inspect and correct as outlined on page 234.
5) Loose steering linkage connections.	5) Inspect, replace damaged parts, if any, and tighten nuts with torque specified on page 207.
6) Loose steering gear, relay lever support or operating rod support (Multipla) at body mountings.	6) Check all mounting nuts for tightness with recommended torque (page 207).
7) Incorrect fitting of steering worm to worm sector or roller.	7) Adjust steering gear as outlined on pages 198 and 204.

Side-to-Side Wander.

POSSIBLE CAUSES	REMEDIES
1) Incorrect tire pressure.	1) Check tire pressure and inflate as specified on page 234.
2) Incorrect front wheel alignment.	2) Check wheel alignment and adjust as specified on pages 156 and 171.
3) Loose steering linkage connections.	3) Check, replace damaged parts and tighten nuts with torque specified on page 207.
4) Loose steering gear, relay lever support or operating rod support (Multipla) at body mountings.	4) Check all mounting nuts for tightness with recommended torque (page 207).
5) Incorrect fitting of steering worm to worm sector or roller.	5) Adjust steering gear as outlined on pages 198 and 204.
6) Distorted steering knuckle pillar or swinging arms.	6) Check knuckle pillar and swinging arms on test equipment as shown under « Front Suspension » and replace knuckle pillar, if distorted, and swinging arms which cannot be straightened correctly.
7) Semi-elliptic springs or coil springs weak or broken.	7) Check springs against data on pages 148, 149 and 169, and replace if damaged or broken.

Rattles.

POSSIBLE CAUSES	REMEDIES
1) Loose steering linkage connections.	1) Inspect, replace worn parts, if any, and tighten nuts with torque recommended on page 207.
2) Loose steering gear, relay lever support or operating rod support (Multipla) at body mountings.	2) Check all mounting nuts for tightness with recommended torque (page 207).
3) Semi-elliptic springs (Sedan) or coil springs (Multipla) weak or broken.	3) Check against data on pages 148, 149 and 169 and replace damaged or broken springs.
4) Leak of lubrication.	4) Lubricate as specified in lubrication diagrams, following recommended procedure.

Section 8

BRAKES
WHEELS AND TIRES

	Page
HYDRAULIC SERVICE BRAKES	216
PARKING BRAKE	225
BRAKE TIGHTENING REFERENCE	227
SERVICE BRAKE SPECIFICATIONS AND DATA	228
PARKING BRAKE SPECIFICATIONS AND DATA	229
BRAKE SERVICE EQUIPMENT	229
HYDRAULIC BRAKE SYSTEM TROUBLE DIAGNOSIS AND CORRECTIONS	231
WHEELS AND TIRES	234
WHEEL SCREW TIGHTENING REFERENCE	236

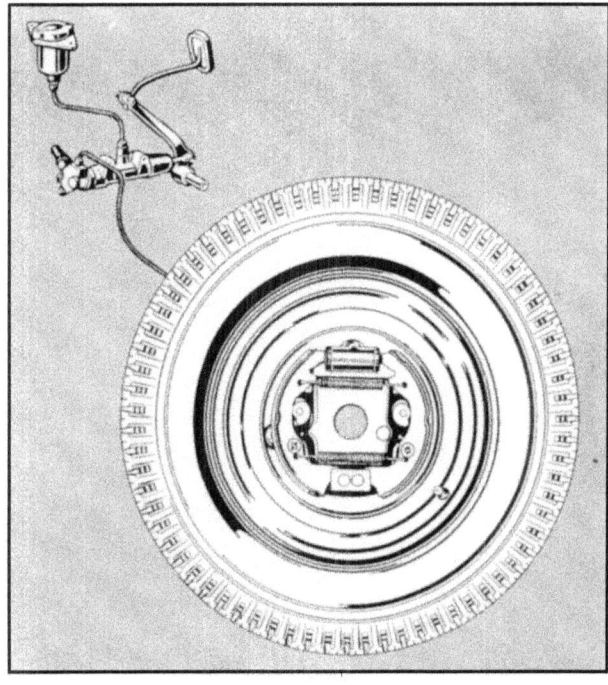

214 FIAT - 600 - 600 D SEDAN AND MULTIPLA

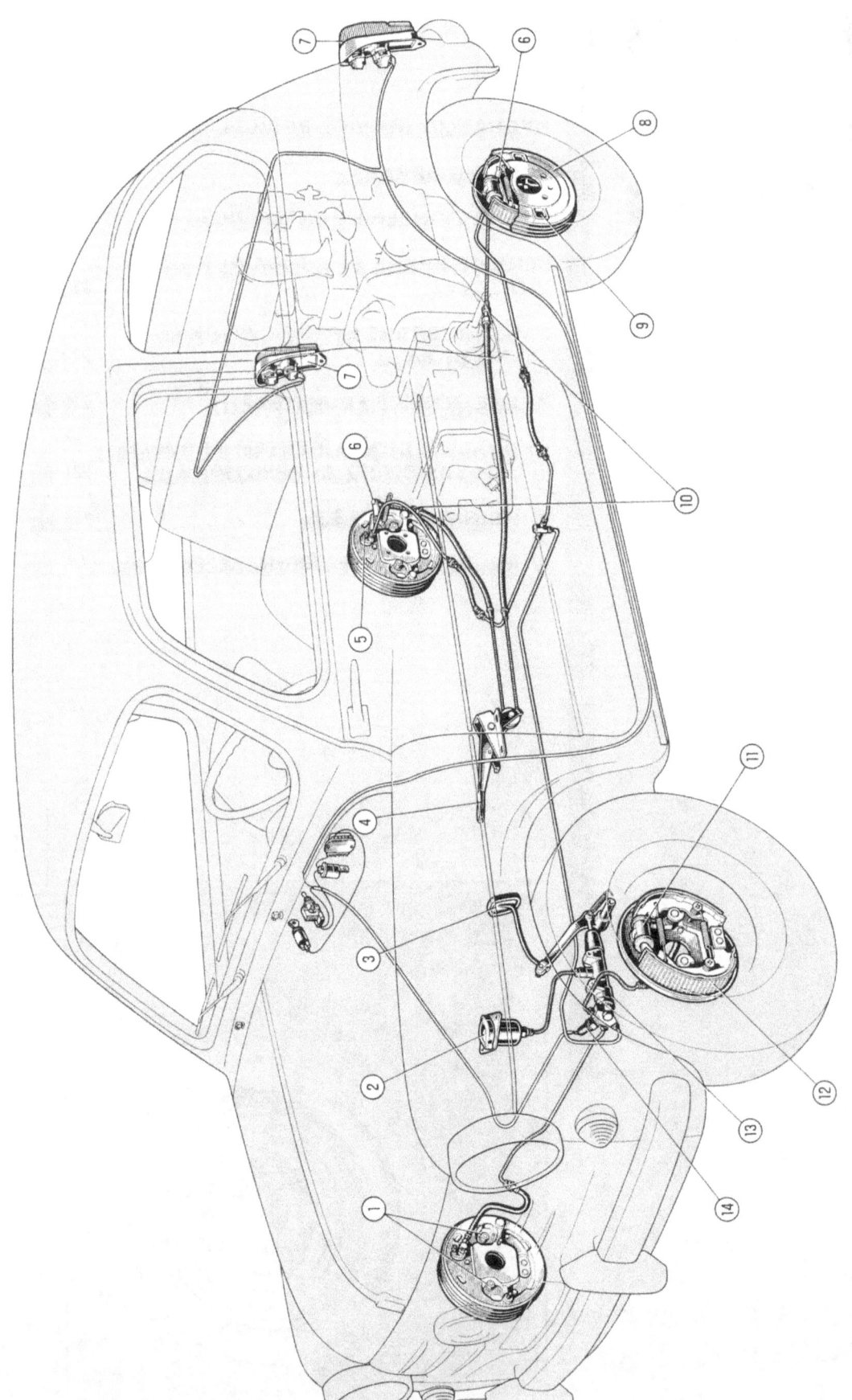

Fig. 346 - Phantom view of hydraulic service brake system on four wheels, and of hand-controlled, parking brake system on rear wheels (Sedan from engine No. 758493).

1. Cams, brake shoe-to-drum clearance adjustment. - 2. Tank, brake fluid. - 3. Pedal, service brake control. - 4. Lever, parking brake manual control. - 5. Connection, line bleeding. - 6. Lever, rear brake shoe operating, driven by parking brake lever (4). - 7. Stop lights, rear. - 8. Brake drum. - 9. Slots, brake shoe-to-drum clearance inspection. - 10. Stretchers, parking brake hand lever travel adjustment. - 11. Wheel cylinder. - 12. Brake shoes. - 13. Master cylinder. - 14. Switch, pedal operated, rear stop light.

BRAKES

Description	page 215
HYDRAULIC SERVICE BRAKES	» 216
Master Cylinder	» 216
Wheel Cylinders	» 216
Hydraulic System Operation	» 216
Inspecting the Hydraulic System	» 217
Servicing the Hydraulic System	» 219
Servicing Shoes and Linings	» 220
Drums	» 221
Adjusting Shoe Clearance	» 222
Bleeding the Hydraulic Lines	» 224
Brake Fluid Reservoir	» 225
PARKING BRAKE	» 225
On Rear Wheels	» 225
On Drive Line	» 226
BRAKE TIGHTENING REFERENCE	» 227
SERVICE BRAKE SPECIFICATIONS AND DATA	» 228
PARKING BRAKE SPECIFICATIONS AND DATA	» 229
BRAKE SERVICE EQUIPMENT	» 229
HYDRAULIC BRAKE SYSTEM TROUBLE DIAGNOSIS AND CORRECTIONS	» 231

Description.

Model 600 has been equipped with two types of brakes, which apply to both « Sedan » and « Multipla » version:

— service, hydraulically operated, on all four wheels;

— auxiliary, mechanically operated, on rear wheels.

Hydraulic brakes are pedal controlled; mechanical brake is controlled by a hand lever on floor tunnel, within easy reach of the driver.

Service brakes are of the drum, expanding shoe type: sheet metal, self-centering shoes for « Sedan »; aluminum, bottom-hinged shoes for « Multipla ». Both type shoes are provided with asbestos woven linings.

When pedal is operated, the master cylinder transmits pressure to the brake line fluid which, in turn, operates the wheel cylinders on the four brake housing flanges. The result is a smooth braking of shoes against drums, through wheel cylinder plungers.

The auxiliary hand brake, which should be used as a normal braking means only in emergency and with great caution, has been basically designed for keeping the car at standstill in parking position. The hand lever operates, through a cable, levers and wedges providing shoe expansion.

NOTE

Auxiliary parking brake on rear wheels has been fitted starting from engine No. 758493, « Sedan », and engine No. 765151, « Multipla » Previously the parking brake developed on the drive line and was of the expanding shoe type, acting on a drum press fitted on the gearbox layshaft.

HYDRAULIC SERVICE BRAKES

MASTER CYLINDER

Master cylinder is of the floating valve ring type, featuring extremely simple construction, strong components and minimum number of parts.

It operates in the following way (fig. 347):

The brake pedal control rod exerts pressure directly on master cylinder plunger (13). On feed chamber rear end, sealing is ensured by front rubber valve (20) identical to valve (18). Valve (20) is fitted on a shoulder of plunger (13), and is squeezed between parts (19) and (13) by return spring (7) with a radial pressure sufficient to give perfect sealing.

When master cylinder is at rest, valve (18) has no radial pressure, and, moreover, it is in such a position as to allow master cylinder to be fed through compensating hole (8).

Valves (18) and (20) have a marked toric section; their maximum free diameter is equal to, or slighty larger than, the cylinder diameter; when not under hydraulic pressure, only their outer face mid portion is in contact with the cylinder wall, while the edges clear it.

When hydraulic pressure, combined with spring reaction, comes into play, it causes valve expansion. The contact area is reduced to a minimum and the rounded fluid-side edge ensures good lubrication to sliding surfaces and drag is negligible.

Compensating hole (8) in master cylinder is .0275" (0,7 mm) in diameter (Sedan) and .039" (1 mm) in diameter (Multipla). This ensures proper compensation in case of fluid expansion due to drum heating, reduces clogging probabilities by foreign matter having entered the system and improves bleeding by facilitating the expulsion of air bubbles from compression chamber.

Inner diameter of master cylinder is 3/4" (Sedan) or 1" (Multipla).

WHEEL CYLINDERS

Diameters of wheel cylinders are:

« Sedan »
— front and rear . . . . 3/4"

« Multipla »
— front . . . . 1 1/8"
— rear . . . . 3/4"

As with the master cylinder, sealing is obtained by two rubber seal rings (5, fig. 348) which expand radially under fluid pressure.

Spring (6), clenched to thrust washers (6), presses seal rings against plungers (2) acting on shoes through stems.

Hydraulic System Operation.

Through hole (12, fig. 347), the fluid is admitted to master cylinder, seeps through gap between valve ring carrier (19) and master cylinder barrel and, flowing through valve ring carrier holes (17), reaches and fills the system.

By depressing the brake pedal, the plunger is moved forward by rod (16).

The forward stroke of plunger (13) and valve carrier (19) brings valve (18) to rest against valve carrier front face, thus closing the passage to valve carrier annular chamber. Continuing in its forward movement, valve ring (18) passes over compen-

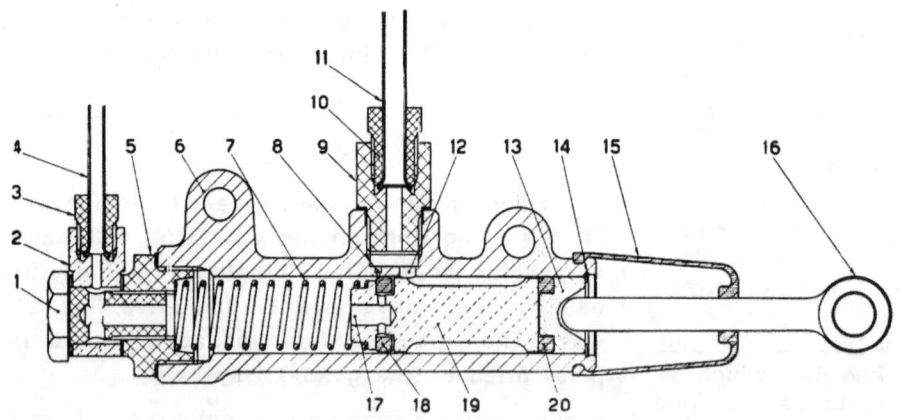

Fig. 347.
Master cylinder section.

1. Drilled screw fixing the connection to master cylinder. - 2. Four-way connection for brake pipe line and stop switch. - 3 and 4. Left front brake pipe and connection. - 5. Master cylinder plug and spring seat. - 6. Master cylinder body. - 7. Plunger return spring. - 8. Compensating hole. - 9. Fluid inlet connection. - 10 and 11. Reservoir-to-master cylinder pipe. - 12. Fluid-to-master cylinder inlet hole. - 13. Plunger. - 14. Plunger stop circlip. - 15. Control rod boot. - 16. Control rod. - 17. Holes on valve shoulder for fluid inlet. - 18. Floating valve. - 19. Floating valve carrier. - 20. Ring valve and seal.

sating hole and cuts off any communication with the fluid reservoir.

Compression of the fluid begins from this instant.

By acting on front and inner faces of valve, it warrants perfect valve sealing even under noticeably high operation pressures.

When pressure reaches the fluid in wheel cylinders (fig. 348) it pushes plungers (2) outward, thus actuating brake shoes.

In wheel cylinders, seal rings (5), also when at rest, are axially compressed by washers (6) under the action of spring. Rings are under the radial and axial action of hydraulic pressure so that their sealing ability is improved as pressure increases.

After releasing the pedal, the combined action of both master cylinder and brake shoe return springs sends the fluid back to master cylinder and all parts resume their original positions, and free intercommunication between system and reservoir is restored.

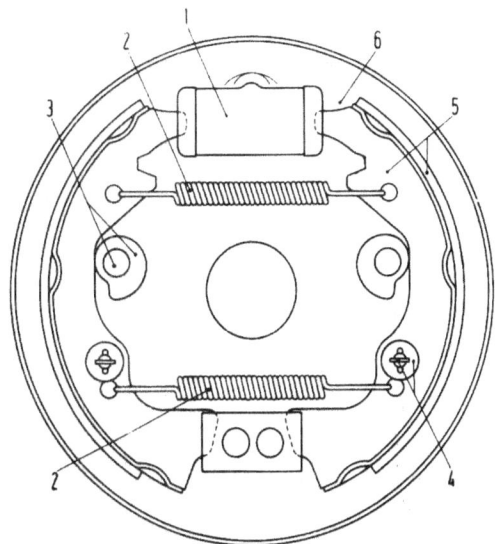

Fig. 349 - Left-hand front brake housing flange, « Sedan », (self-centering shoes).

1. Wheel cylinder. - 2. Shoe return springs. - 3. Brake shoe-to-drum clearance adjusting cams. - 4. Shoe guide spring pins and cups. - 5. Brake shoes and shoe linings. - 6. Brake housing flange.

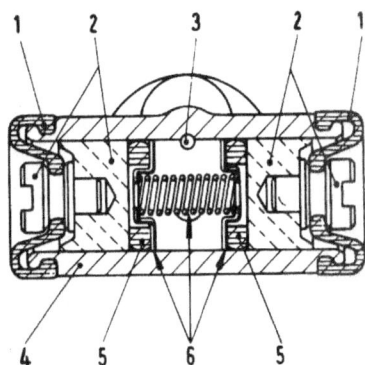

Fig. 348 - Wheel cylinder section.

1. Cylinder boots. - 2. Plungers with stems. - 3. Fluid inlet. - 4. Cylinder body. - 5. Seal rings. - 6. Reaction spring and spring thrust washers.

Since no valves proper are fitted in the brake system and the communication orifice between system and reservoir is amply dimensioned, bleeding is a very simple and easy operation.

In most cases, to eliminate air or vapor locks in the lines it will suffice to pump brake pedal: air will be drawn into master cylinder and discharged through reservoir vent.

Inspecting the Hydraulic System.

Check that:

1) Metal lines are in tip top condition, i. e., without flattenings and cracks and are away from sharp edges.

2) Hoses have not been fouled with oil or grease which would destroy the rubber.

3) All line fastening clips are secure. Should they be loose, this would originate vibrations liable to cause failure of lines.

4) No fluid leaks are noticeable at connections. Should leaks be detected, tighten connections, being careful not to twist pipe during this operation.

5) The fluid level reaches at least 3/4 of reservoir tank height.

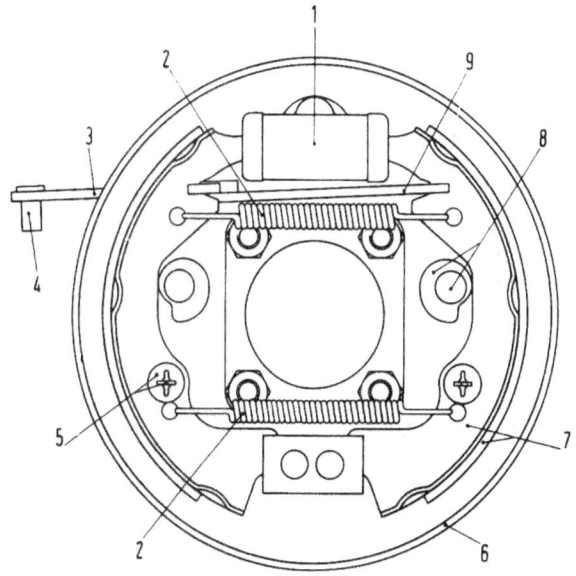

Fig. 350 - Right-hand rear brake housing flange, « Sedan », (self-centering shoes).

1. Wheel cylinder. - 2. Shoe return springs. - 3. Parking brake shoe operating lever, driven by manual lever. - 4. Parking brake cable pin. - 5. Shoe guide spring pins and cups. - 6. Brake housing flange. - 7. Brake shoes and shoe linings. - 8. Brake shoe-to-drum clearance adjusting cams. - 9. Parking brake shoe operating wedge, driven by lever (3).

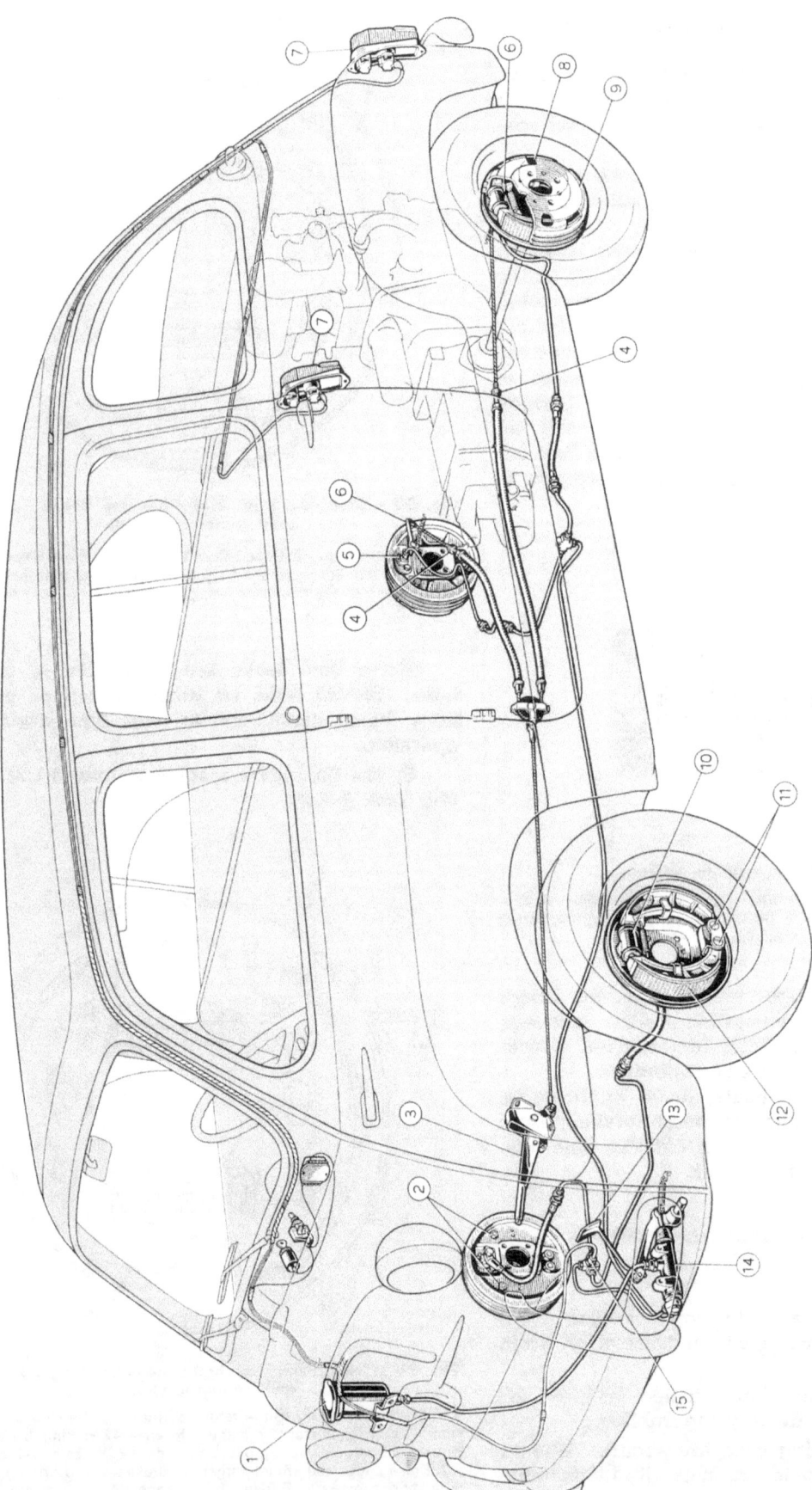

Fig. 351 - Phantom view of hydraulic service brake system on four wheels, and of hand-controlled, parking brake system on rear wheels (Multipla from engine No. 765151).

1. Tank, brake fluid. - 2. Cams, brake shoe-to-drum clearance adjustment. - 3. Lever, parking brake manual control. - 4. Stretchers, parking brake hand lever travel adjustment. - 5. Connection, line bleeding. - 6. Lever, rear brake shoe operating, driven by parking brake lever (3). - 7. Stop lights, rear. - 8. Slots, brake shoe-to-drum clearance inspection. - 9. Brake drum. - 10. Wheel cylinder. - 11. Eccentric pins, shoe pivot and adjustment. - 12. Brake shoes. - 13. Pedal, service brake control. - 14. Master cylinder. - 15. Switch, pedal operated, rear stop light.

The fluid to be used is the FIAT special blue label fluid and it must not be contaminated by any other liquid which, if present, would irreparably damage the special rubber gaskets of the system.

Avoid spilling any fluid over body paint because it is a solvent.

6) Play between rod and master cylinder plunger is .039″ to .059″ (1 to 1,5 mm).

This corresponds approximately to a .20″ to .31″ (5 to 8 mm) pedal free travel.

7) Master cylinder and wheel cylinder boots are in perfect condition and well tight. The accidental admission of foreign matter or of water through master cylinder rear end and in wheel cylinders may cause a locking of plungers resulting in unbalanced or completely inefficient braking.

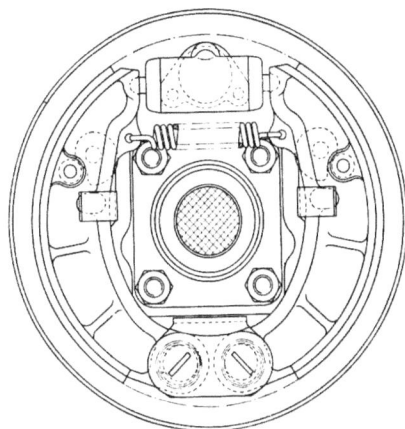

Fig. 352 - Brake housing flange-rear, wheels, « Sedan » (hinged-type shoes).

SERVICING THE HYDRAULIC SYSTEM

Disassembly.

Raise car and place on stands. Remove wheels. Remove front and rear brake drums using puller **A. 6469** or universal puller **A. 40005.**

After taking off reservoir filler cap and strainer, blank lower outlet hole with a suitably sized wooden peg, from inside reservoir.

Next, disconnect and remove:

— the line from reservoir to master cylinder;
— the front and rear brake hoses;
— all metal lines of front and rear brakes;
— the reservoir;
— the rear stop lights pressure-operated switch;
— the master cylinder;
— the wheel cylinders;
— the brake shoes.

Inspection and Service.

Lines and reservoir.

Check the hoses and replace if deteriorated.

As a rule, however, it is advisable to change all hoses after 50,000 miles (80.000 km) or after five years of operation: this will prevent sudden unexpected failures of hoses on account of age and fatigue

Check also metal pipes: they must not be flattened in any point and must be integral. Replace if required

Thoroughly clean the reservoir to eliminate possible sludge deposits.

Take always all necessary precautions and care to avoid contamination of the brake fluid by foreign matter which would seriously compromise hydraulic system operation because the fluid boiling point, freezing point and viscosity will be altered.

Another result may be the deterioration of rubber seals which, by swelling, will block the system and impair the sealing ability or fluid feed of master cylinder.

Master cylinder.

To disassemble master cylinder:

Remove rubber boot (15, fig. 347) and rod (16).

Take off circlip. From master cylinder body (6) the following items may now be removed: plunger (13), seal (20), valve-ring carrier (19), valve-ring (18) and return spring (7)

Remove master cylinder connection and front blanking plug

Carefully check master cylinder inner surface and plunger outer surface: they must be absolutely mirror-like and play must not be excessive.

Smoothen out any roughness present on master cylinder inner surface to prevent fluid leaks or excessive wear of seals or plunger.

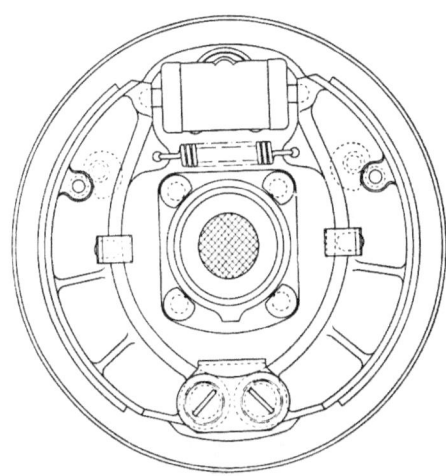

Fig. 353 - Brake housing flange-front wheels, « Multipla ».

It goes without saying that smoothening must not appreciably change master cylinder inner diameter which must be 3/4″ (Sedan) and 1″ (Multipla). If these diameters cannot be preserved, replace master cylinder body.

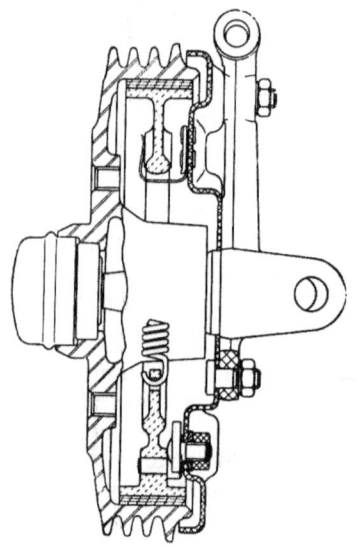

Fig. 354. Section through brake shoes and one of the upper eccentric pins of left front wheel, « Sedan » (hinged-type shoes).

Replace seals.

Inspect master cylinder rear end boot: if damaged, replace.

Make sure plunger return spring has not weakened.

Before installation, clean all parts by washing in clean brake fluid. Avoid any contact with mineral oil, gasoline, kerosene or diesel oil which would irreparably damage rubber seals.

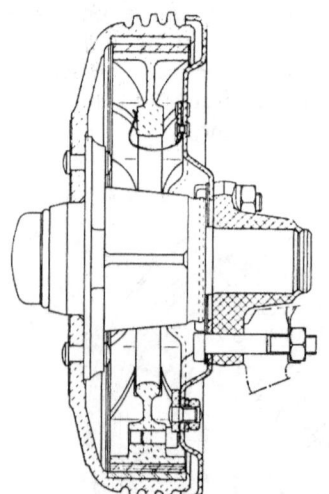

Fig. 355. Section through brake shoes and one of the upper eccentric pins of left front wheel « Multipla ».

Reassembly master cylinder by introducing the parts in reversed disassembly order.

As a lubricant, use exclusively the FIAT special blue label fluid (or equivalent HD non-mineral fluid).

Checking wheel cylinders.

To remove cylinders from brake housing flanges, unfasten and remove rubber boots (1, fig. 348) on cylinder ends. Plungers and stems (2), seal rings (5) and thrust washers (6) (clenched to reaction spring) will be pushed out by the expansion of the spring.

Check that barrel and plunger surfaces have a mirror-like finish and clearance between contacting surfaces is not excessive.

If necessary, polish surfaces, to prevent fluid leaks or excessive plunger and seal ring wear.

During this operation no alteration is permitted in the inner diameter, which is:

« Sedan »
— front and rear . . . . 3/4″

« Multipla »
— front . . . . $1\tfrac{1}{8}$″
— rear . . . . 3/4″

Fig. 356 - Front left wheel brake housing flange assembly, with drum removed, « Sedan » (hinged-type shoes).

Check that the return spring is not weak: replace spring and washers, if required.

Check, and preferably replace, the seals; inspect also wheel cylinder end boots for damages and replace as required.

Before reassembly, lubricate wheel cylinder parts by immersion in brake fluid.

Servicing Shoes and Linings.

Linings.

Check that linings are not dirty or greasy. If necessary, wash with turpentine using a wire brush. Check also that no oil or grease leaks into drum.

Should the lining thickness result excessively reduced, less than .059" (1,5 mm), replace lining.

Brake linings are bonded on shoes by the «Permafuse» process, as described in a FIAT Service Department publication.

In replacing linings, refer to this literature, minding that the pressure band, for fitting and bonding the linings on wheel brake shoes, is the **A. 64002** for «Sedan» and the **A. 64023** for «Multipla».

Bonding of lining to shoe is obtained by the interposition of a synthetic resin which is hardened by baking and that ensures such a bonding of parts that it can be broken only by destroying the linings.

Shoes.

Accurately check brake shoes for any sign of breakage or distortion.

Deformations impede a uniform contact of lining on drums with consequent reduction in braking.

Check the pin (3, fig. 363) for free sliding in the shoe seat, the shoe spring (5) for a sagged condition and the inner and outer cups for distortion. Replace damaged parts.

Furthermore, check that brake shoe return springs, both upper and lower, are not weak and, if necessary, replace.

NOTE

For the early type brake shoes, which are bottom linked, check them for free rotation on lower anchor and eccentric pins, without excessive play.

Drums.

While servicing the brakes, inspect also the drums: if excessively scored or ovalized, recondition on lathe **M. 10** using bush and spindle **A. 10125** (fig. 357) to load the drum on lathe.

After turning, still on lathe **M. 10**, lap the drums using fixture **M. 178** (fig. 358).

This operation, which is carried out with very fine grade abrasive stones, has the purpose of eliminating the marks left over by the tool while turning the drum.

This will eliminate the erosion of linings, thus preventing the formation of lining material dust which is an obstacle to good braking and obtaining, at the same time, longer lining life and more uniform and efficient braking as well.

In the turning and lapping operation, maximum permissible oversizes beyond standard drum diameter are the following:

Fig. 357 - Turning a brake drum on lathe M. 10.
For drum centering, spindle and bushes A. 10125 must be used.

«Sedan»

— standard diameter . 7.2929" to 7.3043"
    (185,24 to 185,53 mm)
— oversize . . . . . . .0315" (0,8 mm)

«Multipla»

— standard diameter . 8.6716" to 8.6830"
    (220,26 to 220,55 mm)
— oversize . . . . . . .0394" (1 mm)

Never exceed this limit or else both drum strength and braking efficiency would be impaired.

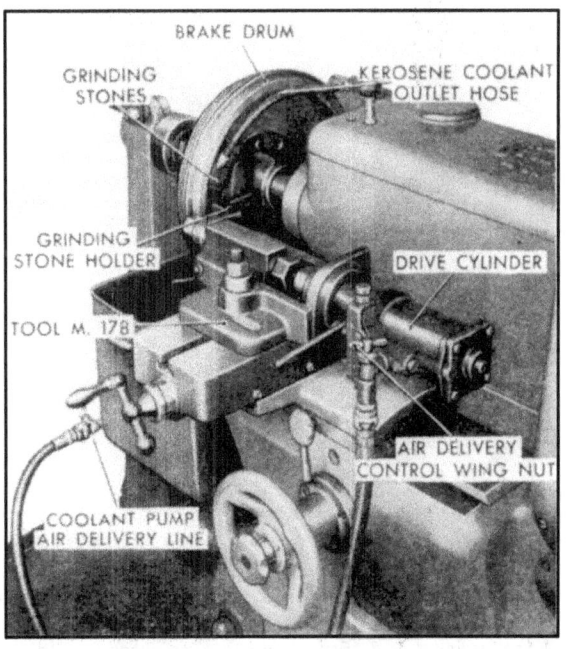

Fig. 358 - Lapping a brake drum using fixture M. 178 installed on lathe M. 10.

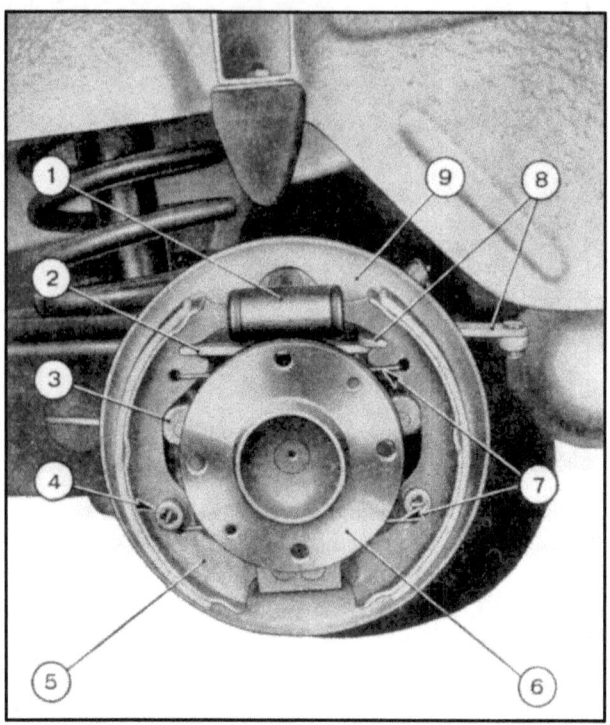

Fig. 359 - Left-hand rear brake housing flange, «Sedan», (with self-centering shoes).

1. Wheel cylinder. - 2. Parking brake wedge, driven by lever (8). - 3. Brake shoe-to-drum clearance adjusting cam. - 4. Shoe guide cups, pin and spring. - 5. Brake shoe. - 6. Wheel shaft. - 7. Shoe return springs. - 8. Parking brake shoe operating lever. - 9. Brake housing flange.

Fig. 360 - Left-hand front brake housing flange, «Sedan», (with self-centering shoes).

1. Wheel cylinder. - 2. Brake shoe-to-drum clearance adjusting cam. - 3. Shoe guide cups, pin and spring. - 4-5. Brake shoes. - 6. Shoe return springs. - 7. Brake housing flange.

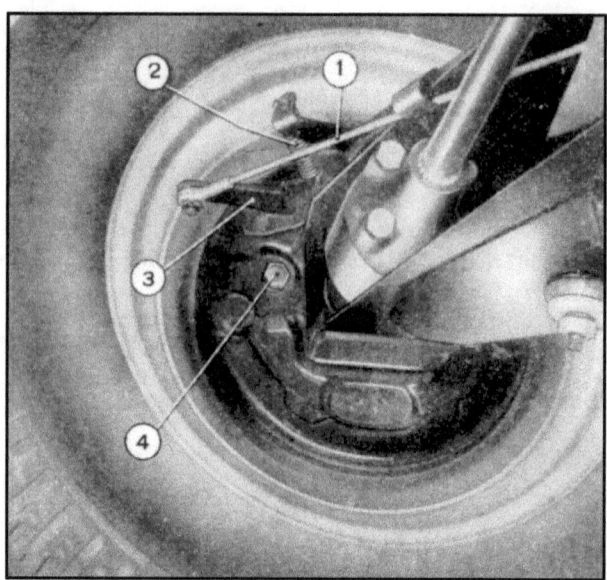

Fig. 361 - Left-hand rear wheel, «Sedan», (with self-centering shoes).

1. Parking brake cable, controlling lever (3). - 2. Lever return spring. - 3. Parking brake shoe operating lever. - 4. Brake shoe-to-drum clearance adjusting cam nut.

The reduction in braking efficiency would result from the increase in shoe expansion travel and the consequent diminished contact pressure.

Adjusting Shoe Clearance.

With pedal at rest, each wheel (clear of ground) must spin freely, i.e., without any drag of linings on drums.

Fig. 362 - Adjusting left-hand rear wheel brake shoe-to-drum clearance, «Sedan», (with self-centering shoes).

1. Brake shoe-to-drum clearance adjusting cam nut. - 2. Wrench for operation of nut 1 and cam rotation. - A. Cam nut rotating angle, from stop position: 20°, seated linings, and some 25°, new linings (corresponding to a .0098"-0,25 mm shoe-to-drum clearance at cams).

BRAKES

With pedal pressed to midtravel, an appreciable effort must be exerted to turn wheels manually.

If wheel braking is unbalanced, or pedal free travel is excessive (which would indicate abnormal lining wear) adjust shoe-to-drum clearance as follows:

SELF-CENTERING SHOES

Self-centering shoe brakes do not demand any adjusting operation for center which, as a matter of fact, is automatically assured through the use of brakes, inasmuch as brake shoes are not mounted on fixed-type anchor pins, but merely on a guide pin and spring (fig. 363) allowing for slight radial movements, and rest on a lower plate (fig. 360).

Brake shoes, under the impending hydraulic pressure from wheel cylinders, are caused to expand and move for such a seating as the braking area of shoes will adhere to the drum face at all points.

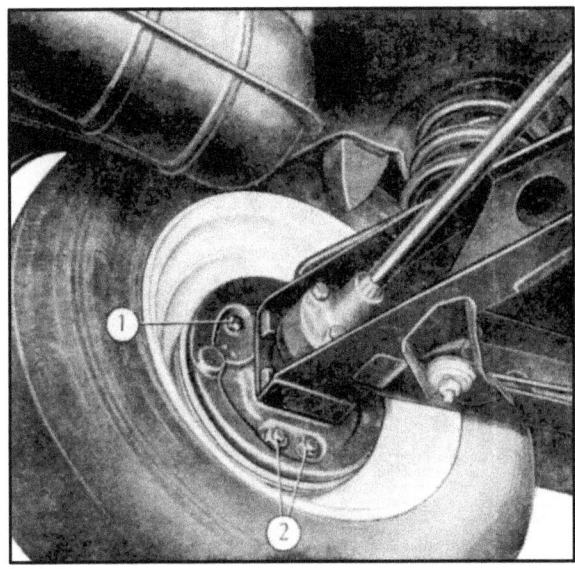

Fig. 364 - Axle end of left rear wheel brake housing flange, « Sedan », (hinged-type shoes).

1. One of the two shoe toe clearance adjustment upper eccentric cams. - 2. Shoe heel clearance adjustment anchor pin nuts.

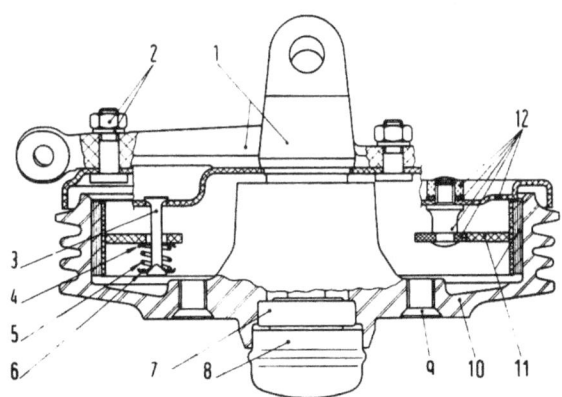

Fig. 363 - Sectional view through left-hand front wheel hub, « Sedan », (with self-centering shoes).

1. Steering knuckle and knuckle arm. - 2. Brake housing flange lock toothed washer and nut. - 3. Pin. - 4. Inner cup. - 5. Shoe guide spring. - 6. Outer cup. - 7. Outer roller bearing. - 8. Cap. - 9. Wheel stud seats. - 10. Brake drum. - 11. Brake shoe and lining. - 12. Brake housing flange with shoe-to-drum clearance adjusting nut, pin and cam.

This clearance can be checked through the drum slots, after the wheel has been removed, of course);

— release the brake pedal and see that the wheel can turn freely.

HINGED-TYPE SHOES

Brake shoe-to-drum clearance should be:

— .0039'' (0,10 mm) at lower eccentric pins;
— .0098'' (0,25 mm) at upper cams.

Prior to adjusting the brake shoe-to-drum clearance, therefore, operate the brakes with running vehicle to assure centering of brake shoes, especially when they have been replaced. Then proceed as follows, at each wheel:

— jack up the vehicle on the side where work is needed;

— depress brake pedal all the way down to hing brake shoes to contact the drum;

— keep the pedal in down position and rotate the nuts (4, fig. 361 and 1, fig. 362) of eccentric pins outward to the last stop;

— next turn nuts in opposite direction (fig. 362) by some 20° for seated linings and same 25° for new linings (which corresponds to a .0098''-0,25 mm brake shoe-to-drum clearance at eccentric pins.

Fig. 365 - Checking shoe-to-drum clearance on front right wheel using feeler gauge C. 114, « Sedan », (hinged type shoes).

Toe clearance: .0098'' (0,25 mm).

Fig. 366 - Checking shoe-to-drum clearance on right front wheel, with feeler gauge C. 114, « Sedan », (hinged-type shoes).

Heel clearance: .0039″ (0,10 mm).

To adjust clearance, operate as outlined hereafter (the brake drum has slots for feeler gauge passage and rotation of lower eccentric pins).

Fig. 367 - Left front wheel brake bleeding.
Use hose A. 10103.

1) Through drum slots insert the .0098″ (0,25 mm) feeler blade of gauge C. 114 (fig. 365) between shoe and drum, in correspondence with the upper eccentric cams.

2) Screw upper eccentric cam hexagon (1, fig. 364) and cause shoe to expand until shoe-to-drum clearance is reduced to .0098″ (0,25 mm).

NOTE - The centering of shoes may be carried out on fixture A. 64024; when linings are replaced, with this same fixture their surface may be reconditioned to smoothen out any roughness.

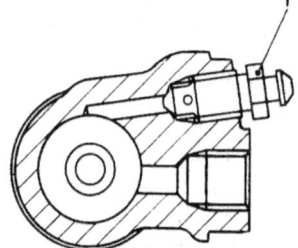

Fig. 368.
Wheel cylinder cross section.
1. Bleeder screw.

3) Insert the .0039″ (0,10 mm) feeler blade (fig. 366) between drum and shoe, in correspondence with the lower anchor pins.
Slacken anchor pin nut (2, fig. 364), push back the pin until it clears the stop plate, and rotate pin of one or two serrations so as to bring drum-to-shoe heel clearance to .0039″ (0,10 mm).

If necessary, operate again on upper eccentric cam so as to set the specified clearance both at shoe heel and toe.

4) Repeat operations 1, 2 and 3 on the other shoe.

An even shoe-to-drum braking contact will thus be obtained.

Bleeding the Hydraulic Lines.

When brake pedal operation becomes spongy or when some connections have had to be unscrewed, bleed system as follows:

1) Top up brake fluid reservoir.

2) Fit one end of bleeder hose A. 10103 on wheel cylinder bleeder screw. Immerse the other hose end in a transparent vessel partially filled with brake fluid (fig. 367).

3) Slacken bleeder screw a few turns and pump pedal repeatedly (depressing quickly and releasing slowly) until fluid issues in a solid stream without bubbles.

4) While keeping brake pedal depressed, tighten bleeder screw and remove bleeder hose.

5) Repeat operations 2, 3 and 4 on the other wheel cylinders.

NOTE - In case brake system has been completely drained, after refilling and before bleeding, proceed as follows:

a) Slacken bleeder screws a few turns on all four wheel cylinders.

b) Pump brake pedal and then tighten the screws when fluid begins to issue.

Should air bubbles continue to issue through bleeder hose ends, though bleeding operation is prolonged, check all connections for air leaks.

If no leaks are found, check master cylinder and wheel cylinder seals for perfect tightness.

WARNING

To prevent air from being drawn in by master cylinder during the bleeding operation, the fluid level in reservoir must never be allowed to fall under the minimum mark.

If bleeding operations have not been carried out properly, master cylinder plunger travel will be greater than .39" (10 mm) and, with pedal fully depressed, a more or less marked sponginess will be felt, depending upon the amount of air that has remained in the system.

In this case, bleeding must be repeated simultaneously on the four bleeder screws.

If the brake system of the car in question has been in service for long, do not re-utilize the fluid.

The fluid bled into vessels, must be carefully filtered, before re-usage.

BRAKE FLUID RESERVOIR

Location: in front compartment next to the battery, on the «Sedan», and inside car ahead of the spare wheel, on the «Multipla».

Before disconnecting the brake line at reservoir, the fluid outlet hole must be blanked by a wooden peg, to be fitted after removing cap and strainer.

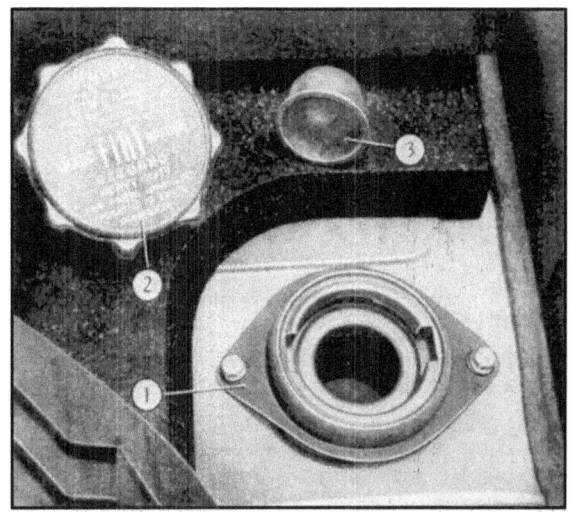

Fig. 369 - Brake fluid reservoir (Sedan).
1. Reservoir. - 2. Cap., vented. - 3. Strainer.

Peg length must be such that reservoir cap may be reinstalled. This precaution is essential to prevent the entrance of foreign matter in the reservoir and the absorption of moisture, oil or kerosene vapors by the fluid, whose properties would otherwise be altered and impaired.

PARKING BRAKE

On Rear Wheels.

The mechanical parking brake on rear wheels is controlled by a hand lever on floor tunnel, amid front seats. The hand lever operates, through a metal cable, the levers and wedges providing shoe expansion at rear wheels.

Two stretchers are located at the end of the metal cable sheath. Stretchers are clamped to swinging arm mountings.

To check the parking brake for correct operation, proceed as follows:

— pull the control lever all the way up;

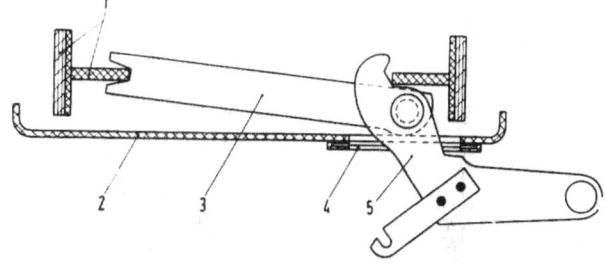

Fig. 370 - Sectional view through «Sedan» parking brake control at right-hand rear wheel.

1. Brake shoe and lining. - 2. Brake housing flange. - 3. Wedge. - 4. Gasket. - 5. Shoe operating lever.

Fig. 371 - Parking brake control at left-hand rear wheel, «Sedan».
1. Control cable. - 2. Plain washer. - 3. Cable lock split pin. - 4. Shoe operating lever. - 5. Lever return spring.

— see whether the vehicle is sufficiently at standstill;

— should the braking strength non be enough, release the hand lever and operate both stretchers (2, fig. 372);

— when adjustment is correct, make sure that the cable ist aut before the control lever has completed its up travel.

NOTE - Pay special care to parking brake adjustment, as any abnormal tension on metal cable may adversely affect the service brake operation on rear wheels as well, the brake shoes being common to both systems.

Fig. 373 - Parking brake mounted on gearbox casing front cover.
1. Operating lever. - 2 and 4. Shoe expansion blocks. - 3. Shoe expansion wedge. - 5. Brake shoe. - 6. Oil seal on cover. - 7. Shoe return springs. - 8. Special shoe reaction bolt.

On Drive Line.

Up to engine No. 758492, «Sedan», and up to engine No. 765150, «Multipla», the parking brake was on the drive line, namely of the expanding shoe type, operating on a drum press fitted on the gearbox layshaft.

Fig. 372 - Close-up view of left-hand rear wheel parking brake cable stretcher.
1. Parking brake control cable and sheath. - 2-3. Cable adjusting sleeve and nut. - 4. Locking nut. - 5. Cable.

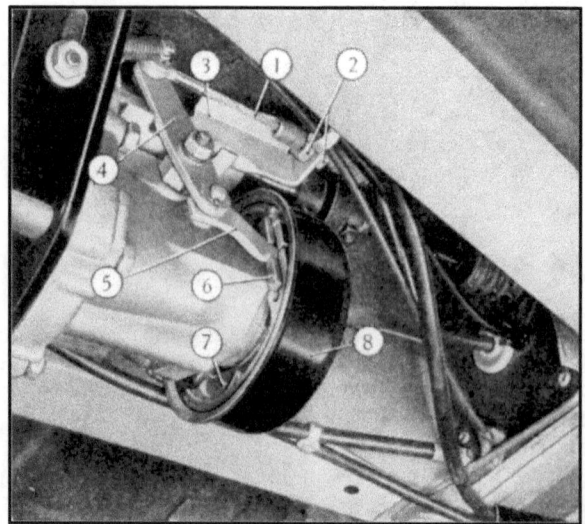

Fig. 374 - Drive line parking brake adjustment.
1. Brake control cable. - 2. Stretcher locking nuts. - 3. Control cable bracket. - 4. Operating lever. - 5. Wedge. - 6. Blocks. - 7. Shoes. - 8. Drum.

BRAKES

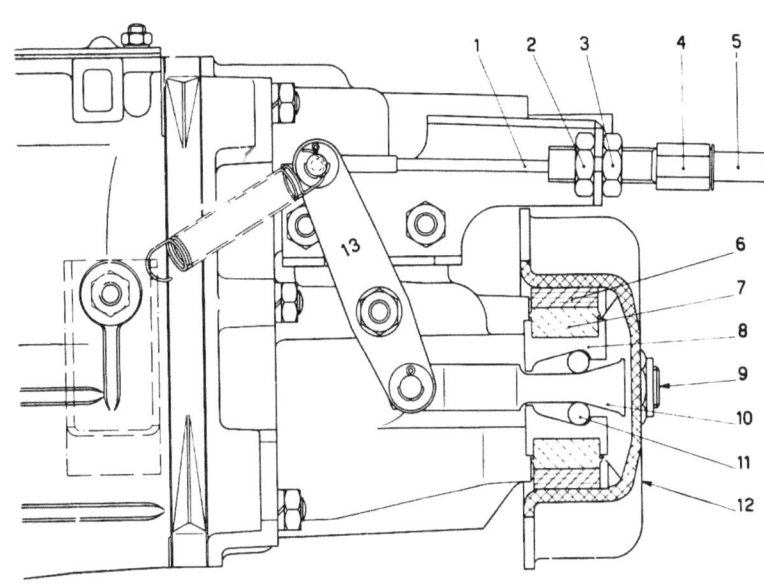

Fig. 375.
Drive line parking brake assembly. Longitudinal section through drum and shoes.

1. Brake control cable. - 2 and 3. Stretcher locking nuts. - 4. Cable stretcher. - 5. Cable sheath. - 6. Shoe lining. - 7. Brake shoe. - 8. Shoe expansion blocks. - 9. Gearbox layshaft. - 10. Shoe expansion wedge. - 11. Rollers. - 12. Drum. - 13. Brake shoe operating lever.

The expanding-shoe drum type hand brake is placed in front of gearbox case on layshaft, that is, on bevel drive pinion shaft. It is controlled by a hand lever on tunnel, within easy reach of driver.

The braking action develops as follows:

When hand lever on floor tunnel is pulled, an adjustable wire rope actuates parking brake expanding shoes through a suitable mechanism consisting of a spring-loaded operating lever, an expansion wedge, two rollers and two blocks.

At assembly, adjust shoe-to-drum clearance by slackening nuts (2 and 3, fig. 375), and screwing or unscrewing sleeve (4) until the prescribed clearance of .0098" (0,25 mm) is obtained.

Then lock nuts.

When lining thickness is reduced to less than .059" (1,5 mm), replace linings following the « Permafuse » process and using pressure band **A. 64021**.

Tighten the nut fixing the drum to layshaft by means of a torque wrench, to 47 ft.lbs (6500 kgmm).

Use tool **A. 62024** to prevent drum and layshaft rotation (fig. 236).

BRAKE TIGHTENING REFERENCE

ITEM	DRWG. OR STD. PART No.	THREAD	MATERIAL	TIGHTENING TORQUE
Nut, securing brake housing flange to:				
— knuckle pillar, « Sedan »	1/17016/11	8 MA (x1,25)	R 50 Cdt (Screw R 50)	14.5 ft.lbs (2.000 kgmm)
— steering knuckle « Multipla »	1/21647/11	10 x 1,25 M	R 50 Cdt (Screw R 50)	32.5 to 39.8 ft.lbs (4.500 to 5.500 kgmm)
Knuckle arm and brake housing flange-to-steering knuckle nut, « Multipla »	1/21647/11	10 x 1,25 M	R 50 Cdt (Screw R 80)	32.5 to 39.8 ft.lbs (4.500 to 5.500 kgmm)
Hub and brake housing flange-to-rear swinging arm nut, « Sedan » and « Multipla »	1/21647/11	10 x 1,25 M	R 50 Cdt (Screw R 80)	43.4 ft.lbs (6.000 kgmm)
Hand brake drum-to-layshaft nut, « Sedan » and « Multipla »	1/25748/11	14 MB (x1,5)	R 50 Cdt (Shaft 14 CN5)	47 ft.lbs (6.500 kgmm)

SERVICE BRAKE SPECIFICATIONS AND DATA

Type	pedal-controlled, hydraulically-operated expanding-shoes
Front and rear drum diameters: 　　　　　　Sedan . . . . 　　　　　　Multipla	7.2929″ to 7.3043″ (185,24 to 185,53 mm) 8.6716″ to 8.6830″ (220,26 to 220,55 mm)

		SEDAN	MULTIPLA
Shoe linings	bonding	by Permafuse process	
	length (developed)	7.09″ (180 mm)	8.19″ (208 mm)
	width	1.18″ (30 mm)	1.57″ (40 mm)
	thickness — hinged-type shoes	.1575″ (4 mm)	.1575″ (4 mm)
	thickness — self-centering shoes . . .	.1654″ to .1772″ (4,2 to 4,5 mm)	—

Shoe-to-drum clearance: 　　self-centering shoes at eccentric pins . . . 　　hinged-type shoes { at upper cams . . . 　　　　　　　　　　　at lower eccentric pins	.0098″ (0,25 mm) .0098″ (0,25 mm) .0039″ (0,10 mm)
Master cylinder diameter: 　　　　　　Sedan . . . . 　　　　　　Multipla	3/4″ 1″
Wheel cylinder diameters { Sedan: 　　— front and rear . 　　Multipla: 　　— front . . . . 　　— rear	3/4″ 1 1/8″ 3/4″
Master cylinder plunger-to-rod clearance	.039″ to .059″ (1 to 1,5 mm)
Brake pedal free travel	.20″ to .31″ (5 to 8 mm)
Brake system fluid . . . . { type . . . . 　　　　　　　quantity { Sedan . . . 　　　　　　　　　　　　Multipla . .	special FIAT blue label fluid 0,280 lt - 0,275 kg 0,370 lt - 0,365 kg
Grinding brake drums: Maximum diameter { Sedan . 　　　　　　　oversize allowance { Multipla	.0315″ (0,8 mm) .0394″ (1 mm)

PARKING BRAKE SPECIFICATIONS AND DATA

	EARLY-TYPE	LATE-TYPE	
Type and location	On drive line, with hand-controlled brake shoes operating on gearbox layshaft-press fitted drum	On rear wheels, with hand operation of service brake shoes	
Shoe linings:			
— shoe anchor system	« Permafuse » bonding process	« Permafuse » bonding process	
		SEDAN	MULTIPLA
— length (developed)	4.72" (120 mm)	7.09" (180 mm)	8.19" (208 mm)
— width	.98" (25 mm)	1.18" (30 mm)	1.57" (40 mm)
— thickness	.1299" to .1378" (3.3 to 3,5 mm)	.1654" to .1772" (4,2 to 4,5 mm)	.1575" (4 mm)
Drum diameter	4.5346" to 4.5433" (115,180 to 115,400 mm)	7.2929" to 7.3043" (185,24 to 185,53 mm)	8.6716" to 8.6831" (220,26 to 220,55 mm)
Shoe lining-to-drum clearance	.0098" (0,25 mm)	.0098" (0,25 mm)	

BRAKE SERVICE EQUIPMENT

- A. 10103   Air bleeder rubber hose.
- A. 64002   Metal pressure band - bonding of service brake shoe linings (Sedan).
- A. 64021   Metal pressure band - bonding of hand brake shoe linings (Sedan and Multipla).
- A. 64023   Metal pressure band - bonding of service brake shoe linings (Multipla).
- C. 114   Feeler gauge - brake shoe centering and clearance adjustment.

Additional equipment.

- A. 6469   Puller - drums and wheel hubs (or puller A. 40005).
- A. 46014   Remover - front wheel hub caps.
- A. 66008   Striker - front wheel hub caps installation.

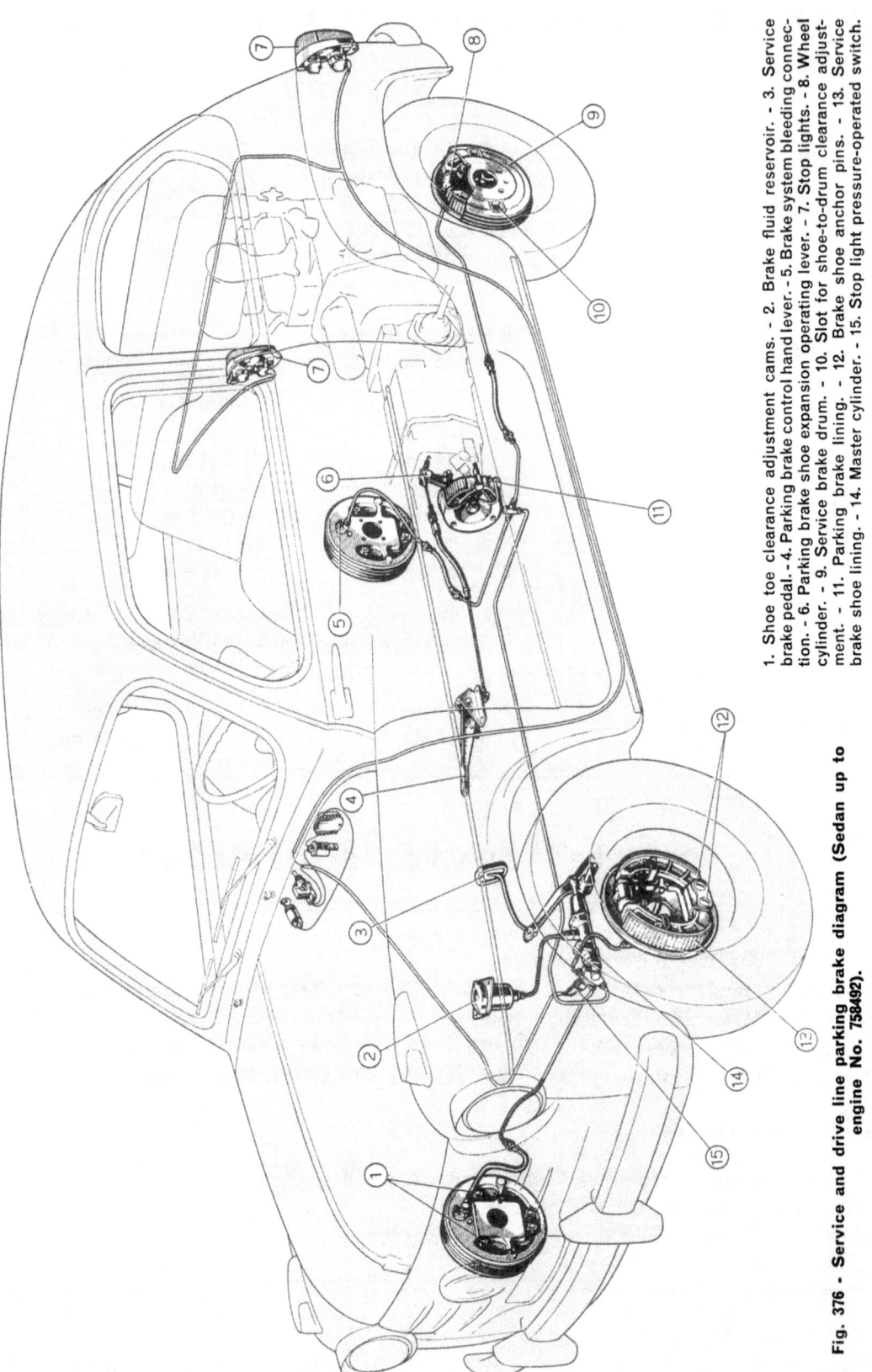

Fig. 376 - Service and drive line parking brake diagram (Sedan up to engine No. 758492).

1. Shoe toe clearance adjustment cams. - 2. Brake fluid reservoir. - 3. Service brake pedal. - 4. Parking brake control hand lever. - 5. Brake system bleeding connection. - 6. Parking brake shoe expansion operating lever. - 7. Stop lights. - 8. Wheel cylinder. - 9. Service brake drum. - 10. Slot for shoe-to-drum clearance adjustment. - 11. Parking brake lining. - 12. Brake shoe anchor pins. - 13. Service brake shoe lining. - 14. Master cylinder. - 15. Stop light pressure-operated switch.

HYDRAULIC BRAKE SYSTEM
TROUBLE DIAGNOSIS AND CORRECTIONS

Locked Brake Pedal.

POSSIBLE CAUSES	REMEDIES
1) Swollen linings because the fluid used is inadequate or contaminated by kerosene, gasoline or mineral oil.	1) Flush the system, replace all rubber parts, refill with new fluid and air bleed the lines.
2) Plungers or valve carriers locked by deposits of fluid, foreign matter, etc.	2) Clean and bleed the system.
3) Master cylinder compensating hole blanked because plunger clearance is misadjusted.	3) Adjust the rod-to-plunger clearance by setting to .039'' to .059'' (1 to 1,5 mm).
4) Clogged compensating hole. No compensation takes place.	4) Disassemble and clean master cylinder.
5) Seized master cylinder piston due to infiltrations of water through rear end because boot has failed or seals are no longer tight.	5) Service the master cylinder, replace the plunger and the boot and/or seals, to prevent water infiltrations.
6) Seized pedal shaft (this is also the cause for hard pedal or locked brakes).	6) Free and smoothen the parts and lubricate.

Spongy Pedal.

POSSIBLE CAUSES	REMEDIES
1) Air in brake system because of imperfect bleeding.	1) Repeat the bleeding operations more accurately.
2) Swollen hose because of deterioration.	2) Replace the hose; bleed the system.
3) Hose swollen under fluid pressure because hose used is of poor quality.	3) Fit new hoses of a quality approved by FIAT and bleed the system.
4) Air in master cylinder on account of insufficient seal tightness.	4) Fit a new valve-ring, checking that the plunger land height is less than ring thickness. Bleed the system.
5) Use of a brake fluid whose boiling point is too low.	5) Change the fluid with the FIAT special blue label fluid (or equivalent non-mineral grade) and bleed the system.
6) Reservoir filler cap vent hole clogged. This promotes a vacuum in master cylinder that sucks in air through rear seal.	6) Clean reservoir filler cap and bleed the system.

Pedal Yields Under Slight Pressure.

POSSIBLE CAUSES	REMEDIES
1) Deteriorated floating valve-ring.	1) Fit a new valve-ring, check that there are no roughness or irregularities in master cylinder and bleed the system.
2) Chips or impurities on valve-ring sealing surfaces.	2) Clean, replace the valve-ring if found deteriorated and bleed the system.
3) Fluid leaks through connections.	3) Tighten connections and, if necessary, replace faulty parts. Bleed the system.
4) Fluid leaks at wheel cylinders.	4) Replace the deteriorated seals and packings. Dry and clean brake shoe linings.
5) Fluid leaks through hoses.	5) Replace the damaged hose, using only FIAT-approved hoses and bleed the system.

Reduced Pedal Free Travel.

POSSIBLE CAUSES	REMEDIES
1) Master cylinder compensating hole blanked on account of misadjusted plunger rod.	1) Adjust the rod-to-plunger clearance and set to .039'' to .059'' (1 to 1,5 mm).
2) Master cylinder compensating hole clogged by impurities.	2) Clean and bleed the system.
3) Master cylinder compensating hole clogged by a swollen valve-ring.	3) Flush the system, replace the valve-ring, refill with new fluid and air-bleed the lines.

Unbalanced Braking.

POSSIBLE CAUSES	REMEDIES
1) Fluid leaks at one wheel cylinder.	1) Dry and clean the brake shoe linings, service the wheel cylinder and bleed the system.
2) Rust corrosion on the edges of a wheel cylinder.	2) Eliminate rust and replace the boots.
3) Seized plunger in one wheel cylinder.	3) Service the wheel cylinder, replace the plunger and bleed the system.
4) Hose obstructed because the inner pipe has swollen or is clogged (if the brakes on one axle are excluded, weak braking may result).	4) Replace or clean the pipe and bleed the system.
5) Obstructed flow in metal pipe which has flattened or is clogged (if the brakes on one axle are excluded, weak braking may result).	5) Replace or clean the pipe and bleed the system.

Excessive Pedal Free Travel.

POSSIBLE CAUSES	REMEDIES
1) System has not been bleed.	1) Bleed the system.
2) Shoe clearance maladjusted.	2) Adjust the brake shoe-to-drum clearance.
3) Fluid level in reservoir is too low.	3) Refill with special FIAT blue brake fluid (or equivalent non-mineral grade); if required, bleed the system.
4) Master cylinder plunger rod misadjusted.	4) Adjust the rod-to-plunger clearance and set to .039" to .059" (1 to 1,5 mm) (this corresponds to a pedal free travel of .20" to .31" - 5 to 8 mm).
5) Deteriorated rubber seals in master cylinder or in wheel cylinders.	5) Replace the seals and bleed the system.
6) Excessive swelling of hoses because the ones used were of poor quality.	6) Replace by FIAT-approved hoses and bleed the system.
7) Thermal expansion of drums because of excessive overheating.	7) Allow drums to cool off. Check brake shoe linings and drums. Replace damaged parts.

Shoes Drag Permanently on Drums.

POSSIBLE CAUSES	REMEDIES
1) Weak return springs.	1) Replace the springs.
2) Brake pedal has no free travel.	2) Adjust the rod-to-plunger clearance and set to .039" to .059" (1 to 1,5 mm).
3) Seized master cylinder plunger.	3) Service the master cylinder, replace the plunger and bleed the system.
4) Master cylinder flooded because compensating hole is clogged.	4) Service the master cylinder, replace the valve-ring if swollen or deteriorated, clean the compensating hole and bleed the system.

Excessive Effort Required on Pedal.

POSSIBLE CAUSES	REMEDIES
1) Swollen rubber seals because the fluid used is inadequate or contaminated by kerosene, gasoline or mineral oil (this may also cause a permanent drag of shoes on brake drum).	1) Flush the system, replace rubber parts, refill with new brake fluid, and bleed the system.

Brakes Locked Even After Releasing the Pedal.

POSSIBLE CAUSES	REMEDIES
1) Weak or broken return springs.	1) Replace inefficient springs.
2) Clogged master cylinder compensating hole.	2) Clean and bleed the system.
3) Rubber seals swollen or stuck because of contamination by kerosene, mineral oil, gasoline, etc.	3) Flush the system, replace all rubber parts, refill with new brake fluid and bleed the system.
4) Insufficient shoe-to-drum clearance.	4) Adjust the clearance.

Weak Braking.

POSSIBLE CAUSES	REMEDIES
1) Fluid leakage from wheel cylinders.	1) Dry and clean the brake shoe linings, service the wheel cylinder replacing damaged parts and bleed the system.

WHEELS AND TIRES

Features	page 234
Wheel Balance	» 234
Tire Inflating Pressures and Wear	» 235
Changing the Wheels	» 236
Wheel Screw Tightening Reference	» 236

Features.

Wheels are of the disc type with $3\frac{1}{2}$x12" rims and 5.20 - 12, low pressure tires.
Tire inflation pressures:

	p.s.i.	kg/cm²
« Sedan »		
— front	14.2	1,00
— rear	22.8	1,60
« Multipla »		
— front	24.2	1,70
— rear	28.5	2,00

WHEEL BALANCE

It is extremely important to check the wheels and eliminate all possible causes of unbalance.

The causes that may affect wheel balance are:

a) wheel lateral runout, resulting from bumps or abnormal lateral strain;

b) out-of-round of wheel due to eccentricity either of rim or tire;

c) static unbalance, due to uneven distribution of weight with respect to rotation axis.

WHEELS AND TIRES

The first two causes may be easily detected by putting into rotation first the rim alone and then the rim and tire against a scriber:

— check that on the rim flange inner edge (accomodating tire beads) and on the well there are no spots off-centre by more than .039" (1 mm);

— when installing tires, remember that the Manufacturer's reference balance mark must be located in correspondence with tire valve.

The rim run-out may be corrected under a hydraulic press.

As to point c), perform balancing on electronic balancer **A. 76002** which ensures best results in the shortest possible time and with very simple operations.

For the use of the balancer, follow the instructions contained in the handbook accompanying every machine.

TIRE INFLATING PRESSURES

Check pressure with cold tires.

Check that tire pressures correspond closely to the specified values since too high pressures cause uncomfortable riding and excessive wear of tire tread central portion, while too low pressures bring about rapid tread wear. Also, care for even inflation of all tires because tires inflated at different pressures affect road holding qualities and stability of car.

Tire Wear.

Abnormal wear of tires may occur on different areas of tread, as follows:

a) **Front tires show an excessive wear only on one side of the tread:** check camber. If it is correct, wear must be ascribed to the habit of negotiating curves at high speeds.

b) **Tires show a wear particularly remarkable on both sides of tread rather on center portion:** tires are inflated at a pressure lower than specified.

Under such condition the tread side surfaces are supporting most of the load, while center portion is deflected upwards.

c) **Tires show wear on tread center portion:** tires are inflated at a pressure higher than specified. Under such condition tread central portion is supporting most of the load.

d) **Remarkable wear on tread inner end of both wheels:** toe-out is the possible cause; check and adjust toe-in as required.

e) **Remarkable wear on tread outer end of both wheels:** excessive toe-in; correct to specified value.

f) **One front tire shows wear on tread inner end and the other on outer end:** steering is maladjusted and causes an excessive toe-in on one wheel, and toe-out on the other.

Check wheel alignment and see that steering and suspension components are not deformed.

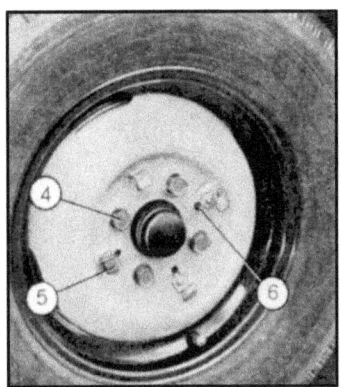

Fig. 377.
Front wheel detail.

Fig. 378 - Jacking up the car.

1. Bracket, for jack application. - 2. Jack. - 3. Chock. - 4. Screw fixing wheel to hub. - 5. Wheel cap fasteners. - 6. Wheel location dowel.

NOTE: Use of chock (3) is unnecessary on cars equipped with rear wheel parking brake.

NOTE - To ensure uniform wear of all tires change wheels in criss cross fashion every 3,000 miles (5.000 km).

CHANGING THE WHEELS

To obtain best results, follow this procedure:

a) If possible, place car on level ground and, to prevent any accidental movement of car while jacked up, fit chock (3, fig. 378) under the rear wheel on ground.

b) Pry wheel cap off with fingers, if possible, or with a screwdriver tip.

Using the speed handle, slacken about one turn the four wheel fixing screws (4, fig. 377).

c) Place jack nub in bracket (1, fig. 378) under body floor, then jack up until wheel to be removed clears ground.

NOTE - On the « Sedan » brackets are two, one on each side, on the « Multipla » brackets are four, two at front and two at rear.

d) Undo and remove the four fixing screws. Pull off wheel.

e) Fit spare wheel. The wheel location dowel (6, fig. 377) on brake drum must fit into the hole provided on wheel disc. Insert wheel fixing screws and tighten uniformly in criss-cross sequence.

f) Lower car and disinsert jack nub from bracket under floor.

g) Tighten wheel fixing screws to a 43.4 - 50.6 ft.lbs (6-7 kgm) torque for both « Sedan » and « Multipla ». Refit wheel caps, checking that fasteners (5, fig. 377) secure a positive grip.

WHEEL SCREW TIGHTENING REFERENCE

ITEM	DRWG. OR STD. PART No.	THREAD	MATERIAL	TIGHTENING TORQUE
Front and rear wheel screws:				
Sedan	1.49.012/ 996225	12 MB (x1,5)	C 35 R (Bon Cdt)	43.4 to 50.6 ft.lbs (6.000 to 7.000 kgmm)
Multipla	1.49.110/ 4052840	12 MB (x1,5)	C 35 R (Bon Cdt)	

Section 9

AIR CONDITIONING
WINDSHIELD WASHER
CHASSIS TIGHTENING REFERENCE

	Page
AIR CONDITIONING, « SEDAN »	239
AIR CONDITIONING, « MULTIPLA »	239
WINDSHIELD WASHER	241
CHASSIS TIGHTENING REFERENCE	242

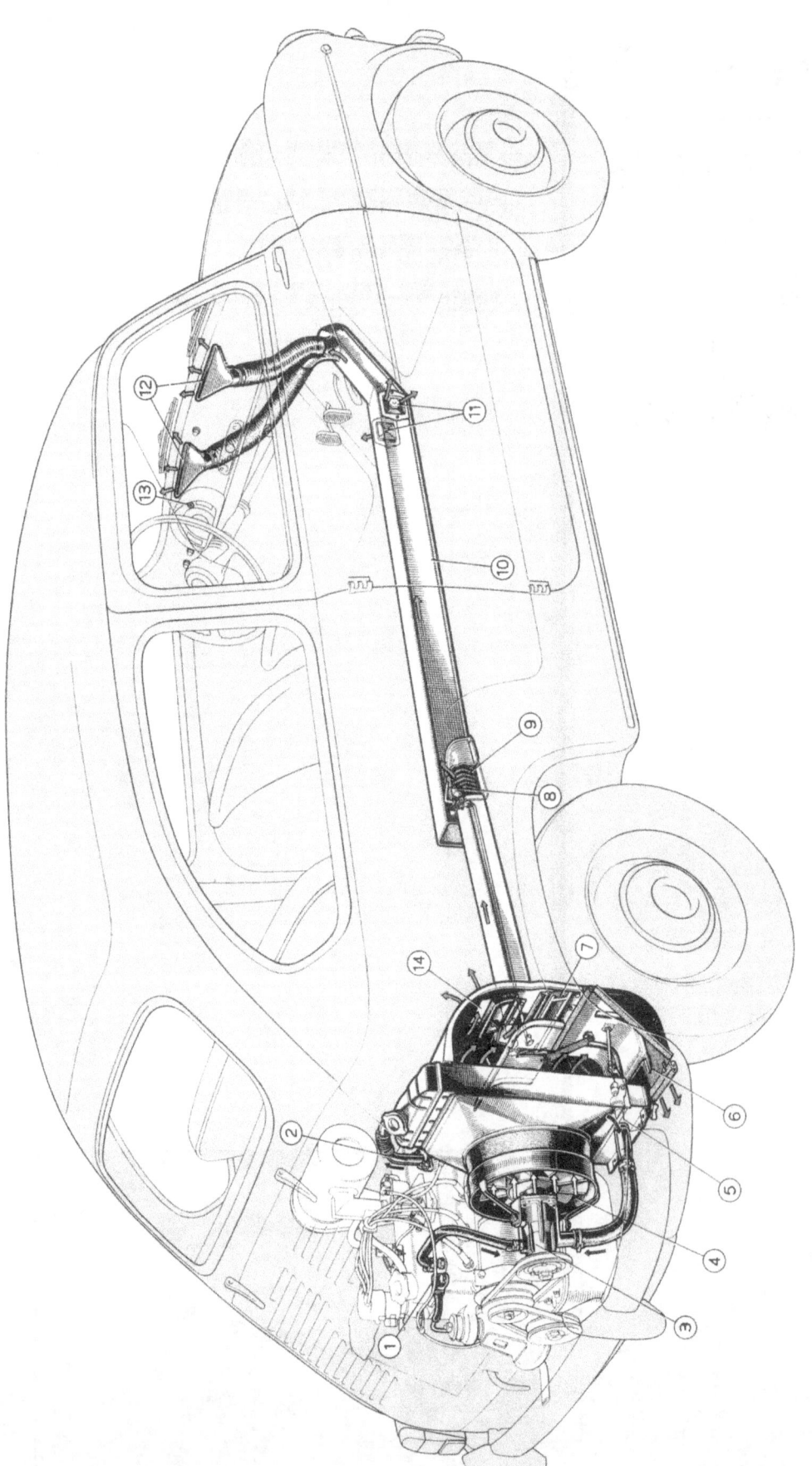

Fig. 379 - Engine cooling and car heating systems (Sedan).

1. Sending unit for excessive water temperature indicator. - 2. Water outlet pipe from cylinders. - 3. Water pump. - 4. Fan. - 5. Thermostat, shutter control. - 6. Shutter, air draft control in engine compartment. - 7. Baffle in open position (warm air enters car). - 8. Baffle control lever. - 9. Warm air filter. - 10. Longitudinal warm air conveyor. - 11. Knobs controlling warm air shutters. - 12. Diffusers sending warm air against windshield. - 13. Excessive water temperature indicator. - 14. Shutter, for warm air admission through luggage space behind rear seat.

AIR CONDITIONING

Sedan . . . . page 239
Multipla . . . . » 239

The air conditioning systems of the two models differ as described below.

Sedan.

Car interior heating and windshield defrosting are accomplished by the air coming from the engine radiator and conveyed inside the car through the floor central tunnel and through an inlet behind rear seat.

To demist or defrost windscreen, turn clockwise the lever (8, fig. 379) under rear seat. This way, a continuous flow of warm air against windscreen and in luggage space behind rear seat (14, fig. 379) is obtained.

To improve heating, after turning the lever, press and turn the two warm air control knobs (11, fig. 379) on tunnel sides.

Lever (8, fig. 379) controlling baffle (7) and shutter (14) may be set at will in any intermediate position so as to regulate the flow of incoming warm air

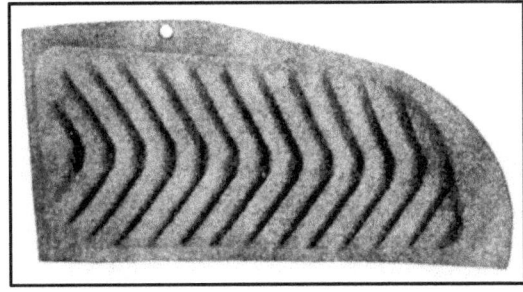

Fig. 380 - Warm air filter (Sedan).

To totally exclude air circulation, push lever (8) back all the way.

A suitable cloth filter (9, fig. 379), in the portion of tunnel from control lever to baffle (7), cleanses the entering air.

Inspection.

Check that the hinges of baffle (7) and of shutter (14, fig. 379), the linkages and their fasteners are not deformed or damaged, otherwise repair or replace.

Check that the windshield warm air diffuser hoses are sound and that their lower spring fasteners are well tight.

The axial spring on control lever (8, fig. 379) must not be weak.

If the conditioned air admitted into car is insufficient, clean the filter (9, fig. 379). To reach the filter, lift floor mat and take off filter cover after removing its three mounting screws.

Pull out filter, clean with a soft brush or with a low-pressure air blast. If filter in excessively dirty, replace.

Multipla.

Conditioned air may either be warm or cold, depending on seasonal requirements, and may be circulated directly on windshield (demisting or defrosting) and in car (heating) simultaneously or separately for either purpose (fig. 381).

Recommendations are:

a) **Summer ventilation**: to admit fresh air, turn the two side butterfly valve control knobs (15) as required. These valves can assume different positions, thus allowing control of admitted air.

b) **Midseason ventilation**: to demist windshield, simply let in some cold air by turning down the baffle lever (12), which will convey air against windshield through the two diffusers (11).

c) **Winter heating**: open first cock (14) on heater radiator inlet pipe to permit re-circulation of some warm water from engine to heater radiator (13) (of the upright-pipes type) in front, behind grille.

Next, turn the two side butterfly valve knobs (15), and turn down the baffle lever (12), so that part of the conditioned air will be utilized for car interior heating and part will be directed by the diffusers on windshield for demisting and defrosting)

By cock (14) the warm water flow in heater radiator may be fully excluded or varied to suit requirements (maximum flow in radiator is obtained when cock handwheel is rotated three full turns); consequently, the conditioned air may be more or less warm to the passengers' comfort.

When temperature drops close to 32°F (0°C) the coolant must be replaced by the special FIAT anti-

FIAT - 600 - 600 D SEDAN AND MULTIPLA

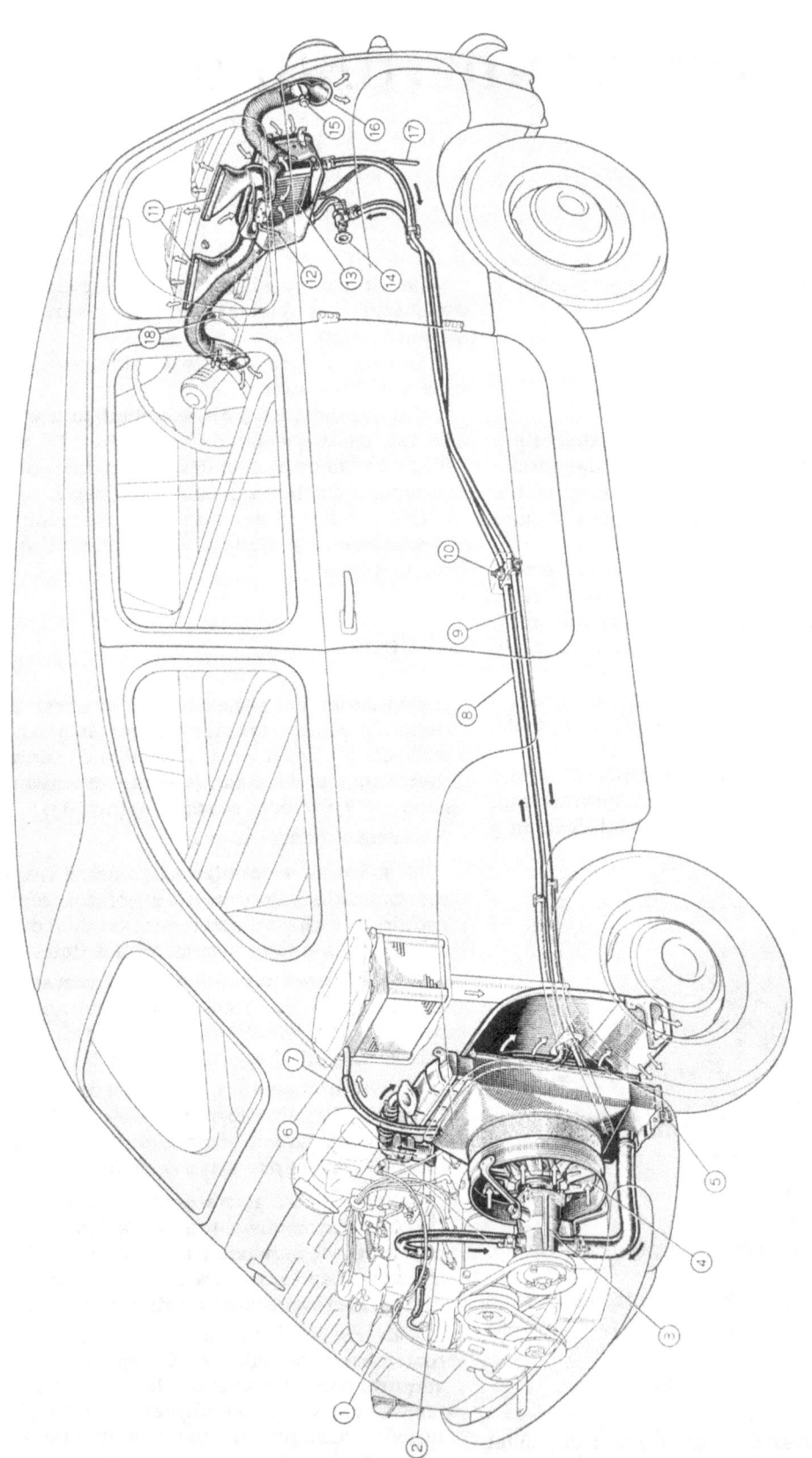

Fig. 381 - Engine cooling and car heating systems (Multipla).

1. Sending unit for excessive water temperature indicator. - 2. Line, water from cylinder block to pump (with cold engine, i.e., when temperature is below 167° F - 75° C). - 3. Water pump. - 4. Fan. - 5. Radiator drain cock. - 6. Line, with incorporated thermostat, water from cylinder block to radiator (with warm engine, i.e., when temperature exceeds 167° F - 75° C). - 7. Line, forced ventilation of battery box. - 8. Line, water to heater radiator. - 9. Line, heater water outlet. - 10. Cock, heating system drain. - 11. Diffusers on windshield. - 12. Heater baffle control lever. - 13. Heater radiator. - 14. Cock, regulating amount of water flow in heater radiator. - 15. One of the two knobs for heater butterfly valve control. - 16. One of the two warm air outlets. - 17. Drain pipe for any water which might collect in heater radiator housing through splashes on front panel. - 18. Excessive water temperature indicator.

freeze mixture (or equivalent) to prevent freezing of water in the cooling system and in heater radiator (13, fig. 381) which is exposed, during vehicle operation, to a strong air draft coming in through the grille. If in winter the car is kept inoperative for some time and the cooling system is not filled with an antifreeze mixture, besides draining the engine and the engine cooling radiator, drain also the heater radiator and lines by opening cock (10, fig. 381).

IMPORTANT

Filling the engine cooling circuit and the air conditioning circuit with the necessary amount of water must be accomplished as follows:

a) open heater radiator water inlet cock (14, fig. 381);

b) fill engine radiator to required level; then fit the cap;

c) turn on engine and allow to run for a while: the water pump will send water all around in the circuit and into the heater radiator. This, of course, will result in a lower engine radiator water level;

d) stop the engine and top up water in radiator to correct level.

Inspection.

Following is a list of all items that must receive care when servicing the air conditioning system. In some cases repairs are possible, in others parts must necessarily be replaced.

To facilitate identification, parts have been subdivided into four groups.

Water delivery to heater: rear hose and relevant bush; central line; front hose to cock; cock with packing and gasket, on central line, for water drain; cock, with gasket, heater water inlet; hose, cock to radiator; collars, water hoses and lines.

Heater: radiator and gasket; baffle; grommets, water inlet and outlet pipes; condensed water drain pipe.

Warm air delivery: butterfly valve on central lever and relevant spring; windshield diffuser hoses and side outlet flexible pipes; butterfly valve for side outlets and relevant control knob and drag spring.

Water return: front hose; central line; rear hose and relevant bush; hose collars; fairlead, delivery and return hoses, in engine bulkhead.

WINDSHIELD WASHER

The « Sedan » is equipped with a windshield washer consisting of:

— reservoir bottle on front compartment bulkhead left side;

— two jets on cowl;

— pump, centrally mounted under facia.

To clean the windshield, depress several times the rubber bulb of washer pump and then switch on the wiper.

For windshield washer jets maintenance, operate as follows:

a) **Jet positioning:** loosen the screw on the jet head, reposition the hexagonal nut so as to direct the water squirt to top of wiper sweep arc and retighten the screw.

b) **Cleaning of jets and filtering gauze in bottle:** remove jet hexagonal nut and clean jet hole accurately. Every 4 or 5 refills it is advisable to clean also the filtering gauze in the lower end of suction pipe.

To replenish the washer, refill the bottle with 0,75 kg of pure water plus 0,017 kg (2.28% in weight) (Summer) or 0,034 kg (4.56% in weight) (Winter) of FIAT D.P./1 liquid or Trico XAW 30 solution.

Make sure there are no leaks in any part of the system.

CHASSIS TIGHTENING REFERENCE

ITEM	DRWG. OR STD. PART No.	THREAD	MATERIAL	TIGHTENING TORQUE
Brake drum-to-layshaft nut (early type)	1/25748/11	14 MB (x1,5)	R 50 Cdt (Shaft 14 CN5)	47 ft.lbs (6.500 kgmm)
Pinion layshaft nut (late type) . . .	1/07934/11	14 MB (x1,5)	R 50 Cdt (Shaft 14 CN5 Cmt 5)	39.8 ft.lbs (5.500 kgmm)
Primary shaft gear nut (early type)	1.28.113/ 977844	14 MC (x1)	R 50 (Shaft 38 NCD 4 Bon)	43.4 ft.lbs (6.000 kgmm)
Primary shaft gear nut (late type)	1.28.113/ 981581	20 MC (x1)	R 50 (Shaft 14 CN 5 Cmt 5)	72.3 ft.lbs (10.000 kgmm)
Ring gear-to-differential case screw	1.45.145/ 869734	10 x 1,25 M	R 100	44.8 ft.lbs (6.200 kgmm)
Differential bearing housing-to-gearbox casing nut	1/61008/11	8 MA (x1,25)	R 50 Cdt (Stud R 80 Cdt)	18 ft.lbs (2.500 kgmm)
Layshaft rear bearing retainment plate screw	1.28.191/ 4065777	8 MA (x1,25)	R 80	18 ft.lbs (2.500 kgmm)
Gearbox casing rear housing-to-central body nut	1/21647/11	10 x 1,25 M	R 50 Cdt (Stud R 50 Cdt)	27.5 ft.lbs (3.800 kgmm)
Gearbox-to-engine bolts: lower upper	1.28.067/ 870058 1.28.068/ 870059	12 MB (x1,5)	R 80 Cdt	57.9 ft.lbs (8.000 kgmm)
Leaf spring-to-body nut (Sedan) . .	1/21647/11	10 x 1,25 M	R 50 Cdt (Screw C21R)	29 ft.lbs (4.000 kgmm)
Knuckle pillar-to-swinging arm nut (Sedan)	1/25747/11	12 MB (x1,5)	R 50 Cdt (Screw R 50 Cdt)	43.4 to 50.6 ft.lbs (6.000 to 7.000 kgmm)
Brake housing flange-to-steering knuckle nut (Sedan)	1/17016/11	8 MA (x1,25)	R 50 Cdt (Screw R 50)	14.5 ft.lbs (2.000 kgmm)

(continued)

CHASSIS TIGHTENING REFERENCE

Chassis Tightening Reference (*continued*).

ITEM	DRWG. OR STD. PART No.	THREAD	MATERIAL	TIGHTENING TORQUE
Leaf spring-to-knukle pillar nut (Sedan)	1/25748/11	14 MB (x1,5)	R 50 Cdt (Screw R 50 Znt)	43.4 to 50.6 ft.lbs (6.000 to 7.000 kgmm)
Front swinging arm-to-body nut (Sedan)	1/21647/11	10 x 1,25 M	R 50 Cdt (Screw R 50)	32.6 ft.lbs (4.500 kgmm)
Bearing-on-steering knuckle nut (Sedan)	1.58.220/ 980498	14 MB (x1,5)	R 50 (Steering knuckle 38NCD4 Bon)	22 ft.lbs (3.000 kgmm) (see page 155)
Steering knuckle-to-swinging arms self-locking nut (Multipla) . . .	1/25748/11	14 MB (x1,5)	R 50 Cdt (steering knuckle 38NCD4 Bon)	86.8 ft.lbs (12.000 kgmm)
Brake housing flange and knuckle arm to steering knuckle bolt nut (Multipla)	1/21647/11	10 x 1,25 M	R 50 Cdt (Screw R 80)	32.5 to 39.8 ft.lbs (4.500 to 5.500 kgmm)
Brake housing flange to steering knuckle bolt nut (Multipla) . . .	1/21647/11	10 x 1,25 M	R 50 Cdt (Screw R 50)	32.5 to 39.8 ft.lbs (4.500 to 5.500 kgmm)
Front wheel bearing retainment nut on steering knuckle (Multipla) .	1/07246/11	18 MB (x1,5)	R 50 Cdt (steering knuckle 38 NCD4 Bon)	22 ft.lbs (3.000 kgmm) (see page 167)
Rear swinging arm pin-to-floor nut	1/25748/11 1/21640/11	14 MB (x1,5)	R 50 Cdt (Screw R 80 Cdt)	43.4 to 50.6 ft.lbs (6.000 to 7.000 kgmm)
Rear swinging arm support-to-floor screw	1.56.589/ 832632	10 x 1,25 M	R 80	29 to 36.2 ft.lbs (4.000 to 5.000 kgmm)
Hub and brake housing flange-to-swinging arm nut	1/21647/11	10 x 1,25 M	R 50 Cdt (Screw R 80)	43.4 ft.lbs (6.000 kgmm)
Differential shaft sleeve-to-flexible joint screw	1.45.579/ 988118	8 MA (x1,25)	R 80 Cdt	22 ft.lbs (3.000 kgmm)
Steering wheel nut	1.62.025/ 743601	18 MB (x1,5)	R 50 Cdt (Shaft C 12 tube)	28.9 to 36.2 ft.lbs (4.000 to 5.000 kgmm)
Steering box mounting self-locking nut: Sedan (and relay lever support)	1/25743/11	8 MA (x1,25)	R 50 Cdt (Screw R 80 Cdt)	14.5 to 18 ft.lbs (2.000 to 2.500 kgmm)
Multipla	1/25745/11	10 x 1,25 M	R 50 Cdt (Screw R 80 Cdt)	27.5 ft.lbs (3.800 kgmm)

(*continued*)

Chassis Tightening Reference (continued).

ITEM	DRWG. OR STD. PART No.	THREAD	MATERIAL	TIGHTENING TORQUE
Pitman arm self-locking nut (Sedan)	1/25748/11	14 MB (x1,5)	R 50 Cdt (Sector 19CN5 Cmt3)	72 to 80 ft.lbs (10.000 to 11.000 kgmm)
Pitman arm nut (Multipla)	1/21641/21	16 MB (x1,5)	R 80 Cdt (Rod 38NCD4 Bon)	80 ft.lbs (11.000 kgmm)
Relay lever pin (or pivot) nut:				
Sedan	1/25747/11	12 MB (x1,5)	R 50 Cdt (Pin R 80 Cdt)	39.8 to 43.4 ft.lbs (5.500 to 6.000 kgmm)
Multipla	1/07924/11	16 MB (x1,5)	R 50 Cdt (Pivot R 100)	101 ft.lbs (14.000 kgmm)
Track rod articulation head ball pin nut:				
Sedan	1/25756/11	10 x 1,25 M	R 50 Cdt (Pin 15 CND 3 Cm 1)	18.1 to 21.7 ft.lbs (2.500 to 3.000 kgmm)
Multipla	1/07933/11	12 MB (x1,5)	R 50 Cdt (Pin 15 CND 3R)	21.7 ft.lbs (3.000 kgmm)
Wheel-to-hub screw:				
Sedan	1.49.012/ 996225	12 MB (x1,5)	C 35 R (Bon Cdt)	43.4 to 50.6 ft.lbs (6.000 to 7.000 kgmm)
Multipla	1.49.110/ 4052840	12 MB (x1,5)	C 35 R (Bon Cdt)	43.4 to 50.6 ft.lbs (6.000 to 7.000 kgmm)

Section 10
ELECTRIC SYSTEM

	Page
BATTERY	246
GENERATOR	250
GENERATOR REGULATOR	263
STARTER	277
IGNITION SYSTEM	285
LIGHTING SYSTEM	295
GAUGES AND CONTROLS	309

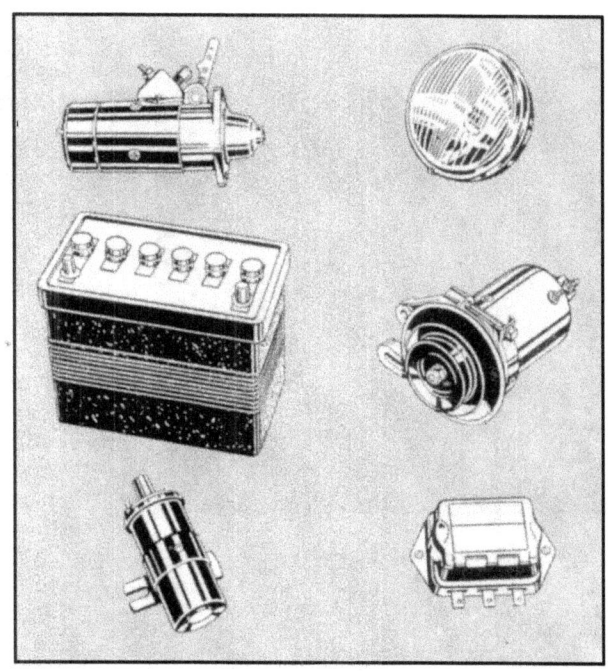

BATTERY

Specifications	page	246
First Use Directions	»	247
Inspection and Upkeep	»	247
Recharging Battery with External Means	»	250

Specifications.

The storage battery as fitted to Model 600 « Sedan » and « Multipla », has the following specifications (the same battery is installed also on versions 140 and 141, applying to cars for export to U. S. A.):

— Tension . . . . 12 Volts
— Capacity (at 20 hrs discharge rate)   32 Amp/h
— Length . . . . 9.252" (235 mm)
— Width . . . . 5.236" (133 mm)
— Height . . . . 7.795" (198 mm)
— Weight (w/electrolyte)   abt. 30 lbs (13,65 kg)

Battery location:

Sedan - in front compartment, next to fuel tank (fig. 382).

Multipla - behind rear seat, on the right (fig. 383).

The battery connectors are sunk in sealant; this design feature improves insulation and reduces current leaks to ground, corrosion, etc.

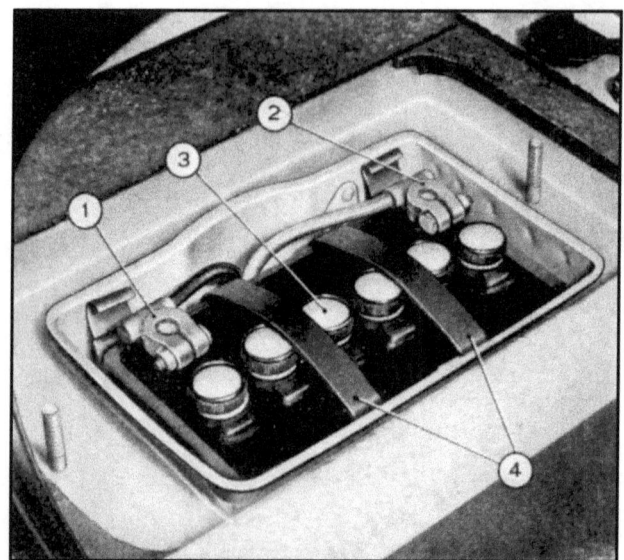

Fig. 383 - Battery (Multipla).

1. Positive post. - 2. Negative post. - 3. Cell plugs (vented). 4. Insulating band for battery removal.

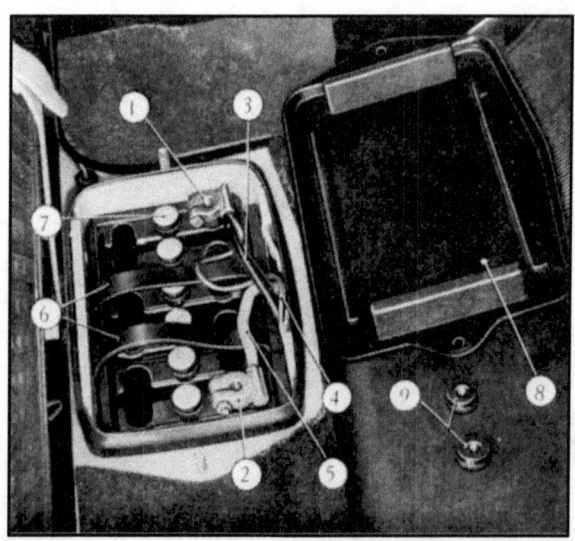

Fig. 382 - Battery (Sedan).

1. Positive post. - 2. Negative post. - 3. Battery-to-starter cable. - 4. Positive post-to-lock switch cable. - 5. Battery ground cable. - 6. Insulating band for battery removal. - 7. Cell plugs (vented). - 8. Cover. - 9. Hold-down knobs.

Model 600 « Sedan » and « Multipla » for export to cold weather countries (Canada, etc.) are equipped with another battery type, the specifications of which are as follows:

— Tension . . . . 12 Volts
— Capacity (at 20 hrs discharge rate)   38 Amp/hrs
— Width . .   5.1968" to 5.2756" (132 to 134 mm)
— Length . .   9.1338" to 9.3701" (232 to 238 mm)
— Height . .   7.7165" to 7.8739" (196 to 200 mm)
— Weight   { with electrolyte .   30.9 lbs (14 kg)
            { without electrolyte 25.4 lbs (11,5 kg)

This battery is of the « winterized » type, that is it was specially designed for use in « cold weather » countries, assuring quick starting even with extremely low temperature.

It is identified with a blue paint stripe on upper edge of battery case, terminal post side.

In this battery, connectors are sunk in sealant, too.

The main feature of this battery is that it is supplied in a **dry charge** condition.

During battery manufacture, battery plates are submitted to a special process of formation, washing and drying, with the result that **battery can be put into service just after filling with electrolyte and a proper relief period, without the necessity of the initial charging work.**

First Use Directions.

1) Prepare electrolyte in a jar of glass or plastic. Electrolyte should be made of extremely pure sulphuric acid diluted in distilled water (specific gravity 1.28). Recall that it is dangerous pouring water on acid.

CAUTION

a) Cell caps should not be removed for any reason other than for filling the battery with acid to put it into service.

b) **Mind to it that distilled water trays, funnels, sticks, etc. should not be of metal. Glass or plastic will do and cleanliness is of utmost importance.**

Above points should be closely observed inasmuch as metals, namely copper and iron, are liable to be attacked by electrolyte which contaminates causing early battery rundown.

2) Remove vent cap seals and screw out vent caps. Withdraw plastic washers which are located under caps, thus clearing vent holes.

3) Fill up with electrolyte as per step 1) the cells of all elements up to 3/16" (5 mm) above the top edge of separators.

4) A relief period of two hours at least should be allowed for the plates to absorb acid.

5) During this time the electrolyte level in each cell is diminishing and therefore acid should be added to compensate for the amount absorbed by plates and separators and restore level to 3/16" (5 mm) above top edge of separators.

6) Screw up vent caps into seat and make sure that vent holes are not plugged.

7) Battery is ready for installation on vehicle. If the vehicle is anticipated to run mostly in town with frequent starts etc., it will be good practice to submit the battery to a 4 Ampere bench charge, as soon as possible.

This procedure is recommended especially with cold weather.

Inspection and Upkeep.

1. - **Access to battery.**

Sedan - Raise front compartment lid and back out the two battery hold-down frame nuts (fig. 382).

Multipla - Lift the mat on engine partition wall, unscrew the two knobs securing the upper right protection panel and the other two knobs holding down the battery cover (fig. 383).

NOTE - Removal of battery is done by grabbing the two insulating bands (6, fig. 382 or 4, fig 383), after disconnecting negative and positive terminal clamps, and pulling up.

---

2. - **Cleaning.**

The battery must always be clean and dry, especially its top.

Use a hard brush and keep out dust or other foreign matter from cells.

Check that sealing compound around battery cell covers has not cracked (with consequent electrolyte leaks). Electrolyte should never spill over battery because highly corrosive. In case leaks have already occurred and some parts are corroded, clean and coat with acidproof paint all serviceable damaged parts and replace the unserviceable ones.

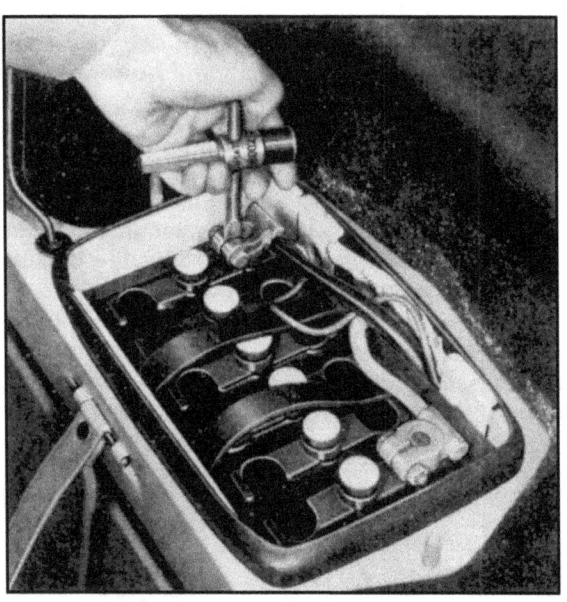

Fig. 384 - Slackening clamps from battery posts by tool A. 68002.

3. - **Posts and terminal clamps.**

To unscrew or tighten terminal clamp nuts, **do not use pliers or hammers** but the specially provided wrenches.

To free clamp, never grab and rotate the cable but use tool **A. 68002** (fig. 384). Jerking the cable stresses and may crack the ebonite cell cover or may tear cable off clamp, thus causing electrolyte dispersion paths, with consequent damages.

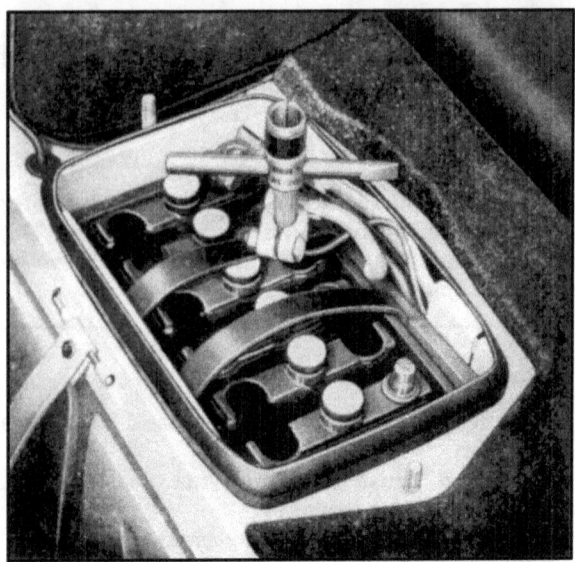

Fig. 385 - Cleaning battery posts by tool A. 68002.

Any corroded terminals, clamps or cables must be replaced.

Corrosion reduces the section of conductor resulting in increased conductor ohmic resistance.

This causes a noticeable voltage drop at terminal clamps of starter whose output will be reduced and starting will not always be successful.

To clean terminals and clamps, use tool **A. 68002** (figs. 385-386).

Well clean terminals and clamps must be coated with pure ropy vaseline. Particular attention must be devoted to the lower end of terminals and clamps where acid is more likely to be present.

Do not use grease because it reacts with the sulphuric acid contained in the electrolyte or in its vapors issuing from plugs with the naturally developed gases and forming conductive salts (green or bluish) which cause current dispersions and favour corrosion of terminals and clamps.

Always use pure ropy vaseline.

If vaseline is not pure, reactions may occur as in the case of grease. If not ropy, it may soften excessively when heated, fall on battery cover and soften also the cover sealing compound.

It is also important not to use vaseline too liberally: a thin uniform coating will do.

After the cleaning and vaseline-coating operations, fix clamps securely on battery posts to reduce contact resistance.

4. - Electrolyte level.

Check level periodically. During battery operation, water is the only element that evaporates. Consequently, only distilled water must be added to top up battery and never any acid.

Electrolyte level must be kept constantly above separators, but not above a given height. Separators must never be allowed to emerge from electrolyte.

NOTE - Addition of distilled water into six battery elements should be made using automatic filler **A 13021**

Refills must always be effected with battery cold (68° F - 20° C), at rest, and up to a level above separators of:

— 3/16'' (5 mm), when battery is charged 100%;

— 1/8'' (3 mm), when battery is in normal operating condition.

This, because during operation the state of charge ranges between 2/3 (density about 1.23) and 3/4 (density about 1.25) of full charge.

Since as temperature and state of charge increase also the electrolyte level increases sensibly, when a normally charged battery is topped up to fully charged battery level, the electrolyte will rise - especially during long runs when battery undergoes heating and charging cycles - up to the lower edge of breathers and overflow.

To check on electrolyte level, use a 3/16''-5/16'' (5-8 mm) dia. glass tube inserted through plug seat down to separator top edge. Blank tube upper end with index finger, lift tube out of cell, and check height of solution drawn up by tube. Reference marks on tube bottom end will facilitate level readings.

The containers, funnels, rods, tubes, etc., for distilled water should be of glass or plastic, never of metal, and must always be perfectly clean.

Fig. 386 - Cleaning battery cable clamps by tool A. 68002.

1. Tool A. 68002. - 2. Negative clamp.

ELECTRICAL

This is essential since if metals of any kind (specially copper and iron) are put in contact with the electrolyte, they react with the latter and cause quick deterioration of battery on account of electrolyte contamination.

Electrolyte level must be checked at 1,500-mile (2500 km) intervals or every 15 days if car is garaged.

If car is not used for a long time, battery must receive proper maintenance care (recharging, topping up, etc.).

Should electrolyte level in one cell be found lower than in the others, check cell for cracks, since this indicates a leak has occurred.

NOTICE - Electrolyte level must never be higher than recommended. When level is too high, gases developed cause the spraying of the electrolyte on battery top with consequent corrosion of clamps, terminals and battery box itself.

5. - Checking the state of charge.

State of charge is determined by measuring the electrolyte specific gravity. The charge measurement by the high-discharge method (Voltmeter individual cell tester) should never be adopted, since cells tested may be damaged seriously and current consumption is very high.

The electrolyte gravity is proportional to the state of charge and relationship is as follows:

Specific gravity	State of charge
1.28 (*)	Fully charged
1.25	Three-fourths charged
1.22	One-half charged
1.19	One-fourth charged
1.16	Barely operative
1.11	Completely discharged

(*) Specific gravity of batteries for export to U.S.A. should be 1.27, with fully charged battery.

To check specific gravity, use the accurate hydrometer **C. 852**.

Readings should be taken at eye level on float graduated stem, with free float and tube held vertical.

Once reading has been taken, return the electrolyte to cell from which it was sucked into hydrometer.

IMPORTANT - Take hydrometer readings away from battery, because any electrolyte (which contains sulphuric acid) dripping onto battery will cause corrosion, current dispersions, etc.

Specific gravity readings **should never be taken** under these conditions:

a) incorrect electrolyte level;

b) too warm ot too cold electrolyte; temperature should be $68°\pm 9°$ F ($20°\pm 5°$ C);

c) soon after topping up (wait until acid solution in electrolyte is uniform: if battery is discharged, wait a few hours);

d) soon after repeated engine starts: also in this case wait until acid dispersion is uniform;

e) bubbling electrolyte: wait until all bubbles sucked in hydrometer with the solution have come up into empty portion of tube.

If the following conditions are found:

— cell gravity readings more than 0.02 apart;

— excessively high specific gravity: 1.30;

— low specific gravity: 1.22;

and at the same time an excessive overheating of battery during regular operation (more than 18°F-10°C above ambient temperature) take the battery for repairs to one of the Battery Manufacturer's Shops.

When car is not used for a long time, recharge periodically once a month.

Recharging must be carried out at low current (4 Amps max.) until all cells boil briskly.

On FIAT cars, **fitted with voltage regulators, the battery does not require a periodical recharge during, operation, inasmuch as the car recharging system is sufficient to keep battery in perfect efficiency.**

If battery runs down during operation (the long standing periods during which battery is selfdischarged should naturally not be taken into account) indicates abnormal operating conditions, the most commonly encountered ones being:

I) **Improper recharging system operation** (generator and regulator.) - See the instructions outlined for generator and regulating units on the following pages.

II) **Current dispersions caused by defective insulation in car system.** - This is a rather frequent case, especially when car owner adds on his own initiative some new user (special horns, fog lamps, etc.) in which case he tampers with the electric system and faulty insulations are very likely to occur.

If a megohmmeter is available, check insulation by placing the instrument between the disconnected battery positive cable and ground (all users totally excluded). Even in the worst test conditions (wet car, etc.) an insulating resistance reading of less than 10,000 Ohms should not be recorded.

A quick check can be carried out using a milliammeter: arrange it in series between battery positive cable clamp and terminal, and make sure that indicated current (without any users inserted in the circuit) is not greater than 1 milliampere.

NOTE - Before connecting or disconnecting the positive clamp from battery terminal, always disconnect the negative cable (grounded on frame) from battery.

III) **Addition of users by the car owner.** - A given proportionate margin is possible with the charging system. Therefore, provided given limits are not exceeded, the addition of a few users can be tolerated.

IV) **Use of car on short runs, with frequent stops and repeated use of 4th gear at very low speeds.** - Because starter is used often, battery discharges quickly. Generator supplies no output or develops only a part of the power it should because its r.p.m. rate is too low.

It will suffice to tell car owner to run car in low gear when travelling at reduced speeds: the generator will then operate at a normal recharging rate.

V) Sulphated battery with shorted or «open» cells.

Recharging Battery with External Means.

Bearing in mind the aforementioned recommendations, recharging the battery by rectifiers or motor-generator converter unit will be necessary only when car is not used for a long time or when the abnormal operating conditions outlined in points 5 I), II), III), IV) have occurred.

Remember the following:

a) after removal from car, clean well the battery, especially its top;

b) check electrolyte level;

c) insert battery in the charging circuit and methodically check, at intervals, the state of charge using a hydrometer;

d) clean battery once more, before installation on car.

GENERATOR

Specifications	page 250
Operation	» 251
Bench Testing Instructions	» 253
Trouble Shooting Instructions	» 255
Servicing	» 258
R 90-180/12-2500 Generator Specifications and Data	» 261
D 90/12/16/3 Generator Specifications and Data	» 262

Specifications.

Model 600 «**Sedan**» and «**Multipla**» are equipped with generator **D 90/12/16/3** having the following characteristics:

— Nominal tension . . . . 12 Volts
— Maximum continued operation output (ammeter limit) . . . . 16 Amperes
— Maximum current output . . . . 22 Amperes
— Maximum power, continued operation . . . . 230 Watts
— Maximum power . . . . 320 Watts
— Initial charging speed at 12 Volts and 68° F (20° C) } *1710 to 1860 r.p.m.
**1710 to 1790 r.p.m.
— 16 Ampere current output speed, at 68° F (20° C) } *2550 to 2800 r.p.m.
**2550 to 2700 r.p.m.
— 22 Ampere current output speed, at 68°F (20° C) . . . . . 3050 to 3200 r.p.m.
— Max. steady speed . . . . 9000 r.p.m.
— Rotation . . . . clockwise, drive end
— Two-pole, shunt field winding.
— Separate regulator assembly (FIAT GN 1/12/16).
— Engine-to-generator drive ratio (with new belt) 1.7

---

* For generators with armature package disc teeth .1732" (4,4 mm) in length (early type).

** For generators with armature package disc teeth .1969" (5 mm) in length.

ELECTRICAL

NOTE - Up to engine No. 573516 was installed the FIAT generator type R 90-180/12-2500. Specifications and data pertaining to this generator are given on page 261.

On drive end the armature rotates on a ball bearing and, on the commutator end, on a self-lubricating bronze bush. An oil lubricator with wick and oil reserve is fitted on commutator end head.

The ball bearing is press fitted in the head and can be slid off from the armature shaft. Bearing is secured to the head by two retaining discs which, together with the two felt seal holding caps, are screwed to the heads.

The heads are fastened to frame by two tie rods passing between the two pole shoes.

Commutator end head is provided with brush holders of the « reaction » type (fig. 387).

Fig. 387 - Commutator end head of generator D 90/12/16/3. « Reaction » type brush holders.

This design feature, with respect to « radial type » brush holders, remarkably reduces the vibration of brushes in their holders and hence the jumping of brushes on commutator during generator operation. Furthermore, with brush section on par, the brush contact surface on commutator increases.

As a result, the following advantages are obtained:

— less sparking and wear of brushes, with added life;

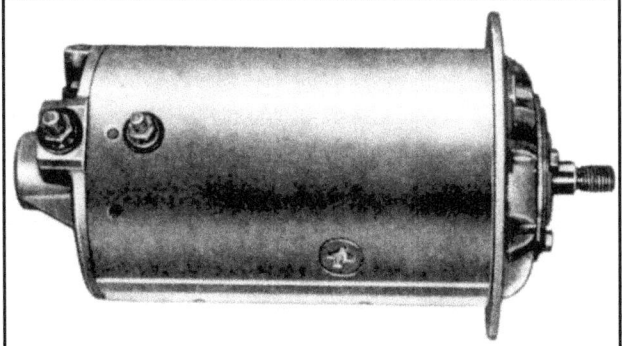

Fig. 388 - FIAT generator D 90/12/16/3.

— less overheating and wear of commutator, with added life;

— less excitation current in generator, resulting in longer life of voltage regulator and current regulator contacts.

Internal generator windings are efficiently cooled by the fan and drive pulley, forming a single unit. Air enters through the openings on the commutator end head and is circulated by the fan.

The generator is provided with the two following numbered terminals:

— Terminal 51 applied and suitably insulated on commutator end head: connected to positive brush. Terminal axis perpendicular to generator axis.

— Terminal 67 applied and suitably insulated on generator frame: connected to one end of field winding. Terminal axis perpendicular to generator axis.

Terminals 51 and 67 must be connected with the regulator terminals bearing the same numbers.

Operation.

When generator connected with its regulator is set into operation, the voltage increases gradually with r.p.m. rate, but there is no output as long as cutout contacts remain open.

As voltage within generator reaches 12.6 ± 0.2 volts, cutout contact close and current flows to battery and users.

As outlined in detail under the heading « Generator Regulator », the current regulator of the FIAT GN 1/12/16 regulator assembly fitting this generator is « thermally stabilized ».

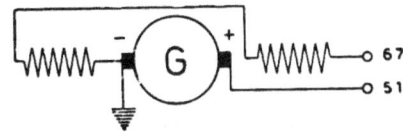

Fig. 389 - Generator wiring diagram.

D 90/12/16/3 GENERATOR

SECTION A-A

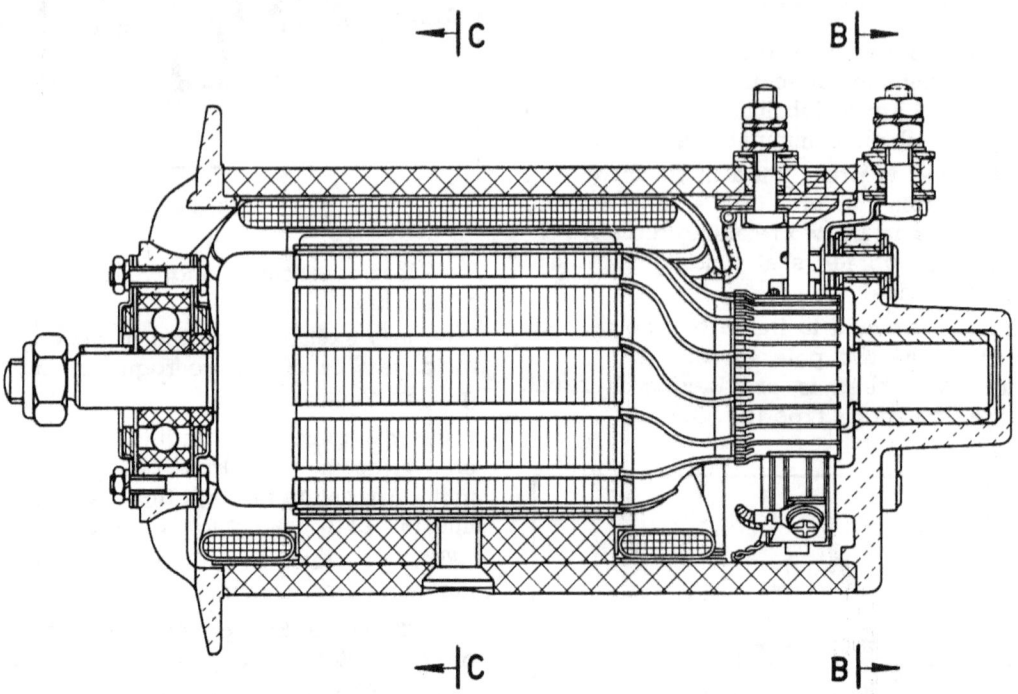

Fig. 390 - D 90/12/16/3 generator longitudinal section.

SECTION B-B

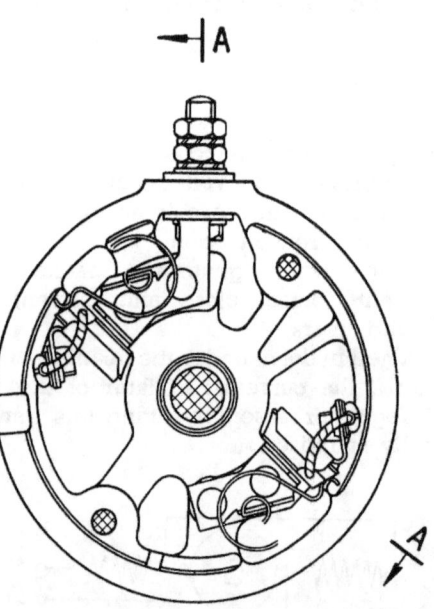

Fig. 391 - Commutator end head of generator D 90/12/16/3. « Reaction » type brush holders are visible.

SECTION C-C

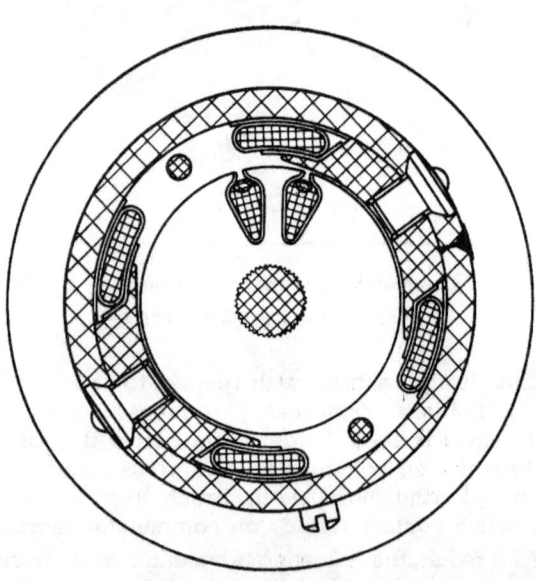

Fig. 392 - Cross section of generator D 90/12/16/3 through armature and pole shoes.

Thanks to this feature, the limiting current of a cold regulator (at the beginning of operation, after a sufficiently long inactivity period), is higher than maximum steady output of generator. Therefore, if current draw from electrical units is heavy, the generator may be overloaded.

The generator, however, can withstand this overload because it, too, is at the beginning of operation and not yet « thermally stabilized », i.e. its windings are still at ambient temperature.

As both regulator and generator warm up due to heat transfer from windings, current regulator reduces (within 20-30 minutes) the limiting current until it reaches a value that the generator can withstand safely in continuous operation. This value varies with ambient temperature and is reached when the unit is thermally « soaked » at rated operation temperature.

It ensues that the overload cannot cause dangerous temperatures within the generator since, as generator temperature increases, the load decreases.

The temporary initial operation in overload of generator permits a quicker battery charging when charge level is lowest due to a difficult cold start or when the car is operated in town with frequent stops and starts and recharge periods are very short.

As said above, the limiting current value with thermally stabilized regulator is variable with ambient temperature.

Therefore in winter the limiting current is lower than in summer.

As a result there will be lesser heat dissipation of generator in winter and better uniformity of generator temperature in both seasons.

However the in-and-out power balance in the system is not compromised as the average current consumption is lower in summer time.

The amount of current delivered depends upon battery state of charge and power of users.

Proper current and voltage regulation is provided by the current and voltage regulators incorporated with the cutout.

The generator must work exclusively with its own regulator.

Therefore, we warn against connecting terminal 67 directly to terminal 51 during generator tests on bench, or on engine, since under such conditions the generator would perform simply as a shunt excited generator in which voltage increases progressively with the increase on generator speed and induces a field current so strong that the field winding might burn.

BENCH TESTING INSTRUCTIONS

Check generator efficiency by carrying out the mechanical and electrical tests described below.

Operation Tests.

Follow strictly the procedure outlined for each test making sure that all instruments and gauges are available for prompt use.

Testing generator as a motor (at 68° F - 20° C).

This is the first and simplest test for a quick generator check.

Wire up according to diagram fig. 393.

Feed generator with a 12 V d.c. supply and check that current draw is 5±0.5 A and speed 1500±100 r.p.m.

Output test at 12 V steady tension (at 68° F - 20° C).

NOTICE - Prior to plotting the output curve, make sure that brushes are thoroughly seated in commutator bore.

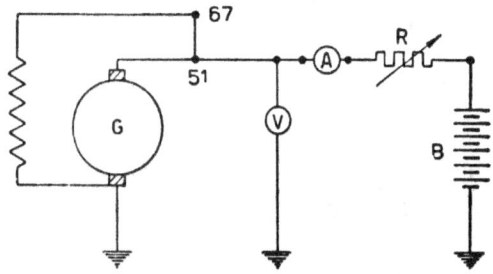

Fig. 393 - Wiring diagram for testing generator as a motor.
G. Generator. - V. Voltmeter, 15 V scale. - A. Ammeter, 10 A scale. - B. Battery capable of supplying a voltage slightly above 12 V during a discharge of 5 A. - R. Plate type rheostat for regulating the battery voltage, 100 A capacity, variable resistance of 0.2 to 20 Ω.

Install generator on test bench and couple it with a motor whose speed may be varied at will by small degrees.

Wire up according to diagram fig. 394.

Before starting the test, carry out either of the following operation, as the equipment may allow:

— run generator, with fan pulley, for about

one hour and 45 minutes at 4500 r.p.m., delivering a 16 ± 0.5 A - 14 V current to a resistor. Stop motor.

Disconnect load rheostat.

Start generator and speed up gradually until voltmeter reading is 12 volts; at this point, determine generator speed by a revolution counter.

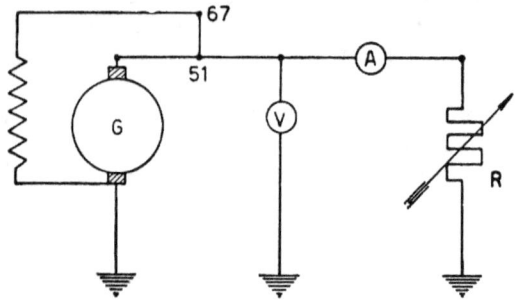

Fig. 394 - Wiring diagram for the determination of the ampere revolution output curve at a steady 12 V voltage (68° F - 20° C).

G. Generator. - V. Voltmeter, 15 V scale. - A. Ammeter, 25 A scale. R. Plate type rheostat, 100 A capacity, variable resistance of 0.20 to 20 Ω.

This represents the cut-in speed at 12 volts output (origin of curve on abscissa axis).

Stop generator and connect load rheostat.

While driving generator at steady speed in different increments, adjust load rheostat to ensure a constant 12 V output at each given r. p. m. rate; at the same time, read the value of current supplied. Each determination will give a point of the output curve.

Note that readings must be taken in a very short period of time, since the curve extends beyond

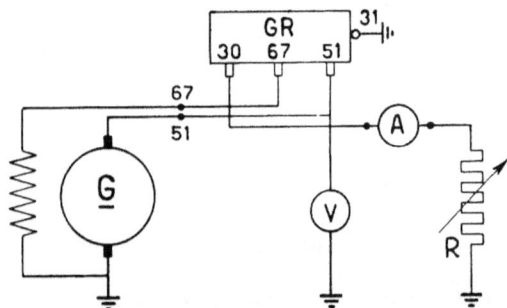

Fig. 395 - Wiring diagram for the generator heating test.

G. Generator. - GR. Regulator. - V. Voltmeter, 15 V scale. - A. Ammeter, 20 A scale. - R. Carbon plate type rheostat, 100 A capacity, 0.2 to 20 Ω variable resistance.

generator nominal power and currents higher than those of the nominal output range impose an overload that generator cannot withstand for long without overheating, with consequent failure of insulations.

The curve plotted by points must lie within the limits indicated in the shaded area shown in fig. 396.

Heating Test.

Wire up the generator complete with fan pulley, according to diagram fig. 395

Carry out either of the following operations, as the equipment may allow:

— run generator for one hour and 45 minutes at 4500 r. p. m., delivering 16 ± 0.5 Amperes and 14 volts to a resistor.

Check that temperatures of frame and commutator do not exceed respectively 86° F (30° C) and 149° F (65° C).

Ohmic Resistance Test.

Resistance at 68° F (20° C) must be 0.145 ± 0.01 Ω for the armature and $8^{+0.1}_{-0.3}$ Ω for field winding.

Field winding ohmic resistance may be determined with assembled generator, by simply measuring the resistance between terminal 67 and ground.

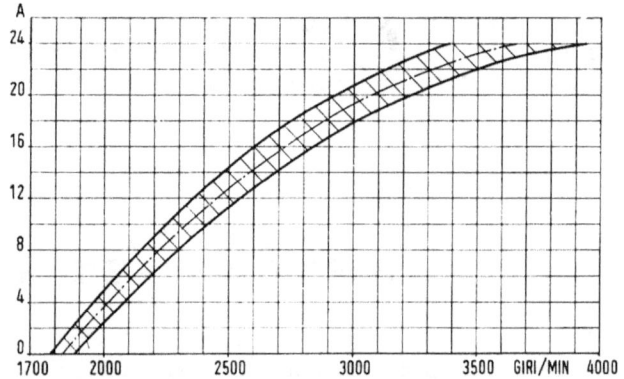

Fig. 396 - Output curve of warm generator D 90/12/16/3. GIRI/MIN = R. P. M.

The recommended measurement method is that of the Volt/Ampere ratio in which a sufficiently high voltage is applied and measured, together with the current drawn by the winding. The ratio of applied voltage to drawn current gives the ohmic resistance, according to the formula: $\frac{V}{I} = R$.

Alternatively, a Wheatstone bridge may be used, provided it is sufficiently accurate.

Determining armature winding resistance is more difficult on account of the low value involved and, therefore, must be made only in exceptional cases, provided proper equipment is available.

In this case proceed as follows:

— solder two wire lengths on the faces of two commutator segments 180° apart;

— apply 2 to 2.5 volts and measure with accuracy the current drawn (Volt and Ampere readings).

Resistance R is still given by $\frac{V}{I}$.

ELECTRICAL

Mechanical Characteristics Check Data.

1) Brush hold-down springs load must be 1.3 to 1.6 lbs (0,60 to 0,72 kg).

2) Maximum commutator out-of-round (on rubbing surface): not more than .0004" (0,01 mm).

3) Commutator mica must be undercut at least .04" (1 mm) throughout its entire length and width.

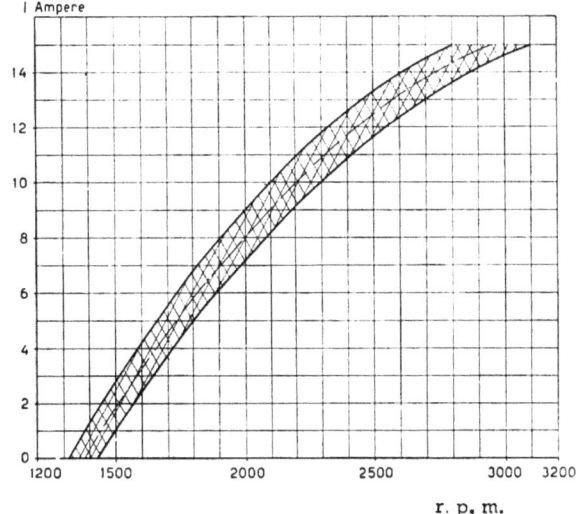

Fig. 397 - Output curve of warm generator R 90-180/12-2500. Steady 12 tension.

TROUBLE SHOOTING

Troubles in battery charging system may originate from:
  a) generator;
  b) other components of system.

Before inspecting generator for faults make sure that no other component in the system is responsible for the trouble.

To detect the trouble observe the charge indicator which may give the following indications:

1. By inserting and rotating lock switch key to ignition ON position, the indicator lights up. It normally goes out when engine reaches the predetermined r.p.m. rate.

This is a sign that generator is efficient.

2. By inserting and rotating the key to ignition ON position, the indicator lights up. It goes out only at a fairly high engine r.p.m. rate.

Generator is faulty and defects may be:

  2.1. Short-circuited coils in field winding.
  2.2. Field winding, or **jumper between the two field windings**, grounded on frame.
  2.3. Large number of armature coils shorted.

These irregularities cause a complete alteration of the cut-in and max. output speed rates which shift to increasingly higher values in proportion to the severity of short circuits.

WARNING - Troubles 2.1 and 2.2 must be **remedied as soon as detected** since they are liable to render unserviceable the entire recharging system, owing to the abnormally high excitation current induced, whose value increases because of the reduction in field winding resistance.

The voltage regulator contacts are required to cut a current higher than the rated one and, therefore, are quickly damaged.

This condition will ultimately result in the unserviceability of the entire regulating unit.

On the other hand, when replacing a regulating unit with oxidized contacts, before setting recharging system into operation, again check the generator (points 2.1, 2.2, 2.3) and repair or replace accordingly, or else also the new regulator might be damaged in a short time.

  2.4. Insulating coat (grease, etc.) between contacts of voltage regulator or current regulator. This results in increased resistance between said contacts and hence in reduced excitation current. Also this trouble causes an increase in generator cutting-in speed and maximum output speed.

3. By inserting and rotating the key to the ignition ON position the indicator lights up but does not go out even with engine running at high r.p.m. rates.

Defects may be:

  3.1. Broken connection between terminal 67 of generator and terminal 67 of regulator.
  3.2. Heavily oxidized or dirty contacts of either voltage or current regulators.
  3.3. Inner regulator connections to terminals 67 and 51 unsoldered or broken.
  3.4. Connection to terminal 51 of regulator broken.
  3.5. Broken field winding.
  3.6. Grounded armature winding.
  3.7. Broken armature winding.

3.8. Grounded field winding.

3.9. Worn brushes not contacting commutator, or commutator coated with an insulating film (grease, oxide, etc.).

3.10. Cutout which does not close (e. g., magnetizing coil broken).

In this case, at a given speed, generator voltage equalizes battery voltage and the indicator goes out; then (the charging circuit being broken), at a higher r.p.m. the generator voltage reaches the no-load adjustment value of voltage regulator (15 V) and the indicator burns again feebly on account of the difference in generator over battery voltage.

3.11. Though cutout armature lowers, contacts do not close the circuit, being excessively worn or heavily oxidized.

Also in this case consequences are as outlined in point 3.10.

4. By inserting and rotating the key clockwise to the ignition ON position, the indicator does not light up, even when engine is speeded up.

Check first the indicator bulb and replace if defective. Check also contact of bulb base with holder.

If bulb is efficient, causes for trouble may be:

4.1. Open circuit between generator terminal 51 and regulator terminal 51.

4.2. Open circuit between regulator terminal 51 and plug-in connection of red indicator in instrument cluster.

4.3. Open circuit between plug-in connection « INTER » in instrument cluster and red indicator.

4.4. Open circuit between instrument cluster plug-in connection « INTER » and plug-in connection « 15/54 » of ignition lock switch.

4.5. Open circuit inside ignition lock switch.

4.6. Open circuit between plug-in connection « 30 » of ignition lock switch and plug-in connection « 30 » of fuseholder.

4.7. Open circuit between plug-in connection « 30 » of fuseholder and + clamp of battery.

5. By inserting and rotating the key clockwise to the ignition ON position, the indicator lights up. After starting and speeding up the engine the indicator goes out but when the engine reaches and exceeds a given r.p.m. rate the indicator lights up again feebly.

This is not an indication of troubles in the recharging system but, rather, that **the indicator bulb is faulty,** i.e., the bulb begins to light up at a too low voltage.

In fact, at the indicator circuit terminal points there is a small voltage differential - due to the normal voltage drops along the circuit - when generator supplies a rather high current (discharged battery, users « ON »).

If the bulb begins to light up when tension is too low, its filament will glow feebly. To remedy this trouble, fit a new indicator bulb which will begin to light up at a voltage of 1.1-1.5 V.

This voltage may easily be checked using a suitable potentiometer and a 2-Volt scale voltmeter.

NOTE - If the above case is met, check the following:

a) The tightening of clamp 30 of generator regulator.

b) The proper coupling of plug-in connections located in the section of circuit between regulator terminal 30 and terminal 30 of ignition lock switch.

Said checks are important because the loosening of regulator terminal 30 or the inadequate coupling of plug-in connections (weakened inserts, etc.) cause an increase in voltage drops along the circuit so that the lamp lights up too soon.

TROUBLE SHOOTING HINTS

Should conditions under point 2. occur, check generator for defects indicated in 2.1, 2.2 or 2.3.

Note that:

1) Troubles of points 2.1 and 2.2 may be detected by a resistance measurement on field winding. The resistance value must be as specified under « Ohmic Resistance Test » or $8^{+0.1}_{-0.3}$ Ohms.

The measurement is made by connecting the tester outlets respectively to terminal 67 and ground.

Under conditions of point 2.1 it is more reliable to use a shorted coil detector, if available. High frequency detectors are the most recommended, but to use them the field windings must be removed from frame.

2) The defect stated under 2.3 causes, besides the troubles indicated in 2. also a commutation trouble in correspondence with the segments connected to shorted coils.

The increased brush wear, due to a worsened

commutation, is accompanied by damages to the involved commutator segments (sinking). This condition further contributes to brush wear.

For shorted coils detection, an armature tester as test benches are equipped with (fig. 398) may be used, but its sensitivity is limited to two or more shorted coils.

After checking generator, check also regulating unit for the reasons stated in point 2. as outlined under « Regulator Bench Testing Instructions », page 268.

3) If conditions correspond to those under point 3., first check the regulator and, if found efficient, single out by elimination the defective item among those indicated in points 3.1 and 3.4 through 3.9 inclusive.

4) If conditions are those of point 4, generator is not faulty. Therefore, check the other items listed in sub-paragraphs of point 4.

5) Possible troubles in generator may also be the quick wear of brushes and damaged commutator. These defects may not be easily detected during operation, at any rate not until brushes are almost worn out. However, a careful inspection of commutator and brushes may prevent further harm.

Causes of this type of trouble may be:

a) loose commutator segments;

b) inadequate quality of brushes;

c) some shorted armature coils.

The defect mentioned in a) seldom occurs and is due to some segment having worked loose under the combined action of centrifugal force and heating-and-cooling cycles. The segments are displaced radially and, by protruding beyond commutator surface, cause an imperfect contact of brushes which cannot follow the commutator irregularities by inertia with consequent heavy arcing. Furthermore, this actually mills the brushes. The defect may easily be detected by a dial indicator (fig. 400), as follows.

Secure generator. Rest the dial indicator plunger on the two edges of commutator surface not rubbed by brushes and, by rotating slowly the armature, determine maximum out-of-round points and their location. If segments are properly seated, out-of-round must not exceed .0004" (0,01 mm).

The fault quoted in b) causes an alteration in commutation and, consequently, an abnormal wear of both commutator and brushes.

Use of genuine FIAT brushes (supplied by the Spare Parts Department) will minimize troubles from this source.

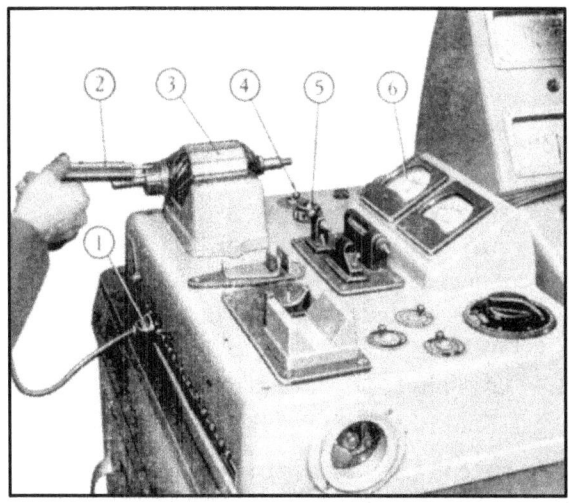

Fig. 398 - Testing the armature on bench, using a twin contact tester.

1. Ammeter plug. - 2. Twin-contact insulated grip. - 3. Armature. - 4. Armature tester throw-in switch. - 5. Pilot lamp. - 6. Ammeter.

In correspondence with an open coil the ammeter reading will be zero.

Trouble c), though not causing an appreciable increase in cut-in and output speeds of generator, and therefore not easily detectable during operation, induces commutation alterations and spot-damaging of commutator.

To single out shorted coils, use a high frequency tester, inserting a voltmeter between segments. Under normal generator operation conditions, life of brushes should range from 20,000 to 30,000 miles (30.000 to 50.000 km) of car service.

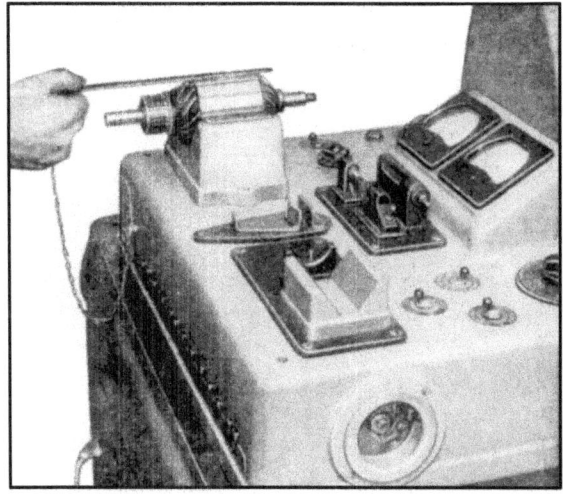

Fig. 399 - Testing the armature on bench, using a lamina.

In correspondence with short-circuited coils the lamina will vibrate.

GENERATOR SERVICING

To remove generator troubles, proceed as outlined hereafter:

1. - The only repairs that may be carried out by Service Station personnel are:
— commutator re-turning;
— repairs of broken or unsoldered field winding connections.

2. - Any other defective part must be replaced.

Generator Disassembly.

Back out the thru bolt nuts.

First raise the spring and then the brushes, sliding the latter in their seats on brush holders.

Arrange the spring end so that it will rest on the brush side, thus exerting a lateral pressure on brush.

Brushes will thus be locked in their holders and cannot be chipped by striking against armature shaft during commutator end head removal.

Pull out commutator end head and remove brushes.

Remove the armature with drive end head assembly: thus, the latter assembly, the frame with field winding and commutator end head are separated.

Remove pulley from armature shaft, after backing out its self-locking nut and plain washer.

Take out the key on armature shaft and separate the drive end head from the armature, pulling the latter out of the ball bearing that remains in head.

Disinsert thru bolts.

On drive end head, back out the nuts of screws securing ball bearing retainment rings.

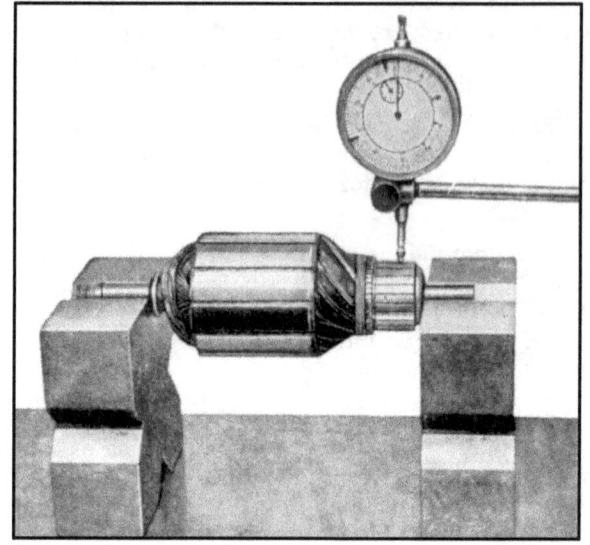

Fig. 400 - Checking commutator out-of-round.
It must not exceed .0004" (0,01 mm).

Remove said retainment rings and remove ball bearing from drive end head using the special tool provided.

Commutator Re-Turning.

The armature assembly must be placed on a lathe and suitably centered, as it is not possible to hold the armature shaft between lathe centers.

This centering must be perfect because commutator out-of-round must not exceed .0004" (0,01 mm) (fig. 400).

After re-turning, undercut the mica (fig. 402).

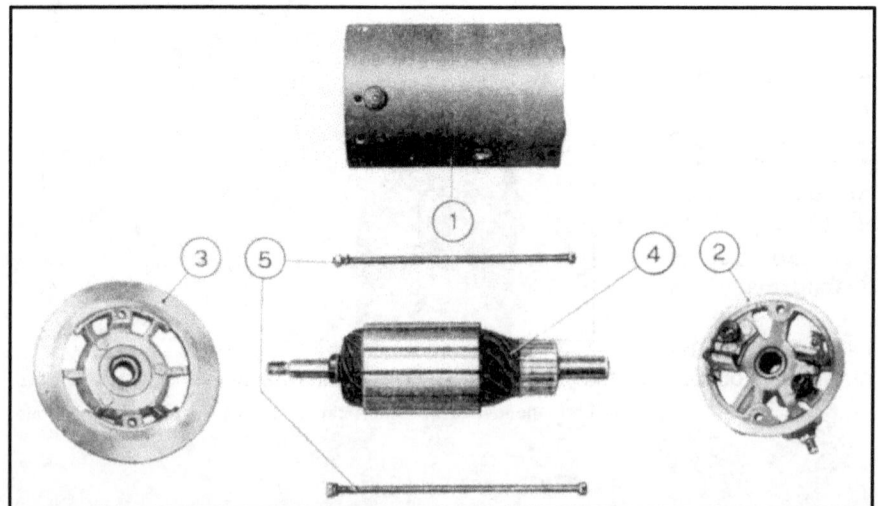

Fig. 401.
Components of generator D 90/12/16/3.

1. Housing. - 2. Commutator end head. - 3. Drive end head. - 4. Armature. - 5. Through bolts.

Broken Field Winding, with Shorted or Grounded Coils.

Repair only if trouble consists in unsoldered or broken connections. In all other cases replace winding with a **genuine one**.

Do not attempt to build a winding since windings are made of a copper wire coated with special insulating material (vinyl acetate) and require, for winding, soldering, impregnation, etc., **special treatment and equipment covered by suitable Process Standards**.

Field winding checks may be carried out using the bench for current feed and instrument reading.

Heat new winding to 122° F (50° C) before installation, to render it slightly flexible, thus facilitating its seating under pole shoes.

Pole shoes must be well set against frame and their screws fully tightened, so as to restore original air gap.

After reassembly, check that pole shoe inner diameter is 2.2952" to 2.2991" (58,3 to 58,4 mm).

If diameter departs from above figures, it is an indication that assembly is incorrect.

In this case, the whole operation must be repeated. **Never ream pole shoes.**

Shorted, Grounded or Open Armature Coil.

If this winding is damaged in its coils, it cannot be repaired by Service Stations for the same reasons given for the field winding but must be replaced as an assembly with the armature.

Brush Replacements.

Only genuine FIAT spares must be used. Brushes with different hardness or composition characteristics would impair commutator life and affect generator and regulator operation adversely.

The use of unsuitable brushes determines poor commutation, followed by accelerated wear rate of commutator segments and brushes, remarkable voltage drops between commutator and brushes and a marked excitation current increase.

Under these conditions the voltage and current regulator contacts of the generator regulator are crossed by a current higher than normal.

This higher current causes material transfer between contacts, generally of voltage regulator, forming build-up on one contact and pit in the other.

The following two cases may be met:

1) The transfer of material between contacts continues to occur until the pitted tungsten contact is pierced through. The build-up on the other

Fig. 402 - Undercutting the mica of a commutator by means of a saw blade.

contact will then touch the support of the pierced-through contact.

Since the support is of iron, arcing in the contact area causes an immediate local oxidation.

Consequently, the two contacts are insulated and the regulating resistance remains in the excitation circuit of the generator that is no longer able to supply any current.

2) The transfer of material between contacts welds them together. Under this condition, the voltage regulator cannot do its part of work (it no longer adjust voltage) and the voltage may rise to excessively high values whereby the generator will supply high current even when battery has reached the «fully charged» condition. A result of this is an overcharging of battery which consequently will be quickly and irreparably damaged.

Also the life of users in car electric system is reduced, particularly the lamps.

Summing it all up, the use of unsuitable brushes, besides a poor life of brushes and quick wear of commutator, also means damages to the generator regulator and, sometimes, to battery on account of overcharging.

Inspection.

Independently of the repair or replacements effected, before reassembling the generator:

a) blow all carbon dust from components;

b) with a dry rag, clean brush holders and commutator end head from all grease an carbon dust;

c) with a dry rag, clean commutator, especially between segments.

Do not use emery cloth or sand paper, or even cloths soaked in oil, gasoline or solvents of any kind;

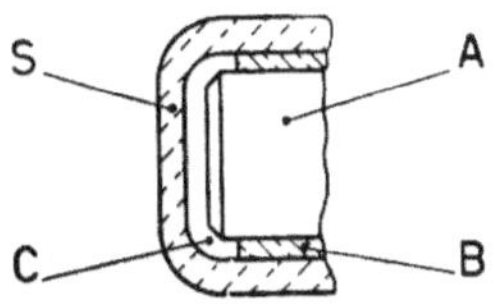

Fig. 403.
Detail of commutator end head.

A. Armature shaft end. - B. Bush. - C. Grease pocket. - S. Head.

d) with FIAT Jota 3 grease, pack ball bearing and pocket at the end of commutator end head bush and, with FIAT VE oil, fill up the commutator end head oiler.

NOTE - Do not use lubricants other than specified, unless of equivalent grade.

Reassembly.

Reverse disassembly operations.

After reassembly, repeat generator operation checks, proceeding as directed under « Bench Testing Instructions ».

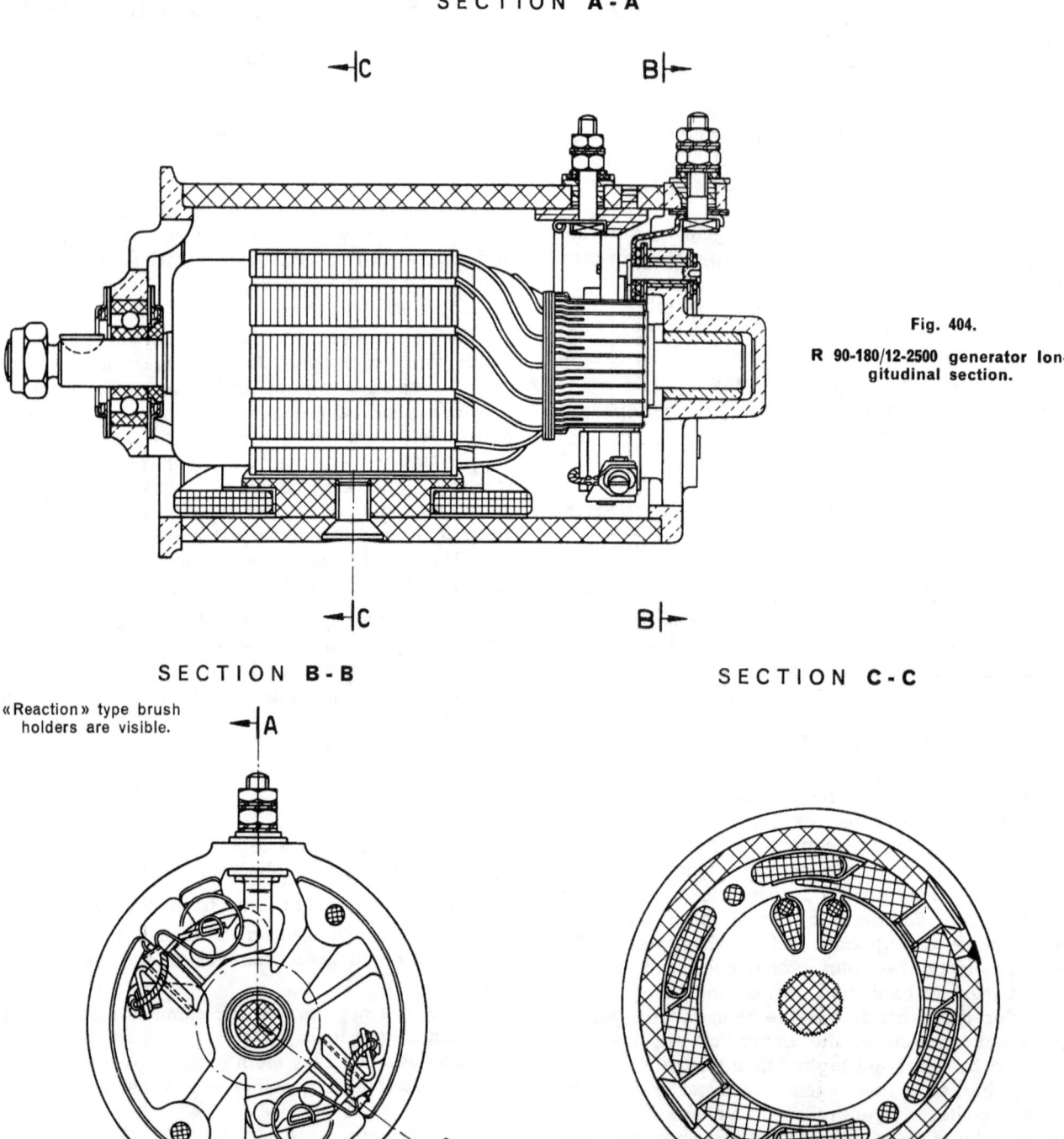

Fig. 404.
R 90-180/12-2500 generator longitudinal section.

Fig. 405 - Cross section through commutator end head of generator R 90-180/12-2500.

Fig. 406 - Cross section of generator R 90-180/12-2500 through armature and pole shoes.

ELECTRICAL

261

GENERATOR SPECIFICATIONS AND DATA
(up to engine No. 573516)

Type	R 90-180/12-2500
Nominal tension	12 Volts
Max. continued operation output	180 Watts
Max. steady current output	13 Amps
Poles	2
Field winding	shunt
Regulator	separate
Cutting-in speed (at 68° F - 20° C)	1300-1380 r.p.m.
Speed at which generator reaches max. continued operation output (tension: nominal; temperature: 68° F - 20° C)	2250-2400 r.p.m.

Mechanical Data.

Max. steady speed	7500 r.p.m.
Rotation, viewed from commutator end	clockwise
Engine-to-generator drive ratio (with new belt)	1.42
Pole shoes I.D.	2.3192" to 2.3259" (58,91 to 59,08 mm)
Armature diameter	2.2814" to 2.2834" (57,95 to 58 mm)
Part No. of brushes	879210

Bench Testing Data.

— Testing generator as a motor (at 68° F - 20° C):

Feed voltage	12 V
Current draw	4.5±0.2 Amps
Speed	1200±100 r.p.m.

— Output test (at 68° F - 20° C):

Steady voltage	12 V
Speed for abt. one hour and 45 min.	3750 r.p.m.
Current delivery to resistor	13±0.5 Amps

After bringing generator to operation temperature by running generator at the above specified speed and time rates, read, at a steady 12 V tension, the values of the current output at every generator speed increment.

— Ohmic resistance test (at 68° F - 20° C):

Armature resistance	0.31±0.01 ohms
Field winding resistance	6.4±0.2 ohms

— Mechanical characteristics test:

Load of springs on new brushes	1.3 to 1.6 lbs (0,600 to 0,720 kg)
Commutator maximum out-of-round	.0004" (0,01 mm)
Mica undercut depth	.04" (1 mm)

Lubrication.

Drive end ball bearing	FIAT Jota 3 Grease
Commutator end head bush pocket	FIAT Jota 3 Grease
Commutator end head oiler	FIAT VE oil

GENERATOR SPECIFICATIONS AND DATA
(from engine No. 573517)

Type	D 90/12/16/3
Nominal tension	12 Volts
Max. continued operation output (ammeter limit)	16 Amperes
Max. current output	22 Amperes
Max. steady power	230 Watts
Max. power	320 Watts
Initial charging speed at 12 Volts and 68° F (20° C)	1710 to 1860 r.p.m. (*) 1710 to 1790 r.p.m. (**)
16 A. max. output delivery speed, at 68° F (20° C)	2550 to 2800 r.p.m. (*) 2550 to 2700 r.p.m. (**)
22 A. max output delivery speed, at 68° F (20° C)	3050 to 3200
Max. steady speed	9000 r.p.m.
Rotation, drive end	clockwise
Poles	2
Field winding	shunt
Regulator, separate	FIAT GN 1/12/16
Drive ratio (new belt), engine-to-generator	1.7
Pole shoe I. D.	2.2952" to 2.2991" (58,3 to 58,4 mm)
Brush part No.	4033762

Bench Testing Data.

— Testing generator as a motor (at 68° F - 20° C):	
Feed voltage	12 V
Current draw	5 ± 0.5 Amps
Speed	1500 ± 100 r.p.m.
— Output test (at 68° F - 20° C):	
Steady voltage	12 V
Speed for abt. one hour and 45 min	4500 r.p.m.
Current delivery to resistor, at 14 Volts	16 ± 0.5 Amps

After bringing generator to operation temperature by running generator at the above specified speed and time rates, at a steady 12 V tension, read the values of the current output at every generator speed increment.

Caution - Before running output tests, check that the brush seating face has formed properly on commutator.

— Heating test:	
Speed for abt. one hour and 45 minutes	4500 r.p.m.
Delivery, on resistor, at 14 Volts	16 ± 0.5 Amperes
Overheating { frame	not above 86° F (30° C)
{ commutator	not above 149° F (65° C)
— Ohmic resistance test (at 68° F - 20° C):	
Armature resistance	0.145 ± 0.01 ohms
Field winding resistance	$8 ^{+0.1}_{-0.3}$ ohms
— Mechanical characteristics test:	
Load of springs on new brushes	1.3 to 1.6 lbs (0,600 to 0,720 kg)
Commutator maximum out-of-round	.0004" (0,01 mm)
Mica undercut depth	.04" (1 mm)

Lubrication.

Drive end ball bearing	FIAT Jota 3 Grease
Commutator end head bush pocket	
Commutator end head oiler	FIAT VE oil

(*) Refers to generators with armature package disc teeth .1732" (4,4 mm) in length (early type).
(**) Refers to generators with armature package disc teeth .1969" (5 mm) in length.

ELECTRICAL

GENERATOR REGULATOR

Description	page 263
Operation	» 264
Bench Testing Instructions	» 268
Trouble Shooting Instructions	» 270
Servicing	» 271
Adjusting the Regulator Assembly	» 273
GN 1/12/16 Regulator Checking and Setting Data	» 275
A/4-180/12 Regulator Checking and Setting Data	» 276

Description.

The GN 1/12/16 regulator to suit Model 600 «Sedan» and «Multipla» consists of three separate units: voltage regulator, current regulator, cutout relay (three-core regulator).

NOTE - Up to engine No. 573516 regulator type A/4-180/12 has been installed. Check-up and setting data relevant to this assembly are contained on page 276.

Fig. 407 - Regulator GN 1/12/16 with cover (terminal numbers are clearly visible).

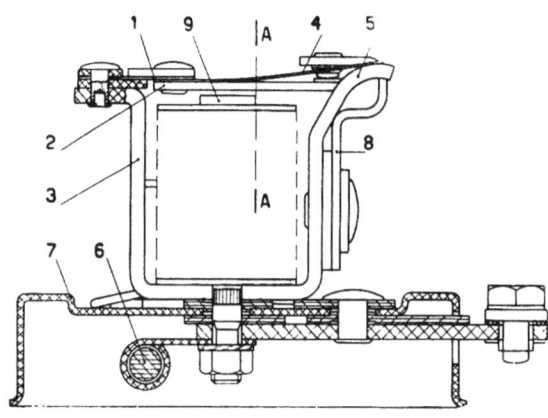

Fig. 408 - Voltage regulator and current regulator for regulator GN 1/12/16.

1. Hinge spring (steel and bimetal for current regulator and bimetal for voltage regulator). - 2. Armature. - 3. Body. - 4. Adjusting spring. - 5. Adjustment arm. - 6. Voltage regulator resistance. - 7. Base. - 8. Stationary contact blade spring. - 9. Core.

Voltage regulator and current regulator relays (fig. 408) consist of a «U» shaped body one of whose arms is bent to form a flange, while the other adjustment arm provides a stop for the hinge spring.

The «U» shaped body is secured to frame by the core threaded shank and carries, on the flanged end, an armature supported by a «hinge» spring (steel leaf and bimetal leaf overimposed in current regulator and bimetal leaf in voltage regulator).

In turn, the armature carries the movable contact.

Fixed contact of both voltage and current regulators are mounted on two blade springs secured to a single bracket riveted to the «U» shaped adjustment arm.

The design of the two fixed contact carrier blade springs is such as to permit the adjustment of the contact position by suitably bending the blade springs.

The cutout is similar in design to the other two relays (fig. 409).

The hinge spring is bi-metallic, same as for the voltage regulator.

All armatures are provided with blade springs, so that their tension may be adjusted to the setting value.

264 FIAT - 600 - 600 D SEDAN AND MULTIPLA

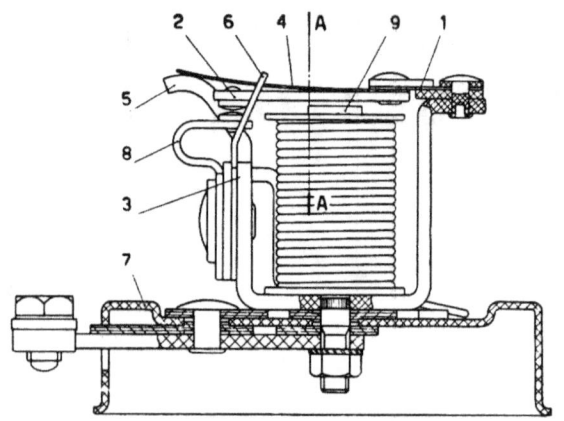

Fig. 409 - Cutout of regulator GN 1/12/16.

1. Bi-metallic hinge spring. - 2. Armature. - 3. Body. - 4. Adjustment spring. - 5. Adjustment arm. - 6. Armature stop. - 7. Base. - 8. Stationary contact blade spring. - 9. Core.

This adjustment is obtained by suitably bending the adjustment arms.

The voltage regulator coil consists of a fine wire winding with a great number of turns, shunt-connected to generator.

The cutout coil consists of a fine wire winding with a great number of turns, shunt-connected to generator, and of a winding consisting of a few turns of heavy wire, connected in series with the generator charge circuit (cutout series winding).

The current regulator coil consists of a few turns of heavy wire series-connected with the generator charge circuit.

The base has three terminals, to which the various cables are connected, and two mounting flanges.

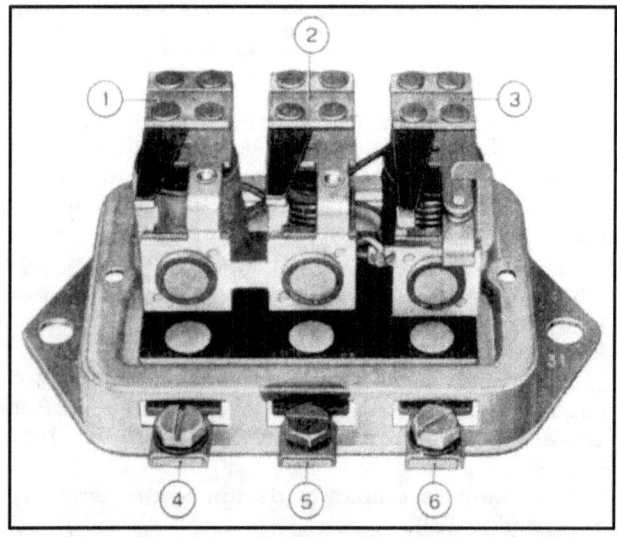

Fig. 410 - Regulator assembly GN 1/12/16.
Front view.

1. Voltage regulator body and armature plate. - 2. Current regulator body and armature plate. - 3. Cutout body and armature plate. - 4. Terminal 51. - 5. Terminal 67. - 6. Terminal 30.

Terminal numbers are stamped on cover:

— No. 51 - connection to generator positive terminal;

— No. 67 - connection to generator field winding;

— No. 30 - connection to electric devices.

The regulator cover is secured to base through the interposition of a rubber gasket which seals the unit against dust and moisture.

A regulating resistor is fitted under the base, and is secured by the voltage regulator and current regulator relay core threaded shanks.

Operation.

At low speeds generator voltage is not sufficient to induce a current strong enough to create in the voltage regulator and cutout relays a magnetic field capable of attracting the armatures.

At this time no current flows through the current regulator winding which, therefore, is not energized.

Under these conditions all armatures are at rest, so that contacts of cutout are open and those of voltage and current regulators are closed.

As generator speed increases, voltage and current rise until, at a given value, the cutout relay is energized enough to pull the armature, thus closing the contacts. This allows a flow of current to circulate from positive brush to users and to positive battery terminal and then to generator negative brush at which it closes the circuit.

This current flows through the series winding of cutout and produces a magnetizing action, which adds to that of the shunt winding, and then passes also in the current regulator winding.

In the cutout, the effect of this current is that of assisting in keeping more strongly closed the contacts.

However, current regulator contacts do not yet open since the current must still rise to higher values, as specified below.

Normally, if after cutout has closed the generator voltage continues to increase, on reaching the voltage regulator setting value the contacts of this relay will open.

As these contacts open due to the magnetic pull exerted on the armature by the cores of the shunt winding, the regulating resistor is automatically inserted in the generator field circuit.

This reduces the field current and, hence, the voltage of the generator and causes the voltage regulator contacts to close; from this instant the field current increases again and, consequently, also the generator voltage rises.

This cycle is repeated many times a second so that the voltage variations result imperceptible and voltage is maintained at the rated values.

When either the current drawn by users exceeds a given limit or battery is in a low state of charge, a heavy output is required of the generator. With this current the magnetic pull on the current regulator armature becomes so strong that, by overcoming armature spring load, it forces down the armature and closes the contacts.

This causes also the insertion of the regulating resistor in the generator field circuit, producing the same effects described above for the voltage regulator, so that current is kept within controlled limits.

Should the current output exceed said limits, the current regulator armature will vibrate continuously, taking the place of the voltage regulator armature that, therefore, will remain inoperative.

In other words, it limits the generator current output, while the voltage regulator controls and maintains tension within the setting limits, so that it supplies to both battery and generator the right amount of power needed to meet operational requirements.

In the case the generator output value falls below the value of the current stored in battery, a « reserve » current will flow back from battery to generator. But this current will circulate in a reverse direction in the series windings of both the current regulator and cutout. This will have no effect on the current regulator, which will not be energized enough to pull down the armature, but on the cutout core it will produce a demagnetizing action with consequent release of the armature and opening of contacts. This way the current flow from battery to generator will be cutout, thus preventing discharge of the battery.

As hinted in the previous chapter, the voltage regulator and cutout relay have a bi-metal hinge-spring and the current regulator is provided with a dual hinge-spring consisting of a steel leaf and a bi-metal leaf set the one upon the other.

As far as the voltage regulator and cutout relay are concerned, the purpose of the bi-metal hinge spring is the thermal compensation of voltage.

In fact, when relay temperature varies, the ohmic resistance of windings varies accordingly and, along with these two factors, also the current absorption of the shunt winding and the magnetic pull on armature are changed.

Precisely, ohmic resistance increases with temperature increase, while magnetic pull becomes weaker and, consequently, the setting voltage (contact opening in voltage regulator, and contact closing in cutout) increases.

To compensate for the weakened magnetic pull, the hinge spring is bi-metallic and is arranged in such a way as to gradually relieve the load of adjustment spring as temperature increases.

In the case of the voltage regulator this is a « thermal overcompensation », namely, the bi-metallic spring action is greater than required to keep voltage temperature steady as ambient temperature varies.

It follows that when ambient temperature increases (summer), the voltage regulator setting voltage is slightly reduced.

The contrary happens when ambient temperature decreases (winter).

This « thermal overcompensation » is necessary, since the voltage of a battery, in which current flows, decreases as electrolyte temperature increases, and vice-versa. On the other hand, the electrolyte temperature is affected by ambient temperature.

Should voltage regulator setting tension not suit ambient temperature conditions of battery, the following troubles would occur:

— with high ambient temperature, setting voltage would become excessive and the battery would be compelled to store too high a current - after reaching the normal charge level - and would « boil » with consequent damages to plates;

— with low ambient temperature, setting voltage would be too low and the battery would fail to reach a correct state of charge.

The task of the dual hinge spring in the current regulator is that of permitting the **thermal correction of the limiting current.**

The spring consists of a steel leaf and a bi-metallic lamina placed one on top of the other and is so arranged as to reduce gradually the reaction of return springs as temperature increases. By this provision the pull of current regulator armature will decrease as temperature increases and the limiting current will therefore be higher with cold regulator and lower with warm regulator.

Purposes are the following:

— at the beginning of operation, after a sufficiently long inactivity period (at least 2 hours), the regulating unit is not « thermally stabilized », i.e., it is at ambient temperature.

Under these conditions the limiting current is higher than maximum permissible generator continuous current and, therefore, if current draw from users is heavy, the generator may be overloaded. The generator, however, can withstand this overload because it too is at the beginning of operation and not yet thermally stabilized, i.e., its windings are still at ambient temperature. As both regulator and generator warm up, the action of the bi-metallic lamina reduces (within 20-30 minutes) the limiting current until it reaches a value that the generator may withstand safely in continuous operation. This value varies with ambient temperature and is reached when the unit is thermally « soaked » at rated operation temperature. It ensues that the overload cannot cause dangerous temperatures within the generator since, as generator temperature increases, the load decreases.

The temporary initial operation in overload of generator permits a quicker battery charging when charge level is lowest due to a difficult cold start or when the car is operated in town with frequent stops and starts and recharge periods are very short.

— As said above, the limiting current value with thermally stabilized regulator is variable with ambient temperature. In fact, under these conditions the bi-metallic lamina temperature will be higher or lower depending on ambient temperature, so that limiting current will be higher at lower ambient temperatures and lower at higher ambient temperatures. Also, the limiting current will be higher in winter and lower in summer with consequent lesser heat dissipation of generator in winter and better uniformity of generator temperature in both seasons.

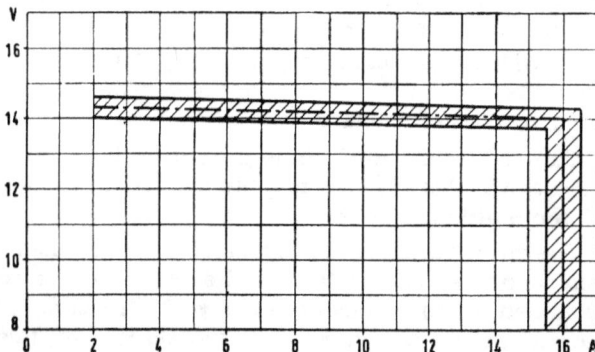

Fig. 411 - Characteristic regulator V-Amp curves on battery. Temperature: 122° ± 5° F (50° ± 3° C). - Generator speed: 4500 r.p.m.

Fig. 411 shown the characteristic curve of the regulating unit. In the diagram the area where the two strips meet indicates the limit of operation between voltage regulator and current regulator.

As it is apparent from the characteristic curve, current remains constant up to a given voltage and then decreases rapidly.

It is just because of this feature that the A/4 regulators, by exploiting in full the generator output capacity, assist in keeping the battery in the best state of charge, even under the most severe service, as required on vehicles whose engines are started very frequently or when there is a great number of users.

In the particular case that a generator operates with a battery almost totally discharged, the regulator will provide for the maximum flow of current to the battery until this has reached a high state of charge (about 14 volts).

As the battery reaches the correct level of charge, the voltage regulator enters into operation to maintain voltage around 14.5 volts, thus determining a rapid decrease in the charging current (provided no users are switched on which draw heavily from the battery). This way, the battery reaches full charge with no risk of being damaged.

When battery is fully charged, the current levels off at a few amperes and there remains, thus maintaining the battery well charged and without causing excessive electrolysis, positive grid sulphation, overheating, damages to separators, etc.

It should be noted that in the case of a battery fully charged left at rest for some time (whereby its voltage drops approximately to the nominal value - 12 Volts, i. e. 2 Volts per cell), when generator resumes delivery the output values will not be those corresponding to the end of charge, but considerably higher, since the battery does not reach full voltage immediately. Under these conditions, only the current regulator will operate. However, as the battery voltage rises, the current diminishes and the voltage regulator takes over, to maintain tension within the rated limits.

In other words, the charging cycle is repeated but in a much shorter time.

WARNING

1. - Connections to terminals 67 and 51 of regulator should **never** be interchanged, otherwise the regulator would **immediately become unserviceable**, since (see figs. 412-413) the current supplied by the generator would flow from generator terminal 51 to regulator terminal 67 through the voltage and current regulator contacts. The effects are readily evident: as soon as generator voltage increases, it causes the voltage regulator contacts (or current regulator contacts, depending on battery state of charge or on the amount of current drawn by users) to open, and since under these conditions the contacts are requested to break the entire current supplied by generator (instead of merely inserting a resistance in the circuit) a heavy arcing will occur, with consequent melting of material, oxidation and charring of contacts, etc.

In a short time this will cause the welding of contacts.

The trouble in this situation is that the unit, though operating abnormally and supplying a reduced voltage, will continue to operate just the same, and a repairman not amply versed in such problems or not provided with proper facilities, may not become aware of the incorrect connection until after unit failure due to welding of contacts. This trouble causes also the generator field winding to burn.

It should be noted that under these conditions an incorrectly wired unit would be damaged even if operated for a few seconds only, since the contacts overheat, undergo trasfer and become oxidized.

ELECTRICAL

It follows that though rewiring connections correctly and restoring normal regulator operation, contacts are irreparably damaged and very soon pitting and build-up will occur (if an initial melting has taken place which primes the phenomenon), or oxidation will become so heavy as to insulate contacts.

Attention is drawn on the fact that the troubles originating from a wrong connection of terminals 67 and 51 are not peculiar to this type of regulator but are common to all types of vibrating regulators, whichever are the construction and the wiring diagram.

Keep in mind that the unit must operate exclusively with its own generator if long life and satisfactory operation of the unit is expected.

Never use this regulator with a third-brush type generator, even if the latter is of the same size as the correct regulator generator, either by simply removing the third brush or, what is worse, by wiring up the third brush generator as if it were designed to operate with a regulator.

If regulator is not used with the generator for which it has been designed, or vice-versa, such condition will result in irregular operation, inadequate performance and poor contact life characteristics.

2. - Be careful not to mishandle the unit during assembly and disassembly operations. This recommendation holds also for regulators in storage.

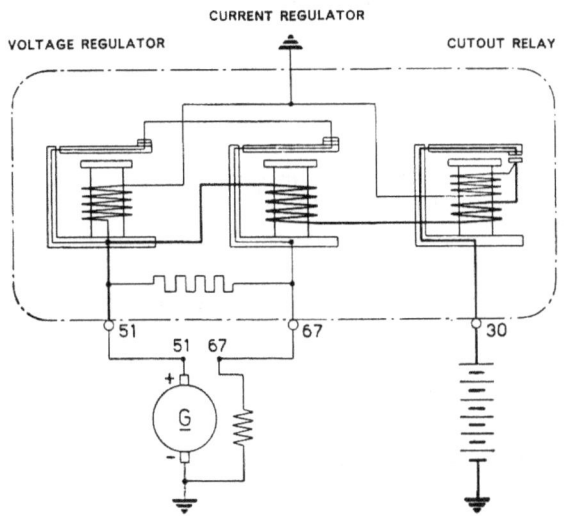

Fig. 412 - Wiring diagram of regulator GN 1/12/16.

Handle regulators always very gently to avoid damages to the more delicate parts.

3. - When installing regulator on test bench, insert an insulating sheet between regulator base and support on which the unit is mounted. During tests, the regulator must be mounted vertically, with terminals lowermost.

4. - During tests wire up generator, regulator, battery and ground, according to the diagrams given further on. **Make sure terminal 51 of generator is connected to terminal 51 of regulator and terminal 67 of generator is connected to terminal 67 of regulator. If connections are interchanged the regulator would be immediately ruined, as explained above.**

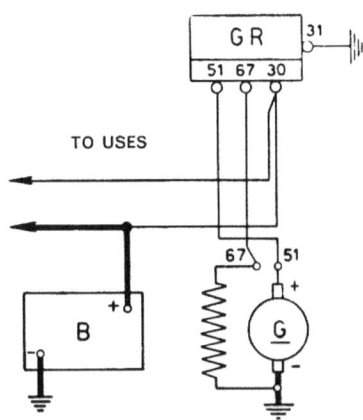

Fig. 413 - Wiring diagram of regulator GN 1/12/16.
GR. Regulator. - B. Battery. - G. Generator.

5. - Connection between regulator base (31) and ground must be such as to ensure a perfect electrical contact, otherwise regulator remains inoperative (no current would pass in shunt windings) and generator voltage would reach values so high as to burn the generator windings and damage seriously the voltage and current regulator contacts.

IMPORTANT

Never insert radio interference suppression condensers of any capacity between:

— terminal 67 and ground;

— terminals 67 and 51, both on generator and on regulator.

If condensers are inserted between said terminals, regulator contacts will be damaged in a very short time.

Normally, regulators do not cause radio interference.

If this recommendation is disregarded, **the regulator will be damaged, as explained above**

BENCH TESTING INSTRUCTIONS

To check the efficiency of GN 1/12/16 type regulator, proceed as follows:

On a test bench, install a FIAT D 90/12/16/3 generator.

Couple this generator to a motor whose speed may be varied at will in small increments.

Prepare all instruments and devices required to test cutout, voltage and current regulators in accordance with the diagrams and instructions given hereunder.

WARNING

All checks must be accomplished without removing the seals from the regulator unit.

— Due to the fact that test bench gauges are subject to being upset from vibrations and the difficulty of detecting any fault in bench circuits, it is good practice to use portable gauges to check the generator regulator, by setting the generator-regulator-gauges wiring circuit through outside electrical connections, which can be inspected more easily.

— Reliable results can be obtained only if tests are run under the exact temperature conditions specified for each single test.

Checking Cutout.

1. - **Closing voltage** (ambient temperature: 77° ± 18° F [25° ± 10° C]).

1-1. Wire as shown in diagram (fig. 414).

1-2. Initially the unit must be at ambient temperature of 77° ± 18° F (25° ± 10° C).

1-3. Operate the unit with no load, at ambient temperature of 77° ± 18° F (25° ± 10° C) for 15-18 minutes, with cover installed and with voltage of:

— 16.5 V for initial temperatures of 59° to 68° F (15° to 20° C);

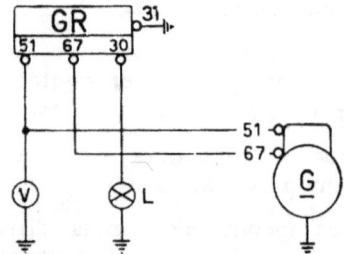

Fig. 414 - **Wiring diagram for checking the cutout closing voltage.**

GR. Regulator GN 1/12/16. - G. Generator FIAT D 90/12/16/3. - V. Voltmeter, 20 V scale (0.5% accuracy). - L. 12 V, 3 to 5 W bulb.

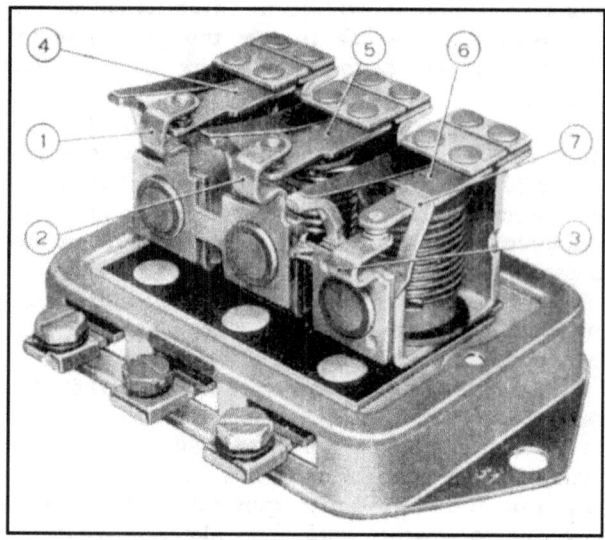

Fig. 415 - **Regulator assembly GN 1/12/16.**

1. Voltage regulator stationary contact carrier arm. - 2. Current regulator stationary contact carrier arm. - 3. Cutout stationary contact carrier arm. - 4. Voltage regulator armature. - 5. Current regulator armature. - 6. Cutout armature. - 7. Cutout armature stop.

Perspective view from cutout side.

— 15 V for initial temperatures of 68° to 95° F (20° to 35° C).

This way, the thermal stabilization of the unit is obtained, i.e., the temperature of both the cutout shunt windings and bi-metallic springs increases due to heat developed by the windings and reaches the « operative value ».

Thermal stabilization is necessary because initially there is a « transient voltage » of some minutes before the setting voltage stabilizes on a steady value, and if this condition is not observed results are liable to be erroneous.

1-4. Soon after reaching thermal stabilization, start the generator, increase its speed gradually and check on voltmeter the value of cutout contact closing voltage. Take reading at the instant at which test lamp glows. Closing contact voltage should be 12.6 ± 0.2 V.

2. - **Reverse current** (ambient temperature: 77° ± 18° F [25° ± 10° C]).

This check must be performed soon after the closing voltage test, so that thermal stabilization remains unaltered (point 1-3).

2-1. Wire as shown in diagram (fig. 416).

2-2. Speed up generator to 4500 r.p.m. for 5 minutes, making sure voltmeter reads at least 14.5 V, then gradually reduce generator r.p.m.

2-3. The ammeter needle, at first indicating a given charging current, will gradually move to zero and then shift to the other side of the scale

ELECTRICAL

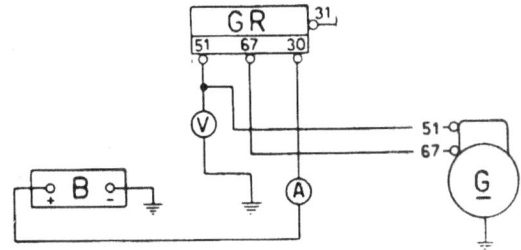

Fig. 416 - Wiring diagram for checking the reverse current of cutout.
GR. Regulator GN 1/12/16. - G. Generator FIAT D 90/12/16/3. - B. Battery, 50 Ah, fully charged. - A. Ammeter, asymmetrical scale 10-0-15 A. - V. Voltmeter, 20 V scale (0.5% accuracy).

to indicate reverse current value. By still reducing generator speed, the reverse current reading will increase to a given value and then abruptly fall to zero (cutout contacts have opened).

This limit indicates max. reverse current value which must not exceed 16 Amp.

NOTE - To obtain the max. reverse current possible, the reduction in generator speed must be so quick as not to give battery voltage sufficient time to drop excessively (10 seconds). Should it be desired to repeat the test, to avoid erroneous readings wich may result from residual magnetism in cutout, wait until generator stops and then re-start.

Checking Voltage Regulator.

Regulating voltage, with half load, on battery (ambient temperature: 122°±5° F [50°±3° C]).

Wire as shown in diagram (fig. 417).

1. **Operate regulator in ambient temperature of 122°±5° F (50°±3° C) for 30 minutes**, by supplying a current half that of regulated current which is 8±2 Amp.

For this test, the thermostat oven **Ap. 5014** should be available, so that regulator can be maintained at the above specified temperature.

2. Soon after this test, keeping regulator always at 122°±5° F (50°±3° C), stop generator and start it again, increasing its speed gradually up to 4500 r.p.m.

3. Adjust rheostat R for a generator output corresponding to half-load current, that is 8±2 Amps.

4. With this generator output, voltage should be 14.2±0.3 V.

Checking Current Regulator.

Regulated current on battery.

Wire in accordance with the same diagram as for voltage regulator.

The regulated current on battery must be checked immediately after testing the half-load regulated voltage (on battery) of the voltage regulator.

1. Instruments are the same as used in determining half-load regulated voltage, excepting the ammeter which must have a 40 Amp scale.

2. Insert maximum rheostat resistance.

3. Operate the regulator at 122°±5° F (50°± ± 3° C) for 30 minutes with regulator-controlled current (**reduce resistor R of rheostat until current is steady** and voltage drops) and 13 Volt tension.

4. After this operating period, check current for a steady delivery (that is rated operation temperature).

5. Stop the generator, restart and speed it up to 4500 r.p.m. Check that the regulated current value corresponds to specified 16±0.5 Amperes.

By still reducing the resistance, the current shall remain constant. The voltage, instead, with the decrease in resistance should drop to as low as 12 V.

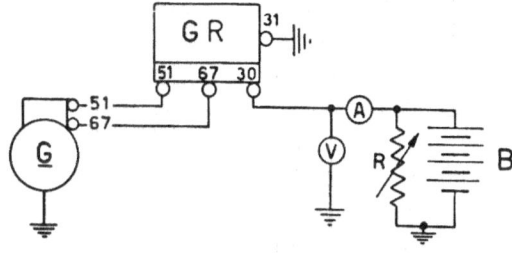

Fig. 417 - Wiring diagram for checking the current and voltage regulators.
GR. Regulator GN 1/12/16. - G. Generator FIAT D 90/12/16/3. - V. Voltmeter, 20 V scale (0.5% accuracy). - A. Ammeter, 20 A scale. - R. Rheostat, 25 A, 3 Ω. - B. Battery, 50 Ah, fully charged.

TROUBLE SHOOTING INSTRUCTIONS

1. - Low recharging rate with fully charged battery.

This indicates that generator-regulator operation is normal.

2. - High recharging rate with fully charged battery.

This condition discloses that voltage regulator does not control generator output as it should. A high recharging rate on a fully charged battery damages the battery and the ensuing high voltage is detrimental to users.

Possibles causes are:

a) Voltage regulator setting too high.

b) Faulty voltage regulator windings.

c) Short circuit, between generator positive terminal and field winding.

This impedes a normal insertion of resistance in generator field circuit when voltage regulator contacts open.

d) Insufficient generator-to-regulator connection through ground.

e) High temperature. This reduces battery emf reaction to the charge, meaning that battery receives a high recharging current even if regulator rated voltage is correct.

f) Welding of voltage regulator or of current regulator contacts.

If this trouble is not ascribable to high temperatures, detect the cause by disconnecting cable terminal 67 from regulator, while generator operates at average speed.

The following conditions may be experienced:

1. Output keeps on high level.

If so, there will be a short circuit between plus terminal and field winding of generator, as already hinted at c) above.

2. Output drops to nil.

If so, defect lies in regulator. Inspect regulator as hinted in previous items a) - b) - d) - f).

NOTE - It may happen that generator output remains very high even after a long recharge period though temperature is not excessive and regulator operation is correct.

In this case the trouble is not due to regulator but to battery being « aged » i. e., it no longer takes the charge and its voltage cannot rise beyond a given limit, whereby generator output cannot decrease.

This trouble is quite frequent and is to be ascribed to poor maintenance, sulphation or misuse of battery.

3. - Discharged battery and high recharging rate.

This indicates that generator-regulator operation is correct.

NOTE - It may happen that, although the generator-regulator system is operating regularly, as the engine is started and revved up to a certain speed, the generator charge light goes out and then glows feebly.

This is not an indication of troubles in the charging system, but merely a consequence of a faulty bulb which has a low lighting voltage.

As a matter of fact, when the generator delivers a certain amount of current (battery discharged, users in), a small power differential occurs at the circuit ends, due to normal voltage drops in the circuit.

If the lighting voltage of the bulb is too low, the bulb filament glows feebly.

To remove this trouble, just replace the indicator bulb by another having the lighting voltage of 1.1 to 1.5 Volts (12 Volt bulb).

To check lighting voltage, use a potentiometer and a voltmeter with a 3 Volt scale.

4. - Discharged battery and low recharging rate, or no recharge at all.

Possible causes are:

a) loose connections, faulty cables;

b) defective battery;

c) high resistance of charging circuit;

d) low setting of voltage or current regulators;

e) oxidized contacts in voltage or current regulators;

f) other defects in generator.

If a) is not the cause, proceed as follows:

To detect whether battery is the cause of trouble, replace it with a fully discharged but efficient battery.

If generator output reaches maximum value, the replaced battery was faulty.

If trouble does not disappear, find out whether the fault originates in generator or in regulator, by temporarily short circuiting regulator terminals 67 and 51 and increasing generator speed.

If the output, which was zero or very low, rises to a given value, the trouble is due to one of the following causes:

a) low voltage or current regulator settings;

ELECTRICAL

b) oxidized voltage or current regulator contacts. This oxidation causes an excessive resistance in generator field circuit and, consequently, the output is very low or even zero;

c) accidental resistance or interruptions in generator field circuit (in the regulator, connections or windings)

No output, instead, reveals a faulty generator.

5. - **Windings damaged from overheating, cutout overheated connections and contacts**

This may be due to inversion of generator polarity.

An inversion of polarity rapidly overheats the cutout and current regulator series windings by inducing a very high reverse current in the generator-regulator-battery circuit (in fact, generator emf and battery emf add up on a low resistance circuit). Overheating involves and damages also the other circuits. Also the current carrier spring, the connections and cutout contacts overheat.

To re-polarize the generator, temporarily connect terminal 51 to terminal 30 on regulator with a jumper.

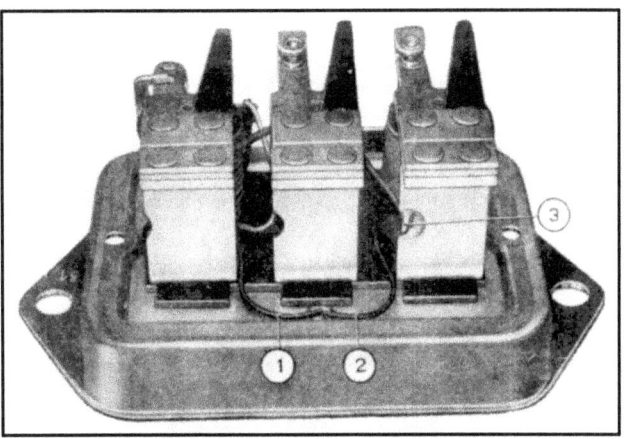

Fig. 418 - Regulator assembly GN 1/12/16.
1. Cutout winding terminal soldered to base. - 2. Voltage regulator winding terminal soldered to base. - 3. Current regulator series winding terminal soldered to voltage regulator frame.
Rear view.

Before connecting the jumper, make sure all connections between generator and battery are as they should be.

A brief flash of current will thus flow through generator field and re-polarization will take place.

REGULATOR SERVICING

As a rule a defective regulator should be replaced. Limit repairs to very exceptional cases

If a repair has to be made on regulator, follow strictly these directions:

Before unit is unsealed, check regulator as directed under « Trouble Shooting » and make perfectly sure that the repair is really necessary and worthwhile.

When servicing a faulty regulator, absolutely abstain from disassembling, replacing or repairing any part of its relays.

Repairs must be limited to the substitution of complete relays besides the resistor or connections between them

Readjust regulator after reassembly.

Opening the Regulator.

Unseal the unit, remove cover-to-base nuts, cover and gasket.

CAUTION

Always bear in mind that most troubles, especially the serious ones like:

— excessive wear or welding of cutout contacts;

— oxidation of voltage and current regulator contacts;

— contact pitting and build-up in voltage regulator and current regulator;

— contact welding in voltage regulator and current regulator;

— short-circuited coils;

— overheated windings;

are often due to causes not ascribable to regulator and which generally originate from troubles in the generator, such as alteration of field winding resistance, use of improper brushes, damaged circuits (wires, etc.).

Especially use of improper brushes brings about a poor commutation, with rapid wear of commutator segments and brushes themselves, high voltage drop between commutator and brushes and remarkable increase of field current.

In such conditions voltage regulator and current regulator contacts are affected by a current which is above the standard value.

This causes stock transfer between contacts, generally in the voltage regulator, with the result that one contact is pitted and the other built up.

Stock transfer will grow until pitting of tungsten contact turns into a hole. Therefore the tip of the

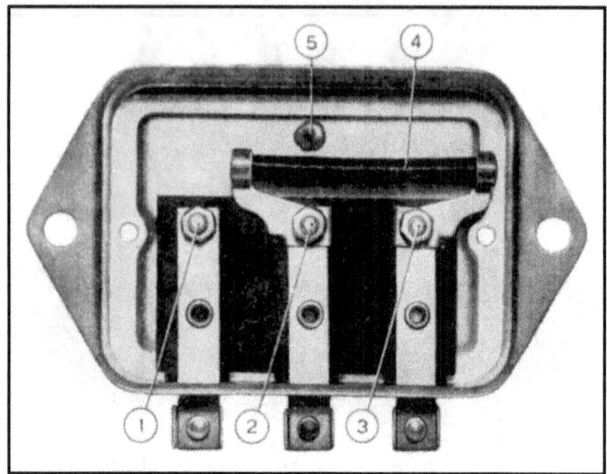

Fig. 419 - Regulator assembly GN 1/12/16. - Bottom view.
1. Nut, cutout fixing. - 2. Nut, current regulator and resistance fixing. - 3. Nut, voltage regulator and resistance fixing. - 4. Resistance. - 5. Soldering on base of cutout and voltage regulator shunt windings.

built up contact reaches the bracket of the pierced contact.

As the bracket is of iron, sparkling at the contact area will cause local oxidation.

So both above contacts are isolated and the regulating resistance of the unit is all the time in the filed winding of the generator, which delivers no output.

As a rule, regulator operation and life are most satisfactory. **For this reason, the serviceman must not simply restore unit to efficiency but should also test generator and the entire recharging system.**

Replacement of Cover.

If the cover has to be replaced, check the regulator before a new cover is installed (see « Bench Testing Instructions »).

This is important because usually a broken cover is an indication that regulator has received a blow and this, generally, upsets regulator setting. When a new cover is fitted, always remember to re-install properly the gasket between cover and base so as to ensure adequate watertightness.

Next, install lockwashers under cover fixing nuts and tighten nuts until lockwasher end gap closes.

Finally, apply sealing paint on cover nuts and screws.

Regulating Resistance Replacement.

If it has been found that the voltage and/or current regulator settings have been altered, namely:

— regulated voltage is low or reduced to negligible values;

— voltage is no longer under control, but rises to high values;

— regulated current no longer ranges within rated limits and is excessive;

the trouble may be ascribed to an open regulating resistor or to an alteration in resistance value, which possibly induces the following damages:

— oxidation of voltage or current regulator contacts (« low » or « very low » no-load voltage);

— welded voltage regulator contacts (uncontrolled voltage reaching very high values);

— welded current regulator contacts (uncontrolled current reaches very high values).

Inspect the resistor and make sure that the wire is neither broken nor disconnected from terminals and that no coils are shorted or with damaged insulation.

In doubtful cases, remove the resistor and test at 68° F (20° C); its value must be 105 ± 3 Ohms.

This operation can be performed without taking off resistor from regulator. Just insert a lintless paper between current and voltage regulator contacts and take the reading across terminals 51 and 67.

If a different value is found, replace resistor by taking off nuts (2 and 3, fig. 419) with lock washers.

The resistor **must not be repaired**. A repair is never satisfactory since special methods and equipment are required. Replace with a new resistor.

Caution. - If the resistor is found damaged, remember that to restore regulator efficiency it will not suffice to simply replace the resistor, but it is **indispensable** to inspect the whole regulator; if any damage is detected, regulator must be replaced.

To reassemble resistor on regulator, refit nuts (2 and 3, fig. 419), being careful not to forget lock washers which must be fitted as before removal. During assembly, do not damage the wire with the screwdriver or wrench.

Subsequently, check armature-to-core air gap of current and voltage regulators, taking the measurement on core edge towards contacts. Gap should equal .0391" to .0437" (0,99 to 1,11 mm).

Finally check regulator setting in accordance with the instructions given under « Regulator Setting ».

The above checks are indispensable since the voltage and current regulator cores, and relevant frames, are interconnected and mounted on base by the same nuts that secure the regulating resistor. Therefore, when handling the unit to replace regulating resistor, the arrangement of relays may be altered. For this reason, make sure that, after tightening the nuts, no asymmetry, if any, is left. In any case, the operation should be performed

ELECTRICAL

with maximum care and **regulating resistor mounting nuts should be tightened securely**.

If, after adjustment, armature-to-core air gaps are not within specified tolerance, it will be necessary to bend blade spring (8, fig. 408) carrying the stationary contact so as to bring air gap again within recommended limits. During this operation, it is essential to maintain the parallelism of both the movable and stationary contacts, that is to say, the two contacts should touch each other at their centers. This condition should be checked using a magnifying glass.

NOTE - Even if cutout is not involved when regulating resistor is removed, it is always advisable to inspect cutout just the same, checking that:

— armature-to-core air gap, **with contacts closed**, measured at core edge towards contacts (A-A, fig. 409) is .0138″ (0,35 mm);

— contact gap, **when open**, is .0177″ ± .0023″ (0,45 ± 0,06 mm).

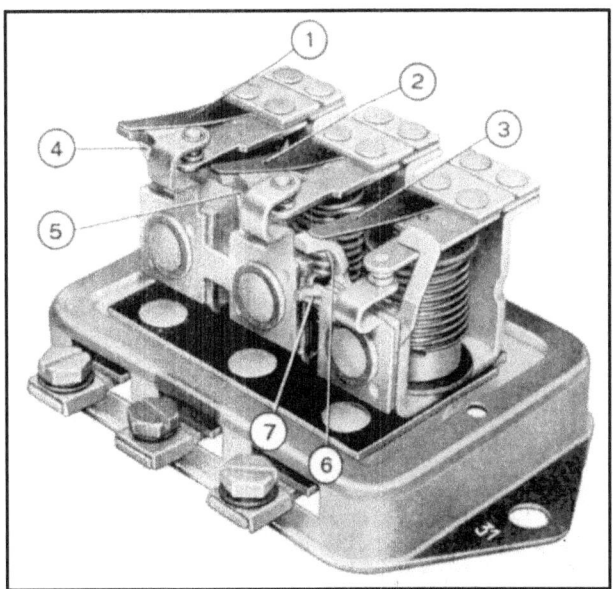

Fig. 420 - Regulator assembly GN 1/12/16.

1. Voltage regulator adjusting spring. - 2. Current regulator adjusting spring. - 3. Cutout adjusting spring. - 4. Voltage regulator adjustment arm. - 5. Current regulator adjustment arm. - 6. Cutout adjustment blade spring. - 7. Soldering of cutout shunt and series winding.

Perspective view from cutout relay side.

ADJUSTING THE REGULATOR ASSEMBLY

The adjustment of regulator assembly must be carried out placing the unit upright on bench with terminals lowermost.

WARNING - If the regulator assembly has remained for a certain while in a room below 59° F (15° C) or above 95° F (35° C), prior to proceeding as outlined hereafter, keep the regulator for at least one hour at 77° ± 18° F (25° ± 10° C) room temperature.

Adjusting Cutout Setting.

Wire as shown in diagram (fig. 421 for GN 1/12/16 and fig. 423 for A/4-180/12).

The setting of instruments before inserting the unit should be:

— P at minimum (Voltmeter reads zero);
— T open;
— R all inserted (max resistance);
— T_1 open.

1. - **Contacts closing voltage** (ambient temperature: 77° ± 18° F [25° ± 10° C]).

a) Close switch T.

b) Stabilize regulator thermally by feeding current for 15-18 minutes at 16.5 V (obtained by suitably adjusting P) for initial regulator operating temperatures of 59° to 68° F (15° to 20° C), or at 15 V for initial operating temperatures of 68° to 95° F (20° to 35° C).

c) Immediately after stabilizing regulator, bring voltage to 12.6 ± 0.2 V by adjusting P.

d) Adjust load on setting spring by bending the relevant arm, until pilot lamp S goes out.

e) Reset P to minimum.

f) Again increase voltage by P and check that pilot lamp goes out at the specified voltage.

2. - **Reverse current** (ambient temperature: 77° ± 18° F [25° ± 10° C]).

This test must be run soon after the closing voltage test, so as to maintain regulator thermal stabilization.

a) With switch T closed, using P bring voltage to 14.5 V. Cutout contacts should be closed, pilot lamp S off.

b) Close T_1.

c) Increase reverse current by means of rheostat R, and check that pilot lamp S glows as contacts part.

Opening may also be unsteady: such condition is evidenced by a slight buzz.

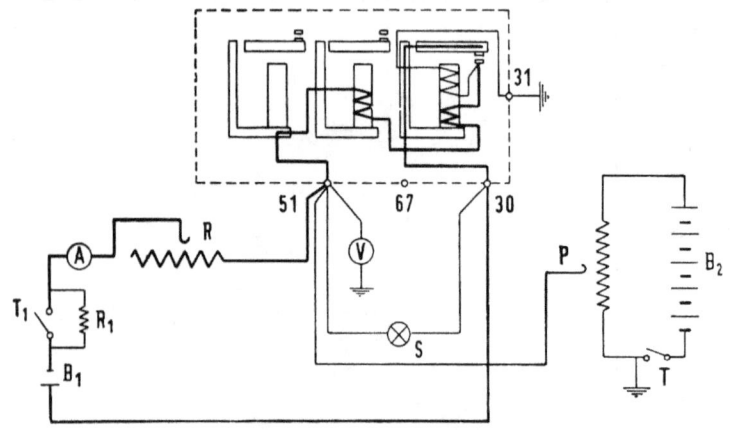

Fig. 421.

Wiring diagram for setting the cutout relay.
(GN 1/12/16 regulator assembly).

B_1. 2-V battery. - B_2. 20-V battery. - A. Ammeter, 15 A scale (1% accuracy). - V. Voltmeter, 20 V scale (0.5% accuracy), directly connected to terminals 31-51. - P. Potentiometer for voltage adjustment, having such a capacity that the current draw of the cutout shunt winding does not cause sensible variations in the voltage readings (voltmeter under no load). - S. Test lamp, with 2 V, 3 W bulb, to signal opening and closing of contacts. - R. Rheostat, 4 Ω, 12 A. - R_1. Voltage drop resistor, suitable to allow turning on of S with T_1 open and cutout contacts open.

Setting of instruments before inserting the unit: P. At minimum (voltmeter reads zero). - T. Open. - R. All inserted (max. resistance). - T_1. Open.

d) Check on ammeter the value of the reverse current causing the opening of contacts: it should not exceed 16 Amps.

e) If reading is unstable, or S lights up at tolerance limit, reset reverse current to the minimum value and repeat operation c).

f) Open switches T and T_1 and again adjust rheostat R and potentiometer P to minimum settings.

Adjusting Voltage Regulator Setting

(ambient temperature: 122°±5° F [50°±3° C]).

NOTE - This test requires adequate equipment within which the regulator can be maintained and operate.

a) Wire as shown in diagram (fig. 422).

b) Load voltage regulator adjusting springs by suitably bending the relevant arm.

c) With the unit at 122°±5° F (50°±3° C) room temperature, close I, start generator and stabilize regulator thermally by feeding current for 30 minutes at 15 V (obtained by suitably adjusting generator speed).

d) With unit still at 122° F (50° C), stop generator, open I, start generator again and speed it up to 4500 r.p.m.

e) Set voltage regulator adjustment spring load by suitably bending the relevant adjusting arm and by rheostat R so as to have a voltage of 14.2±0.3 V and half-load current of 8±2 Amps.

f) Check steadiness and accuracy of voltage regulator setting by stopping the generator and starting it off again after a short while, and speeding it up to 4500 r.p.m.

Adjusting Current Regulator Setting

(ambient temperature: 122°±5° F [50°±3° C]).

To be performed immediately after adjusting voltage regulator, using the same wire diagram (fig. 422) and instruments, except ammeter, which should have a 40 A scale.

a) With the regulator at 122°±5° F (50°±3° C), room temperature, close I, start the generator and set its speed and rheostat R for a 13 Volt tension and 16±0.5 Ampere output.

b) Operate in above conditions for 30 minutes with the regulator at 122°±5° F (50°±3° C), stop the generator and open I. Again run the generator at 4500 r.p.m.

c) Adjust the load of current regulator setting spring by bending the spring tab, and rheostat R, in order that regulated current and voltage are respectively 16±0.5 Amperes and 13 Volts.

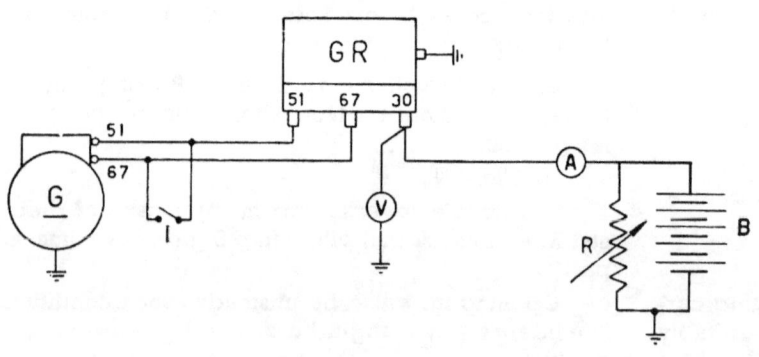

Fig. 422.

Wiring diagram for setting the voltage and current regulators.

GR. Regulator assembly GN 1/12/16. - G. Generator D 90/12/16/3. - V. Voltmeter, 20 V scale (0.5% accuracy). - A. Ammeter, 15 Amp. scale. - R. Rheostat, 25 Amps., 3 Ohms. - B. 50 Amp/h battery, fully charged. - I. Switch.

ELECTRICAL

d) Check regulated current for stability and precision by stopping generator and running it again as hinted in step b).

OPERATION TEST AND SEALING

After the regulator has been set, close the assembly in a warm condition (see « Warning » beside) byfting cover and gasket, and check as outlined under « Bench Testing Instructions ». Next apply the paint seal.

The unit must never be returned to the Customer without this seal since **only FIAT authorized dealers should service the unit.**

WARNING

Whenever the unit has been opened and kept open for servicing, it must be operated for a while and the cover fitted only after a suitable warm up period.

Close cover carefully on warm unit and check that rubber gasket between cover and base is properly seated and ensures adequate sealing.

This eliminates the moisture usually deposited on windings and prevents the formation of moisture occurring when cover is applied on a cold unit. If any moisture is trapped in the unit, during operation when the unit is warm moisture will evaporate and deposit on armatures, thus causing highly detrimental oxidation of contatcs.

GN 1/12/16 REGULATOR CHECKING AND SETTING DATA

(Sedan and Multipla starting from engine No. 573517)

Cutout Relay.

Feed voltage for thermal stabilization:
- regulator initial (59° - 68° F (15° - 20° C) . . .   16.5 V
- operating temperature) 68° - 95° F (20° - 35° C) . . .   15 V

Closing voltage . . . . 12.6 ± 0.2 V
Voltage-contact stroke variation: below . . . .   1 V/mm
Reverse current: up to and not above . . . .   16 Amps
Air gap (closed contacts) . . . .   .0138" (0,35 mm)
Point gap . . . . $.0177" \pm .0023"$ ($0,45 \pm 0,06$ mm)

Voltage Regulator.

Battery . . . .   50 A/h
Half-load current . . . . 8 ± 2 Amps
Setting voltage after thermal stabilization with room at 122° ±
5° F (50° ± 3° C) for 30 minutes, half-load on battery . . 14.2 ± 0.3 V
Feed voltage for thermal stabilization . . . .   15 V
Air gap . . . .   .0391" to .0437" (0,99 to 1,11 mm)

Current Regulator.

Regulated current on battery . . . . 16 ± 0.5 Amps
Voltage for regulated current inspection . . . .   13 V
Air gap . . . .   .0391" to .0437" (0,99 to 1,11 mm)

Regulating Resistor . . . . 105 ± 3 Ω

A/4 - 180/12 REGULATOR CHECKING AND SETTING DATA
(Sedan and Multipla up to engine No. 573516)

Cutout Relay.

Feed voltage for thermal stabilization:
- regulator initial } 59°-68° F (15°-20° C) . . . . . 16.5 V
- operating temperature } 68°-95° F (20°-35° C) . . . . . 15 V

Closing voltage . . . . 12.6 ± 0.2 V
Voltage-contact stroke variation: below . . . . 1 V/mm
Reverse current: up to and not above . . . . 10 Amps
Air gap (closed contacts) . . . . .0138″ (0,35 mm)
Point gap . . . . .0177″ ± .0023″ (0,45 ± 0,06 mm)

Voltage Regulator.

Battery . . . . 50 A/h
Half-load current . . . . 6.5 ± 0.5 Amps
Setting voltage after thermal stabilization with room at 122° ± 5° F (50° ± 3° C) for 30 minutes, half-load on battery . . . 14.5 ± 0.3 V
Feed voltage for thermal stabilization . . . . 15 V
Air gap . . . . .0391″ to .0437″ (0,99 to 1,11 mm)

Current Regulator.

Regulated current on battery . . . . 13 ± 0.5 Amps
Air gap . . . . .0391″ to .0437″ (0,99 to 1,11 mm)

Regulating Resistor . . . . 105 ± 3 Ω

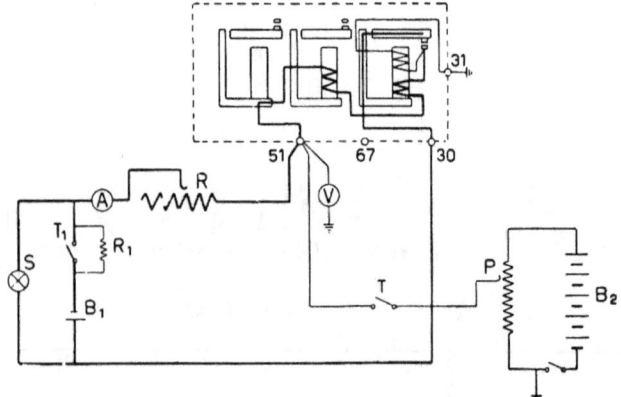

Fig. 423 - Wiring diagram for setting the cutout relay. (A/4 - 180/12 regulator assembly).

B_1. 2 V battery. - B_2. 20 V battery. - A. Ammeter, 15 A scale (1% accuracy). - V. Voltmeter, 20 V scale (0.5% accuracy), directly connected to terminals 31-51. - P. Potentiometer for voltage adjustment, having such a capacity that the current draw of the cutout shunt winding does not cause sensible variations in the voltage readings (voltmeter under no load). - S. Test lamp, with 2 V, 3 W bulb, to signal opening and closing of contacts. - R. Rheostat, 4 Ω, 12 A. - R_1. Voltage drop rheostat, suitable to allow turning on of S with T_1 open and cutout contacts open.

Setting of instruments before inserting the unit:
P. At minimum (voltmeter reads zero). - T. Open. - R. All inserted (max resistance). - T_1. Open.

STARTER

Description	page 277
Operation	» 277
Bench Testing Instructions	» 279
Trouble Shooting Instructions	» 280
Servicing	» 283
Specifications and Data	» 284

Description.

The B 76-0,5/12 S type starter is fitted on both 600 « Sedan » and 600 « Multipla » models.

— Tension . . . . 12 Volts
— Nominal power . . . . 0.5 kW
— Rotation (pinion end) . . . counterclockwise
— Pole shoes . . . . four
— Excitation . . . . series

The armature rotates on self-lubricating bronze bushes.

Heads are joined to frame by tie rods passing in the space between pole shoes.

Commutator and brushes may be reached after removing the cover band.

The switch is mounted on frame. The stationary contact is directly connected to battery; the other stationary contact is connected to one end of field winding whose other end is wired to the positive brush (see diagram fig. 424).

The negative brush is grounded.

The two switch stationary contacts are electrically insulated from grounded parts and are interconnected by a movable contact only when starting control is actuated.

The switch may be inspected after removing the two mounting screws.

The overrunning clutch type drive unit consists of (figs. 425 and 426):

— a pinion, integral with overrunning clutch outer race;

— a hub carrying, on one end, four lugs alternated with four races which, through four rollers, drive the pinion along when the hub rotates in a given direction; the hub slides on armature shaft through a straight spline coupling;

— a sleeve sliding on the hub and on which the forked lever works;

— coil spring;

— a sleeve retainer pressed against the sleeve by the coil spring.

NOTE - Vehicles for export to U.S.A., starting from the serial No. 816159, Sedan, and No. 072211, Multipla, are equipped with starting motor type E 76-0,5/12/S, solenoid engaged from the ignition switch on the instrument panel.

Features and specifications of this starting motor are tabulated on page 392, 600 D section.

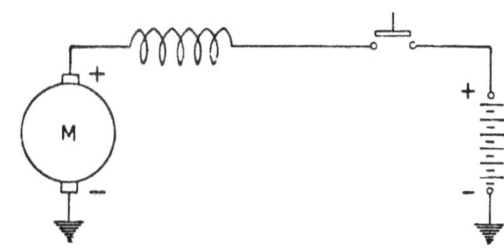

Fig. 424 - Operation diagram of starter B 76-0,5/12 S.

Operation.

When pulling the starter hand lever through a flexible transmission, this operates the lever controlling the pinion engagement with the flywheel.

During this stage two cases may occur:

1) The pinion tooth finds immediately the corresponding space betweend the ring gear teeth and, assisted by the chamfering provided on the edges, goes into mesh with ring gear.

As the shift lever completes its travel, it closes the starter motor switch so that cranking takes place.

2) The pinion tooth finds, instead, a flywheel tooth and cannot mesh.

The shift lever, however, completes its travel since the sleeve slides on the hub and compresses the interposed spring.

Under these conditions, the spring, besides allowing the lever rotation, forces also the pinion against the flywheel.

As the lever completes its travel, it closes the starter switch contacts.

STARTER B 76 - 0,5/12 S

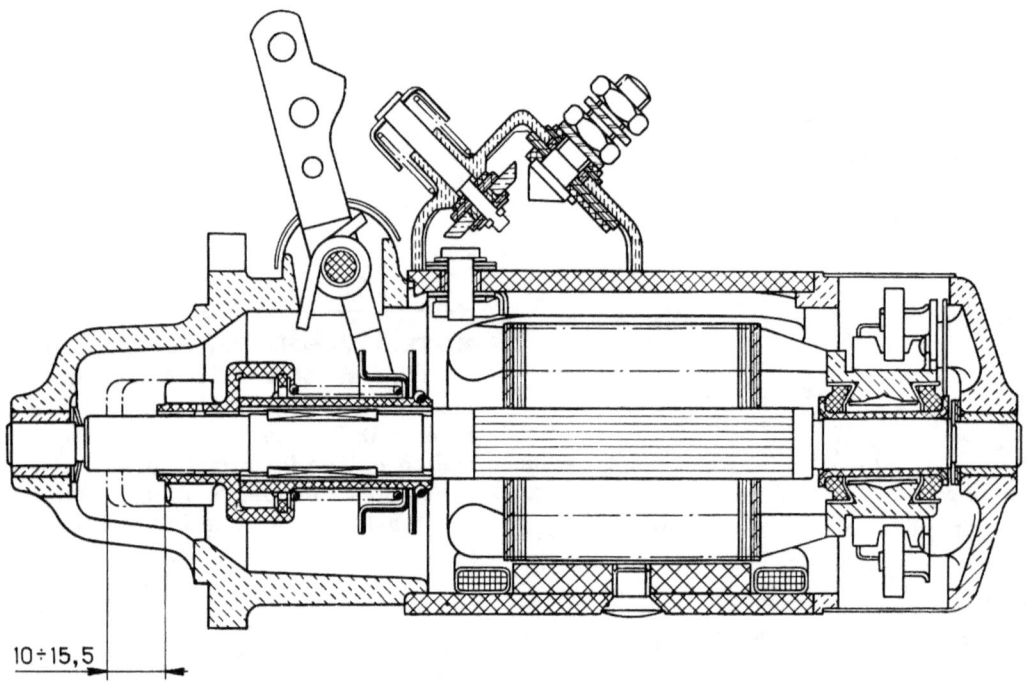

Fig. 425 - Starter assembly longitudinal section.

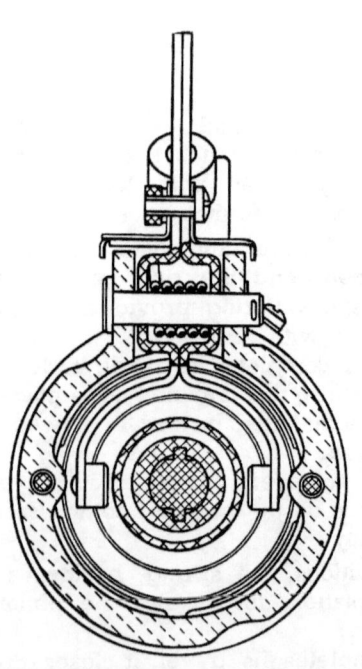

Fig. 426 - Cross section on drive unit.

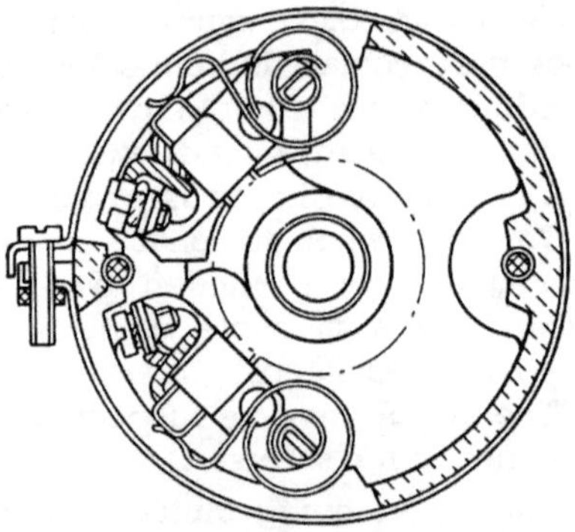

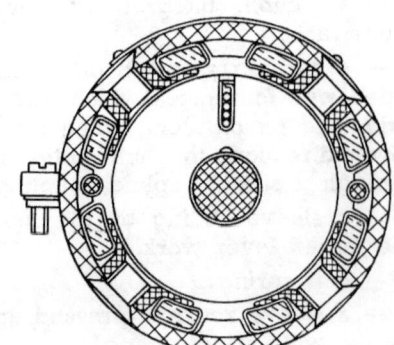

Fig. 427.
Section through commutator end head, showing the brushes.

Fig. 428.
Section through pole shoes and armature wiring.

ELECTRICAL

The starter is thrown into rotation, driving along the pinion, which, forced by the spring, goes into mesh with the ring gear after completing a small angle.

As soon as the engine fires, the starter hand lever must be released.

This action opens the starter switch contacts, the starter stops, and, under the return spring action, the pinion is unmeshed from ring gear.

Should the hand lever not be immediately released after the engine fires, owing to the high ratio between starter pinion and ring gear, the pinion, and hence the armature, would be spun at a terrific speed, with consequent centrifugation of coils and commutator segments. This excessive speed, however, is prevented by the overrunning clutch of the drive unit which allows the pinion to be momentarily driven by the ring gear, while the armature, instead, runs at the normal « no load » speed.

Nevertheless, the engine should never be accelerated during starting, when the pinion is still engaged with the flywheel, to prevent an excessive strain on the overrunning clutch and a premature wear.

The characteristic curves of starter B 76-0,5/12 S are shown in fig. 429.

The performances represented by these curves are obtained using either the specified batteries in the required state of charge and temperature, or any other suitable d. c. current supply characterized by the voltage-current curve shown in fig. 429.

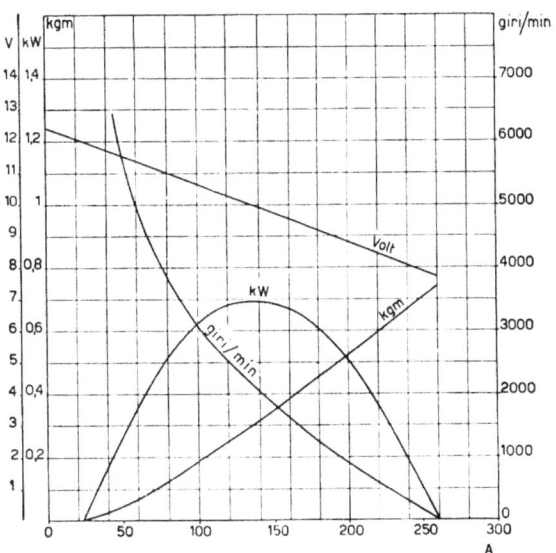

Fig. 429 - Characteristic curves of starter B 76-0,5/12 S.
Readings at 68° F (20° C). - giri/min. = R.p.m.

If the voltage-current characteristic differs, only the torque-current curve will not suffer considerable variations, while, on the contrary, the speed will vary along with power and performance.

If a suitable means to obtain the required voltage-current characteristics is not available, the test should be limited to the torque-current curve. Even in this case, results will only be approximate.

BENCH TESTING INSTRUCTIONS

Check starter efficiency by carrying out the mechanical and electrical tests described below. Follow strictly the procedure outlined, making sure that all instruments and gauges are properly adjusted.

1. - **Operation test** (ambient temperature 68° F - 20° C).

Connect starter to a high capacity 12-V battery, so as to avoid current fluctuations during the test.

Adjust the rheostat so that the voltage at starter terminals correspond exactly to the specified current draw.

This is an essential condition to obtain reliable results which, otherwise, would be true only for the torque (and even in this instance only approximately).

Wire up as per diagram fig. 430.

Install starter on a bench provided with a ring gear (whose ratio to pinion is not less than 10 to 1) and a dynamometric brake.

By pushing starter switch lever to travel **end**, carry out ten 4-second starts at intervals of 30 seconds.

Braking the motor when supplied with a 130 A, 10 V current, the torque should be $2 \pm .14$ ft.lbs $(0,28 \pm 0,02$ kgm) at 2250 ± 100 r. p. m.

2. - **Stall torque** (ambient temperature 68° F - 20° C).

With the same wiring and installation layout described above, lock the ring gear and actuate starter lever.

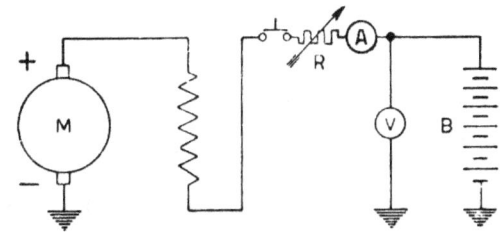

Fig. 430 - Wiring diagram for B 76-0,5/12 S starter operation test.
M. Starter. - V. Voltmeter, 15 V scale. - A. Ammeter, 350 A scale.
B. Battery 32 Ah, 12 V. - R. Rheostat, 200 A capacity.

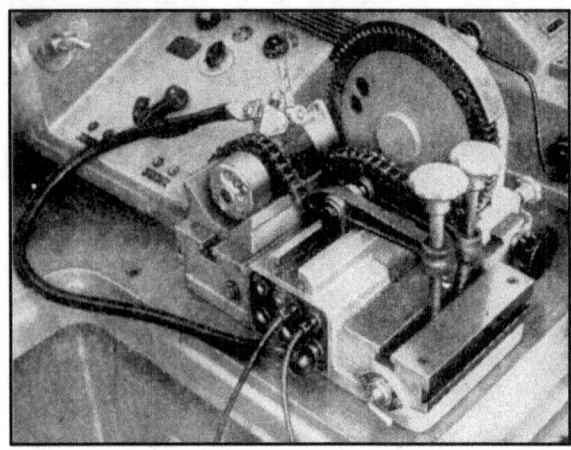

Fig. 431 - Brake test of a starter.

The starter should draw 258 A at a 7.7±0.3 V current and give a 5.3±0.4 ft.lbs (0,73±0,05 kgmm) torque.

3. - **No-load test** (ambient temperature 68°F - 20°C).

Same wiring layout.

Move starter out from ring gear so that pinion cannot mesh even when travelling its full forward stroke.

Actuate starter lever.

With a 12 V current at terminals, the starter should draw not more than 30 Amperes and turn at 8500±1000 r.p.m.

Ohmic Resistance Test.

From the data obtained during the **stall torque test** and by computing the ratio of voltage to drawn current, the starter internal resistance may be directly determined. Its value, with starter at 68° F (20° C) must be 0.03±0.001 Ω.

Mechanical Characteristics Check Data.

1) Brush hold down springs load must be (with new brushes) 2.5 to 2.9 lbs (1,15 to 1,3 kg).

2) Armature shaft axial play must be .0059" to .0256" (0,15 to 0,65 mm).

3) Commutator mica must be undercut at least .04" (1 mm) throughout its entire length and width.

4) The efficiency of drive unit free wheel must be such that the static torque required to rotate the pinion slowly is not greater than .35 in-lbs (0,4 kgcm).

TROUBLE SHOOTING

Operation troubles in starting system may originate from:

— starter;
— other components of system.

First locate the source of trouble, then inspect the starter.

Possible causes are:

1. - On pulling the hand lever, starter fails to function.

Causes:

1.1. Oxidized battery terminals and clamps.

1.2. Loose starter switch or battery clamps.

1.3. Dead battery.

1.4. Excessively worn brushes which do not contact commutator.

1.5. Starter switch contacts heavily oxidized, worn or insulated by foreign matter.

1.6. Grounded field or armature windings.

1.7. Thrown armature or commutator.

2. - On pulling the hand lever, starter rotates very slowly. This trouble is also revealed by a characteristic noise.

Causes:

2.1. Worn brushes not contacting commutator.

2.2. Field or armature windings partially grounded.

2.3. Oxidized battery terminals and clamps.

2.4. Loose starter switch or battery clamps.

2.5. Battery barely operative or with one or more cells damaged (short circuited, sulphated, no longer capable of retaining the charge, etc.).

3. - On pulling the hand lever, starter runs regularly but develops unusual noises.

Causes:

3.1. Self-lubricating bushes of both armature and pinion excessively worn.

3.2. Pinion that does not unmesh from ring gear soon after releasing starter lever.

3.3. Oxidation of drive unit, particularly of the collar on which the forked lever that causes the axial displacement of drive unit is working.

ELECTRICAL

TROUBLE SHOOTING HINTS

4.1. Should conditions under point 1 occur, inspect the system, including battery and starter, so as to single out the faulty component by process of elimination.

4.1.1. First inspect battery posts and clamps (point 1.1) for oxidation. Check that they are evenly coated with pure ropy vaseline. The coating must be renewed at regular intervals. If posts and clamps are oxidized, remove clamps (using exclusively a wrench and, if required a puller; never pliers or other tools that might damage irreparably the battery). Wipe clean both the posts and the clamps.

Refit and tighten clamps and coat with pure ropy vaseline.

4.1.2. If terminals are not oxidized, check clamp tightening (point 1.2) on both battery and starter.

4.1.3. If connections are found in order, check state of battery charge (point 1.3), using a hydrometer. If electrolyte density is found very low (1.16 or even less) the cause for starter failure is in the battery.

Note, however, that the total battery discharge originates from a faulty insulation at some point which grounds the system. In this case look for the dispersion point which might be located in cables, users, or even within the battery cells.

Though less likely, the trouble may be attributed to the recharging system that must be inspected as directed in the relevant Chapter.

Changing or recharging the battery without locating the discharging cause would be useless.

4.1.4. If inspections relevant to points 1.1, 1.2, 1.3, have unearthed no irregularities, the starter is at fault. Remove it from car and inspect all its components carefully.

4.1.5. Lack of contact between brushes and commutator due to brush wear (see 1.4) is normal if it occurs after a long period of starter operation.

At maximum starter power, with fully charged battery and normal temperature, brushes may withstand nearly 5000 starts of 2 seconds each before wearing out.

The above conditions, however, are much more severe than those of actual operation, since four or more times the number of starts are actually obtained during normal car service.

In terms of mileage, the life of brushes depends on the type of service in which the vehicle is used.

In any case, even with very frequent starts, brushes last for more than 12,000 miles (20.000 km).

If wear is abnormal, it may be due to the causes stated in point 5.3.3. After determining that this is the origin of starter failure, replace brushes.

Note, however, that the commutator may also have suffered damages and must be inspected very carefully.

If wear is normal, commutator may be trimmed by a simple re-turning followed by proper undercutting of the mica. If, instead, wear is abnormal and damages as those quoted under 5.3.2. have been induced, replace the armature.

4.1.6. After checking that both brushes and commutator are in good condition, inspect starter switch (point 1.5) which may show:

a) **Oxidized contacts.** - If may happen that on account of short circuited coils in the starter windings, the current draw exceeds given values with an ensuing overheating and/or charring of contacts.

Reconditioning of contacts is not sufficient to restore starter efficiency. Therefore, inspect the starter to single out the cause of contact oxidation.

b) **Presence of insulating particles between stationary and movable contacts.** - Disassemble switch and clean contacts.

4.1.7. Possible grounding of field and/or armature windings (point 1.6).

If this trouble is present when the switch is closed, a strong current flow towards ground will occur with considerable risk of damaging switch contacts and cables.

Disassemble starter. The grounded point will be readily identified by blackened insulations.

If grounding is in the armature, the commutator segments connected to the grounded coils will also be badly damaged.

Replace faulty parts.

4.1.8. Thrown armature (1.7) or commutator.

Causes may be:

a) Seizing of overrunning clutch.

b) Loosening of slot stopping wedges or of commutator segments under combined action of centrifugal force and heating-and-cooling cycles.

Trouble b) is normally due to trouble a), but sometimes originates from erroneous starting maneuvers.

During manufacture, overrunning clutches are submitted to the static sliding torque, whose value must not exceed .35 in-lbs (0,4 kgcm), as specified under « Mechanical Characteristics Check Data », point 4 (page 280).

The overrunning clutch may be damaged, however, by the following erroneous starting maneuvers:

i) too long meshing of pinion with ring gear after engine has started;

ii) speeding up of the engine before starter control hand lever is released;

iii) defective operation of starting control such as: seizing of bowden, of tie rod or of levers, weakened springs, etc.

If maneuvers i) and ii) are repeated a number of times, the overrunning clutch overheats, the grease is quickly burnt, rollers and plungers wear, and finally, the whole drive unit seizes.

Under these conditions the pinion can no longer free-wheel and therefore drives along the armature at such a high speed that coils and commutator will be thrown.

This trouble, however, can be prevented if drive units are inspected and overhauled when servicing the starter.

As for loose and missing commutator segments, see point 5.3.2. for probable causes.

4.2. In case trouble 2 occurs, look for the source by following the procedure outlined under 4.1.

4.2.1. For causes indicated under 2.3. and 2.4, see respectively 4.1.1. and 4.1.2.

4.2.2. After ascertaining that connections are in order, check battery and its state of charge (points 2.5).

If electrolyte density is less than 1.22, the battery is 50% discharged and must be recharged.

The battery may have one or more cells damaged, shorted or sulphated, so that it can no longer retain the charge.

Battery must be replaced.

4.2.3. If nothing abnormal is found relevant to 2.3, 2.4, 2.5, the source must be looked for exclusively in the starter according to the following procedure.

4.2.4. Brush wear (point 2.1): see point 4.1.5.

4.2.5. If brushes and commutator are in good condition, inspect armature and field windings (point 2.2), which may have some shorted coils.

By reducing the number of useful coils, the short circuit in armature winding brings about a reduction in starter power. Furthermore, by causing commutation troubles is correspondence with segments connected to shorted coils, the shorting stresses brush wear owing to both the worsened commutations and to the damage on commutator (sinking in correspondence with said segments).

An armature tester may be used to locate shorted coils, though its sensitivity is limited to two or more shorted coils. More accurate readings may be obtained by using high-frequency detectors in conjunction with a voltmeter connected across segments.

Should the field winding have one or more shorted coils, the starter power would also be noticeably reduced.

Accurate determinations are possible only by removing the field winding and measuring its electrical characteristics with a high-frequency instrument.

4.3. If trouble under point 3 occurs, no check of electric system is required. Possible causes must be looked for in the starter, proceeding as follows:

4.3.1. Remove starter from car and inspect the drive unit and related parts. If the drive unit or the collar (on which the engagement fork acts) are found oxidized (3.3), lubricate thoroughly with FIAT Jota 3 G grease.

4.3.2. If engagement unit is in working order, check bushes for excessive wear. These bushes are of self-lubricating bronze and require special equipment for press fitting in their seats.

4.3.3. If troubles described in 3.1 and 3.3 are not present, noisiness should be attributed to the faulty operation of the drive unit engagement control (see 3.2).

First, lubricate the splined coupling and the pins of control levers. Check for weakened or oxidized return springs of both switch and levers.

When reinstalling starter on car, check that starting control bowden does not bind in its sheath (due to kinks, twisting, etc.), that it is adequately lubricated and, finally, that when at rest it allows the pinion to clear the flywheel ring gear.

If the bowden is damaged, replace.

5. - Some of the troubles described above cannot be easily detected when starter is installed on car but may be revealed by:

— the operation tests described previously;

— the inspection of starter inner components.

Such troubles may be traced to:

5.1. Poor commutation, accompanied by an excessive brush wear with respect to the period and type of car service.

Possible causes:

5.1.1. Shorted armature winding coils.

5.1.2. Loose commutator segments.

5.1.3. Incorrect grade brushes.

5.2. Reduction in the torque and power developed by the motor.

Possible causes:

5.2.1. Shorted field winding coils.

5.2.2. Shorted armature winding coils.

5.3. If trouble indicated under 5.1. occurs, detect its source as follows:

5.3.1. Check for shorted coils (5.1.1) as described in 4.2.5.

5.3.2. If armature winding is found in order, check commutator.

The defect mentioned in 5.1.2, is normally due to some segments having worked loose under the combined action of centrifugal force and heating-and-cooling cycles.

Segments are displaced radially, and protruding beyond the commutator surface cause an imperfect contact of brushes (which cannot follow the commutator irregularities because of inertia), with consequent heavy arcing.

Furthermore, this actually mills the brushes.

In some cases, conditions may be so bad that a loose segment is dislodged by striking against the brushes.

The defect may be easily detected with a dial indicator as follows:

Fix the starter firmly. Rest the dial indicator plunger on the commutator surface not rubbed by brushes, and by rotating the armature slowly, determine the maximum out-of-round points and their location.

If segments are properly seated, out-of-round must not exceed .0004" (0,01 mm).

5.3.3. If commutator is found undamaged, check brushes. They should be genuine FIAT parts.

6. - If trouble corresponds to 5.2.1 or 5.2.2, follow the procedure described under 4.2.5.

STARTER SERVICING

1. - The only repairs that may be carried out by Service Stations are:

— commutator returning;

— repairs to field winding connections damaged in insulation, broken or unsoldered.

2. - Any other part must be replaced.

Commutator Returning.

For this operation install on lathe the armature, having care that it rotates on its own shaft axis, so that shaft out-of-round does not add to commutator out-of-round.

Brush Replacement.

Take off cover band and remove old brushes. Fit original FIAT brushes whose hardness and composition is such as to ensure best performance of starter and long life of commutator.

Removal of Commutator Assembly.

Remove cover band. Lift brush hold-down springs and take off commutator end head.

Slide off armature assembly from drive unit and from shoe poles. If inspection shows that armature is efficient, reassemble the latter by reversing

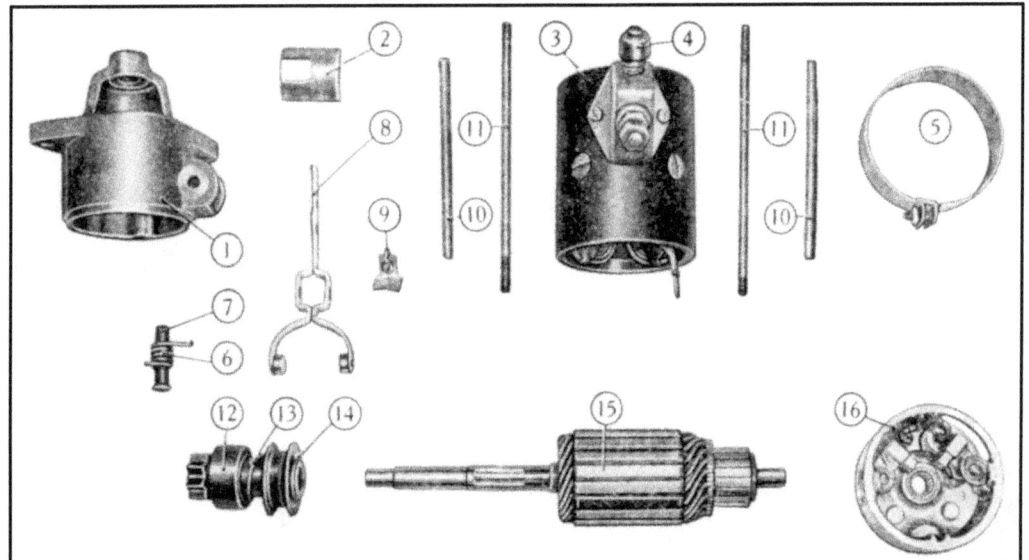

Fig. 432.

Components of starter.

1. Drive end head. - 2. Head shield. - 3. Frame. - 4. Switch. - 5. Commutator cover band. - 6 and 7. Pin and spring for lever 8. - 8. Starting engagement lever. - 9. Head shield. - 10 and 11. Head fixing tie rods and sheath. - 12. Pinion, complete. - 13. Starting engagement spring. - 14. Drive unit sleeve and free wheel hub. - 15. Armature. - 16. Commutator end head.

STARTER MOTOR SPECIFICATIONS AND DATA

Type	B 76-0,5/12 S
Voltage	12 V
Nominal power	0.5 kW
Rotation (pinion end)	counterclockwise
Pole shoes	4
Field winding	in series
Engagement	by free wheel
Mechanical Data.	
— Pole shoes I. D.	2.0697 to 2.0768 in. (52,57 to 52,75 mm)
— Armature diameter	2.0394 to 2.0413 in. (51,80 to 51,85 mm)
— Part No. of brushes	805581
Bench Test Data.	
— Operation test at 68° F (20° C):	
Current	130 Amp
Torque developed	2 ± .14 ft.lbs (0,28 ± 0,02 kgm)
Speed	2250 ± 100 r.p.m.
Tension	10 Volt
— Stall torque at 68° F (20° C):	
Current	258 Amp
Tension	7.7 ± 0.3 Volts
Torque developed	5.3 ± .36 ft.lbs (0,73 ± 0,05 kgm)
— No-load test:	
Current	≤ 30 Amp
Tension	12 Volts
Speed	8500 ± 1000 r.p.m.
— Ohmic resistance during stall torque test, at 68° F (20° C)	0.03 ± 0.001 Ω
Mechanical Characteristic Test.	
— Load of spring on new brushes	2.5 to 2.9 lbs (1,15 to 1,30 kg)
— Armature shaft axial play	.0059" to .0256" (0,15 to 0,65 mm)
— Mica undercut depth ... not more than	.04" (1 mm)
— Drive unit free wheel efficiency: static torque required to rotate pinion slowly	≤ .35 in.lbs (0,4 kgcm)
Lubrication.	
— Drive unit splines	FIAT VS 10 W oil
— Sleeve-to-engagement lever surfaces	FIAT Jota 2/M grease
— Free wheel components	FIAT Jota 2/M grease

ELECTRICAL

the disassembly operations. Before reassembly blow clean the armature, the drive end head and the frame, also lubricating the armature shaft splined end with FIAT VS 10 W oil and polishing the commutator with a clean cloth free of grease, gasoline or other substances.

Replacing Drive Unit.

Take off armature as described above. Remove drive end head and then withdraw the drive unit from the head by rotating the lever as far as it will go. Before reassembling the drive unit, lubricate the inner splined face with FIAT VS 10 W oil and the contact face between lever sleeve and rollers with FIAT Jota 2/M grease.

Replacing Starter Switch.

Take off switch by removing the two mounting screws. Install a new switch, being careful to tighten well the field winding terminal clamping nuts.

Replacing Field Winding.

Remove armature from frame, free pole shoes by slackening their mounting screws, and take off field winding.

Heat new winding to 122° F (50° C) to render it slightly flexible thus facilitating its seating under pole shoes.

Pole shoes must be correctly seated on frame by tightening their mounting screws until the original air gap is restored.

After reassembly, check that pole shoe inner diameter is 2.0697" to 2.0768" (52,57 to 52,75 mm).

If diameter departs from the above figures it is an indication that assembly is incorrect.

In this case, the whole operation must be repeated.

Never ream pole shoes to obtain correct diameter.

Check also that armature diameter is 2.0394" to 2.0413" (51,80 to 51,85 mm).

IGNITION SYSTEM

Description	page 285
Operation	» 286
Distributor	» 286
Coil	» 290
Spark Plugs	» 291
Timing	» 293
Ignition System Specifications and Data	» 294

Description.

The ignition system consists of:

— ignition coil;

— ignition distributor with breaker, centrifugal automatic advance and condenser;

— low and high tension wiring;

— spark plugs;

— a power supply provided by generator-and-battery.

The system is subdivided into two circuits (fig. 433), namely:

— **the low tension circuit** or primary circuit, which includes: the power supply, breaker, condenser and ignition coil primary winding;

— **the high tension circuit** or secondary circuit, which includes: the ignition coil secondary winding, distributor rotor, distributor cap with terminals and central brush, high tension cables and spark plugs,

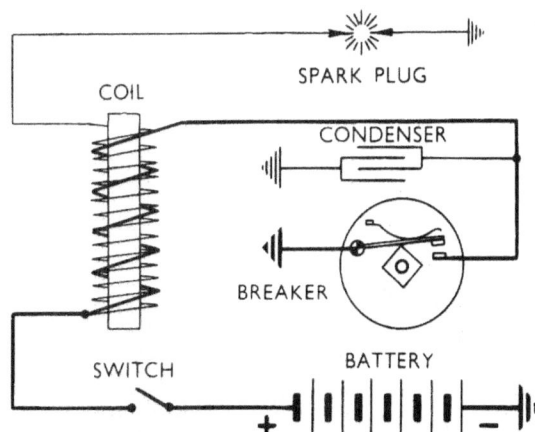

Fig. 433 - Ignition system wiring diagram.

Operation.

The circuit breaker in the distributor interrupts the primary circuit by opening the contacts.

The current flow, broken in the primary winding, does not arc the contact gap because it discharges into the condenser, which is connected in parallel to contacts.

Thus, the primary current flow instantly collapses, producing a sudden drop of intensity in the magnetic field.

This collapse induces a voltage surge in the ignition coil secondary winding.

The high e. m. f. is distributed to spark plugs (in firing sequence: 1-3-4-2) by the ignition distributor rotor.

IGNITION DISTRIBUTOR

The centrifugal automatic advance device, the low-tension circuit breaker, condenser and rotor are all incorporated in this unit.

The automatic advance device consists of a plate carrying two weights, symmetrically hinged on plate at one end, articulated on cam carrier shaft and provided with return springs.

Due to the action of centrifugal force, a more or less high rotational speed moves the weights outwards. Since weights pivot on cam carrier shaft, the latter moves angularly, resulting in a rotation of cams with respect to distributor drive shaft.

The breaker consists of the cam on drive shaft and of two contacts, one of which is stationary while the other rotates with breaker arm and is provided with rubbing block.

The cam has four lobes to control the opening and closing of contact points. The stationary contact is mounted on an adjustable support to make possible the adjustment of contact gap.

From the ignition coil, the H. T. current reaches the distributor cap central terminal, and through the rotor (which may be considered as a revolving contactor), it is distributed ot each of the spark plugs in turn.

Manifold Vacuum-Operated Advance Control.

To improve engine performance under part-loads (on level, on moderately steep climbs, etc.) and low r. p. m. rates, a device has been added which makes possible increases in ignition advance angle as a function of vacuum in carburetor.

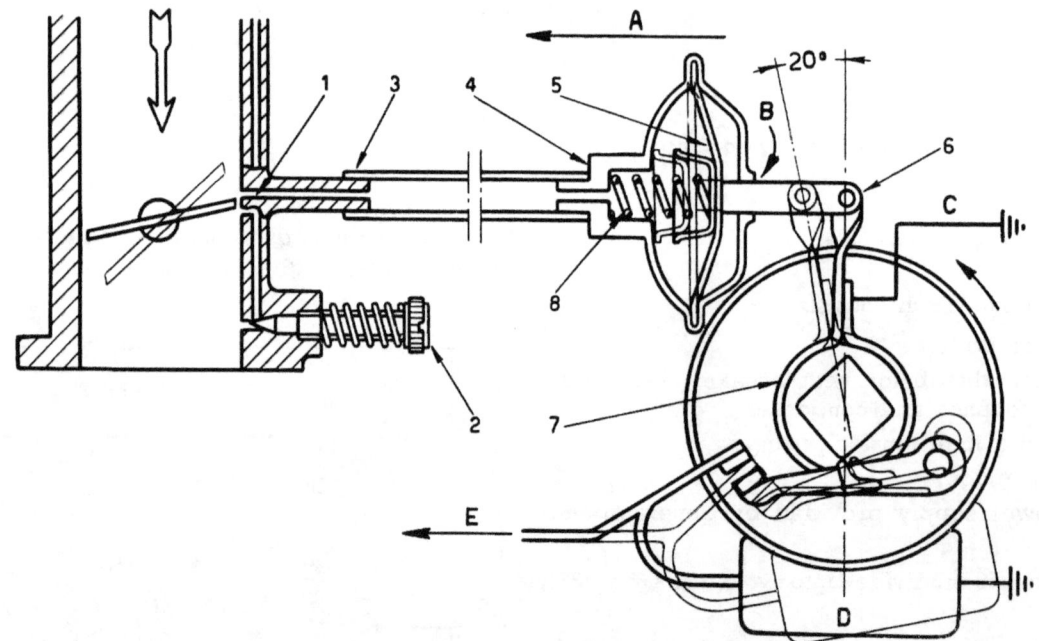

Fig. 434 - Vacuum advance control operation diagram.

1. Vacuum hole. - 2. Idle speed mixture richness setscrew. - 3. Connecting hose. - 4. Vacuum advance device case. - 5. Control diaphragm. 6. Lever 7 operating tie rod. - 7. Ignition distributor rotating lever. - 8. Diaphragm retracting spring.

A. Advance. - B. Area to be lubricated. - C. Ground braid. - D. Condenser. - E. To ignition coil.

ELECTRICAL

In fact, the ignition advance angle must not only be proportionate to engine speed but also to many other very important factors as cylinder head temperature, fuel mixture temperature and the effective pressure in cylinder when compression ends.

The device is operated by the vacuum promoted beneath throttle in carburetor by engine suction.

The vacuum hole (1, fig. 434) in carburetor is drilled next to idle speed mixture richness setscrew (2), right under the throttle when in closed position.

Because of this arrangement, during idle speed operation the vacuum in intake manifold cannot act on the advance control.

This device consists of an outer case (4) enclosing a special diaphragm (5) which is connected on one side by tie rod (6) and lever (7) to ignition distributor and, on the other side, is subjected to the action of manifold vacuum through a rubber hose (3).

As soon as accelerator pedal is depressed and throttle begins to open, hole (1) will remain past the throttle and vacuum acts on diaphragm of vacuum-operated advance control. Under these conditions the diaphragm overcomes the load of reactionary spring (8), deflects leftwards and through tie rod (6) connected to lever (7) fastened to distributor body, causes the distributor to rotate. This way, a maximum 11° advance may be obtained in addition to the original advance of 10° set at assembly.

By further depressing the accelerator pedal the throttle opens of a further amount: vacuum in carburetor decreases and consequently also the advance is reduced, until the diaphragm returns to rest position. Contemporaneously, since the engine r. p. m. rate has gone up, the centrifugal automatic advance device has already taken over; the automatic advance reaches a value of 30°.

Initial advance	10°
Automatic advance	30°
Vacuum advance	20°

NOTE - 600 engines up to No. 758492, Sedan, and No. 765150, Multipla, are fitted with 11° vacuum advance in respect of the engine.

Checking the Distributor on Test Bench.

1. - Operation test.

Install distributor on tester and connect it to the variable-speed motor. Wire with an ignition coil and a battery, and connect the four peripheral cap terminals to four terminals of an adjustable point gap spark tester.

Rotate distributor for some minutes in the prescribed direction at a speed of about 2000 r. p. m., keeping the spark tester point gap at .2" (5 mm).

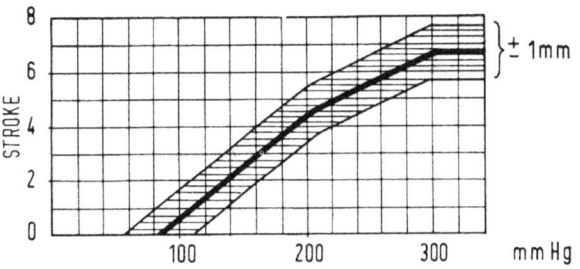

Fig. 435 - Vacuum advance device diagram.
Stroke variation as a function of vacuum.

Then, widen gap to .4" (10 mm) and check if any sparking takes place in distributor. Aside from the particular noise produced, such sparks are revealed either by a drop in intensity or total lack of one or more sparks at the tester.

2. - Checking the automatic advance curve.

Install distributor on tester and connect terminal D of an ignition coil to the ignition distributor low tension terminal; next, connect the coil H. T. terminal to the graduated disc of tester.

Operate distributor at a speed of 300 ÷ 400 r.p.m., and on the graduated disc, record the value in degrees at which one of the four sparks is produced. Increase distributor r.p.m.; if the increase is very slight in comparison to that of the preceding test, the same reading should be recorded.

Continue to increase the rotational speed: by taking readings at every 200 ÷ 300 r.p.m. increment, it will be possible to record the new values in degrees of spark advance (referred to distributor), with respect to initial advance setting and as a function of distributor rotational speed.

Since the distributor rotational speed is half that of engine, the values obtained must be doubled (both the r.p.m. and advance in degrees) to properly plot the distributor automatic advance versus engine diagram and to compare it with fig. 436.

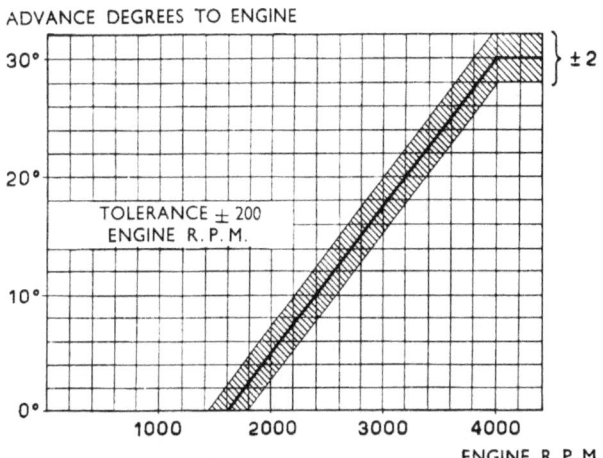

Fig. 436 - Centrifugal advance device diagram.

Fig. 437 - Ignition distributor with vacuum advance device, in place on engine.

1. Ignition distributor. - 2. Ground connection cable. - 3. Condenser. - 4. Lubrication fitting. - 5. Distributor support mounting screws. - 6. Vacuum advance lever screw. - 7. Vacuum advance lever. - 8. Distributor support. - 9. Vacuum advance device. - 10. Carburetor inlet line-to-vacuum advance hose. - 11. Ignition coil. - 12. Ignition distributor-to-spark plug high tension cables. - 13. Ignition coil-to-distributor high tension cable. - 14. Ignition coil-to-distributor low tension cable.

The automatic advance to engine reaches a value of 30°.

3. - Checking the vacuum-operated advance device.

Check that distributor is free to rotate in its support because if rotation is hindered by a binding of the distributor-support assembly or by the cables to spark plugs, the advance device will not operate properly.

The above troubles, besides hindering the advance device, would also cause knocking of the engine in the case that the distributor remains blocked in the position corresponding to the maximum advance angle when engine operates at its maximum r.p.m. rate.

On the contrary, if the distributor remains blocked in the position corresponding to the minimum advance angle, the trouble is not so serious, since the engine performs as if it were not provided with vacuum operated advance device.

The ground cable (2, fig. 437) must be firmly fastened so as to ensure a good grounding because, otherwise, ignition would be defective. Also, the cable must not impede the free rotation of distributor.

Check for tightness also the connections of hose (10).

4. - Checking the timing.

With distributor mounted on test bench as described under «Checking the automatic advance curve», operate it at approximately 400 r.p.m.

By properly adjusting the distributor on the bench support, align one of the our sparks occurring between the rotating point and the graduated disc with the 0° mark.

The four sparks should thus correspond to 0°, 90°, 180° and 270° on the disc with a $\pm 1°$ tolerance.

5. - Checking the breaker contact points opening-closing rate.

Install distributor on test bench and connect primary circuit with a battery and a test lamp.

Rotate distributor by hand in the prescribed direction and read on the graduated disc, in correspondence with the reference index, the value in degrees corresponding to the instant at which contacts begin to part.

This instant is revealed by the lamp going out; continue to rotate distributor until the lamp lights up again meaning that contacts have closed. Record at this instant the degrees read on the graduated disc.

Still rotate distributor until contacts open (lamp going out). The difference between the second and the first value recorded gives the opening angle; the difference between the third value (corresponding to the last lighting up of the lamp) and the second value recorded, indicates the closing angle.

Check the values o the recorded opening and closing angles taking the average of several readings.

The value of the ratio between closing angle and opening angle must be about 1.3:

— closing angle magnitude: $51° \pm 3°$;
— opening angle magnitude: $39° \pm 3°$.

6. - Checking distributor noises.

No matter at what speed the car is driven, the distributor should not be noisy.

Generally, the presence of marked noises can be attributed to the following sources:

  a) contact points pressure lower than 16.8 ± 1.8 oz (475 ± 50 gr.);

  b) worn shaft bushes;

  c) excessively worn weight pivots;

  d) weakened weight springs.

Trouble a) will also account for a difficult ignition at high speeds.

Instead, higher contact point pressure values will result in a marked wear of contacts, cam and movable contact rubbing block.

In case d) also a consequent alteration in automatic advance will be present and ignition will be advanced on specified r. p. m. rate.

7. - Checking mechanical components.

Contacts should be checked for pitting, oxidation and charring.

Ascertain that rotor, cap stationary contacts, H.T. central brush are not worn by more than .0118" (0,3 mm).

Check breaker arm rubbing block. Its wear must not be such as to upset breaker timing by more than 2° with respect to ignition distributor setting.

Check also that contact gap is .0185" to .0209" (0,47 to 0,53 mm) (fig. 439) and contact points pressure 16.8 ± 1.8 oz (475 ± 50 gr.).

8. - Checking insulation resistances.

The insulating resistance between different terminals and ground must exceed 10 MΩ at a 500 Volts d.c., and can be controlled with a megohmmeter.

The measurement between breaker terminal and ground must be taken while breaker contact points are kept open.

9. - Checking the condenser.

Condenser capacity - measured at a frequency ranging from 50 to 100 Hz. - should be from 0.15 to 0.20 μF.

Trouble Shooting.

Ignition faulty or completely absent.

Possible causes:

a) **Condenser shorted or with low insulation resistance.**

Voltage built up in the secondary circuit is insufficient to produce sparks, or sparking is poor.

b) **Defective distributor cap (cracks, carbonized inner surface or deposited moisture).**

In this case, current leaks to ground along cracks, burnt paths and moisture.

c) **Cracks, carbon or moisture traces on rotor plastic portion.**

Leaks occur as described in b).

d) **Distributor cap central brush worn or broken, brush spring deformed or burnt.**

Arcing occurs between rotor and central brush, with consequent voltage drop and low tension at spark plug electrodes.

The breakage of the central sprung brush may be detected by ocular inspection.

The excessive wear of the brush or the deformation of its spring is evidenced by the corrosion traces and oxidation on the brush central portion, which are caused by the arcing between brush and contact on rotor due to unsteady contact of the two parts.

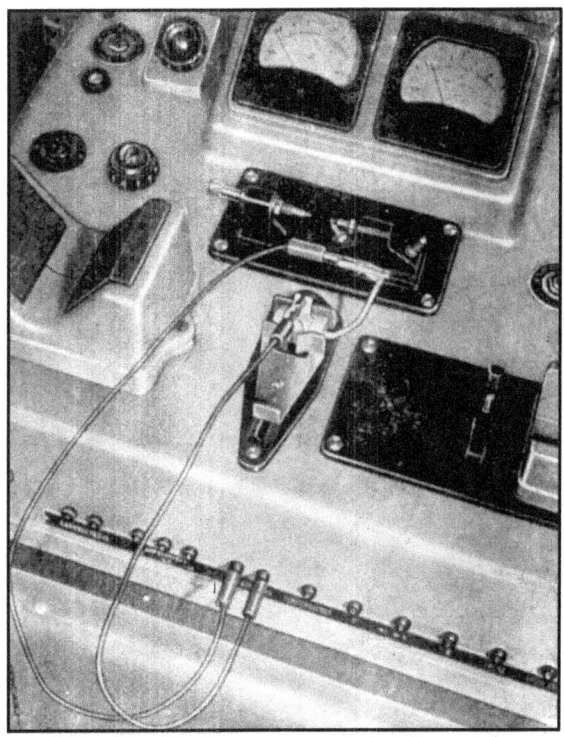

Fig. 438 - Checking a condenser on tester bench C. 905.

e) **Build-up and pitting on contact points.**

Generally, this is caused by contact points gap being less than specified, due to wear of breaker arm contact carrier lever rubbing block.

Since build-up causes improper opening of primary circuit, the secondary circuit will supply an inefficient spark.

f) **Burnt or oxidized contact points.**

Excessive resistance in condenser circuit, caused by improper connections or broken cables. In turn, this accounts for poor ignition both when starting and at high speeds:

— oiled or soiled contact surfaces;

— in some cases (less frequently) a too high setting of regulator (much above max. allowable rate).

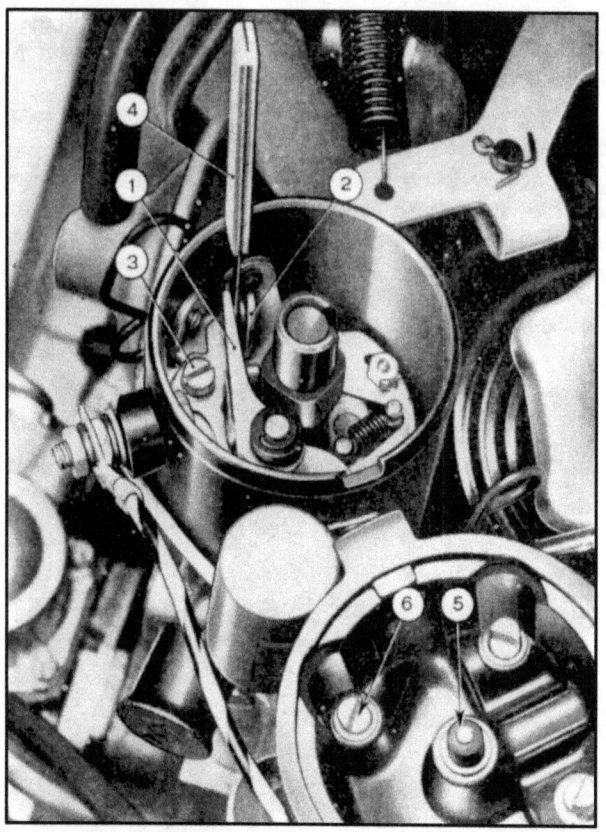

Fig. 439 - Checking distributor breaker point opening.

1. Breaker arm. - 2. Stationary contact carrier. - 3. Stationary contact carrier adjusting screw. - 4. Feeler gauge, for checking point opening. - 5. Current contact carbon. - 6. Distributor cap terminal.

The oxidation or burning of contacts determines a high resistance between contact points and hence permanently cuts out the primary circuit, with consequent exclusion of the ignition system.

g) **Excessive contact opening.**

The spark is weak, particularly at high speeds, since the closing time of contacts is too brief and the primary current cannot reach the value required for proper operation in such a short interval.

Extremely Advanced Ignition.

This is caused by weakened centrifugal weight springs.

Repairs.

Replace distributor caps which are cracked or have traces of carbon.

Cap terminals, rotor and breaker contacts (when oxidized, corroded or burnt) can be cleaned with a fine cut file.

Never use emery cloth in these cases.

When terminal and rotor wear exceeds .0118″ (0,3 mm), rotor and distributor cap must be replaced.

Also, replace the breaker arm if the rubbing block turns out to be excessively worn. Breaker arm should be replaced, too, when points are worn to such an extent as the gap exceeds the last setting limit of .0209″ (0,53 mm), so that adjustment through stationary contact carrier screw (3, fig. 439) is no longer possible.

To adjust point opening, loosen screw (3, fig. 439) and move the stationary contact carrier (2) as required. After the adjustment has been made, use a feeler gauge and check it against the gap specification (.0185″ to .0209″ - 0,47 to 0,53 mm). Again tighten the contact carrier screw (3).

If distributor drive shaft play is excessive, replace the distributor shaft and body.

Weak centrifugal weight springs must be replaced by genuine ones.

When servicing the ignition distributor, check the lubrication of the drive shaft bushes. If these lack lubricant, refill the fittings with the prescribed amount of Jota 3 grease.

Furthermore, wet the felt in cam carrier shaft with FIAT engine oil.

IGNITION COIL

The ignition coil consists of a soft iron core around which both primary and secondary windings are wound.

These two windings are embedded in insulating compound.

The unit is housed in a metal casing provided with a bakelite insulating cap for winding end outlets.

On the coil cap are found two side terminals and a central terminal. The two side terminals constitute the primary winding inlet and outlet while the central terminal is for secondary winding outlet.

Bench Testing.

Proceed as follows to check ignition coil efficiency:

1. - **Ohmic resistances.**

The ohmic resistance of the primary circuit at $68° \pm 9°$ F ($20° \pm 5°$ C) must not be lower than 3.2 Ohms. If it is, this indicates the presence of a short. Secondary circuit resistance must be instead 5000 ± 100 Ohms.

ELECTRICAL

2. - Grounding insulation.

Ignition coil must withstand, without any sparking, an alternate tension of 500 V. r. m. s., 50 Hz, applied for three minutes between one end of the primary winding and the metal casing. Insulation resistance, with respect to ground, must be greater than 50 MΩ at 500 V. d. c. This can be measured with a megohmmeter.

3. - Measuring spark length.

Run the ignition coil with the distributor without using H. T. distribution, and send all sparks to a standard ionising point spark tester for measurement of maximum spark length.

After the coil has been operating for approximately two hours at a rate of 50 sparks per second and is warm, spark length at 12 Volts should be at least .47" (12 mm).

4. - Test with shunted spark tester.

Insert a 1 MΩ resistance in parallel with spark tester. Under these conditions, the spark length should not be less than $^3/_4$ the length of the spark obtained in previous test.

5. - Over-voltage test.

Feed the ignition coil with a 17 V. battery at 60 sparks per second, connecting the H.T. lead directly to spark tester with .3150" (8 mm) spark gap adjustment. The coil must withstand this test without damage for 15 minutes.

Trouble Shooting and Servicing.

Possible ignition coil defects are:

a) Open circuits - check this by a simple circuit tester (test lamp, bell tester, etc.).

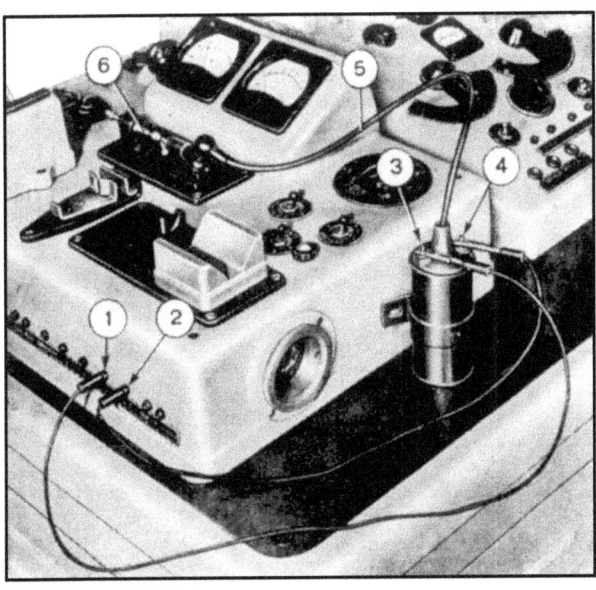

Fig. 440 - Checking an ignition coil on tester bench.
1. Breaker. - 2. 12 Volt power socket. - 3. Low tension cable terminal. - 4. Power cord terminal. - 5. High tension cable. - 6. Spark issuing between tester points.

b) Shorted inner winding turns - check this by measuring the circuit resistance (provided a great number of turns are shorted).

c) Insulating compound squeezed out on account of excessive filling - this may insulate the H. T. terminal.

d) Water leaking in through a defective seal. Check by measuring ground insulation.

e) Loose or dirty connections.

Only in case e) can ignition coil be restored to proper efficiency. In all other cases, coil must be replaced.

SPARK PLUGS

Technical Data.

Type: M 14 - 12/225.
Code: CW 225 N.
Thread (metric): 14 x 1,25 mm.
Manufacturer: F. I. Magneti Marelli.
Mark: CW 225 A.
Electrode gap: .020" to .024" (0,5 to 0,6 mm).

NOTE - Vehicles for export to U.S.A. and Canada are equipped with the following spark plugs:
— **Type:** M 14-13;
— **Code:** L 7 (Champion);
— **Gap:** .024" to .028" (0,6 to 0,7 mm).

Fig. 441 - Sanding a spark plug.
The spark plug is washed in the device to the right.

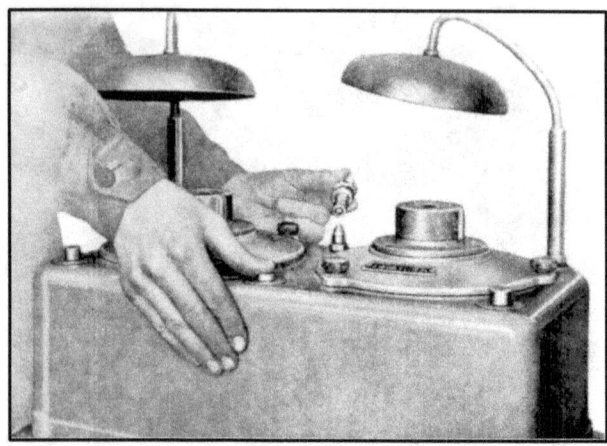

Fig. 442 - Blowing a spark plug after sanding and washing.

To remove and install plugs on engine, use wrench A. 50022 (fig. 444).

Tightness Test.

The tightness test of the parts which compose a spark plug, that is insulator body and center electrode, is made on test bench as shown in fig. 443.

Screw the spark plug on to the Service Center seat, then operate the manual pump lever until a 284 to 356 p. s. i. (20 to 25 kg/cm^2) pressure is obtained.

Using a distributor, pour some drops of oil or kerosene on spark plug (fig. 443). If the plug is leaky, oil or kerosene will bubble out, most likely between the insulator and metal body.

Inspection and Repair.

Should ignition troubles and misfiring occur in one or more cylinders, check spark plug condition.

For a perfect cleaning of spark plugs, use the proper Service Center where the spark plug is first sanded (fig. 441) then washed by gasoline under pressure and, finally, blown dry (fig. 442).

Check electrode gap and adjust to .0197" to .0236" (0,5 to 0,6 mm).

To adjust the gap, bend the outer electrode towards the central one; never try to move the central electrode towards the outer one, since this would break the porcelain, with consequent failure of spark plug.

If the porcelain appears black and coated with carbon deposits, pour some alcohol or gasoline in the capsized spark plug and after a while scrub with a wire brush.

After these operations, check spark plugs for gas tightness.

Fig. 444 - Removal of a spark plug by means of wrench A. 50022.

Electrical Test.

Screw the spark plug, without copper seal, on to the Service Center seat; tightness is assured by the connection seal on seat.

Adjust the tester spark meter point gap at .315" (8 mm), then operate the manual pump lever. Take care to push the lever all the way down at each time, to have the pressure gauge dial read as tabulated hereafter:

Tester spark meter point gap		Spark plug gap		Tester cell pressure reading					
				Very good plug		Good plug		Faulty plug	
in	mm	in	mm	p.s.i.	kg/cm²	p.s.i.	kg/cm²	p.s.i.	kg/cm²
.315	8	.020	0,5	85	6	71	5	57	4
.315	8	.024	0,6	71	5	57	4	50	3,5

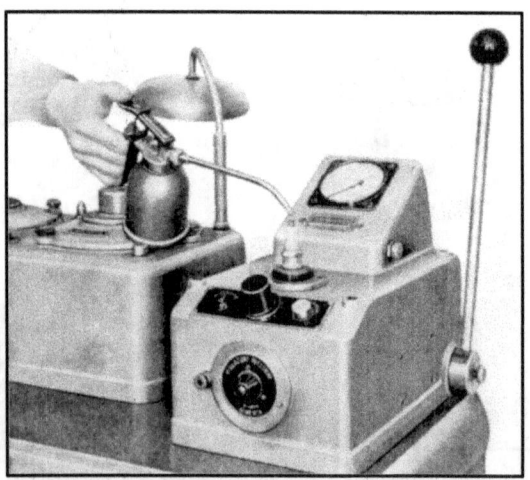

Fig. 443 - Testing a spark plug for gas tightness.

ELECTRICAL

Place the **high tension** cable socket on the spark plug and depress the switch button.

The following condition may be experienced:

1) Looking through the eye piece, a vivid spark is seen to issue through the plug electrodes; if so, the plug is serviceable.

2) Spark occurs at the meter points. Decrease the tester pressure and see at what pressure spark issues through plug electrodes. To judge on the efficiency of the spark plug under test, compare data with those in the table.

NOTE - Some sparks at the meter points can be tolerated.

Should no spark be seen either at the plug or at the meter, this is an indication that the plug insulator is cracked and the spark occurs internally between ground and electrode. As a result, the spark plug is unserviceable.

IGNITION TIMING

This timing is necessary when the distributor shaft and/or camshaft have been removed.

Proceed as follows:

On timing sprocket cover, fit fixture **A. 13065/B** (for shops equipped with fixture **Ap. 5030**, the tester plate is identified by code **Ap. 5030/2, fig. 445**). Make sure cylinder No. 1 is in the compression stroke, i. e., with both valves closed. Bring crankshaft to the position in which **the mark** on drive pulley will line up with the white 10° mark on fixture: this corresponds to a 10° static advance B.T.D.C.

Remove distributor cap and rotate drive shaft by hand until rotor points to contact for firing in cylinder No. 1.

In this position contacts are about to snap open (check first if maximum contact distance is .0185" to .0209" [0,47 to 0,53 mm]).

Fig. 446 - Timing marks.

The arrow points to the reference marks on timing gear cover and on crankshaft pulley that line up when pistons of cylinder Nos. 1 and 4 are at T.D.C. For the 10° static advance setting the reference mark on pulley must be placed .32"-.35" (8-9 mm) ahead of index mark on timing cover.

Fig. 445 - Tester plate Ap. 5030/2, in place for inspection of ignition advance to engine.

Without disturbing distributor shaft, insert lower coupling on its toothed end, install support and tighten the lock screw on crankcase.

To check if ignition distributor is properly timed to engine and if centrifugal automatic advance and total advance angles are as specified (30° and 40°, respectively) proceed as follows:

Connect the testing apparatus **Ap. 5030** to a single-phase 220 Volt power outlet, fitted with grounding insert. The grounding of the tester must be made positively, before or when plugging in the tester service cord.

Connect ground terminal with an unpainted metal portion of car under test.

Connect the equipment cable with the spark plug No. 1, then insert the plug terminal on cable end in order to restore the ignition circuit.

Chalk off the T.D.C. mark on drive pulley.

Start the engine and aim the winking light beam on the chalk mark drawn on pulley. If ignition is timed, **at slow running speed** the mark on pulley must be seen aligned with the first white line (10º) on the fixture. By speeding up the engine so as to bring the automatic advance into operation, the chalked mark will be seen to move counterclockwise until, at maximum r.p.m., it will reach the second white mark on fixture (40º).

If fixture **A. 13065** is not available, ignition timing is made as follows:

See that cylinder No. 1 piston is in the compression stroke; rotate crankshaft clockwise so that the cast reference mark on generator drive pulley (fig. 446) is set .32" to .35" (8 to 9 mm) ahead of the mark cast on timing sprocket cover.

This setting corresponds to a static advance of 10º B.T.D.C.

Next carry out the distributor timing, proceeding as directed previously.

IGNITION SYSTEM SPECIFICATIONS AND DATA

Ignition Distributor.	
Static advance	10º
Centrifugal advance	30º
Vacuum advance:	
up to engine No. 758492, Sedan, and No. 765150, Multipla	11º
from engine No. 758493, Sedan, and No. 765151, Multipla	20º
Breaker contact pressure	16.8±.9 oz. (475±25 gr.)
Contacts gap	.0185" to .0209" (0,47 to 0,53 mm)
Terminal-to-ground insulation at 500 V d.c.	over 10 MΩ
Condenser capacity at 50-100 Hz	0.15 to 0.20 µF
Condenser insulation resistance at 212º F (100º C) and 100 V d.c.	over 1 MΩ/µF
Distributor shaft lubricant	Jota 3 grease
Cam carrier shaft felt lubricant	FIAT VE oil
Ignition Coil.	
Primary winding ohmic resistance at 68º±9º F (20º±5º C)	$\geq$ 3.2 Ω
Secondary winding ohmic resistance at 68º±9º F (20º±5º C)	5000±100 Ω
Ground insulation resistance at 500 V d.c.	$\geq$ 50 MΩ
Spark Plugs.	
Type	M 14 - 12/225
Thread metric	14 x 1,25 M
Code	CW 225 N
Electrode gap	.020" to .024" (0,5 to 0,6 mm)
Vehicles for Export to U.S.A. and Canada.	
Type	M 14-13
Thread metric	14 x 1,25 M
Code (Champion)	L 7
Electrode gap	.024" to .028" (0,6 to 0,7 mm)

LIGHTING SYSTEM

Description	page	295
Headlamps	»	296
Front Parking and Direction Indicator Lamps	»	299
Side Direction Indicator Lamps	»	299
Rear View Mirror Light	»	299
Rear Parking, Direction Indicator, Stop Lamps and Reflector Lens	»	301
Number Plate Lamp	»	301
Engine Compartment Light	»	303
Indicators in the Instrument Cluster	»	303
Fuses	»	303
Lighting System Specifications and Data	»	305
LIGHTING SYSTEM - U. S. A. AND CANADA VEHICLES	»	306
Headlamps	»	306
Tail Parking, Direction Indicator, Stop Lamps and Reflector Lens	»	306
Bulb Specifications	»	306
Fuses	»	307

Description.

The lighting system consists of:

— Two headlamps, with double-filament globe bulbs (45 Watts for high beam and 40-Watts for low beam).

— Front parking and direction indicator lamps provided with double-filament globe bulbs (5 Watts for parking lights and 20 Watts for winking direction indicator lights).

— Two side direction indicator lamps fitted with 2.5 W tubular bulb (these lamps have been adopted starting from No. 723664, «Sedan», and No. 062188, «Multipla»).

— Number plate lamp with 5-Watt globe bulb.

— The three-purpose rear lights (parking, winking direction indicators, stop) with reflex reflector, are provided with one single filament 20-W globe bulb (direction) and one double filament globe bulb (5-W parking and 20-W stop lights).

— 3-Watt cylindrical bulb for interior lighting, incorporated in rear view mirror and controlled by a lever switch.

— 2.5-Watt instrument panel light, with switch on facia.

— 5-Watt engine compartment light, with incorporated switch automatically controlled by engine compartment lid.

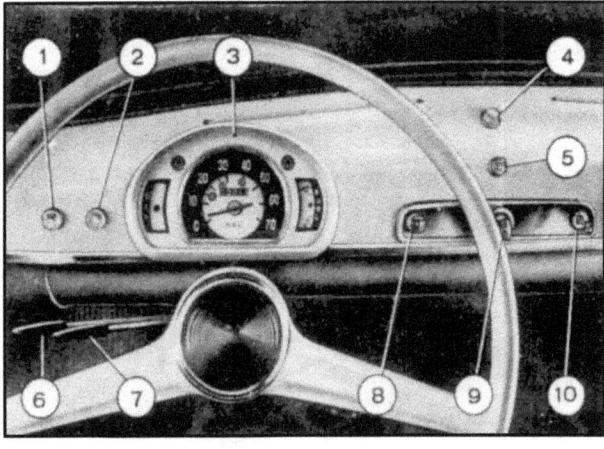

Fig. 447 - Instrument panel (Sedan).

1. High beam indicator (blue light). - 2. Parking light indicator (green light). - 3. Instrument cluster. - 4. Direction indicator pilot light (green). - 5. External light switch. - 6. External light shifting lever switch. - 7. Direction indicator control lever switch. - 8. Instrument cluster light switch. - 9. Ignition and sundry signals lock switch. - 10. Windshield wiper switch.

— Four tubular 2.5-W bulbs, in instrument cluster, for:

— generator charge indicator;
— fuel reserve supply indicator;
— insufficient oil pressure indicator;
— engine water temperature indicator.

— One tubular 2.5-W bulb for direction indicators green pilot light.

HEADLAMPS

Removal and Disassembly.

a) Sedan.

— Up to parts serial No. 842099.

Loosen lower screw (1, fig. 448) securing lamp unit to lamp shell.

Withdraw the lamp unit by lowering it slightly to facilitate extraction.

Rotate upward bulb holder-to-reflector spring (2).

Remove the bulb holder (3) from reflector.

Remove the double-filament bulb (4) from bulb holder (symmetrical headlights). Bulb is secured by bayonet coupling.

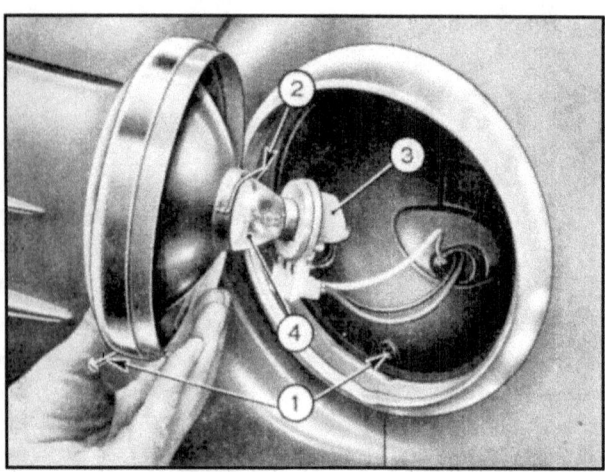

Fig. 448 - Opening the headlamp (Sedan).

1. Screw to be slackened to open headlamp. - 2. Bulb holder-to reflector fastener spring. - 3. Bulb holder. - 4. Double-filament bulb.

— (Only « Multipla »). Two cylindrical 3-W bulbs for pillar lamps with incorporated switch.

— One 2.5-W tubular bulb for parking lamp green pilot light (on « Sedan » this light has been adopted starting from car No. 723664).

— One 2.5-W tubular bulb for high beam blue pilot light (this light has been adopted starting from No. 723664 « Sedan », and No. 062188, « Multipla »).

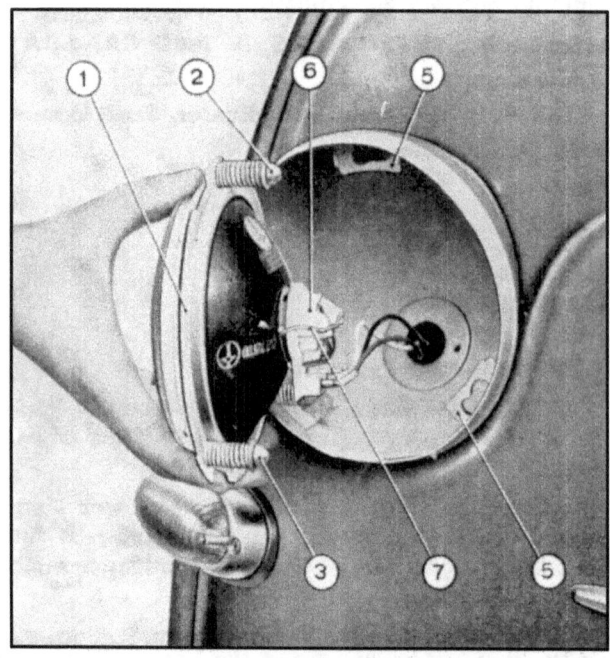

Fig. 450 - Disassembly of the headlamp (Multipla).

1. Lamp unit. - 2. Upper screw, for beam vertical aiming. - 3. One of the two screws for beam horizontal aiming. - 5. One of the three lamp unit-to-shell mounting plates. - 6. Bulb holder. - 7. Bulb holder spring fastener.

NOTE - On asymmetrical headlights, bulb and bulb holder are one unit which cannot be separated.

— Starting from parts serial No. 842100.

Remove the headlamp rim, press fitted on three spring fasteners (A, fig. 452).

Push the spring fastener (B) outward and slide off the lamp unit from two stationary retainers (C).

The lens cannot be separated from the reflector.

To replace the bulb, raise the spring fastener and withdraw the socket retaining the bulb.

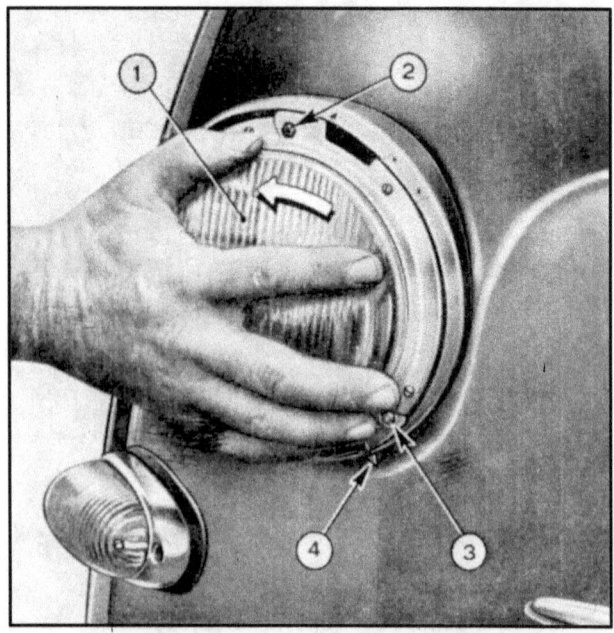

Fig. 449 - Opening the headlamp (Multipla).

1. Lamp unit (for removal rotate as indicated by arrow). - 2. Upper screw, for beam vertical aiming. - 3. One of the two screws for beam horizontal aiming. - 4. Rim spring fastener.

ELECTRICAL

The bulb and bulb holder are secured to the socket by bayonet coupling.

b) **Multipla.**

Pry off the rim with a screwdriver (rim is simply secured to the shell by spring fasteners - 4, fig. 449). Then, apply pressure on the lens of lamp unit while rotating it counterclockwise through an angle of about 15° (fig. 449). Remove the lamp unit.

For the disassembly procedure, proceed as hinted under a) (Sedan).

NOTE - Headlights to suit Model 600 « Sedan » and « Multipla », are different according to whether they are of the symmetrical or asymmetrical type and, also, according to their aiming procedure.

Some minor variations from the description above may be met on disassembly of headlights, according to the make.

Aiming Headlights.

Headlight aiming should be made in a no-load condition.

Check tires for correct inflating pressure.

Locate the car on a level floor, 16'5" (5 m) apart from an opaque, white wall screen in the shade (fig. 451) and make sure that the car centerline is square to the screen face.

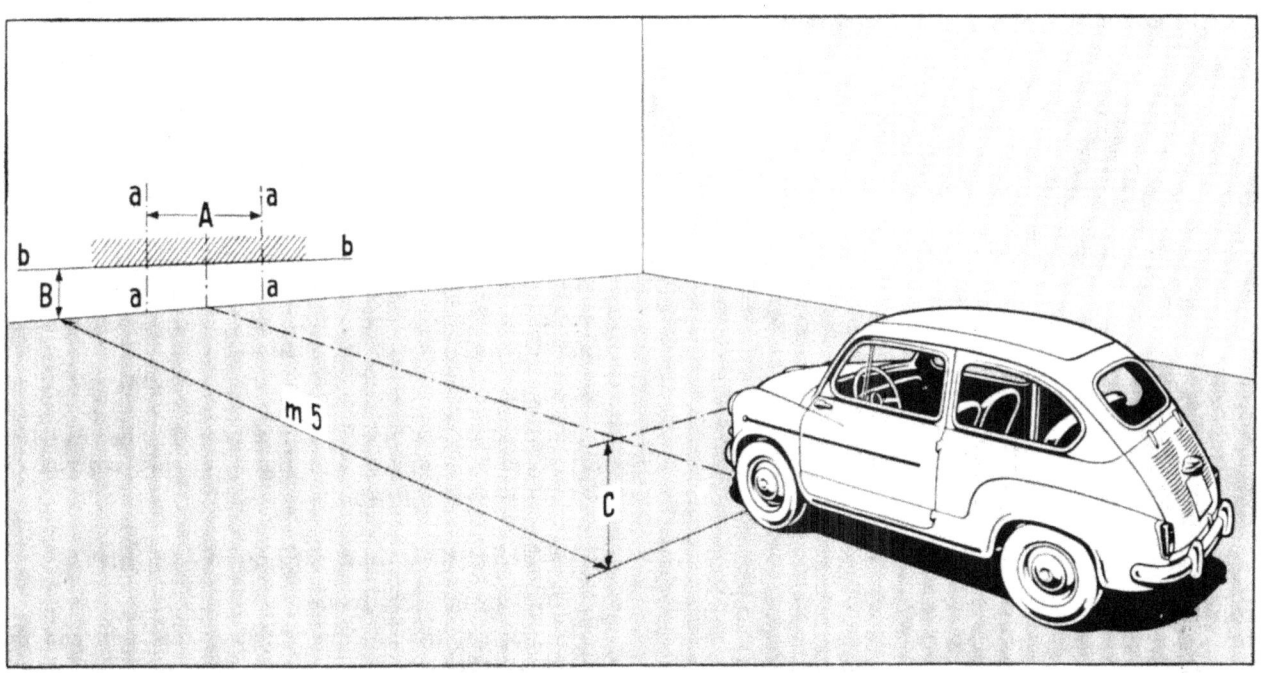

Fig. 451 - Headlamp low beam aiming chart.

HEADLIGHT AIMING CHART

TYPE OF VEHICLE	TYPE OF HEADLIGHTS	A	B	
			New Vehicle	Seated Vehicle
« Sedan »	asymmetrical	38 3/16" (970 mm)	C minus 1 25/32" (45 mm)	C minus 1 37/64" (40 mm)
« Multipla »	»	36 5/8" (930 mm)	C minus 1 31/32" (50 mm)	C minus 1 31/32" (50 mm)
« Sedan »	symmetrical	38 3/16" (970 mm)	C minus 1 25/32" (45 mm)	C minus 1 37/64" (40 mm)
« Multipla »	»	36 5/8" (930 mm)	C minus 1 31/32" (50 mm)	C minus 1 31/32" (50 mm)

A = Headlight center-to-center distance (interaxis).
B = Light pool ground clearance (separation line between lit and unlit area) at a distance of 16'5" (5 m).
C = Headlight center ground clearance.

Jounce the vehicle both sides to set suspensions.

Draw a pair of vertical lines a-a on the screen. These lines should be equally spaced throughout (distance A, corresponding to the headlight interaxis, as shown in the chart).

Draw a horizontal line b-b (fig. 451) at the height B specified in the chart for either a new vehicle and a vehicle with suspension renewed (not yet seated), or a seated vehicle. Vehicles are seated in practice when they have run the mileage covering the first voucher service.

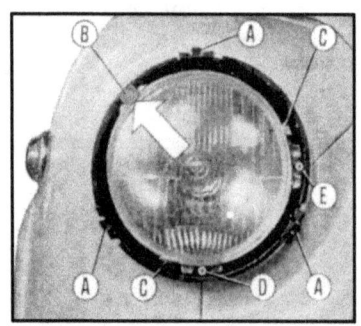

Fig. 452 - Headlamp in position, with rim removed (Sedan starting from serial No. 842100).

A. Rim spring fasteners. - B. Lamp unit spring fastener. - C. Lamp unit stationary retainers. - D. Light beam vertical adjusting screw. E. Light beam horizontal adjusting screw.

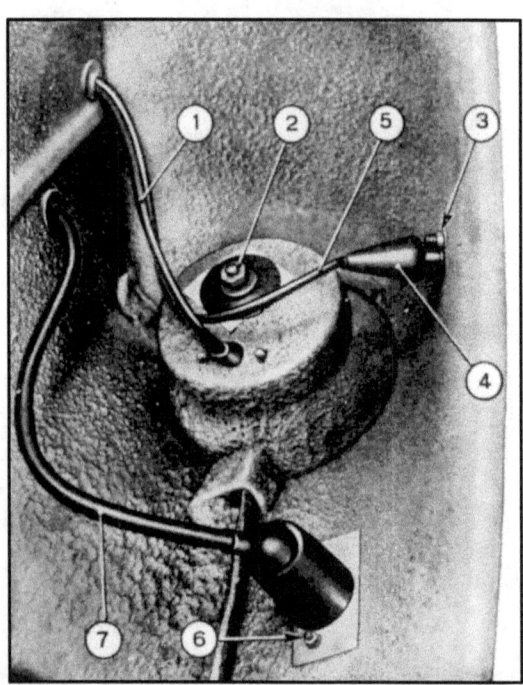

Fig. 453 - Inside view of right-hand front fender (Sedan, from serial No. 723664).

1. Headlamp lead. - 2. Headlamp locking and adjusting nut. - 3. Side direction indicator lamp casing nuts. - 4. Bulb holder socket boot. - 5. Side direction indicator lamp lead. - 6. Front parking and direction indicator lamp casing nuts. - 7. Parking and direction indicator lamp lead.

To check and correct headlight aiming, adhere to the following procedures which cover the asymmetrical and symmetrical headlights, separately.

ASYMMETRICAL LOW BEAM HEADLIGHTS

Turn on the low beam:

— the horizontal separation line between the unlit and the lit area should be on line b-b and never above it (fig. 451);

— the upward slanting (some 15°) separation lines should start from the meeting points of vertical lines a-a with the horizontal line b-b (fig. 451) or just outside of them. A $10\,^{15}/_{64}''$ (26 cm) increase in distance A specification, corresponding to a 3° aggregate beam divergence, is permissible.

If the above conditions are not observed, aim the headlights as follows.

Sedan.

— Up to parts serial No. 842.099.

Slightly turn out the headlamp shell center shank nut on body and, working on the shank, move the headlamp in its housing until correct aiming is obtained. Tighten down on the shank nut.

— Starting from parts serial No. 842.100.

To aim the light beam vertically (inclination), work on screw (D, fig. 452), and horizontally (divergence), work on screw (E).

Multipla.

Turn in or out the upper screw (2, figs. 449-450) for vertical aiming, and the two side screws (3) for horizontal aiming.

SYMMETRICAL LOW BEAM HEADLIGHTS

Turn on the low beam:

— the separation line between the unlit and the lit area should be on line b-b (fig. 451) and never above it.

Turn on the high beam:

— the center of the zone of highest intensity (hot spot) of each headlight should fall on line a-a or just outside thereof. Allowance is made for the distance A to be extended by $10\,^{15}/_{64}''$ (26 cm) corresponding to a 3° aggregate divergence of light pools.

If above conditions are not observed, aim the headlights following the directions given for the asymmetrical type.

IMPORTANT

Headlamp reflectors are aluminized; therefore, during disassembly, be careful not to soil or touch the reflecting surface with fingers. Should reflector be dusty, clean preferably with an air blast or a

ELECTRICAL

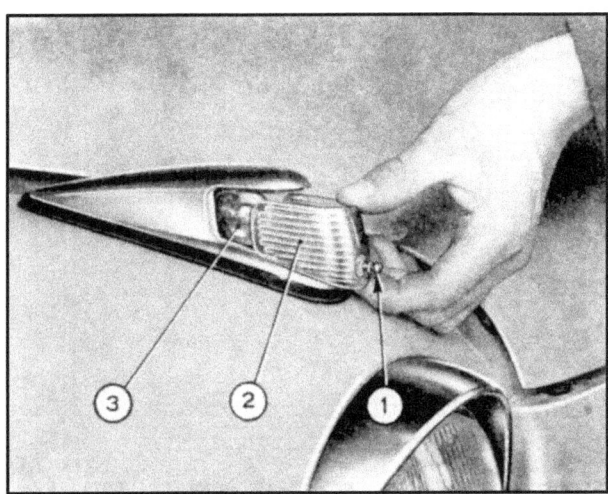

Fig. 454 - Disassembling front parking and direction indicator lamp (Sedan, up to car No. 723663).
1. Lens screw. - 2. Lens. - 3. Bulb, bayonet coupling.

feather duster. Never use a cloth, which would impair the reflecting surface brilliancy.

Bulbs must not be replaced by others of a different type or wattage, as this would result, in the first case, in decreased headlamp efficiency, and in the second, in an excessive consumption of current, more than generator can deliver, which would cause gradual discharging of the battery.

Front Parking and Direction Indicator Lamps.

To replace the double filament bulb (5/20 W), undo the screws (figs. 454, 455 and 456) securing the lens to lamp casing; bulb is secured by bayonet coupling.

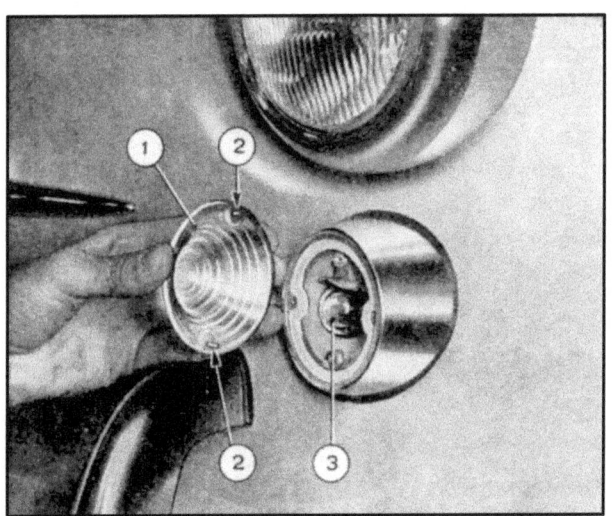

Fig. 455 - Disassembling front parking and direction indicator lamp (Multipla, from car No. 062188).
1. Lens. - 2. Lens retaining screws. - 3. Bulb, bayonet coupling, parking and direction indicator lights.

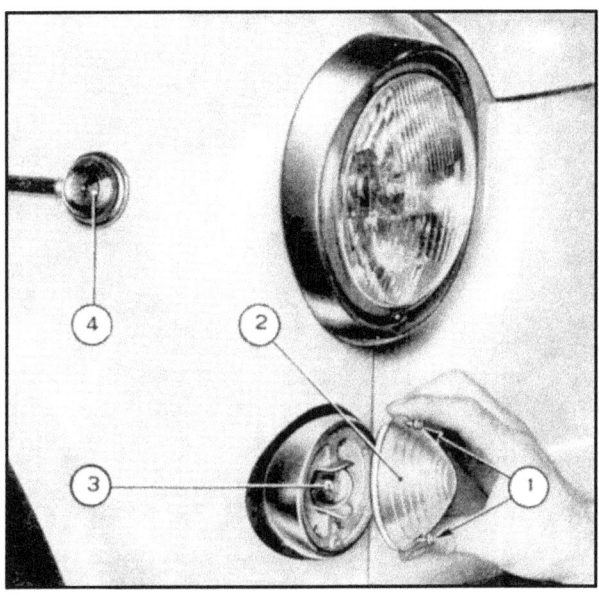

Fig. 456 - Disassembling front parking and direction indicator lamp (Sedan, from car No. 723664).
1. Lens retaining screws. - 2. Lens. - 3. Bulb, bayonet coupling, parking and direction indicator lights. - 4. Side direction indicator lamp.

Side Direction Indicator Lamps.

To replace the 2.5 W tubular bulb, operate from below fender (fig. 453) and slide off bulb holder from rubber socket. Bulb is secured by bayonet coupling.

Rear View Mirror Light.

On underside of rear view mirror frame, centrally located above windscreen, is controlled by an incorporated toggle switch and by a jam switch, placed between driver's side door and pillar which automatically turns on the light when door is opened.

Fig. 457 - Side direction indicator lamp (Multipla, from car No. 062188).

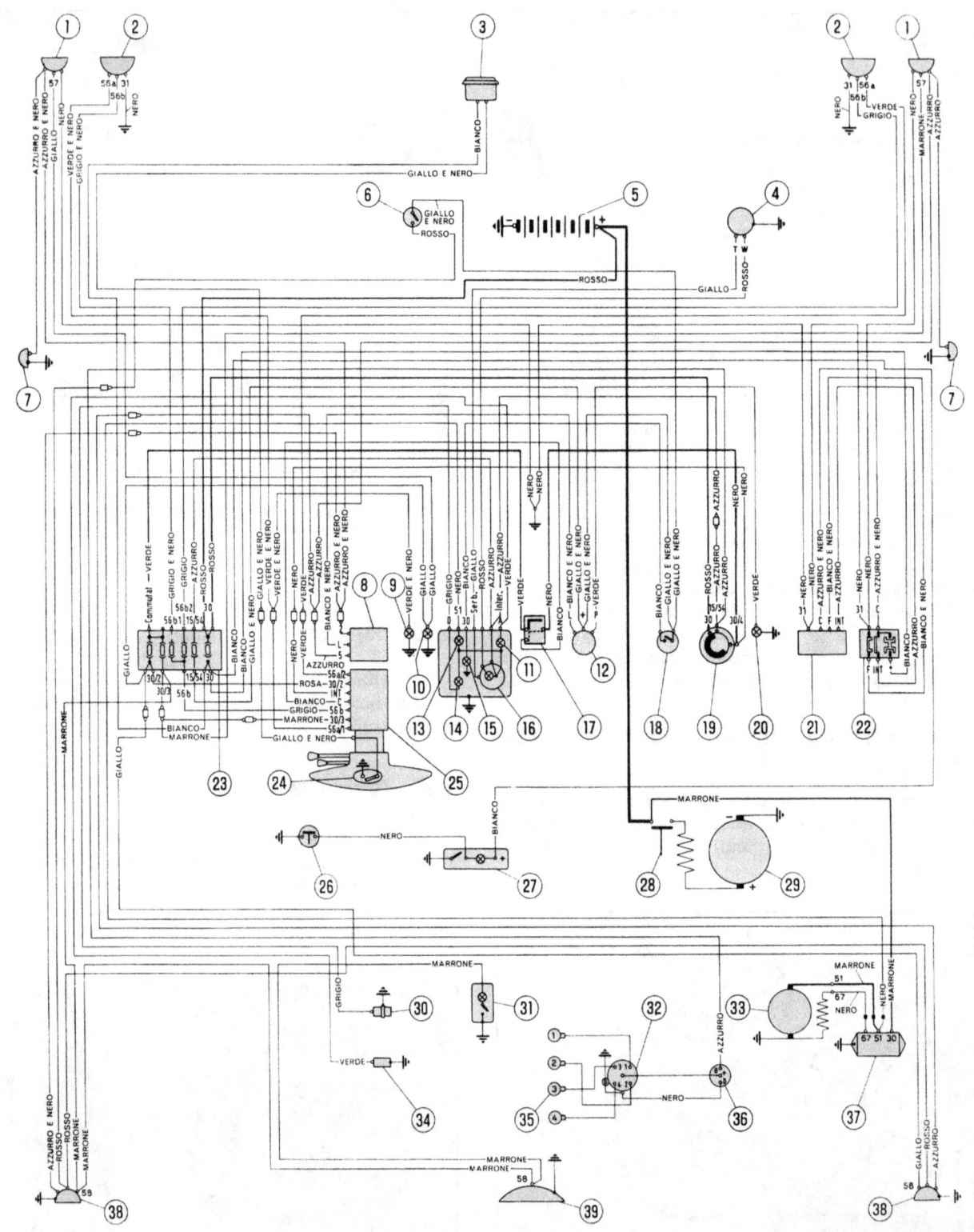

Fig. 458 - Wiring diagram - Sedan.

KEY TO CABLE COLORS

Azzurro	=	**Blue**	Grigio	=	**Grey**	Rosa	=	**Rose**	Azzurro e Nero	=	**Black and Blue**	Grigio e Nero	=	**Black and Grey**
Bianco	=	**White**	Marrone	=	**Brown**	Rosso	=	**Red**	Bianco e Nero	=	**Black and White**	Commutat.	=	**Switch**
Giallo	=	**Yellow**	Nero	=	**Black**	Verde	=	**Green**	Giallo e Nero	=	**Black and Yellow**	Serb.	=	**Tank (Fuel)**
									Verde e Nero	=	**Black and Green**	INT - Inter.	=	**Switch**

(Specifications on opposite page)

ELECTRICAL

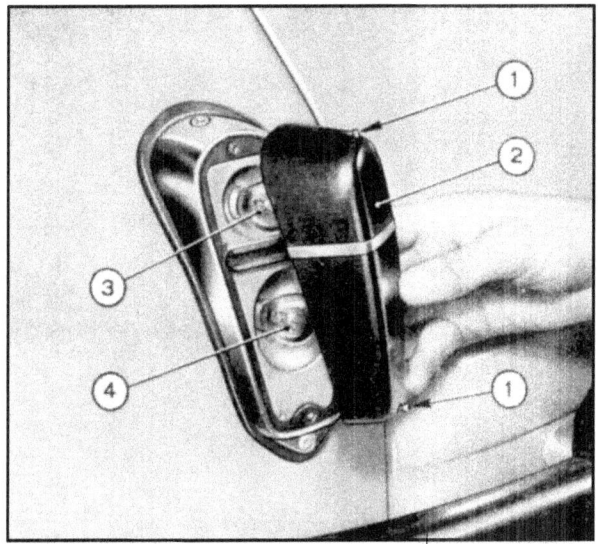

Fig. 459 - Disassembling tail parking, stop and direction indicator lamp (Sedan, up to car No. 723663).

1. Lens screws. - 2. Lens. - 3. Bulb, bayonet coupling, direction indicator light. - 4. Bulb, bayonet coupling, parking and stop lights.

NOTE - Lens is all red in colour.

Bulb replacement.

1. - Back out the two mirror frame mounting screws.

2. - Separate the mirror frame from body.

3. - Pull out bulb from the two retaining spring fingers.

Rear Parking, Direction Indicator, Stop Lamps and Reflector Lens.

To replace bulbs, undo the two screws (1, figures 459 and 460) securing the lens to lamp casing; bulbs are fixed by bayonet coupling.

Number Plate Lamp.

To replace bulb, undo both screws (1, fig. 461) securing the screen, lens and lining assembly to lamp casing; bulb is retained by bayonet coupling.

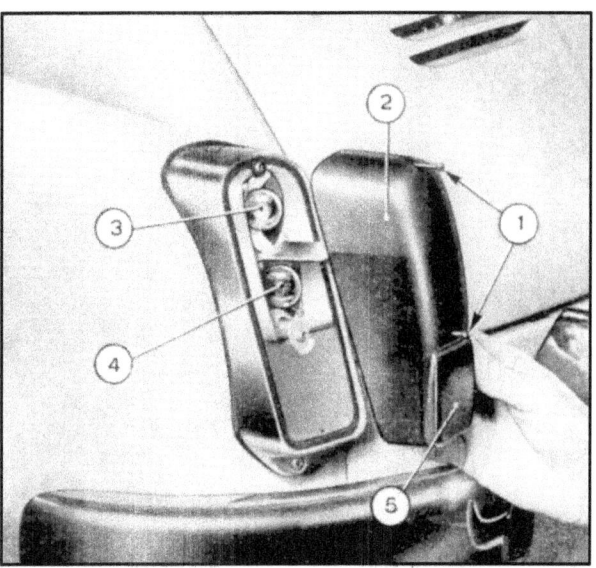

Fig. 460 - Disassembling tail parking, stop, direction indicator lamp and reflector lens (Sedan, from car No. 723664).

1. Lens retaining screws. - 2. Lens. - 3. Bulb, bayonet coupling, direction indicator lights. - 4. Bulb, bayonet coupling, parking and stop lights. - 5. Reflector lens.

NOTE - Lens is orange-coloured on upside and red-coloured on underside.

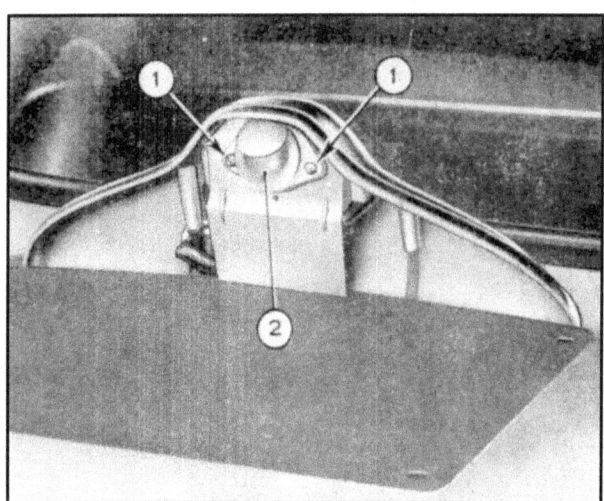

Fig. 461 - Number plate lamp.
1. Light screen and lens screws. - 2. Lens.
Bulb is inserted by bayonet coupling.

Specifications of fig. 458 (page 300).

1. Front parking and direction indicator lamps. - 2. Headlamps (high and low beam). - 3. Horn. - 4. Fuel gauge sending unit. - 5. Battery. - 6. Stop lamp pedal-operated switch. - 7. Side direction indicator lights. - 8. Direction indicator switch. - 9. High beam indicator. - 10. Parking light indicator. - 11. High water temperature indicator. - 12. Winking device (flasher unit). - 13. Generator charge indicator. - 14. Low engine oil pressure indicator. - 15. Instrument cluster light. - 16. Fuel gauge, with reserve supply indicator. - 17. Outer lighting switch. - 18. Instrument cluster light switch. - 19. Ignition lock switch. - 20. Direction indicator pilot light. - 21. Windshield wiper motor. - 22. Windshield wiper switch. - 23. 8-A fuses. - 24. Horn button. - 25. Outer lighting change-over switch. - 26. Jam switch, between door and pillar, for rear view mirror light. - 27. Lamp incorporated in rear view mirror, for car interior illumination, with toggle switch. - 28. Starter switch. - 29. Starter. - 30. Sending unit, for low oil pressure indicator. - 31. Engine compartment light, with automatic switch. - 32. Ignition distributor. - 33. Generator. - 34. Thermostatic sending unit for excessive water temperature indicator. - 35. Spark plugs. - 36. Ignition coil. - 37. Generator regulator. - 38. Rear parking, stop and direction indicator lamps. - 39. Number plate lamp.

NOTE - Mark ■ means that cable is provided with numbered strip or ferrule.

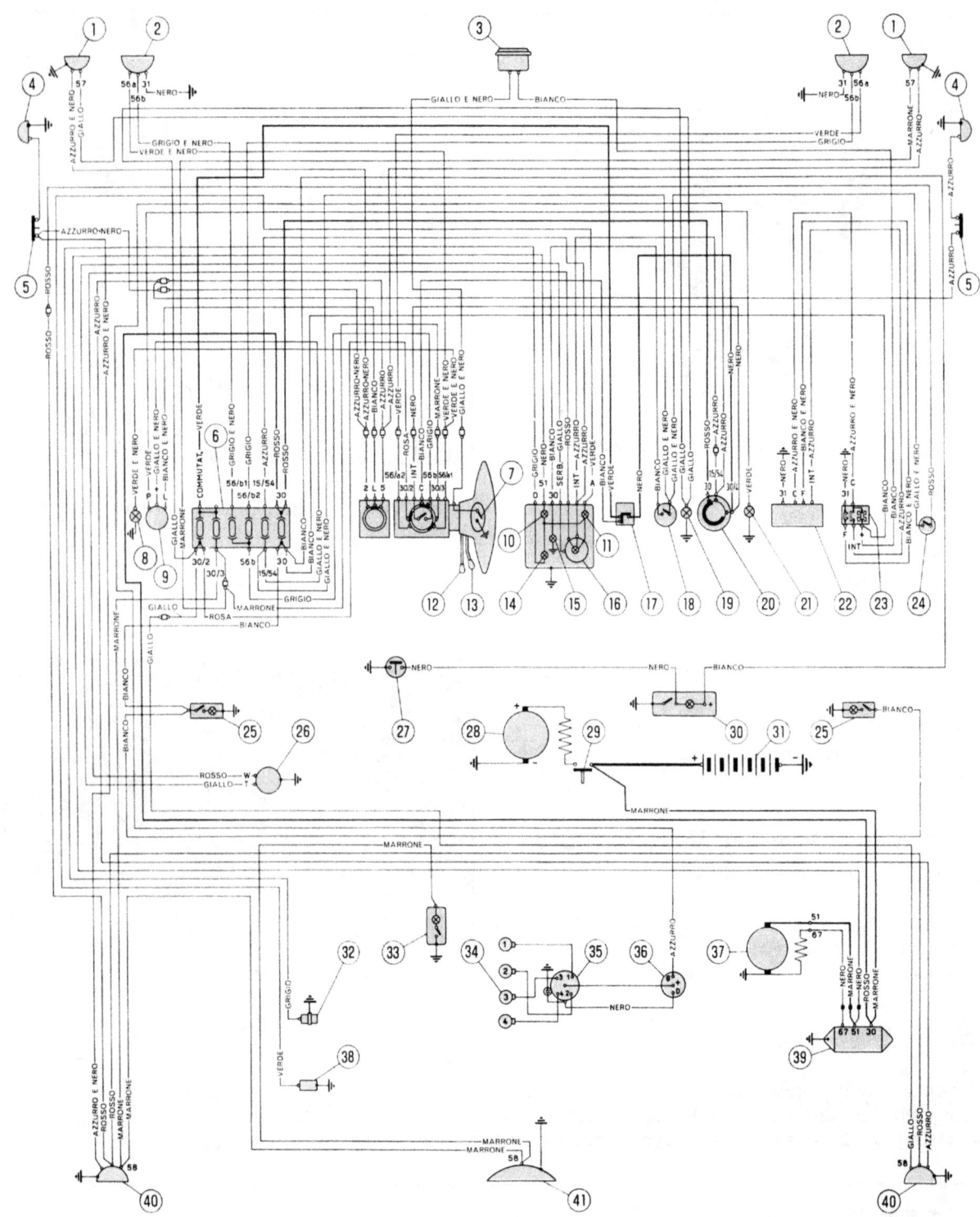

Fig. 462 - Wiring diagram - Multipla.

NOTE - Mark ■ means that clabe is provided with numbered strip or ferrule.

KEY TO CABLE COLORS

Azzurro = **Blue**	Grigio = **Grey**	Rosa = **Rose**	Azzurro e Nero = **Black and Blue**	Grigio e Nero = **Black and Grey**
Bianco = **White**	Marrone = **Brown**	Rosso = **Red**	Bianco e Nero = **Black and White**	Commutat. = **Switch**
Giallo = **Yellow**	Nero = **Black**	Verde = **Green**	Giallo e Nero = **Black and Yellow**	Serb. = **Tank (Fuel)**
			Verde e Nero = **Black and Green**	INT - Inter. = **Switch**

(Specifications on opposite page)

ELECTRICAL

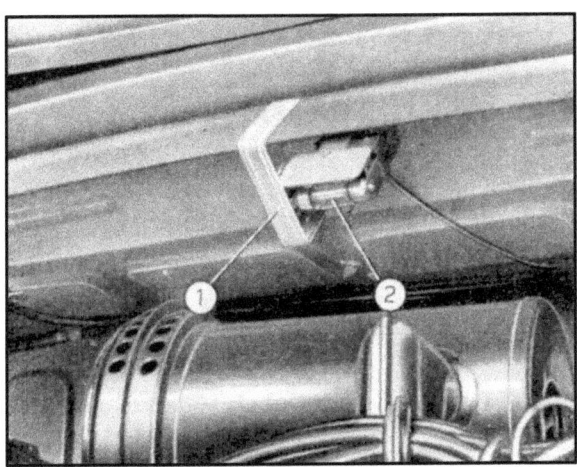

Fig. 463 - Engine compartment light.
1. Switch lever. - 2. Bulb (5 watt, cylindrical).

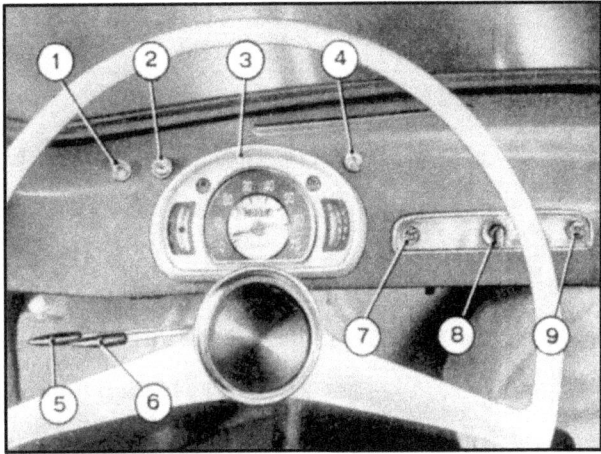

Fig. 464 - Instrument panel (Multipla from car No. 062188).
1. Headlight high beam indicator (blue). - 2. Parking light indicator (green). - 3. Instrument cluster. - 4. Direction indicator tell-tale light (green). - 5. External light shifting lever switch. - 6. Direction indicator control lever switch. - 7. Instrument cluster light switch. - 8. Ignition and sundry signals lock switch. - 9. Windshield wiper switch.

Engine Compartment Light.

To replace the cylindrical 5-Watt bulb, just pull it out of the two spring fingers (fig. 463).

Indicators in the Instrument Cluster.

To replace any of these tubular 2.5-Watt bulbs, disinsert bulb holders from their sockets and then the bulbs.

Bulbs are secured by bayonet coupling.

FUSES

The electric system is protected by six 8-A fuses.
Before replacing a burnt fuse, locate the cause of blowing, or short circuit. Reference to the wiring diagram (figs. 458 and 462) will be most useful to this purpose.

«Sedan».

The six fuses are contained in a fuse holder which is located on vertical wall of cowl, below the dashboard (fig. 465). Fuses protect the electrical circuits as shown on table, page 304.

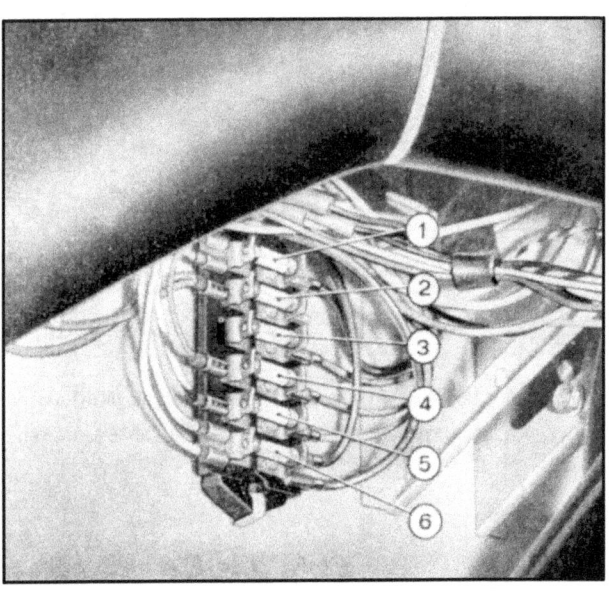

Fig. 465 - Location of electrical system fuses (Sedan).
1. Fuse No. 30. - 2. Fuse No. 15/54. - 3. Fuse No. 56/b 2. - 4. Fuse No. 56/b 1. - 5. Fuse No. 30/3. - 6. Fuse No. 30/2.

Specifications of fig. 462 (page 302).

1. Front parking and direction indicator lights with 5-Watt (parking) and 20-Watt (direction indicator) double-filament bulb. - 2. High and low beam headlights with 45-Watt (high beam) and 40-Watt (low beam) double filament bulb. - 3. Horn. - 4. Side direction indicator lights. - 5. Side direction indicator winking device. - 6. 8-A fuses. - 7. Horn button. - 8. Headlight high beam indicator, blue (2.5-Watt bulb). - 9. Direction indicator flasher unit. - 10. Generator charge indicator (2.5-Watt bulb). - 11. High water temperature indicator (2.5-Watt bulb). - 12. Headlight shifting switch. - 13. Direction indicator switch. - 14. Low oil pressure indicator (2.5-Watt bulb). - 15. Instrument cluster light (2.5-Watt bulb). - 16. Fuel gauge with reserve supply indicator (2.5-Watt bulb). - 17. Outer lighting switch. - 18. Instrument cluster, light, switch. - 19. Front parking light indicator, green (2.5-Watt bulb). - 20. Ignition lock switch. - 21. Direction indicator tell-tale light green (2.5-Watt bulb). - 22. Double arm windshield wiper. - 23. Windshield wiper switch. - 24. Stop light pedal-operated switch. - 25. Dome lights (3-Watt bulbs) with built-in toggle switch. - 26. Fuel gauge sending unit. - 27. Courtesy light jam switch between driver's door and pillar. - 28. Starting motor. - 29. Starting motor switch. - 30. Rear view mirror courtesy light (3-Watt bulb). - 31. Battery. - 32. Low oil pressure indicator sending unit. - 33. Engine compartment light (5-Watt bulb) with automatic switch. - 34. Spark plugs. - 35. Ignition distributor. - 36. Ignition coil. - 37. Generator. - 38. High water temperature indicator sending unit. - 39. Generator regulator. - 40. Parking, stop and direction indicator lights with 5-Watt (parking) and 20-Watt (stop) double filament bulb and 20-Watt (direction indicator) bulb. - 41. License plate light (5-Watt bulb).

ELECTRICAL SYSTEM FUSES, « SEDAN »

FUSES	CONTROLLED CIRCUITS
1 - Fuse No. 30	Horn - Windshield wiper - Rear view mirror light.
2 - Fuse No. 15/54	Winking direction indicators with pilot light - Instrument cluster light - Stop light.
3 - Fuse No. 56/b 2	Right headlamp low beam.
4 - Fuse No. 56/b 1	Left headlamp low beam.
5 - Fuse No. 30/3	Left headlamp high beam - Right front parking light - Left rear parking light - Number plate light - Engine compartment light - High beam indicator.
6 - Fuse No. 30/2	Right headlamp high beam - Left front parking light with indicator - Right rear parking light.

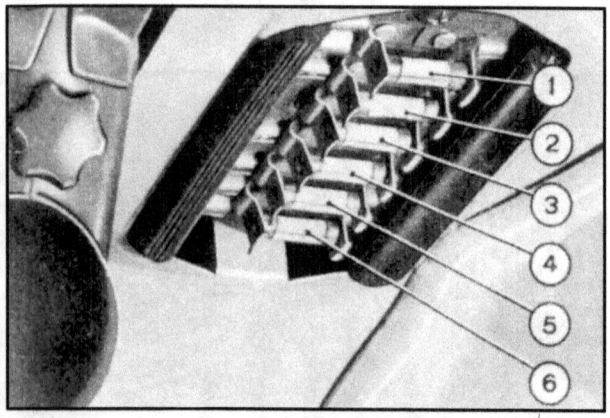

Fig. 466 - Location of electrical system fuses (Multipla).
1. Fuse No. 30. - 2. Fuse No. 15/54. - 3. Fuse No. 56/b 2. - 4. Fuse No. 56/b 1. - 5. Fuse No. 30/3. - 6. Fuse No. 30/2.

« Multipla ».

The six fuses are contained in a fuse holder which is located below the dashboard on left-hand side of steering column (fig. 466).

Fuses protect the electrical circuits as shown on table, below.

NOTICE - The following circuits are not fuse-controlled:

— generator charge with pilot light;
— ignition;
— starting;
— low oil pressure indicator;
— fuel gauge and reserve supply light;
— excessive water temperature indicator.

ELECTRICAL SYSTEM FUSES, « MULTIPLA »

FUSES	CONTROLLED CIRCUITS
1 - Fuse No. 30	Windshield wiper - Horn - Rear view mirror light. - Dome lights.
2 - Fuse No. 15/54	Blinking direction indicators with pilot light - Instrument cluster light - Stop light.
3 - Fuse No. 56/b 2	Right headlamp low beam.
4 - Fuse No. 56/b 1	Left headlamp low beam.
5 - Fuse No. 30/3	Left headlamp high beam - Right front parking light - Left rear parking light - Number plate light - Engine compartment light - High beam indicator.
6 - Fuse No. 30/2	Right headlamp high beam - Left front parking light with indicator - Right rear parking light.

LIGHTING SYSTEM SPECIFICATIONS AND DATA*

Headlamps	2
Double filament globe bulb:	
high beam	45 W
low beam	40 W
Front parking and direction indicator lamps	2
Double filament globe bulb:	
parking	5 W
direction indicator (flashing)	20 W
Side direction indicator lamps	2
Tubular bulb	2.5 W
Rear parking, direction indicator and stop lamps (with reflex reflector)	
Globe bulbs:	2
single filament (direction indicators)	20 W
double filament { parking	5 W
stop	20 W
Rear number plate lamp	1
Globe bulb	5 W
Inner lighting	
Cylindrical bulb incorporated in rear view mirror	3 W
switch { toggle type	on mirror frame
jam type	on steering wheel side door pillar
Dome lamps (only Multipla), 2, cylindrical, with incorporated switch	3 W
Instrument cluster light	
Tubular lamp with toggle switch on panel	2.5 W
Engine compartment light	
Cylindrical lamp with jam switch actuated by the opening of lid	5 W
Indicators - 4 tubular bulbs in instrument cluster, each	2.5 W
Tell-tales on dashboard	
— direction indicator, green	
— parking light, green } tubular bulb	2.5 W
— high beam, blue	
Headlamp aiming	
Car distance from screen	16.4 ft (5 m)
Fuses, six	8 Amps

(*) For lighting system to suit « Sedan Version 140 » and « Multipla Version 141 », see covering data on pages 306, 307 and 308.

LIGHTING SYSTEM - U.S.A. AND CANADA VEHICLES

The lighting system to suit «Sedan Version 140» and «Multipla Version 141» vehicles for export to U.S.A. and Canada, includes the lamps and bulbs specified below.

Headlamps.

Removal of lamp unit.

To remove the lamp unit, proceed as follows:

1) Back out the screw (2, fig. 467) and slide off the rim from its lodging.

2) Using a screwdriver, disengage the four spring fingers (3, fig. 467) retaining the lamp unit and mounting ring assembly.

3) Withdraw the lamp unit from its seat and slide off the lamp unit tripolar receptacle.

Headlamp aiming.

Using proper wrench, work on two screws (1 and 2, fig. 468). The upper screw (1) is to adjust beam vertically, the lower screw (2) adjusts beam horizontally.

For aiming specifications, comply with S.A.E. headlight aiming Standards.

Tail Parking, Direction Indicator, Stop Lamps and Reflector Lens.

To replace bulbs, back out both screws securing lens to lamp casing.

Bulbs are inserted by bayonet coupling.

BULB SPECIFICATIONS

Q.ty	LOCATION	TYPE ORIGINAL EQUIPMENT	TYPE SAE EQUIVALENT
2	Headlamps (high beam and low beam)	«Sealed beam» headlamp unit 5400	
2	Front lamps: direction indicators .. parking lights	12 V - 5/20 W FIAT Norm. 1/08569/90	No. 1016 - 12.8 V 21/6 Cp
2	Tail lamps: stop lights ...... parking lights		
2	Tail lamps: direction indicators ...	12 V - 20 W FIAT Norm. 1/08562/90	No. 1141 - 12 V - 21 W
1	License plate light	12 V - 5 W FIAT Norm. 1/08577/90	No. 89 - 13 V - 6 Cp
1	Engine compartment light	12 V - 5 W FIAT Norm. 1/08630/90	—
1	Dome lights and rear view mirror courtesy light	12 V - 3 W FIAT Norm. 1/08595/90	—
1	Instrument cluster light		
1	Direction indicator pilot light (green)		
1	Headlamp high beam indicator: Sedan Version 140: green .. Multipla Version 141: blue ..	12 V - 2.5 W FIAT Norm. 1/08583/90	—
1	Generator charge indicator (red) ..		
1	Low oil pressure indicator (red) ..		
1	Reserve supply indicator (red) ...		
1	Parking light indicator (green) ...		
1	Excessive water temperature indicator (red)		
2	Dome lights (Multipla Version 141) .	12 V - 3 W FIAT Norm. 1/08595/90	—

ELECTRICAL

FUSES

The electric system is protected by six 8-A fuses. Before replacing a burnt fuse, locate the cause of blowing, or short circuit. Reference to the wiring diagram (fig. 469) will be most useful to this purpose.

a) « Sedan ».

The six fuses are contained in a fuse holder which is located on vertical wall of cowl, below the dashboard (fig. 465). Fuses protect the following electrical circuits:

FUSES	CONTROLLED CIRCUITS
30	Horn - Windshield wiper - Rear view mirror light.
15/54	Blinking direction indicators with pilot light - Instrument cluster light - Stop light.
56/b 2	Right headlamp low beam.
56/b 1	Left headlamp low beam.
30/3	Left headlamp high beam - Right front parking light - Left rear parking light - License plate light - Engine compartment light - Parking light indicator.
30/2	Right headlamp high beam - Left front parking light - Right rear parking light - Headlamp high beam pilot light.

b) « Multipla ».

The six fuses are contained in a fuse holder which is located below the dashboard on left-hand side of steering column (fig. 466). Fuses protect the following electrical circuits:

FUSES	CONTROLLED CIRCUITS
30	Windshield wiper - Horn - Rear view mirror light - Dome lights.
15/54	Blinking direction indicators with pilot light - Instrument cluster light - Stop light.
56/b 2	Right headlamp low beam.
56/b 1	Left headlamp low beam.
30/3	Left headlamp high beam - Right front parking light with indicator - Left rear parking light - License plate light - Engine compartment light.
30/2	Right headlamp high beam - Left front parking light - Right rear parking light - Headlamp high beam pilot light.

NOTICE

The following circuits are not fuse-controlled:

— generator charge with pilot light;
— ignition;

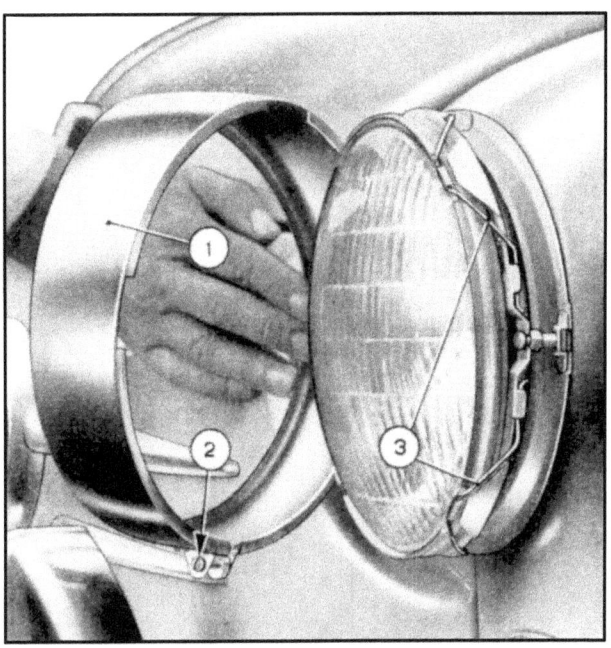

Fig. 467 - Removing headlamp rim (Version 140).
1. Rim. - 2. Rim retaining screw. - 3. Unit mounting spring fingers.

— starting;
— low oil pressure indicator;
— fuel gauge and reserve supply light;
— excessive water temperature indicator.

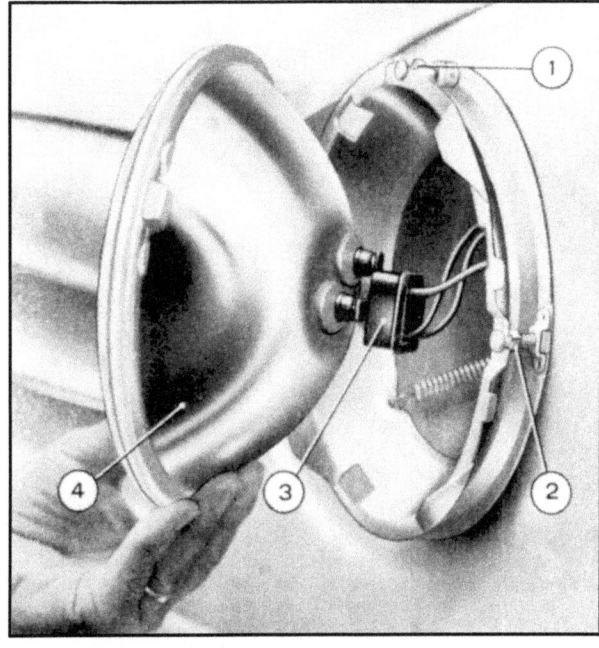

Fig. 468 - Opening headlamp (Version 140).
1. Beam vertical aiming adjustment screw. - 2. Beam horizontal aiming adjustment screw. - 3. Headlamp terminal plug. - 4. Sealed beam unit.

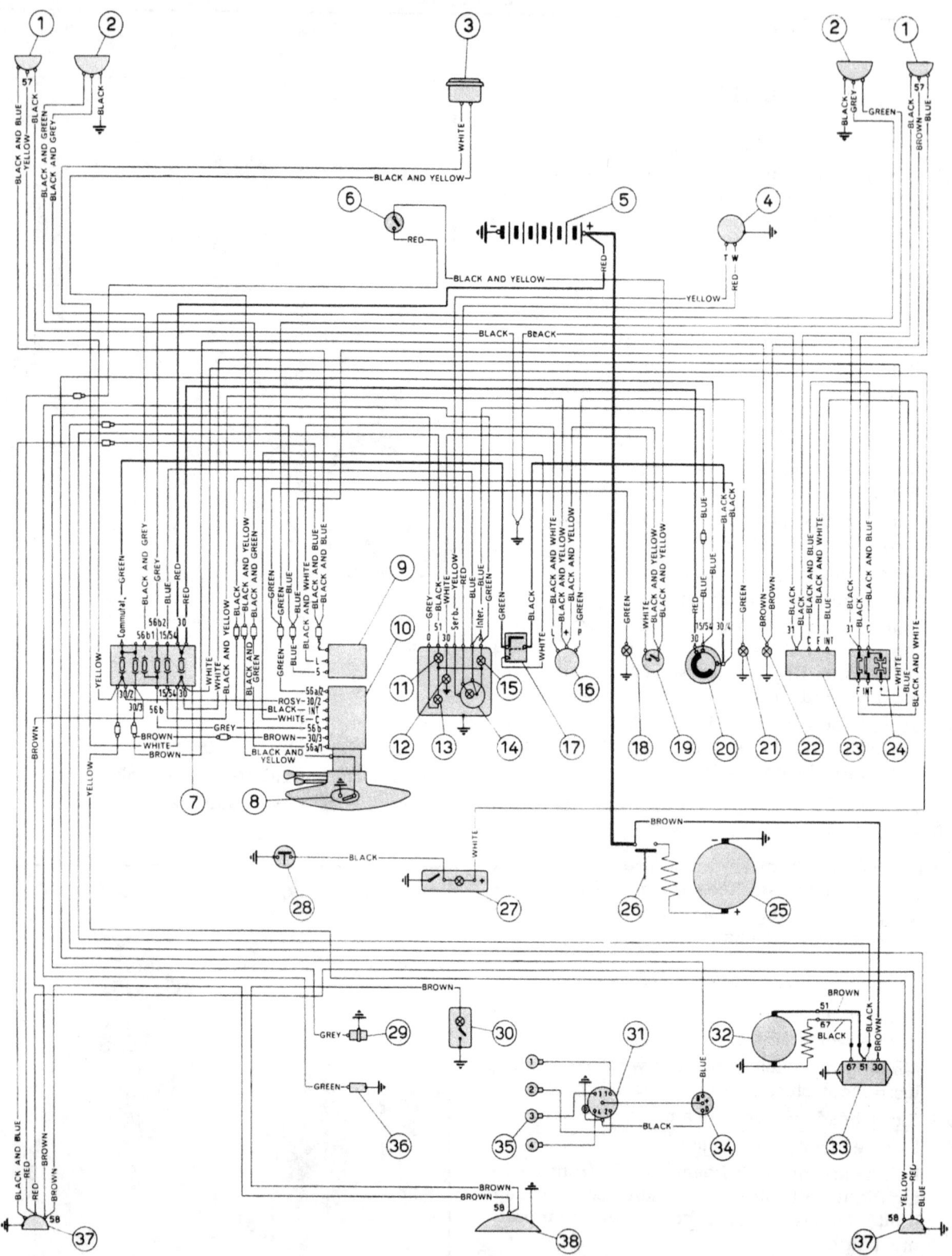

Fig. 469 - Wiring diagram. - Sedan Version 140.

1. Front parking and direction indicator lights. - 2. Headlights (high and low beam). - 3. Horn. - 4. Fuel gauge sending unit. - 5. Battery. - 6. Stop light pedal-operated switch. - 7. 8-A fuses. - 8. Horn button. - 9. Direction indicator switch. - 10. Outer light shifting switch. - 11. Generator charge indicator. - 12. Instrument cluster light. - 13. Low oil pressure indicator. - 14. Fuel gauge, with reserve supply indicator. - 15. High water temperature indicator. - 16. Flasher unit. - 17. Outer light switch. - 18. Headlamp high beam indicator. - 19. Instrument cluster light switch. - 20. Ignition lock switch. - 21. Direction indicator pilot light. - 22. Front parking light indicator. - 23. Windshield wiper motor. - 24. Windshield wiper switch. - 25. Starting motor. - 26. Starting motor switch. - 27. Courtesy light, with toggle switch. - 28. Courtesy light jam switch, between door and pillar. - 29. Low oil pressure indicator sending unit. - 30. Engine compartment light, with automatic switch. - 31. Ignition distributor. - 32. Generator. - 33. Generator regulator. - 34. Ignition coil. - 35. Spark plugs. - 36. High water temperature indicator sending unit. - 37. Tail parking, stop and direction indicator lights. - 38. License plate light.

NOTE - Mark ■ means that cable is provided with numbered strip or ferrule.

GAUGES AND CONTROLS

Instrument Cluster	page	309
Lock Switch	»	310
Hand Controls	»	310
Excessive Water Temperature Indicator Sending Unit	»	311
Fuel Gauge Sending Unit with Suction Tube	»	312
Flashing Direction Indicator System	»	315
Directional Signal and Outer Lighting Change-over Switch	»	317
Windshield Wiper	»	320
Windshield Wiper Toggle Switch	»	322
Horn	»	323
Electrical Accessory Items Specifications and Data	»	325

INSTRUMENT CLUSTER

All gauges are clustered in a single instrument mounted on facia, incorporating: insufficient engine oil pressure indicator, generator charge indicator, excessive water temperature indicator, fuel level gauge with reserve supply indicator, and speedometer with mileage recorder.

Low Engine Oil Pressure Indicator.

Shows red only when ignition is turned on. Goes out when operating oil pressure reaches at least 7.1 to 21.3 p.s.i. (0,5 to 1,5 kg/cm^2). With very warm engine, at an r.p.m. rate lower than 1000, indicator may light up even if pressure is under control and operation regular. (See page 95 for the description).

Generator Charge Indicator.

Shows red only when ignition is turned on. Goes out when generator output is sufficient for battery charge (engine at about 1100 r.p.m.; car at 14.3 m.p.h. - 23 km/h [Sedan] and 12.4 m.p.h. - 20 km/h [Multipla] in top gear).

Excessive Water Temperature Indicator.

Shows red only when ignition is turned on and water temperature at engine outlet is 230° F (110° C).
At this temperature the sending unit contacts close (see page 311).
During normal car operation the indicator should never light up. If the indicator lights up, this is a warning of danger. Stop engine immediately, let it cool off, and inspect:

Fig. 470 - Instrument cluster.

1. Insufficient engine oil pressure indicator. - 2. Generator charge indicator. - 3. Speedometer-mileage recorder. - 4. Excessive water temperature indicator. - 5. Fuel level gauge. - 6. Fuel reserve supply indicator.

« Sedan ».

a) Generator, water pump and fan drive belts tension.

b) Opening of engine compartment air discharge control shutter and thermostat.

c) Cooling system for steam leaks.

d) Engine lubrication system efficiency.

« Multipla ».

a) Generator, water pump and fan drive belts tension.

b) Cooling system for steam leaks (hoses, cap, etc.).

c) Lubrication system efficiency.

If items inspected are not at fault, check thermostat installed in engine-to-radiator line for correct operation.

The thermostat should open when cooling water temperature reaches 162° to 171° F (72° to 77° C).

NOTE - The great importance of this indication in ensuring satisfactory engine operation within safe temperature limits, calls for a periodical efficiency test. This check can be performed on car, by simply inserting the ignition circuit and connecting sending unit terminal (after removing its rubber hood) to ground (cylinder head) by a jumper. The indicator bulb should glow; if it does not, check bulb and replace, if necessary.

Fig. 471 - Lock switch key positions.

Position 0: all circuits OFF (permits withdrawal of key). - Position 1: engine ignition and services ON (key cannot be withdrawan). Position 2: parking lights ON, with outer lighting switch lever in position 1 (permits withdrawal of key).

Fuel Level Gauge, with Reserve Supply Indicator.

Gives level readings only when ignition is turned on.

A red indicator incorporated in gauge, glows when .9 to 1.3 U. S. Gals. - .7 to 1.1 Imp. Gals. (3,5 to 5 liters) of fuel remain in reserve. Refer to the directions given under « Fuel Gauge Sending Unit » on page 312 also for servicing of fuel level gauge.

Speedometer-Mileage Recorder.

Maximum speed limits corresponding to the different gears (after 1800 miles [3000 km] running-in) era indicated by red spots on dial.

LOCK SWITCH

This switch (fig. 471) is provided with two keys (one is a spare). Insert and rotate key rightwards (position 1) to control ignition and various service circuits, and leftwards (position 2) for night parking (change-over switch lever in position 1) (fig. 477). With key in position 1 the following circuits are energized: fuel level gauge and relevant reserve supply indicator, generator charge indicator, insufficient oil pressure indicator, excessive engine water temperature indicator, direction indicators and their pilot light, stop lights, instrument panel light, headlamps (high and low beams), number plate light, parking lights and engine compartment light.

The key may be withdrawn from switch only when set in positions 0 and 2.

NOTE - The vehicles for export to U.S.A., starting from the serial number 816159, « Sedan », and number 072211, « Multipla », have been fitted with an ignition key-switch (on instrument panel) which controls also the engine starting and can be set in the following positions (see fig. 523 on 600/D section):

Position 0: engine stationary; all lights off.

Position 1 (rightward): ignition and sundry lights on (key not withdrawable).

Position 2 (rightward): engine starting (key returns automatically to position 1).

Position 3 (leftward): engine stationary; parking, tail and license plate lights on, with the main switch in « on » position (key can be withdrawn).

Repairs.

The lock switch has been designed to warrant long life of components, both electrical and mechanical, and best possible performance and therefore troubles are unlikely to occur.

The switch is of the fully enclosed type and, therefore, should be replaced rather than attempt any repair.

HAND CONTROLS

Starter motor and carburetor starting device control levers are located on tunnel between the two front seats.

Starter Control Lever.

This lever controls starter pinion engagement on flywheel ring gear and switch on starter.

ELECTRICAL

Carburetor Starting Device Lever.

For the use of this lever see Chapter « Carburetor » on page 81.

Throttle Control.

Generally, this control (placed below the facia) should be used only if engine shows a tendency to stop when idling, after cold starts. In this case the control may be pulled out slightly as a temporary remedy.

Horn Button.

On steering wheel hub a push button is provided, for horn control. To disassemble the push button, insert a screwdriver tip between button and chromium plated frame and pry it off. Then, disconnect the cable (3, fig. 325) from socket on button.

EXCESSIVE WATER TEMPERATURE INDICATOR SENDING UNIT

Description.

The unit consists mainly of the following parts:
— Metal container.
— Bi-metallic lamina, cantilever-mounted on container bottom.
— Silver ground contact, secured to bi-metallic lamina free end.
— Stationary contact, also of silver, fixed to the end of a threaded dowel.
— Thermo-setting plastic insulating bush, applied to the open end of container by a conical coupling and form-locked over the container itself.
Coaxially mounted with insulating bush is a threaded hollow metal sleeve on which the stationary contact carrier dowel is screwed.
— Plug-in receptacle, arranged in a special cylindrical seat on bush outer face and connected to stationary contact.
To prevent water infiltrations into container, the bush-to-container coupling area is made tight with sealing compound. In the same manner, also the outer end of stationary contact carrier dowel is adequately sealed after sending unit setting.
Furthermore, the receptacle is protected by a heat-resistant rubber boot, press-fitted on bush outer end.

Fig. 473 - Engine compartment (Sedan).
1. High water temperature indicator sending unit. - 2. Cylinder head-to-water pump hose. - 3. Cylinder head-to-radiator water hose. - 4. Water radiator and filler cap. - 5. Fan. - 6. Engine ground cable. - 7. Water pump.

Location.

The sending unit is placed on engine cylinder head as shown in fig. 473.
Cylinder head and sending unit mating faces are perfectly smooth and level, to ensure good thermal conductivity.

Operation.

When engine is cold, and up to rated engine operations temperature, contacts are open.
When temperature exceeds a predetermined value of 230° to 248° F (110° to 120° C) the bi-metallic lamina bows and brings contacts together, this closing the circuit and lighting up the indicator on instrument panel.

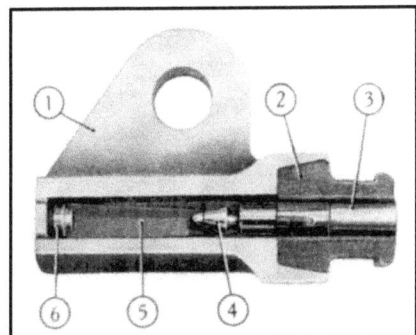

Fig. 472 - Excessive engine water temperature indicator sending unit.
1. Metal container. - 2. Insulating bush. - 3. Plug-in receptacle. - 4. Stationary contact. - 5. Bi-metallic lamina (its free end carries the ground contact). - 6. Lamina mounting.

Insulation resistance.

The insulation between terminal and ground (with open contacts) should be not less than 20 MΩ at 500 V, direct current; the measurement may be carried out by a megohmmeter.

Operation test.

Secure sending unit on a 3.937" (100 mm) diameter, .78" (20 mm) thick aluminum plate having a flat and smooth surface.

Connect switch terminals to a 12 V electrical circuit including a 5-W bulb.

Immerse the plate partially in an oil bath, so that the sending unit does not touch the oil. Heat slowly oil so that its temperature increases 1.8° F (1° C) per minute. Check temperature by dipping an accurate thermometer in an oil-filter pocket machined in plate.

The test bulb should glow when plate temperature reaches 230° to 248° F (110° to 120° C). No re-setting of sending unit is permitted.

Should the unit fail to operate correctly at specified value during the test, discard and install a new unit.

NOTE - If it is found that sending unit is inaccurate, that is, indicator glows at temperatures other than 230° to 248° F (110° to 120° C) replace sending unit, without attempting any re-setting.

Directions for installation.

Maximum care is required in the installation of the sending unit since, with this device, heat transfer from the cylinder head takes place by conduction.

Therefore, before installation, check that resting surfaces of casing and cylinder head on which the unit is mounted are perfectly flat, smooth and clean, and free of any oil or grease.

Secure sending unit to cylinder head by tightening the mounting nuts and making sure that metal casing is true to copper plate.

Connect cable terminal to receptacle and install rubber boot.

CAUTION - To insure sending unit water-tightness, the rubber boot lower end provided with lip must be force-fitted on its seat on casing.

FUEL GAUGE SENDING UNIT WITH SUCTION TUBE

General.

This electrically-operated tank unit consists of a variable-resistor with movable contact arm, having an additional contact for the panel-mounted reserve supply indicator bulb.

Through a rod, the contact arm is operated by a cork float and calibrates the ohmic resistance according to fuel level, i. e., depending on the amount of fuel present in the tank.

At a given float position, corresponding to the level of fuel reserve supply, the contact arm makes

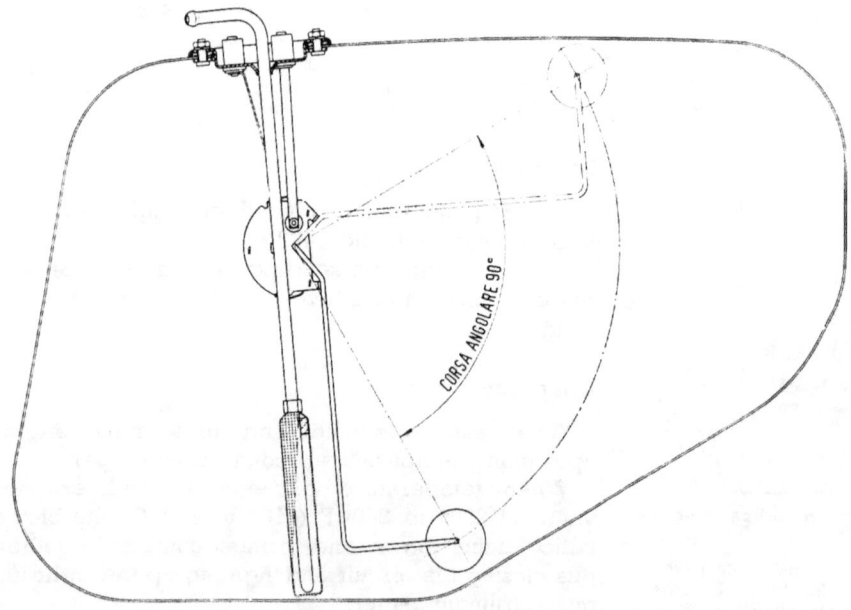

Fig. 474.

Fuel gauge sending unit with suction tube (Sedan).

Corsa angolare 90° = Travel angle: 90°.

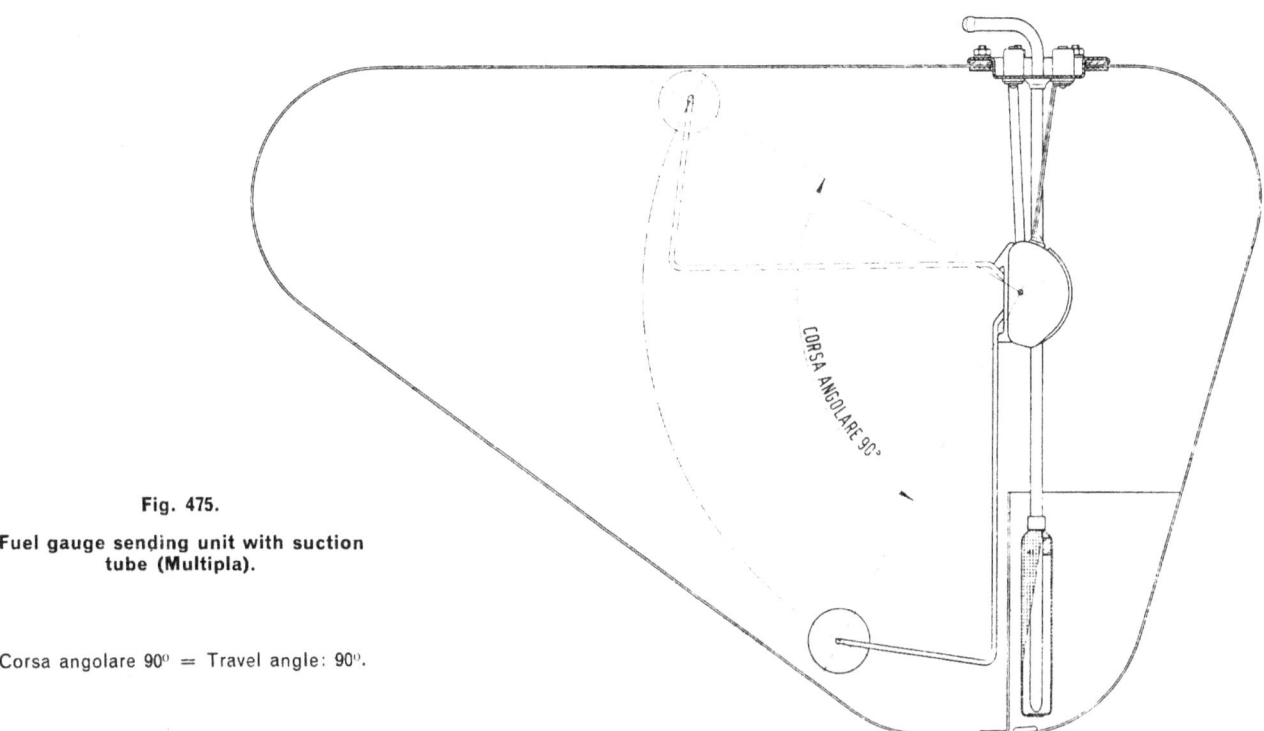

Fig. 475.

Fuel gauge sending unit with suction tube (Multipla).

Corsa angolare 90º = Travel angle: 90º.

the circuit with the additional contact and causes the reserve supply indicator bulb to light up.

The rheostat consists of an arc curved insulating mounting, around which the resistor wire is wound. Wire is insulated, although it is stripped at the touching area with the arm movable contact. The contact arm is a dual rotor being carried by a lever arm welded to the rotor pivot. The rotor pivot is the float rod which has been bent by 90º.

The dual rotor is made up of two lamina springs, namely:

— the first lamina spring has at an end the silver movable contact resting on rheostat;

— rue other lamina spring has at an end the additional brass movable contact for the reserve supply indicator circuit.

The rheostat is secured to and inclosed in a sheet metal casing being welded straight to the fuel tank suction tube, which is one piece with the sending unit.

The lower end of the fuel suction tube is provided with a filter gauze.

The sending unit and suction tube assembly is secured to the fuel tank through a metal flange with a rubber lining for sealing purposes.

The metal flange is welded straight to the bottom end of fuel suction tube and carries two plug-in sockets.

The electrical circuit between rheostat and socket is provided by a brass lamina connector. The same applies to the circuit between reserve supply indicator brass stationary contact and its socket.

The assembly has been designed for long life and reliability both from mechanical and electrical viewpoint, as well as operation safety.

Considering the above, the sending unit is of the locked type and removal of rheostat cannot be made other than by unfastening the metal casing cover.

Therefore, in case of internal failures (see following paras), the whole sending unit should be replaced.

The sending unit wiring diagram is shown in figs. 458, 462 and 469.

Check Data.

1) Following is a chart tabulating the sending unit ohmic resistance values (between terminal « T » and ground) in respect of the amount of fuel contained in the tank:

Fuel amounts in tank (referred to tank capacity)	Sending unit resistance values Ω
Empty	3 to 8
One fourth	25 to 32
A half	42 to 50
Three quarters	59 to 68
Full	86 to 91

2) The contact for fuel reserve supply indication must close when .9 to 1.3 U. S. Gals. - .7 to 1.3 Imp. Gals. (3,5-5 litres) of gasoline remain in tank.

Trouble Shooting.

The following conditions may be experienced:

a) **After bringing the lock switch key to «ignition ON» position, the level gauge pointer moves to the end of the scale even if tank is only partially filled.**

Possible causes are:

1) Interruption of the gauge coil shunted off the sending unit rheostat.

2) Broken connection between rheostat and sending unit control arm brush. Causes of this interruption may be:

— weak or broken brush pressure spring, which serves also as current lead;

— wear of movable contact beyond a certain limit;

— contamination, by oxides or other insulating deposits, of the movable contact or of the stripped resistor wire.

3) Broken connection of the sending unit rheostat at the attachment point on terminal «T».

4) Broken circuit between sending unit terminal «T» and the «Serb» plug-in connection on gauge.

5) Insufficient grounding between rheostat and metal container or between container and tank.

In cases 1), 2) and 3), replace the fuel level gauge or the sending unit.

In case 4) just restore circuit integrity, while in case 5), if the external part of unit is at fault - restore grounding efficiency.

b) **After bringing the lock switch key to «ignition ON» position, the level gauge pointer remains on the «zero» reading even if tank is partially filled.**

Possible causes are:

1) Broken connection of the gauge coil in series with sending unit rheostat.

2) Seizure of gauge moving parts.

3) Sending unit terminal «T» or rheostat end connected to it, short-circuited to ground.

4) Connection between sending unit terminal «T» and «Serb» plug-in connection on gauge, short-circuited to ground.

In cases 1) and 2) replace the level gauge, while in case 3) replace the sending unit.

In case 4) simply eliminate the short circuit.

c) **Fuel level gauge readings are incorrect beyond the tolerance range.**

Main possible causes are:

1) Misadjustment of fuel level gauge (loosening of coils in their seats, excessive drag of moving parts, etc.).

2) Distortion of float-carrying rod in tank.

In case 1) replace the gauge. In case 2), just restore rod to specified configuration followed by a check of sending unit ohmic resistances, as outlined in point 1) under «Check Data» (page 313).

d) **The fuel reserve supply indicator does not light up, even when level in tank has fallen to less than .9 U. S. Gals - .7 Imp. Gals (3,5 liters) (reserve minimum).**

First of all, check the bulb. If found inefficient, fit a new one and make sure operation is again normal.

Instead, if the bulb is not at fault, the trouble may be due to one of the following causes:

1) Poor contact of bulb in holder.

2) Broken circuit between sending unit terminal «W» and bulb terminal.

3) Movable arm contact lamina pressure spring for reserve supply indicator weak or broken, or excessive wear of movable contact.

If one of the troubles above mentioned occurs, a discontinuity will result in the circuit from movable to stationary contact on terminal «W».

4) Inadequate electrical continuity in the circuit between reserve supply indicator stationary contact and terminal «W».

5) Inefficient grounding between sending unit and tank.

In case 1) repair or, if necessary, replace the bulb holder.

In case 2) restore the connection between sending unit terminal «W» and bulb holder connection.

In cases 3) and 4), replace the sending unit.

In case 5) restore an adequate grounding.

Repairs.

The sending unit has been designed to warrant long life of components, both electrical and mechanical, and best possible performance.

In case of a faulty operation not ascribable to the cause in point c-2) under «Trouble Shooting», it is recommended to replace the complete sending unit.

FLASHING DIRECTION INDICATOR SYSTEM

The flashing light directional signal system utilizes the higher wattage filament (20-W) of front parking lamps and, at rear, the 20-Watt bulb of parking, direction indicators and stop lamps.

The system consists of: a directional signal switch, a winking device, the front and rear lamps mentioned above and a pilot light (5-W) incorporated in switch.

The directional signal switch is connected to flasher and signal lamps.

The flasher (fig. 476) is of the hot wire type and consists of:

— a magnetic core with winding A, in series with lamp circuits, and an additional auxiliary winding - formed of a few turns of wire - in series with the pilot light circuit;

— a main armature A_p, which opens and closes intermittently a contact by inserting and disinserting and additional resistor R in the circuit;

— an additional resistor R;

— a secondary armature A_1, that switches on and off the pilot light synchronously with the directional signal by closing and opening an auxiliary contact;

— a hot wire f, in series with resistor R.

The flasher is connected to the directional signal switch and to terminal 15/54 of ignition lock switch.

Operation.

In the « neutral » position (direction indicator toggle switch at centre circuit OFF) current does not flow in any part whatever of the system and the flasher armature contacts are open because main armature is held back by stretched wire f in series with resistor R, and the auxiliary armature by the relevant preload spring. Therefore, resistor R is inserted and pilot light is off.

By shifting toggle switch lever (to the right or left), one of the two circuits closes (either the right or the left one).

The current, coming from battery, flows through the main armature A_p, wire F, resistor R, winding A of flasher (fig. 476), the 20-Watt lamp bulb filaments and ground. Since flow is limited by resistor R, the current is not sufficient to cause filaments to glow, but it does heat wire f which lengthens and allows main armature to close the contact and shorts the wire itself and resistor R.

Then, current increases and filaments glow. Wire f, through which no current now flows, cools off and shortens, and hence opens the main armature contact again, thus inserting resistor R in the circuit.

Current drops, filaments go out, and the cycle is repeated.

The auxiliary contact for the pilot light operates as follows: when current in main circuit increases (phase in which signal lamp bulb filaments glow), winding A attracts auxiliary armature A_1 and closes the contact of pilot light S, which will light up and flash with direction indicator lamp signals; when current drops (the higher wattage filaments fade

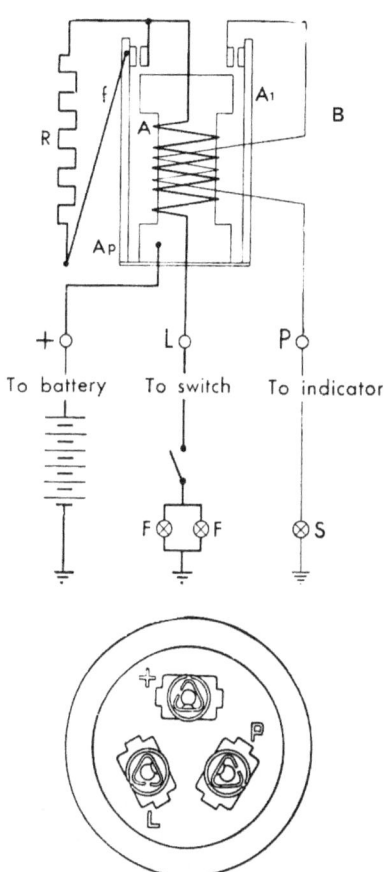

Fig. 476 - Winking device operation diagram, for bench testing, and flasher connection end view.

A. Series winding. - A_p. Main armature. - A_1. Auxiliary armature. - B. Auxiliary winding. - F. Front and rear parking and direction indicator lamps. - L. Clamp. - P. Terminal. - R. Additional resistance. S. Pilot light. - f. Thermostatic wire. - +. Terminal for connection to terminal 15/54 of lock switch.

out), the auxiliary armature return spring overcomes the magnetic attraction of winding A, opens contacts of pilot light S, which will go out. The duration of each cycle is less than 1 second.

Winding B in series with auxiliary circuit has the purpose of preventing auxiliary armature contacts from damage (welding) in case of short circuit between terminal P and ground. This shorting could take place when, for any reason whatever, clamp P is accidentally connected to ground. Were it not for winding B, this occurrence would originate a marked arcing when contacts open and heavy welding when contacts close while the fuse cannot interrupt the circuit before contacts become completely stuck together, at which time it would be too late.

As a matter of fact, since one flash takes less than a second, the ON-cycle is too short to blow the direction indicator fuse on account of its thermal inertia.

Thanks to winding B, instead, the short circuit current magnetically locks the auxiliary armature, while its contacts are closed until the fuse blows.

Flasher Bench Testing.

This device must be bench-tested according to the operation diagram shown in fig. 476.

The two bulbs F, connected in parallel, must have the same power as the one fitted on the car (20-Watts), because the flasher is connected in series with these lamps and operation cannot be regular if the load is not the standard one and, what is more, the device is liable to be damaged if the current is too high.

WARNING

Never insert terminal « L » directly to ground without having first connected in series the bulbs specified, or else the flasher will be irreparably damaged.

For the same reason terminal « L » must never be shorted to ground nor must there be any short-circuits in all leads from said terminal to bulbs.

The flasher must never receive blows of any kind, since the very delicate components could easily be damaged with consequent breakages, misadjustments, etc.

Flasher operation characteristics are:

1) At a nominal tension of 12 V and with a nominal bulb load totalling 40-Watts, the number of flashing cycles per minute at 68º F (20º C) must be 78 ± 8.

2) During the first two seconds of operation it should provide at least two flashing signals.

3) Bulb filaments must glow fully and immediately in the first part of the cycle, and must cease glowing almost entirely in the second part.

4) The time taken to glow must be almost equal to that taken to fade out.

5) With a tension 1.25 times the nominal one (15 V), at a temperature of 104º F (40º C), the cycles must not exceed 100 per minute.

6) With a tension 0.8 times the nominal one (9.5 V), at a temperature of —4º F (—20º C), the cycles must not be less than 45 per minute.

7) The contact of pilot light must flash the bulb synchronously with the cycles, when both bulbs F are operative.

When one of the two bulbs on the same side fails, the pilot light should not flash; if this occurs, the driver is warned of one of the following faults in the system:

— broken or burnt filament in one of the bulbs;

— faulty contact between lamp and socket due to weakening, failure or oxidation of the current carrier spring lamina;

— open circuit between lamp and switch;

— defective grounding of one of the lamps.

Trouble Shooting.

Troubles that may arise during direction indicator operation are many and different in nature.

The following instructions refer both to right and left signalling circuits:

1. - **Both lamps are regularly operative but pilot light does not glow.**

Possible causes independent of flasher are:

— burnt pilot light bulb;

— broken connection between terminal « P » and pilot light bulb;

— defective contact of pilot bulb in socket.

Possible causes in flasher are:

— shorted turns in winding « A »;

— auxiliary contacts oxidized or worn to such an extent that bulb circuit can no longer be closed;

— unsoldering of auxiliary armature « A_1 » movable contact or of fixed contact;

— unsoldering of auxiliary winding « B » end from stationary contact support;

— unsoldering of auxiliary winding « B » end from terminal « P »;

— excessive core-to-auxiliary armature « A_1 » air gap;

— excessive load of auxiliary armature « A » spring;

— broken auxiliary winding « B ».

2. - **Only one lamp is operative (front or rear) and pilot light does not glow (see point 7 under « Warning » above).**

Possible causes:

— broken 20-Watts filament in the bulb of the inoperative lamp;

— broken cable between the inoperative lamp and the directional signal switch;

— defective contact between inoperative lamp bulb and socket lamina;

— defective grounding of inoperative lamp.

3. - **Lamps (front, rear and pilot light) are all inoperative.**

Possible causes independent of flasher are:

— blown fuse, caused by a short circuit (see paragraph « Operation »);

— broken main lead between ignition lock switch terminal « 15/54 » and flasher positive (« + ») terminal;

— broken cable between flasher terminal « L » and directional signal switch terminal « L »;

— broken cables between directional signal switch and lamps;

— defective grounding of lamps;

— dirty, oxidized or worn directional signal switch contacts;

— both lamps on the same side burnt;

— defective contact with socket of both lamps on the same side.

Possible causes in flasher are:

— resistor « R » broken;

— unsoldering of resistor « R » from main stationary contact support;

— main contacts strongly oxidized;

— unsoldering of main armature « A_p » movable contact or unsoldering of stationary contact from its support;

— winding « A » broken;

— winding « A » end unsoldered from main stationary contact support;

— unsoldering of winding « A » end from terminal « L ».

4. - **Direction indicator lamps and pilot light flash with abnormal intermittence or flashing times (on - off) are much different.**

The flasher is misadjusted; mainly, this occurs after the flasher receives a blow; less frequently the cause may be a weakening or breakage of wire « f ».

5. - **Indicator lamps and pilot light glow but do not flash.**

Causes are located in flasher and may be:

— breaking or weakening of wire « f », in which case main contacts remain permanently closed;

— welding of main contacts.

6. - **Indicator lamps glow but do not flash; pilot light remains off.**

Causes are located in flasher and are due to the main winding being directly in contact with the core owing to poor insulation.

In case the cause for trouble is located in the system and not in the flasher, repairs do not require any special instructions (replacement of bulbs, cleaning of contacts, proper arrangement of connections, etc.).

Before replacing a burnt fuse, look for the cause, i. e., the short circuit from which the blowing originated.

If the short circuit is detected in a portion of lead between terminal « L » of flasher and the lamps, install a new flasher, since most likely the old one is damaged.

To determine whether or not the trouble is in flasher, when all indications from inspection point to this unit as the source of trouble, check flasher on test bench as outlined above.

Flashers are delicate units and, for this reason, cannot be repaired. Therefore, always replace faulty flashers, without even attempting any repairs.

SELF-CANCELLING DIRECTIONAL SIGNAL SWITCH-OUTER LIGHTING CHANGE OVER SWITCH

Description.

These two switches form a centralized control unit consisting of:

— directional signal switch, which returns automatically to rest position after negotiating the turn, when steering wheel is brought back to straightforward drive position;

— change-over switch, controlling the outer lights (parking, high and low beams) and the headlamp flashes.

The unit is located on steering column, under steering wheel.

Directional Signal Switch.

Is controlled by the upper (shorter) lever (blue, fig. 477) of the unit. The lever may take three positions determined by a click, the central position being the neutral. The upward or downward movement of the lever controls a revolving drum which, by establishing proper contacts, sends a pulsating current from flasher to front and rear directional lamps on the side of the turn to be negotiated. At the same time the drum brings one of the two triggers to the latching position.

The return of the lever to neutral is automatic with the return of wheels to straightforward drive, and is controlled by a two-lobe cam spring mounted at center of steering wheel.

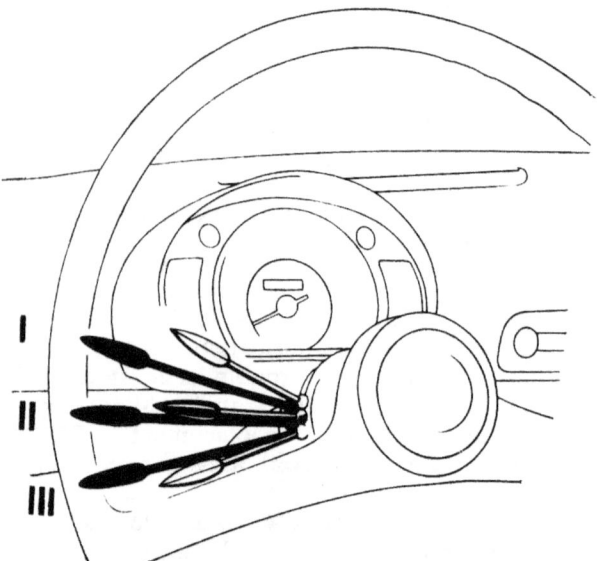

Fig. 477 - **Positions of outer lighting and direction indicator control levers.**

Direction indicators control lever (blue): D. Lever in position for right turn signalling; S. Lever in position for left turn signalling.
Outer lighting switch control lever (red): I. Parking and number plate lights ON; II. Low beam, parking and number plate lights ON; III. High beam, parking and number plate lights ON.

NOTE - On installation of directional signal switch-outer lighting change-over switch unit, lay a coat of vaseline on the horn control lamina contact, fitted on the unit, and on the contact ring, fitted on steering wheel hub. Do not overstretch cables.

When the wheels are steered, one of the two lobes catches the drum control trigger which rotates around its fulcrum. The further rotation of the steering shaft causes the trigger disengagement from the lobe and its return to rest position under the action of its coil load spring. The latching mechanism is thus « loaded ». Subsequently, when the steering wheel is brought back to straightforward drive position, the spring lobe catches the trigger, which rotates about its fulcrum and exerts a pressure on the inner wall of a seat provided in the drum. Under this pressure the drum revolves and returns to rest position together with the control lever. After this movement, also the trigger frees the spring lobe and returns to rest position.

Change-Over Switch.

Is controlled by the lower (longer) lever (red, fig. 477) which may be set in the following three positions being shifted by a click:

1 - Front and rear parking lamps, and number plate lamp ON.

2 - Headlamp low beam, parking and number plate lamps ON.

3 - Headlamp high beam, parking and number plate lamps ON.

NOTE - Outer lighting change-over switch is energized by operating the outer lighting switch on instrument panel.

Furthermore, by pushing the lever towards the steering wheel, from any lever position excepting No. 2, the flashing of low beams is obtained.

The connection of the electric circuits is obtained by sprung contacts carried on the two revolving drums, and by stationary contacts mounted on the two relevant plastic insulating supports.

Switch Unit Removal.

1) By a screwdriver pry off the horn push-button at steering wheel center.

2) Disconnect the plug-in contact.

3) Unscrew the steering wheel hold-down nut.

4) Remove steering wheel from shaft.

5) Slacken the bolt securing the steering column support to body.

6) Disinsert all plug-in contacts of the switch unit.

7) Remove the switch unit from steering column.

Switch Unit Installation.

Reverse the removal operations. After installation check that, with steering wheel in straightforward drive position and directional signal switch lever in neutral, the reference index on the outer face of the directional signal switch drums is in line with the index on steering wheel hub.

Trouble Shooting.

Possible causes for faulty operation are:

A) **Directional Signal Switch.**

1. - **The lever does not return automatically to neutral after straightening the wheels.**

   The trouble may originate from:
   a) defects in the latching mechanism such as:
      i) failure or weakening of trigger return spring;

ii) seizing of triggers;

iii) excessive play of triggers on fulcrum pin;

iv) failure of trigger fulcrum pins;

v) deformations of triggers;

vi) excessive wear of trigger rollers.

Any of the above defects call for the replacement of the complete unit.

b) Failure, weakening or wear of the two-lobe spring fixed at center of steering wheel.

Replace the spring.

2. - Lever rotation clicks not marked or practically inexistent.

The trouble may originate from:

a) Failure of the seat in revolving drum for positioning ball.

b) Wear, or failure, of positioning rack teeth.

In either case, replace the complete unit.

3. - With lever in the upper of lower position, the directional signal flashes occasionally or does not glow at all.

After checking external connections, flasher, lamps and bulbs, and all are faultless, the trouble may be due to:

a) Seizure of movable contact in its seat in revolving drum, so that it does not close the circuit on the fixed contacts.

b) Excessive wear of movable and fixed contacts.

c) Failure or weakening of the movable contact coil load spring.

d) Excessive clearance of revolving drum in its seat. This clearance determines an inadequate rocking of revolving drum, such that in some cases the movable contact clears the fixed contacts.

e) Disconnected fixed contact current leads.

In all the above cases, replace the complete unit.

4. - Remarkable effort required to shift the lever or seizing of the lever in any of the three positions.

The trouble may originate from:

Excessive projection of positioning ball (more than its diameter) from its seat. In this case, instead of entering its seat and compressing the load spring, the ball remains squeezed between the seat edge and a tooth of the rack, thus acting as a wedge. This requires a much greater effort to shift the lever and in some cases may also lock the control. Should this occur, replace the complete unit.

B) Outer Lighting Change-Over Switch.

1. - While tripping the lever for headlamp flashes, abnormal opening or closing of the circuits takes place.

The trouble may originate from:

a) Excessive clearance of revolving drum in its seat. This clearance, during the above lever shifts. determines an excessive rocking of revolving drum, whereby the movable contacts will not close the circuit with fixed contacts.

b) Excessive wear of movable and fixed contacts.

c) Seizure of the movable contact in its seat in the revolving drum.

d) Failure or weakening of the movable contact coil spring.

In these cases replace the complete unit.

2. - In whichever position the lever is tripped, the headlamp low beams keep staying ON.

The trouble may originate from:

a) Seizure of the flashing control spring contact trigger in its seat.

b) Loss in flashing control movable contact flexibility.

In either case replace the complete unit.

3. - When tripping the lever for headlamp flashes, the low beams are not switched ON.

The trouble may originate from:

a) Failure of the flashing control movable contact.

b) Oxidation of the flashing control movable and fixed contacts.

c) Wear of the flashing control trigger.

d) Wear of flashing control trigger seat surface in revolving drum.

e) Disconnection of fixed contact current leads.

In all the above cases, replace the complete unit.

4. - Lever rotation clicks not marked or practically inexistent.

Causes for trouble and relevant remedies are the same as outlined under point 2. for the Directional Signal Switch.

5. - Remarkable effort required to shift the lever, or seizing of the lever in any of its positions.

The cause of this trouble is the same as outlined under 4. for the Directional Signal Switch.

Replace the complete unit.

WINDSHIELD WIPER

It consists of a motor unit that drives wiper blades back and forth through a reduction gearing and linkage. The reduction gear includes a worm screw on armature shaft and a helical pinion. The motor, blade pivots and linkages are mounted on a sheet metal bracket, conferring the necessary rigidity to the system.

The unit is provided with an automatic parking device ensuring the return of blades to the position where visibility impairments are negligible. Below is a diagram (fig. 478) where the operation of this unit can be seen.

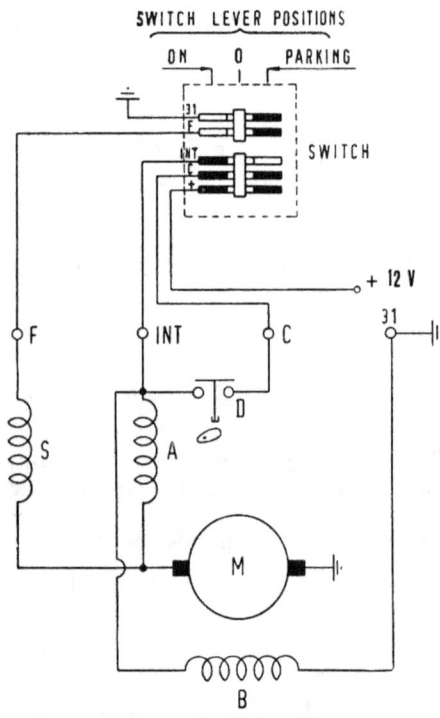

Fig. 478 - Windshield wiper wiring diagram.
A. Series winding. - B. Shunt winding. - D. Switch. - M. Motor. - S. Additional winding. — F. - INT. - C. = Terminals.

The windshield wiper is controlled by a lever switch which may assume the following three positions:

— **Up (position 1 or « ON »).** - Excited by windings A (series) and B (shunted), the motor runs the wipers at a 50-60 sweeps per min. rate.

— **Center (position 0 or « OFF »).** - Blades stop immediately, regardless of their position. All motor windings are excluded.

— **Down (position 2 or « PARKING »).** - With switch lever pressed down, blades are automatically parked. In this position also auxiliary winding S is energized.

When released, lever snaps back to OFF position. Winding S is formed by a few coils of heavy wire; it hence has low resistance and high current absorption, such as to produce a strong excitation e. m. f.

Since, as it is known, by strenghtening a d. c. motor magnetic field the motor rotational speed decreases and torque increases, following the insertion of winding S, the wiper motor will sensibly reduce the speed of blade sweep though still retaining such a torque as to enable blades to overcome possible obstacles on the glass (snow, ice, etc.).

Blades will park when switch D, incorporated in motor, is opened by the sliding sector fitted on rotating arm (for diagram simplicity, in fig. 478 said sector is represented as a cam).

The reduction in speed is necessary to prevent the sliding sector from overriding the opening position of switch D, since this position corresponds to blades parked against cowl.

This ensures best conditions of visibility.

Bench Testing.

Windshield wiper unit check data.

By feeding a 14-V current to the motor and by braking with a stall torque of .43 ft.lbs (6 kgcm) - obtained by a friction brake - the following should not be exceeded: a temperature increase of 122º F (50º C), a 60 r.p.m. speed when warm, and a current draw of 1.7 to 1.8 Amp. Stall torque at 14 V must not be less than 5 ft.lbs (70 kgcm) (warm and with shaft locked).

Trouble Shooting.

If wiper unit operation is faulty, or it does not operate at all, possible causes are:

   a) improper assembly on body;
   b) irregularities of motor unit.

An improper assembly on body may bring about a distortion of wiper mounting bracket.

The consequences of this are abnormal stresses on pivots and linkages resulting in irregular and difficult blade sweep.

In this case, check the unit for proper assembly on body, referring to « Wiper Assembly Instructions » as a guide.

As to point b), some of the most commonly encountered wiper motor troubles are:

1) With switch lever pressed down (parking position), the automatic parking of blades does not take place. Instead, blades keep on sweeping at reduced speed.

ELECTRICAL

The trouble is in this case caused by the sliding sector that fails to open switch D (fig. 478). Check by backing out the four reduction gear cover mounting screws, and uncover the sliding sector. If possible, suitably deform the sector to bring it again into contact with the rod tip of switch D.

2) **With switch lever pressed down (parking position), the automatic parking of blades does not take place. Instead, blades stop in whatever position.**

Cause: switch D does not close and, consequently, no current flows between terminals « C » and « INT ».

The trouble may originate from:

a) foreign matter lodged between the movable contact and the fixed contact of switch D;

b) sticking of movable contact operating pushrod in its seat;

c) weakening or failure of movable contact load spring.

In all cases replace the complete unit.

3) **The motor unit, though operating regularly, is remarkably noisy.**

This is due to abnormal reduction gear operation (out-of-true, tooth defects, excessive wear of pinion or worm, excessive play between brush and its holder, etc.).

Replace the motor unit.

4) **With switch lever pushed up (« ON » position) or pressed down (parking position), the wiper is inoperative.**

After ascertaining that the trouble is not imputable to wiring defects or switch, failure of wiper operation may be due to one of the following causes:

a) Shorted or interrupted windings A, B or S.

Replace the motor as an assembly.

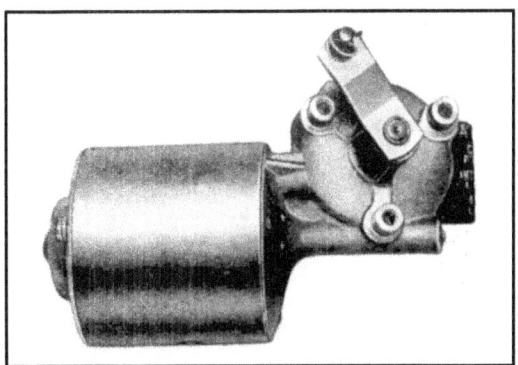

Fig. 479 - Windshield wiper motor unit.

b) Broken or unsoldered inner connections. If possible, repair very carefully, due attention being given to the soldering and insulation of contacts.

c) Failure of brush-to-commutator contact on account of the following causes:

c-1. Excessive brush wear.

c-2. Commutator fouling.

c-3. Locking of brush in brush-holder owing to poor clearance between the two parts.

In case c-1 replace the complete motor unit.

In case c-2 washing the commutator and then polishing it with very fine emery cloth is sufficient.

In case c-3 restore the brush-to-brush holder clearance to correct value.

Reassembly on Body.

When reinstalling the unit, follow carefully the sequence and directions given. For partial reassemblies, proceed as instructed in the relevant paragraphs. However, remember that checking also the parts that have not been disassembled is a good practice which will prove useful.

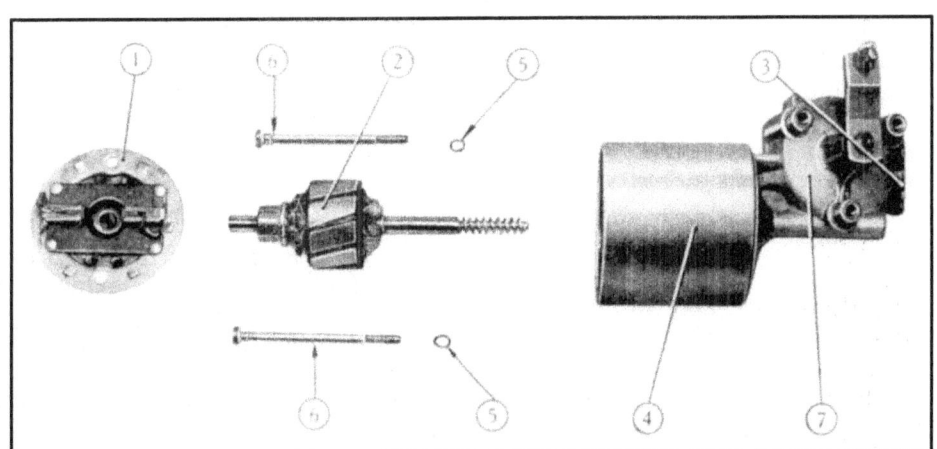

Fig. 480 - Windshield wiper motor components.

1. Commutator end head. - 2. Armature with worm screw. - 3. Terminal insulated carrier. - 4. Frame. - 5. Lockwashers. - 6. Screws, commutator end head and reduction gear to frame. - 7. Reduction gear.

1) Mount wiper on body by fully tightening the nuts fixing the pivots on which arms are fitted. Ensure that rubber sealing bushes between pivots and body are correctly assembled, to prevent water infiltrations.

Next, secure mounting bracket lower edge to body by means of the special square bracket. Do not deform mounting bracket to provide proper mating with body surface. Instead, resort to the square bracket which, to this end, is provided with adjusting slots. In this way, linkages will not be bent and will not undergo abnormal stresses during operation.

2) To fit motor unit on mounting bracket there is no particular rule to be followed excepting: a proper tightening of screws, a correct assembly of the main link on pivot lever, and a proper locking of fastener on pivot lever to prevent its unseating during operation.

3) After having established all electrical connections, taking into due account cable identification markings, switch on and run the motor for a few seconds at the same time checking all switch positions, including the automatic parking (position 2), so that stopping of the sweep will take place with pivots in parking position, which is the one for wiper arm mounting. If no assembly defects are found, check the motor unit. This does not require the removal of wiper unit assembly. To remove motor unit alone, disconnect the motor rotating lever-to-main link connection by taking off, either with fingers or screwdriver, the spring fastener clipped on link pin groove. Then, take off the screws fixing motor on mounting bracket.

If wiper unit operation is noisy, particularly on a dry windscreen, it is advisable to replace the complete unit. This noisiness must be ascribed to irregular operation of motor reduction gearing. In time, gears will wear and may seize, or break, thus rendering the unit unserviceable.

4) On pivots (see point 1), install the spring washer, pivot cover and wiper arms. Then, fully tighten the nuts **with wiper arms parked** (to the left, looking at windshield).

These nuts must be properly and carefully tightened, or else blades may become misadjusted and give rise to the previously described trouble of stopping the motor under tension and its subsequent burning, unless switch is immediately turned OFF.

5) Check that wiper arms may be tilted 100° downwards without striking against cowl or front compartment lid.

6) Check that blade pressure on glass is 10.6 to 12.3 oz. (300 to 350 grams).

7) Run wiper for approximately two minutes and check for smooth and quiet operation.

WINDSHIELD WIPER TOGGLE SWITCH

The switch may assume the following three positions:

— **Up**: wiper is switched ON even if ignition is OFF.

— **Center**: blades stop immediately in whatever position they are on glass.

— **Down**: blades will automatically park. To obtain this, switch lever must be kept down by finger pressure. As soon as released, lever will snap back to **Center** position.

Wiper Switch Trouble Shooting.

The more common troubles that might be met are:

1) Excessive effort needed to operate switch lever.

Cause: seizure of lever in its seat on account of poor lubrication, accumulation of foreign matter, etc.

Remedy: take down switch from instrument panel, wash movable contacts control mechanism in gasoline and lubricate the control lever and its sliding seat, with pure ropy vaseline.

2) One of the two rollers (movable contacts) does not exert sufficient pressure on its stationary contacts, thus determining a poor or non-existent electrical circuit.

This is generally attributed to an excessively reduced radial clearance of switch control lever in its seat.

In this case, in fact, the seat of the lever, at whose end is fitted the plastic support guiding the movable contacts, does not permit the support to slide a sufficient amount to evenly distribute the spring load on both movable contacts.

Repairs.

The switch has been designed to ensure trouble-free operation and maximum possible electrical and mechanical life.

In case of faulty operation not ascribable to cause 1) of the previous paragraph, it is advisable to replace the switch as an assembly without attempting any repair.

HORN

The horn circuit comprises: the horn, pushbutton at center of steering wheel and ground (obtained through car body).

One terminal is connected to battery; the other, having the function of closing the circuit through ground, is connected to pushbutton on steering wheel.

The horn includes a diaphragm that is caused to vibrate rapidly by an electromagnet. When current flows through the electromagnet winding, the induced magnetic field attracts an armature towards the winding core. The armature is fixed to the horn diaphragm so that a movement of the armature causes a distortion of the diaphragm. At the same time the horn points open so that the horn winding circuit is also opened. The magnetic field of the winding collapses, the armature is released, and returns to its original position as the distortion of the diaphragm is relieved. When this takes place, the point close, the winding is again energized, the armature is once more attracted and the cycle is then repeated for a number of times.

The repeated distortion of the diaphragm causes its vibration which produces the warning signal.

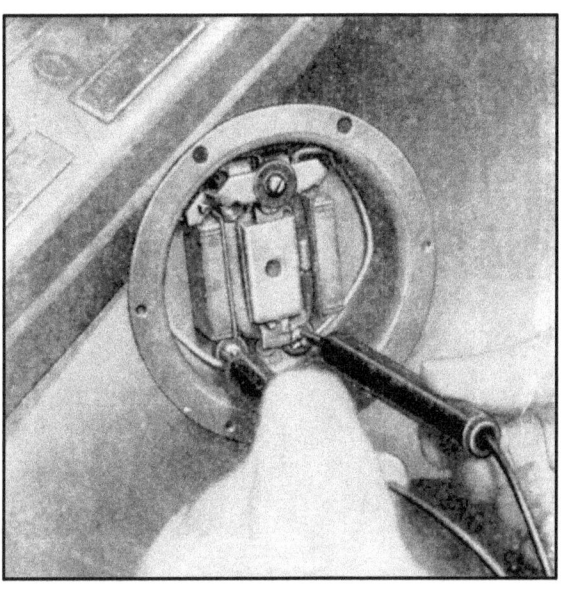

Fig. 482 - Checking magnetizing coil soundness.

Trouble Shooting.

If horn is inoperative, possible causes are:

1) Damaged horn.

2) Broken connection between battery and horn.

3) Broken connection between horn and pushbutton.

4) Damaged push button mechanism.

5) Directional signal and outer lighting change over switch blade contact failing to adhere to steering wheel hub ring contact.

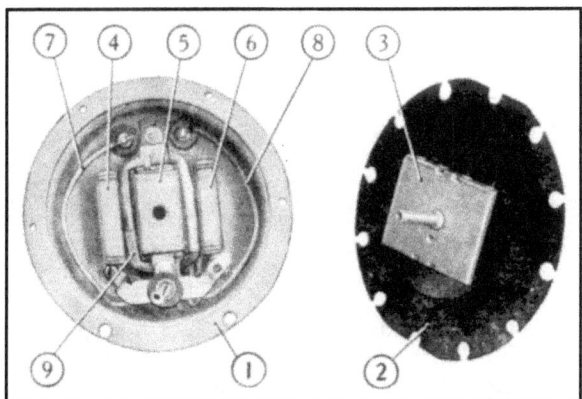

Fig. 481 - Partially disassembled horn.

1. Horn body. - 2. Diaphragm. - 3. Armature. - 4, 5 and 6. Core. - 7. Cable: terminal-condenser-stationary contact. - 8. Cable: terminal-magnetizing coil. - 9. Electromagnet winding.

6) Current lead off horn blade contact on directional signal and outer lighting switch.

Damages to horn may be:

1-a) Distorted or broken diaphragm.

1-b) Connections, or inner windings, broken or burnt.

1-c) Electromagnet contact points deteriorated or excessively worn.

In each of these cases a replacement of the horn will be necessary.

In case 1-c) if wear or deterioration of contacts is not excessive, an adjustment may be made by the adjusting screw after having cleaned the contact points with a fine-cut file.

After adjustment, apply some paint on the screw for a twofold purpose: as a check on any unwanted tamperings and as a seal against possible water infiltrations to horn through screw threads.

In case the horn itself seems to be in perfect order, look for troubles described in points 2), 3) and 4).

The trouble mentioned in point 2) may be checked by means of a jumper connection. That is, connect battery directly to horn and press the pushbutton: if horn signals, the defect will be due to a broken connection between battery and horn.

A similar procedure may be followed for the defect mentioned in point 3).

If even after all these checks no sound is heard, check pushbutton.

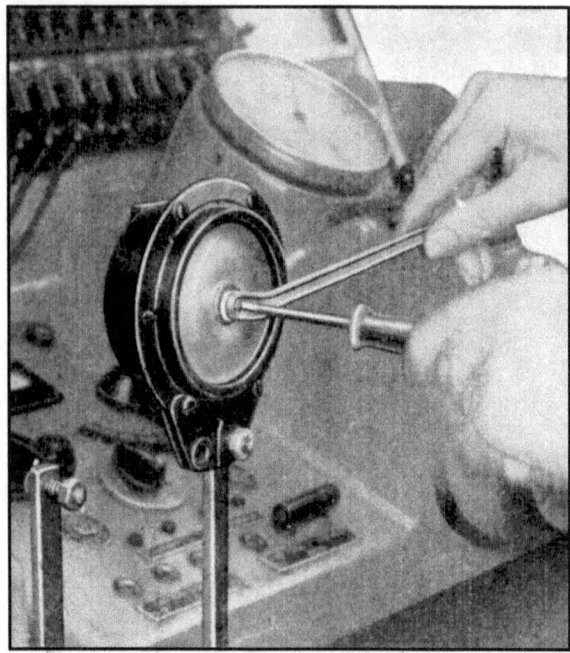

Fig. 483 - Horn sound adjustment.
Obtained by adjusting the armature air gap.

It will then be necessary to single out the trouble among the following causes:

4-1) Fixed and movable contacts oxidized or dirty.

4-2) Ring on which lower end of spring rests is oxidized or dirty.

Fig. 484 - Horn sound adjustment.
1-2. Current plugs. - 3. Contact setscrew.

If both defects are noticed, it will be convenient to check that return spring has not weakened through use, since this can bring about improper opening of the circuit with consequent smelting of contacts and their oxidation.

If trouble is to be traced to point 5), causes may be as follows:

5-1. Blade contact weak or broken.

5-2. Blade contact point worn.

5-3. Steering wheel ring contact worn at blade contact point.

In cases 5-1 and 5-2, replace the directional signal and outer lighting change-over switch assembly. In case 5-3, just replace the steering wheel hub ring contact.

If trouble is to be traced to point 6), replace the directional signal and outer lighting change-over switch assembly.

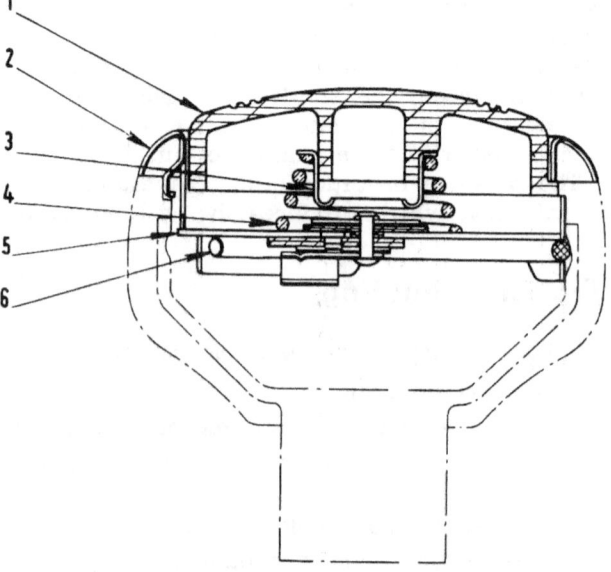

Fig. 485 - Horn control assembly.
1. Horn button. - 2. Horn control stationary contact nut. - 3. Movable contact. - 4. Spring. - 5. Stationary contact assembly. - 6. Stationary contact nut snap ring.

NOTE - Under any circumstances, prior to reassembling, remember recommendations as per « **NOTE** » under « Directional Signal and Outer Lighting Change-over Switch Trouble Shooting » (page 318).

Still to be pointed out is the fact that, at times, even with horn operating and with its components (including the contacts) in good condition, the signal obtained may not be pure and not sufficiently loud: in such cases, the breaker is misadjusted. It will suffice to act conveniently on the adjusting screw until the desired sound is obtained.

ELECTRICAL

Removal and Installation.

No special instructions are required for horn removal and installation.

The only precaution to take is that the rubber gasket bonded to horn body must not be detached.

If horn must be replaced, before installing the new horn bond on the latter the rubber gasket, with adhesive, in the same position as on the replaced horn.

ELECTRICAL ACCESSORY ITEMS SPECIFICATIONS AND DATA

Insufficient oil pressure indicator	red light
Signals when engine oil pressure is less than	7.1 to 21.3 p.s.i. (0,5 to 1,5 kgcm)
Generator charge indicator	red light
Signals when:	
Generator voltage is less than	12.6 V
Engine speed, below (*)	1100 r.p.m.
Car speed in 4th gear below (*) Sedan	14.3 mph (23 km/h)
Multipla	12.4 mph (20 km/h)
Excessive cooling water temperature indicator	red light
Signals when engine temperature at cylinder head is above	230° F (110° C)
Excessive water temperature indicator sending unit.	
Temperature for closing of contacts	230° to 248° F (110° to 120° C)
Insulation resistance between terminal and ground (with contacts apart) at 500 V d. c. not below	20 MΩ
Fuel reserve supply indicator	red light
Signals when the fuel in tank is below	3.5 to 5 lt
Direction indicators pilot light.	
Number of cycles per minute of flasher with a nominal load of 40 W:	
— at a nominal tension of 12 V and at 68° F (20° C)	78 ± 8
— at a tension 1.25 times the nominal one (15 V) and at 104° F (40° C) not above	100
— at a tension 0.8 times the nominal one (9.5 V) and at —4° F (—20° C) above	45
Windshield wiper unit	crank gear type
Sweeps per minute	50 to 60
Motor unit bench test data:	
Feed voltage	14 V
Stall torque	.43 ft.lbs (6 kgcm)
Stator overheating temperature below	122° F (50° C)
Speed, when warm not above	60 r.p.m.
Current draw below	1.8 Amps
Starting torque (with locked shaft, warm), at 14 V not below	5 ft.lbs (70 kgcm)
Wiper blade pressure on windshield	10.6 to 12.3 oz. (300 to 350 gr.)
Wiper arm tilting angle	100°

(*) NOTE - Starting from the serial number 848536, minimum charging speeds for the U.S.A. version vehicles are the following: engine 920 r.p.m., car in high gear 12 m.p.h. (19 km/h), all lights off.

Section 11
BODY

	Page
CONSTRUCTION OF BODY SHELL	328
DOORS	329
GLAZING	333
INNER TRIMMINGS	334
FRONT COMPARTMENT LID	334
ENGINE COMPARTMENT LID	336
FOLDING TOP FOR CONVERTIBLE	336
BUMPERS	337
OUTER TRIM MOLDINGS AND ORNAMENTS	337
REPAIRING ACCIDENTED CARS	337
BODY UPKEEP	341

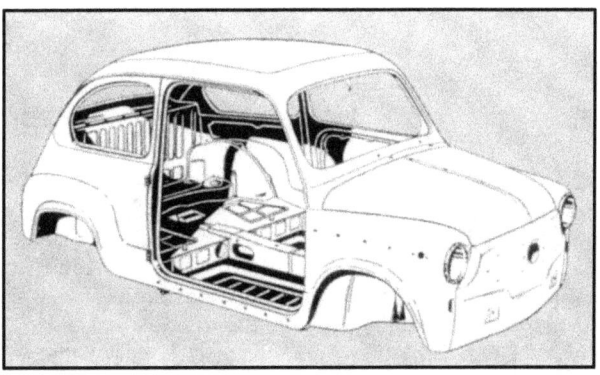

BODY

Foreword	page	328
CONSTRUCTION OF BODY SHELL	»	328
Spare Parts	»	329
DOORS	»	329
Weatherstrips	»	330
Inner Panellings	»	330
Handles and Locks	»	331
Window Regulator	»	331
GLAZING	»	333
Windshield and Back Window	»	333
Multipla Sliding Glasses	»	333
Rear Quarter Windows	»	334
BODY INNER TRIMMINGS	»	334
Tarred Felt Pads	»	334
Mats	»	334
Imitation-Leather Inner Panellings	»	334
FRONT COMPARTMENT LID - SEDAN	»	334
Lid Ornament Molding and Nameplate	»	335
ENGINE COMPARTMENT LID	»	336
FOLDING TOP FOR CONVERTIBLE	»	336
BUMPERS	»	337
OUTER TRIM MOLDINGS AND ORNAMENTS	»	337
REPAIRING ACCIDENTED CARS	»	337
Alignment	»	338
Fixtures A. 66036 and A. 66036/2 for Body Floor Alignment Check-up	»	338
Water and Dust Tightness	»	341
BODY UPKEEP	»	341
Cleaning the Cloth Upholstery of Seats and Rear Compartment Lining	»	341
Cleaning of Imitation-Leather	»	343
Chrome Parts	»	343
Glass Panels	»	343
Washing the Car	»	343

Foreword.

The bodies of the « Sedan » and of the « Multipla » are substantially different.

This chapter will deal with some parts entirely different from each other.

For other parts which, though different, are similar, general rules applicable to both the « Sedan » and the « Multipla » will be given.

CONSTRUCTION OF BODY SHELL

The compact and sturdy integral body is made up of the following structural assemblies.

« Sedan »:

— front floor;

— rear floor and wheelboxes;

BODY

— front frame, dashboard and front wheelboxes;
— rear panel frame;
— right side panel;
— left side panel;
— front panel;
— roof panel;
— rear lower panel.

In the «Convertible» version, some of these parts are reinforced to compensate for the absence of the hard top.

«Multipla»:

— front floor frame;
— front floor and wheelboxes;
— central floor;
— rear floor and wheelboxes;
— front panel;
— right side panel;
— left side panel;
— roof panel;
— rear lower panel.

These assemblies are joined by electric spot welding.

Spare Parts.

Replacement of damaged parts is in many cases more convenient than attempting repairs.

Therefore, spares for those parts that are liable to be damaged or deformed in case of accident are provided for repair and replacement purposes.

The list of these spares may be checked on the «Body Spares Catalogue».

Small sections may be cut from the new part when damage does not require the integral replacement of the whole part.

NOTE - Parts must be joined by electric spot welding; when a spot welder is not available, an electric arc welder may be used. It is not advisable to use torch welding since parts may be deformed by heat.

It shall be the repairman's task to judge case by case the extent of the repair. No detailed rules can be given here, since too many are the cases that may be met. However, it should be kept in mind that the purpose of body repairs is not only that of restoring the car to its original appearance but, and mainly, that of restoring the car to the original sturdiness.

It is easily realized that if the repair has been made with the only purpose of masking the damage, neglecting the structural function of the bodywork, weak spots will develop in time liable to affect the car sturdiness and riding safety.

NOTE - The following descriptions covering some of the major body parts are sufficient to make the operator understand his work, so that he may safely carry out the assembly and disassembly of parts. If damaged parts, or parts whose function is impaired, are found during the vehicle overhaul, it is a good practice to replace such parts.

DOORS

«Sedan».

The two forward-opening doors have welded-on upper and lower hinge halves joined by articulation pins to the other halves welded on the body. Hinge pins must be fitted with ball head uppermost.

Opening of the door is limited by a check strap fixed by four self-tapping screws (two on door and two on body).

The check strap shall be mounted as follows:

— Put some sealing compound on the check strap mounting holes.
— Insert the screws in the plates and in the strap.
— Interpose a washer, one on each screw, between: body and strap, door and strap.
— Lock the screws.

«Multipla».

Has four doors, all hinged on central pillar. Hinges are similar to those of the «Sedan».

Every door is provided with a check arm consisting of two plates articulated on a pin and secured to the body by a screw and to the door by two screws. On its front end the check arm is provided with a rubber pad.

To remove the check arm, undo the screw on body and then the screws on door.

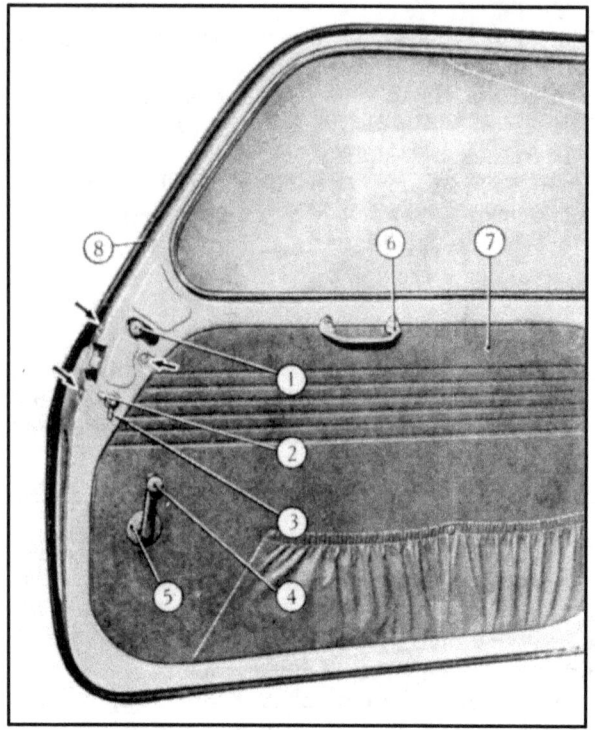

Fig. 486 - Passenger's side door locking system - Sedan.

1. Knob, controlling door lock. - 2. Door lock safety lever («free» position). - 3. Door lock safety lever («locked» position). - 4. Window regulator crank. - 5. Escutcheon. - 6. Grab handle. - 7. Imitation leather trim panel. - 8. Weatherstrip.

Arrows point to lock mounting screws.

Bonding a partially detached weatherstrip will not suffice to avoid water leakage. Weatherstrip must be removed completely or, at least, for a long portion around leaking points and bonded again following the instructions given above.

IMPORTANT

Allow the weatherstrip bonding compound to dry well before closing the door.

Water leakages are often caused by closing the doors too soon.

Inner Panellings.

Imitation leather panels are applied on the doors of both models. The panels are secured to the doors by stiff clips at top and by spring clips at bottom. For their removal see « Window Regulator » on next page.

To prevent water leakages through door lock, it is advisable to use some adhesive tape which must be placed on inner outline of door, only on lock end. Before inserting the panels, put also some sealing compound on its fastening hooks.

Weatherstrips.

Rubber weatherstrips are bonded with a special compound around the doors of both models.

To replace weatherstrips, proceed as follows.

Detach the old weatherstrip and clean carefully its seat with gasoline to remove all rubber, bonding compound and rust traces.

This operation will ensure a firm bonding of the new weatherstrip.

Clean new weatherstrips from graphite or talc, used to prevent aging in storage; if necessary, wash with gasoline the side to be bonded, then let it dry.

By a brush, apply a coat of « bonding compound » on the side to be fixed. Let it dry for about 15 minutes (drying time depends upon the type of compound used).

Next, fit the weatherstrip on door without pulling or forcing. The joint must always be located as at original assembly (to this end, refer to the « Spare Parts Catalogue » where the exact location of joints is shown).

Press weatherstrip, starting from center to ends.

Same directions shall be followed when replacing door opening weatherstrip. Join parts at bottom on rear end.

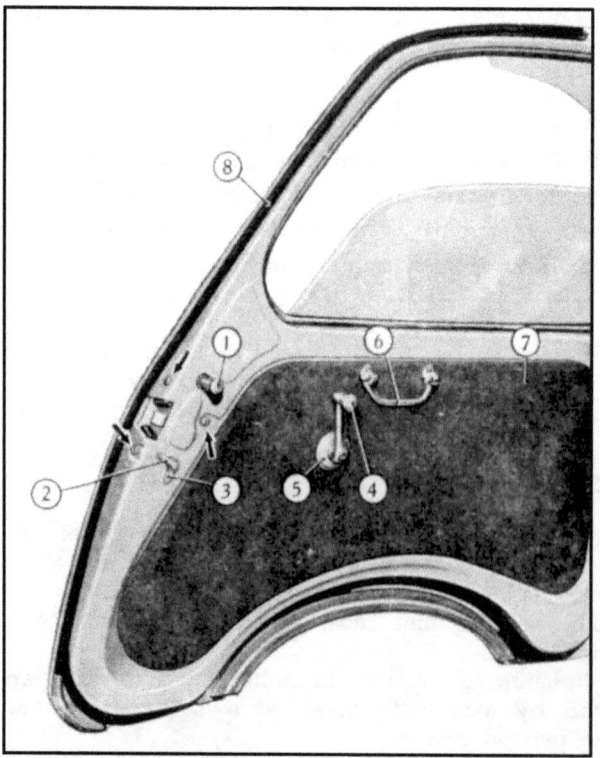

Fig. 487 - Passenger's side door locking system - Multipla.

1. Knob, controlling door lock. - 2. Door lock safety lever («free» position). - 3. Door lock safety lever («locked» position). - 4. Window regulator crank. - 5. Escutcheon. - 6. Grab handle. - 7. Imitation leather trim panel. - 8. Weatherstrip.

Arrows point to lock mounting screws.

BODY

Handles and Locks.

Doors are provided with locks which may be opened by handles either from inside or outside.

The driver's side door handle is provided with a key-controlled lock.

The door on opposite side («Sedan» and «Multipla») and the rear doors («Multipla») may be locked from inside by a safety device.

On both models the door opposite steering wheel side is locked by a handle controlled device. The door may be opened when the handle is horizontal and is locked when the handle is turned down vertically (figs. 486 and 487).

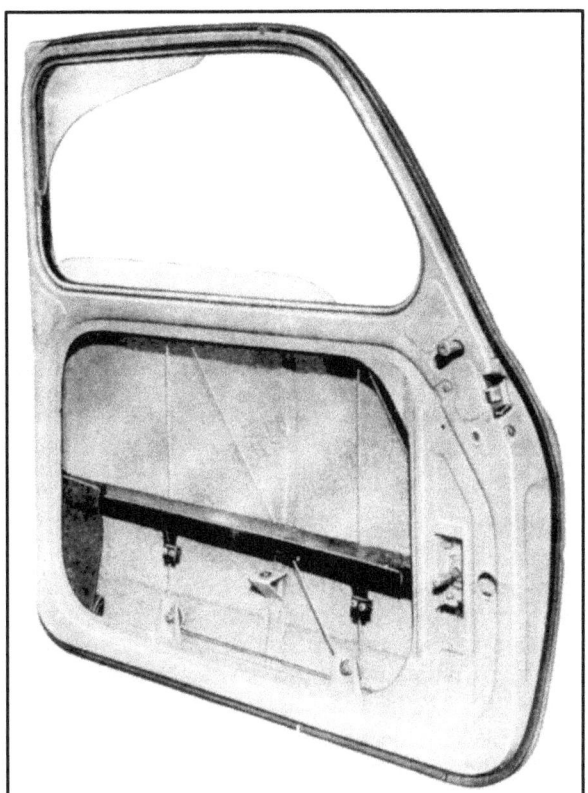

Fig. 489 - Driver's side door (inner panel removed) - Sedan.
Exposed are: glass pane frame, rope, sheaves and low glass position stop pad.

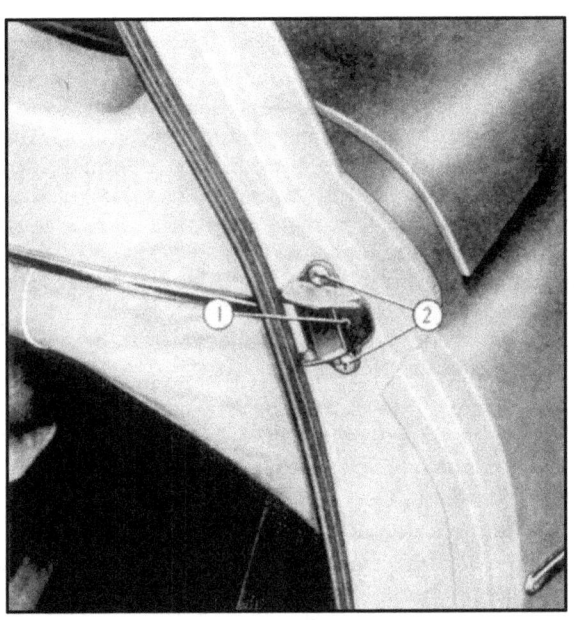

Fig. 488 - Door striker plate (Sedan).
1. Striker plate. - 2. Mounting screws of striker plate and shim (if any).

The «Multipla» rear doors are locked by turning down the handle.

No particular rules are required for door lock removal and installation.

However, when replacing a lock care shall be taken to locate exactly the position of the striker which is secured to the body by two self-tapping screws (fig. 488).

If the door does not close well, relocate the striker as required.

Window Regulator.

Sedan».

The window regulator is of the rope type and is secured, at front, to the door frame (fig. 489).

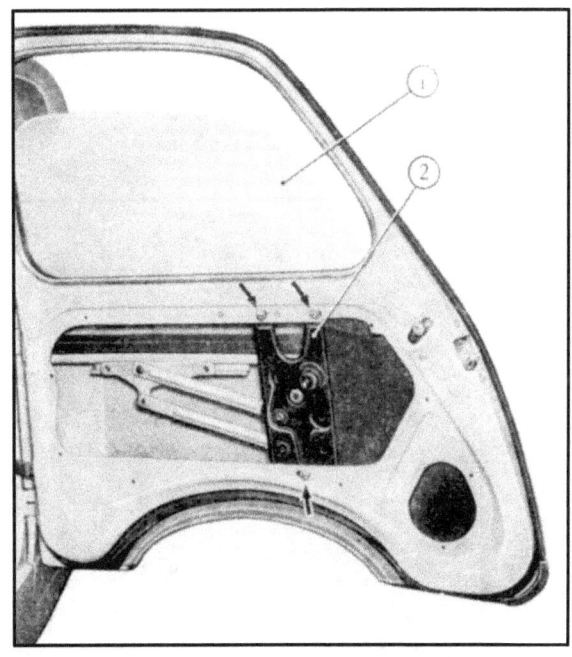

Fig. 490 - Front left door, driver's side (inner panel removed) - Multipla.
1. Glass pane. - 2. Window regulator mounting plate.
Arrows point to window regulator mounting screws.

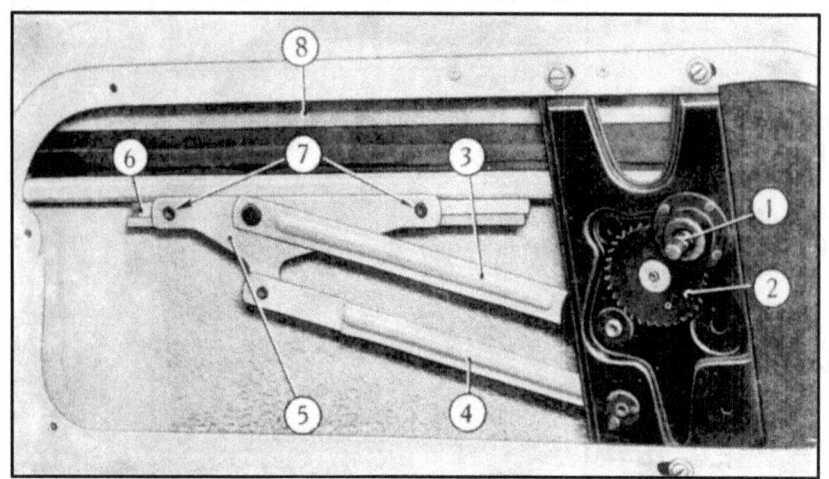

Fig. 491.

Front door window regulator assembly - Multipla.

1. Shaft. - 2. Intermediate gear. - 3. Control lever arm. - 4. Link. - 5. Support. - 6. Guide rail. - 7. Guide pins. - 8. Glass.

The rope is guided by 5 sheaves fixed to the door by screws and washers. Two are fixed at top and two at bottom. The lower intermediate sheave provides a second vertical passage to the rope.

The glass pane is held in a frame through the interposition of a rubber strip; the frame is in turn secured to the rope in two points by plates, each locked by two screws. Laterally the glass pane slides in a guide channel.

At bottom, on a support integral with door frame, is fitted a stop rubber pad.

Two rubber pads mounted in the upper portion act as vibration dampeners so as to prevent any noisiness of the glass.

Owing to the simplicity of this unit, its disassembly and reassembly does not require any special instructions.

During overhauls inspect carefully the rope for wear; even a single torn strand may cause in time the lengthening of the rope with consequent irregular operation of the window regulator. If the rope results slack, restore it to the correct tension by slackening the lower pulley screws and relocating the pulleys in their slots. Retighten the screws and lubricate the unit.

To reach the window regulator, remove the door lining panel as follows:

— Remove the regulator crank (4, fig. 486) by exerting a pressure on the plastic escutcheon (5), so as to uncover the key securing the regulator crank to shaft.

— Remove the key using a screwdriver.

— Pry off the panel by inserting a screwdriver tip between panel and door frame in correspondence with the spring clips.

Fig. 492 - Sedan body shell assembly.

To check door alignment, during service, verify the door-to-shell distances (all gaskets or weaterstrips removed).

A = .24'' (6 mm). - B = .20'' (5 mm).

Be careful, during this operation, not to scratch the door paint.

« Multipla ».

Front door window regulator is of the lever type with gear control.

The constructional simplicity of this system makes it highly reliable and operation troubles should be very unlikely.

The unit consists of a train of gears which transmits the crank movement to the lifting lever with a high reduction ratio. When the crank is rotated, it actuates a pinion integral with its shaft. The pinion is in mesh with a gear (2, fig. 491), on the hub of which is mounted a second pinion that meshes with the toothed sector of lever arm (3, fig. 491).

The arm end is linked to support (5) at the end of which are fixed the guide pins (7).

A link rod (4) is mounted between regulator and support, having the function of maintaining the support constantly parallel to the guide during the movement.

The two pins mounted on the support are housed in a suitable guide rail (6), on top of which is secured the glass pane (8); depending on the crank rotation direction, the pins move the pane up or down while, at the same time, they slide in their guide.

To disassemble the window regulator, proceed as follows:

— Bring the glass pane up and then remove the screws securing the window regulator to door (fig. 490).

— Drive the crank on to the control shaft and turn it until the pins can be disinserted from the guide and the assembly removed from door.

To reinstall the window regulator, place the glass pane in its seat and then reverse the disassembly operations.

Since this type of regulator is unlikely to develop operation troubles, no separate spare parts are supplied. Therefore, in case of malfunctioning due to wear or damages, replace the complete unit.

On reassembling the regulator, lubricate carefully the several parts.

GLAZING

Windshield and Back Window.

Windshield and back window on « Sedan » and « Multipla » models are curved to improve visibility and are provided with weatherstrips.

For assembly proceed as follows:

— fit weatherstrip on glass;

— insert a draw-cord completely around weatherstrip outer lip.

Cord ends shall come out at center of glass lower side (see fig. 493);

— press windshield assembly against body opening from outside; then, pull cord ends from inside to overlap weatherstrip on body opening lip.

The rear view mirror bulb cable, coming out from dashboard right end next to windshield, must be worked into and under the weatherstrip lip all the way around, and then brought to the rear view mirror at center top of windshield.

Next, inject some sealing compound under weatherstrip outer lip.

The removal of glass panes is not difficult. In fact, for the windshield, just tilt first wiper arms, then push glass outwards and remove complete windshield assembly.

Multipla Sliding Glasses.

Rear doors.

Rear doors are provided with sliding glasses whose locking in position is controlled by a push-button (fig. 494). The glass panes are mounted on metal frames provided with a guide, in which are drilled the positioning holes. The frame is surrounded by a weatherstrip.

To install the glasses, proceed as directed for the windshield and for the fixed glasses.

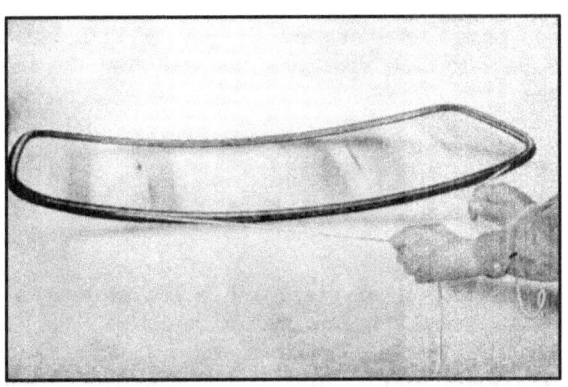

Fig. 493 - Installing draw-cord in windshield glass weatherstrip.

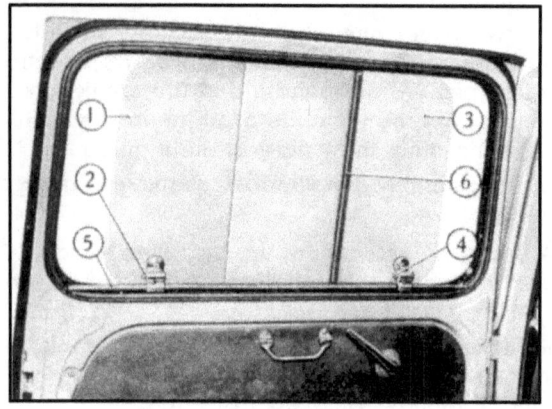

Fig. 494 - Detail of rear left door - Multipla.
1 and 3. Sliding glass panes. - 2 and 4. Release buttons. - 5. Slotted guide for control pin positioning. - 6. Retainer, with reveal, for rear glass.

After installation the glass frame is secured to body by self-tapping screws.

Rear Quarter Windows.

These glass panes are provided with weatherstrips and, additionally, with metal reveals.

To remove glass, push it outwards, exerting pressure from inside, close to the weatherstrip.

To install the glass, proceed as follows:

— fit the rubber weatherstrip on glass; place the metal reveal with fishplate in the seat on weatherstrip;

— insert a cord in the weatherstrip groove and, after placing from the outside the assembly so prepared in the body seat, pull from inside the wo cord ends.

BODY INNER TRIMMINGS

To deaden mechanical component vibrations and make car inside more comfortable, it has been lined with special sound deadening material.

Tarred Felt Pads.

They are bonded on various sections of the body by a special, sound deadening, bonding compound.

When bonding compound is applied by a spray gun, mask off control tunnel and seat fixed guide rails.

Mats.

The mats lining the car floor are secured by special rubber studs.

The mat arrangement and the fastening method are clearly illustrated in the « Spare Parts Catalogue ».

The rubber studs have a hollow fir-tree shank. To install the studs, insert a peg in the blind hole and then press down. For removal, insert the peg and while pressing it down, grab the stud head and pull the stud out.

Imitation Leather Inner Panellings.

They are located as follows:

« Sedan »:

    a) right door;

    b) left door;

    c) rear quarter right side;

    d) rear quarter left side.

« Multipla »:

    a) front right door;

    b) front left door;

    c) rear right door;

    d) rear left door;

    e) rear quarter right side;

    f) rear quarter left side.

These panels are secured in position by metal plates and spring fasteners; on the taxi models, fixing is obtained by rubber studs.

For panel removal, simply pry off in a manner adequate to free the fasteners and then the metal plates.

FRONT COMPARTMENT LID - SEDAN

This two-point rear-hinged lid is in a single piece.

The two hinges are welded on cowl; their passage into dashboard is lined with a gasket (fig. 495).

On the rear underside of lid are welded two plates, each provided with two threaded pins, which are inserted in the relevant holes in hinges on cowl and then secured with locknuts.

Lid is held open by a prop (2, fig. 495) inserted in a bracket welded to dashboard and loaded with a spring (3), which has also the task of fastening the prop.

Lid is kept closed by a locking catch (2, fig. 496). A safety hook (3) is provided to avoid accidental opening.

The catch release mechanism is controlled by a handle, at left under instrument panel and connected to a bowden.

The bowden is arranged inside of front compartment and is secured to catch lower end by a screw.

A return spring is fitted on the catch and on the support plate welded on body front panel, and pivots on a clenched pin. To lift the lid, insert

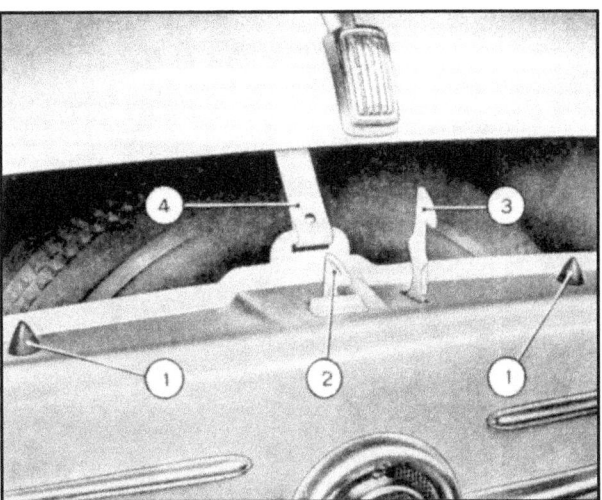

Fig. 496 - Close-up view of front compartment lid locking system, « Sedan ».

1. Lid lift rubber cones. - 2. Lid locking catch. - 3. Safety hook. - 4. Spare wheel fastening strap.

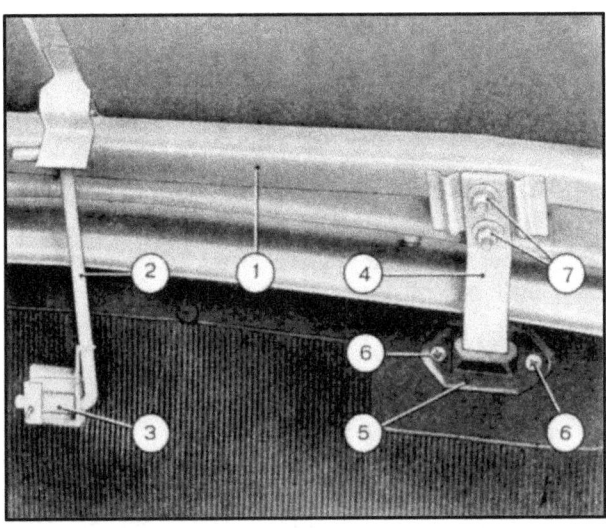

Fig. 495 - Close-up view of front compartment lid staying and hinging system, « Sedan ».

1. Front compartment lid. - 2. Lid prop. - 3. Reaction spring. - 4. Hinge. - 5. Lining. - 6. Lining screws. - 7. Hinge-to-lid nuts.

fingers and push in the safety hook (3, fig. 496) which is pivoted on a hollow clenched pin. A spring is provided for hook return.

Around the edges of front compartment on which the lid rests when closed, are fitted six rubber bumper pins (fig. 497) so located: two at front (3) and four on the sides (2). Two bumper pins, too, are placed laterally under the lid (2).

Bumper pins are simply pressure-mounted.

On body front panel are fitted two cones (1, fig. 496) for lid lifting.

Lid front end is provided with a weatherstrip, which is secured to the lid by six fasteners snapping into lid holes.

Lid Ornament Molding and Nameplate.

Four clips are fitted along lid longitudinal centerline to accomodate an ornament molding mounted in place by pressure.

Also the nameplate is mounted and held by a clip in the same way.

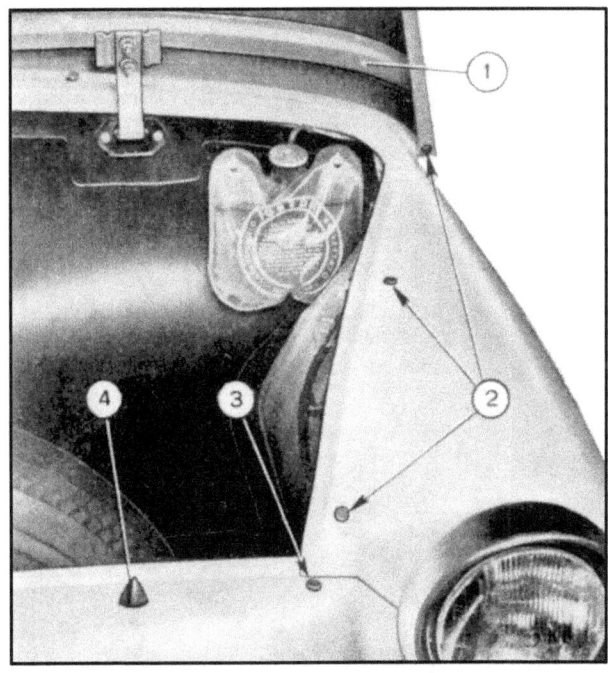

Fig. 497 - Front compartment lid bumper pins, « Sedan ».

1. Front compartment lid. - 2. Side bumper pins. - 3. Front side bumper pin. - 4. Lift rubber cone.

ENGINE COMPARTMENT LID

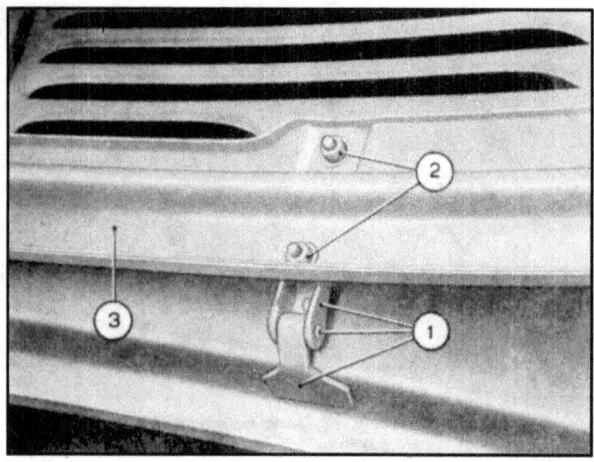

Fig. 498 - Close-up view of engine compartment lid hinging system.
1. Hinge. - 2. Hinge-to-lid mounting nuts. - 3. Engine compartment lid.

Opening and closing of lid is controlled by a handle.

To keep the lid closed, a catch is engaged in a slot in engine rear support.

The lid is articulated at its upper end on two hinges; the hinge fixed half is welded on roof panel rear lower end, while the movable half is secured by nuts on lid threaded studs (fig. 498).

Four rubber bumpers are fitted on lid corners and simply pressed into the relevant mounting holes in lid.

Two more rubber bumpers are placed on body lower rear panel.

The « FIAT 600 » nameplate is secured on lid by two clips.

When installing the lid, check the engine compartment light switch for correct operation.

FOLDING TOP FOR CONVERTIBLE

The folding top assembly consists of:

a) imitation-leather top with vinylite back window;

b) front end frame, complete with two handles and latches, and three bows (with rubber bumper pads) articulated on frame side rails;

c) front hold-down molding;

d) hold-down strip securing top on roof panel;

e) two bow articulation screws;

f) strap, for rolled top retainment on outer holder bracket;

g) front weatherstrip, with hold-down molding, secured on windshield top.

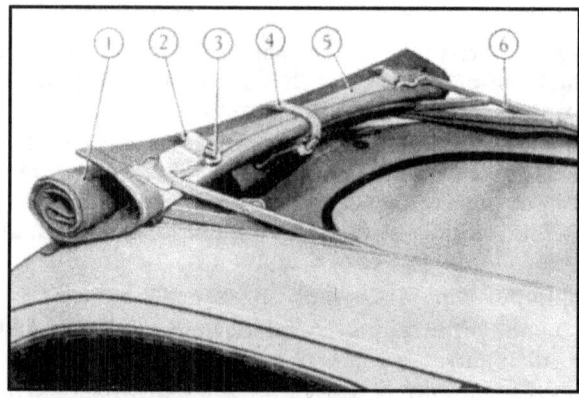

Fig. 500 - Securing the rolled top.
1. Top. - 2. Front latch. - 3. Handle. - 4. Rolled top fastening strap. - 5. Front end frame. - 6. Bows.

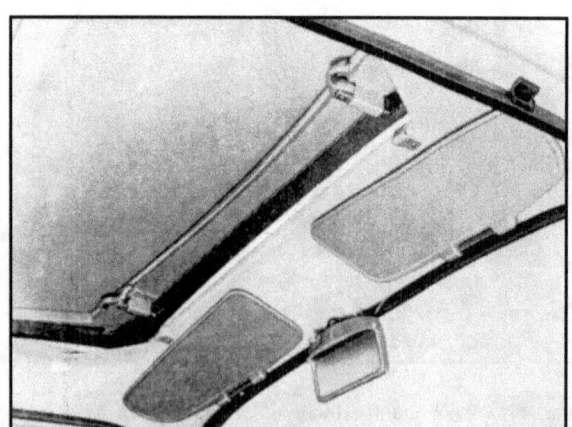

Fig. 499 - Detail of unlatched top.

The installation of roof assembly is not difficult: simply secure the top rear end and then fix the frame rails to the inner edge of body side panels.

BUMPERS

Front and rear bumpers consist of a single bar provided with two ornaments.

The «Multipla» rear bumper is without ornaments.

The front bumper of the «Sedan» is secured, through the ornament stud screws and nuts, on two brackets welded on body; behind the brackets are mounted two reinforcement struts, also welded on body. Two spacers are located between bumper bar and body front panel and have a thru hole to permit passage of the mounting stud screws.

Fig. 502 - Multipla front view (up to car No. 062187).

Fig. 501 - Sedan front view (starting from car No. 723664).

The front bumper of the «Multipla», instead, is secured directly on body front panel by the bumper ornament stud screws and nuts. A rubber gasket is interposed between ornament upper end and body panel, while two drilled spacers are interposed between bumper bar and body panel.

On both «Sedan» and «Multipla» models, the rear bumper is secured by screws (for «Sedan» it is the ornament screw itself) on two mounting brackets bolted to body rear floor assembly. Two drilled spacers are interposed between bumper bar and body rear lower panel.

OUTER TRIM MOLDINGS AND ORNAMENTS

The metal moldings and ornaments on body sides, doors, door sills, and front panel are secured by clips or spring fasteners engaged in suitably located slots. It is advisable to stopper the clips or fasteners with some «Vidradamp» sealing compound.

REPAIRING ACCIDENTED CARS

The damages a car may undergo in an accident may be different in nature and severity.

For this reason it is rather difficult to give specific and detailed instructions on body repair, covering the many possible cases, as each blow and/or bump may lead to given deformations, which must be eliminated in accordance with the best method suggested by the type of damage.

A thorough knowledge of body construction and welding seams is however an essential condition before any repair of body parts is attempted.

In most of such cases it will be necessary to remove some parts in order to gain access to the distorted items to permit straightening and aligning operations.

If body is very badly damaged, it will be advisable to take off all easily removable inner panellings.

This will provide a clearer vision of parts during repair and alignment operations, at the same time facilitating measurements, checks and the application of hydraulic jacks for panel straightening and squaring.

Alignment.

The car is of the intregral construction type and, therefore, the floor is in a single unit with body.

On a bumped car first check the alignment of front and rear wheels. Any misalignment will be revealed by a lack of parallelism between front and rear wheel axes or between front and rear wheel track widths.

It is essential to check that the misalignment is not due to distortion of front and rear swinging arms, of track rods, etc.

If misalignment is caused by deformations of body panels, these must be reshaped and the mounting points of mechanical units on floor muts be rechecked, using the reference data given in figs. 506 and 509 or the specially designed fixtures for floor checks (figs. 503, 504, 505 and 507).

Body floor must be checked very accurately and any deformation must be fully corrected until floor alignment and squareness will correspond to the recommended data, and fixtures will fit on floor in the manner described and illustrated in the following paragraphs.

FIXTURES A. 66036 AND A. 66036/2 FOR BODY FLOOR ALIGNMENT CHECK-UP

To check the floor alignment and the location of the front and rear suspension attachment points, as well as the stabilizer bar attachment and steering control operating rod on the « Multipla », use the following fixtures:

— **A. 66036** for the « Sedan » (figs. 503, 504, and 505);

— **A. 66036/2** for the « Multipla ».

This fixture must be used with tool fixture **A. 66036**, of which it replaces the front portion (fig. 507).

« Sedan » - Fixture A. 66036.

Fixture front end checks the mounting position of leaf spring and swinging arm pin fixing studs.

The rear end checks the position of rear swinging arm mountings.

The central part joins the fixture front and rear ends and serves to check floor alignment.

To check alignment, proceed as follows:

Position fixture front end on floor and fix its two brackets (A, fig. 504) on leaf spring mounting

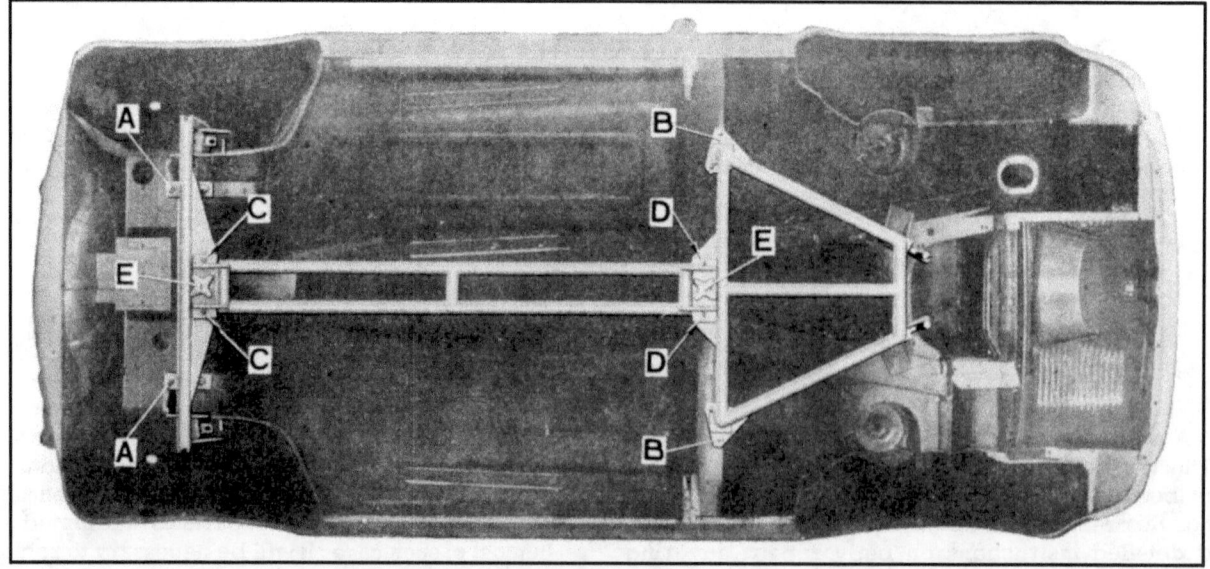

Fig. 503 - Checking alignment of floor and front and rear suspension mountings with fixture A. 66036.

A. Brackets, attachment of fixture to leaf spring mounting studs. - B. Brackets, attachment of fixture to rear swinging arm outer supports. - C and D. Pins, fixture central portion centering on front and rear elements. - E. Clamp-screw knobs, joining the three fixture elements.

BODY

Fig. 504.

Checking floor front end by fixture A. 66036.

A. Brackets, attachment of fixture to leaf spring mounting studs. - a. Fixture hollow pins must fit the swinging arm pin mounting studs.

studs; then, check alignment of the two fixture side arm hollow pins with right and left swinging arm pin mounting studs (a, fig. 504).

Position fixture rear end on floor and fix its outermost ends to mounting holes (B, fig. 505) of rear suspension swinging arm outer supports. The two fixture articulated joints must be inserted into the pins (b, fig. 505) placed in swinging arms inner mounting brackets.

After having carried out the above two checks, install fixture central part. Fixture front and rear ends are provided with two holes (C and D, fig. 503), in which the relevant centering dowels must be inserted and fixed by two clamp-screw knobs (E).

If no difficulty is encountered in installing the fixture on floor and check points (a, fig. 504 at front; b, fig. 505 at rear) coincide, it is an indication that floor has not undergone any deformation and is aligned.

If misaligned, proceed with the necessary corrections.

To straighten out or reshape deformed body or floor parts, use the specially designed equipment which includes a pump-controlled hydraulic jack.

Floor and body panel straightening are operations that call for a thorough knowledge of the construction of parts involved and the know-how required to quickly locate joint areas and welding seams.

« Multipla » - Fixture A. 66036/2.

To check the « Multipla » floor alignment, use the rear and central portions of fixture **A. 66036** (intended for « Sedan ») and replace its front portion with fixture **A. 66036/2** (fig. 507).

Fig. 505.

Checking floor rear end by fixture A. 66036.

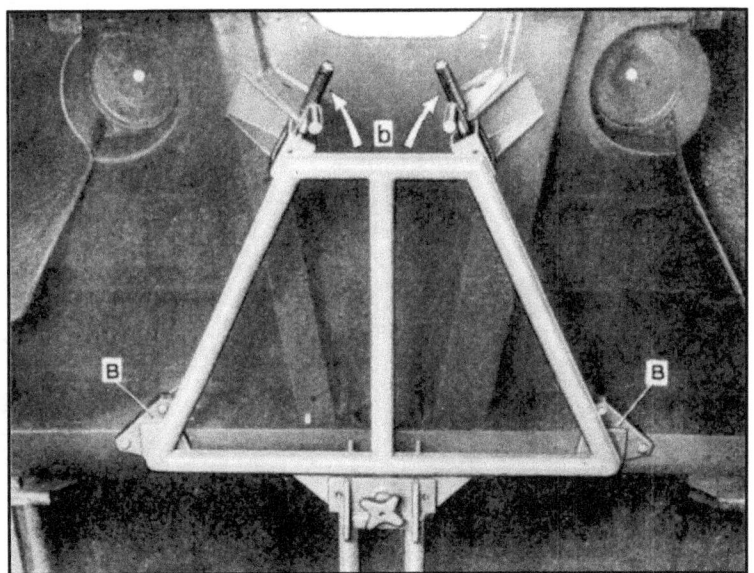

B. Brackets, attachment of fixture to rear swinging arm outer supports. - b. Pins, swinging arm inner mounting holes alignment check.

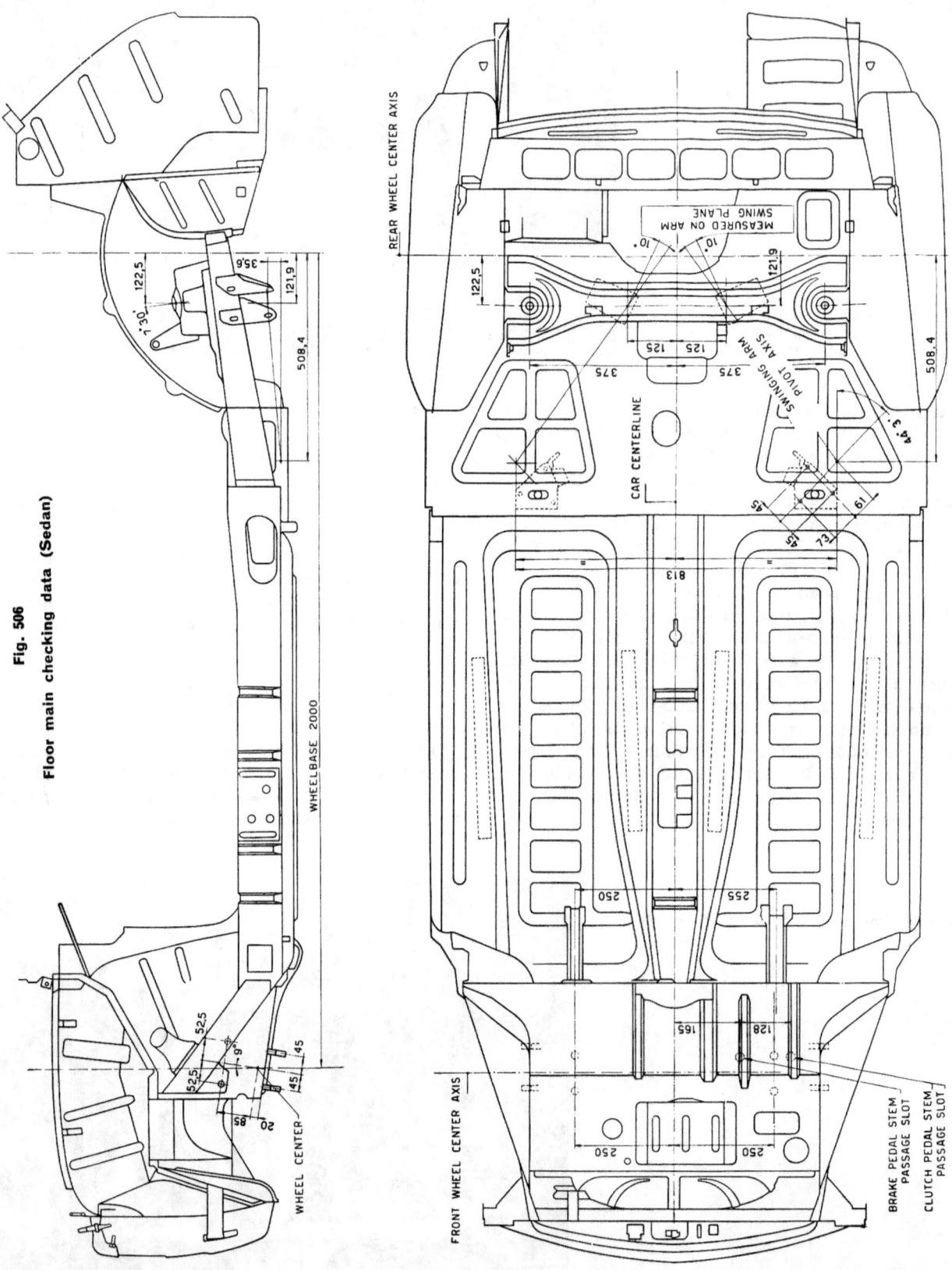

Fig. 506 Floor main checking data (Sedan)

Fixture **A. 66036/2** permits to check the position of:
— suspension upper support (1, fig. 507) attachment studs and holes;
— suspension lower supports (2, 3, fig. 507) mounting holes;
— steering control operating rod support (4, fig. 507) mounting holes;
— stabilizer bar (5, fig. 507) mounting holes.

For the checks to be carried out with the central and rear portions of the fixture, follow the directions outlined for the «Sedan».

The same rule holds also for the correction of deformations.

Water and Dust Tightness.

After body repairs and before re-installation of inner panellings, inspect accurately all points (joints and welds) where water and dust infiltrations are likely to occur. In case any of such points are found faulty, remedy by sealing compound applied with a suitable gun.

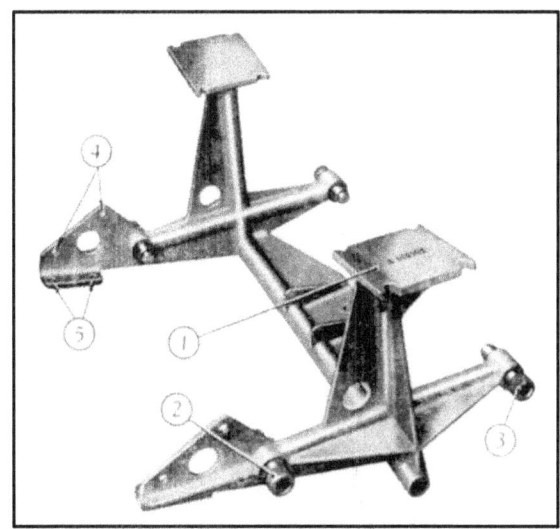

Fig. 507 - Checking floor front end by fixture A. 66036/2 Multipla.

1. Slotted plate for checking the position of front suspension upper support-to-body screws. - 2-3. Pins for lower swinging arm supports mounting checks. - 4. Holes for steering control operating rod support mounting check. - 5. Holes for stabilizer bar mounting check.

BODY UPKEEP

Cleaning the Cloth Upholstery of Seats and Rear Compartment Lining.

A periodical cleaning based on specially devised methods is a «must» to ensure long life and preserve the attractive appearance of upholstery cloth.

Dust and dirt blown into the car when windows are open settle on the upholstery and tend to wear the cloth causing an unsightly appearance. For this reason, it is extremely important to do some rather frequent cleaning (about every 15 days), shortening this interval as the car accumulates mileage.

Fig. 508. 600 Model «Sedan».

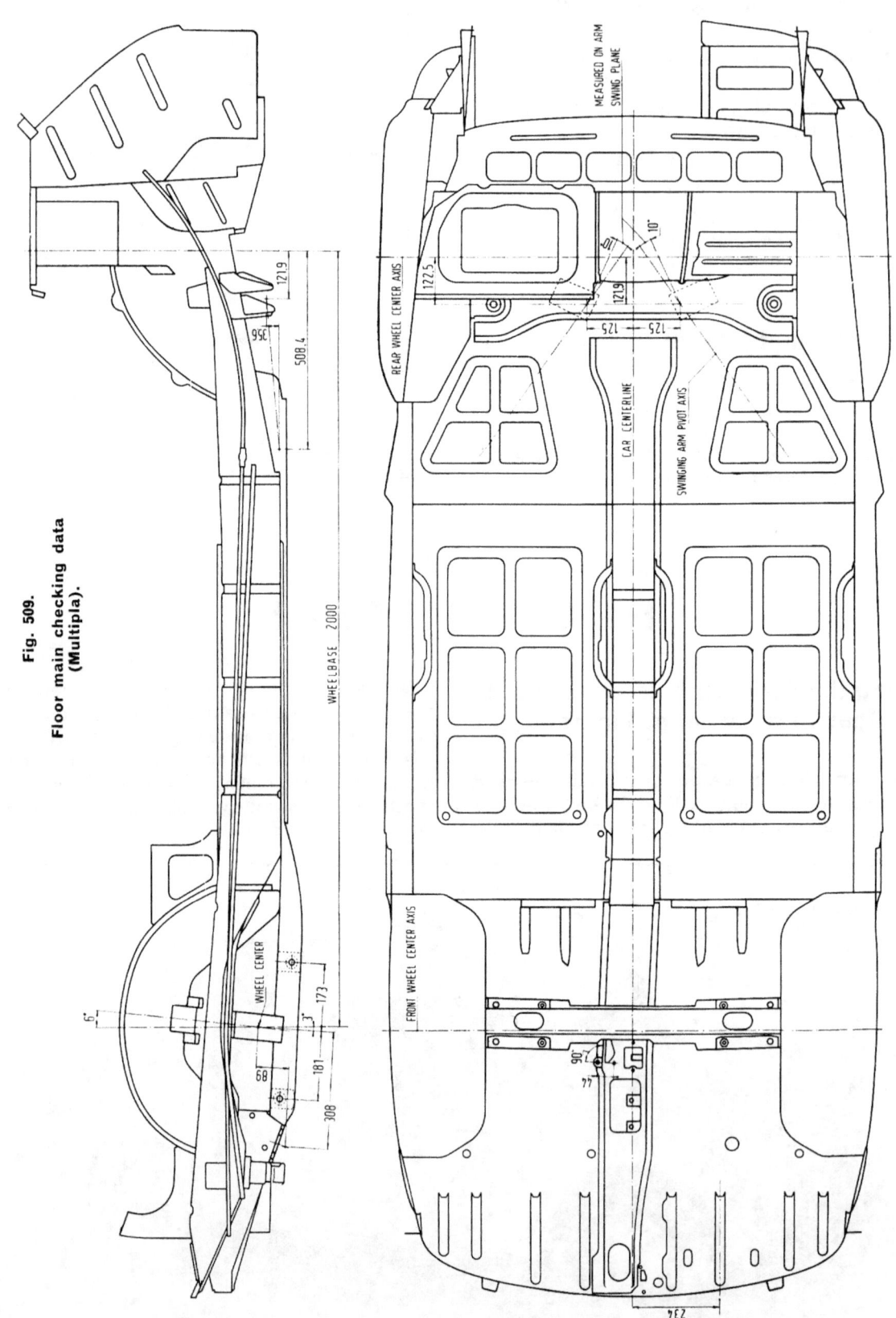

Fig. 509. Floor main checking data (Multipla).

BODY

Wipe off dust using a brush or, better still, use the household vacuum cleaner, if available.

To remove ordinary soiling of the upholstery cloth, proceed as follows:

— lukewarm water and a neutral soap should be used, applying to surface on a piece of clean cloth or brush, wiping in the direction of upholstery nap rather than against it;

— repeat the operation using only a clean damp cloth and no soap;

— when upholstery cloth is dry, brush back against nap to restore a « fresh », fluffy look.

To obtain good results, stains must be removed in the least possible time after they are made, becauses spots that are allowed to remain for long on cloth will set and their removal will be very difficult, if not impossible. Some types of stains call for specific spot removers.

Use those of reliable repute and follow label instructions.

Cleaning of Imitation-Leather.

Never use oil, paints or ammonia solutions.

The cause for any alteration or loss of imitation leather softness or luster, should generally be ascribed to the use of unsuitable or harmful cleaners.

To keep imitation leather clean, simply wash with a soap-sudded moist cloth. Then, wipe clean with a moist cloth and no soap.

Finally, rub with a clean dry cloth and stop when original luster is restored.

Chrome Parts.

To preserve the enduring finish of chrome parts, wash periodically using a cloth dampened with kerosene, dry, and rub with a cloth moistened in fluid oil. Next, remove any trace of oil using a clean woolen cloth.

This procedure will not alter the brilliancy of chromium-plated parts and will preserve them from the detrimental action of atmospheric agents like climate dampness or saline air.

Glass Panels.

Glass panels must be cleaned with a chamois or rag: in either case utmost cleanliness is an essential condition, inasmuch as, if already used to clean the car, they might be soiled with dust or contain sand. This foreign matter is abrasive and will eventually scratch glass panels to the point where perfect visibility is impaired.

Washing the Car.

Body will call for washings at variable intervals depending on driving conditions. If a car washing tunnel is not available, proceed as follows:

Using an ordinary garden hose (with nozzle), wash first the bottom of car, including the wheels. If required, caked road grime should be softened with a sponge. Do not allow the water spout to strike wheel paint finish too violently.

Wash all body panels with running water, moderating the pressure of the water spout. Complete

Fig. 510 - 600 Model « Multipla ».

the washing with a sponge, rubbing gently at first to prevent scratching the finish with the entrained dirt (rinse sponge often) and then more vigorously, using plenty of running water all the time.

Dry car thoroughly with a clean chamois. No trace of water must remain on the finish.

To prevent damages to windshield wiper during the washing operation, pass the sponge or chamois under wiper blades which must be lifted and tilted towards cowl; never displace blades angularly.

If after washing and drying with chamois the original luster of the finish is not restored, use one of the many polishing compounds of good commercial grade. A slight amount of color showing up on the cloth while polishing should not be cause for alarm, as this is a natural condition having no consequence on the luster and life of the finish. Grease, oil and tar stains on the body finish may be removed with some gasoline followed by an immediate wiping with a dry cloth.

Section 12

MAINTENANCE TOOL EQUIPMENT CAR SPECIFICATIONS

	Page
MAINTENANCE	346
LUBRICANT SPECIFICATIONS	347
TOOL EQUIPMENT	348
TOOL KIT	352
GENERAL SPECIFICATIONS OF VEHICLES	352

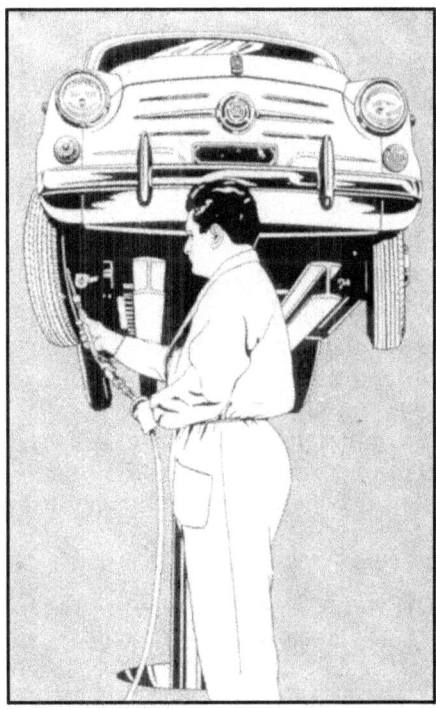

MAINTENANCE

OPERATIONS	Miles	6,000	12,000	18,000	25,000	31,000	37,000	44,000	50,000
	Kms.	10.000	20.000	30.000	40.000	50.000	60.000	70.000	80.000

LUBRICATION

	6,000	12,000	18,000	25,000	31,000	37,000	44,000	50,000
1. Lubricate ignition distributor	★	★	★	★	★	★	★	★
2. Check gearbox-differential unit oil level	★	★		★	★		★	★
3. Replace oil in gearbox-differential unit			★			★		
4. Lubricate generator ball bearings			★			★		
5. Lubricate starter free wheel and electro-magnet plunger				★		★		
6. Lubricate door hinges		★		★		★		★

Every 300 miles (500 km): Check oil level in sump.

Every 1,500 miles (2.500 km): Inject grease in lubricators.

Every 6,000 miles (10.000 km): Replace oil in sump.

CHECKS AND INSPECTIONS

	6,000	12,000	18,000	25,000	31,000	37,000	44,000	50,000
1. Replace by-pass oil filter cartridge	★	★	★	★	★	★	★	★
2. Replace air cleaner cartridge	★	★	★	★	★	★	★	★
3. Check ignition distributor breaker contacts	★	★	★	★	★	★	★	★
4. Clean spark plugs and check gap	★	★	★	★	★	★	★	★
5. Clean carburetor filter	★	★	★	★	★	★	★	★
6. Check brake fluid level	★	★	★	★	★	★	★	★
7. Check tappet clearance	★	★	★	★	★	★	★	★
8. Check and adjust front wheel bearing play		★			★		★	★
9. Check and adjust rear wheel bearing play			★			★		
10. Clean and lubricate battery terminals and clamps and check tension	★	★	★	★	★	★	★	★
11. Check generator and starter brushes for wear				★		★		
12. Tighten all bolts and nuts fixing units to body		★		★		★		★

Every 300 miles (500 km): Check water level in radiator and tire pressure.

Every 1,500 miles (2.500 km): Check electrolyte level in battery.

Every 6,000 miles (10.000 km): **Road test car.**

LUBRICANT SPECIFICATIONS

FIAT VS 40 Oil, for engine (above 86°F - 30°C) (SAE 40, approx.)	Flash point (in open cup) Pour point Viscosity at 122°F (50°C) { Engler units / Kinematic cSt Viscosity at 212°F (100°C) { Engler units / Kinematic cSt	not below 464°F (240°C) not above 18.4°F (−8°C) 11.4 to 12.6 86.6 to 95.6 not below 2.22 not below 14
FIAT VS 30 Oil, for engine (above 32°F - 0°C) (SAE 30, approx.)	Flash point (in open cup) Pour point Viscosity at 122°F (50°C) { Engler units / Kinematic cSt Viscosity at 212°F (100°C) { Engler units / Kinematic cSt	not below 456°F (230°C) not above −.4°F (−18°C) 8 to 9 60.8 to 68.4 not below 1.92 not below 10.90
FIAT VS 20 Oil, for engine (32° to 5°F - 0° to −15°C) (SAE 20, approx.)	Flash point (in open cup) Pour point Viscosity at 122°F (50°C) { Engler units / Kinematic cSt Viscosity at 212°F (100°C) { Engler units / Kinematic cSt	not below 428°F (220°C) not above −.4°F (−18°C) 4.7 to 5.5 35 to 41.3 not below 1.58 not below 7.20
FIAT VS 10 W Oil, for engine (below 5°F - −15°C) (SAE 10 W, approx.)	Flash point (in open cup) Pour point Viscosity at −4°F (−18°C) { Engler units / Kinematic cSt Viscosity at 122°F (50°C) { Engler units / Kinematic cSt Viscosity at 212°F (100°C) { Engler units / Kinematic cSt	not below 404°F (200°C) not above −13°F (−25°C) not above 330 not above 2500 2.7 to 3.3 18.5 to 23.7 not below 1.38 not below 4.80
W 90 Oil (SAE 90 EP, approx.)	Flash point (in open cup) Viscosity at 122°F (50°C) { Engler units / Kinematic cSt Viscosity at 212°F (100°C) { Engler units / Kinematic cSt	not below 374°F (190°C) 14.4 to 15.6 110.2 to 118 not below 2.4 not below 15.7
FIAT Jota 1 Grease	Drop point (Ubbelhode) Worked penetration (after 60 strokes) Colour Appearance	not below 356°F (180°C) 310 to 340 dark yellow creamy
FIAT MR Grease	Drop point (Ubbelhode) Worked penetration (after 60 strokes) Colour Appearance	not below 356°F (180°C) 235 to 250 light brown creamy
FIAT Jota 2/M Grease	Drop point (Ubbelhode) Worked penetration (after 60 strokes) Colour Appearance	not below 356°F (180°C) 265 to 295 black creamy
FIAT Jota 3 Grease	Drop point (Ubbelhode) Worked penetration (after 60 strokes) Colour Appearance	not below 374°F (190°C) 220 to 250 green creamy
Special FIAT blue label fluid	Heavy Duty non-mineral type (SAE 70 R 3)	

SPECIAL TOOL EQUIPMENT

Service tools in this list being common to «Sedan» and «Multipla» bear no indication, whereas tools particular to «Sedan» are identified by the wording (600) and those particular to «Multipla» by the wording (600 M).

NOTE - This list does not include tools and sets of general use but merely special tools, some of which are common to other car Models.

Therefore, for thorough knowledge of all tool equipment recommended for performance of maintenance work, see the «Service Tool Catalogue» published by FIAT Service Dept.

For reasons of standardization, the catalogue number of some tools has been varied. In the text and illustrations of this manual, tools are identified with the previous numbering.

The following list reports, in the first column, the old number of tools and, in the second column, the covering up-to-date number.

Previous Number	New Number	Description
		ENGINE
Arr. 2067	A. 60510	Sling - engine support during removal of gearbox-differential unit.
Arr. 2069	A. 60511	Sling - engine and engine-gearbox unit lifting.
Arr. 2205/3	Arr. 22205/3	Arms - engine fixing on rotating stand.
A. 8110	A. 50049	Wrench - exhaust manifold nuts.
A. 8262 bis	A. 50053	Wrenches, tappet clearance adjustment.
A. 50023	A. 50023	
A. 8302	A. 50064	Bush (14 mm), special - cylinder head central hold-down screw.
A. 10114	A. 60182	Installer and remover - piston rings.
A. 11475	A. 94069	Spindle - valve seat refacing grinding stone.
A. 11482	A. 94058	Spindle - valve seat refacing cutter.
A. 40005	A. 40005	Universal puller.
A. 40006/1/2	A. 40006/1/2	Puller - pilot bush removal.
A. 50021	A. 50021	Wrench - thermostat locking nut on cylinder head water outlet pipe (600 M).
A. 50050	A. 50050	Wrench - thermostat nut (600).
A. 60018	A. 60018	Tool - spark plug seat blanking during valve tightness test.
A. 60041	A. 60041	Fixture - cylinder head support during decarbonizing.
A. 60045	A. 60045	Plate - cylinder head support during valves removal and installation.
A. 60057	A. 94014	Taper grinder - valve seats.
A. 60058	A. 94015	Pilots (set) - valve seat refacing cutter guide.
A. 60059	A. 60059	Drift rod - valve guide installation and removal.
A. 60066	A. 94016	Spindle - crankcase plug seat cutter.
A. 60068	A. 94018	Cutter - crankshaft plug seat (dia. 14 mm) (late type).
A. 60075	A. 60075	Staking punch - crankcase plug caulking.
A. 60076	A. 60076	Striker - connecting rod bush installation and removal.
A. 60077	A. 60077	Reamer - small end bushing.
A. 60078	A. 60078	Installer - pistons.
A. 60079	A. 60079	Tester - valve seat tightness.
A. 60080	A. 60080	Fixture - crankshaft mounting on grinder.
A. 60081	A. 60081	Fixture - cylinder head water tightness tests.
A. 60082	A. 60082	Plate - cylinder liner installation.
A. 60083	A. 60083	Striker - piston pin installer and remover.
A. 60084	A. 60084	Tool - valve installer and remover.
A. 60092	A. 60092	Punch - crankshaft plug installation.
A. 60096	A. 94027	Cutter, 20° - valve seat refacing.
A. 60159	A. 94030	Cutter, 75° - intake and exhaust valve seat refacing.
A. 60162	A. 60162	Gauge - oil pressure test.

(continued)

SPECIAL TOOL EQUIPMENT

Special Tool Equipment (continued).

Previous Number	New Number	Description
A. 60163	A. 60163	Fixture - sump gasket installation.
A. 60165	A. 60165	Tool - flywheel retainment during crankshaft installation.
A. 60166	A. 60166	Tool - flywheel end seal centering.
A. 60262	A. 60262	Plate for removing cylinder liners by means of a press.
A. 72020 bis	D. 15166	Covers - engine protection during car wash.
A. 86028	A. 86028	Drift rods (dia. 28 mm) crankase welsh plugs installation.
A. 90326	A. 90326	Chuck camshaft bushing refacing.
C. 110	A. 95110	Feeler gauge - tappet clearance adjustment (.0039'' - 0,10 mm).
C. 111	A. 95111	Feeler gauge - tappet clearance adjustment (.0059'' - 0,15 mm).
C. 316	A. 95316	Feeler gauge - piston-to-cylinder clearance checks.
C. 631	A. 95631	Ring gauge - zeroing of dial indicator C. 687.
C. 645	A. 95645	Tester - engine T.D.C.
C. 673	A. 95673	Graduated sector - valve gear timing.
U. 0313	A. 90313	Reamer - valve guide bore.
U. 0318/1	A. 90318/1	Reamer - tappet guide bore (oversize).
U. 0318/2	A. 90318/2	
U. 0320	A. 90320	Expansible reamer - piston pin bore and bush.
D. 15802	D. 15802	Shield - fan belt protection during tappet adjustment.
I. 31790	A. 60208	Hose and connection - to be joined to muffler during tappet adjustment.

CLUTCH

Previous Number	New Number	Description
A. 62022	A. 70022	Fixture - clutch assembly and adjustment.
A. 62023	A. 70023	Bar - clutch driven plate alignment on engine transmission installation.

GEARBOX AND DIFFERENTIAL

Previous Number	New Number	Description
Arr. 2067	A. 60510	Hook - engine support on car during gearbox-differential unit removal.
Arr. 2076	A. 70508	Support - to be mounted on garage jack for gearbox-differential installation and removal.
Arr. 2206/6	Arr. 22206/6	Support - gearbox-differential unit retainment on rotating stand Arr. 2204.
A. 8560	—	Wrench - sleeve-to-side gear screw (early type).
A. 42013	A. 45013	Remover - final drive pinion ball bearing (600).
A. 42014	A. 45014	Plate, differential case bearing inner ring removal (to be used with puller A. 40005).
A. 42016	A. 45016	Remover - final drive pinion ball bearing (600 M).
A. 52020	A. 55020	Wrench - differential bearing adjuster rings (early type).
A. 55034	A. 55034	Pin wrench - differential case bearing adjuster (late type).
A. 62024	—	Tool - parking brake drum retainment during tightening of final drive pinion nut (early type).
A. 62026	A. 70026	Dummy pinion fixture - drive pinion shim thickness determination (to be used with fixture C. 689).
A. 62027	A. 70027	Tool - differential case roller bearing outer rings remover and installer and inner ring installer.
A. 62028	A. 70028	Tool - bevel drive pinion rear ball bearing.
A. 62029	—	Rubber boots (pair of) - to prevent oil leakage from gearbox casing with axle shaft removed (early type).
A. 62030	A. 70030	Expander - differential boot retainer collars installation and removal.
A. 62031	A. 70031	Installer - differential bearing oil seal.
A. 70071	A. 70071	Rubber boots (pair of) - to prevent oil leakage from gearbox casing with axle shaft removed (late type).

(continued)

Special Tool Equipment (continued).

Previous Number	New Number	Description
C. 688	A. 95688	Fixture, with dial indicators - for bevel drive pinion-to-ring gear backlash adjustment and differential bearing preload checks.
C. 689	A. 95690	Dial indicator - thrust ring thickness determination (to be used with A. 62026).

FRONT SUSPENSION

Previous Number	New Number	Description
A. 40005/V	A. 40005/V	Puller - swing. arm rubber bushes.
A. 56001	A. 57002	Wrench - lower swinging arm spider self-tapping bush installation (600 M).
A. 56015	A. 57015	Wrench - upper swinging arm spider self-tapping bush installation (600 M).
A. 66003	A. 74083	Fixture - coil spring compression (600 M).
A. 66015	A. 74095	Tool - spider bush remover and installer (600 M).
A. 66016	A. 74016	Installer and remover - bushes on knuckle pillar (600).
A. 66023	A. 74023	Fixture - installation and removal of swinging arm pins and spiders (600 M).
A. 66029	Arr. 22229	Rotating stand - suspension assembly and disassembly (600 M).
A. 66038	A. 74038	Fixture - swinging arm checks, assembly and disassembly (600).
A. 66039	A. 74039	Installer and remover - front suspension leaf spring estendblocks (600).
A. 66042	A. 74042	Installer and remover - estendblock in knuckle pillar.
A. 66044	A. 74044	Installer - bushes on swinging arms.
A. 66061	A. 74061	Fixture - leaf spring flexing to static load setting (600).
U. 0360/25B	A. 90316	Reamer - knuckle pillar bushes (600).
C. 1003	A. 96003	Fixture - knuckle pillar alignment checks (600).
U. 0361	A. 90361	Reamer - front suspension spider bushing (600 M).

REAR SUSPENSION

Previous Number	New Number	Description
A. 66033	A. 74033	Pilot pin - swinging arm shims mounting.
A. 66037	A. 74037	Fixture - swinging arm checks and adjustments.
A. 66045	A. 74045	Tool - swinging arm estendblock removal and installation.

HYDRAULIC SHOCK ABSORBERS

Previous Number	New Number	Description
A. 10228	A. 74019	Adapter - rear shock absorber assembly.
A. 56020	A. 57020	Wrench - front and rear shock absorber (600) installation and removal.
A. 56024	A. 57024	Wrench - front shock absorber plug (600 M).
A. 56031	A. 57031	Wrench - inner sleeve top plug, rear shock absorbers (600 and 600 M).
A. 57034	A. 57034	Wrench - front shock absorber stem pilot nut (600).
A. 57035	A. 57035	Wrench - front and rear shock absorber removal and installation (600 M).

STEERING GEAR

Previous Number	New Number	Description
A. 8065	A. 57003	Wrench - worm screw bearing adjuster sleeve (600).
A. 8279	A. 57005	Wrench - steering wheel-to-shaft nut (600).
A. 10110	A. 74017	Tool - worm screw seal remover (600).
A. 46004	A. 47004	Puller - worm screw upper bearing outer ring (600 M).
A. 46019	A. 47019	Puller - worm screw bearing inner rings (600).
A. 46021	A. 47021	Puller - pitman arm (600).
A. 46022	A. 47022	Puller - steering rod head pins.
A. 57033	A. 57033	Wrench - steering gear casing oil level inspection plug.

(continued)

Special Tool Equipment (continued).

Previous Number	New Number	Description
A. 66009	A. 74089	Tool - installer and remover - roller shaft bushes (600 M).
A. 66032	A. 74032	Support - steering box servicing (600).
A. 66040	A. 74040	Puller - worm screw upper bearing outer ring (600).
A. 66043	A. 74043	Tool, installer and remover - for sector shaft bushes (600).
A. 66046	A. 74046	Installer - worm screw roller bearing inner rings and upper bearing outer ring (600).
A. 66050	A. 74050	Support - steering box servicing (600 M).
U. 0336	A. 90336	Reamer - roller shaft bushing (600 M).

BRAKES

Previous Number	New Number	Description
A. 10103	A. 72206	Hose - air bleeding.
A. 64002	A. 72210	Pressure band - bonding of service brake shoe linings (600).
A. 64021	—	Pressure band - bonding of drive line hand brake shoe linings.
A. 64023	A. 72212	Pressure band - bonding of service brake shoe linings (600 M).
C. 114	—	Feeler gauge - brake shoe centering and clearance adjustment.

HUBS AND WHEELS

Previous Number	New Number	Description
A. 6463	A. 47026/2	Item - to be used with puller A. 6511 - wheel inner roller bearing outer ring removal (600).
A. 6469	A. 47015	Puller - wheel drums (alternative with A. 40005).
A. 6511	A. 47026/1	Puller - front wheel hub bearing outer rings.
A. 46014	A. 47014	Puller - front wheel hub caps.
A. 66000	A. 74094	Installer - front wheel outer and inner roller bearing outer rings (Multipla).
A. 66008	A. 74088	Installer - front wheel hub caps.
A. 66034	A. 74034	Remover - rear wheel roller bearing outer rings.
A. 66035	A. 74035	Installer - rear wheel roller bearing inner and outer rings.
A. 66041	A. 74041	Installer - front wheel inner bearing inner ring and front wheel inner and outer bearings outer rings (Sedan).
A. 66051/1/2	A. 74051	Fixture - leaf spring setting during front end geometry checks (Sedan).
A. 66052	A. 74052	Fixture (set) - rear springs compression and rear wheels holding in vertical position during front and rear end geometry checks (to be used with gauge C. 696).
A. 74003	A. 89854	Spanner wrench (to be used with A. 66051/1/2 and A. 66052).
A. 95697	A. 95697	Dynamometer - bearing rotation torque.
A. 95697/3	A. 95697/3	Item - wheel bearing rotation torque measurements (to be used with dynamometer A. 95697).
C. 696	Ap. 5110/1/2	Gauge - rear wheel toe-in checks.
C. 696/2	Ap. 5110/3	Bracket (to be used with C. 696) - rear wheel toe-in checks (600 M).

ELECTRIC SYSTEM

Previous Number	New Number	Description
A. 13021	A. 76010	Filler - battery (automatic).
Ap. 5030	Ap. 5030	Timing tester.
Ap. 5030/1	Ap. 5030/1	Fixture - to be used with Ap. 5030.
A. 50022	A. 50022	Wrench - spark plugs.
A. 68002	A. 76002	Tool - battery posts and terminals cleaning.

BODYWORK

Previous Number	New Number	Description
Arr. 2072	A. 74503	Cross member - car jacking up at front and rear (early type) (to be used with hydraulic jacks Arr. 2034 bis or Arr. 2027).
A. 58004	—	T-wrench, 12 mm - engine and bumper support rear cross member.
A. 66036	A. 74036/1	Fixture - body floor alignment checks (Sedan).
A. 66036/2	A. 74036/2	Fixture - body floor alignment checks (Multipla).
A. 70005	A. 78005	Pliers - molding clips.

TOOL KIT

The set of wrenches and tools allotted for servicing operations the Owner can do himself, is contained in a bag located in front compartment, on the «Sedan», and inside the car ahead of spare wheel, on the «Multipla».

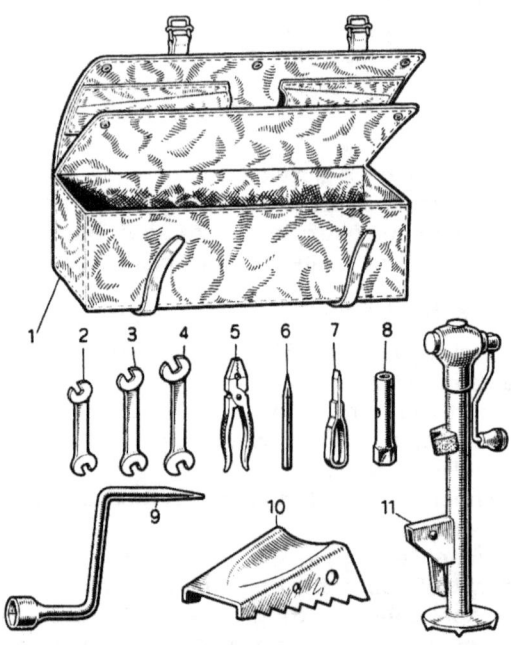

Fig. 511.

Wrenches and tools.

1. Bag, containing:
2. Wrench, double end, 8 x 10 mm.
3. Wrench, double end, 12 x 14 mm.
4. Wrench, double end, 17 x 19 mm.
5. Cutting pliers.
6. Punch, straight.
7. Screwdriver, medium.
8. Wrench, pipe, for spark plugs.
9. Speed handle.
10. Chock (*).
11. Jack.

(*) Chock is no longer included in tool kits to suit rear wheel parking brake cars.

GENERAL SPECIFICATIONS OF VEHICLES

ENGINE

Number and arrangement of cylinders . . . . . 4, in line
Bore and stroke . . . . 2.36" x 2.20" (60 x 56 mm)
Total piston displacement . . . . 633 cc
Compression ratio . . . . 7.5 to 1
Max. power, without fan, silencer and water pump 24.5 HP
Max. power, S. A. E. standards . . . . 28.5 HP
Corresponding r. p. m. rate 4600
Max. torque (without silencer, fan and water pump) 28.9 ft.lbs
(400 kgcm)
Corresponding r. p. m. rate 3000

Cast iron cylinder block and crankcase.
Aluminum cylinder head with cast iron valve seat inserts and incorporated intake manifold.
Steel crankshaft on three supports.
Thin wall, babbitt-lined main bearings and 4 thrust washers on central support.
Steel connecting rods with babbitt metal-lined thin wall type bearings and bronze bush.
Aluminum alloy pistons, shaped as an oval truncated cone, with three compression rings and oil scraper ring. The third ring is of the slotted type.

Power plant elastically mounted on car: by a central rear support with rubber pad at rear and by a crossmember with two lateral rubber mountings at front.

Valve Gear.

Overhead valves, controlled by chain-driven camshaft through pushrods and rockers.
Timing data (for engines up to No. 466800, see page 57):
— Tappet clearance adjustment for valve
timing .0177" (0,45 mm)
— Intake { Opens: B.T.D.C. . . . . . 4°
         { Closes: A.B.C.D. . . . . . 34°
— Exhaust { Opens: B.B.D.C. . . . . . 29°
          { Closes: A.T.D.C. . . . . . 1°
— Final tappet operation clearance adjustment, with cold engine:
Intake and Exhaust . . . . .0059" (0,15 mm)

Fuel System.

Mechanical, diaphragm-type fuel pump controlled by camshaft. Fuel tank mounted: in front compartment on the Sedan and behind the rear seats, against the left side of engine compartment bulkhead, on the Multipla.

GENERAL SPECIFICATIONS OF VEHICLES

Fig. 512.

Power plant, right hand side view («Sedan», from engine No. 758493).

Engine is the 100.000 type.

Fig. 513.

Power plant, left hand side view (starting from engine No. 758493, «Sedan» and from engine No. 765151, «Multipla»).

Air intake fitted with pleated paper cartridge cleaner, with intake silencer and with warm air scoop.

Weber 26 IM downdraught carburetor, with starting device.

Carburetor data:
— Air horn diameter . . . . 1.0236″ (26,00 mm)
— Venturi diameter . . . . .7480″ (19,00 »)
— Main jet diameter . . . . .0382″ (0,97 »)
— Idle jet diameter . . . . .0177″ (0,45 »)
— Starting jet diameter . . . . .0394″ (1,00 »)
— Air bleed jet . . . . .0748″ (1,90 »)

For data referring to Weber 22 IM carburetor, previously adopted, see page 88.

Lubrication.

Forced circulation by camshaft-driven gear pump.
Oil pressure relief valve on main circuit. By-pass cartridge oil filter.
Insufficient oil pressure indicator.
Normal lubrication pressure: 35.5 to 42.6 p.s.i. (2,5 to 3 kg/cm^2).
Engine oil filler cap on cylinder head cover.
Oil level indicator rod on engine left side.
Vent line from crankcase and cylinder head to carburetor air cleaner duct.

Cooling.

Sedan:

— Forced circulation by centrifugal-type water pump.
— Upright pipe radiator, cooled by belt-driven fan.
— Temperature control of water in radiator through thermostatic regulation of air draft in engine compartment.
— Excessive water temperature indicator sending unit.

Multipla:

— Forced circulation by centrifugal-type water pump.
— Upright pipe radiator cooled by belt-driven fan.
— Water temperature control through thermostat in the line from engine to radiator.
— Excessive water temperature indicator sending unit.

Ignition

by battery and ignition coil; ignition distributor with incorporated automatic advance and additional vacuum-operated diaphragm advance control.

Key ignition lock switch.

Firing order . . . . 1 - 3 - 4 - 2
Static advance . . . . 10°
Centrifugal advance . . . . 30°
Vacuum advance . . . . 20°
Ignition point gap . . . . .0185″ to .0209″ (0,47 to 0,53 mm)

Spark plugs:
— type . . . . M 14-12/225
— code . . . . CW 225 N
— thread (metric) . . . . 14 x 1,25 M
— gap . . . . .0197″ to .0236″ (0,5 to 0,6 mm)

Spark plugs (cars for export to U.S.A.):
— type . . . . M 14-13
— code (Champion) . . . . L 7
— thread (metric) . . . . 14 x 1,25 M
— gap . . . . .0236″ to .0275″ (0,6 to 0,7 mm)

Starting

by electric starter motor.

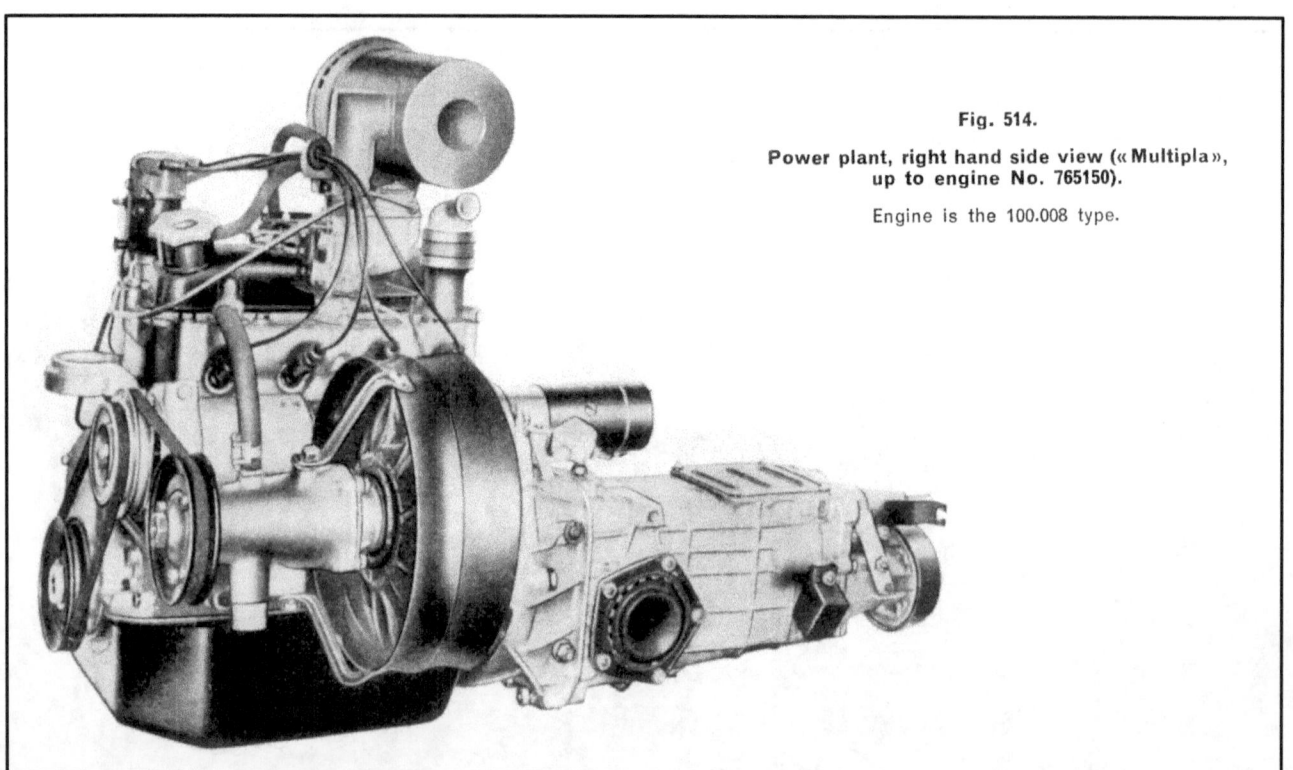

Fig. 514.

Power plant, right hand side view («Multipla», up to engine No. 765150).

Engine is the 100.008 type.

GENERAL SPECIFICATIONS OF VEHICLES

POWER TRAIN

Clutch.

Single-plate, dry, with spring-cushioned hub.
Ferodo facings: outer diameter . . . . . . 6.10" (155 mm)
Pedal free travel . . . . abt. .8" (20 mm)

Gearbox and Differential.

Gearbox with four speeds forward and one reverse, controlled by gearshift lever on tunnel. Constant mesh second, third and fourth speeds, all with synchromesh devices.

Ratios:	Sedan	Multipla
— 1st gear	3.384	3.384
— 2nd »	2.055	2.055
— 3rd »	1.333	1.280
— 4th »	0.896	0.838
— Reverse	4.275	4.275

Differential unit and final drive bevel couple incorporated in gearbox casing.

Reduction ratio { Sedan 8/43
                 { Multipla 7/45

Drive is transmitted to rear wheels through two swing half axle shaft coupled to differential by a slip joints and to wheel shaft by a flexible joint.

CHASSIS

Sedan:	in.	mm
— Wheelbase	78.75	2000
— Front track, on ground	45.30	1150
— Rear track	45.67	1160
— Ground clearance, minimum	6.30	160
Multipla:		
— Wheelbase	78.75	2000
— Front track, on ground	48.42	1230
— Rear track	45.55	1157
— Ground clearance, minimum	5.90	150

Front End Geometry (fully laden):

Sedan:	in.	mm	degrees
— Camber	.20 to .24	5 to 6	1°±20'
— Caster	—	—	9°±1°
— Kingpin inclination	—	—	5° 30'
Multipla:			
— Camber	.0984 to .1181	2,5 to 3	0°30'±20'
— Caster	—	—	6°±30'
— Kingpin inclination	—	—	7°

Front Wheel Toe-in or Toe-out:

Sedan:

— up to car No. 071086, toed-in by
  .2362" to .3149" (6 to 8 mm)
— from car No. 071087 and up to No. 377800,
  toed-in by .1181" to .1968" (3 to 5 mm)
— from car No. 377801 and up to car No. 698914,
  toed-out by .0787" (2 mm)
— from car No. 698915, toed-in by
  .0000" to .0787" (0 to 2 mm)

Multipla:

— Wheels straight with ±.039" (1 mm) tolerance.

Front Suspension.

Sedan:

Wheels independently sprung by a transversal semielliptic spring and upper swinging arms. The transversal spring performs also as an anti-roll stabilizer.
Double-acting, telescopic, hydraulic shock absorbers.
Shock absorber inner cylinder inner diameter 1.06" (27 mm).
Rubber buffers.

Multipla:

By independently sprung wheels, with swinging arms, coil springs and double-acting, telescopic, hydraulic shock absorbers.
Shock absorber inner cylinder inner diameter 1.26" (32 mm).
Transversal stabilizer bar connected to lower swinging arms and to body floor.

Rear Suspension.

Wheels independently sprung by coil springs and swinging arms.
Double-acting, telescopic, hydraulic shock absorbers.
Shock absorber inner cylinder inner diameter 1.06" (27 mm)
Rear wheel toe-in, fully laden . . . . 0°20' ± 15'
Rubber buffers.

Steering.

Sedan:

Standard: left-hand drive; RHD optional.
Control by worm screw and helical sector: ratio 2/26
Independent and symmetric track rods with central link rod and relay lever.
Turning circle diameter . . . . 28' 6" (8,70 m)

Multipla:

Standard: left-hand drive; RHD optional.
Control by worm screw and roller, operating rod, pitman arm, link rod, relay lever and independent track rods.
Worm screw/roller ratio 1/16.4
Turning circle diameter . . . . 28' 10" (8,80 m)

Service Brakes

of the expanding-shoe type, on all four wheels, hydraulically operated by master cylinder and wheel cylinders on brake housing flanges (F. B. Patent).

Drum diameters:
- Sedan . . . 7.2929" to 7.3043" (185,24 to 185,53 mm)
- Multipla . . . 8.6716" to 8.6831" (220,26 to 220,55 mm)

Lining developed lengths:
- Sedan . . . . 7.08" (180 mm)
- Multipla . . . . 8.19" (208 mm)

Lining widths:
- Sedan . . . . 1.18" (30 mm)
- Multipla . . . . 1.57" (40 mm)

Lining thickness:
- Sedan { hinged-type shoes . . . . .1575" (4 mm)
  self-centering shoes .1654" to 1772" (4,2 to 4,5 mm)
- Multipla . . . . .1575" (4 mm)

Master cylinder diameters:
- Sedan . . . . 3/4"
- Multipla . . . . 1"

Front wheel cylinder diameters:
- Sedan . . . . 3/4"
- Multipla . . . . 1 1/8"

Rear wheel cylinder diameter:
- Sedan and Multipla . . . . 3/4"

Brake shoe clearance.

Self-centering shoes:
— at adjusting cams . . . . .0098" (0,25 mm)

Hinged-type shoes:
— at upper cams . . . . .0098" (0,25 mm)
— at lower eccentric pins . . . . . .0039" (0,10 mm)

Mechanical Parking Brake

through expanding-shoes, controlled by hand lever on floor tunnel.

Late type. - On rear wheels. The bowden cable operates rear wheel shoes through a leverage.

Early type. - On drive line. The bowden cable operates, through a leverage, brake shoes expanding against a drum press fitted on to layshaft front end.

Drum diameter . . 4.5347" to 4.5433" (115,180 to 115,400 mm)
Lining developed length . . . . 4.72" (120 mm)
Lining width . . . . .984" (25 mm)
Lining thickness . . . . . . .130" to .137" (3,3 to 3,5 mm)
Shoe-to-drum clearance . . . . .0098" (0,25 mm)

Wheels and Tires.

Disc wheels with rims type . . . . 3 1/2 x 12"
Low pressure tires 5,20-12
Low pressure tires (only for Multipla and for private body builders):
- Pirelli . . . . 5,20-12 Trasporto
- Ceat . . . . 5,20-12 TL 52
- Michelin . . . . 5,20-12 C

Tire pressures:	FRONT		REAR	
	p.s.i.	kg/cm²	p.s.i.	kg/cm²
Sedan	14.2	1	22.8	1,60
Multipla	24.2	1,70	28.5	2
Multipla for body builders	27.0	1,90	Pirelli & Ceat 35.6 / Michelin 39.1	2,50 / 2,75

Fig. 515.

Gauges and controls (LHD), « Sedan ».

1. Horn button. - 2. Instrument cluster. - 3. Ignition and sundry signals lock switch. - 4. Directional signal pilot light. - 5. External light switcht. - 6. Windshield wiper switch. - 7. Instrument cluster light switch. - 8. Windshield washer pump control. - 9. Hand accelerator control. - 10. Clutch pedal. - 11. Brake pedal. - 12. Accelerator pedal. - 13. Warmed air outlet shutters. - 14. Gearshift lever. - 15. Rear wheel parking brake control lever. - 16. Choke control lever. - 17. Starter control lever.

GENERAL SPECIFICATIONS OF VEHICLES

ELECTRIC SYSTEM

Tension . . . . 12 volts

Generator.
FIAT: type D 90/12/16/3, crankshaft belt driven,
  power, maximum, steady . . . . 230 watts
Cut-in speed (lights off):
  — engine, abt. (*) . . . . 1100 r.p.m.
  — car in top gear (*) { Sedan . . . 14.3 m.p.h. (23 km/h)
                         { Multipla . . 12.5 m.p.h. (20 km/h)

(*) NOTE - Starting from the serial No. 848536, minimum charging speeds for the U.S.A. version vehicles are the following: engine 920 r.p.m., car in high gear 12 m.p.h. (19 km/h), all lights off.

Regulating Unit.
Type GN 1/12/16, three core.
Cutout, voltage regulator and current regulator in a single unit.

Battery.
Capacity (at 20 hrs discharge rate) . . . . . . 32 Ah
Location { Sedan . . . . in front compartment
         { Multipla . . . . on the right, behind rear seats
Battery to suit vehicles for export to cold weather countries (Canada, etc.) - capacity (at 20 hrs discharge rate) 38 Ah

Starter.
Type B 76-0,5/12 S; controlled by lever on tunnel. Pinion provided with free-wheel unit.
Power . . . . 0.5 kW

(*) NOTE - Starting from the serial No. 816159 (Sedan) and No. 072211 (Multipla), the vehicles for export to U.S.A. have been equipped with the starting motor type E 76-0,5/12/S. Starting motor drive by solenoid controlled from the ignition lock switch on the instrument panel.

Instrument cluster, incorporating: insufficient engine oil pressure indicator; generator charge indicator; speedometer-mileage recorder; excessive water temperature indicator; fuel level gauge with fuel reserve indicator.

Lock Switch.
Self-cancelling directional signal switch and outer lighting change-over switch unit.
Under steering wheel, lever controlled.

Windshield wiper, twin blade with three-position switch on instrument panel.

Horn - in front compartment on Sedan and on body front panel on Multipla.

Fig. 516 - **Gauges and controls (LHD), « Multipla ».**

1. External lighting changeover lever switch. - 2. Directional signal lever switch. - 3. High beam indicator (blue light). - 4. Horn button. - 5. Parking light indicator (green light). - 6. Instrument cluster. - 7. Directional signal light indicator (green light). - 8. Instrument cluster light switch. - 9. Ignition and sundry signals lock switch. - 10. External light switch. - 11. Windshield wiper switch. - 12. Heating system outlet valve control knob (two). - 13. Gearshift lever. - 14. Windshield air diffuser baffle lever. - 15. Heater radiator water passage control. - 16. Hand accelerator control. - 17. Clutch pedal. - 18. Service brake pedal. - 19. Accelerator pedal. - 20. Choke control lever. - 21. Starter control lever. - 22. Rear wheel parking brake control lever. - 23. Tool kit.

Lighting Equipment (*).

Headlamps	2
double-filament bulb:	
high beam	45 W
low beam	40 W
Front parking and direction indicator lamps	2
double filament bulb:	
parking light	5 W
turning signal	20 W
Side direction indicator lights	2
bulb	2.5 W
Rear parking, direction indicator and stop lamps with reflex reflector	2
turning signal bulb	20 W
double filament bulb:	
parking light	5 W
stop light	20 W
Rear number plate lamp	1
bulb	5 W
Inner lighting:	
bulb incorporated in rear view mirror	3 W
control switch, of the toggle type . .	on rear view mirror body
automatic jam switch	on driver's side door pillar
Inner lighting (only Multipla):	
two pillar lamps w/incorporated switch	3 W bulb
Panel light (in instrument cluster), toggle switch on instrument panel	2.5 W bulb
Engine compartment light:	
lamp with automatic switch	5 W
Indicators:	
4, in instrument cluster, each with . .	2.5 W bulb
Direction indicators flashing pilot light .	2.5 W bulb
High beam indicator light	2.5 W bulb
Parking light indicator	2.5 W bulb
Fuses: 8-Amp.	six

(*) For lighting equipment to suit vehicles « Sedan-Version 140 » and « Multipla-Version 141 », see specifications on page 306.

BODY

Sedan:

Integral construction.
Two forward-opening doors, with drop windows and anti-draught panels; safety lock on door opposite driver's seat. Driver's door locked by key.
Fixed-pane back and rear quarter windows.
Front compartment, housing the spare wheel, battery, fuel tank, brake fluid reservoir, windshield washer bottle, tool kit and a space for luggage.
Engine compartment lid at rear.
Front, adjustable, forward folding, bucket-type seats.
Rear, fixed, bench-type seat with forward-folding back.
Luggage space behind rear seat, whose back may be folded over cushion to increase luggage accomodation.
Two pockets on door inner panellings.
Rear-view mirror with incorporated bulb for car interior illumination by reflection.
Two adjustable sun visors.
Front and rear bumpers with ornaments.
Two-tone body finish is optional.

Multipla:

Integral construction.
Two front forward-opening doors, with drop windows controlled by regulator.
Two rear rear-opening doors, with two horizontally sliding window glass panes.
Driver's door locked by key and the others by safety lock.
Fixed-pane back and rear quarter windows.
Engine compartment lid at rear.
Front bench-type seat with forward-tiltable back adjustable in three positions and:
— Rear bench-type seat with forward-folding back to increase luggage space (4-5 passenger version) or serve as a bed.
— Two intermediate and two rear forward-folding seats (6-passenger version).
Imitation leather seat upholstery.
Pocket on driver's door inner panelling.
Rear-view mirror with incorporated bulb for car interior illumination by reflection.
Two adjustable sun visors.
Spare wheel, with imitation leather cover, arranged under dashboard, opposite the steering wheel side.
Tool bag and jack arranged ahead of spare wheel.

DIMENSIONS

	in.	mm
Sedan:		
Overall length with bumpers	129.33	3285
Overall length with bumpers, Version 140	130.51	3315
Width	54.33	1380
Height, unladen	55.32	1405
Multipla:		
Overall length with bumpers	139.17	3535
Overall length with bumpers, Version 141	141.14	3585
Width	57.10	1450
Height, unladen	62.21	1580

WEIGHTS

Sedan:

Curb weight . . . . 1334 lbs (605 kg)
Useful load: 4 passengers plus 66 lbs (30 kg) of luggage.
Total weight, full load . . . . 2017 lbs (915 kg)

Multipla:

Curb weight . . . . 1653 lbs (750 kg)
Curb weight, Version 141 . . . . . . 1664 lbs (755 kg)
Useful load:
— 6 passengers;
— 5 passengers plus 154 lbs (70 kg) of luggage;
— 4 passengers plus 309 lbs (140 kg) of luggage;
— 2 passengers plus 618 lbs (280 kg) of luggage;
— driver plus 772 lbs (350 kg) of luggage.
Total weight, full load . . . . 2579 lbs (1170 kg)

GENERAL SPECIFICATIONS OF VEHICLES

FUEL CONSUMPTION

According to CUNA (*) Standards (on highway, at 2/3 max. speed):

	m.p.g.	l/100 km
Sedan	41.25 (U.S.) 49.50 (G.B.)	5,7
Multipla	35 (U.S.) 42 (G.B.)	6,7

Average cruising range:

	miles	km
Sedan	260	420
Multipla	250	400

Fuel tank capacity:

	Gals	lt
Sedan	7.13 (U.S.) 5.94 (G.B.)	27
Multipla	7.6 (U.S.) 6.4 (G.B.)	29

(*) Italian Committee for Automotive Industry Standards.

PERFORMANCES

Speeds.

Maximum permissible speeds after running-in:

	Sedan		Multipla	
	m.p.h.	km/h	m.p.h.	km/h
1st gear, abt.	15.5	25	12.5	20
2nd » »	25	40	22	35
3rd » »	40.3	65	34	55
4th » »	62.1	100	56	90

Climbable Gradients.

Maximum, fully laden:

	Sedan %	Multipla %
1st gear abt.	27	23
2nd »	15	13
3rd »	9	7.5
4th »	5	4
Reverse »	30	29

CONVERTIBLE

The differences between the **Convertible** and the **Standard Sedan** are briefly described here.

For all other data refer to the information given for the **Standard Sedan** in this Manual.

Body.

Essentially the difference consists in the imitation leather folding top which may be easily rolled up and strapped on roof rear edge.

Dimensions.

Maximum height (unladen) . . . . 55.7" (1415 mm)

TAXI CAB

The differences between the **Taxi Cab** and the **Multipla** are briefly described here.

For all other data refer to the information given for the **Multipla** in this Manual.

Fig. 517 - 600 Model «Convertible».
Top rolled up.

Electric System.

The only differences are:
— Two passenger compartment pillar lamps (with cylindrical 5-Watt bulbs) without incorporated switch that, instead, is mounted on the instrument panel, next to the instrument cluster.
— A taximeter light switch, centrally located on panel lower edge.

Body.

Main differences are:
— Fixed, single, bucket-type front seat.
— Two central, forward-facing, folding seats.
— Rear bench type seat, fixed.
— Metal partition dividing the driver's and passengers' compartments provided with two glass panes. Driver's side glass is sliding and has a circular window cut in it to permit inter-communication.
— Luggage accomodation next to driver's seat.
— Luggage rack on roof.

Dimensions.

Maximum height, unladen, with luggage rack 65.75″ (1670 mm).

Weights.

Curb weight . . . . 1,698 lbs (770 kg)
Payload . . . . . 5 persons plus 88 lbs (40 kg) of luggage.

Section 13
MODEL 600 D

	Page
MAIN SPECIFICATIONS	362
CAPACITIES	363
SERVICE DIRECTIONS	365
ENGINE	365
CLUTCH	382
BRAKES	382
ELECTRICAL	382
BODY	386

MAIN SPECIFICATIONS

(Differences in respect of Model 600)

NOTE - For all the data and instructions not covered by this section, refer to the previous sections of this manual.

SEDAN AND MULTIPLA

— Engine: type 100 D.000 (Sedan) and 100 D.008 (Multipla); power output 29 HP at 4800 r.p.m.; centrifugal oil filter; Weber 28 ICP 1 or Solex C 28 PIB-2 carburetor and greater capacity water pump.
— Cooling system radiator with larger diameter inlet and outlet.
— Air cleaner: pan type, with paper cartridge and warm and cold air intake to suit climatic conditions.
— External crankcase oil vent: line from cylinder head cover.
— Starter motor: with electromagnetic switch controlled from ignition lock switch key.
— Rear axle final drive ratio { Sedan: 8/39. Multipla: 8/43.
— Rear wheel toe-in (both wheels): 0° 0' to 0° 25'.
— Brake wheel cylinders with the following inner diameters:

« Sedan » { front 7/8''. rear 3/4''.

« Multipla » { front 1 1/8''. rear 3/4''.

— Battery: of larger dimensions and fitted with electrolyte « level sight » at filler necks.
— Front doors swivelling ventipane (Sedan).

ENGINE Type 100 D. 000 (Sedan) and 100 D. 008 (Multipla)

No. of cylinders	4, in line
Bore	2.450'' (62 mm)
Stroke	2.500'' (63,5 mm)
Displacement	767 cc
Compression ratio	7.5 to 1
Maximum horsepower (less silencer, fan and water pump)	29 HP
Maximum horsepower, SAE rating	32 HP
Maximum rate at max. power	4800 r.p.m.

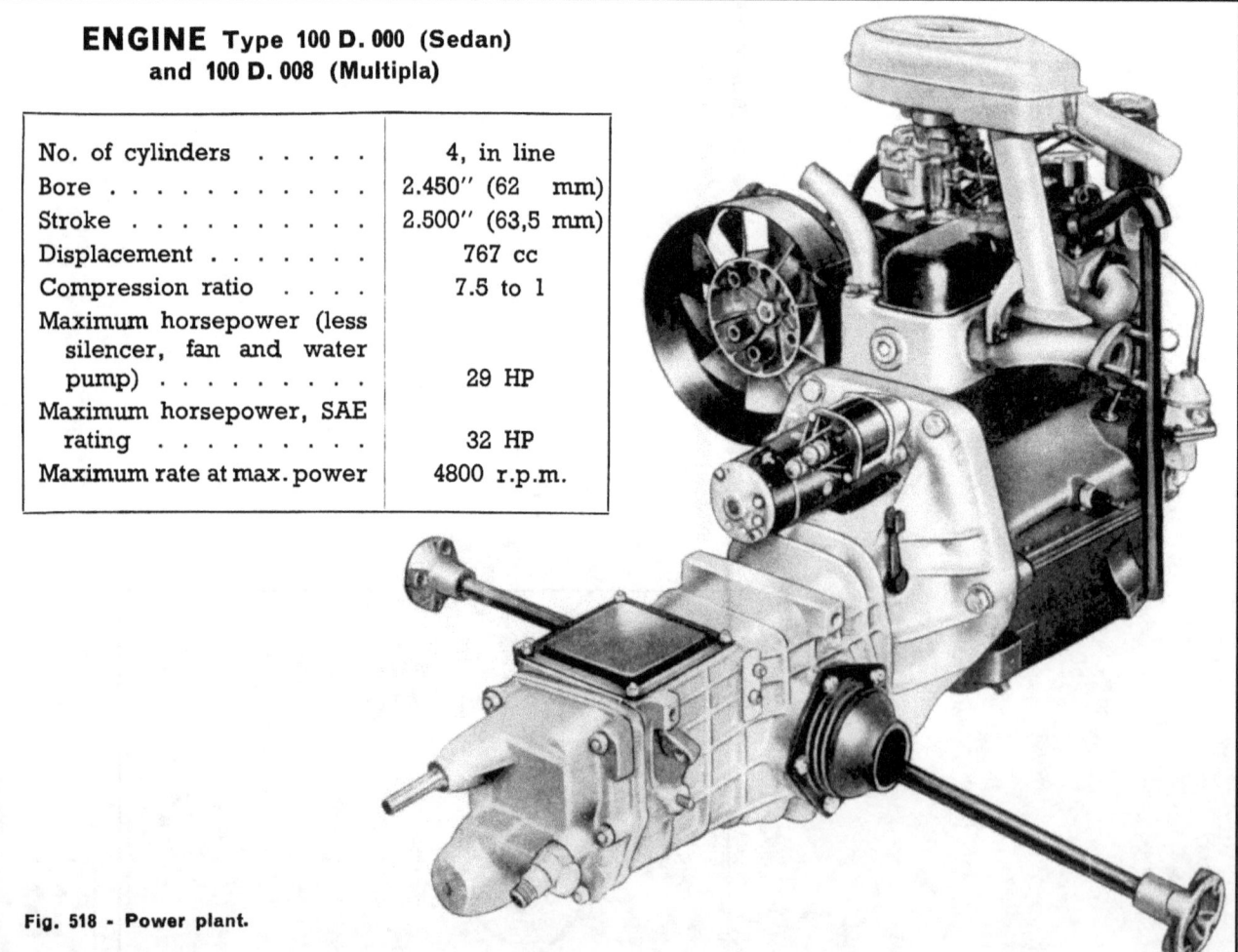

Fig. 518 - Power plant.

VEHICLE SPECIFICATIONS

PERFORMANCES	Sedan		Multipla	
	m.p.h.	km/h	m.p.h.	km/h
Maximum speed under full load, on level, with good road conditions and run-in engine:				
In 1st gear	19	30	16	25
In 2nd gear	28	45	25	40
In 3rd gear	44	70	40	65
In 4th gear . . . abt.	68	110	65	105
In reverse	16	25	12	20
Maximum climbable gradients, under full load, with good road conditions and run-in engine:				
In 1st gear	30%		24%	
In 2nd gear	17%		14%	
In 3rd gear	10%		8%	
In 4th gear	5.5%		4.5%	
In reverse gear	36%		30%	
Weights:				
Curb weight	1334 lbs (605 kg)		1654 lbs (750 kg)	
Useful load	4 persons plus 110 lbs (50 kg) luggage		1 person plus 882 lbs (400 kg) or 6 persons plus 132 lbs (60 kg)	
Gross vehicle weight	2035 lbs (925 kg)		2712 lbs (1230 kg)	

CAPACITIES

UNIT	QUANTITY				FILL-IN
	Imp.units	U.S. units	lt	kg	
Fuel tank	5.94 gals	7.13 gals	27	—	Gasoline: Oct. Rat. 83 (Research Meth.)
Radiator and engine	1 gal	1.2 gals	4,5		Water (^{1})
Oil pan (^{2})	2.64 qts	3.16 qts	3,0	2,700	FIAT oil (^{3})
Transmission and differential	1.32 qts	1.59 qts	1,505	1,400	FIAT W 90 oil (SAE 90 EP)
Steering gear	.21 pts	.25 pts	0,120	0,110	
Hydraulic brakes	.48 pts	.58 pts	0,275	0,275	Special FIAT blue label brake fluid
Front shock absorbers, each	.24 pts	.29 pts	0,135	0,120	FIAT S. A. I. fluid
Rear shock absorbers, each	.21 pts	.25 pts	0,120	0,110	
Windshield washer bag	(^{4})	(^{4})	—	(^{4})	Water and FIAT D. P./1 fluid mixture (concentrated solution).

(^{1}) When temperature approaches 32° F (0° C), replace radiator water by **special Fiat anti-freezing mixture**.
(^{2}) Total capacity of oil pan, filter and pipings is 3.16 Imp. qts - 3.6 U. S. qts (3,25 kg). The figure given in the chart corresponds to the amount required for periodical oil changes, excluding replacement of by-pass filter cartridge (see note).
(^{3}) Recommended oil grades are chartered on page 375.
(^{4}) Pure water .66 Imp. qts - .80 U. S. qts (0,75 kg) plus .60 oz (17 g) (Summer) or 1.2 oz (34 g) (Winter) cleaner.
NOTE - The replacement of engine oil should be made every 6,000 miles (10.000 km). The new routine is valid when FIAT oil for service MS (VS series) or FIAT multigrade oil are used.
Should these FIAT oils not be available, recourse should be made to the supplement 1 type of oil which fills service MS requirements, provided Suppliers indicate it to be suitable for replacement every 6,000 miles (10.000 km).

TRANSMISSION-DIFFERENTIAL UNIT

Transmission and final drive ratios are the following:

SPEED	I	II	III	IV	Reverse
Gearshift ratios:					
— «Sedan»	$\frac{44}{13} = 3.384$	$\frac{37}{18} = 2.055$	$\frac{32}{24} = 1.333$	$\frac{26}{29} = 0.896$	$\frac{24}{13} \times \frac{44}{19} = 4.275$
— «Multipla»	$\frac{44}{13} = 3.384$	$\frac{37}{18} = 2.055$	$\frac{32}{25} = 1.280$	$\frac{26}{31} = 0.838$	$\frac{24}{13} \times \frac{44}{19} = 4.275$
Final drive ratios:					
— «Sedan» (8/39)	16.497	10.018	6.498	4.368	20.840
— «Multipla» (8/43)	18.189	11.045	6.880	4.504	22.978

LOCK SWITCH

Controls ignition, starting and services:

— Position 0: all OFF (key can be pulled out).
— Position 1: ignition ON and services energized.
— Position 2: starter ON.
— Position 3: parking and number plate lights ON, with outer lighting change-over switch lever in upper position (key can be pulled out).

Fig. 519 - Ignition lock switch - Controls ignition, starting and services.

INSTRUMENT CLUSTER

The 5-indication instrument cluster shown in figure 520, incorporates:

a) Excessive water temperature indicator.
b) Generator charge indicator.
c) Speedometer-mileage indicator.
d) Insufficient oil pressure indicator.
e) Fuel level gauge.
f) Fuel reserve supply indicator.

Fig. 520 - Instrument cluster.
a. Excessive water temperature indicator. - b. Generator charge indicator. - c. Speedometer-mileage recorder. - d. Insufficient oil pressure indicator. - e. Fuel level gauge. - f. Fuel reserve supply indicator.

DOOR VENTIPANES

Door ventipanes consist of the following parts (see fig. 559 - 560 - 561):

— glass pane;
— metal reveal;
— glass frame;
— weatherstrip frame;
— weatherstrip;
— lock handle;
— lock handle pin;
— lockwasher, handle.

MAIN SERVICING DIRECTIONS

ENGINE

PISTONS

Pistons are of the aluminum-alloy, slipper-type as shown in fig. 521.

Pistons as well as cylinder liners are selected into classes A-B-C based on skirt diameter meas-

CONNECTING RODS

The steel connecting rods are of the standard type, i. e., they are not offset (see fig. 522).

Connecting rod small end and bush are milled to ensure adequate lubrication of bush and pin.

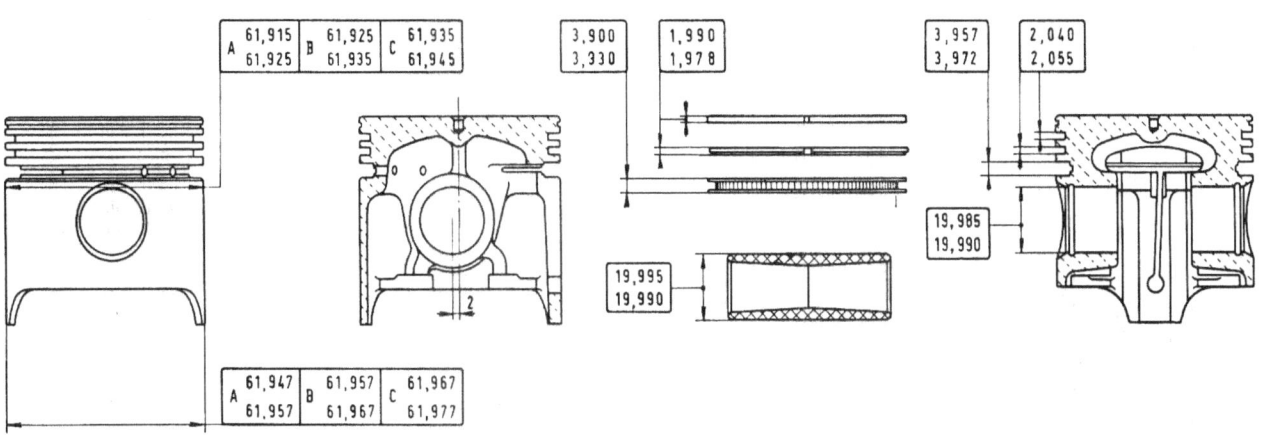

Fig. 521 - Piston, pin and rings data.

NOTE - The heights of ring grooves on piston have been lately modified as follows (see table page 371):

1st groove from 2,040 to 2,055 mm to 2,035 to 2,050 mm

2nd groove from 2,040 to 2,055 mm to 2,015 to 2,030 mm

ured on axis perpendicular to piston pin, as follows :

— at skirt top :

Class A 2.4375″ to 2.4379″ (61,915 to 61,925 mm)
Class B 2.4379″ to 2.4383″ (61,925 to 61,935 mm)
Class C 2.4383″ to 2.4387″ (61,935 to 61,945 mm)

— at skirt bottom :

Class A 2.4388″ to 2.4392″ (61,947 to 61,957 mm)
Class B 2.4392″ to 2.4396″ (61,957 to 61,967 mm)
Class C 2.4396″ to 2.4400″ (61,967 to 61,977 mm)

Pistons and liners must always be paired class by class. Cylinder liner diameters are tabulated on page 369.

Pistons and liners of the same class must have the following fit clearances :

— at skirt top   .0030″ to .0037″ (0,075 to 0,095 mm)
— at skirt bottom .0017″ to .0025″ (0,043 to 0,063 mm)

When replacing small end bushes the new bush must first be press-fitted into place and then milled

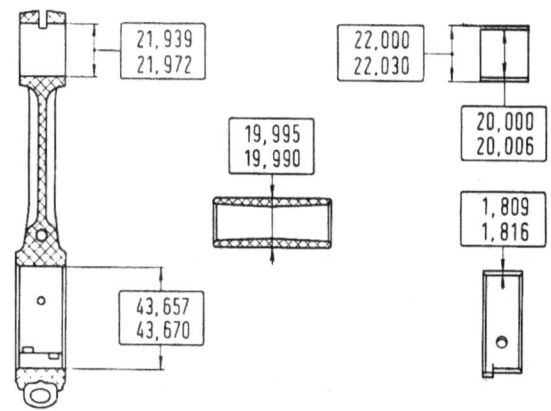

Fig. 522 - Connecting rod, piston pin, bush and bearing data.

by a suitable cutter. Use a cutter having a diameter of 2.1654" (55 mm) and a width of .1181" (3 mm) whose center - during the milling operation - shall be at 1.3780" (35 mm) from small end bore axis.

After the milling operation, ream bush I. D. to .7874" to .7876" (20,000 to 20,006 mm) using expansible reamer **U. 0307**.

Piston pin-to-bush fit clearance: .00020" to .00063" (0,005 to 0,016 mm).

GRINDING JOURNALS AND CRANKPINS

Before regrinding, measure the diameter of crankpins and journals by micrometer and determine, with respect to bearing undersizes, the diameter to which they must be reduced, bearing in mind the following fit clearances:

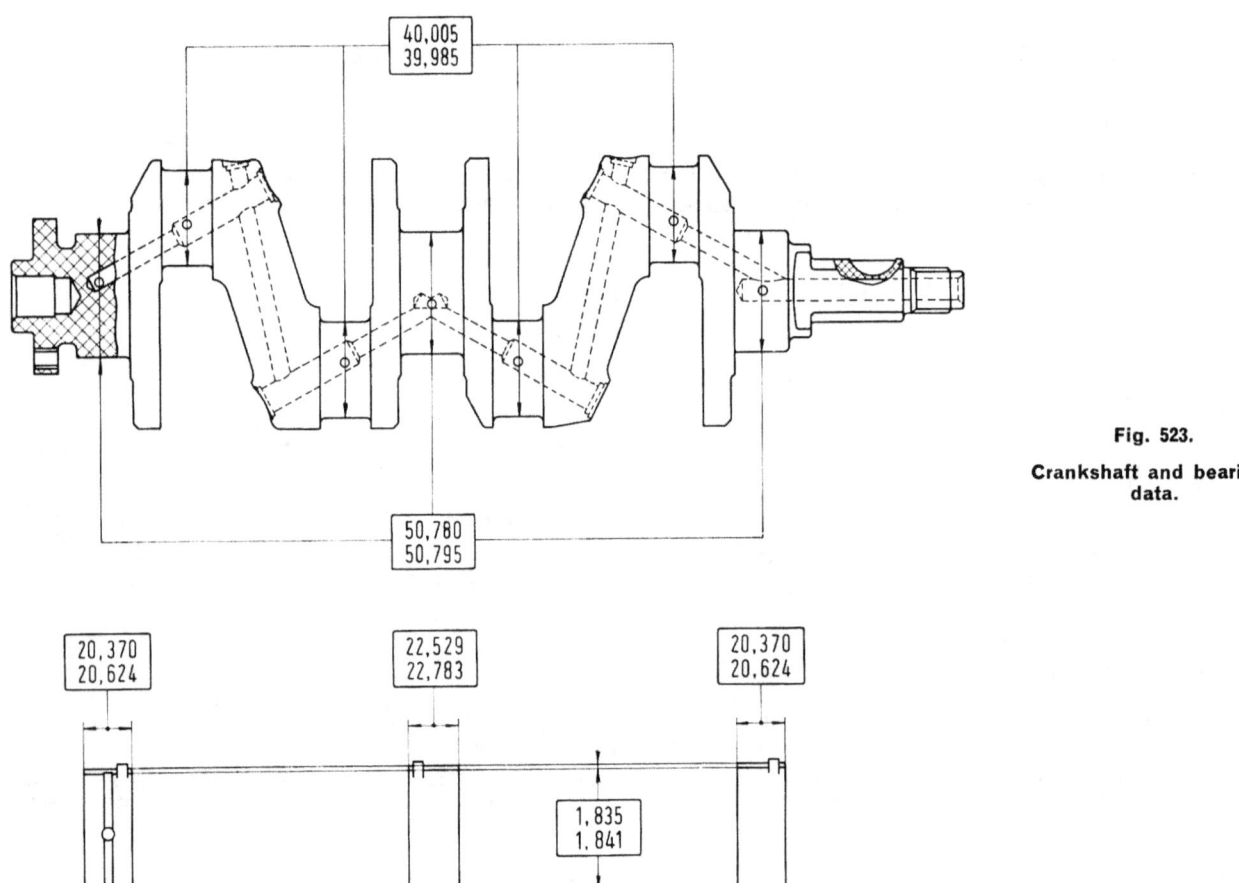

Fig. 523.

Crankshaft and bearings data.

PISTON-CONNECTING ROD ASSEMBLY AND INSTALLATION

The rod and piston sets must be mated in such a way that the cylinder identification number stamped on connecting rod stem and cap faces the side opposite the expansion slot in piston.

Then install the rod-piston assembly with identification numbers facing the camshaft.

CRANKSHAFT

The three-bearing crankshaft has rifle holes to ensure proper lubrication of bearings. Two special rings on central journal take up axial thrusts.

— journal-to-main bearing .00118" to .00276" (0,030 to 0,070 mm);
— crankpin-to-connecting rod bearing .00079" to .00264" (0,020 to 0,067 mm).

VALVES

Mushroom head max. dimensions: 1.00" to 1.008" (25,4 to 25,6 mm) for intake valves and .921" to .929" (23,4 to 23,6 mm) for exhaust valves.

Smaller diameter of valve seats in cylinder head: .866" to .874" (22 to 22,2 mm) for intake valve and .787" to .795" (20 to 20,2 mm) for exhaust valves.

For all other data covering valve guides, springs, etc., refer to the table on page 373.

JOURNAL DIAMETERS

Standard	Undersizes			
	.01″ (0,254 mm)	.02″ (0,508 mm)	.03″ (0,762 mm)	.04″ (1,016 mm)
1.9992″ (50,780 mm)	1.9892″ (50,526 mm)	1.9792″ (50,272 mm)	1.9692″ (50,018 mm)	1.9592″ (49,764 mm)
1.9998″ (50,795 mm)	1.9898″ (50,541 mm)	1.9798″ (50,287 mm)	1.9698″ (50,033 mm)	1.9598″ (49,779 mm)

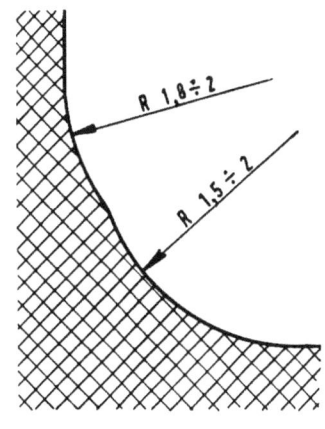

Fig. 524.
Specified fillet radius on front journal shoulders (timing gear end).

CRANKPIN DIAMETERS

Standard	Undersizes			
	.01″ (0,254 mm)	.02″ (0,508 mm)	.03″ (0,762 mm)	.04″ (1,016 mm)
1.5742″ (39,985 mm)	1.5642″ (39,731 mm)	1.5542″ (39,477 mm)	1.5442″ (39,223 mm)	1.5342″ (38,969 mm)
1.5750″ (40,005 mm)	1.5650″ (39,751 mm)	1.5550″ (39,497 mm)	1.5450″ (39,243 mm)	1.5350″ (38,989 mm)

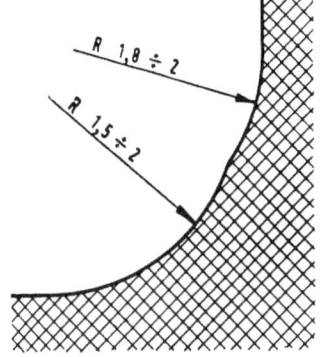

Fig. 525.
Specified fillet radius on rear journal shoulders (flywheel end).

THICKNESS OF MAIN BEARING HALVES

Standard	Undersizes			
	.01″ (0,254 mm)	.02″ (0,508 mm)	.03″ (0,762 mm)	.04″ (1,016 mm)
.0723″ (1,835 mm)	.0772″ (1,962 mm)	.0822″ (2,089 mm)	.0872″ (2,216 mm)	.0923″ (2,343 mm)
.0725″ (1,841 mm)	.0774″ (1,968 mm)	.0824″ (2,095 mm)	.0874″ (2,222 mm)	.0925″ (2,349 mm)

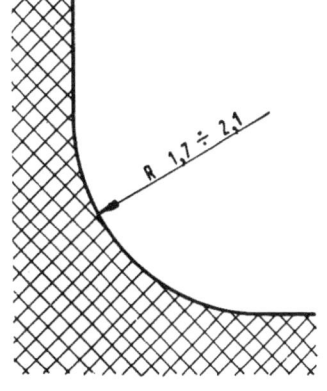

Fig. 526.
Specified fillet radius on central journal shoulders.

THICKNESS OF CONNECTING ROD BEARING HALVES

Standard	Undersizes			
	.01″ (0,254 mm)	.02″ (0,508 mm)	.03″ (0,762 mm)	.04″ (1,016 mm)
.0713″ (1,809 mm)	.0763″ (1,936 mm)	.0813″ (2,063 mm)	.0863″ (2,190 mm)	.0913″ (2,317 mm)
.0715″ (1,816 mm)	.0765″ (1,943 mm)	.0815″ (2,070 mm)	.0865″ (2,197 mm)	.0915″ (2,324 mm)

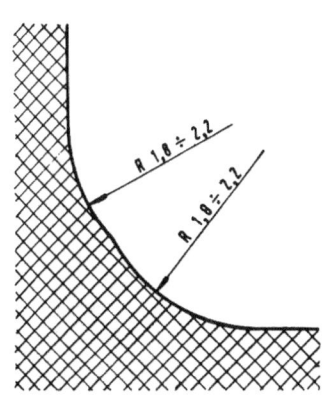

Fig. 527.
Specified fillet radius on crankpin shoulders.

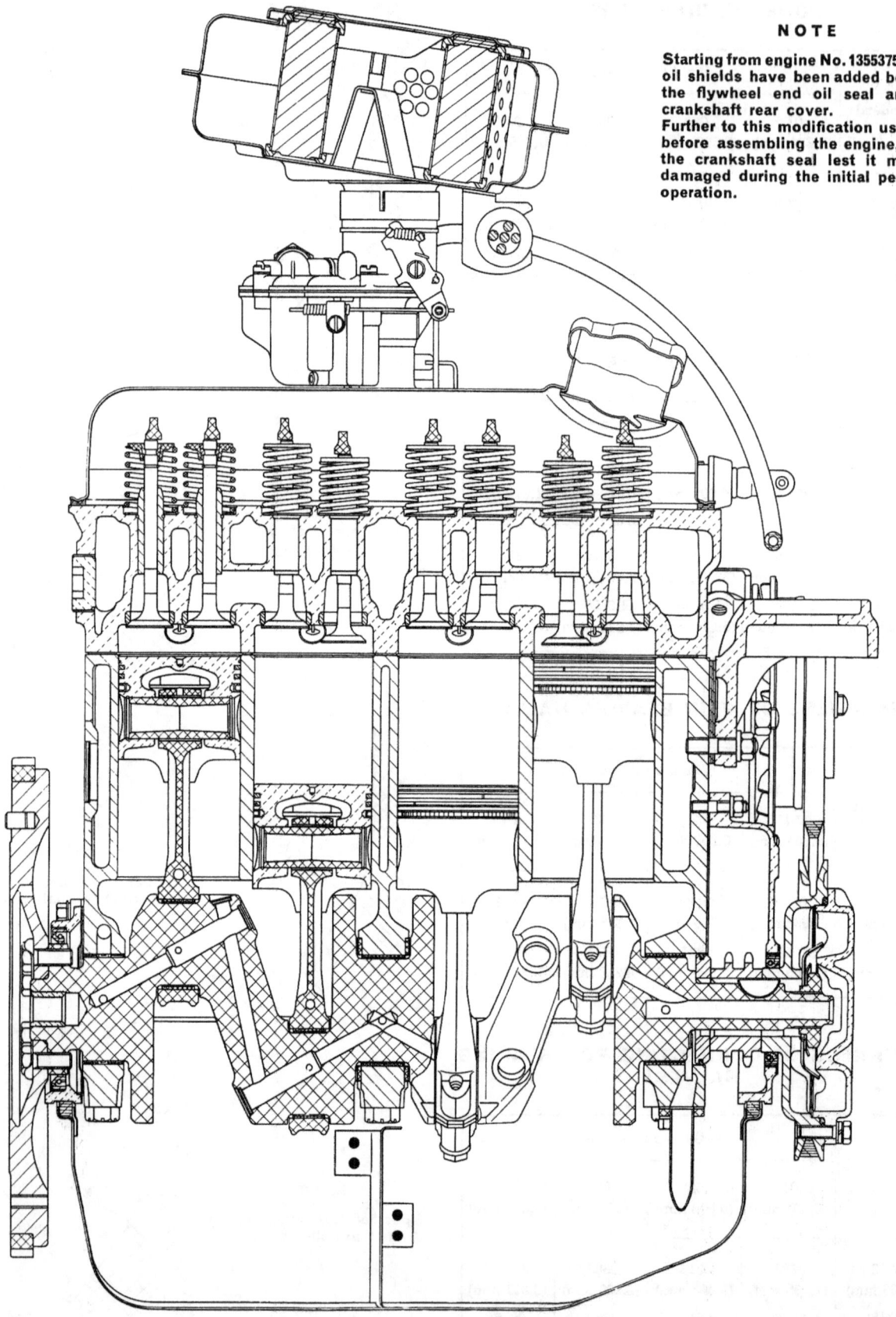

NOTE

Starting from engine No. 1355375, metal oil shields have been added between the flywheel end oil seal and the crankshaft rear cover.
Further to this modification use care, before assembling the engine, to oil the crankshaft seal lest it may be damaged during the initial period of operation.

Fig. 528 - Engine longitudinal section.

CRANK GEAR DATA

CYLINDER BLOCK AND CRANKCASE

		in	mm
Cylinder liner diameter	Class A	2.4409 to 2.4413	62,000 to 62,010
	Class B	2.4413 to 2.4417	62,010 to 62,020
	Class C	2.4417 to 2.4421	62,020 to 62,030
Camshaft bush seat diameters:			
— chain end	Class A	1.8900 to 1.8904	47,990 to 48,000
	Class B	1.8904 to 1.8908	48,000 to 48,010
	Class C	1.8908 to 1.8912	48,010 to 48,020
— central		1.6504 to 1.6516	41,920 to 41,950
— flywheel end		1.4143 to 1.4155	35,921 to 35,951
Standard tappet seat diameter		.5516 to .5523	14,010 to 14,028
Main bearing seat diameter		2.1459 to 2.1464	54,507 to 54,520
Central main bearing width		.9249 to .9273	23,24 to 23,20

CONNECTING RODS - C/ROD BEARINGS AND BUSHES

	in	mm
Connecting rod bearing seat diameter	1.7188 to 1.7193	43,657 to 43,670
Connecting rod small end bush seat diameter	.8638 to .8651	21,939 to 21,972
Connecting rod standard bearing thickness	.0713 to .0715	1,809 to 1,816
Connecting rod bearing undersizes	.01-.02-.03-.04	0,254-0,508-0,762 1,016
Connecting rod small end bush O. D.	.8661 to .8673	22,00 to 22,03
Connecting rod small end bush I. D. (to be obtained after press fitting)	.7874 to .7876	20,000 to 20,006
Piston pin-to-bush fit clearance	.00020 to .00063	0,005 to 0,016
Bush-to-connecting rod small end (pinch fit at all times)	.0011 to .0036	0,028 to 0,091
Connecting rod bearing-to-crankpin fit clearance	.00079 to .00264	0,020 to 0,067

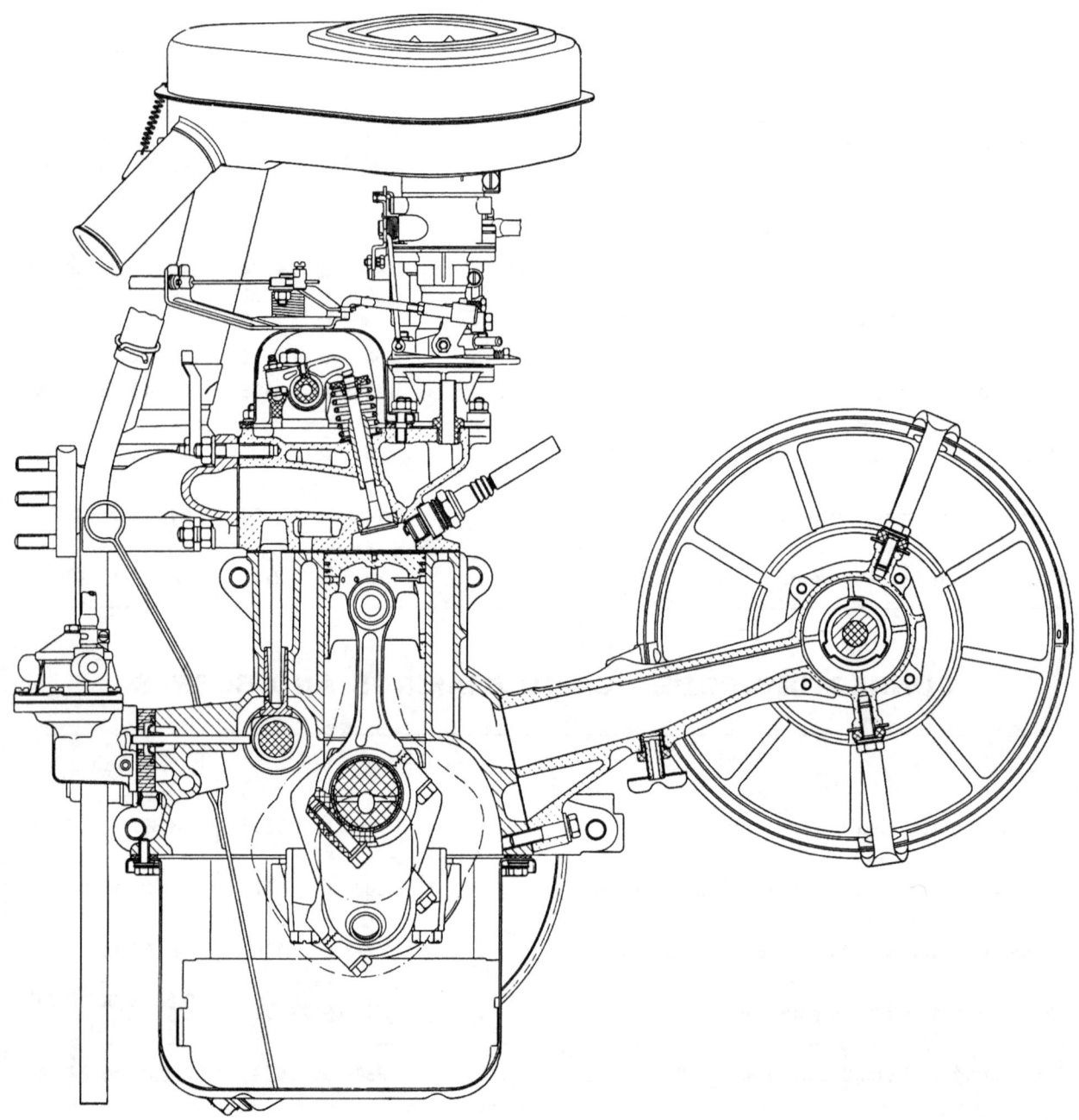

Fig. 529 - Section of power plant through crank gear, valve gear and water pump.

PISTONS - PISTON RINGS - PINS

		in	mm
Piston diameter, on axis perpendicular to pin:			
— at skirt top — Class A		2.4375 to 2.4379	61,915 to 61,925
Class B		2.4379 to 2.4383	61,925 to 61,935
Class C		2.4383 to 2.4387	61,935 to 61,945
— at skirt bottom — Class A		2.4388 to 2.4392	61,947 to 61,957
Class B		2.4392 to 2.4396	61,957 to 61,967
Class C		2.4396 to 2.4400	61,967 to 61,977
Piston pin bore diameter		.7866 to .7868	19,985 to 19,990

	in LATE TYPE mm		EARLY TYPE	
Ring groove height — 1st groove	.0801 to .0807	2,035 to 2,050	.0803 to .0809	2,04 to 2,055
2nd groove	.0793 to .0799	2,015 to 2,030	.0803 to .0809	2,04 to 2,055
3rd groove	.1552 to .1564	3,957 to 3,972	.1558 to .1564	3,957 to 3,972

	in	mm
Piston standard pin diameter	.7872 to .7868	19,995 to 19,990
Spare piston pin oversizes	.0079	0,2
Piston ring thickness:		
— 1st compr. ring and 2nd oilscraper ring	.0784 to .0779	1,990 to 1,978
— 3rd radial-slotted oilscraper ring	.1535 to .1547	3,90 to 3,93
Piston to cylinder liner fit clearance, on axis perpendicular to pin:		
— at skirt top	.0030 to .0037	0,075 to 0,095
— at skirt bottom	.0017 to .0025	0,043 to 0,063
Piston pin to boss bore (pinch fit at all times)	0 to .00039	0 to 0,010

	in LATE TYPE mm		EARLY TYPE	
Ring-to-piston groove land fit clearance:				
— 1st grove	.00177 to .00283	0,045 to 0,072	.00197 to .00303	0,050 to 0,077
— 2nd groove	.00092 to .00205	0,025 to 0,052	.00197 to .00303	0,050 to 0,077
— 3rd groove	.00106 to .00283	0,027 to 0,072	.00106 to .00283	0,027 to 0,072

	in	mm
Ring gap, with rings in barrel:		
— 1st and 2nd ring	.00787 to .01378	0,20 to 0,35
— 3rd ring	none	none
Spare piston oversizes	.0079-.0157-.0236 .0315	0,2-0,4-0,6-0,8
Piston ring oversizes: 1st and 2nd	.0079-.0157-.0236	0,2-0,4-0,6-0,8
3rd	.0315-.0157	0,4

CRANKSHAFT - MAIN BEARING HALVES

	in	mm
Standard crankpin diameter	1.5751 to 1.5743	40,008 to 39,988
Main bearing seats diameter	2.1460 to 2.1465	54,507 to 54,520
Thickness of standard main bearing halves	.0723 to .0725	1,835 to 1,841
Main bearing halves undersizes	.01-.02-.03-.04	0,254-0,508-0,762 1,016
Standard journal diameter	1.9992 to 1.9998	50,780 to 50,795
Main bearing halves-to-journals fit clearance	.00118 to .00276	0,030 to 0,070
Central journal shoulder-to-shoulder width	1.1055 to 1.1071	28,08 to 28,12
Central journal support width across thrust ring seats	.9149 to .9173	23,24 to 23,30
Thickness of standard central main bearing thrust rings	.0909 to .0929	2,31 to 2,36
Central main bearing thrust ring oversize	.0039	0,10
Clearance to crankshaft shoulder	.0102	0,26

VALVE GEAR DATA

CAMSHAFT AND ITS BUSHES

		in	mm
Camshaft bush seat diameters:			
— chain end { Class A*		1.8894 to 1.8898	47,990 to 48,000
Class B		1.8898 to 1.8902	48,000 to 48,010
Class C		1.8902 to 1.8906	48,010 to 48,020
— central		1.6504 to 1.6516	41,920 to 41,950
— flywheel end		1.4143 to 1.4155	35,921 to 35,951
Camshaft bush O.D.	in Free mm	Press fitted	
— chain end { Class A*	1.8886 to 1.8894 47,970 to 47,990	—	—
Class B	1.8892 to 1.8896 47,985 to 47,995	—	—
Class C	1.8896 to 1.8900 47,995 to 48,005	—	—
— central	1.6550 to 1.6565 42,037 to 42,075	1.6504 to 1.6516	41,920 to 41,950
— flywheel end	1.4185 to 1.4200 36,030 to 36,068	1.4143 to 1.4155	35,921 to 35,951
Camshaft bush I.D.	Press fitted	Finished in seat	
— chain end	1.4870 to 1.4910 37,770 to 37,871	1.4971 to 1.4976	38,025 to 38,037
— central	1.4850 to 1.4890 37,719 to 37,821	1.4970 to 1.4978	38,024 to 38,044
— flywheel end	1.2069 to 1.2110 30,657 to 30,759	1.2215 to 1.2223	31,026 to 31,046
Bush-to-seat fits:			
— chain end (clearance)		.00020 to .00098	0,005 to 0,025
— central (pinch)		.00343 to .00610	0,087 to 0,155
— flywheel end (pinch)		.00311 to .00579	0,079 to 0,147
Camshaft journals diameters:			
— chain end		1.4961 to 1.4951	38,000 to 37,975
— central		1.4961 to 1.4951	38,000 to 37,975
— flywheel end		1.2205 to 1.2195	31,000 to 30,975
Camshaft journals-to-bush fits:			
— chain end		.00098 to .00244	0,025 to 0,062
— central		.00094 to .00272	0,024 to 0,069
— flywheel end		.00102 to .00283	0,026 to 0,071

(*) Crankcases of early production.

CYLINDER HEAD - VALVES - VALVE GUIDES AND SPRINGS

	in	mm
Valve guide seat diameter in cylinder head	.5098 to .5108	12,950 to 12,977
Valve guide O.D.	.5118 to .5130	13,000 to 13,030
Valve guide I.D. (press fitted)	.2765 to .2772	7,022 to 7,040
Valve guide to cylinder head	pinch fit at all times of	
	.00091 to .00315	0,023 to 0,080
Valve stem diameter	.2756 to .2750	7,000 to 6,985
Valve stem-to-guide clearance	.00079 to .0021	0,020 to 0,055
Valve seat inclination angle on cylinder head	45° ± 5′	
Valve face inclination angle	45° 30′ ± 5′	
Intake valve head max. diameter	1.000 to 1.008	25,4 to 25,6
Exhaust valve head max. diameter	.921 to .929	23,4 to 23,6
For a complete valve revolution, guided by stem, T.I.R. with plunger on face center	.00079	0,02
Valve seat height above cylinder head	.0512 to .0591	1,3 to 1,5
Valve seats minor diameter:		
— intake	.866 to .874	22 to 22,2
— exhaust	.787 to .795	20 to 20,2
Valve spring I.D.	.795	20,2
Valve spring free height	2.04	51,7
Valve spring height under a 53.4 lbs (24,2 kg) load (closed valve)	1.26	32
Valve spring height under a 73.6 lbs (33,4 kg) load (open valve)	.96	24,5
Minimum permissible load referred to a 1.26 in (32 mm) height	41.9 lbs	19 kg
Valve lift { intake	.295	7,55
exhaust	.278	7,05

VALVE PUSHRODS - ROCKERS - ROCKER SHAFT AND SUPPORTS

	in	mm
Pushrod seat dia. in crankcase	.5516 to .5524	14,010 to 14,028
Standard pushrod O.D.	.5513 to .5502	14,000 to 13,982
Pushrod oversizes	.00197 - .00394	0,05 - 0,10
Pushrod-to-seat clearance	.00039 to .00181	0,010 to 0,046
Rocker shaft support bore dia.	.5910 to .5917	15,010 to 15,028
Rocker shaft diameter	.5906 to .5901	15,000 to 14,988
Rocker shaft-to-support clearance	.00039 to .00157	0,010 to 0,040
Rocker bore diameter	.5910 to .5918	15,010 to 15,030
Rocker-to-shaft clearance	.00039 to .00165	0,010 to 0,042

TIGHTENING REFERENCE

ITEM	Drwg. or Std. Part No.	Thread	Material	Tightening torque	
				ft.lbs	kgm
Flywheel-to-crankshaft screw	1/60434/30	M 8 x 1,25	R 100	25.3 to 28.9	3,5 to 4
Main bearing cap-to-crankcase screw	4052463	M 10 x 1,25	R 100	44.8	6,2
Cap-to-connecting rod bolt	4101608	M 8 x 1	R 100	25.3	3,5
Sprocket-to-camshaft screw	1/59707/20	M 10 x 1,25	R 80	36.2	5
Cylinder head-to-crankcase and thermal switch screw	1/60444/30 1/60450/30 1/60451/30	M 8 x 1,25	R 100	20.3 to 21.7	2,8 to 3
Rocker support-to-cylinder head stud nut	1/61008/20	M 8 x 1,25	R 80 (stud R 100)	14.5	2
Fan and generator drive pulley-to-crankshaft nut	4064759	M 18 x 1,5	R 50 Cdt (crankshaft C 40 Bon.)	72.3	10
Air conveyor-to-water pump screw	898514	M 8 x 1	R 80 Cdt	18.1	2,5
Drive pulley cover screw	1/38236/21	M 6 x 1	R 80 Cdt	5.8	0,8
Spark plug	4012866 4067805	M 14 x 1,25	—	18.1 to 21.7	2,5 to 3

LUBRICATION

Forced, by gear pump. Besides the pump, the lubrication system includes:

— a suction scoop with filter screen, connected to pump by a pipe;
— a centrifugal filter on delivery line;
— a pressure regulating valve in crankcase;
— a sending unit for insufficient oil pressure indicator.

Specified normal oil pressure is 35.6 to 42.7 psi (2,5 to 3 kg/cm^2).

Fig. 530 - Bottom view of engine with oil sump removed.

Fig. 531 - Centrifugal filter details.
1. Cover (removed). - 2. Seal ring. - 3. Centrifugal hub. - 4. Deflector ring. - 5. Lockplate. - 6. Mounting nut. - 7. Oil duct.

NOTE - Starting from engine No. 1101669, Sedan, and engine No. 1101681, Multipla, provision has been made for a supplementary oil filter of the cartridge-element type on the crankcase, shunt-connected to the main delivery circuit.

Filter cartridge replacement is recommended to take place every 6,000 miles (10.000 km).

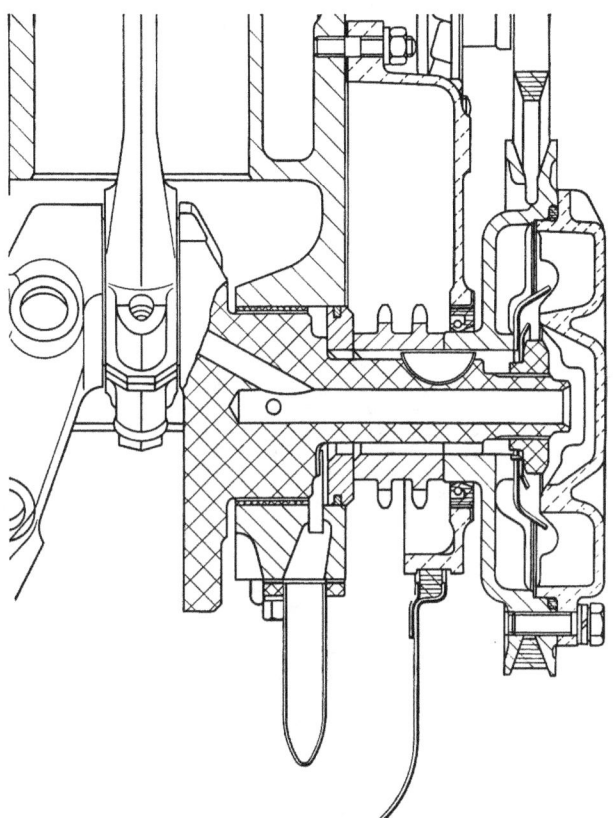

Fig. 532 - Longitudinal engine section showing the centrifugal oil filter detail.

CENTRIFUGAL OIL FILTER

The centrifugal oil filter consists essentially of a cover with pulley groove, a hub for pulley-cover and an annular deflector (see figs. 531 and 532).

The deflector has a diameter smaller than the pulley with relevant hub, but it is so dimensioned as to cause the oil to circulate radially up to an area where the centrifugal force has such a magnitude as to separate the impurities.

The radial ribs on pulley inner face hold the impurities and convey the oil to the center of filter.

The oil coming from crankshaft front tang through the two grooves machined in the tang itself is forced to the filter periphery by the deflector. After having been clarified, the oil returns to filter center and flows into crankshaft inner duct through the hole in crankshaft tang (fig. 531).

The pulley drives the generator, water pump and fan.

The hub-to-shaft nut must be tightened to a 72.3 ft.lbs (10.000 kgmm) torque.

NOTE - Starting from engine No. 1115841, the drive pulley and the centrifugal oil filter hub are one cast-iron piece; moreover provision has been made for an aluminum cover to clean the centrifugal filter.

FIAT VS Oil (Detergent Series).

For the gasoline motor car engine lubrication, the use of a detergent type oil, namely the FIAT VS series oil, is now specified.

The VS detergent oil, which comes in the entire SAE grade range, is capable of withstanding the type of service identified as MS in the API classification.

MS service involves the most severe lubricating requirements for Otto-cycle engines operating in extremely unfavorable and burdensome conditions (frequent starts and stops at low temperature, high speed, heavy load at high temperature).

The use of the new type of oil on Model 600 D can be safely extended to the vehicles of previous manufacture, although it demands some special attention when shifting to the detergent oil on engines having already run with conventional-type oil.

To change the oil type, proceed as follows:

— thoroughly flush the engine using FIAT L 20 flushing oil;

— clean all filters, especially the by-pass filter on Model 600 D.

If the engine was previously filled with Multigrade oil, the use of this oil, which is also detergent, of course, can be continued. When changing from Multigrade to VS detergent oil, engine flushing is not required.

Use the following oil grades:

Temperature	FIAT MS Service Oil (API)	FIAT Multigrade Oil
Below +5° F (—15° C), minimum	VS 10 W (SAE 10 W)	—
+32° F to +5° F (0° C to —15° C), minim.	VS 20 (SAE 20)	10 W - 30
Above 32° F (0°C), minimum	VS 30 (SAE 30)	10 W - 30
Above 86° F (30° C), average	VS 40 (SAE 40)	20 W - 40

FUEL SYSTEM

Fig. 533 - Removal of cartridge from cleaner.
A. Cover wingnut. - B. Cartridge.

AIR CLEANER

The air cleaner is of the caked type with paper cartridge and is fitted with cold and warm air intake.

The cartridge must be replaced every 6,000 miles (10.000 km). Obviously, if the car is operated under extreme dust conditions the cartridge must be replaced more often.

Fig. 535 - Engine assembly. The centrifugal oil filter and the generator and fan drive are visible in the foreground.

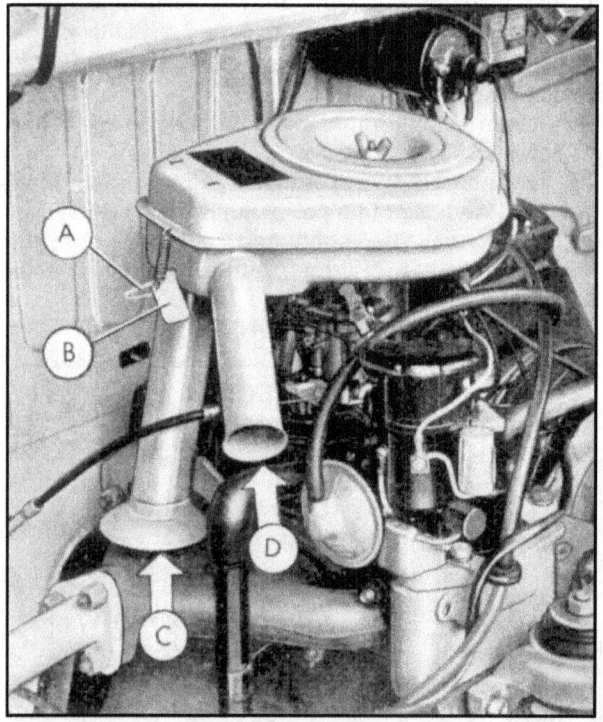

Fig. 534 - Adjustment of air intake of air cleaner to suit seasonal requirements.
A. Lever in « Winter » position. - B. Lever in « Summer » position. - C. Winter air intake. - D. Summer air intake.

To remove the cartridge undo wingnut (A, figure 533).

In winter, to obtain a better performance from engine shut off the entrance of cold air into engine by rotating 120° the lever (fig. 534) located on conveyor. « Summer » and « Winter » positions are indicated on cleaner body by letters « E » and « I », respectively.

MODEL 600 D

NOTE - For countries or areas in prevailingly dusty road conditions provision has been made for fitting a special dry suction air cleaner without warmed air intake.

Fig. 536 - Engine compartment.

WEBER CARBURETOR TYPES « 28 ICP » - « 28 ICP 1 »

The single-throat, downdraft, Weber carburetors type « 28 ICP » and « 28 ICP 1 » are built with an air horn diameter of 1.1024" (28 mm) at throttle height.

The fuel/air mixture is metered by the throttle which is in turn controlled by the accelerator pedal through a proper linkage.

These units are provided with starting device (choke) of the mechanically-controlled strangler valve type, mixture leaner and accelerating pump.

NOTE - The above carburetor types differ as far as the setting is concerned and moreover:

— the type « 28 ICP » is fitted with the needle valve resting on a float arm;

— the type « 28 ICP 1 » has the needle valve spring-fastened to the float arm.

The new carburetor type « 28 ICP 1 » has been adopted in production starting from engine No. 1118557.

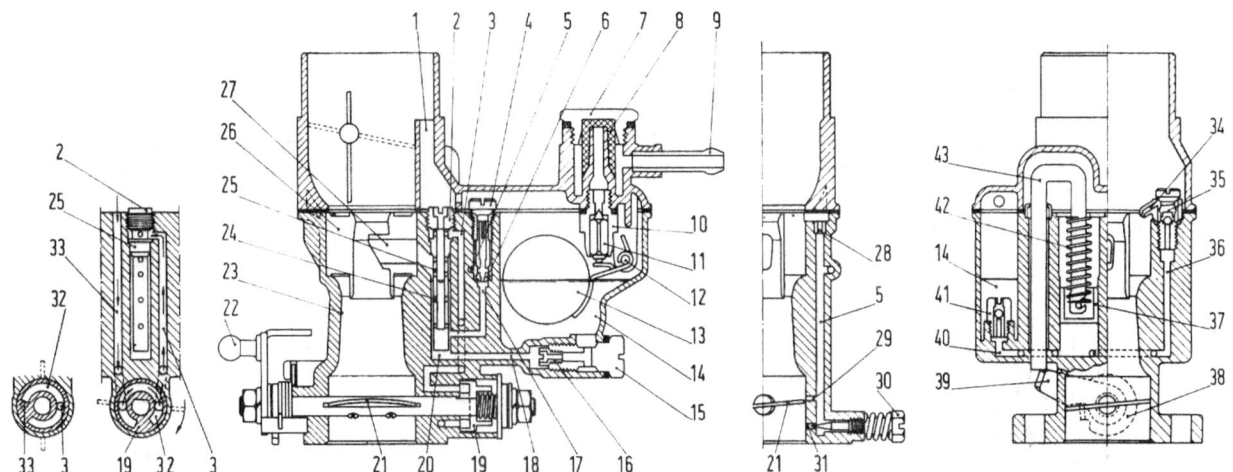

Fig. 537 - Weber 28 ICP carburetor - Schematic diagram.

1. Air inlet. - 2. Air corrector screw. - 3. Air duct to mixture leaner. - 4. Idle speed jet holder. - 5. Idle speed mixture duct. - 6. Idle speed jet. - 7. Filter access plug. - 8. Filter gauze. - 9. Fuel inlet connection. - 10. Needle valve. - 11. Valve needle. - 12. Float pivot. - 13. Float. - 14. Fuel bowl. - 15. Main jet holder. - 16. Main jet. - 17. Duct, idle speed well-to-jet. - 18. Duct, main jet-to-well. - 19. Mixture leaner diaphragm. - 20. Emulsion tube well. - 21. Throttle. - 22. Throttle lever. - 23. Primary Venturi. - 24. Emulsion orifices. - 25. Emulsion tube. - 26. Auxiliary Venturi. - 27. Spray nozzle. - 28. Calibrated bush, idle speed air. - 29. Transition orifice. - 30. Idle speed mixture adjustment screw. - 31. Idle speed orifice. - 32. Diaphragm. - 33. Mixture leaner air duct. - 34. Accelerating pump jet. - 35. Accelerating pump delivery valve. - 36. Accelerating pump delivery duct. - 37. Pump plunger. - 38. Pump fixed lever. - 39. Pump idle lever. - 40. Pump suction duct. - 41. Pump suction valve. - 42. Pump delivery booster spring. - 43. Pump control rod.

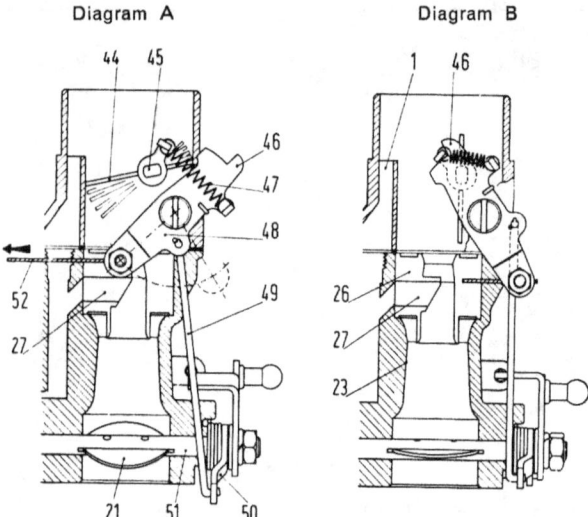

Fig. 538 - Weber 28 ICP carburetor - Schematic diagram.

1. Air inlet. - 21. Throttle. - 23. Primary Venturi. - 26. Auxiliary Venturi. - 27. Spray nozzle. - 44. Strangler valve, starting device. - 45. Strangler spindle. - 46. Starting lever lug. - 47. Strangler valve return spring. - 48. Choke lever. - 49. Link. - 50. Lever, throttle to strangler. - 51. Throttle spindle. - 52. Choke wire.

General Description.

Referring to diagram fig. 537, the air from above flows through Venturi (26) in air horn where it mixes with the fuel issuing from spray nozzle (27) and, via the restriction in primary Venturi (23), is then conveyed to the cylinders through the opening adjusted by throttle (21).

From fuel feed lines, joined to carburetor by connection (9), gasoline flows across gauze filter and then, through needle valve (10) it arrives at bowl (14) where float (13) - pivoting on pin (12) - keeps fuel at a constant level by adjusting needle (11).

From bowl (14) - via metered main jet (16) and duct (18) - the fuel passes on to emulsion well (20) whence, mixed with the air coming from orifices (24) in emulsion tube (25), air corrector screw (2) and duct (3) in leaner, it flows through spray nozzle (27) and finally reaches the carburetion area formed by auxiliary (26) and primary (23) Venturis.

For idle speed operation, through duct (17) fuel is conveyed from well (20) to idle speed jet (6). Here, it blends with the air coming from metered bush (28) through duct (5) and idle speed orifice (31) - adjustable by taper point screw (30) - whence it reaches carburetor duct downstream of throttle (21) and mixes with the engine-promoted air stream flowing through the gap around throttle in idle speed position.

Through idle speed duct (5) the mixture reaches air horn also via transition orifice (29) located at throttle height and having the purpose of allowing a gradual uniform increase in engine angular speed from idle, when throttle is opened.

The mixture leaner is formed by throttle spindle-operated diaphragm (19), duct (33) in communication with carburetor air intake and duct (3) whose outlet is located in the well downstream of air corrector screw (2).

When throttle is partially opened, diaphragm (19) puts ducts (33) and (3) into communication: under these conditions, the air coming from ducts (33) and (3) is added to the air flowing through corrector screw (2), thus leaning the mixture sprayed from nozzle (27). This arrangement provides maximum possible fuel economy.

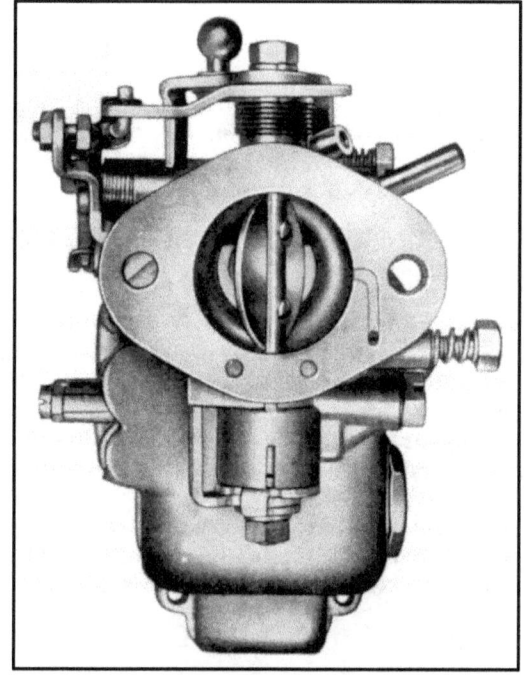

Fig. 539 - Carburetor bottom view.

When throttle is fully open, diaphragm (19) blanks the passage between ducts (33) and (3): when this occurs, the only emulsion air is the one supplied by the corrector screw, thus enriching the mixture sprayed from nozzle (27) and providing full power operation of engine.

The **accelerating pump** provides a regular increase in engine angular speed even when throttle is suddenly opened. This pump consists of a metal plunger (37) actuated by rod (43) through idle lever (39).

As the throttle is closed, lever (39) - pulled by fixed lever (38) - lifts plunger (37) by means of rod (43). As a result, fuel is sucked from bowl (14) into pump barrel through ball valve (41) and duct (40).

When throttle is opened, rod (43) remains free and plunger (37) under the action of spring (42) moves downwards: through duct (36) and ball valve (35) the fuel is delivered to metered jet (34) whence it is injected into carburetor throat.

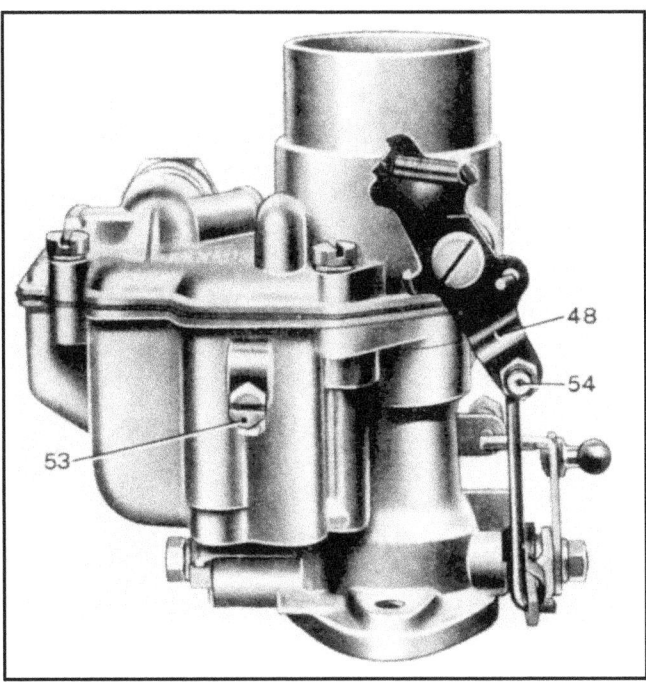

Fig. 540 - Side view - starting device lever end.

48. Starting device (choke) operating lever. - 53. Bowden screw. - 54. Bowden wire screw.

To reduce the amount of fuel delivered by the accelerating pump, ball valve (41) may be provided

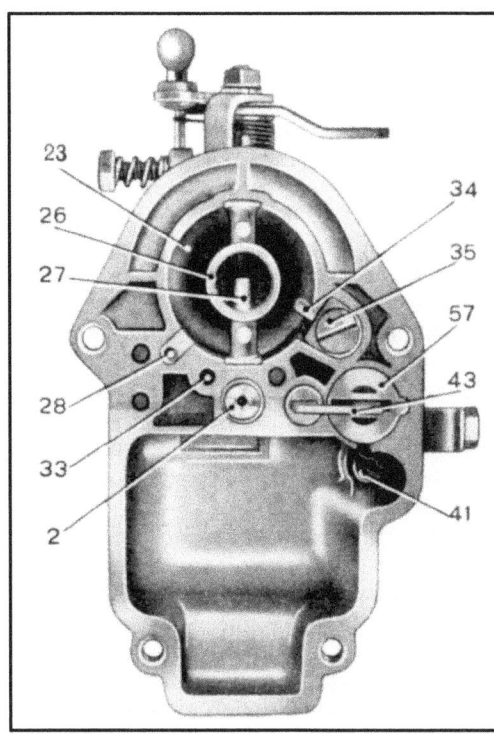

Fig. 542 - Top view (cover removed).

2. Emulsion tube, complete with air corrector screw. - 23. Venturi. - 26. Venturi. - 27. Spray nozzle. - 28. Idle speed air calibrated bush. - 33. Mixture leaner air duct. - 34. Pump jet. - 35. Pump delivery valve. - 41. Pump suction valve. - 43. Pump control rod. - 57. Pump spring retainment plate.

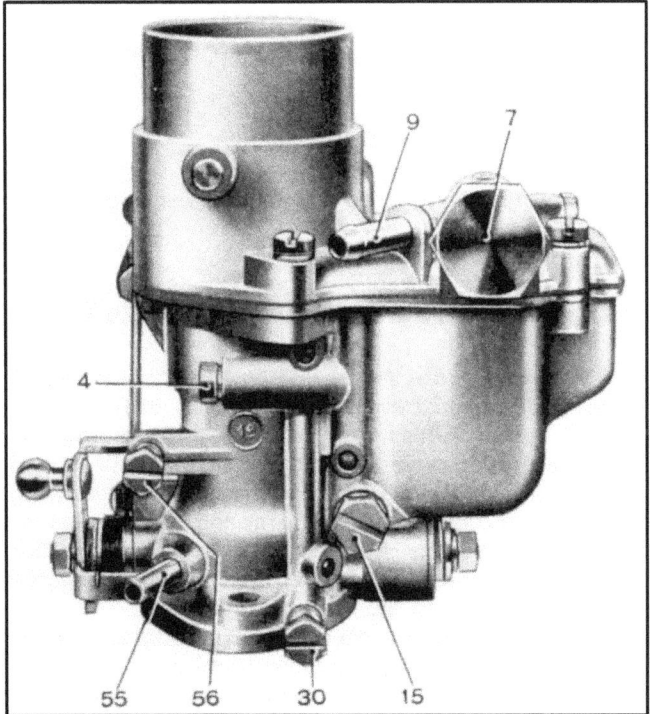

Fig. 541 - Side view - fuel inlet, jets and adjustment screw end.

4. Idle speed jet holder. - 7. Filter access plug. - 9. Fuel arrival connection. - 15. Main jet holder. - 30. Idle speed mixture adjustment screw. - 55. Connection to vacuum advance device. - 56. Idle speed adjustment screw.

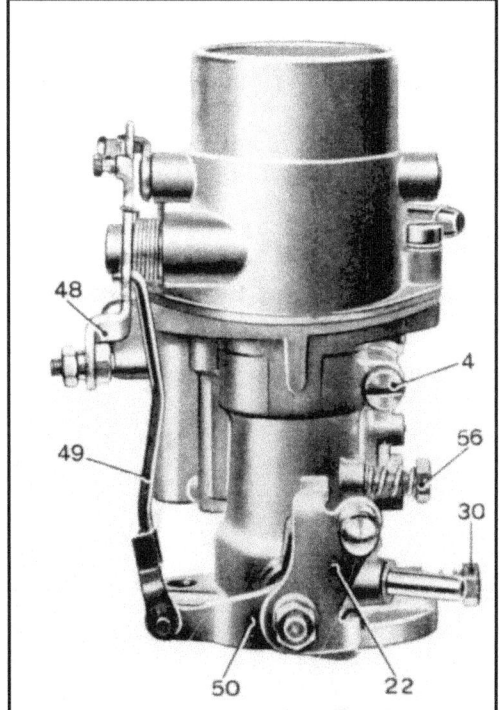

Fig. 543 - Side view - throttle lever end.

4. Idle speed jet holder. - 22. Throttle operating lever. - 30. Idle speed mixture adjustment screw. - 48. Strangler valve operating lever. - 49. Starting device link. - 50. Link lever. - 56. Idle speed adjustment screw.

with a metered side orifice discharging the excess fuel into bowl.

The starting device (choke) consists of strangler valve (44) offset on spindle (45) connected by spring (47) to control lever (48).

When the choke lever on car floor tunnel is pulled for engine cold starts, lever (48) is brought into the position shown in **diagram A** (fig. 538) and strangler (44) therefore « chokes » carburetor air intake while throttle (21) is positioned at a given opening through link (49) connecting lever (48) and lever (50) on throttle spindle (51).

The vacuum promoted by the starter-cranked engine reaches noticeable values as a result of the « choking » by strangler (44) and a rich mixture is thus forced out of spray nozzle (27) and a prompt starting of engine is had.

Once the engine is started, under the action of the vacuum in carburetor, strangler (44) opens partially against the opposing spring (47); this provides a sufficiently rich mixture to ensure regular and smooth engine operation.

While engine warms up, the opening of strangler (44) must be progressively increased and at the same time throttle (21) must be closed through link (49) until, as engine reaches the rated operation temperature, the starting device is fully cut-off - **diagram B** - strangler (44) is kept fully open by lug (46) of lever (48) while throttle (21) is shifted to idle speed position.

STARTING DEVICE OPERATING INSTRUCTIONS

To obtain the best possible results from this progressive-action starter, proceed as follows:

Engine Starts.

Fully insert the device by its control lever (figure 544).

Fig. 544 - Choke lever on floor tunnel.

Fig. 545 - Carburetor on engine.

A. Idle speed setscrew. - B. Idle speed mixture adjustment screw. - C. Main jet holder. - D. Idle speed jet holder. - E. Filter access plug.

Engine Warm-up.

During engine warming up period, even when car is running, the device should be gradually disinserted; thus the mixture will progressively lean out to ensure smooth engine operation.

Normal Operation.

Fully disinsert the device as soon as engine runs smoothly.

IDLE SPEED ADJUSTMENT

Carburetor idle speed is adjusted by setscrew A (fig. 545) and mixture setscrew B (fig. 545). Taper-point screw A has the purpose of metering the amount of mixture coming from the idle speed passage which will then blend with the air flowing past the throttle that, in idle speed setting, leaves a gap between its edge and the throat walls. This permits a rating of mixture best suited to engine requirements and smooth operation.

Always adjust idle speed with running and warm engine by first setting throttle to minimum opening by setscrew A so as to ensure steady operation.

Next, by turning setscrew (B) in or out, set mixture richness to the most suitable ratio with respect to said throttle opening - thus accomplishing a fast steady idling - and reduce minimum throttle opening a little more until best idling is obtained.

FLOAT LEVELLING

To correctly level the float proceed as follows:

Check that needle valve (fig. 546) (V) is screwed well tight in its seat.

Keep carburetor cover (C) vertical to prevent the weight of float (G) from lowering ball (Sf) mounted on needle (S).

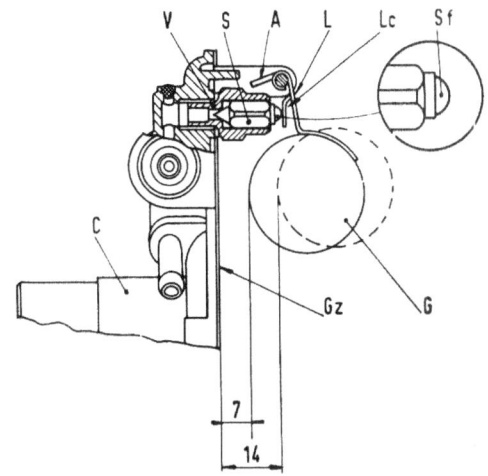

Fig. 546 - Diagram and data for float levelling.

With carburetor cover vertical and arm (Lc) slightly in contact with ball (Sf) of needle (S), float (G) should clear the cover with gasket (Gz) by .276" (7 mm).

After this check that the float travel is .276" (7 mm); if necessary bend end (A) as required.

NOTE - As far as the Weber carburetor type 28 ICP 1 is concerned, check that the needle return hook does not hamper the needle from moving freely in seat.

If float (G) is not correctly positioned bend float arms (L) until obtaining the correct adjustment.

See that arm (Lc) is perpendicular to the needle axis and does not show rough spots or indents impairing the free sliding of the needle.

Check that float (G) swings freely around its pivot.

WARNING - In the event that needle valve (V) must be replaced, tighten firmly the new needle, with which a new gasket shall be used, and repeat the float levelling operations.

SOLEX CARBURETOR TYPE C 28 PIB - 2

For the setting data of Solex carburetor type « C 28 PIB-2 » which is fitted alternatively with Weber carburetor type « 28 ICP 1 », see the chart on bottom of this page.

SETTING DATA OF CARBURETORS

	Weber 28 ICP	Weber 28 ICP 1	Solex C 28 PIB - 2
Air horn diameter	1.1024" (28 mm)	1.1024" (28 mm)	1.1024" (28 mm)
Primary Venturi diameter	.7480" (19 mm)	.7480" (19 mm)	.7874" (20 mm)
Main jet diameter	.0394" (1,00 mm)	.0394" (1,00 mm)	.0421" (1,07 mm)
Idling speed jet diameter	.0177" (0,45 mm)	.0177" (0,45 mm)	.0157" (0,40 mm)
Starting jet diameter	rotary	rotary	.0394" (1,00 mm)
Accelerating pump jet diameter	.0157" (0,40 mm)	.0157" (0,40 mm)	.0197" (0,50 mm)
Main air jet diameter	.0748" (1,90 mm)	.0787" (2,00 mm)	.0630" (1,60 mm)
Needle seat	.0492" (1,25 mm)	.0591" (1,50 mm)	.0591" (1,50 mm)

BENCH TEST RANGE OF REBUILT ENGINES

A rebuilt engine should be submitted to a proper testing range on test bench.

When doing so, adhere to the procedure shown in the following chart:

Engine Test Speed - r.p.m.	Time-Minutes	Braking Load
500	15	no
2,000	15	half
2,000	5	full
Total minutes	35	

When bench testing a rebuilt engine, it is recommended not to race it at top speed in an attempt to accomplish the data specified in the power curve. Engine run-in will be completed on the vehicle to the care of the Owner, who should keep within the speed limits for the initial period of use.

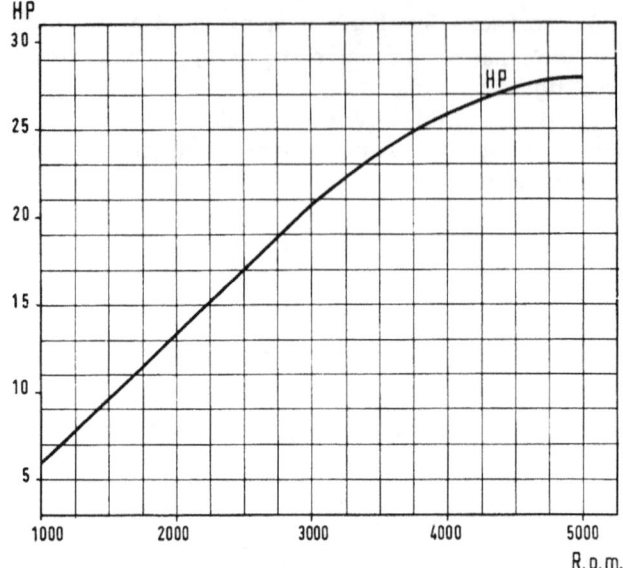

Fig. 547 - Performance curve of engines 100 D.000 and 100 D.008.

CLUTCH

Clutch spring main data are:

- Part No. 4061230
- Wire diameter .... .134″ (3,4 mm)
- Spring O.D. .... .984″ (25 mm)
- Number of active coils 7.9
- Total number of coils 9
- Free height .... 2.087″ (53 mm)
- Seated spring:
  — height .... 1.339″ (34 mm)
  — corresponding load ..... 82±4.2 lbs (37,2±1,9 kg)
- minimum load .... 71 lbs (32 kg)
- spring height with shut coils . 1.204″ (30,6 mm)

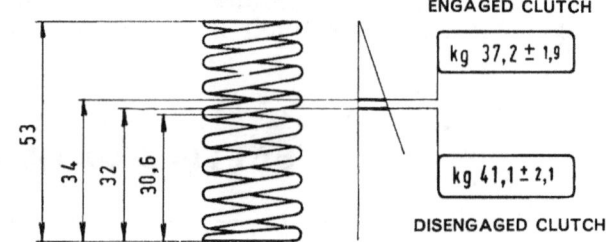

Fig. 548 - Clutch spring data.

BRAKES

The « Sedan » brake master cylinder has a 7/8″ I.D. All other data are the same as for the 600 « Sedan » and « Multipla » described and illustrated in the relevant Section.

ELECTRIC SYSTEM

BATTERY

The battery equipping Model 600 D « Sedan » and « Multipla » has the following characteristics.

Up to the serial No. for spare parts 1343327 (Sedan) and 104023 (Multipla):

- Tension .... 12 Volts
- Capacity (at 20-hrs discharge rate) 32 Amp/hr
- Length .... 9.3″ (237 mm)
- Width .... 5.5″ (139 mm)
- Height (at posts) .... 8.9″ (225 mm)
- Weight { dry .... 26 lbs (11,8 kg)
           w/ electrolyte ... 33 lbs (14,8 kg)

MODEL 600 D

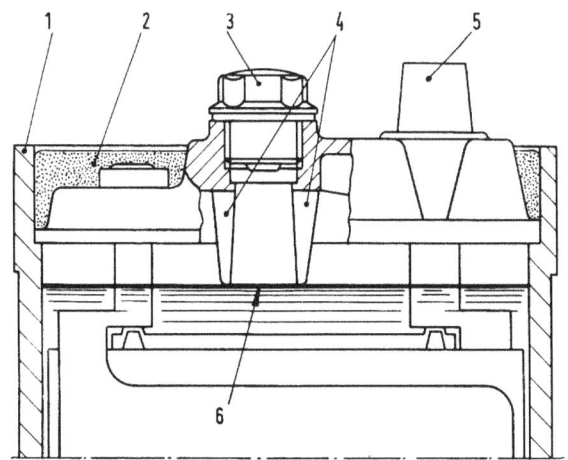

Fig. 549 - Section view through a battery fitted with electrolyte «level sight» at filler necks.

1. Battery case. - 2. Sealing compound. - 3. Plug. - 4. Filler neck with vent slots. - 5. Post. - 6. Electrolyte level sight on the filler neck.

Starting from the serial No. for spare parts 1343328 (Sedan) and 104024 (Multipla):

— Tension . . . . 12 V
— Capacity (at 20 hr discharge rate) 36 Amp/hr
— Length . . . . 9.0'' (228 mm)
— Width . . . . 6.8'' (172 mm)
— Height (at posts) . . . . . . 8.9'' (225 mm)
— Weight { dry . . . . 29 lbs (13 kg)
         { w/ electrolyte . . . 37 lbs (17 kg)

Minimum speed for battery charge (lights off):
— engine abt. . . . . 920 r.p.m.
— car in 4th gear { Sedan 12.7 m.p.h. (20,5 km/h)
                  { Multipla 11.8 m.p.h. (19 km/h)

NOTE - Starting from the month of December 1960, 600 D cars have been equipped with generator regulator type **GN 2/12/16**, in the place of the previous type **GN 1/12/16**.

STARTER MOTOR

The starter motor is the type E 76-05/12/S (see figs. 553 thru 556) with engagement by electro-magnet. Control is by the lock switch key as described on page 364.

Starter motor specifications are listed in the table on next page.

IGNITION TIMING

Time distributor to engine as follows:

Make sure cylinder No. 1 is in the compression stroke, i. e., with both valves closed.

Bring crankshaft to the position in which **the mark** on generator and fan drive pulley will be located .51'' to .55'' (13-14 mm) ahead of the **mark** on timing gear cover (see fig. 551); this corresponds to a 10° B. T. D. C. advance.

Then proceed as directed on page 293.

Fig. 551 - Reference marks for ignition timing.

To set the 10° static advance, the pulley must be so rotated that its reference mark is brought .51''-.55'' (13-14 mm) ahead of mark on cover, in the normal rotation direction. Cylinder No. 1 must be in the compression stroke.

Vacuum Advance.

NOTE - Starting from engine No. 1038311, vacuum advance versus engine has been varied to 13°.

In case of vacuum advance unit replacement, install:

— the late type (13°) on 600 D Sedan and Multipla;
— the early type (20°) on 600 Sedan and Multipla.

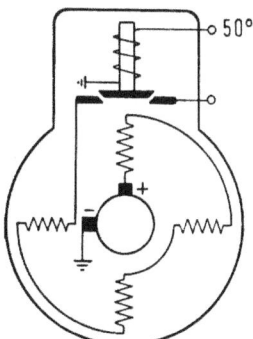

Fig. 550.
Starter motor E 76-0,5/12/S operation diagram.

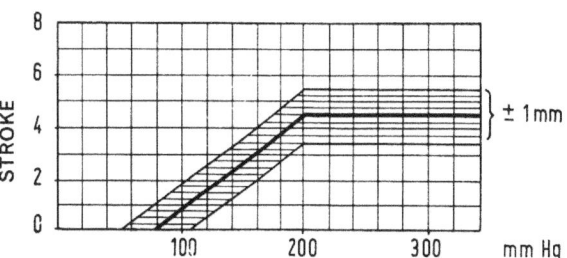

Fig. 552 - Vacuum advance diagram.
Stroke variation after vacuum amount: stroke .1772'' (4,5 mm) corresponding to a 13° advance to engine.

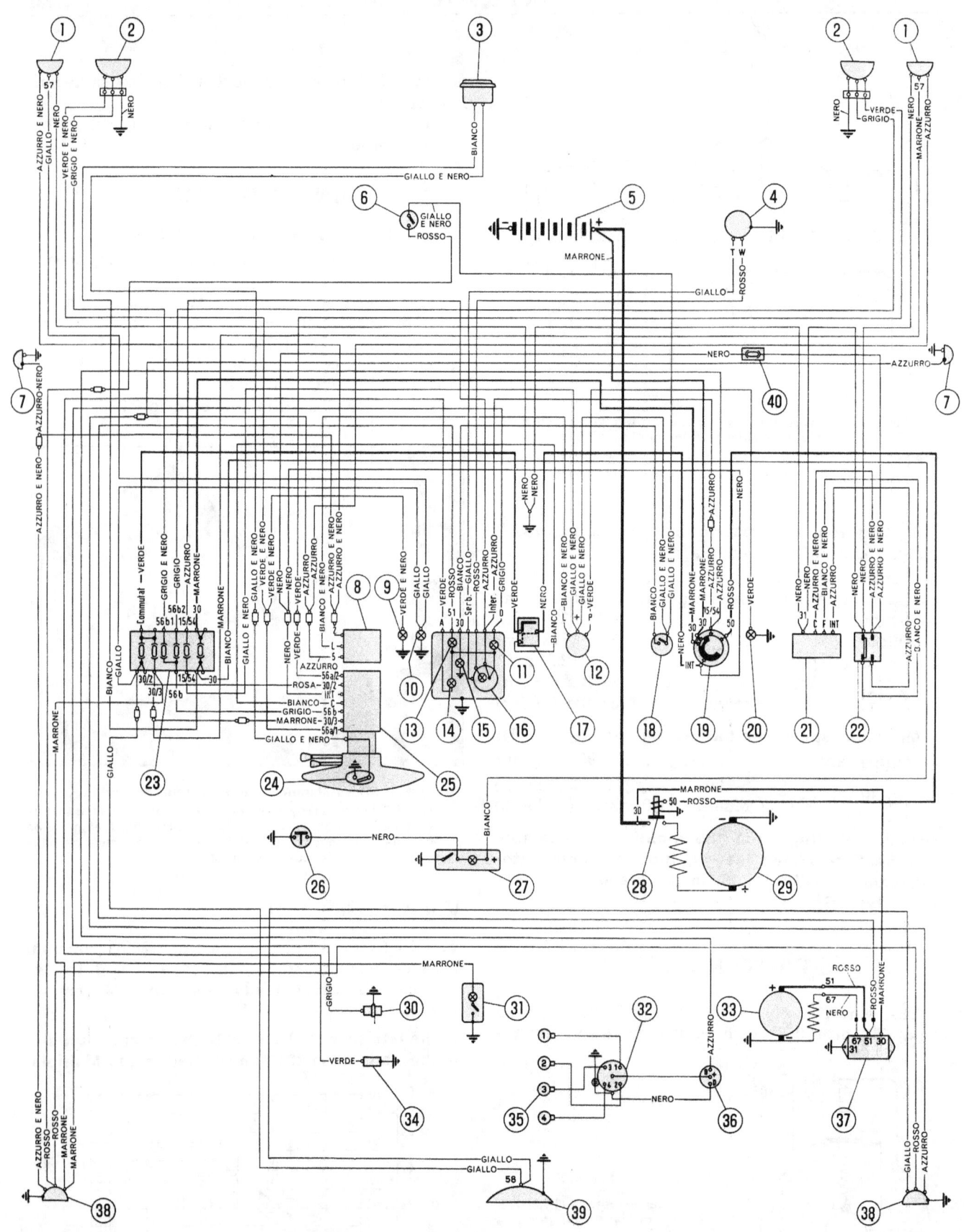

Fig. 553.

FIG. 553 - WIRING DIAGRAM - 600 D SEDAN

1. Front parking and direction indicator lamps (double-filament bulb; 5-W parking and 20-W direction).
2. Headlamps (double-filament bulb; 45-W high beam and 40-W low beam).
3. Horn.
4. Fuel level gauge sending unit.
5. Battery.
6. Stop lights pressure-operated switch.
7. Direction indicator side repeaters (3-W bulb).
8. Direction indicators switch.
9. High beam indicator (blue, 3-W bulb).
10. Parking lights indicator (green, 3-W bulb).
11. Insufficient engine oil pressure indicator (3-W bulb).
12. Winking device (flasher).
13. Generator charge indicator (3-W bulb).
14. Excessive water temperature indicator (3-W bulb).
15. Panel light bulb (3-W bulb).
16. Fuel level gauge, with reserve supply indicator (3-W bulb).
17. Outer lighting switch.
18. Panel light switch.
19. Ignition lock switch.
20. Direction indicators pilot light (green, 3-W bulb).
21. Windshield wiper motor.
22. Windshield wiper switch.
23. 8-A fuses.
24. Horn button.
25. Outer lighting changeover switch.
26. Jam switch, between door and pillar, for lamp in rear view mirror.
27. Bulb (3-W) incorporated in rear view mirror, for courtesy light, with toggle switch.
28. Starter switch (electromagnetic).
29. Starter.
30. Sending unit for insufficient oil pressure indicator.
31. Engine compartment light (5-W) with automatic switch.
32. Ignition distributor.
33. Generator.
34. Thermostatic sending unit for excessive water temperature indicator.
35. Spark plugs.
36. Ignition coil.
37. Generator regulator.
38. Rear parking and stop (double filament bulb, 5-W and 20-W) and direction indicator (single-filament bulb, 20-W) lamps.
39. Number plate lamp (5-W).
40. Windshield wiper fuse.

Note - Mark ▬ means that cable is provided with numbered strip or ferrule.

KEY TO CABLE COLORS

Azzurro	= Blue
Bianco	= White
Giallo	= Yellow
Grigio	= Grey
Marrone	= Brown
Nero	= Black
Rosa	= Rose
Rosso	= Red
Verde	= Green
Azzurro e Nero	= Black and Blue
Bianco e Nero	= Black and White
Giallo e Nero	= Black and Yellow
Verde e Nero	= Black and Green
Grigio e Nero	= Black and Grey
Commutat.	= Switch
Serb.	= Tank (Fuel)
INT - Inter.	= Switch

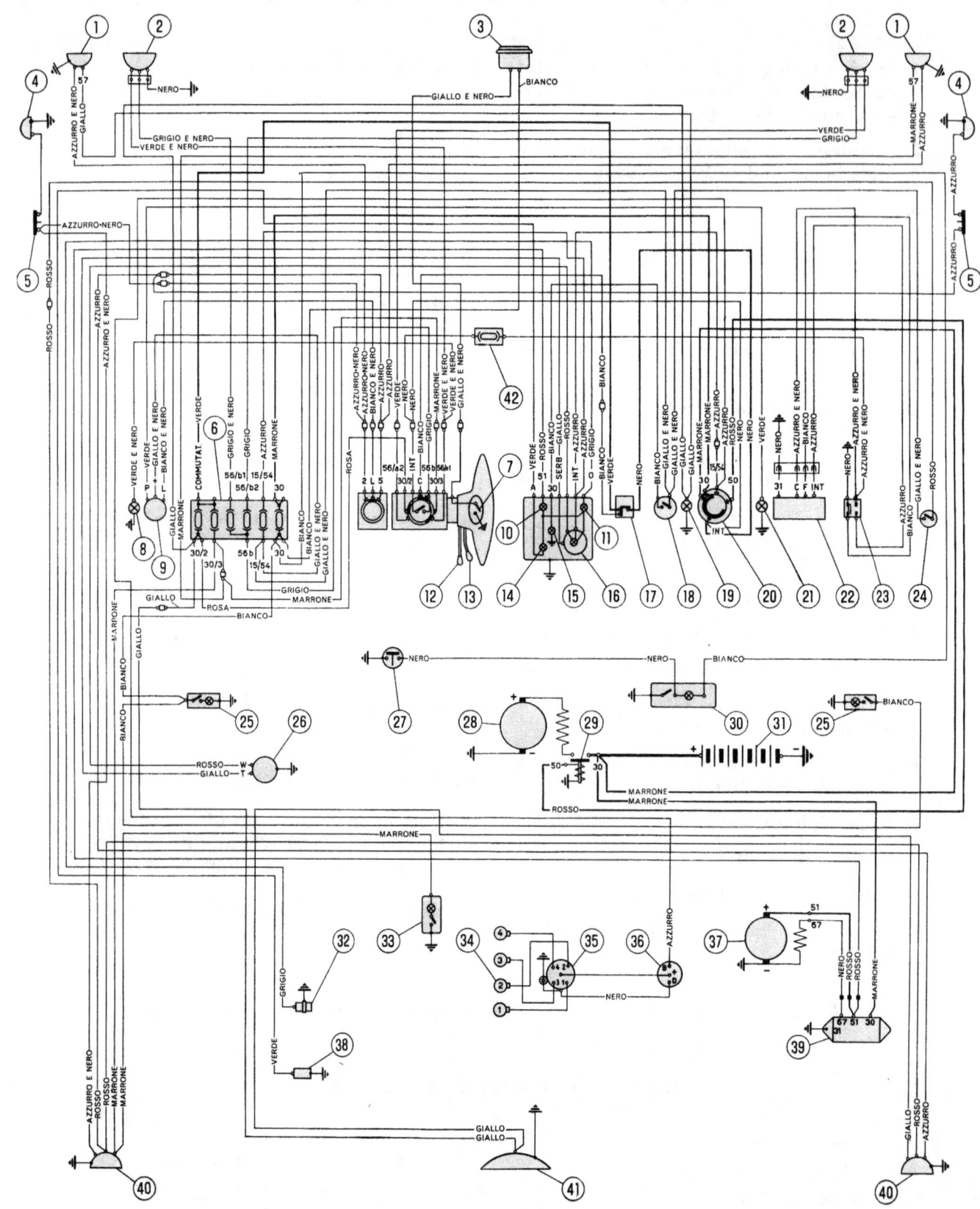

Fig. 554

FIG. 554 - WIRING DIAGRAM - 600 D MULTIPLA

1. Front parking and direction indicator lamps (double-filament bulb; 5-W parking; 20-W direction).
2. Headlamps (double-filament bulb; 45-W high beam and 40-W low beam).
3. Horn.
4. Direction indicator side repeaters (3-W bulb).
5. Movable contact for direction indicators side repeaters.
6. 8-A fuses.
7. Horn button.
8. High beam indicator (blue, 3-W bulb).
9. Winking device (flasher).
10. Generator charge indicator (3-W bulb).
11. Insufficient engine oil pressure indicator (3-W bulb).
12. Outer lighting change-over switch.
13. Direction indicators switch.
14. Excessive water temperature indicator (3-W bulb).
15. Panel light bulb (3-W bulb).
16. Fuel level gauge, with reserve supply indicator (3-W bulb).
17. Outer lighting switch.
18. Panel light switch.
19. Parking light indicator (green, 3-W bulb).
20. Ignition lock switch.
21. Direction indicator pilot light (green, 3-W bulb).
22. Windshield wiper motor.
23. Windshield wiper switch.
24. Stop lamps pressure-operated switch.
25. Pillar lamps (3-W bulb) with incorporated switch.
26. Fuel level gauge sending unit.
27. Jam switch, between door and pillar, for lamp in rear view mirror.
28. Starter.
29. Starter electromagnetic switch.
30. Bulb (3-W) incorporated in rear view mirror, for car interior illumination, with toggle switch.
31. Battery.
32. Sending unit, for insufficient oil pressure indicator.
33. Engine compartment light (5-W bulb), with automatic switch.
34. Spark plugs.
35. Ignition distributor.
36. Ignition coil.
37. Generator.
38. Thermostatic sending unit for excessive water temperature indicator.
39. Generator regulator.
40. Rear parking and stop (double-filament bulb, 5 and 20-W) and direction indicator (20-W single-filament bulb) lamps.
41. Number plate lamp (5-W bulb).
42. Windshield wiper fuse.

Note - Mark ▬ means that cable is provided with numbered strip or ferrule.

KEY TO CABLE COLORS

Azzurro	= Blue	Verde	= Green
Bianco	= White	Azzurro e Nero	= Black and Blue
Giallo	= Yellow	Bianco e Nero	= Black and White
Grigio	= Grey	Giallo e Nero	= Black and Yellow
Marrone	= Brown	Verde e Nero	= Black and Green
Nero	= Black	Grigio e Nero	= Black and Grey
Rosa	= Rose	Commutat.	= Switch
Rosso	= Red	Serb.	= Tank (Fuel)
		INT - Inter.	= Switch

STARTER MOTOR DATA

Type	E 76-0.5/12 S
Voltage	12 V
Nominal power	0.5 kW
Rotation (pinion end)	counterclockwise
Pole shoes	4
Field winding	in series
Engagement	by free wheel
Engagement control	by electromagnet

Mechanical Data.

— Pole shoes I. D.	2.0697 to 2.0768 in (52,57 to 52,75 mm)
— Armature diameter	2.0394 to 2.0413 in (51,80 to 51,85 mm)
— Part No. of brushes	805581

Bench Test Data.

— Operation test at 68° F (20° C):	
Current	130 Amp
Torque developed	2±.14 ft.lbs (0,28±0,02 kgm)
Speed	2250±100 r.p.m.
Tension	10 Volts
— Stall torque at 68° F (20° C):	
Current	258 Amp
Tension	7.7±0.3 Volts
Torque developed	5.3±.36 ft.lbs (0,73±0,05 kgm)
— No-load test at 68° F (20 C°):	
Current	≤ 30 Amp
Tension	12 Volts
Speed	8500±1000 r.p.m.
— Ohmic resistance during stall torque test, at 68° F (20° C)	0.03±0.01 Ω
— Field winding resistance at 68° F (20° C)	0.0152±0.0015 Ω
— Electromagnet coil resistance at 68° F (20° C)	0.404±0.05 Ω

Mechanical Characteristics Test.

— Load of springs on new brushes	2.5 to 2.9 lbs (1,15 to 1,30 kg)
— Armature shaft axial play	.0059 to .0256 in (0,15 to 0,65 mm)
— Mica undercut depth . . . not more than	.04 in (1 mm)
— Drive unit free wheel efficiency: static torque required to rotate pinion slowly	.35 in.lbs (≤ 0,4 kgcm)
— Electromagnet contact stroke	.49" to .58" (12,32 to 14,67)
— Electromagnet winding stroke	.40" to .51" (10,04 to 13,02)

Lubrication.

— Drive unit splines	FIAT Jota 2/M grease

STARTER TYPE E 76-0,5/12/S

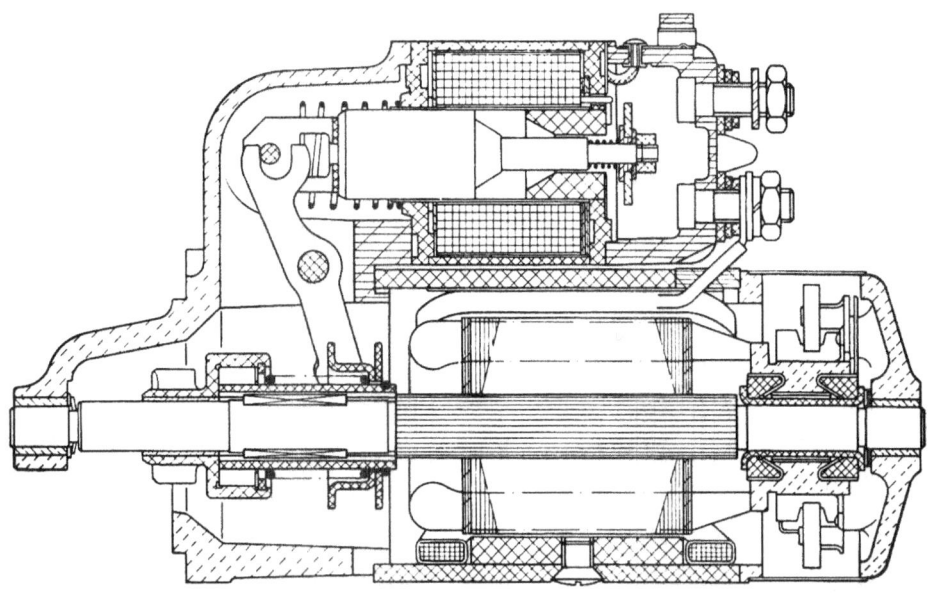

Fig. 555 - Starter assembly longitudinal section.

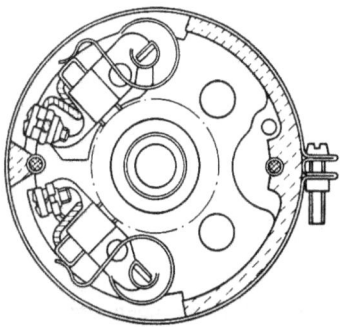

Fig. 557 - Section through commutator end head, showing the brushes.

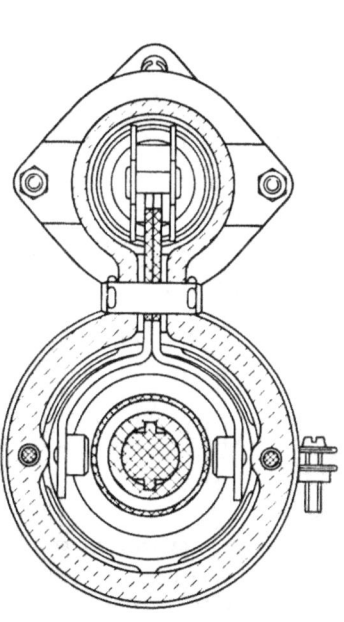

Fig. 556 - Cross section on drive unit.

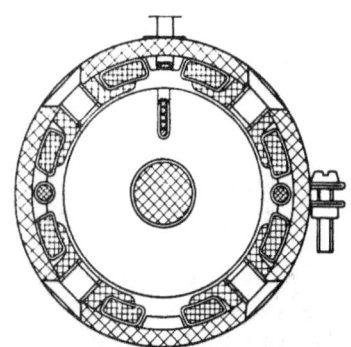

Fig. 558 - Section through pole shoes and armature winding.

BODY

Disassembly of Swivelling Ventipane.

Disassembly operations are as follows:

Remove door inner trim panel by forcing out the spring fasteners from their seats in door frame.

Back out the drop pane front guide channel lower screw and disinsert the channel upper tongue from ventipane frame.

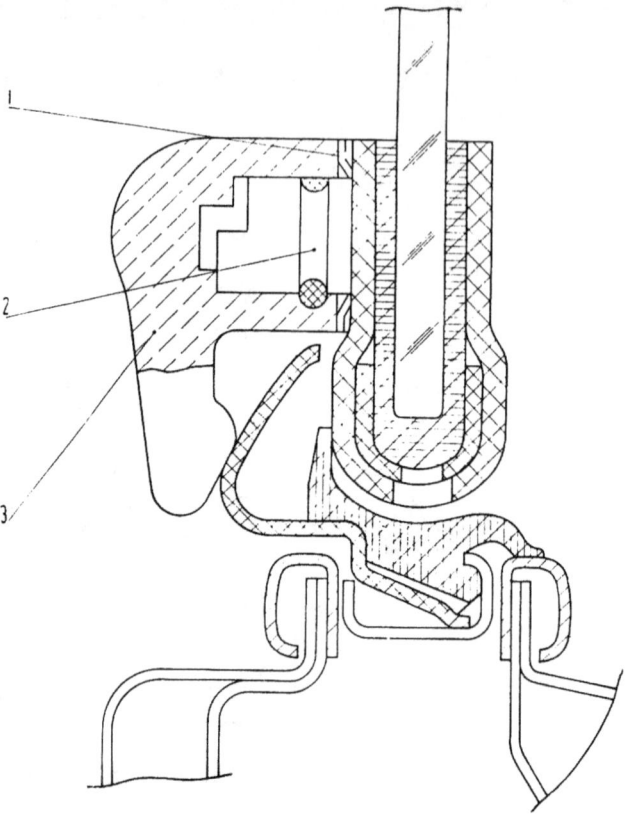

Fig. 560 - Section on ventipane lock handle.
1. Lockwasher. - 2. Handle lock pin. - 3. Handle.

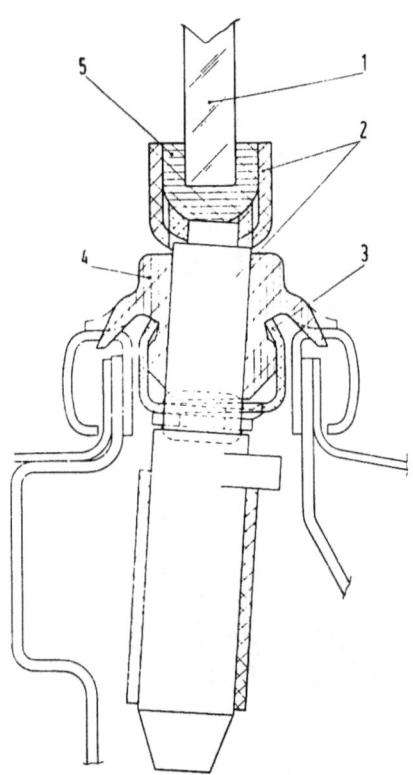

Fig. 559 - Section on ventipane lower articulation.
1. Glass pane. - 2. Frame complete with articulation pin. - 3. Weatherstrip frame. - 4. Weatherstrip. - 5. Glass rubber strip.

Back out the two upper screws, located under door weatherstrip, fixing the ventipane assembly.

After this operation, tilt ventipane assembly slightly backwards and pull out.

Remove the upper articulation rivet and back out the lower articulation pin mounting screw.

Take out the ventipane glass by exerting a slight pressure to unseat the lower articulation pin from its retainment plate.

Finally, remove the ventipane lock handle.

To reassemble the ventipane, suitably reverse the sequence of the above operations.

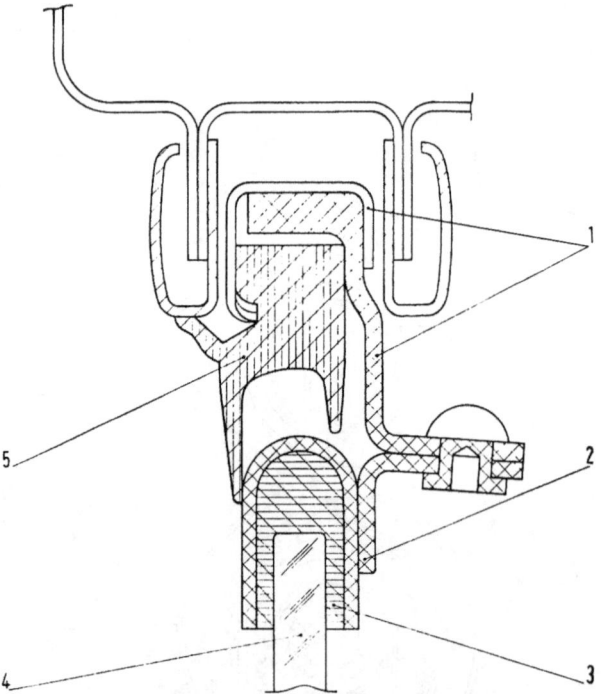

Fig. 561 - Section on ventipane upper articulation.
1. Frame, complete. - 2. Mounting channel. - 3. Glass rubber strip. 4. Glass pane. - 5. Weatherstrip.

VELOCEPRESS MANUALS - MOTORCYCLE

1930'S BRITISH MOTORCYCLE CARBS & ELEC COMPONENTS (BOOK OF)
1930'S BRITISH MOTORCYCLE ENGINES (OVERHAUL & MAINTENANCE)
1930'S BRITISH MOTORCYCLE GEARBOXES & CLUTCHES (BOOK OF)
AJS 1932-1948 SINGLES & TWINS 250cc THRU 1000cc (BOOK OF)
AJS 1945-1960 SINGLES 350cc & 500cc MODELS 16 & 18 (BOOK OF)
AJS 1955-1965 SINGLES 350cc & 500cc (BOOK OF)
ARIEL 1932-1939 PREWAR MODELS (BOOK OF)
ARIEL 1933-1951 (WORKSHOP MANUAL)
ARIEL 1939-1960 4 STROKE SINGLES (BOOK OF)
ARIEL 1958-1964 LEADER & ARROW (BOOK OF)
BMW R26 R27 (1956-1967) FACTORY WORKSHOP MANUAL
BMW R50 R50S R60 R69S (1955-1969) FACTORY WORKSHOP MANUAL
BRIDGESTONE 90 SERIES FACTORY WSM & PARTS CATALOGUE
BRIDGESTONE 175 SERIES FACTORY WSM & PARTS CATALOGUE
BSA BANTAM ALL MODELS FROM 1948 ONWARDS (BOOK OF)
BSA SINGLES & V-TWINS UP TO 1927 (BOOK OF)
BSA SINGLES & V-TWINS UP TO 1935 (BOOK OF)
BSA SINGLES & V-TWINS 1936-1939 (BOOK OF)
BSA SINGLES & V-TWINS 1936-1952 (BOOK OF)
BSA OHV & SV SINGLES 250-600cc 1945-1954 (BOOK OF)
BSA OHV & SV SINGLES 250cc 1954-1970 (BOOK OF)
BSA OHV SINGLES 350 & 500cc 1955-1967 (BOOK OF)
BSA TWINS 1948-1962 (BOOK OF)
BSA TWINS 1962-1969 (SECOND BOOK OF)
DOUGLAS 1929-1939 PREWAR ALL MODELS (BOOK OF)
DOUGLAS 1948-1957 POSTWAR ALL MODELS FACTORY SHOP MANUAL
DUCATI 160cc, 250cc & 350cc OHC MODELS FACTORY SHOP MANUAL
HONDA 50 ALL MODELS UP TO 1970 INC MONKEY & TRAIL (BOOK OF)
HONDA 90 ALL MODELS UP TO 1966 (BOOK OF)
HONDA 125-150cc TWINS C/CS/CB/CA FACTORY WORKSHOP MANUAL
HONDA 250-305 TWINS C/CS/CB FACTORY WORKSHOP MANUAL
HONDA C100 SUPER CUB FACTORY WORKSHOP MANUAL
HONDA C110 SPORT CUB 1962-1969 FACTORY WORKSHOP MANUAL
HONDA TWINS & SINGLES 50cc THRU 305cc 1960-1966 (BOOK OF)
HONDA TWINS ALL MODELS 125cc THRU 450cc UP TO 1968 (BOOK OF)
J.A.P. ENGINES 1927-1952 & MOTORCYCLES 1934-1952 (BOOK OF)
LAMBRETTA 1947-1957 ALL 125 & 150cc MODELS (BOOK OF)
LAMBRETTA 1957-1970 LI & TV MODELS (SECOND BOOK OF)
MATCHLESS 1931-1939 ALL MODELS 250cc THRU 990cc (BOOK OF)
MATCHLESS 1945-1956 350 & 500cc SINGLES (BOOK OF)
MATCHLESS 1955-1966 350 & 500cc SINGLES (BOOK OF)
NEW IMPERIAL ALL SV & OHV FROM 1935 ONWARDS (BOOK OF)
NORTON 1932-1939 PREWAR MODELS (BOOK OF)
NORTON 1932-1947 (BOOK OF)
NORTON 1938-1956 (BOOK OF)
NORTON 1945-1963 MODELS 19, 50 & ES2 (BOOK OF)
NORTON 1955-1965 DOMINATOR TWINS (BOOK OF)
NORTON 1957-1970 TWINS FACTORY WORKSHOP MANUAL
NSU PRIMA 1956-1964 ALL MODELS (BOOK OF)
NSU QUICKLY 1953-1963 ALL MODELS (BOOK OF)
PANTHER 1932-1958 LIGHTWEIGHT MODELS 250 & 350cc (BOOK OF)
PANTHER 1938-1966 HEAVYWEIGHT MODELS 600 & 650cc (BOOK OF)
RALEIGH MOPEDS 1960-1969 (BOOK OF)
RALEIGH MOTORCYCLES 1919-1933 (BOOK OF)
ROYAL ENFIELD 1934-1946 SINGLES & V TWINS (BOOK OF)
ROYAL ENFIELD 1937-1953 SINGLES & V TWINS (BOOK OF)
ROYAL ENFIELD 1946-1962 SINGLES (BOOK OF)
ROYAL ENFIELD 1958-1966 250cc & 350cc SINGLES (SECOND BOOK OF)
ROYAL ENFIELD 736cc INTERCEPTOR FACTORY WORKSHOP MANUAL
RUDGE 1933-1939 (BOOK OF)
SUNBEAM 1928-1939 (BOOK OF)
SUNBEAM 1946-1957 S7 & S8 (BOOK OF)
SUZUKI 50cc & 80cc UP TO 1966 (BOOK OF)
SUZUKI T10 1963-1967 FACTORY WORKSHOP MANUAL
SUZUKI T20 & T200 1965-1969 FACTORY WORKSHOP MANUAL
TRIUMPH 1935-1939 PREWAR MODELS (BOOK OF)
TRIUMPH 1935-1949 (BOOK OF)
TRIUMPH 1937-1951 (WORKSHOP MANUAL)
TRIUMPH 1945-1955 FACTORY WORKSHOP MANUAL
TRIUMPH 1945-1958 TWINS (BOOK OF)
TRIUMPH 1956-1969 TWINS (BOOK OF)
VELOCETTE 1925-1970 ALL SINGLES & TWINS (BOOK OF)
VESPA 1951-1961 (BOOK OF)
VESPA 1955-1963 125 & 150cc & GS MODELS (SECOND BOOK OF)
VESPA 1955-1968 GS & SS (BOOK OF)
VESPA 1963-1972 90, 125 & 150cc (THIRD BOOK OF)
VILLIERS ENGINE UP TO 1959 INC. 3 WHEELERS (BOOK OF)
VILLIERS ENGINE UP TO 1969 (BOOK OF)
VINCENT 1935-1955 (WORKSHOP MANUAL)

VELOCEPRESS TECHNICAL BOOKS – MOTORCYCLE

CATALOG OF BRITISH MOTORCYCLES (1951 MODELS)
INDIAN PONYBIKE, BOY RACER & PAPOOSE ILL PARTS LIST & SALES LIT
MOTORCYCLE ENGINEERING (P.E. Irving)
SPEED AND HOW TO OBTAIN IT (Motor Cycle Magazine UK)
TUNING FOR SPEED (P.E. Irving)

VELOCEPRESS MANUALS - THREE WHEELER'S

BSA THREE WHEELER (BOOK OF)
VINTAGE MORGAN THREE WHEELER (BOOK OF)

VELOCEPRESS MANUALS - AUTOMOBILE

AUSTIN-HEALEY 6-CYLINDER WORKSHOP MANUAL
AUSTIN-HEALEY SPRITE & MG MIDGET WORKSHOP MANUAL 1958-1971
BMW 600 LIMOUSINE FACTORY WORKSHOP MANUAL
BMW 600 LIMOUSINE OWNERS HAND BOOK & SERVICE MANUAL
BMW 2000 & 2002 1966-1976 WORKSHOP MANUAL
BMW ISETTA FACTORY WORKSHOP MANUAL
CORVAIR 1960-1969 WORKSHOP MANUAL
CORVETTE V8 1955-1962 WORKSHOP MANUAL
FIAT 500 FACTORY WORKSHOP MANUAL 1957-1973
FIAT 600, 600D & MULTIPLA FACTORY WORKSHOP MANUAL 1955-1969
JAGUAR E-TYPE 3.8 & 4.2 SERIES 1 & 2 WORKSHOP MANUAL
JAGUAR MK 7, 8, 9 & XK120, 140, 150 WORKSHOP MANUAL 1948-1961
METROPOLITAN FACTORY WORKSHOP MANUAL
MGA & MGB OWNERS HANDBOOK & WORKSHOP MANUAL
MG MIDGET TC, TD, TF & TF1500 WORKSHOP MANUAL
PORSCHE 356 1948-1965 WORKSHOP MANUAL
PORSCHE 912 WORKSHOP MANUAL
TRIUMPH TR2, TR3, TR4 1953-1965 WORKSHOP MANUAL
VOLKSWAGEN TRANSPORTER, TRUCKS & WAGONS 1950-1979 WSM
VOLVO 1944-1968 ALL MODELS WORKSHOP MANUAL

VELOCEPRESS TECHNICAL BOOKS - AUTOMOBILE

FERRARI 250/GT SERVICE AND MAINTENANCE
FERRARI GUIDE TO PERFORMANCE
FERRARI OWNER'S HANDBOOK
FERRARI TUNING TIPS & MAINTENANCE TECHNIQUES
HOW TO BUILD A FIBERGLASS CAR
HOW TO BUILD A RACING CAR
HOW TO RESTORE THE MODEL 'A' FORD
MASERATI OWNER'S HANDBOOK
OBERT'S FIAT GUIDE
PERFORMANCE TUNING THE SUNBEAM TIGER
SOUPING THE VOLKSWAGEN
SOLEX CARBURETORS (EMPHASIS ON UK & EU AUTOMOBILES)
SU CARBURETORS (EMPHASIS ON UK AUTOMOBILES)
WEBER CARBURETORS (EMPHASIS ON ALFA & FIAT)

VELOCEPRESS BOOKS & GUIDES - AUTOMOBILE

ABARTH BUYERS GUIDE
COMPLETE CATALOG OF JAPANESE MOTOR VEHICLES
FERRARI 308 SERIES BUYER'S AND OWNER'S GUIDE
FERRARI BERLINETTA LUSSO
FERRARI BROCHURES AND SALES LITERATURE 1946-1967
FERRARI BROCHURES AND SALES LITERATURE 1968-1989
FERRARI OPP, MAINTENANCE & SERVICE H/BOOKS 1948-1963
FERRARI SERIAL NUMBERS PART I - ODD NUMBERS TO 21399
FERRARI SERIAL NUMBERS PART II - EVEN NUMBERS TO 1050
FERRARI SPYDER CALIFORNIA
HENRY'S FABULOUS MODEL "A" FORD
MASERATI BROCHURES AND SALES LITERATURE

VELOCEPRESS BOOKS – RACING

CARRERA PANAMERICANA - MEXICAN ROAD RACE (BOOK OF)
DIALED IN - THE JAN OPPERMAN STORY
IF HEMINGWAY HAD WRITTEN A RACING NOVEL
LE MANS 24 (THE BOOK THAT THE FILM WAS BASED ON)
VEDA ORR'S NEW REVISED HOT ROD PICTORIAL

AUTOBOOKS WORKSHOP MANUALS & BROOKLANDS ROAD TEST PORTFOLIOS

FOR A COMPLETE LISTING OF THE AUTOBOOKS & BROOKLANDS TITLES THAT WE CURRENTLY HAVE AVAILABLE, PLEASE VISIT OUR WEBSITE.

For A Detailed Description Of Any Of The Titles Listed Above Please Visit Our Website
www.VelocePress.com

Please visit our website

www.VelocePress.com

for a complete up-to-date list of titles, descriptions, and secure online ordering using PayPal.

www.ingramcontent.com/pod-product-compliance
Lightning Source LLC
Chambersburg PA
CBHW060243240426
43673CB00047B/1872